create™

AF861222

Course Includes SIMnet Access

create™

http://create.mheducation.com

ISBN-10: 1260105660 ISBN-13: 9781260105667

Contents

Credits

chapter 1

Essential Skills for Office 2016

In this chapter, you will learn the following skills:

- Learn about Microsoft Office 2016 and its applications Word, Excel, PowerPoint, and Access
- Demonstrate how to open, save, and close files
- Recognize Office 2016 common features and navigation elements
- Use Microsoft Help and Tell Me feature
- Create new files
- Share files through OneDrive
- Modify account information and the look of Office
- Customize the Quick Access Toolbar

introduction

This chapter introduces you to Microsoft Office 2016. You will learn about the shared features across the Office 2016 applications and how to navigate common interface elements such as the Ribbon and Quick Access Toolbar. You will learn how to open and close files as well as learn how to create new blank files. You will search for help and use the new *Tell Me* feature as well as work with messages that appear when you first open files. You will learn about the different ways to save and share files, including through your OneDrive account. You will become familiar with the Office account and learn how to modify the account as well as the look of Office.

Skill 1.1 Introduction to Microsoft Office 2016

Microsoft Office 2016 is a collection of business "productivity" applications (computer programs designed to make you more productive at work, school, and home). The most popular Office applications are:

Microsoft Word—A word processing program. Word processing software allows you to create text-based documents, similar to how you would type a document on a typewriter. However, word processing software offers more powerful formatting and design tools, allowing you to create complex documents, including reports, résumés, brochures, and newsletters.

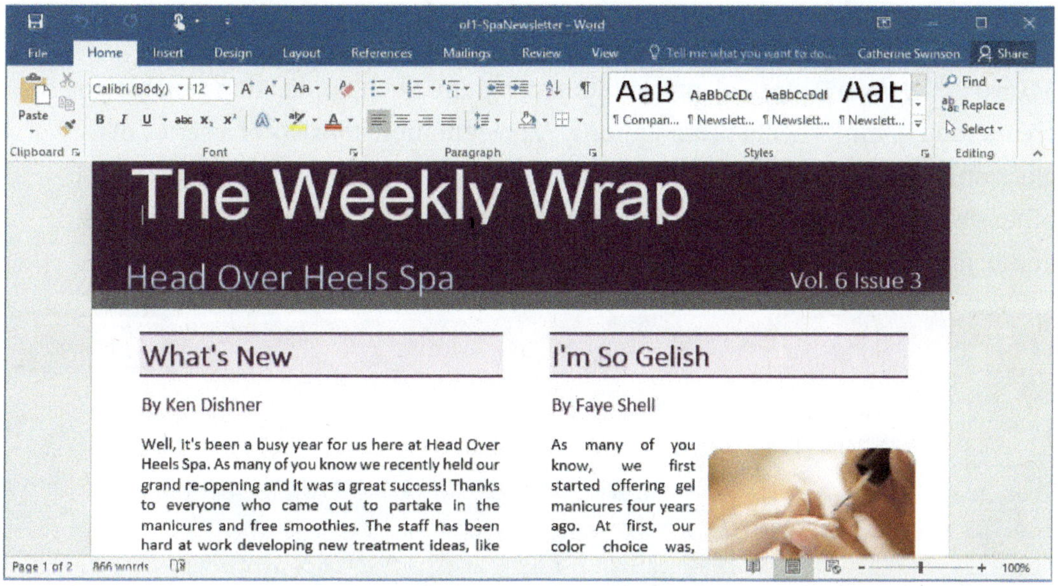

FIGURE OF 1.1

Microsoft Excel—A spreadsheet program. Originally, spreadsheet applications were viewed as electronic versions of an accountant's ledger. Today's spreadsheet applications can do much more than just calculate numbers—they include powerful charting and data analysis features. Spreadsheet programs can be used for everything from managing personal budgets to calculating loan payments.

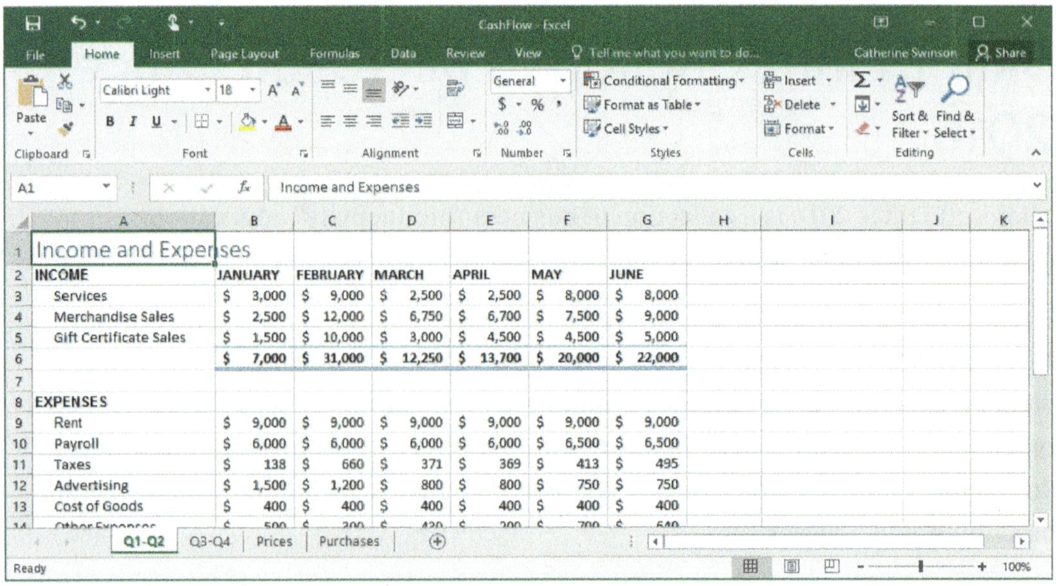

FIGURE OF 1.2

Microsoft PowerPoint—A presentation program. Such applications enable you to create robust, multimedia presentations. A presentation consists of a series of electronic slides. Each slide contains content, including text, images, charts, and other objects. You can add multimedia elements to slides, including animations, audio, and video.

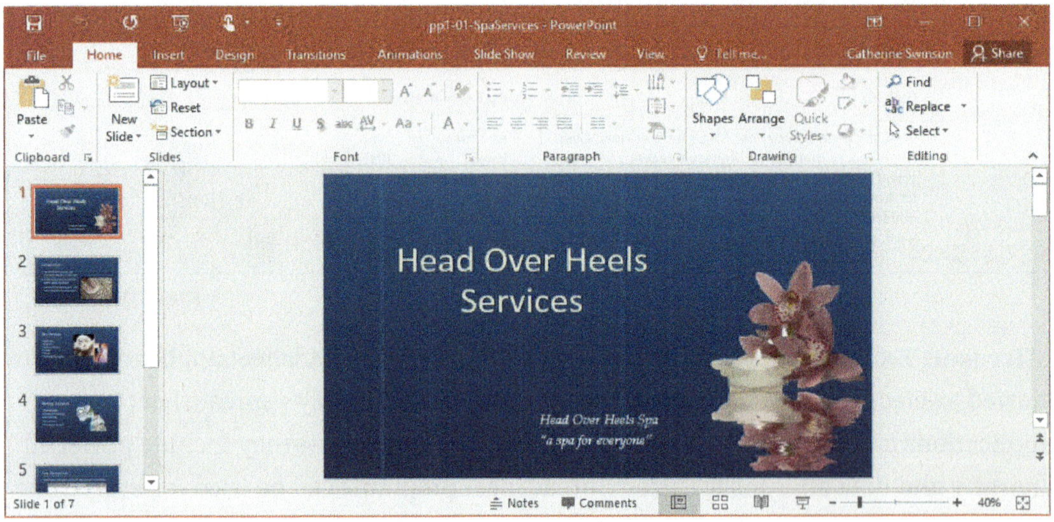

FIGURE OF 1.3

Microsoft Access—A database program. Database applications allow you to organize and manipulate large amounts of data. Databases that allow you to relate tables and databases to one another are referred to as *relational* databases. As a database user, you usually see only one aspect of the database—a *form*. Database forms use a graphical interface to allow a user to enter record data. For example, when you fill out an order form online, you are probably interacting with a database.

The information you enter becomes a record in a database *table*. Your order is matched with information in an inventory table (keeping track of which items are in stock) through a *query*. When your order is filled, a database *report* can be generated for use as an invoice or a bill of lading.

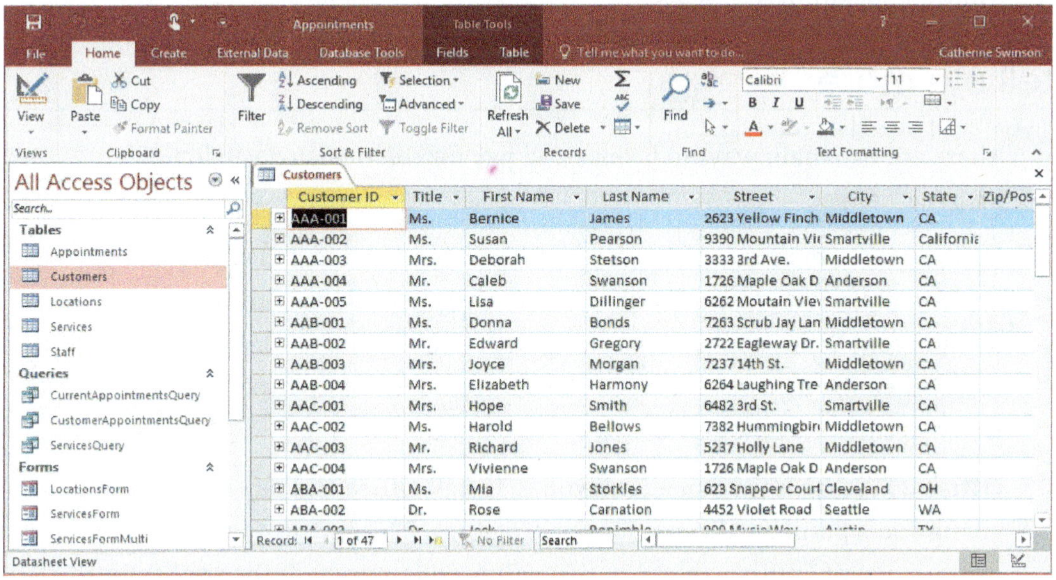

FIGURE OF 1.4

To open one of the Office applications in Windows 10:

1. Click the Windows **Start** button (located in the lower left corner of your computer screen).
2. Click **All Apps**.
3. Find the application in this list and click the application you want to open.

In addition to the different applications available in the Office suite, there are also a number of versions of each application:

- Desktop app—Full-featured version of the Office applications that you download and install on your computer. If you are creating complex documents or presentations or performing complicated calculations on large amounts of data, you will most likely need the desktop version of the application.
- Universal app—Installed for free with Windows 10. These apps are included in the Windows 10 operating system. They are optimized for touch screen interaction and have fewer features than the desktop app versions, but if all you need to do is review and edit files, this version may work well for you.
- Online app—Available at https://office.com. These apps are accessed through a Web browser (no install required) and allow you to create and save files online using your OneDrive account (Microsoft's cloud storage service). Like the

Universal apps, the Online apps have a limited set of features, but depending on your needs that may be enough.

- Mobile app—Free apps available for your tablet device. Similar in features and functionality to the Universal app, these apps are designed to run on the iOS and Android operating systems.

tell me **more**

There are two main ways to license and pay for the installed version of Microsoft Office:

Office 365—This version allows you to download and install Office and pay for it on a yearly or monthly subscription basis. It includes full versions of the different Office applications along with online storage services for your files. When the next version of Office is released, the subscription can be transferred to the new version.

Office 2016—This version allows you to install Office and pay for it once, giving you a perpetual license for the programs. This means that when the next version of Office is released, you will need to purchase the application suite again. You can associate a Windows account with Office 2016, giving you access to online storage for your files.

If you are a home user, business, or a student, there are different purchasing options for both Office 365 and Office 2016. Both versions require that you are running the Windows 7, Windows 8, or Windows 10 operating system.

Skill 1.2 Opening Files

Opening a file retrieves it from storage and displays it on your computer screen. Files can be stored online, such as in your OneDrive, or on the hard drive of your computer. The steps for opening a file are the same for Word documents, Excel spreadsheets, PowerPoint presentations, and Access databases.

To open a recently opened file:

1. Click the **File** tab to open Backstage view.
2. Click **Open**.
3. The *Open* page displays listing the recently opened files by default.
4. Click a file in the list to open it.

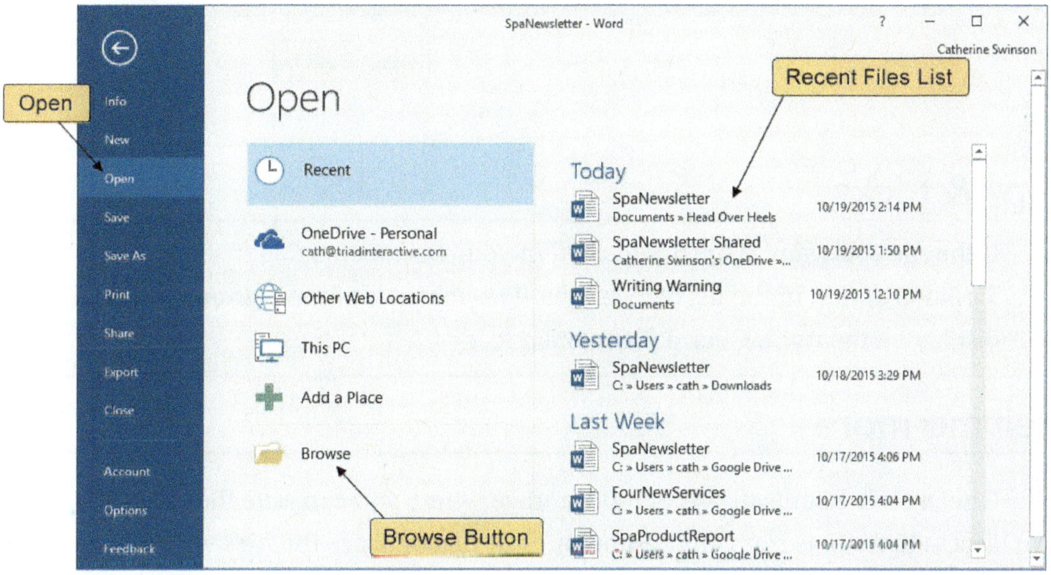

FIGURE OF 1.5

If you do not see the file you want to open in the *Recent Files* list, you can navigate to find the file you want to open:

1. Click the **Browse** button to open the *Open* dialog.
2. Navigate to the folder containing the file you want to open.
3. Select the file name you want to open and click the **Open** button.

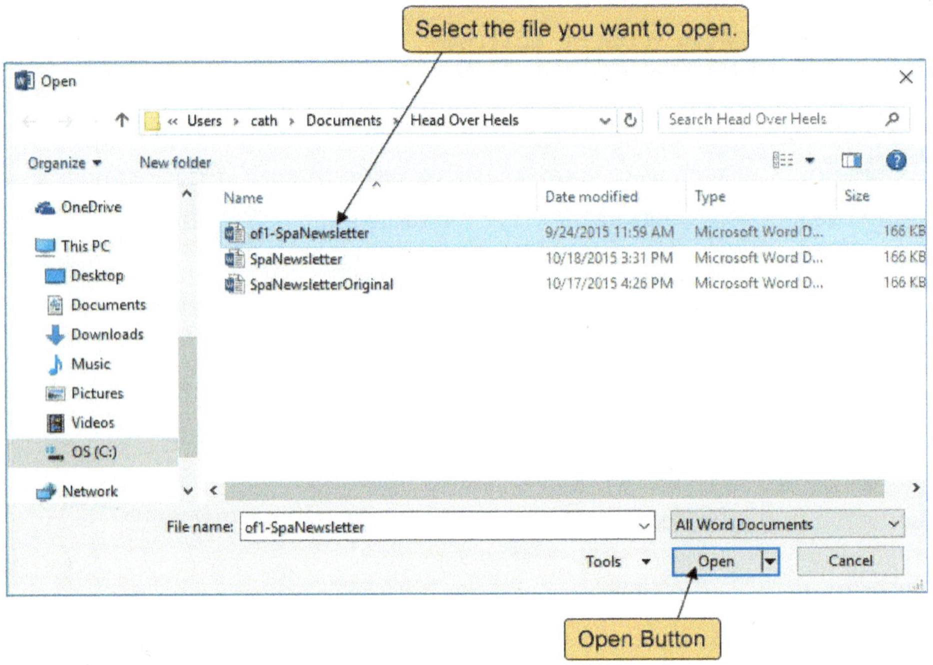

FIGURE OF 1.6

tips & tricks

If the file you want to open is located in your *Documents* folder, click the **This PC** option in the list of locations. The contents of the *Documents* folder display on the right. Click a file to open it.

tell me more

OneDrive is Microsoft's free cloud storage where you can save files and access those files from any computer or device or share the files with others. When you save files to your OneDrive, they are stored locally on your computer and "synched" with your OneDrive account and stored online where you can then access the files from another computer or device that has OneDrive capability.

another method

- To display the *Open* page in Backstage view, you can also press Ctrl + O on the keyboard.
- To open the *Open* dialog from the *Open* page in Backstage view, you can also click **This PC** and then click the **Documents** folder at the top right side of the window.

let me try *Live!*

Try this skill on your own:

1. Open the student data file **of1-SpaNewsletter** .

   NOTE: You may see a yellow security message at the top of the window. See the skill *Working in Protected View* to learn more about security warning messages.

2. Keep the file open to work on the next skill.

Skill 1.3 Closing Files

Closing a file removes it from your computer screen and stores the last saved version for future use. If you have not saved your latest changes, most applications will prevent you from losing work by asking if you want to save the changes you made before closing.

To close a file and save your latest changes:

1. Click the **File** tab to open Backstage view.
2. Click **Close**.
3. If you have made no changes since the last time you saved the file, it will close immediately. If changes have been made, the application displays a message box asking if you want to save the changes you made before closing.

Click **Save** to save the changes.

Click **Don't Save** to close the file without saving your latest changes.

Click **Cancel** to keep the file open.

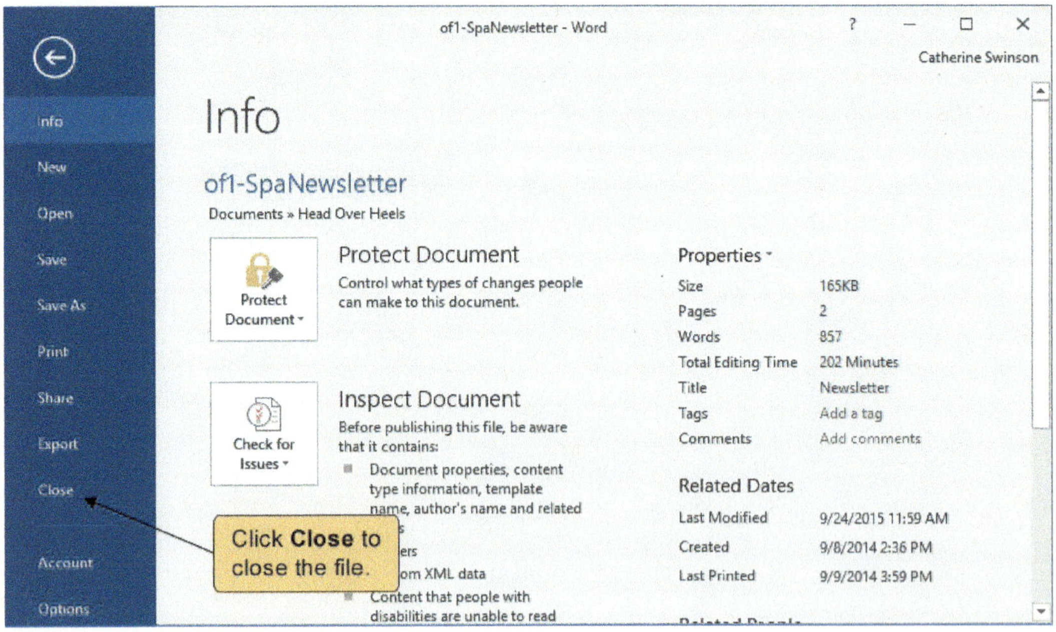

FIGURE OF 1.7

another method

To close a file, you can also press Ctrl + W on the keyboard.

let me try *Live!*

If you do not have the data file from the previous skill open, open the student data file
of1-SpaNewsletter and try this skill on your own:

1. Close the file
2. Keep the application open to work on the next skill.

Skill 1.4 Closing the Application

When you close a file, the application stays open so you can open another file to edit or begin a new file. Often, when you are finished working on a file, you want to close the file and exit the application at the same time. In this case, you will want to close the application.

To close an application:

1. Click the **Close** button in the upper right corner of the application.
2. If you have made no changes since the last time you saved the file, it will close immediately. If changes have been made, the application displays a message box asking if you want to save the changes you made before closing.

Click **Save** to save the changes.

Click **Don't Save** to close the file without saving your latest changes.

Click **Cancel** to keep the file open.

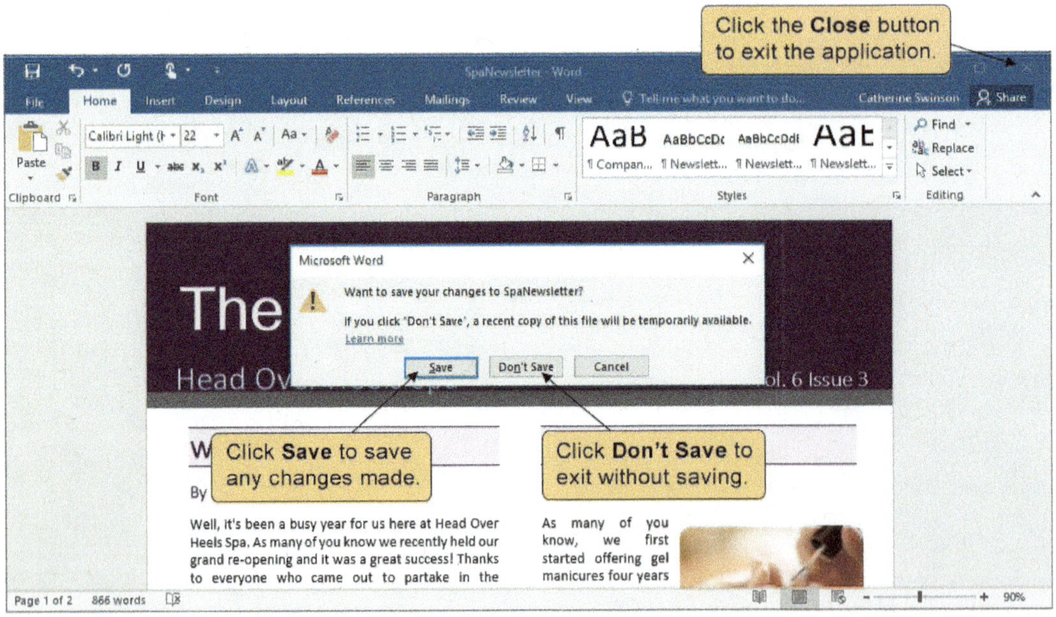

FIGURE OF 1.8

tips & tricks

Next to the **Close** button in the upper right corner of the application you will see two other buttons:

Minimize —hides the window from view, but does not close the application. The application button is still active on the Windows taskbar. Click the button on the taskbar to display the window again.

Maximize —resizes the application window so it fills the screen. When the window is maximized, the window cannot be moved around the screen and the *Maximize* button is replaced with the *Restore* button. Click the **Restore** button to reduce the size of the window and move it around on the screen.

another method

To close the application, you can also right-click the title bar and select **Close**.

let me try *Live!*

Open the student data file **of1-SpaNewsletter** and try this skill on your own:

1. Make a change to the document.
2. Close the application.
3. Do not save the change you made.

Skill 1.5 Using the Start Page

When you launch an Office 2016 application you are first taken to the **Start page**. Before you can begin working in an application, you must have a file to work on. This can be a file you have worked on in the past, a new blank file, or a new file based on a template. The left side of the *Start* page displays a list of recently opened files. You can choose a file from this list or create a new file using one of the file templates displayed on the right side of the *Start* page.

To open a recent file from the *Start* page:

1. Launch the application.
2. The *Start* page displays.
3. Click a file in the left pane to open the file.

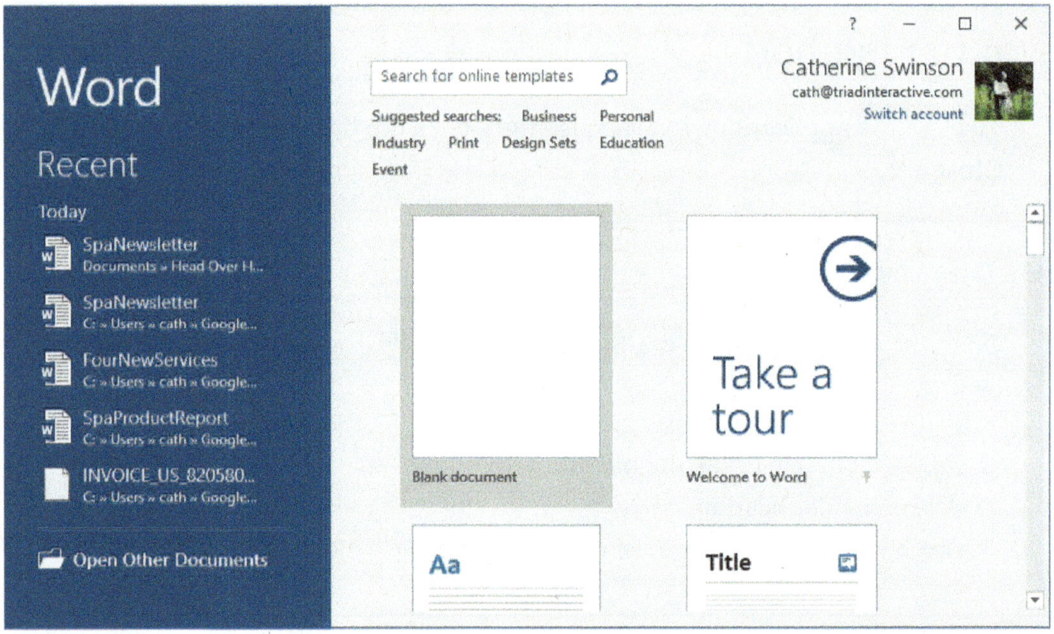

FIGURE OF 1.9

tips & tricks

If you do not see the file you want to open in the list of recent files, click **Open Other Documents** at the bottom of the left pane. This will display the *Open* page that includes buttons for finding and opening files from other locations such as your computer or your OneDrive.

tell me **more**

In previous versions of Office when you launched an application, a blank file opened ready for you to begin working. If you want to start a new blank file, click the blank file template in the list of templates. It is always listed as the first option.

let me **try** *Live!*

To try this skill on your own:

1. Launch **Microsoft Word**.
2. Click the **of1-SpaNewsletter** file in the list of recently opened files. If you do not see this file, open a file of your choice.
3. If you will be moving on to the next skill in this chapter, leave the document open to continue working. If not, close the file.

Skill 1.6 Getting to Know the Office 2016 User Interface

THE RIBBON

Beginning with Office 2007, Microsoft redesigned the user experience for the Office applications—replacing the old menu bar/toolbar interface with a new Ribbon interface that makes it easier to find application functions and commands.

The **Ribbon** is located across the top of the application window and organizes common features and commands into tabs. Each **tab** organizes commands further into related **groups**. The dialog launcher appears in the lower right corner of some groups. Clicking this button opens the primary dialog for working with commands in the group. For example, clicking the dialog launcher in the *Font* group will open the *Font* dialog.

When a specific type of object is selected (such as a picture, table, or chart), a contextual tab will appear. **Contextual tabs** contain commands specific to the type of object selected and are visible only when the commands might be useful.

Each application includes a **Home tab** that contains the most commonly used commands for that application. For example, in Word, the *Home* tab includes the following groups: *Clipboard*, *Font*, *Paragraph*, *Styles*, and *Editing*, while the Excel *Home* tab includes groups more appropriate for a spreadsheet program: *Clipboard*, *Font*, *Alignment*, *Number*, *Styles*, *Cells*, and *Editing*.

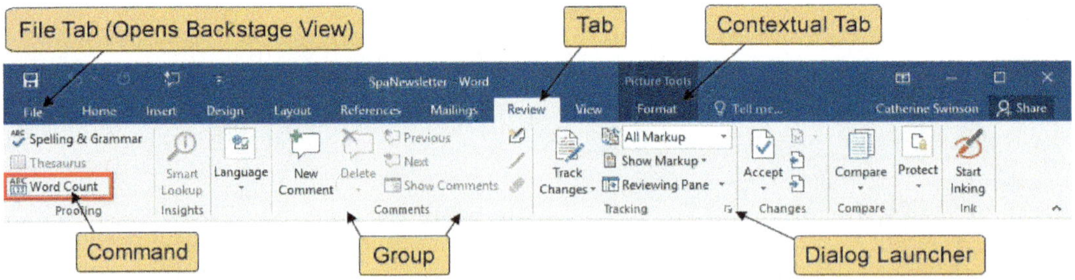

FIGURE OF 1.10

tips & tricks

If you need more space for your file, you can minimize the Ribbon by clicking the **Collapse the Ribbon** button in the lower right corner of the Ribbon (or press Ctrl + F1). When the Ribbon is minimized, the tab names appear along the top of the window (similar to a menu bar). When you click a tab name, the Ribbon appears. After you select a command or click away from the Ribbon, the Ribbon hides again. To redisplay the Ribbon permanently, click the **Pin the Ribbon** button in the lower right corner of the Ribbon. You can also double-click the active tab to hide or display the Ribbon.

BACKSTAGE

Notice that each application also includes a **File tab** at the far left side of the Ribbon. Clicking the File tab opens **Backstage view**, where you can access the commands for managing and protecting your files, including *Save*, *Open*, *Close*, *New*, *Print*, and *Share*.

To return to your file from Backstage view, click the **Back** button located in the upper left corner of the window. 

KEYBOARD SHORTCUTS

Many commands available through the Ribbon and Backstage view are also accessible through keyboard shortcuts and shortcut menus.

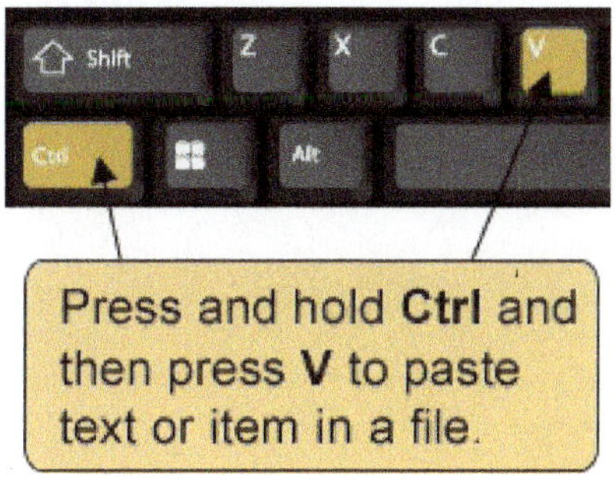

FIGURE OF 1.11

Keyboard shortcuts are keys or combinations of keys that you press to execute a command. Some keyboard shortcuts refer to **F** keys or function keys. These are the keys that run across the top of the keyboard. Pressing these keys will execute specific commands. For example, pressing the F1 key will open Help in any of the Microsoft Office applications. Keyboard shortcuts typically use a combination of two keys, although some commands use a combination of three keys and others only one key. When a keyboard shortcut calls for a combination of key presses, such as Ctrl + V to paste an item from the *Clipboard*, you must first press the modifier key Ctrl holding it down while you press the V key on the keyboard.

tell me **more**

Many of the keyboard shortcuts are universal across all applications—not just Microsoft Office applications. Some examples of universal shortcut keys include:

Ctrl + C = Copy

Ctr + X = Cut

Ctr + V = Paste

Ctr + Z = Undo

Ctr + O = Open

Ctr + S = Save

SHORTCUT MENUS

Shortcut menus are menus of commands that display when you right-click an area of the application window. The area or object you right-click determines which menu appears. For example, if you right-click in a paragraph, you will see a shortcut menu of commands for working with text; however, if you right-click an image, you will see a shortcut menu of commands for working with images.

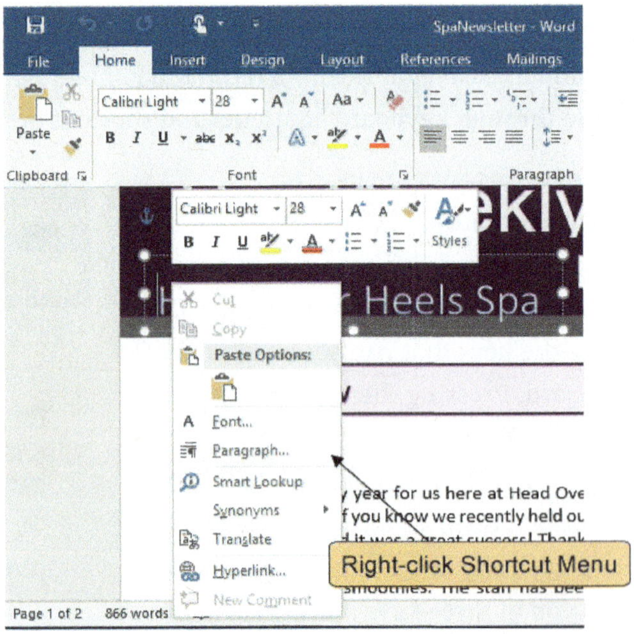

FIGURE OF 1.12

THE MINI TOOLBAR

The **Mini toolbar** gives you access to common tools for working with text. When you select text and then rest your mouse over the text, the Mini toolbar fades in. You can then click a button to change the selected text just as you would on the Ribbon.

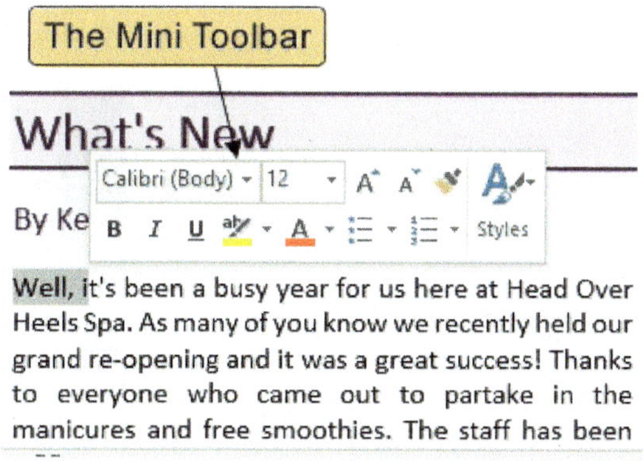

FIGURE OF 1.13

another method

> To display the Mini toolbar, you can also right-click the text. The Mini toolbar appears above the shortcut menu.

QUICK ACCESS TOOLBAR

The **Quick Access Toolbar** is located at the top of the application window above the *File* tab. The Quick Access Toolbar, as its name implies, gives you quick one-click access to common commands. Some of the commands include *Save*, *Undo*, and *Redo*.

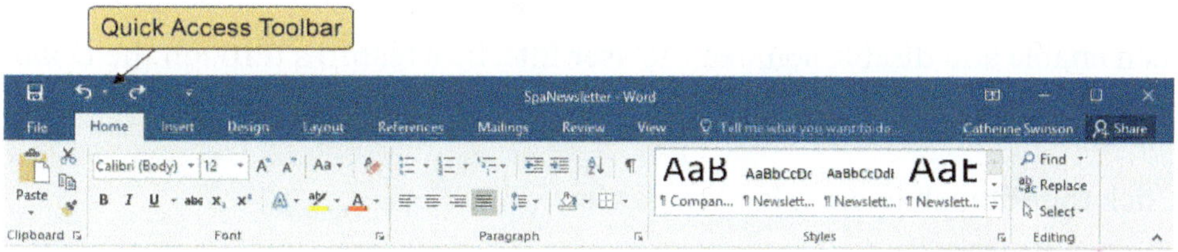

FIGURE OF 1.14

ENHANCED SCREENTIP

A **ScreenTip** is a small information box that displays the name of the command when you rest your mouse over a button on the Ribbon. An **Enhanced ScreenTip** displays not only the name of the command, but also the keyboard shortcut (if there is one) and a short description of what the button does and when it is used. Certain Enhanced ScreenTips also include an image along with a description of the command.

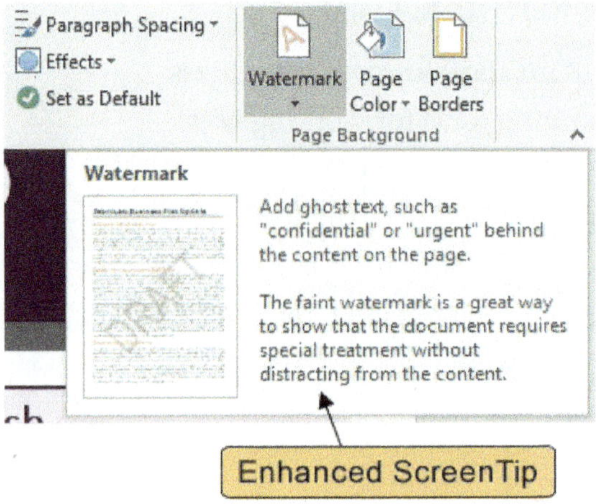

FIGURE OF 1.15

THE OPTIONS DIALOG

The Options dialog is where you can control settings for the Office application. When you make a change in the *Options* dialog, the setting applies to the application, not the current active file. This means when you exit the application and open it again, any changes you made in the *Options* dialog will remain.

Although each application has a slightly different set of controls, the *Options* dialog includes areas for controlling proofing options, save options, language, the Ribbon, and Quick Access Toolbar, as well as a general section where you can control some of the user interface features.

You can enable and disable some of the user interface features through the *Options* dialog:

1. Click the **File** tab to open Backstage view.
2. Click **Options**.
3. Make the changes you want, and then click **OK** to save your changes
   - Check or uncheck **Show Mini toolbar on selection** to control whether or not the Mini toolbar appears when you hover over selected text. (This does not affect the appearance of the Mini toolbar when you right-click.)
   - Check or uncheck **Enable Live Preview** to turn the live preview feature on or off.
   - Make a selection from the *ScreenTip style* list:
     - **Show feature descriptions in ScreenTips** displays Enhanced ScreenTips when they are available.
     - **Don't show feature descriptions in ScreenTips** hides Enhanced ScreenTips. The ScreenTip will still include the keyboard shortcut if there is one available.
     - **Don't show ScreenTips** hides ScreenTips altogether, so if you hold your

mouse over a button on the Ribbon, nothing will appear.

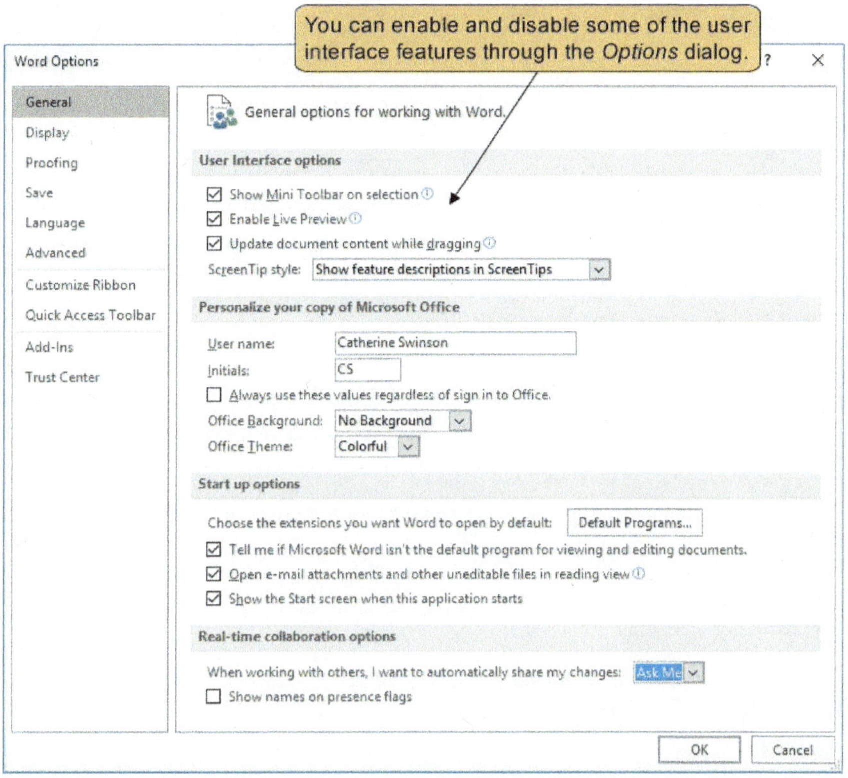

FIGURE OF 1.16

LIVE PREVIEW

The **Live Preview** feature in Microsoft Office 2016 allows you to see formatting changes in your file before actually committing to the change. When Live Preview is active, rolling over a command on the Ribbon will temporarily apply the formatting to the currently active text or object. To apply the formatting, click the formatting option.

Use Live Preview to preview the following:

Font Formatting—Including the font, font size, text effects, and font color

Paragraph Formatting—Including numbering, bullets, line spacing, and shading

Styles and Themes Table Formatting—Including table styles and shading

Picture Formatting—Including correction and color options, picture styles, borders, effects, positioning, brightness, and contrast

SmartArt—Including layouts, styles, and colors

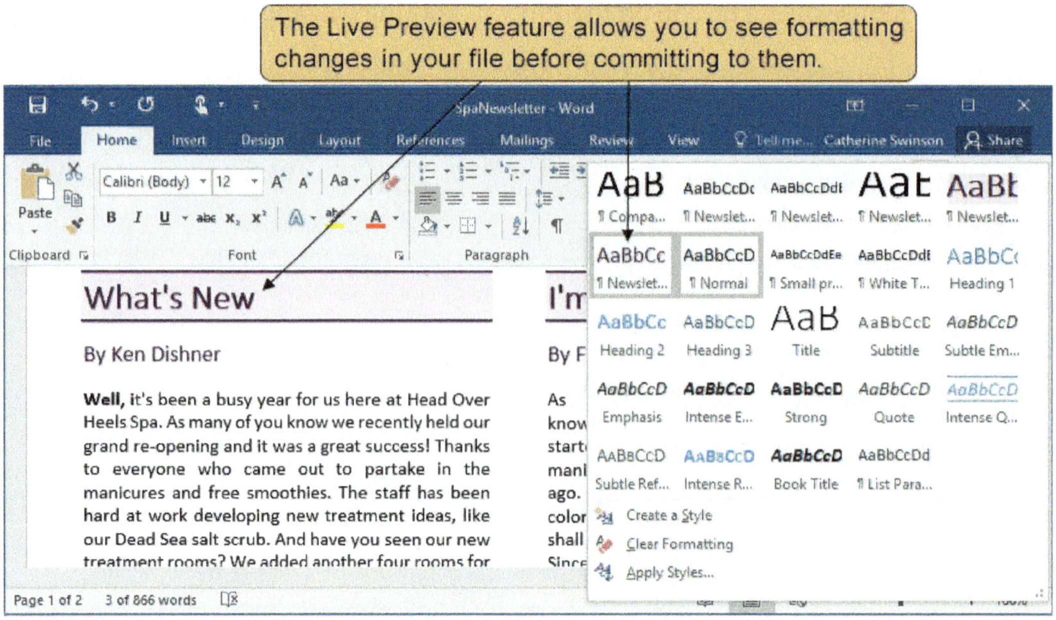

FIGURE OF 1.17

let me try *Live!*

If you do not have the data file from the previous skill open, open the student data file **of1-SpaNewsletter** and try this skill on your own:

1. Explore the Ribbon. Click on different tabs and note how commands are arranged together in groups.
2. Click the picture to display the *Picture Tools* contextual tab.
3. Right-click an area of the file to display the shortcut menu.
4. Explore the Mini Toolbar at the top of the shortcut menu. Click away from the menu to hide it.
5. Click the **Insert** tab. In the *Pages* group, roll your mouse over the **Cover Page** button to display the Enhanced ScreenTip.
6. Display **Backstage** view.
7. Click **Options** to open the *Options* dialog.
8. Disable **Live Preview** and change the **ScreenTips** so they don't show feature descriptions. Close the *Options* dialog and save your changes.
9. Click the **Back** button to return to the document.
10. If you will be moving on to the next skill in this chapter, leave the document open to continue working. If not, close the file.

Skill 1.7 Getting Help

In Office 2016, Microsoft introduced the **Tell Me** feature. This feature offers a quick way to access commands that you do not know how to find in the Office interface or that take several clicks to get to. By using the *Tell Me* box to access commands, you can save time and frustration by quickly getting to the features you need.

To use *Tell Me* to access a command:

1. Type the word or phrase you want to look up in the **Tell me what you want to do...** box at the top of the window.
2. Office displays a list of commands that match your search.
3. Options with a triangle have a gallery or menu of options associated with it. Point to the option to display more commands from which to choose.
4. Click an option on the list to access that command.

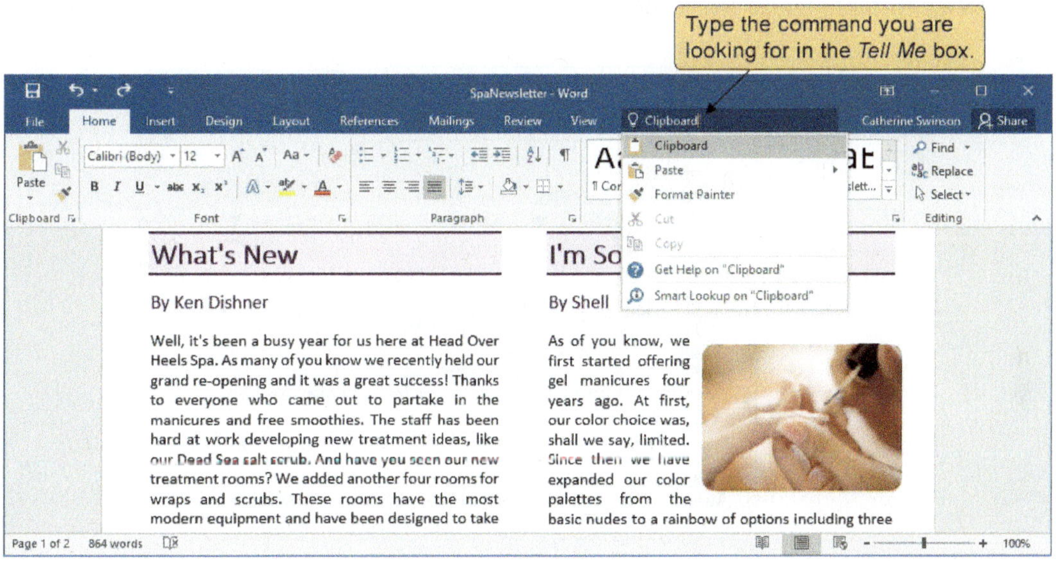

FIGURE OF 1.18

If you want to learn more about a command, you can look it up in the **Office Help** system. Each application comes with its own Help system with topics specifically tailored for working with that application.

To look up a topic using the Microsoft Office Help system:

1. Type the word or phrase you want help on in the *Tell Me* box.
2. At the bottom of the list of options, you will see an option for getting help on the topic. Click the **option** to open the *Help* window.

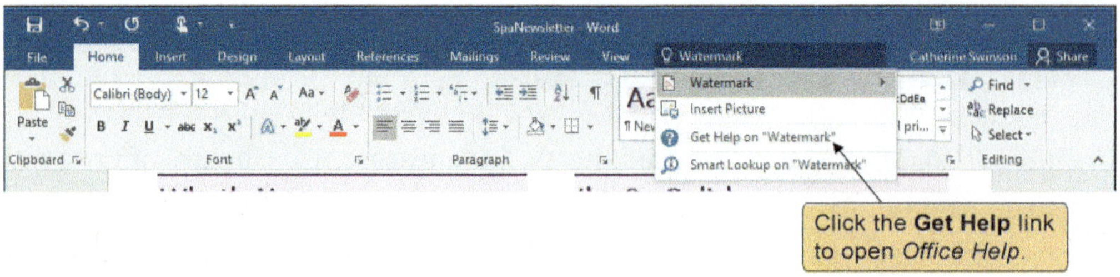

FIGURE OF 1.19

3. The *Help* window displays topics on the word or phrase you typed.
4. Click a link to display the help topic.

From the *Help* window, you can search for more topics:

1. Click in the **Search** box and type a word or phrase describing the topic you want help with.
2. Click the **Search** button.
3. A list of results appears.
4. Click a link to display the help topic.

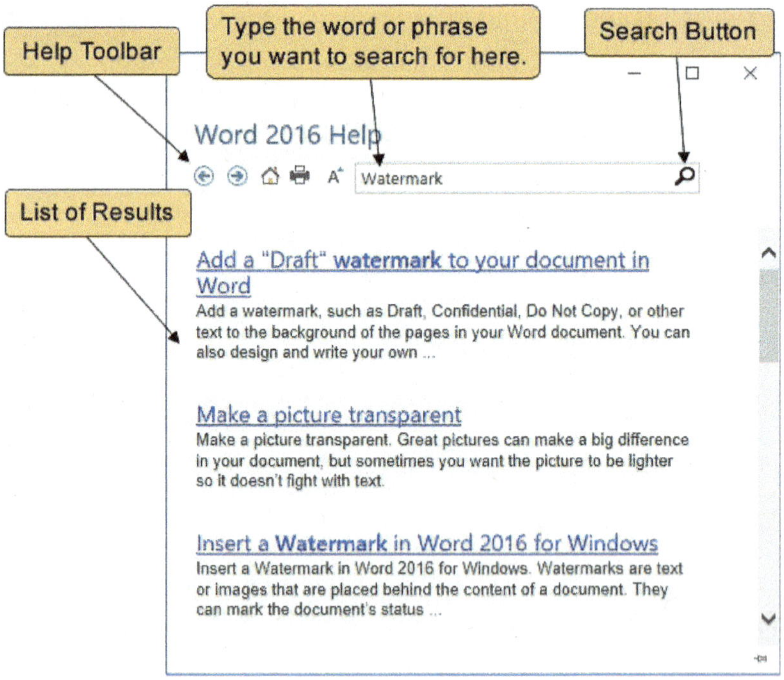

FIGURE OF 1.20

tips & tricks

At the bottom of the list of options, you will see options for **Smart Lookup**. Click the **Smart Lookup** link to search for information on the Internet on the word or phrase you typed.

tell me more

The *Help* toolbar is located at the top of the *Help* window. This toolbar includes buttons for navigating between screens, changing the size of text, and returning to the *Help Home* page. Click the **printer icon** on the toolbar to print the current topic. Click the **pushpin icon** to keep the *Help* window always on top of the Microsoft Office application.

another method

To open the *Help* window, you can also:

- Click the **File** tab and then click the **Microsoft Office Help** button. It is the question mark located at the far right side of the Window above the user profile information.
- Press F1 on the keyboard.

let me try *Live!*

If you do not have the data file from the previous skill open, open the student data file
of1-SpaNewsletter and try this skill on your own:

1. Type `Clipboard` in the *Tell Me* box and display the *Clipboard* task pane.
2. Click the **X** in the upper right corner of the task pane to close it.
3. Type `Watermark` in the *Tell Me* box and open the **Office Help** window to learn more about adding a watermark in Word.
4. Click a link of your choice.
5. Close the **Help** window.
6. Close the file.

from the perspective of . . .

A BUSY PARENT

Learning Microsoft Office was one of the best things I did to help manage my family's busy lifestyle. I use Word to write up and print a calendar of everyone's activities for the week. I keep a handle on the family finances with a budget of all expenses in an Excel spreadsheet. I used PowerPoint to create a presentation for my family of our summer vacation pictures. Once I became more familiar with Access, I used it to help organize my family's busy schedule. I created a database with one table for activities, another for parent contact information, another one for carpooling, and another one for the schedule. Being able to organize all the information in a database has been invaluable. And the best part is now I can share and view these files with everyone, even on my tablet. I always thought Office was only for businesses, but now I can't imagine running my household without it!

Skill 1.8 Using Smart Lookup

The **Smart Lookup** tool allows you to quickly search the Internet about any word or phrase in a document, spreadsheet, or presentation. When you look up a word or phrase, the *Insights* task pane displays. This task pane has two tabs—*Explore* and *Define*. The *Explore* tab displays search results powered by Microsoft's Bing search engine. The *Define* tab displays a definition of the word or phrase from the Oxford Dictionaries.

To look up information about a word or phrase using the *Smart Lookup* tool:

1. Select the word or phrase you want more information on.
2. Click the **Review** tab.
3. In the *Insights* group, click the **Smart Lookup** button.
4. The *Insights* task pane opens displaying information about the word.

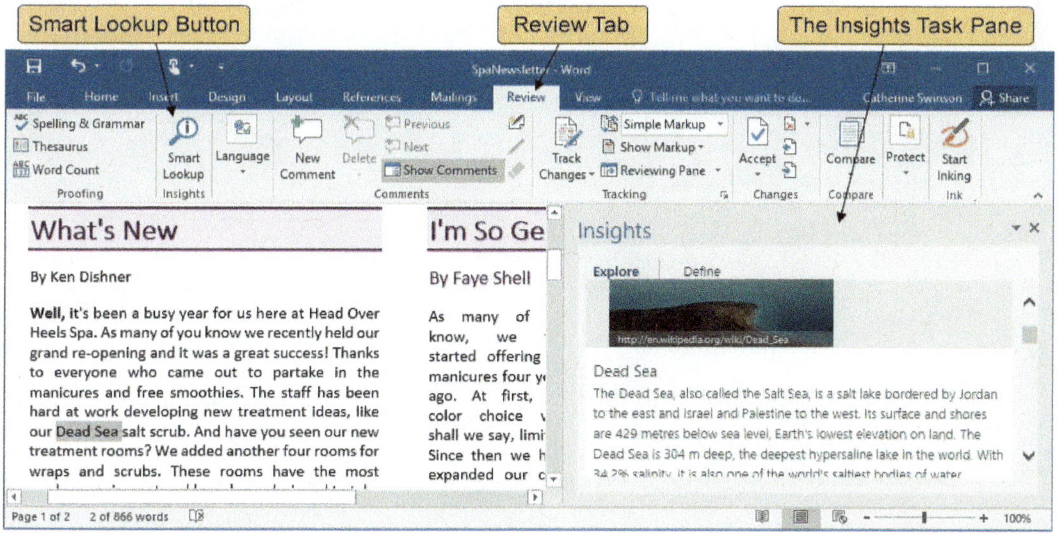

FIGURE OF 1.21

tips & tricks

You can also display the *Insights* task pane from the *Tell Me* box. First, type the word or phrase you want more information on in the *Tell Me* box at the top of the screen. Click the **Smart Lookup on** link on the menu. The *Insights* task pane opens with the information displayed.

tell me **more**

The *Insights* task pane displays results from Wikipedia at the top of the pane. It will also return images found through a Bing image search and other sources on the Web.

let me **try** *Live!*

If you do not have the data file from the previous skill open, open the student data file
of1-SpaNewsletter and try this skill on your own:

1. Select the words **Dead Sea** in the middle of the first paragraph of the newsletter.
2. Display the **Insights** task pane.
3. Review the information on the *Explore* tab.
4. Click the **X** in the upper right corner of the task pane to close it.
5. Close the file.

Skill 1.9 Working in Protected View

When you download a file from a location that Office considers potentially unsafe, it opens automatically in **Protected View**. Protected View provides a read-only format that protects your computer from becoming infected by a virus or other malware. Potentially unsafe locations include the Internet, e-mail messages, or a network location. Files that are opened in Protected View display a warning in the Message Bar at the top of the window, below the Ribbon.

To disable Protected View, click the **Enable Editing** button in the Message Bar.

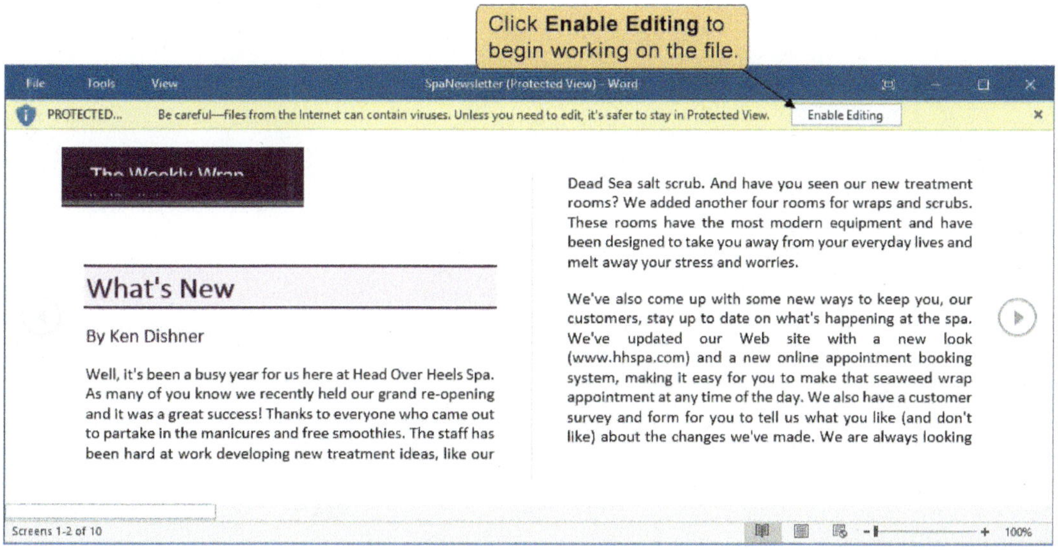

FIGURE OF 1.22

You can also enable editing from the *Info* page in Backstage view.

1. Click the **File** tab to open Backstage view.
2. Click **Info**.
3. The *Info* page provides more information about the file. If you are sure you want to remove it from Protected View, click the **Enable Editing** button.

tips & tricks

To learn more about the security settings in Office 2016, open the Trust Center and review the options. To open the Trust Center, click the **File** tab and select **Options**. In the *Options* dialog, click **Trust Center** on the left side of the dialog. We do not recommend changing any of the default Trust Center settings.

let me try *Live!*

Open the student data file **of1-SpaNewsletter** and try this skill on your own:

1. If you downloaded the file from the Internet, the file will open in Protected View.
2. Click the **Enable Editing** button to begin working with the file.
3. Navigate to the second page of the document.
4. Close the file.

Skill 1.10 Picking Up Where You Left Off

When you are working in a long document or a presentation and reopen it to work on it, you may not remember where you were last working. The **Pick up where you left off**feature automatically bookmarks the last location that was worked on when the file was closed.

To pick up where you left off in a document or presentation:

1. Open the document or presentation.
2. A message displays on the right side of the screen welcoming you back and asking if you want to pick up where you left off. The message then minimizes to a bookmark tag.
3. Click the **bookmark tag** to navigate to the location.

FIGURE OF 1.23

tips & tricks

The bookmark tag displays only until you navigate to another part of the document. If you scroll the document, the bookmark tag disappears.

tell me more

The bookmark tag is available only in Word and PowerPoint. This feature is not necessary in Excel, since Excel automatically opens to the last active cell position when the workbook was last closed.

let me try *Live!*

Open the student data file **of1-SpaNewsletter** and try this skill on your own:

1. Navigate to the last location of the file when it was last closed.
2. If you will be moving on to the next skill in this chapter, leave the document open to continue working. If not, close the file.

Skill 1.11 Working with File Properties

File Properties provide information about a file such as the location of the file, the size of file, when the file was created and when it was last modified, the title, and the author. Properties also include keywords, referred to as **tags**, that are useful for grouping common files together or for searching. All this information about a file is referred to as **metadata**.

To view a file's properties:

1. Click the **File** tab to open Backstage view.
2. Properties are listed at the far right of the *Info* page.
3. To add keywords to a file, click the text box next to *Tags* and type keywords that describe the file, separating each word with a comma.

The Author property is added automatically using the account name entered when you installed and registered Office. You can change the author name or add more names by editing the Author property.

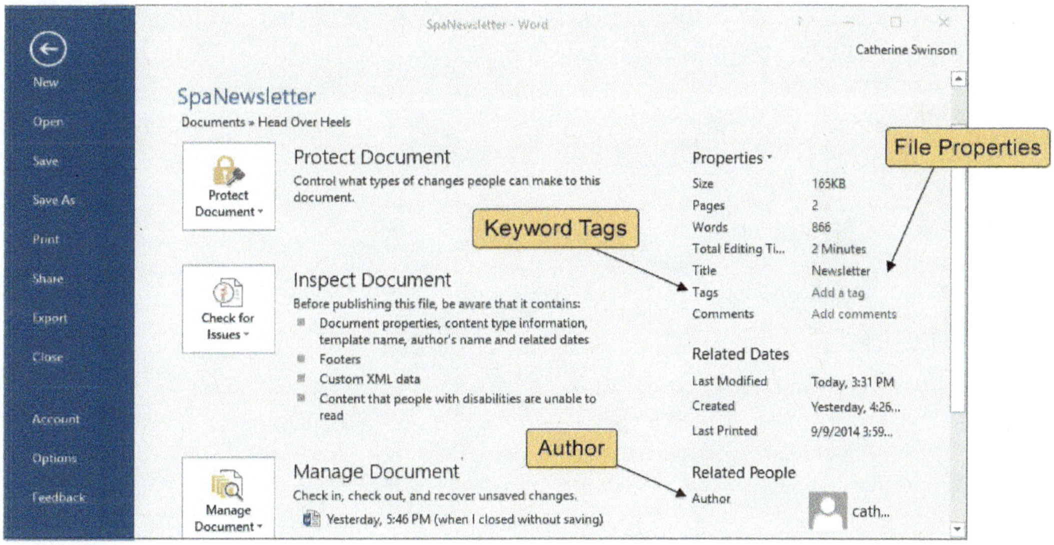

FIGURE OF 1.24

tips & tricks

Some file properties are generated automatically by Windows and cannot be edited by the user, such as the date the file was created and the size of the file.

let me try *Live!*

If you do not have the data file from the previous skill open, open the student data file **of1-SpaNewsletter** and try this skill on your own:

1. Add a tag to the document that reads **newsletter**.
2. If you will be moving on to the next skill in this chapter, leave the document open to continue working. If not, close the file.

Skill 1.12 Creating a New Blank File

When you first open an Office application, the *Start* page displays giving you the opportunity to open an existing file or create a new blank file or one based on a template. But what if you have a file open and want to create another new file? Will you need to close the application and then launch it again? The **New command** allows you to create new files without exiting and reopening the program.

To create a new blank file:

1. Click the **File** tab to open Backstage view.
2. Click **New**.
3. The first option on the *New* page is a blank file. Click the **Blank document** thumbnail to create the new blank file.

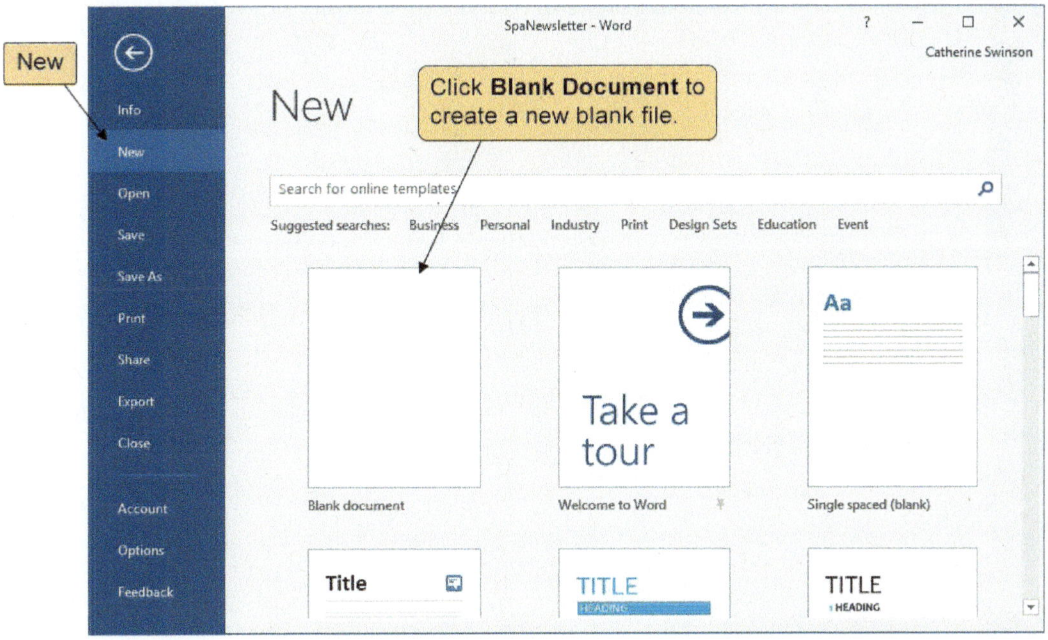

FIGURE OF 1.25

tell me more

In addition to a blank file, you can create new files from templates from the *New* page.

another method

To bypass the Backstage view and create a new blank file, press insert Ctrl + N on the keyboard.

let me try *Live!*

If you do not have the data file from the previous skill open, open the student data file
of1-SpaNewsletter and try this skill on your own:

1. Create a new blank file.
2. If you will be moving on to the next skill in this chapter, leave the document open to continue working. If not, close the file.

Skill 1.13 Saving Files to Your PC

As you work on a new file, it is displayed on-screen and stored in your computer's memory. However, it is not permanently stored until you save it as a file to a specific location. The first time you save a file, the *Save As* page in Backstage view will display. Here you can choose to save the file to your OneDrive, your local computer, or another location.

To save a file to your PC:

1. Click the **Save** button on the Quick Access Toolbar.
2. The *Save As* page in Backstage view appears.
3. On the left side of the page, click **This PC** to save the file to a local drive.
4. At the top of the right side of the page, you will see the name of the folder the file will be saved in. If you want to save the file in this location, type the name of the file in the *Enter file name here* box and click the **Save** button.

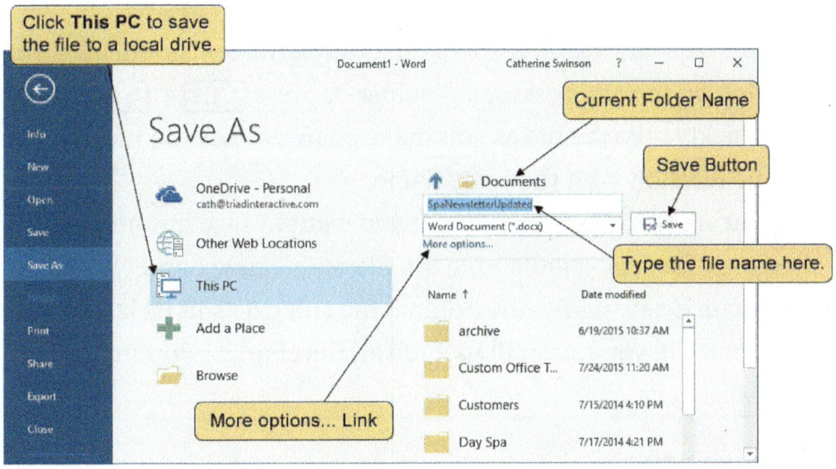

FIGURE OF 1.26

To save the file to a new folder:

1. On the *Save As* page, click the **More options...** link under the *Enter file name here* box.
2. The *Save As* dialog opens.
3. If you want to create a new folder, click the **New Folder** button near the top of the file list. The new folder is created with the temporary name *New Folder*. Type the new name for the folder and press Enter.
4. Double-click the folder to open it.
5. Click in the **File name** box and type a file name.
6. Click the **Save** button.

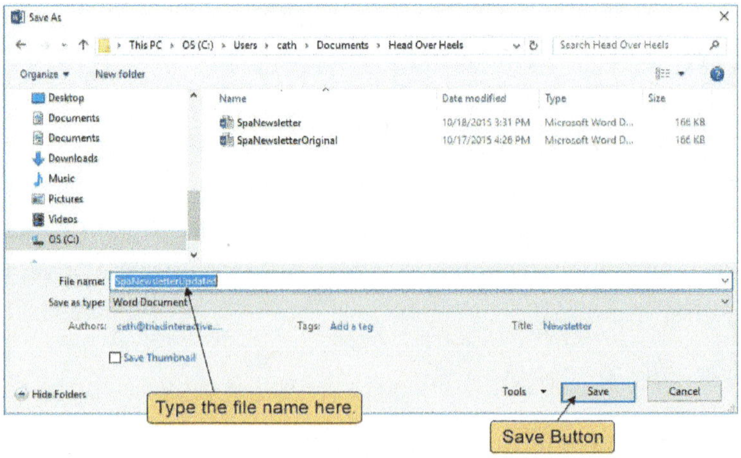

FIGURE OF 1.27

tips & tricks

- If the location where you want to save the file is not listed on the right side of the *Save As* page, click the **Browse** button to open the *Save As* dialog. Navigate to the location where you want to save the file.
- If you are working on a file that has already been saved, click the **Save** button on the Quick Access Toolbar or press Ctrl + S on the keyboard to quickly save the file as you make changes. The file will be saved to the same location with the same name.
- If you are working on a file that you want to save but not overwrite the original file, you should save the file with a new name. When you save a file with a new name, the original file still exists in its last saved state and the new file you save will include all the changes you made.

another method

To save a file, you can also:

- Press Ctrl + S on the keyboard.
- Click the **File** tab, and then select **Save**.
- Click the **File** tab, and then select **Save As**.

let me try *Live!*

If you do not have the data file from the previous skill open, create a new blank document and try this skill on your own:

1. Save the file to a new folder inside the **Documents** folder. Name the new folder **`Newsletters`**.
2. Name the file **`SpaNewsletterUpdated`**.
3. Close the file.

Skill 1.14 Saving Files to OneDrive

OneDrive is Microsoft's free cloud storage where you can save documents, workbooks, presentations, videos, pictures, and other files and access those files from any computer or share the files with others. When you save files to your OneDrive, they are stored locally on your computer and then "synched" with your OneDrive account and stored in the "cloud" where you can then access the files from another computer or device that has OneDrive capability.

To save a file to your OneDrive:

1. Click the **File** tab.
2. Click **Save As**.
3. Verify the OneDrive account is selected on the left side of the page.
4. A list of OneDrive folders appears on the right. Click the **folder** you want to save to.
5. Type the name of the file in the *Enter file name here* box and click the **Save** button.

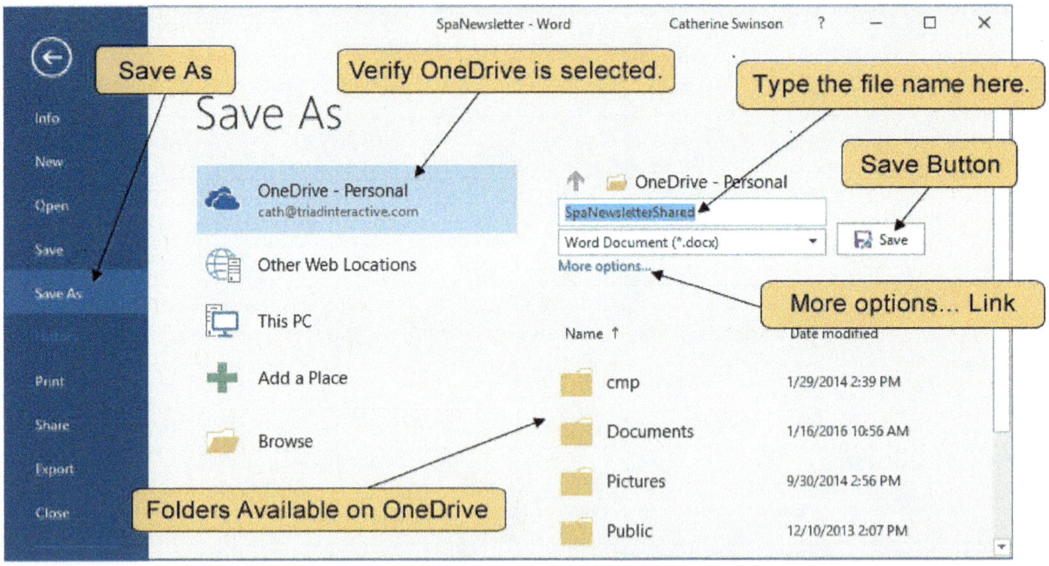

FIGURE OF 1.28

You can also save the file through the *Save As* dialog:

1. On the *Save As* page, click the **More options...** link under the *Enter file name here* box.
2. The *Save As* dialog opens to your OneDrive folder location on your computer.
3. Click in the **File name** box and type a file name.
4. Click the **Save** button.

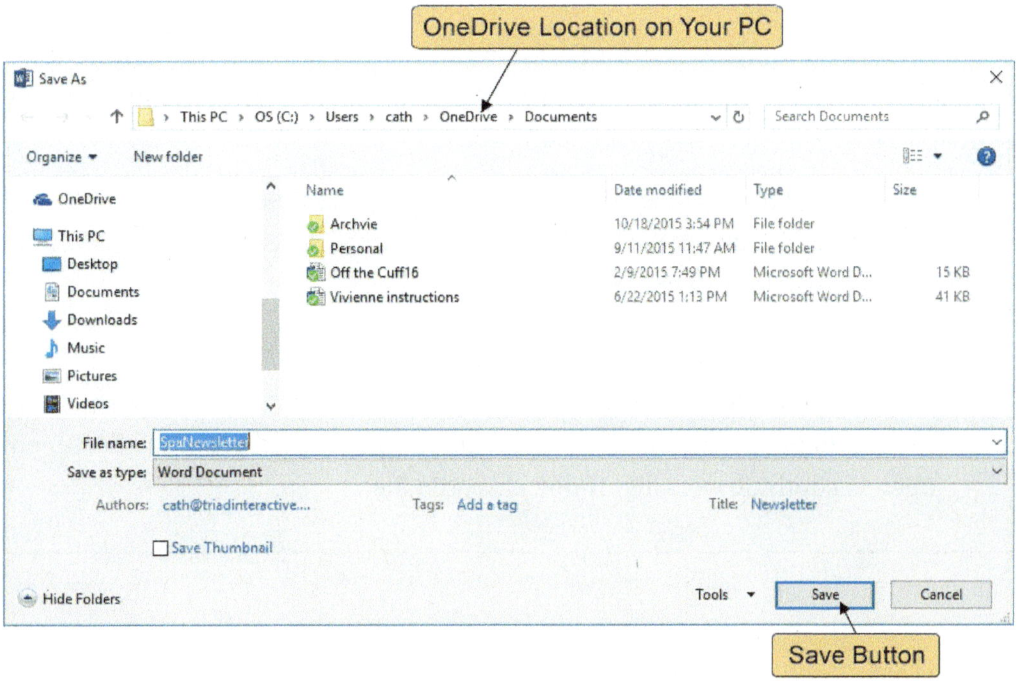

FIGURE OF 1.29

tips & tricks

By default, your OneDrive includes folders for documents, pictures, and files you want to make public. You can save your files in any of these folders or create your own. To create a new folder in your OneDrive, click the **New Folder** button near the top of the file list in the *Save As* dialog. The new folder is created with the temporary name *New Folder*. Type the new name for the folder and press Enter.

tell me more

When you are working on a file that has been saved to your OneDrive, others can work on the file at the same time as you. The application will mark the area being worked on as read only so others cannot modify the same information you are working on.

let me try *Live!*

Open the student data file **of1-SpaNewsletter** and try this skill on your own:

NOTE: You will need a OneDrive account to complete this exercise. In addition, if you are using this in class or in your school's computer lab, check with your instructor before completing this exercise.

1. Save the file to the **Documents** folder on your OneDrive.
2. Name the file `SpaNewsletterShared`.
3. If you will be moving on to the next skill in this chapter, leave the document open to continue working. If not, close the file.

Skill 1.15 Sharing Files using OneDrive

One of the benefits of saving files to your OneDrive is the ability to share files with others. The first step in sharing a file using OneDrive is to save the file to your OneDrive folder. To learn how to save a file to a OneDrive account, see *Saving Files to OneDrive*. Once the file is saved to your OneDrive, you can share it with others from the Ribbon.

To share a file using OneDrive:

1. Click the **Share** button at the far right side of the Ribbon next to the user profile name.
2. The *Share* task pane displays.
3. Type the e-mail address of the person you want to share the file with in the *Invite people* box.
4. Click the drop-down arrow under the box and select whether the recipient(s) can edit or only view the file.
5. If you want to include a note to the recipient(s), click in the message box and a type a message.
6. Click the **Share** button.

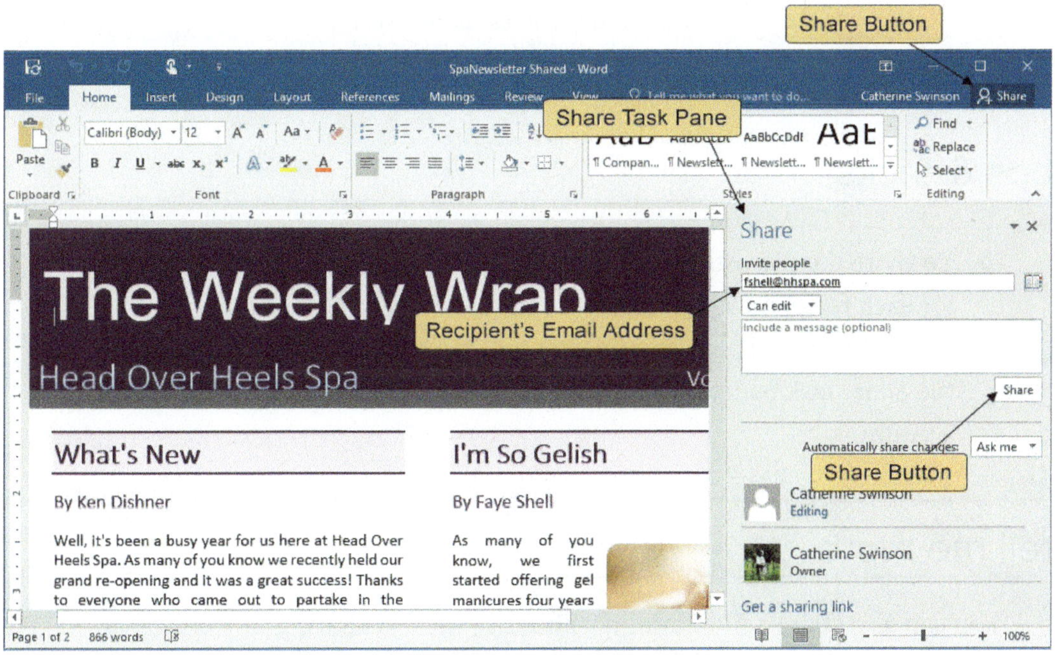

FIGURE OF 1.30

REAL-TIME COLLABORATION IN WORD

When you share Word documents through OneDrive, multiple people can work on a file at the same time and all the changes are made to one file. When people work on a shared document, Office locks any section of the file currently being worked on. This prevents overlapping changes when multiple people are working on the same file.

The *Share* button above the Ribbon displays the number of users editing the file in real time. Click the **Share** button to display the *Share* task pane to see who is editing the document. Word marks the area being worked on by others and displays a flag at the site of the change with the user's name.

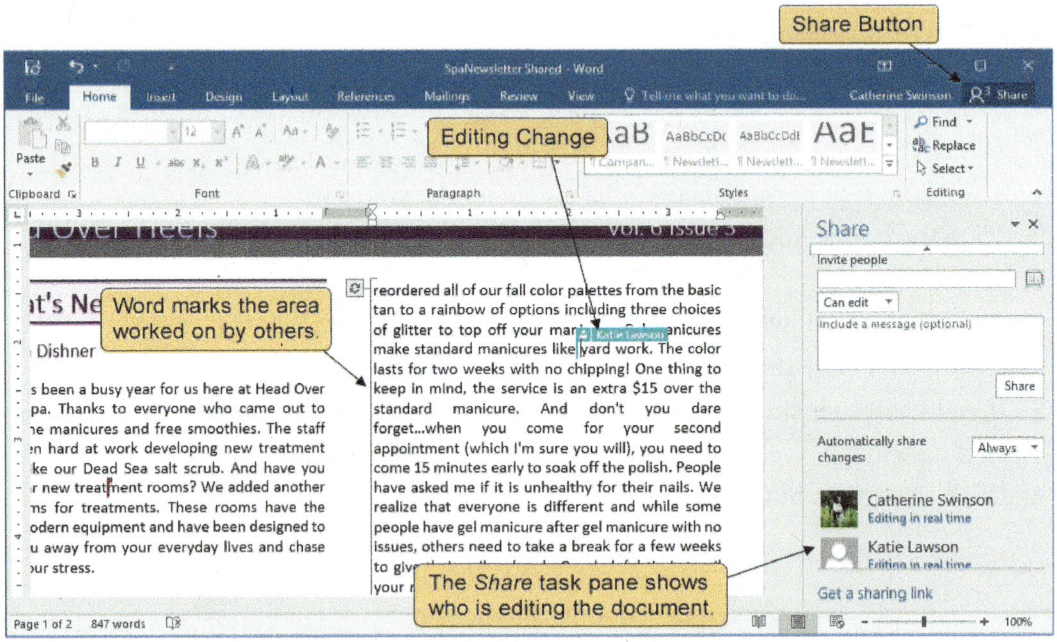

FIGURE OF 1.31

tips & tricks

- To share the file with more than one person, enter the e-mail addresses for each recipient separated by a comma.
- If the file has not been shared, you will see a **Save to Cloud** button in the *Share* task pane. Click the button to save the file to your OneDrive account.

tell me more

You can also share a file through a **sharing link**. A sharing link creates a link on your OneDrive that others can access to either view or edit the file. Click the **Get a sharing link** option at the bottom of the *Share* task pane to create a sharing link you can send to others.

another method

To open the *Share* task pane, you can also:

1. Click the **File** tab.
2. Click **Share**.
3. Verify *Share with People* is selected on the left side of the page. Click the **Share with People** button on the right side of the page.

let me try *Live!*

If you do not have the data file from the previous skill open, open a file you have saved to your OneDrive account and try this skill on your own:

NOTE: You will need a OneDrive account to complete this exercise. In addition, if you are using this in class or in your school's computer lab, check with your instructor before completing this exercise.

1. Display the **Share** task pane.
2. Share the document with **fshell@hhspa.com** and include the message **`Please review and edit.`** The recipient should be able to edit the document.
3. If you will be moving on to the next skill in this chapter, leave the document open to continue working. If not, close the file.

Skill 1.16 Using the Account Page

In the upper right corner of any Office application, you will see the name of the person who is currently logged into Office. The **Account page** lists more information for that user. This account information comes from the Microsoft account you used when installing Office. From the *Account* page, you can view your Microsoft user profile, switch between user accounts, view your product information, and connect to online services, such as Twitter and YouTube.

To view user information:

1. Click the **File** tab.
2. Click **Account**.
3. The current user profile is listed under *User Information*.

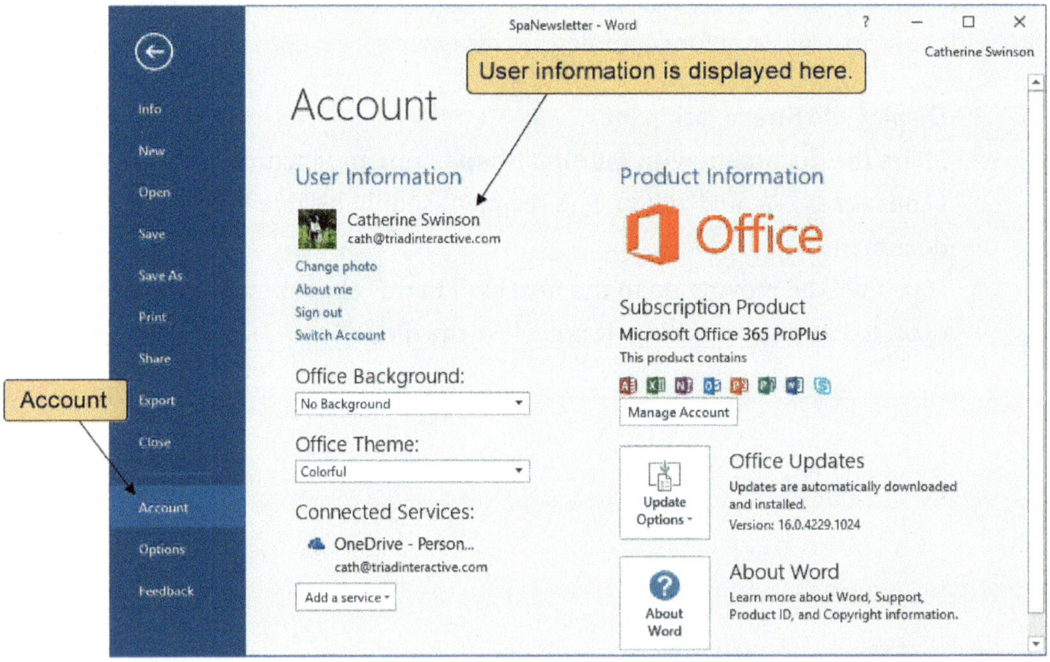

FIGURE OF 1.32

There are a number of connected services that you can add to your Office account. A **connected service** is an online service that you can access directly from an Office application. Connected services allow you to add images and videos from your favorite sites such as YouTube or Flickr, store files on online storage sites such as OneDrive and SharePoint, and share files on social media sites such as Twitter and Facebook.

To add a service to Office:

1. Display the **Account** page.
2. Click the **Add a Service** button at the bottom of the screen.
3. Point to a service option and select an option to add.
4. In most cases, a new window will open asking you to connect to the selected service.
5. Enter your information and follow the prompts to add the service to Office.

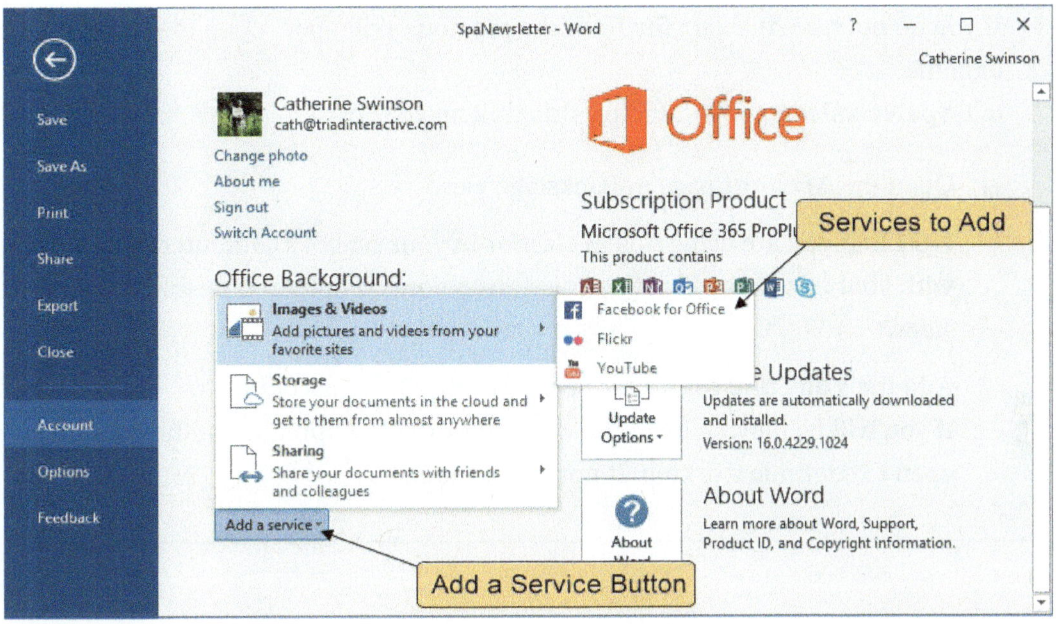

FIGURE OF 1.33

tips & tricks

Click **Change photo** or **About me** under user information to navigate to *live.com* where you can change the image that appears with the user profile and change information for that user as well.

tell me more

Depending on the version of Office 2016 you have, multiple accounts can use the same installation of Office. When you switch accounts, any personalization that person has done to Office will be applied. The account will also have access to that person's OneDrive account and all files that have been saved there.

another method

To display the *Account* page, you can also click the user name in the upper right corner of the window and select the **Account Settings** link.

let me try *Live!*

If you do not have the data file from the previous skill open, open the student data file
of1-SpaNewsletter and try this skill on your own:

1. Open the **Account** page in Backstage view.

   NOTE: If you are using this in class or in your school's computer lab, check with your instructor about permissions before completing the following steps.

2. Add the **YouTube** connected service to the Office account.
3. If you will be moving on to the next skill in this chapter, leave the document open to continue working. If not, close the file.

Skill 1.17 Changing the Look of Office

In addition to managing the Office account, you can also control the look of Office from the *Account* page. Changing the **Office background** changes the background image that displays in the upper right corner of the window near the user profile. Changing the **Office theme** changes the color scheme for Office, affecting the look of the Ribbon, task panes, and main working areas.

To change the look of Office:

1. Click the **File** tab to open Backstage view.
2. Click **Account**.
3. Click the **Office Background** drop-down list and select an option to display as the background.
4. Click the **Office Theme** drop-down list and select a color option for your applications.

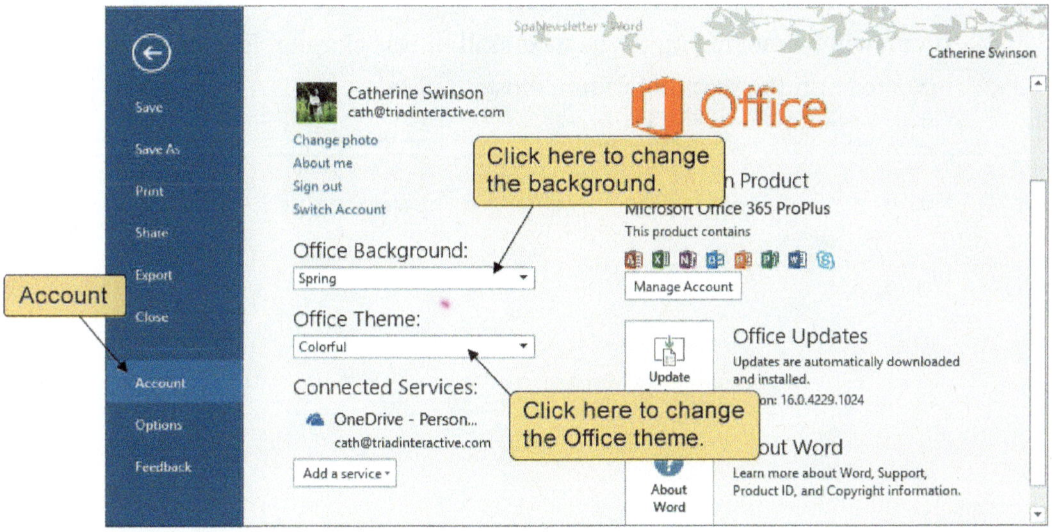

FIGURE OF 1.34

tell me more

In Office 2016, Microsoft added a number of new backgrounds and themes for Office. The new default theme is the *Colorful* theme. This theme recolors parts of the user interface to match the color of the application. For example, in Word the area above the Ribbon appears blue when the *Colorful* theme is applied.

another method

To display the *Account* page, you can also click the user name in the upper right corner of the window and select the **Account Settings** link.

let me try *Live!*

If you do not have the data file from the previous skill open, open the student data file
of1-SpaNewsletter and try this skill on your own:

1. Open the **Account** page in Backstage view.

   NOTE: If you are using this in class or in your school's computer lab, check with your instructor about permissions before completing the following steps.

2. Change the Office background to the **Spring** background.
3. Change the Office theme to **Colorful**.
4. If you will be moving on to the next skill in this chapter, leave the document open to continue working. If not, close the file.

Skill 1.18 Customizing the Quick Access Toolbar

The Quick Access Toolbar gives you a fast way to access commands that you use often. By default, the Quick Access Toolbar displays the *Save*, *Undo*, and *Redo* commands. If you use different commands often, you can add commands to and remove commands from the Quick Access Toolbar.

To modify the Quick Access Toolbar:

1. Click the **Customize Quick Access Toolbar** button located on the right side of the Quick Access Toolbar.
2. Options with checkmarks next to them are already displayed on the toolbar. Options with no checkmarks are not currently displayed.
3. Click an option to add it to or remove it from the Quick Access Toolbar.

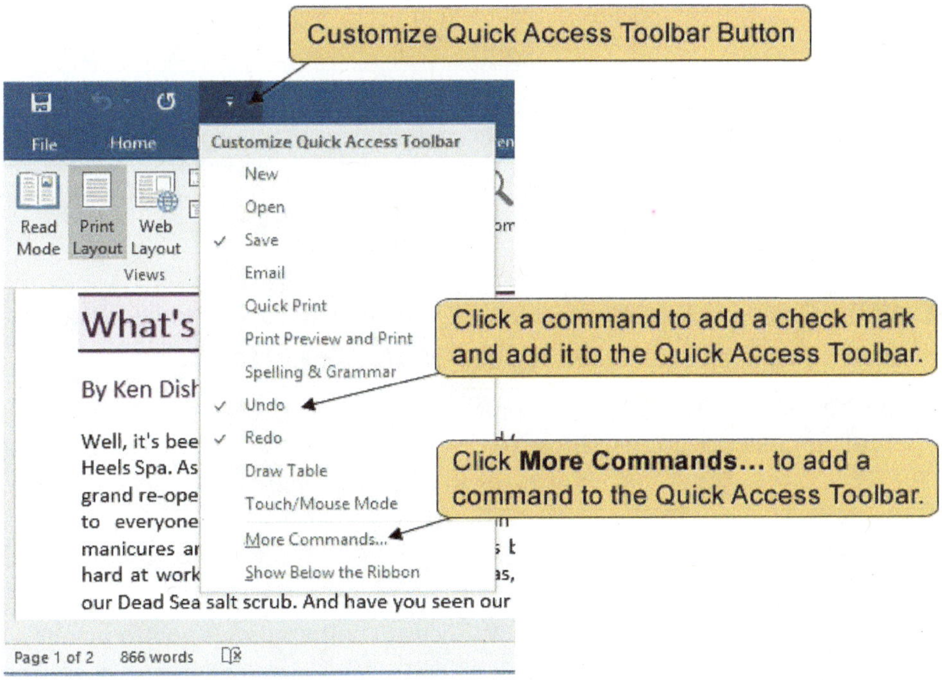

FIGURE OF 1.35

If a command does not appear on the *Quick Access Toolbar* list, you can still add it to the Quick Access Toolbar:

1. Click the **Customize Quick Access Toolbar** button and select **More Commands...**
2. The *Options* dialog opens to the *Customize the Quick Access Toolbar* page.

3. Scroll the list of popular commands or expand the **Choose commands from** list and select an option.
4. Select the command you want to appear on the Quick Access Toolbar and click the **Add** button.
5. You can reorder commands by selecting a command in the list and using the **Move Up** and **Move Down** buttons.
6. When you are finished customizing the Quick Access Toolbar, click **OK**.

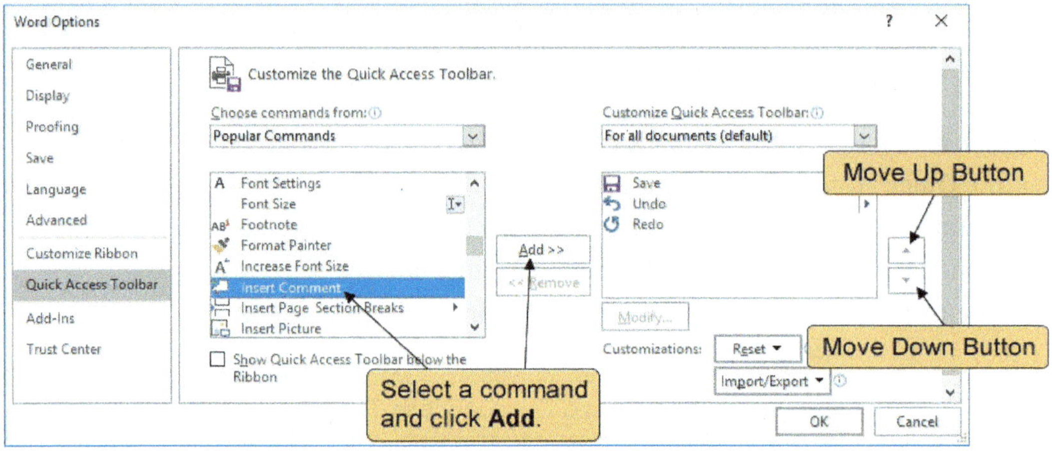

FIGURE OF 1.36

tips & tricks

To reset the Quick Access Toolbar to its original state:

1. In the *Options* dialog, *Customize the Quick Access Toolbar* page, click the **Reset** button and select **Reset only Quick Access Toolbar**.
2. A message displays to verify that you want to reset the Quick Access Toolbar customizations. Click **Yes**.

tell me more

The **Quick Print** option on the Quick Access Toolbar allows you to print with a single mouse click. If you do not need to change any print settings, this is by far the easiest method to print a file because it doesn't require opening Backstage view first.

another method

To open the *Customize Quick Access Toolbar* page:

- Click the **File** tab and click **Options** to open the *Options* dialog. Click **Quick Access Toolbar**.
- Right-click the **Quick Access Toolbar** and select **Customize Quick Access Toolbar...**

let me try *Live!*

If you do not have the data file from the previous skill open, open the student data file
of1-SpaNewsletter and try this skill on your own:

NOTE: If you are using this in class or in your school's computer lab, check with your instructor about permissions before completing the following steps.

1. Add the **Quick Print** command to the Quick Access Toolbar.
2. Open the **Word Options** dialog to the *Quick Access Toolbar* page.
3. Add the **Insert Comment** command to the Quick Access Toolbar.
4. Close the file.

key terms

- Microsoft Word
- Microsoft Excel
- Microsoft PowerPoint
- Microsoft Access
- Start page
- Ribbon
- Tab
- Groups
- Contextual tabs
- Home tab
- File tab
- Backstage view
- Keyboard shortcuts
- Shortcut menus
- Mini toolbar
- Quick Access Toolbar
- ScreenTip
- Enhanced ScreenTip
- Live Preview
- Office Help
- Smart Lookup
- Protected View
- File Properties
- Tags
- Metadata
- New command
- OneDrive
- Account page

concept review

1. Which Microsoft Office application is a spreadsheet program?
   a. Word
   b. Excel
   c. Access
   d. PowerPoint
2. Which tab do you click to display Backstage view?
   a. File
   b. Home
   c. View
   d. Contextual
3. To display a shortcut menu ________________ an area of the file.
   a. left-click
   b. right-click
   c. double-click
   d. drag over
4. If you have downloaded a file from the Internet and it opens in Protected View, you should never open the file.
   a. true
   b. false
5. Which part of the Office interface is located across the top of the application window and organizes common features and commands into tabs.
   a. Menu bar
   b. Toolbar
   c. Title bar
   d. Ribbon
6. The ________________ provide(s) information about a file such as the location of the file, the size of file, when the file was created and when it was last modified, the title, and the author.
   a. file properties
   b. user profile
   c. account information
   d. Options dialog
7. When you save files to your OneDrive, they are available to access from other computers that have OneDrive capability. If you are working on an Excel or Word file, others can be working on the same file at the same time you are working on the file.

a. true
b. false

8. You can change user information from which page in Backstage view?
   a. Account
   b. Options
   c. Share
   d. Info
9. Which keyboard shortcut allows you to paste an item from the *Clipboard*?
   a. Ctrl + C
   b. Ctrl + X
   c. Ctrl + V
   d. Ctrl + P
10. Which part of the Office interface gives you quick one-click access to common commands and is located at the top of the application window above the *File* tab?
   a. Ribbon
   b. Quick Access Toolbar
   c. *Options* dialog
   d. Backstage view

chapter 1

Getting Started with Excel 2016

In this chapter, you will learn the following skills:

- Identify the elements of a Microsoft Excel 2016 workbook
- Navigate a workbook
- Enter and format text, numbers, and dates in cells
- Enter simple formulas
- Understand relative and absolute cell references
- Understand the concept of a function
- Use AutoSum and the Quick Analysis tool to add totals
- Use the status bar to display totals and other values
- Change the zoom level to view more or less of the worksheet
- Create a new workbook from a template
- Arrange multiple workbook windows
- Spell check a worksheet
- Preview and print a worksheet

introduction

This chapter provides you with the basic skills necessary to start working with Excel 2016. The first step is to become familiar with the Excel interface and learn how to navigate a workbook. Next, you'll learn how to enter data and apply simple number and date formats. This chapter introduces the concepts of formulas, functions, and absolute and relative references. Pay close attention to the skill *Understanding Absolute and Relative References*. These concepts are used throughout Excel. You will add totals to worksheet data using the SUM function with a variety of methods including AutoSum and the Quick Analysis tool. To help you start using Excel for your own purposes, you will learn how to create a new workbook from a template and how to manage multiple workbooks at the same time. Finally, the chapter covers how to check a worksheet for spelling errors and how to preview and print.

Skill 1.1 Introduction to Excel 2016

Microsoft Excel 2016 is a spreadsheet program in which you enter, manipulate, calculate, and chart numerical and text data. An Excel file is referred to as a **workbook**, which is a collection of worksheets. Each worksheet (also called a "sheet") is made up of rows and columns of data on which you can perform calculations. It's these calculations that make Excel such a powerful tool. Some of the basic elements of a Microsoft Excel workbook include:

- **Worksheet** — an electronic ledger in which you enter data. The worksheet appears as a grid where you can enter and then manipulate data using functions, formulas, and formatting. Excel workbooks have one worksheet by default named *Sheet1*. You can rename, add, and delete worksheets as necessary.
- **Row** — a horizontal group of cells. Rows are identified by numbers. For example, the third row is labeled with the number *3*.
- **Column** — a vertical group of cells. Columns are identified by letters. For example, the fourth column is labeled with the letter *D*.
- **Cell** — the intersection of a column and a row. A cell is identified by the **cell address** — its column and row position. For example, the cell at the intersection of column D and row 3 has a cell address of *D3*.
- **Cell range** — a contiguous group of cells. A cell range is identified by the address of the cell in the upper left corner of the range, followed by a colon, and then the address of the cell in the lower right corner of the range. The cell range *B3:B5* includes cells B3, B4, and B5. A cell range can incorporate multiple columns and rows as long as the cells are all contiguous. The range *B3:D5* includes cells B3, B4, B5, C3, C4, C5, D3, D4, and D5.
- **Formula bar** — data entry area directly below the Ribbon and above the worksheet grid. Although you can type any data in the formula bar, the *Insert Function* button at the left side of the formula bar was designed to make it easier to create complex formulas.
- **Name box** — appears at the left side of the formula bar and displays the address of the selected cell. If a group of cells is selected, the *Name* box displays the address of the first cell in the group.
- **Status bar** — appears at the bottom of the worksheet grid and can display information about the selected data, including the number of cells selected that contain data (count) and the average and sum (total) of the selected values.

You can use Excel for a wide variety of purposes, from calculating payments for a personal loan, to creating a budget, to tracking cash flow for your business. Excel is not limited to numerical calculations.

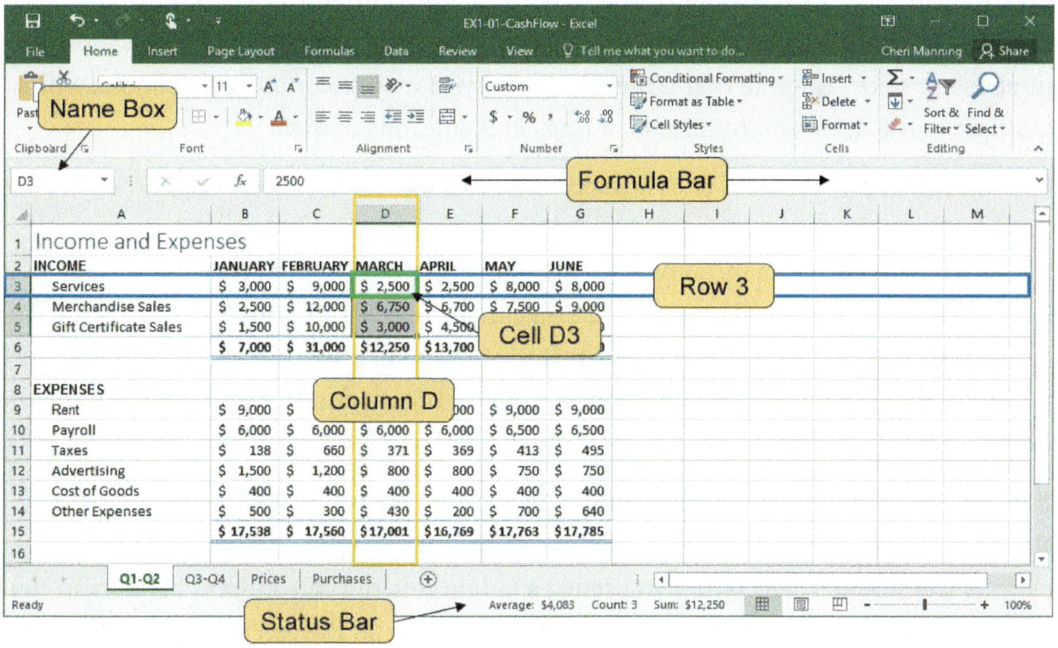

FIGURE EX 1.1

let me try *Live!*

Open the student data file **EX1-01-CashFlow** and explore the Excel workbook on your own:

1. If necessary, click the **Q1-Q2** worksheet tab at the bottom of the workbook.
2. Click anywhere in **column D**.
3. Click anywhere in **row 3**.
4. Click cell **D3**.
5. Click the **formula bar**.
6. Click the **Name box**.
7. Click the **status bar**.
8. If you will be moving on to the next skill in this chapter, leave the workbook open to continue working. If not, save the file as directed by your instructor and close it.

Skill 1.2 Navigating a Workbook

An Excel 2016 worksheet can include more than one million rows and more than sixteen thousand columns. That's a lot of potential data to navigate! Luckily, most spreadsheets are not quite that large. However, you may encounter workbooks with multiple worksheets and hundreds of rows and columns of data.

The Excel window includes both a **vertical scroll bar** (at the right side of the window) and a **horizontal scroll bar** (at the bottom of the window). Click the arrows at the ends of the scroll bars to move up and down or left and right to see more cells in an individual worksheet. You can also click and drag the scroll box to reposition your view of the spreadsheet. Notice that when you use the scroll bars, the selected cell does not change. Using the scroll bars changes only your view of the worksheet.

The most obvious way to select a cell in a worksheet is to click it with the mouse. Notice that Excel highlights the appropriate column letter and row number to identify the selected cell. When you select a single cell, the cell address appears in the *Name* box in the upper left corner of the spreadsheet, and the cell content appears in the formula bar (immediately below the Ribbon).

To navigate to another worksheet in the workbook, click the appropriate tab at the bottom of the worksheet grid. If the worksheet tab is not visible, use the navigation arrows located at the left side of the first sheet tab to show one worksheet at a time to the left or the right. These arrows are active only when there are worksheets not visible in your current view.

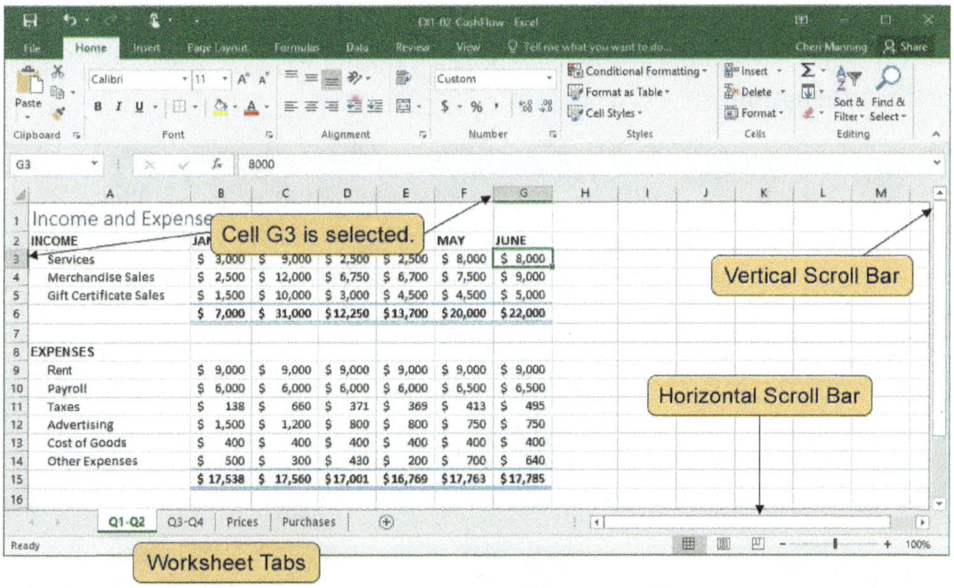

FIGURE EX 1.2

To navigate from cell to cell, use the mouse to click the cell you want to go to. You can also use keyboard shortcuts to navigate around or between worksheets.

↑	Move up one cell
↓	Move down one cell
→	Move one cell to the right
←	Move one cell to the left
Home	Move to the first cell in the row
Ctrl + Home	Go to cell A1
Ctrl + PageDown	Move one worksheet to the right
Ctrl + PageUp	Move one worksheet to the left

To select a range of cells, click the first cell in the range and drag the mouse until the cells you want are selected. Release the mouse button. You can also click the first cell in the range, press Shift, and then click the last cell in the range.

To select an entire row, point to the **row selector** (the box with the row number at the left side of the worksheet grid). When the mouse pointer changes to an arrow, click the left mouse button.

To select an entire column, point to the **column selector** (the box with the column letter at the top of the worksheet grid). When the mouse pointer changes to an arrow, click the left mouse button.

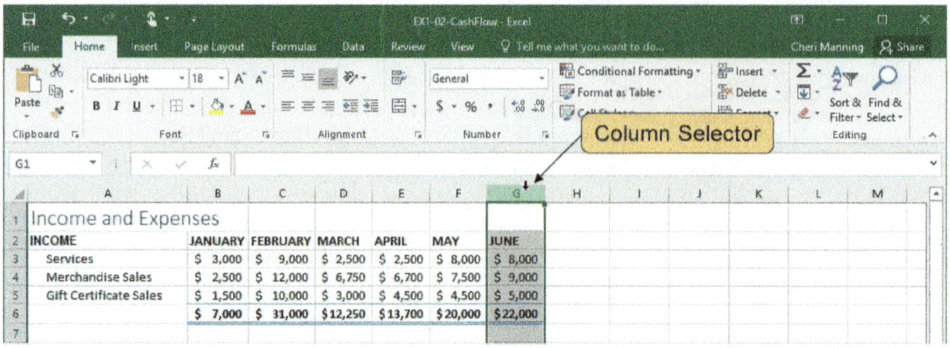

FIGURE EX 1.3

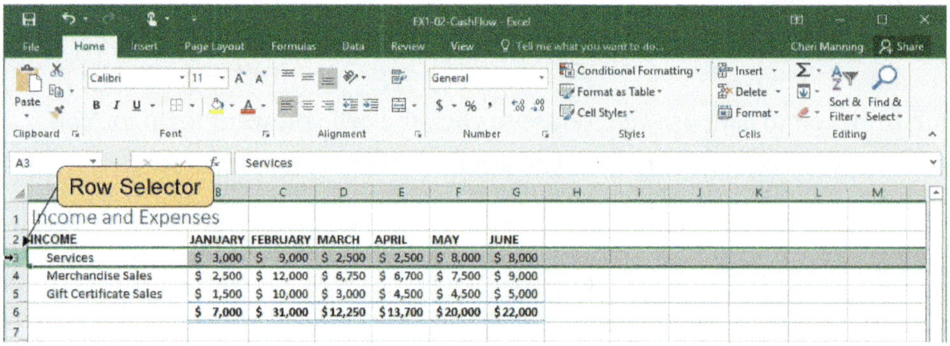

FIGURE EX 1.4

tips & tricks

To make more worksheets visible at one time, adjust the size of the horizontal scroll bar by clicking the dotted line that appears immediately to the left of the scroll bar. Notice that the cursor shape changes to a double-sided arrow. Click and drag to the right to make the horizontal scroll bar shorter and reveal more worksheet tabs.

tell me more

- Another way to navigate to a specific cell location is to type the cell address in the *Name* box, and then press Enter.
- Use the *Go To* dialog to navigate to a specific cell. On the *Home* tab, in the *Editing* group, click the **Find & Select** button and select **Go To** from the menu. In the *Reference* box, type the cell address and then click **OK**.

let me try *Live!*

If you do not have the data file from the previous skill open, open the student data file **EX1-02-CashFlow** and try this skill on your own:

1. On the *Q1-Q2* worksheet, select cell **G3**.
2. Select column **G**.
3. Select row **3**.
4. Navigate to the **Q3-Q4** worksheet.
5. Select cells **B3:G5**.
6. If you will be moving on to the next skill in this chapter, leave the workbook open to continue working. If not, save the file as directed by your instructor and close it.

from the perspective of . . .

SPORTS CLINIC OFFICE MANAGER

I couldn't do my job without Microsoft Excel. All the clinic financial data are kept in Excel spreadsheets, and I use Excel's analysis and formatting tools to visualize our cash flow. Any problem areas are easy to find. We sell rehab equipment directly to our patients, and I also use Excel to track the progress of our orders and sales.

Skill 1.3 Working in Protected View

When you download a workbook from a location that Excel considers potentially unsafe, it opens automatically in Protected View. **Protected View** provides a read-only format that protects your computer from becoming infected by a virus or other malware. Potentially unsafe locations include the Internet, e-mail messages, or a network location. Files that are opened in Protected View display a warning in the **Message Bar** at the top of the window, below the Ribbon.

To disable Protected View, click the **Enable Editing** button in the Message Bar.

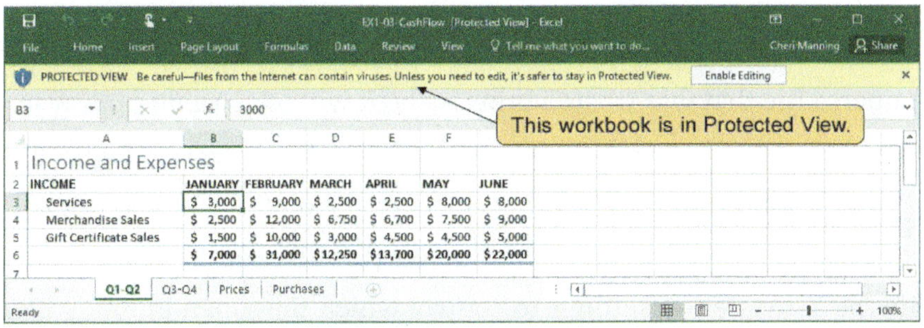

FIGURE EX 1.5

You can also enable editing from the Info page in Backstage view.

1. Click the **File** tab to open Backstage view.
2. Click **Info**.
3. The Info page provides more information about the file. If you are sure you want to remove it from Protected View, click the **Enable Editing** button.

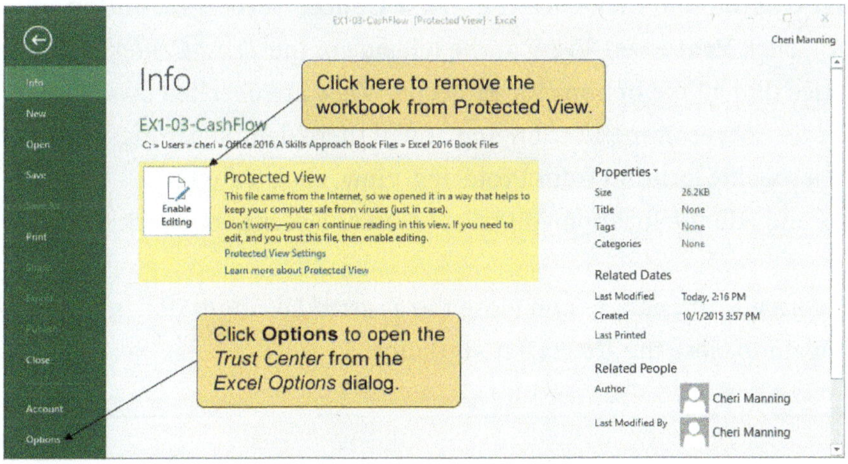

FIGURE EX 1.6

Once you enable editing for a file, it is added to the **Trusted Documents** list and will not appear in Protected View again unless you clear the *Trusted Documents* list.

To remove all files from the *Trusted Documents* list:

1. Click the **File** tab, and then click the **Options** button to open the *Excel Options* dialog.
2. Click **Trust Center**, and then click the **Trust Center Settings...** button to open the *Trust Center* dialog.
3. If necessary, click **Trusted Documents** at the left side of the *Trust Center* dialog.
4. Click the **Clear** button to clear all Trusted Documents so that they are no longer trusted.
5. Click **Yes**.
6. Click **OK** to close the *Trusted Locations* dialog.
7. Click **OK** again to close the *Excel Options* dialog.

The next time you open a file that was trusted previously, it will once again appear in Protected View.

tell me **more**

You can modify the Trust Center settings to control which files open in Protected View.

If you are currently in Protected View, the Info page will include a link to go to the Protected View settings. If you are not currently in Protected View, open the Trust Center from the *Excel Options* dialog.

1. Click the **File** tab, and then click the **Options** button to open the *Excel Options* dialog.
2. Click **Trust Center**, and then click the **Trust Center Settings...** button.
3. If necessary, click **Protected View** at the left side of the *Trust Center* dialog. Notice that all the options for Protected View are checked by default. We do not recommend changing any of these default settings.
4. To exempt a specific location from Protected View, click **Trusted Locations**, and add the location you trust (such as a secure network folder).
5. Click **OK** to save your changes and close the *Trusted Locations* dialog.
6. Click **OK** again to close the *Excel Options* dialog.

let me try *Live!*

If you do not have the data file from the previous skill open, open the student data file **EX1-03-CashFlow** and try this skill on your own:

1. This workbook came from a trusted source. If the workbook opens in Protected View, disable Protected View and allow editing.
2. Open the *Trust Center* dialog and review the settings.
3. Close the *Trust Center* and *Excel Options* dialogs without making any changes.
4. If you will be moving on to the next skill in this chapter, leave the workbook open to continue working. If not, save the file as directed by your instructor and close it.

Skill 1.4 Entering and Editing Text and Numbers in Cells

The most basic task in Excel is entering data in your workbook. Entering numerical data is as easy as typing a number in a cell. Numbers can be displayed as dates, currency values, percentages, or other formats. (Later skills discuss number formatting and using functions and formulas to automate numerical calculations.)

Excel is not just about numbers, though. Without text headers, descriptions, and instructions, your workbook would consist of numbers and formulas without any structure. Adding text headers to your rows and columns creates the structure for you to enter data into your workbook.

To enter data in a cell:

1. Click the cell where you want the data to appear.
2. Type the number or text.
3. Press Enter or Tab.
   Pressing Enter after entering text will move the cursor down one cell.
   Pressing Tab will move the cursor to the right one cell.

Excel gives you different ways to edit the data in your worksheet. If you want to change the contents of the entire cell, use **Ready mode**. If you want to change only part of the cell data, use **Edit mode**. The status bar, located at the lower left corner of the Excel window, displays which mode you are in—Ready or Edit.

To use Ready mode to change text:

1. Click the cell you want to change.
2. Type the new contents for the cell.
3. Press Enter or Tab when you are finished.
4. The old contents are completely removed and replaced with what you've typed.

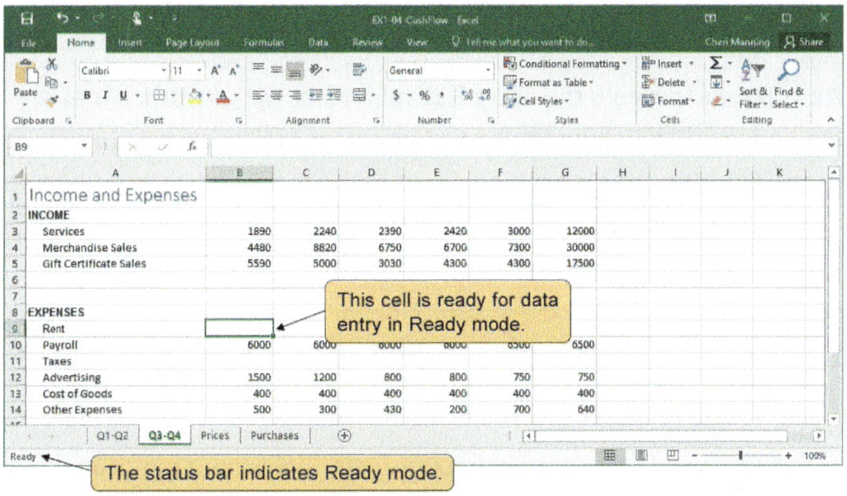

FIGURE EX 1.7

To use Edit mode to change text:

1. Double-click the cell you want to change.
2. You should now see a blinking cursor in the cell.
3. Move the cursor to the part of the entry you want to change and make your changes. Use Backspace to delete characters to the left of the cursor, use Delete to delete characters to the right of the cursor. You can also click and drag your mouse to select a section of text to delete.
4. Press Enter or Tab when you are finished making your changes.

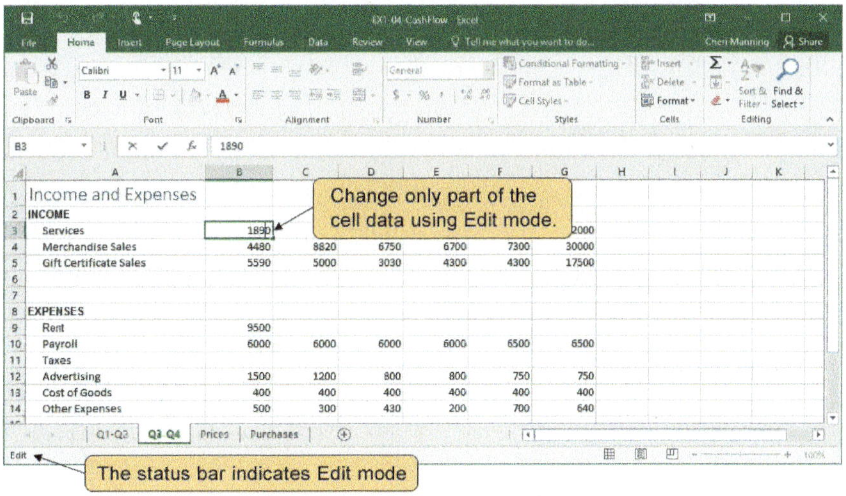

FIGURE EX 1.8

tips & tricks

To add a line break within the cell, press Alt while pressing Enter.

another method

As you type in a cell, the entry is displayed in the formula bar as well as in the active cell. Clicking the **Enter** icon next to the formula bar accepts your entry. Clicking the **Cancel** icon next to the formula bar removes your entry.

let me try *Live!*

If you do not have the data file from the previous skill open, open the student data file **EX1-04-CashFlow** and try this skill on your own:

1. On the *Q3-Q4* worksheet, add the number **9500** to cell **B9**.
2. Add the word **JULY** to cell **B2**.
3. Change the text in cell **B3** to **1870**. You can use Ready mode or Edit mode.
4. If you will be movingon to the next skill in this chapter, leave the workbook open to continue working. If not, save the file as directed by your instructor and close it.

Skill 1.5 Applying Number Formats

When you first type numbers in a worksheet, Excel applies the **General number format** automatically. The General format right-aligns numbers in the cells but does not maintain a consistent number of decimal places (43.00 will appear as 43, while 42.25 appears as 42.25) and does not display commas (so 1,123,456 appears as 1123456). For consistency, and to make your worksheet easier to read, you should apply the specific number format that is most appropriate for your data. Excel provides several number formats for you to choose from.

Figure EX 1.9 shows common Excel number formats. All numbers in row 2 contain the number 0.567. All numbers in row 3 contain the number 1234. Formatting numbers changes the appearance of the data in your worksheet but doesn't change the numerical values. The formatted number is displayed in the cell, and the actual value is displayed in the formula bar.

To apply the most common number formats, go to the *Home* tab, *Number* group, and click one of the following buttons:

$ ▾	Click the **Accounting Number Format** button to apply formatting appropriate for monetary values. The **Accounting Number Format** aligns the $ at the left side of the cell, displays two places after the decimal, and aligns all numbers at the decimal point. Zero values are displayed as dashes (-).
%	Click the **Percent Style** button to have your numbers appear as %. For example, the number .02 will appear as 2%. By default, **Percent Style format** displays zero places to the right of the decimal point.
,	Click the **Comma Style** button to apply the same format as the Accounting Number Format but without the currency symbol. **Comma Style format** is a good number format to use if your worksheet includes many rows of numbers, summed in a total row (like a budget or cash flow projection), where too many $ symbols could be distracting. Use Comma Style formatting for all numbers except the total row. Use Accounting Number Format for the total row.

Use *Increase Decimal* and *Decrease Decimal* to increase or decrease the number of digits that appear to the right of the decimal point. For example, if a cell contains the number 1.234 and you click the **Decrease Decimal** button twice, the cell will display 1.2. The formula bar will still display 1.234 because that is the number stored in the worksheet.

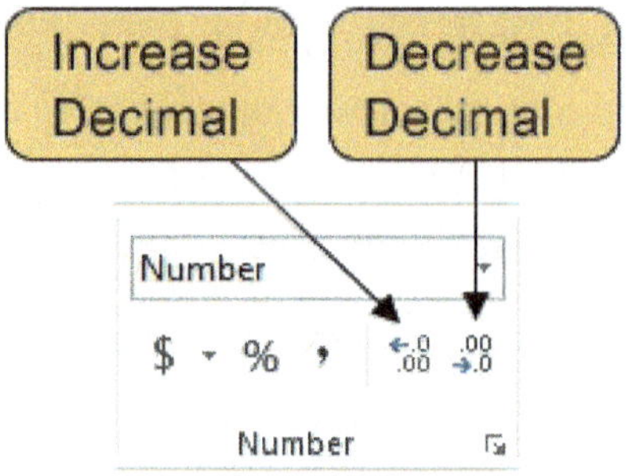

FIGURE EX 1.10

For other common number formats, click the **Number Format** arrow above the buttons in the *Number* group to display the *Number Format* menu.

Number— The default **Number format** shows two decimal places by default so 43 displays as 43.00 but does not include commas.

Currency— With the **Currency format**, columns of numbers do not align at the $ and at the decimal as they do with Accounting Number Format. Instead, the Currency format places the $ immediately to the left of the number.

Percentage— The *Percentage* option on the *Number Format* menu does not apply the same Percent Style format as clicking the *Percent Style* button. The *Percentage* option from the *Number Format* menu displays two digits to the right of the decimal.

More Number Formats...— This option opens the *Format Cells* dialog to the Number tab, where you can select from even more number formats and customize any format, including adding color, specifying the number of decimal places to display, and setting whether or not negative numbers should be enclosed in parentheses.

tips & tricks

If you type $ before a number, Excel automatically applies the Currency number format.

tell me **more**

On the *Home* tab, in the *Styles* group, click the **Cell Styles** button to expand the *Styles* gallery. At the bottom of the gallery are five number styles. Applying one of these cell styles is the same as applying a number format. However, be aware that applying the Currency cell style actually applies the Accounting Number Format, not the Currency format.

- **Comma**— applies the default Comma Style format, with two digits to the right of the decimal.
- **Comma [0]**— applies the Comma Style format, but with no digits to the right of the decimal.
- **Currency**— applies the default Accounting Number Format, with two digits to the right of the decimal.
- **Currency [0]**— applies the Accounting Number Format, but with no digits to the right of the decimal.
- **Percent**— applies the default Percent Style format.

another method

When you right-click a cell, these formats are available from the Mini toolbar: Accounting Number Format, Percent style, and Comma style.

The *Increase Decimal* and *Decrease Decimal* buttons are also available from the Mini toolbar.

To apply the Percent Style, you can use the keyboard shortcut Ctrl + Shift + 5.

let me try *Live!*

If you do not have the data file from the previous skill open, open the student data file **EX1-05-CashFlow** and try this skill on your own:

1. On the *Q3-Q4* worksheet, select cells **B3:G5**.
2. Apply the **Accounting Number Format**.
3. Modify the number format so no decimal places are visible after the decimal point.
4. Go to the **Prices** worksheet and select cells **C2:C106**.
5. Apply the **Currency** number format.
6. If you will be moving on to the next skill in this chapter, leave the workbook open to continue working. If not, save the file as directed by your instructor and close it.

Skill 1.6 Entering Dates and Applying Date Formats

When you enter numbers in a date format such as 9/5/1966 or September 5, 1966, Excel detects that you are entering a date and automatically applies one of the date formats. Excel treats dates as a special type of number, so cells formatted as dates can be used in calculations. There are many types of date formats available, but the underlying number for the date will always be the same.

There are two number formats available from the *Number Format* menu. To apply one of these formats, from the *Home* tab, click the **Number Format** arrow above the buttons in the *Number* group, and then click the format you want:

- **Short Date format**—Applies a simple format displaying the one- or two-digit number representing the month, followed by the one- or two-digit number representing the day, followed by the four-digit year 9/5/1966.
- **Long Date format**—Applies a longer format displaying the day of the week, and then the name of the month, the two-digit date, and the four-digit year Monday, September 05, 1966.

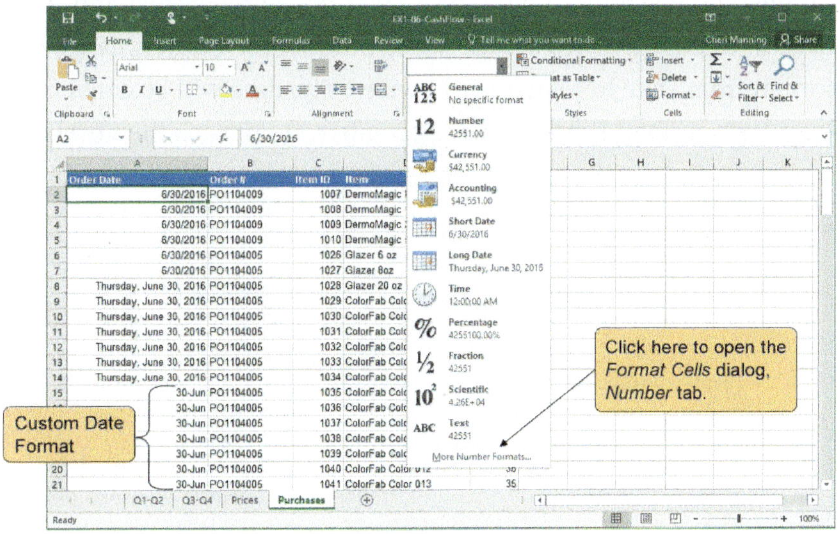

FIGURE EX 1.12

If you would like to use a different date format:

1. Select **More Number Formats...** from the *Number Format* list.
2. In the *Format Cells* dialog, from the *Number* tab, if necessary, click **Date** in the *Category* list. Excel offers a variety of prebuilt date formats to choose from.

3. Notice that as you click each format in the *Type* list, the *Sample* box shows how the active cell will display with the selected format.
4. Click the date format you would like, and click **OK**.

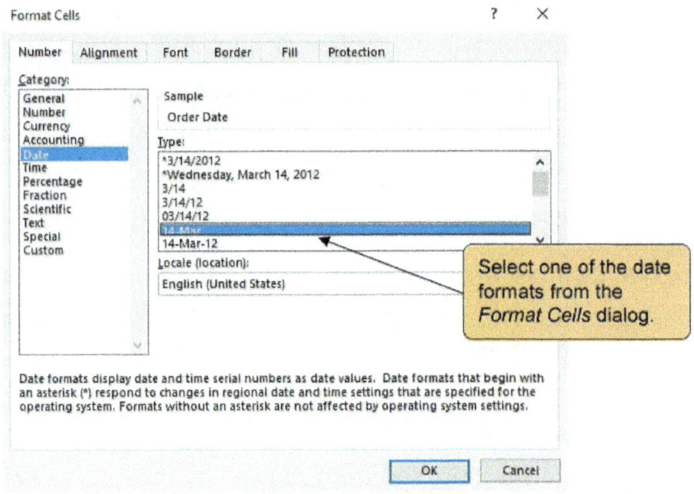

FIGURE EX 1.13

tips & tricks

Only dates from January 1, 1900, through December 31, 9999, are stored as numbers. Dates prior to January 1, 1900, are stored as text and cannot be used in calculations. To see the serial number for a date, change the cell format from Date to *General* or *Number*. The date will be converted to a "regular" number. For example, December 31, 2009, is the number 40178.

tell me **more**

Every date format can be expressed as a code. The code for the Short Date format is **m/d/yyy**. The code for the Long Date format is more complicated: **[$ -F800]dddd, mmmm dd, yyyy**. If Excel does not offer the exact date format you want to use, you can modify the date code using the Custom number option.

1. Select **More Number Formats...** from the *Number* list.
2. In the *Format Cells* dialog, from the *Number* tab, click **Custom** in the *Category* list.
3. The *Custom* list includes the code for every number format offered. Click the code for the format closest to the format you want, and then make adjustments to the code in the *Type* box. The *Sample* box shows how the number format will look in your worksheet.
4. Click **OK** to apply your new custom number format.

let me **try** ***Live!***

If you do not have the data file from the previous skill open, open the student data file **EX1-06-CashFlow** and try this skill on your own:

1. On the *Purchases* worksheet, review the date formats used in column A.
2. Select column A, and apply the **Long Date** format.
3. With column A still selected, apply the **Short Date** format.
4. With column A still selected, apply the format to display dates in the format similar to **14-Mar**.
5. If you will be moving on to the next skill in this chapter, leave the workbook open to continue working. If not, save the file as directed by your instructor and close it.

Skill 1.7 Inserting Data Using AutoFill

Use the **AutoFill** feature to fill a group of cells with the same data or to extend a data series.

With AutoFill, you can copy the same value or formula to a group of cells at once. This is much more efficient than using copy and paste over and over again.

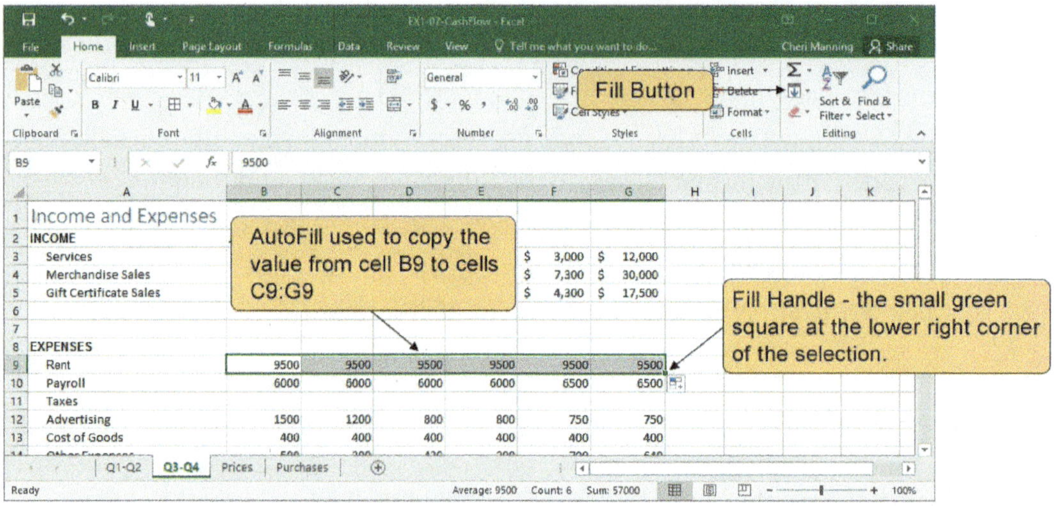

FIGURE EX 1.14

The easiest way to use AutoFill is to use the **Fill Handle** to fill data up or down in a column or to the left or right in a row.

To use the Fill Handle:

1. Select the cell(s) that contain(s) the data you want to use in the AutoFill.
2. Click and drag the **Fill Handle** in the direction you want to fill the data. The Fill Handle is the very small green square at the lower right corner of the cell(s) you selected. As you drag the Fill Handle, a tool tip appears displaying the suggested value for each highlighted cell.
3. Release the mouse button when you have highlighted the last cell you want to fill.

If you have a difficult time using the Fill Handle, use the *Fill* command from the Ribbon instead:

1. Select the entire range you want to fill, beginning with the cell(s) containing the data.
2. On the *Home* tab, in the *Editing* group, click the **Fill** button and select the type of fill you want. The options available will vary depending on the data you selected to use as the source for the fill.

If you have a group of cells with similar data in a series, AutoFill can extend the series automatically. A **data series** is any sequence of cells with a recognizable pattern like those shown in Figure EX 1.15.

	A	B	C	D	E
1	Numeric Patterns				
2	1	2	3	4	
3	3	5	7	9	
4	Student 1	Student 2	Student 3	Student 4	
5					
6	Date Patterns				
7	January	February	March	April	
8	1/1/2016	2/1/2016	3/1/2016	4/1/2016	
9	1/1/2016	1/1/2017	1/1/2018	1/1/2019	
10					

FIGURE EX 1.15

Excel attempts to detect automatically if the data appear to be a series. Sometimes, however, the series doesn't fill with the data you expect or want. To change the type of data AutoFill inserts, click the **AutoFill Options** button and select a different option. From the *AutoFill Options* button, you can choose to copy the cells or fill the series. By default, Excel includes formatting when copying or filling a series; however, you can choose to copy only the cell formatting or to fill or copy the data series without formatting.

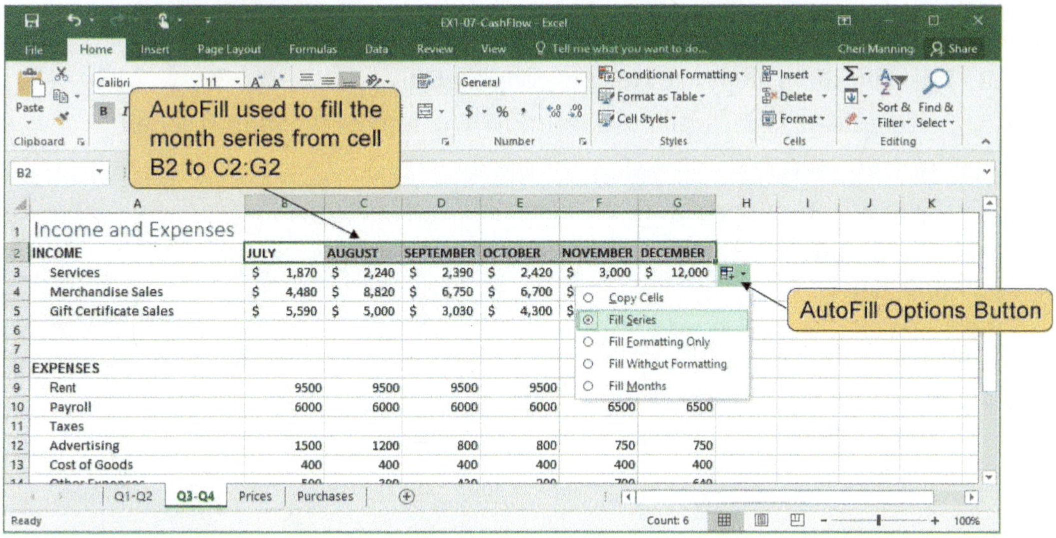

FIGURE EX 1.16

tips & tricks

Use AutoFill to enter repetitive data in your worksheet to avoid errors from entering data manually.

tell me **more**

The Fill Handle tool can be used to fill a series of dates by month as well as year. For example, if you start the series with Jan-2016 and Feb-2016, the Fill Handle will fill in the next cells with Mar-2016, Apr-2016, May-2016, and so on. When the series reaches Dec-2016, the next cell will be filled in with Jan-2017. If you are filling a series of dates, the *AutoFill Options* button will give you the options to fill by day, weekday, month, or year.

another method

1. Pressing Ctrl + D will fill the selected cell(s) with the value from the cell above it.
2. Pressing Ctrl + R will fill the selected cell(s) with the value from the cell to the left of it.

let me **try** *Live!*

If you do not have the data file from the previous skill open, open the student data file **EX1-07-CashFlow** and try this skill on your own:

1. On the *Q3-Q4* worksheet, select cell **B9** (the rent value for July).
2. Use AutoFill to copy the value of cells **C9:G9**.
3. Select cell **B2** (JULY) and use AutoFill to complete the month series through cell **G2**.
4. If you will be moving on to the next skill in this chapter, leave the workbook open to continue working. If not, save the file as directed by your instructor and close it.

Skill 1.8 Entering Simple Formulas

A **formula** is an equation used to calculate a value. A formula can perform a mathematical calculation, such as displaying the sum of **35 + 47**, or a formula can calculate a value using cell references, such as displaying a value equal to the value of another cell (**=B15**) or calculating an equation based on values in multiple cells (**=B17+B18-B19**).

In Figure EX 1.17, cell B19 contains the formula **=B15**. This formula directs Excel to make the value of cell B19 equal to the value of cell B15. If the value in cell B15 changes, the value displayed in cell B19 will update accordingly.

Notice that when the cell is selected, the result of the formula is displayed in the cell, while the formula is displayed in the formula bar.

To enter a formula:

1. Click the cell in which you want to enter the formula.
2. Press = and begin typing the formula. The = tells Excel that you are entering a formula, not standard text or numeric data.
3. Use the following symbols for mathematical operations:

Addition	+
Subtraction	-
Multiplication	*
Division	/

4. To add a cell reference to a formula, you can type the cell address or click the cell. If you are in the middle of typing a formula and you click another cell in the worksheet, Excel knows to add that cell reference to the formula instead of moving to it.
5. Press Enter or click the **Enter** button to the left of the formula bar when you are finished entering the formula.

When you edit the formula in the cell or the formula bar, any referenced cells are highlighted in the same color as the cell reference in the formula. When you have a formula with multiple cell references, such as the one in Figure EX 1.18, the colors make it easier to troubleshoot any errors.

tell me more

When you enter a formula with more than one mathematical operation, the formula is not necessarily calculated from left to right. Excel calculations follow the mathematical rules called the **order of operations** (also called **precedence**).

The rules state that mathematical operations in a formula are calculated in this order:

1. Exponents and roots
2. Multiplication and division
3. Addition and subraction

Adding parentheses around part of a formula will override the order of operations, forcing Excel to perform the calculation within the parentheses first.

- 4 + (5 * 2) = 14—Excel calculates 5 * 2 first (10), and then adds 4.
- (4 + 5) * 2 = 18—Excel calculates 4 + 5 first (9), and then multiples by 2.
- 4 + 5 ^ 2 = 29—Excel calculates 5 to the 2nd power first (25), and then adds 4.
- (4 + 5) ^ 2 = 81—Excel calculates 4 + 5 first (9), and then raises that number to the 2nd power.

let me try *Live!*

If you do not have the data file from the previous skill open, open the student data file **EX1-08-CashFlow** and try this skill on your own:

1. On the *Q1-Q2* worksheet, enter a formula in cell **B19** to display the value of cell **B15** (the total expenses for January).
2. In cell B20, enter a formula to calculate the cash balance for the month: the cash available at the beginning of the month (cell **B17**) + income for the month (cell **B18**) – expenses for the month (cell **B19**).
3. On the *Q3-Q4* worksheet, enter a formula in cell **B11** to calculate the value of merchandise sales (cell **B4**) multiplied by **5.5%**
4. If you will be moving on to the next skill in this chapter, leave the workbook open to continue working. If not, save the file as directed by your instructor and close it.

Skill 1.9 Understanding Absolute and Relative References

A cell's address, its position in the workbook, is referred to as a **cell reference** when it is used in a formula. In Excel, the $ character before a letter or number in the cell address means that part of the cell's ***address*** is absolute (nonchanging). Cell references can be relative, absolute, or mixed.

- A **relative reference** is a cell reference that adjusts to the new location in the worksheet when the formula is copied.
- An **absolute reference** is a cell reference whose location remains constant when the formula is copied.
- A **mixed reference** is a combination cell reference with a row position that stays constant with a changing column position (or vice versa).

- Relative reference—A1
- Absolute reference—$A$1
- Mixed reference with absolute row—A$1
- Mixed reference with absolute column—$A1

Here's how relative and absolute references work:

When you type a formula into a cell, it uses ***relative*** references by default. Excel notes the position of the referenced cell ***relative*** to the active cell. For example, if cell B19 is the active cell and you type the formula **=B15**, Excel displays the value of the cell that is up four rows from the active cell.

- If you change the structure of the worksheet by adding or removing rows or columns, Excel will automatically update all relative cell references. In this example, Excel will update the formula to reflect the new address of the cell that is up four rows from the cell containing the formula.
- If you copy the formula **=B15** from cell B19 and paste it into cell C19, the pasted formula will update automatically to **=C15** to reflect the cell address that is up four rows from the pasted formula.

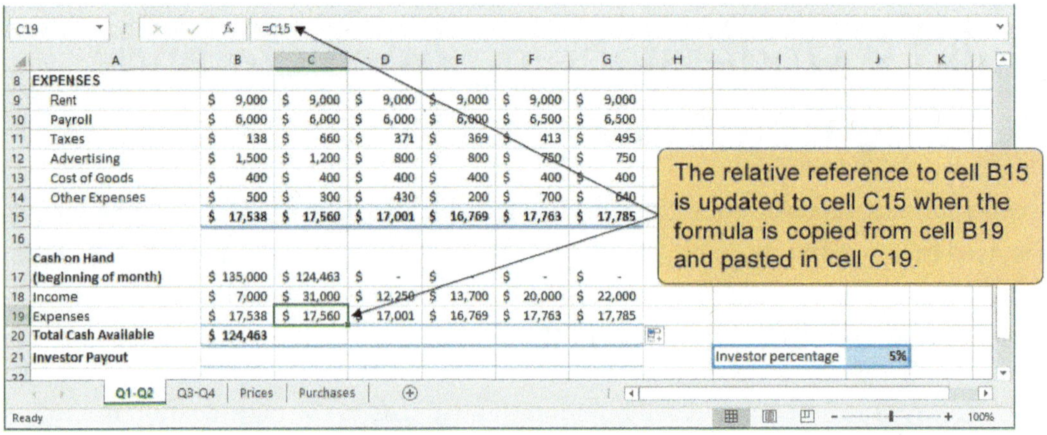

FIGURE EX 1.19

But what if you don't want the cell reference to adjust? For example, in Figure EX 1.20 cell J21 contains a value that you want to use in calculations for multiple cells in a row. If you were to copy the formula **=B20*J21** from cell B21 to cell C21, the formula would update to **=C20*K21** (not what you intended) because both of the cell references are relative. Instead, you want the reference to cell J21 to be ***absolute***, so it does not update when you copy it. If you use the formula **=B20*$J$21** instead and copy it from cell B21 to cell C21, the pasted formula will update only the relative reference **B20**. The absolute reference **$J$21** will remain constant. The formula in cell C21 will be **=C20*$J$21**.

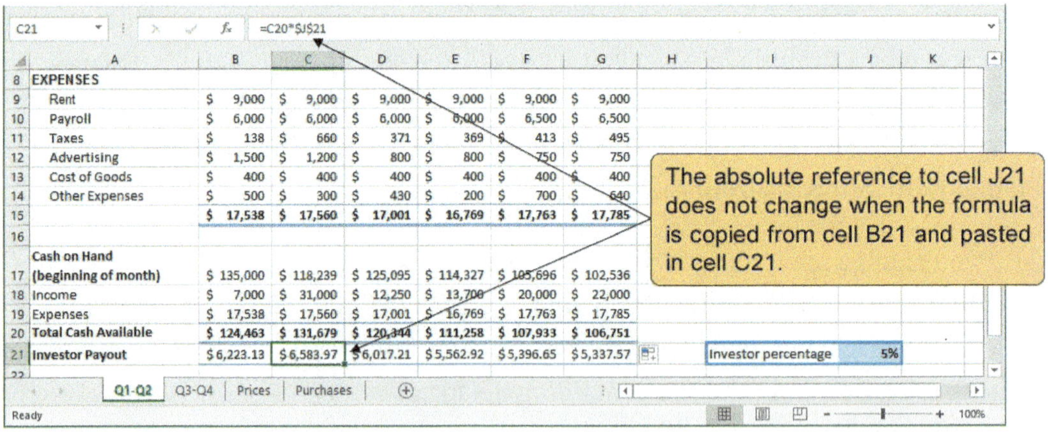

FIGURE EX 1.20

tips & tricks

If you cut and paste a formula, Excel assumes that you want the formula to maintain its previous value and treats the formula as if it had included absolute references, pasting the formula exactly as it was in the original cell.

another method

Another way to change the cell reference type is to select the cell reference in the formula bar, and then press **F4** to cycle through the various reference types until you find the one you want (absolute, mixed with absolute row, mixed with absolute column, and then back to relative).

let me try *Live!*

If you do not have the data file from the previous skill open, open the student data file **EX1-09-CashFlow** and try this skill on your own:

1. On the *Q1-Q2* worksheet, use AutoFill to copy the formula from cell **B19** to cells **C19:G19**. Now copy the formula in cell **B20** to cells **C20:G20**. Note how the relative reference in the formulas update.
2. In cell **B21**, enter a formula to calculate the investor payout for the month: the cash balance (cell **B20**) multiplied by the investor percentage (cell **J21**). In the next step, you will copy the formula across the row, so be sure to use an absolute reference for cell J21.
3. Use AutoFill to copy the formula in cell **B21** to cells **C21:G21**. If you entered the formula in B21 correctly, the cell reference to J21 will remain constant.
4. On the *Q3-Q4* worksheet, use AutoFill to copy the formula in cell **B11** to cells **C11:G11**. Observe that the relative reference updates as the formula is copied across the row.
5. If you will be moving on to the next skill in this chapter, leave the workbook open to continue working. If not, save the file as directed by your instructor and close it.

Skill 1.10 Using Functions in Formulas

Functions are preprogrammed shortcuts for calculating equations. Functions can simplify a straightforward computation such as figuring the total of a list of values. They can also calculate the answer to a complicated equation such as figuring the monthly payment amount for a loan.

Most functions require you to provide input called the **arguments**. For example, when writing a formula using the SUM function to calculate the total of a list of values, each value or range of values to be included in the calculation is an argument. Multiple arguments are separated by commas [,].

- This formula will calculate the total of the values in cells B9 through B14: **SUM(B9, B10, B11, B12, B13, B14)**
- In this example, each cell reference is an argument.
- An easier way to write the arguments for this formula is: **SUM(B9:B14)**

In the second example, the function requires only one argument—the cell range containing the values. Both formulas will return the same total value.

The easiest way to enter a formula using a simple function like SUM is to type the formula directly in the cell or the formula bar. Begin the formula by typing =, and then type the function name. After the function name, type (followed by the function arguments, separated by commas, and then). Press Enter to complete the formula.

tell me more

You can also enter functions in formulas using AutoSum, Formula AutoComplete, and the *Function Arguments* dialog. These methods are covered in later skills.

let me try *Live!*

If you do not have the data file from the previous skill open, open the student data file **EX1-10-CashFlow** and try this skill on your own:

1. On the *Q1-Q2* worksheet, review the formulas in rows **6** and **15**.
2. On the *Q3-Q4* worksheet, in cell **B6**, enter the formula using the SUM function to calculate the total of cells **B3** through **B5**.
3. If you will be moving on to the next skill in this chapter, leave the workbook open to continue working. If not, save the file as directed by your instructor and close it.

Skill 1.11 Using AutoSum to Insert a SUM function

If your spreadsheet includes numerical data organized in rows or columns, **AutoSum** can enter totals for you. When you use AutoSum, Excel enters the SUM function arguments using the most likely range of cells based on the structure of your worksheet. For example, if you use AutoSum at the bottom of a column of values, Excel will assume that you want to use the values in the column as the function arguments. If you use AutoSum at the end of a row of values, Excel will use the values in the row. To insert a SUM function using AutoSum:

1. Select the cell in which you want to enter the function.
2. On the *Home* tab, in the *Editing* group, click the **AutoSum** button.
3. Excel automatically inserts a formula with the SUM function, using the range of cells contiguous to (next to) the selected cell as the arguments for the function. You can increase or decrease the range of cells selected by clicking and dragging the corner of the highlighted cell range.
4. Press Enter to accept the formula.

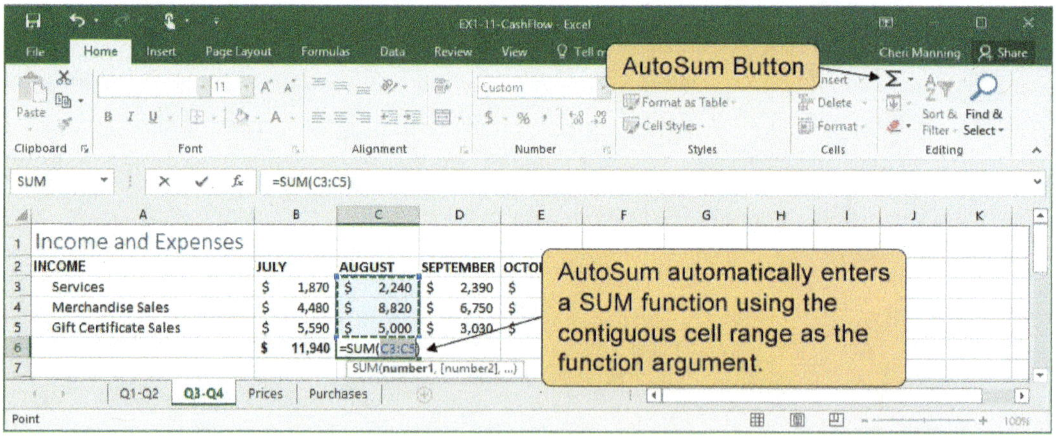

FIGURE EX 1.22

another method

- AutoSum is also available on the *Formulas* tab, in the *Function Library* group.
- You can also click the **AutoSum** button arrow and select **SUM** from the list.
- Another way to use the AutoSum function is to select a range of cells, and then click the **AutoSum** button. Excel will insert the SUM function in the next available (empty) cell.

let me try *Live!*

If you do not have the data file from the previous skill open, open the student data file **EX1-11-CashFlow** and try this skill on your own:

1. On the *Q3-Q4* worksheet, select cell **C6**.
2. Use AutoSum to enter a formula to calculate the total of cells **C3:C5**.
3. If you will be moving on to the next skill in this chapter, leave the workbook open to continue working. If not, save the file as directed by your instructor and close it.

Skill 1.12 Calculating Totals with the Quick Analysis Tool

When you have a range of cells selected, you can use the Quick Analysis tool to calculate totals down entire columns or across entire rows at once. The **Quick Analysis tool** includes five types of calculations:

- **Sum** — calculates the total of the values in each row or column.
- **Average** — calculates the average of the values in each row or column.
- **Count** — counts the number of cells that contain values in each row or column.
- **% Total** — calculates the percentage of the overall total for the total of each row or column: the sum of values in the row or column divided by the sum of the values in the entire selection.
- **Running Total** — calculates a total for each row or column that includes the values in the row or column plus the values in all the previous rows or columns. Notice that the formula for the running total uses an absolute reference for the first cell in the range and a relative reference for the last cell in the range.

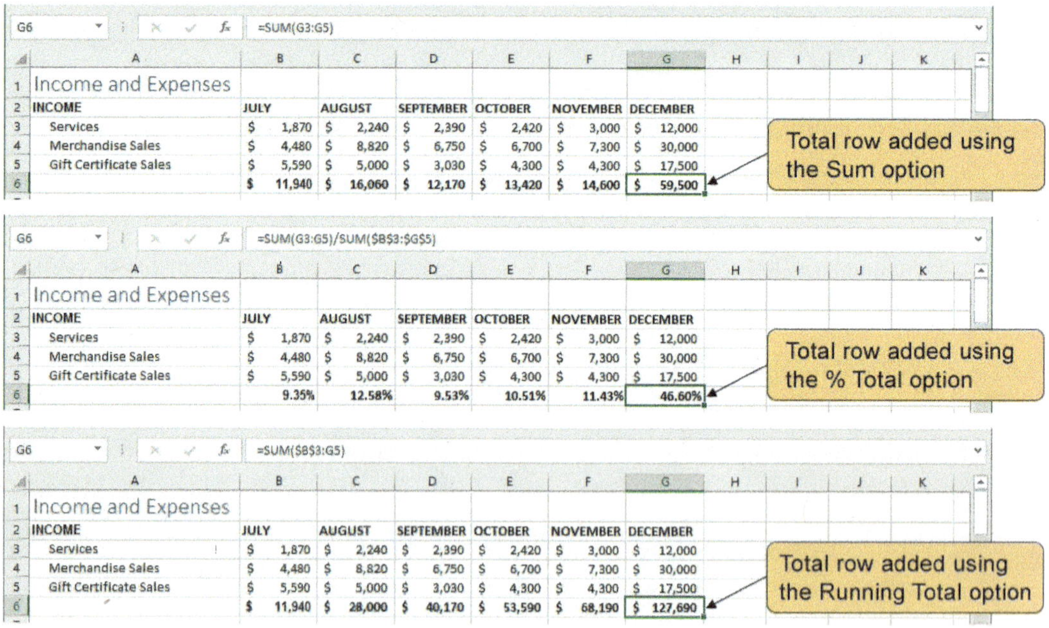

FIGURE EX 1.23

To use the Quick Analysis tool to calculate totals:

1. Select the range of cells. Totals can be inserted below or to the right of the selected cells.
2. The Quick Analysis tool button appears near the lower right corner of the selected range. Click the **Quick Analysis tool** button, and then click the **Totals** tab.

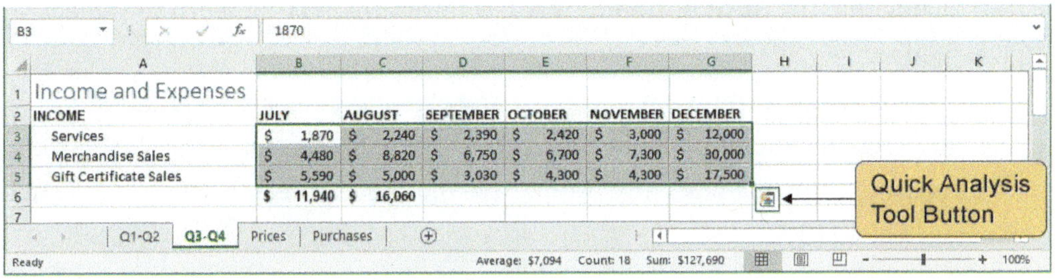

FIGURE EX 1.24

3. Notice that Excel displays a preview of the formulas as you hover the mouse pointer over each option. As showin in Figure EX 1.24, the images in the Quick Analysis tool shows where the formulas will be inserted. The first set of buttons shows a blue highlight along the bottom, indicating that the formulas will be inserted below the selected range. The second set of buttons shows a yellow highlight along the right side, indicating that the formulas will be inserted to the right of the selected range.

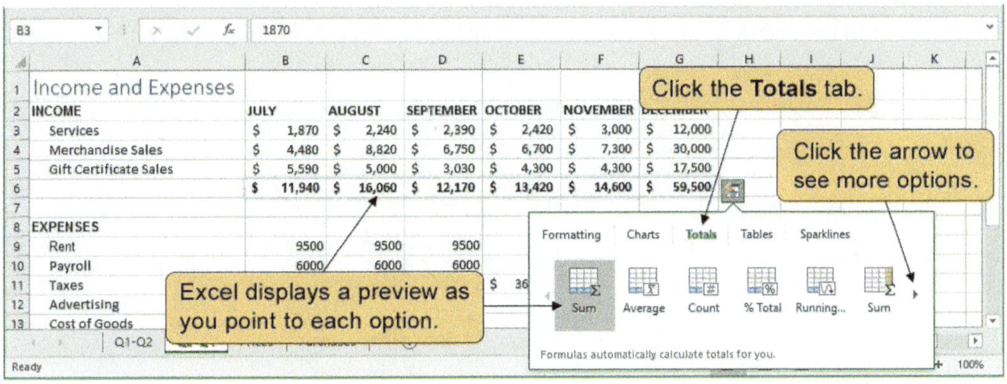

FIGURE EX 1.25

4. Click the button that represents the type of calculation you want to insert.
5. If there are data in any of the cells where the total formulas will be inserted, Excel asks if you want to replace them. Click **OK**.

tips & tricks

If the Quick Analysis tool button is not visible, move your mouse cursor over the selected cell range, without clicking. This action should make the button appear.

let me try *Live!*

If you do not have the data file from the previous skill open, open the student data file **EX1-12-CashFlow** and try this skill on your own:

1. On the *Q3-Q4* worksheet, select the cell range **B3:G5**.
2. Click the **Quick Analysis tool** button, and then click the **Totals** tab.
3. Click the first **Sum** button to insert totals in the row beneath the selected cell range.
4. If Excel asks if you want to replace the existing data, click **OK**.
5. If you will be moving on to the next skill in this chapter, leave the workbook open to continue working. If not, save the file as directed by your instructor and close it.

Skill 1.13 Using the Status Bar

The **status bar** appears at the bottom of the Excel window and displays information about the current worksheet. By default, the status bar displays whether you are in Ready or Edit mode and information about the selected cells (such as the number of cells selected, the sum of the values in the selected cells, or the average of the values in the selected cells). You can customize the status bar to show other information about the worksheet, the minimum or maximum value in the selected cells, and whether Caps Lock is on or off.

To change the information shown on the status bar:

1. Right-click anywhere on the status bar.
2. The *Customize Status Bar* menu appears. Options with checkmarks next to them are currently active. Options without a checkmark are not currently active.
3. Click an item on the menu to add it to or remove it from the status bar display.

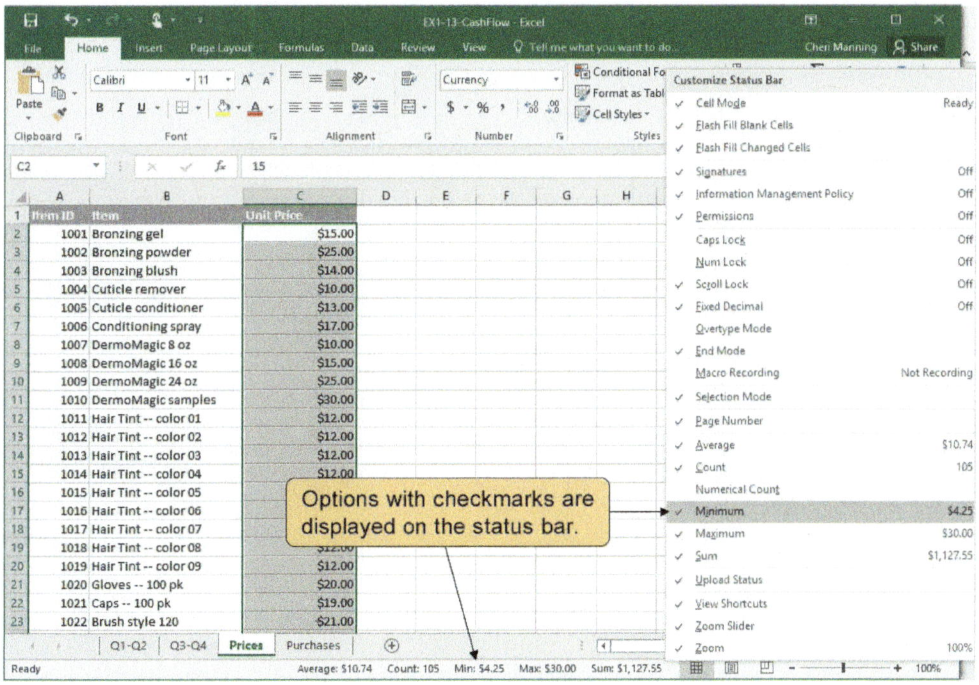

FIGURE EX 1.26

let me try *Live!*

If you do not have the data file from the previous skill open, open the student data file **EX1-13-CashFlow** and try this skill on your own:

1. On the *Prices* worksheet, select cells **C2:C106** and observe the calculations displayed on the status bar. You should see the average, count, and sum of the selected cells.
2. Add the minimum and maximum values to the status bar.
3. Observe the changes, and then remove the minimum and maximum values from the status bar so it is back to its original state.
4. If you will be moving on to the next skill in this chapter, leave the workbook open to continue working. If not, save the file as directed by your instructor and close it.

Skill 1.14 Changing the Zoom Level

If you are working with a large spreadsheet, you may find that you need to see more of the spreadsheet at one time or that you would like a closer look at a cell or group of cells. You can use the **zoom slider** in the lower right corner of the window to zoom in and out of a worksheet, changing the size of text and images on screen. As you move the slider, the zoom level displays the percentage the worksheet has been zoomed in or zoomed out. Zooming a worksheet affects only how the worksheet appears on-screen. It does not affect how the worksheet will print.

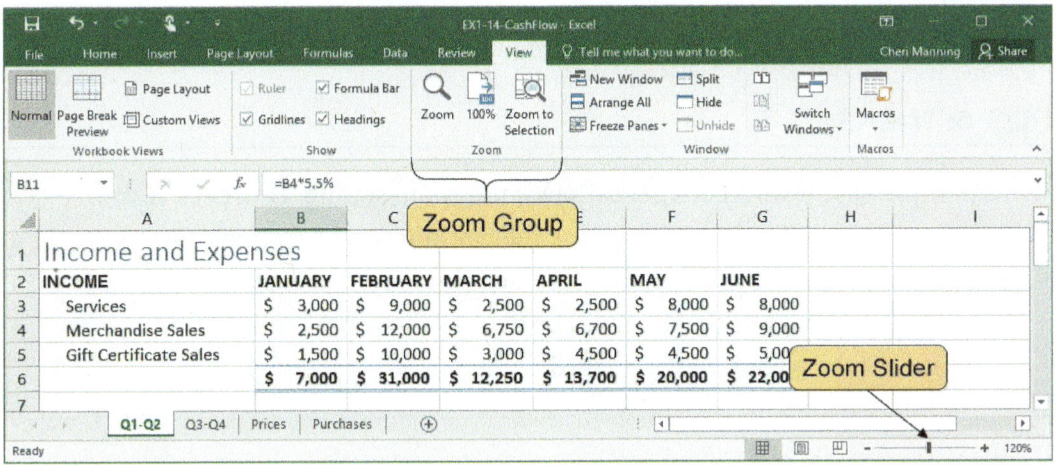

FIGURE EX 1.27

To zoom in on a worksheet, making the text and graphics appear larger:

- Click and drag the zoom slider to the right.
- Click the **Zoom In** button on the slider.

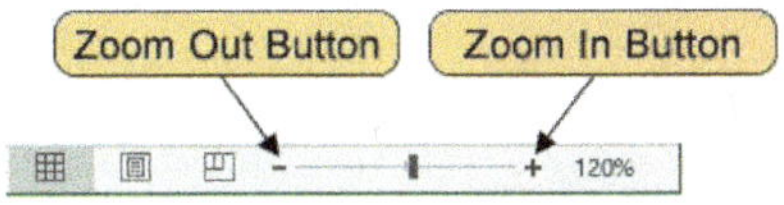

FIGURE EX 1.28

To zoom out of a worksheet, making the text and graphics appear smaller:

- Click and drag the zoom slider to the left.
- Click the **Zoom Out** button on the slider.

On the *View* tab, the *Zoom* group includes buttons for two of the most common zoom options:

- Click the **Zoom to Selection** button to zoom in as close as possible on the currently selected cell(s).
- Click the **100%** button to return the worksheet back to 100% of the normal size.

You can also change the zoom level through the *Zoom* dialog.

1. On the *View* tab, in the *Zoom* group, click the **Zoom** button.
2. In the *Zoom* dialog, click the radio button for the zoom option you want, and then click **OK**.

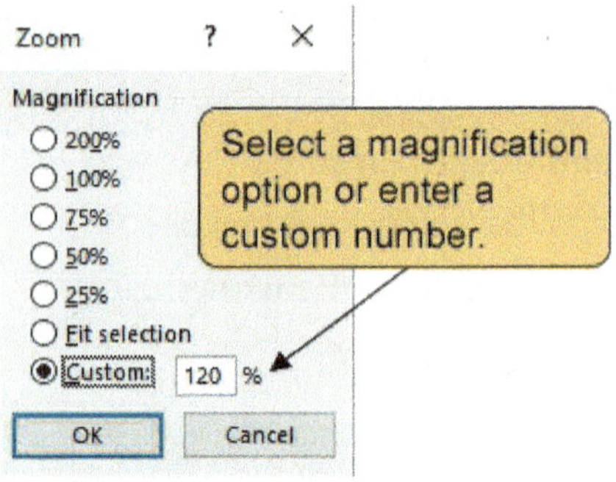

FIGURE EX 1.29

tips & tricks

When you save a workbook, Excel saves the zoom setting. However, if you change the zoom level and then close the workbook without making any other changes, Excel will not warn you about saving your change. The next time you open the workbook, it will be back to the zoom level that was set at the time the workbook was last saved.

another method

You can also open *Zoom* dialog by clicking the zoom level number that appears at the right side of the zoom slider.

let me try *Live!*

If you do not have the data file from the previous skill open, open the student data file **EX1-14-CashFlow** and try this skill on your own:

1. Change the zoom level to **110%**.
2. Change the zoom level back to **100%**.
3. Change the zoom level to **90%**.
4. If you will be moving on to the next skill in this chapter, leave the workbook open to continue working. If not, save the file as directed by your instructor and close it.

from the perspective of . . .

ACCOUNTING FIRM INTERN

My boss works on two 24" monitors. She always has her files set at 150% or higher because she has the room to spread the worksheet across two large monitors. I work on a laptop with a 15" screen. When I open her files, I can only see part of the worksheet until I set the zoom level back to 100%. It is harder to see details when the zoom level is set lower, but for me, it's more important to see the whole worksheet without having to scroll.

Skill 1.15 Creating a New Workbook Using a Template

A **template** is a file with predefined settings that you can use as a starting point for your workbook. Using an Excel template makes creating a new workbook easy and results in a professional appearance. Many templates use advanced techniques that you may not have learned yet—but you can take advantage of them in a template where someone else has created the workbook framework for you. Templates are available for every imaginable task: from creating budgets to tracking exercise to calculating your grade point average.

To create a new workbook using a template:

1. Click the **File** tab to open Backstage view.
2. Click **New**. Excel 2016 includes a variety of templates that are copied to your computer when you install the application. These templates are always available from the *New* page. Additional templates that you download are also displayed on the *New* page, so your screen may look different than the one in Figure EX 1.30.

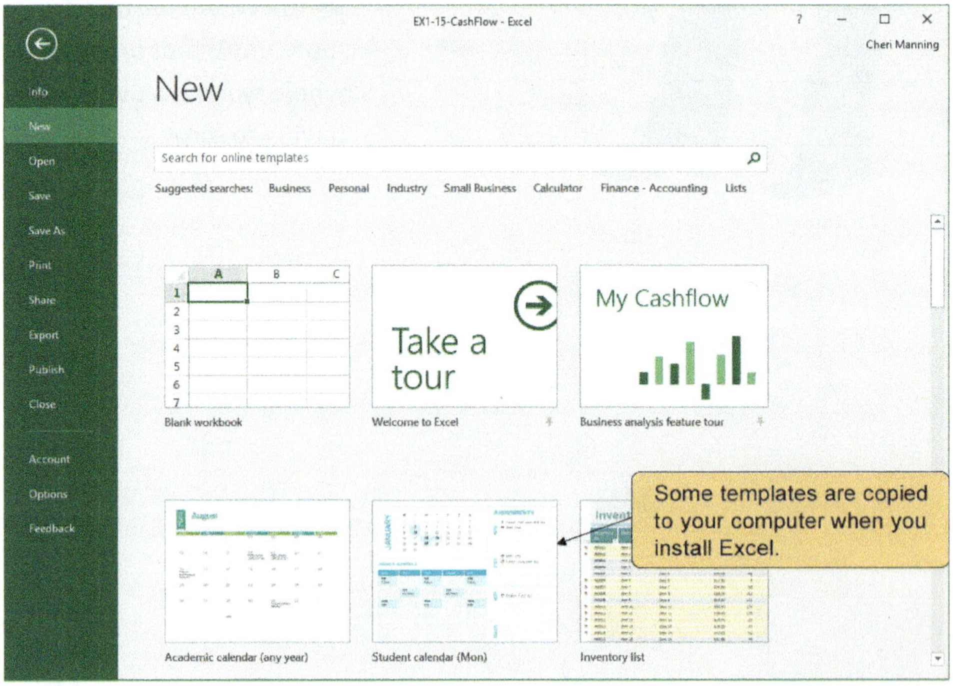

FIGURE EX 1.30

3. Click a template picture to open the template preview including a brief description of the template.
4. You can cycle through the template previews by clicking the arrows that appear on either side of the preview.
5. When you find the template you want to use, click the **Create** button.
6. A new workbook opens, prepopulated with all of the template elements and sample data. Work through the template, replacing the sample data with your own.
7. Don't forget to save the file.

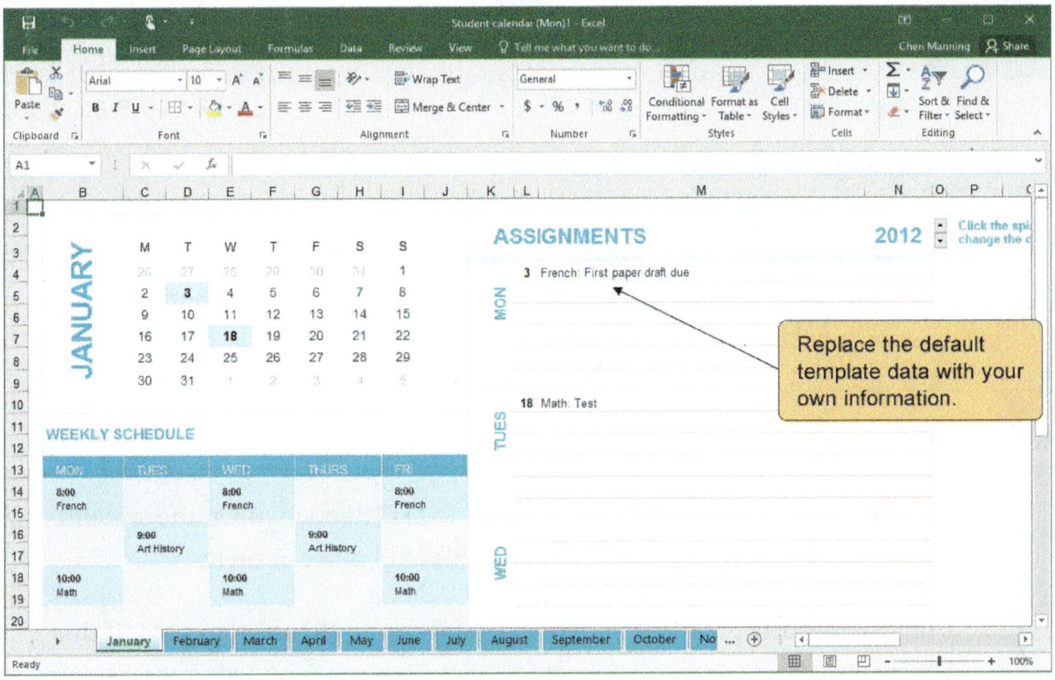

FIGURE EX 1.31

You can search for additional workbook templates online. (You must have an active Internet connection.)

1. Near the top of the *New* page, in the *Search online templates* box, type a keyword or phrase that describes the template you want.
2. Click the **Start searching** button (the magnifying glass image at the end of the *Search online templates* box).
3. The search results display previews of the templates that match the keyword or phrase you entered. To further narrow the results, click one of the categories listed in the *Filter by* pane at the right side of the window. Notice that each category lists the number of templates available.
4. When you find the template you want, click it to display the larger preview with detailed information about the template, and then click **Create**.

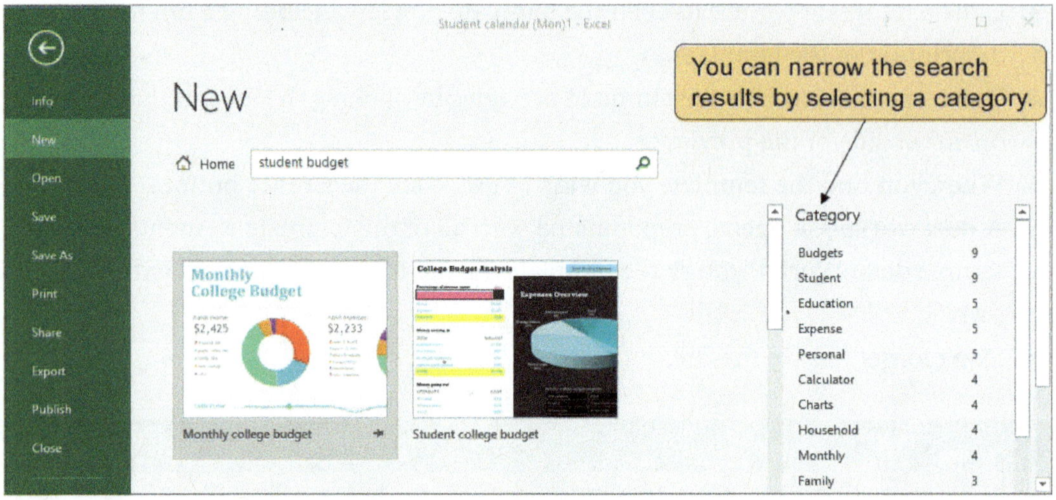

FIGURE EX 1.32

tips & tricks

Many Excel templates have a special worksheet labeled Settings, Instructions, or something similar. Be sure to read all of the instructions before entering data.

let me try *Live!*

If you do not have the data file from the previous skill open, open the student data file **EX1-15-CashFlow** and try this skill on your own:

1. Create a new file based on the **Student calendar (Mon)** template. If this template does not appear on your *New* page, search for it using the *Search online templates* feature. You may find more than one template named Student calendar. Select one that appeals to you.
2. Create another new file by searching for a template based on the phrase **student budget**. Use any template you want.
3. If you will be moving on to the next skill in this chapter, leave the workbooks open to continue working. If not, save the files as directed by your instructor and close them.

from the perspective of . . .

COLLEGE STUDENT

I thought Excel was only for business. It's not! I found some really useful templates —one for tracking my day-to-day expenses and another one to help me budget my expenses for the semester. And even though some of the templates look fancy and complicated, I find that I can use them easily by reading the instructions and taking a little bit of time to personalize the data with my own information.

Skill 1.16 Arranging Workbooks

If you are working with multiple workbooks, you may want to arrange them so you can see them all at the same time. You can arrange workbooks so they are tiled, horizontal, vertical, or cascading windows.

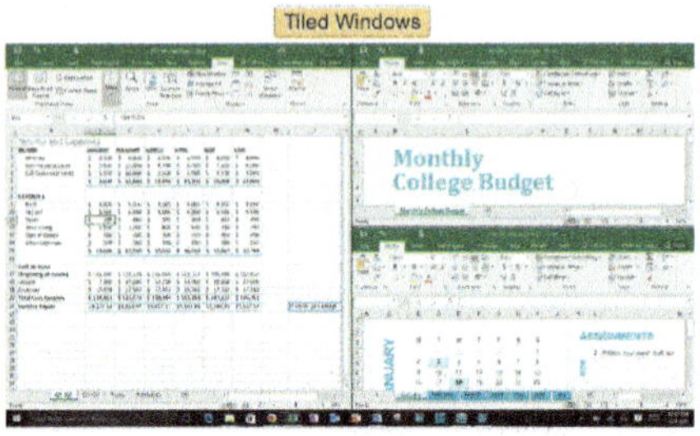

FIGURE EX 1.33

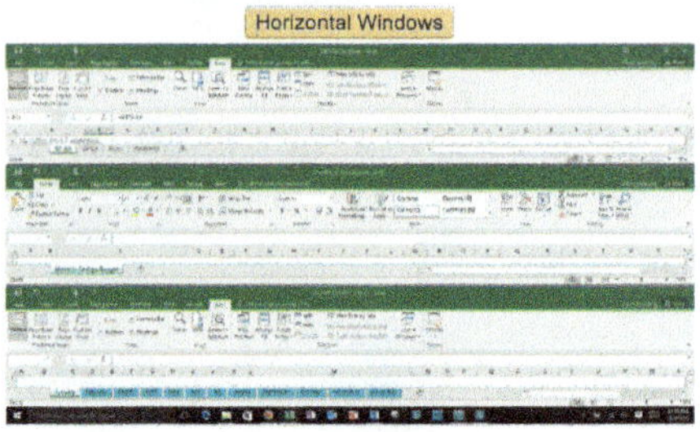

FIGURE EX 1.34

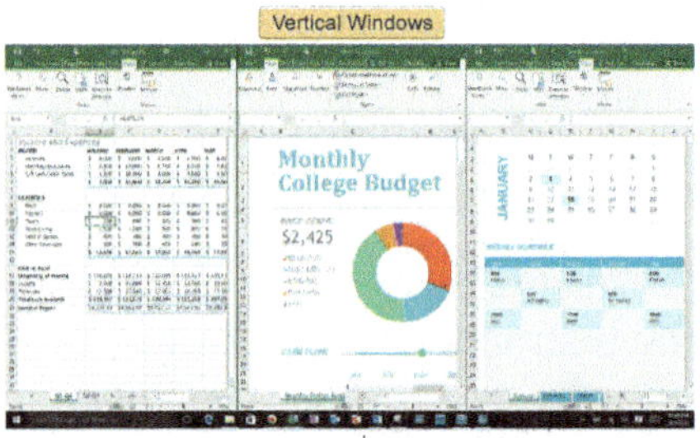

FIGURE EX 1.35

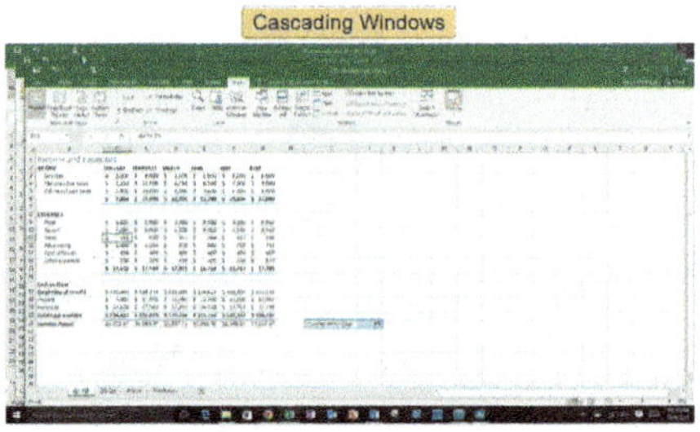

FIGURE EX 1.36

To change the arrangement of workbooks:

1. On the *View* tab, in the *Window* group, click the **Arrange All** button.
2. In the *Arrange Windows* dialog, select an arrangement option:
   - **Tiled** — places the windows in a grid pattern.
   - **Horizontal** — places the windows in a stack one on top of the other.
   - **Vertical** — places the windows in a row next to each other.
   - **Cascade** — places the windows in a staggered, overlapping, diagonal arrangement.
3. Click **OK**.

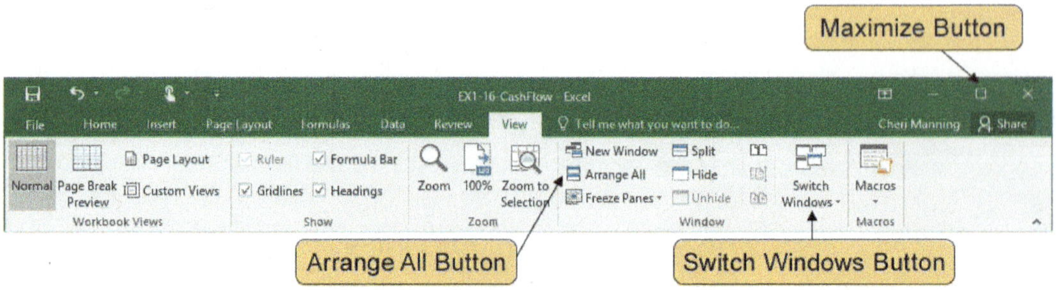

FIGURE EX 1.37

To switch between workbooks, you can:

- Click anywhere in the workbook you want to make active.
- On the *View* tab, in the *Window* group, click the **Switch Windows** button, then click the name of the workbook you want.

To undo the arrangement and put the workbooks back into separate windows, maximize any of the workbooks by clicking the **Maximize** button on the title bar.

tell me more

If you have two workbooks with similar data, you may want to compare their data row by row. Excel's *Compare Side by Side* feature allows you to compare two workbooks at the same time. When you compare workbooks, the *Synchronous Scrolling* feature is on by default. This feature allows you to scroll both workbooks at once. If you scroll the active workbook, the other workbook will scroll at the same time, allowing you to carefully compare data row by row.

1. Open the workbooks you want to compare.
2. On the *View* tab, in the *Window* group, click the **View Side by Side** button.
3. The two workbooks are displayed one on top of the other.
4. Scroll the active window to scroll both workbooks at once.
5. Click the **View Side by Side** button again to restore the windows to their previous positions.

let me try *Live!*

If you do not have the data files from the previous skill open, open the student data file **EX1-16-CashFlow** and a few other Excel files to try this skill on your own:

1. Arrange the Excel windows so they are in a staggered arrangement.
2. Arrange the Excel windows so they are in a row next to eachother.
3. If you will be moving on to the next skill in this chapter, close all of the workbooks except the *Sales* workbook. If not, save the files as directed by your instructor and close them.

Skill 1.17 Checking Spelling

Regardless of the amount of work you put into a workbook, a spelling error or typo can make the entire workbook appear sloppy and unprofessional. All the Office applications include a built-in spelling checker. In Excel, the *Spelling* command analyzes the current worksheet for spelling errors. It presents any errors it finds in a dialog, enabling you to make decisions about how to handle each error or type of error in turn.

To check a worksheet for spelling errors:

1. On the *Review* tab, in the *Proofing* group, click the **Spelling** button or use the keyboard shorcut F7.
2. The first spelling error appears in the *Spelling* dialog.
3. Review the spelling suggestion and then select an action:
   - Click **Ignore Once** to make no changes to this instance of the word.
   - Click **Ignore All** to make no changes to all instances of the word.
   - Click **Add to Dictionary** to make no changes to this instance of the word and add it to the spelling checker dictionary, so future uses of this word will not show up as misspellings. When you add a word to the dictionary, it is available for all the Office applications.
   - Click the correct spelling in the *Suggestions* list, and click **Change** to correct just this instance of the misspelling in your worksheet.
   - Click the correct spelling in the *Suggestions* list, and click **Change All** to correct all instances of the misspelling in your worksheet.

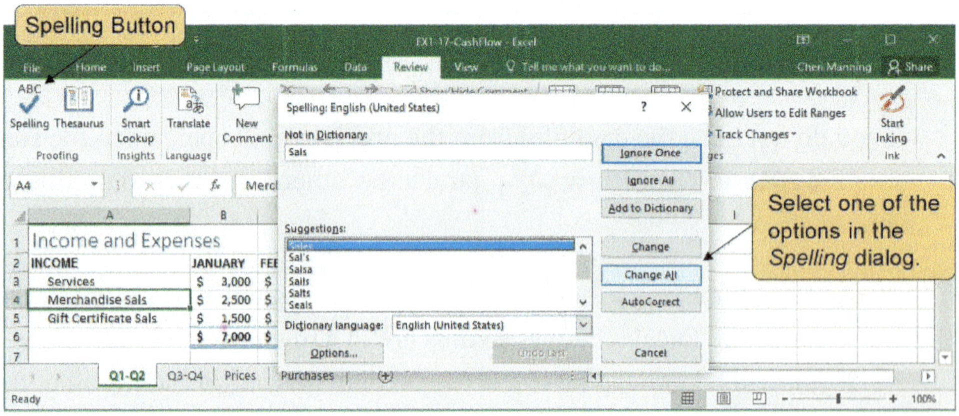

FIGURE EX 1.38

4. After you select an action, the spelling checker automatically advances to the next suspected spelling error.
5. When the spelling checker finds no more errors, it displays a message telling you the check is complete. Click **OK** to close the dialog and return to your worksheet.

tips & tricks

Whether or not you use the Spelling tool, you should always proofread your files. Spelling checkers are not infallible, especially if you misuse a word yet spell it correctly—for instance, writing "bored" instead of "board."

If you misspell a word often, the next time the spelling checker catches the misspelling, use this trick: Click the correct spelling in the *Suggestions* list and then click the **AutoCorrect** button. Now, when you type the misspelled version of the word, it will be corrected automatically as you type.

let me try *Live!*

If you do not have the data file from the previous skill open, open the student data file **EX1-17-CashFlow** and try this skill on your own:

1. Spell check the *Q1-Q2* worksheet and correct any errors you find.
2. If you will be moving on to the next skill in this chapter, leave the workbook open to continue working. If not, save the file as directed by your instructor and close it.

Skill 1.18 Previewing and Printing a Worksheet

In Excel 2016, all the print settings are combined in a single page along with a preview of how the printed file will look. As you change print settings, the preview updates. To preview and print the current worksheet:

1. Click the **File** tab to open Backstage view.
2. Click **Print**.
3. At the right side of the page is a preview of how the printed file will look. Beneath the preview there is a page count. If there are multiple pages, use the *Next* and *Previous* arrows to preview all the pages in the file. You can also use the scroll bar to the right to scroll through the preview pages.
4. Set the number of copies to print by changing the number in the *Copies* box.
5. Click the **Print** button to send the file to your default printer.

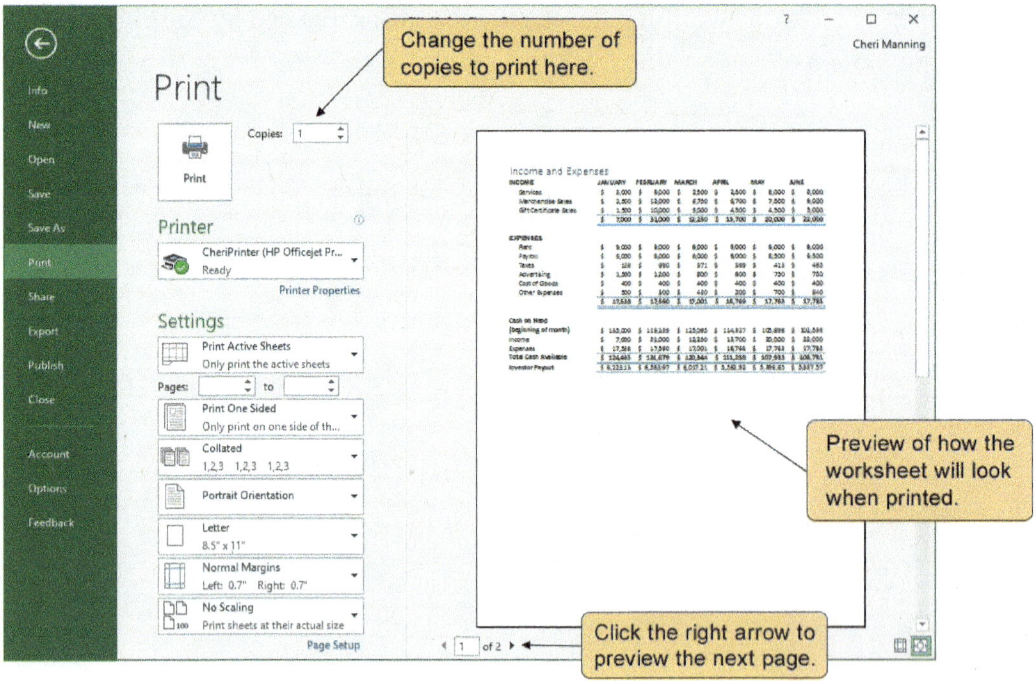

FIGURE EX 1.39

tips & tricks

Add the *Quick Print* command to the Quick Access Toolbar so you can print with a single mouse click. If you do not need to change the default print settings, you can click the *Quick Print* button instead of going through the *Print* tab in Backstage view.

tell me more

To open the *Print* page in Backstage view, you can use the keyboard shortcut Ctrl + P.

let me try *Live!*

If you do not have the data file from the previous skill open, open the student data file **EX1-18-CashFlow** and try this skill on your own:

1. Preview how the worksheet will look when printed.
2. If you can, print the worksheet and compare the printed page to the preview.
3. Save the file as directed by your instructor and close it.

key terms

- Workbook
- Worksheet
- Row
- Column
- Cell
- Cell address
- Cell range
- Formula bar
- Name box
- Status bar
- Vertical scroll bar
- Horizontal scroll bar
- Row selector
- Column selector
- Protected View
- Message Bar
- Trusted Document
- Ready mode
- Edit mode
- General number format
- Accounting Number Format
- Percent Style format
- Comma Style format
- Number format
- Currency format
- Short Date format
- Long Date format
- AutoFill
- Fill Handle tool
- Data series
- Formula
- Order of Operations (precedence)
- Cell reference
- Relative reference
- Absolute reference
- Mixed reference

- **Function**
- **Argument**
- **AutoSum**
- **Quick Analysis tool**
- **Status bar**
- **Zoom slider**
- **Template**
- **Tiled window arrangement**
- **Horizontal window arrangement**
- **Vertical window arrangement**
- **Cascade window arrangement**

concept review

1. How many worksheets does a new Excel 2016 workbook have?
   a. one
   b. two
   c. three
   d. four
2. The cell B2 refers to the cell at ______________.
   a. the intersection of row B and column 2
   b. the intersection of column B and row 2
   c. the first cell on the B2 worksheet
   d. none of the above
3. Which of these dates uses the Long Date format?
   a. 1/1/2000
   b. January 1, 2000
   c. 01/01/200
   d. Saturday, January 1, 2000
4. Formulas begin with which character?
   a. $
   b. @
   c. =
   d. *
5. Which of these cell references is an absolute reference?
   a. $D4
   b. D4
   c. $D$4
   d. none of the above
6. Which of these formulas uses a function?
   a. =B4
   b. =B4 + B5
   c. =SUM(B4:B5)
   d. =B4*B5
7. AutoSum is located ______________.
   a. on the Home tab, in the Editing group
   b. on the Insert tab, in the Formulas group
   c. on the Home tab, in the Formulas group
   d. on the Insert tab, in the Tables group

8. The zoom slider is located ________________.
   a. at the lower right corner of the status bar
   b. on the View tab, in the Zoom group
   c. in the Zoom dialog
   d. on the Ribbon
9. The keyboard shortcut to begin the spelling checker is ________________.
   a. F5
   b. F7
   c. F4
   d. F9
10. Which of these tasks can you *not* perform in Backstage view?
   a. Enable Editing when a workbook is in Protected View.
   b. Preview how a workbook will look when printed.
   c. Create a new workbook from a template.
   d. None of the above.

projects

Data files for projects can be found by logging into your SIMnet account and going to the *Library* section.

skill review 1.1

The workbook for this project generates client bills from staff hours in multiple worksheets. In this project, you will complete the worksheet for staff member Swinson to calculate the daily bill, the total billable hours per week, and the total weekly bill. The worksheet for staff member Stevens has been completed. You may use it for reference as necessary.

Skills needed to complete this project:

- Working in Protected View (Skill 1.3)
- Navigating a Workbook (Skill 1.2)
- Entering and Editing Text and Numbers in Cells (Skill 1.4)
- Applying Number Formats (Skill 1.5)
- Entering Dates and Applying Date Formats (Skill 1.6)
- Inserting Data Using AutoFill (Skill 1.7)
- Understanding Absolute and Relative References (Skill 1.9)
- Entering Simple Formulas (Skill 1.8)
- Calculating Totals with the Quick Analysis Tool (Skill 1.12)
- Previewing and Printing a Worksheet (Skill 1.18)

1. Open the start file **EX2016-SkillReview-1-1** and resave the file as: `[your initials]EX-SkillReview-1-1`
2. If the workbook opens in Protected View, click the **Enable Editing** button in the Message Bar at the top of the workbook so you can modify the workbook.
3. Explore the workbook. If you accidentally make changes while exploring, press Ctrl + Z to undo the change.
    a. Click the worksheet tab labeled *Stevens Hours.*
    b. If necessary, use the vertical scroll bar to scroll down so you can see both weeks of billable hours. (If necessary, use the vertical scroll bar again to return to the top of the worksheet.)
    c. Click cell **B2** (the cell displaying the staff member's last name, Stevens). This is the cell at the intersection of column B and row 2.
        i. Note that the column B and row 2 selector boxes highlight.
        ii. Note that the status bar displays Ready, indicating that you are in Ready mode.
        iii. On the *Home* tab, in the *Number* group, look at the *Number Format* box at the top of the group. Note that the format for this cell is *General.*

iv. Double-click cell **B2** to switch to Edit mode. Note that the status bar now displays *Edit*, and the blinking cursor appears within the cell. If you needed to, you could edit the text directly in the cell.

d. Press Esc to exit Edit mode and return to Ready mode.

e. Press Enter twice to move to cell **B4** (the cell displaying the staff member's billable rate). This cell is formatted with the Accounting Number Format number format.

   i. Look in the *Number Format* box and note that the format for this cell is *Accounting*.

   ii. On the *Home* tab, in the *Styles* group, look in the *Cell Styles* gallery, and note that the cell style *Currency* is highlighted. (If the *Cell Styles* gallery is collapsed on your Ribbon, click the **Cell Styles** button to display it.)

f. Click cell **B9** (the cell displaying the number of hours for Monday, August 8). This cell is formatted with the Comma Style number format.

   i. Look in the *Number Format* box and note that the format for this cell is also *Accounting*.

   ii. On the *Home* tab, in the *Styles* group, look in the *Cell Styles* gallery, and note that the cell style *Comma* is highlighted for this cell. (If the *Cell Styles* gallery is collapsed on your Ribbon, click the **Cell Styles** button to display it.)

   iii. Note the style differences between cell **B4** (Accounting Number Format) and cell **B9** (Comma Style format).

g. Click cell **B7** (the cell displaying the date 8/8/2016). This cell is formatted using the Short Date format. Note that the *Number Format* box displays *Date*.

h. Double-click cell **B15**.

   i. Note that the status bar now displays *Edit*, indicating that you are in Edit mode.

   ii. This cell contains a formula to calculate the daily bill for Monday, August 8: **=B13*$B$4**

   iii. Note that cells B13 and B4 are highlighted with colors matching the cell references in the formula.

   iv. Note that the reference to cell B4 is an absolute reference ($B$4).

i. Press Esc to exit Edit mode.

j. Double-click cell **B13**.

   i. Note that once again the status bar displays *Edit*, indicating that you are in Edit mode.

   ii. This cell contains a formula using the SUM function to calculate the total billable hours for Monday, August 8: **=SUM(B9:B12)**

   iii. In this case, the SUM function uses a single argument **B9:B12** to indicate the range of cells to total.

iv. Note that the cell range **B9:B12** is highlighted with the color matching the argument in the SUM function formula.

v. Note that the reference to the cell range **B9:B12** uses relative references.

k. Press [Esc] to exit Edit mode.

l. Press [Tab] to move to cell **C13**. Look in the formula bar and note that this cell contains a similar formula to the one in cell **B13: =SUM(C9:C12)**

m. Press [→] to move through cells **D13 through H13**. Note the formula in the formula bar for each cell.

n. Did you notice that the cell references in the formulas in cells **C34 through H13** all use relative references?

4. Now you are ready to complete the worksheet for David Swinson. Navigate to the *Swinson Hours* worksheet by clicking the **Swinson Hours** worksheet tab.

5. The staff member's last name is spelled incorrectly. Navigate to cell **B2** and edit the text so the last name is spelled correctly (Swinson – with an *i* instead of an *a*). Use Edit mode.

   a. Double-click cell **B2**.

   b. Edit the text to: `Swinson`

   c. Press [Enter] to accept your changes.

6. The billable rate amount is missing. Navigate to cell **B4** and enter the rate. Use Ready mode.

   a. Click cell **B4**.

   b. Type: `175`

   c. Press [Enter].

7. Modify the billable rate to use the Accounting Number Format.

   a. Press the [↑] to return to cell **B4**.

   b. On the *Home* tab, in the *Number* group, click the **Accounting Number Format** button.

8. The dates are missing from the timesheet. Enter the first date, August 8, 2016.

   a. Click cell **B7**.

   b. Type: `8/8/2016`

   c. Press [Enter].

9. Use Autofill to complete the dates in the timesheet.

   a. Click cell **B7**.

   b. Click the **Fill Handle**, and drag to cell **H7**. Release the mouse button.

10. Change the date format to the 8/8/2016 format.

    a. The cell range **B7:H7** should still be selected. If not, click cell **B7**, press and hold [Shift], click cell **H7**, and then release the [Shift] key.

    b. On the *Home* tab, in the *Number* group, expand the *Number Format* list, and click **Short Date**.

11. Use the Quick Analysis tool to enter total hours for each day.

a. Select cells **B9:H12**. Click cell **B9**, hold down the left mouse button, and drag the mouse to cell **H12**. Release the mouse button. The cell range B9 through H12 should now appear selected.

b. The Quick Analysis tool button should appear near the lower right corner of the selected cell range. (If the Quick Analysis tool button is not visible, move your mouse cursor over the selected cell range again, without clicking. This action should make the button appear.)

c. Click the **Quick Analysis tool** button, and then click **Totals**.

d. Click **Sum** (the first option).

12. Format the hours billed section to use the Comma Style number format. Be sure to include the total row.

    a. Select cells **B9:H13**. Try another method: Click cell **B9**, press and hold Shift, click cell **H13**, and release the Shift key.

    b. On the *Home* tab, in the *Nubmer* group, click the **Comma Style** button.

13. Enter a formula in cell **B15** to calculate the daily bill for Monday, August 8. The formula should calculate the total billable hours for the day (cell B13) times the billable rate (B4).

    a. Click cell **B15**.

    b. Type: =

    c. Click cell **B13**.

    d. Type: *

    e. Click cell **B4**.

    f. Press F4 to change the cell reference **B4** to an absolute reference **($B$4)**.

    g. Press Enter

    h. The formula should look like this: **=B13*$B$4**

14. Use AutoFill to copy the formula to the remaining days in the timesheet.

    a. Click cell **B15** again.

    b. Click the **AutoFill handle**. Hold down the left mouse button and drag to cell **H15**. Release the mouse button.

    c. The formulas in cells B15 through H15 should look like this.

	B	C	D	E	F	G	H
15	=B13*$B$4	=C13*$B$4	=D13*$B$4	=E13*$B$4	=F13*$B$4	=G13*$B$4	=H13*$B$4

FIGURE EX 1.40

Notice that when the AutoFill copied the formula, it updated the relative reference (B13) to reflect the new column position, but it did not change the relative reference ($B$4).

15. Now you can calculate the bill total for the week by summing the daily bill amounts. Enter a formula using the SUM function with the cell range **B15:H15** as the argument.

a. Click cell **B16**.
b. Type: `=SUM(B15:H15)`
c. Press Enter.

16. Preview how the worksheet will look when printed.
    a. Click the **File** tab to open Backstage view.
    b. Click **Print** to display the print preview.
    c. Click the left arrow to close the Backstage view.
17. Save and close the workbook.

projects

Data files for projects can be found by logging into your SIMnet account and going to the *Library* section.

skill review 1.2

In this project you will create a new workbook to track the cost of books for your college classes. For each book, you will enter the purchase price, the potential sell-back price, and the cost difference. You will calculate totals using AutoSum. You will then create a new workbook from a template, and practice changing the zoom level and arranging the workbooks.

Skills needed to complete this project:

- Entering and Editing Text and Numbers in Cells (Skill 1.4)
- Navigating a Workbook (Skill 1.2)
- Inserting Data Using AutoFill (Skill 1.7)
- Applying Number Formats (Skill 1.5)
- Using the Status Bar (Skill 1.13)
- Using AutoSum to Insert a SUM Function (Skill 1.11)
- Entering Simple Formulas (Skill 1.8)
- Creating a New Workbook Using a Template (Skill 1.15)
- Checking Spelling (Skill 1.17)
- Arranging Workbooks (Skill 1.16)
- Changing the Zoom Level (Skill 1.14)

1. Start a new blank Excel workbook. Save the file as:
   `[your initials]EX-SkillReview-1-2`
2. The new workbook opens with one sheet (*Sheet1*). Cell **A1** is selected.
3. In cell **A1**, type the title for the worksheet: **`Textbooks`**
4. Enter data in the worksheet as follows:

	A	B	C	D	E
1	Textbooks				
2					
3	Book	Cost	Value	Difference	
4	Book 1	75	35		
5	Book 2	100	80		
6	Book 3	250	100		
7	Book 4	80.95	24.75		
8					

FIGURE EX 1.41

5. Use AutoFill to add two additional books to the list.
   a. Click cell **A4**, hold down the left mouse button and drag the mouse to cell **A7**. Release the mouse button. The cell range A4 through A7 should now appear selected.

    b. Click the **Fill Handle** (located at the lower right corner of the selected cell range).
    c. Drag down to cell **A9**, and release the mouse button.
    d. Excel adds Book 5 and Book 6 to the list.
6. Book 5 cost **`$115.00`** and can be sold for **`$60.00`**. Book 6 cost **`$175.00`** and can be sold for **`$90.00`**. Add these data to the worksheet.
    a. Click cell **B8** and type: **`115`**
    b. Press Tab and type: **`60`**
    c. Click cell **B9** and type: **`175`**
    d. Press Tab and type: **`90`**
    e. Press Enter.
7. Modify the **status bar** to display the minimum value.
    a. Right-click anywhere on the **status bar**.
    b. Click **Minimum** to add a checkmark.
    c. Click anywhere to dismiss the menu.
8. Use the status bar to check the total value of the books and the minimum value.
    a. Click cell **C4**. Press and hold Shift and click cell **C9**. Release the Shift key.
    b. Look at the status bar and find the *Sum* value (**389.75**).
    c. Look at the status bar and find the *Min* value (**24.75**).
9. Use AutoSum to calculate total cost and total value. The totals should be placed in cells **B10** and **C10**.
    a. Click cell **A10** and type: **`Total`**
    b. Press Tab.
    c. Cell **B10** should be selected. Press and hold Shift and click cell **C10**. Release the Shift key.
    d. On the *Home* tab, in the *Editing* group, click the **AutoSum** button.
10. Change the number format for the cost and value numbers to the Accounting Number Format.
    a. Click cell **B4**. Press and hold Shift. Click cell **C10**. Release Shift.
    b. On the *Home* tab, in the *Number* group, click the **Accounting Number Format** button.
11. Enter a formula in cell **D4** to calculate the difference between the cost and the value for Book1. The formula will use only relative references because in the next step, you will use AutoFill to copy the formula down the column.
    a. Click cell **D4**.
    b. Type: =
    c. Click cell **B4**.
    d. Type: –
    e. Click cell **C4**.
    f. Press Enter

12. Use AutoFill to copy the formula to calculate the difference for books 2 through 6 and the total.
    a. Click cell **D4**.
    b. Click the **AutoFill handle**. Hold down the left mouse button and drag to cell **D10**. Release the mouse button.
13. Save the workbook. Do not close it or exit Excel.
14. Create a new file from a template called *Student grade and GPA tracker*.
    a. Click the **File** tab to open Backstage view.
    b. Click **New**.
    c. Open a new file based on the *Student grade and GPA tracker* template. (This step may require an active Internet connection.)
        i. The *Student grade and GPA tracker* template may appear in the list of templates automatically. If it does not, you will need to search for it. In the *Search online templates* box, type: `student grade tracker`
        ii. Click the template preview.
        iii. Click **Create**.
15. The new workbook based on the *Student grade and GPA tracker* template opens. This is a complex workbook using many advanced techniques. The good news is that you don't have to understand how this workbook was created in order to use it.
    a. The workbook includes four worksheets. The first worksheet, *Score Tracker*, lists all assignments the student has completed. Navigate to the other worksheets by clicking each of the sheet tabs and review the content of each. When you are finished, return to the first sheet, *Score Tracker*, by clicking that **worksheet** tab.
    b. Click cell **C4** (the cell displaying the text *Modern French*).
    c. Click the arrow that appears at the right side of the cell. The list of available classes appears. If you were using this template to actually create your own grade and GPA tracker, this list would display your classes. But where does this list come from?
    d. Click the **Settings** tab to go to the *Settings* worksheet.
    e. Note the classes listed in cells C9:C15. These are the same classes displayed in the list you saw in the *Score Tracker* sheet.
    f. Change the *Modern French* class name to *Conversational Latin*.
        i. Click cell **C9**. Verify that the status bar displays *Ready* to indicate that you are in Ready mode.
        ii. Type: `Conversational Latin`
        iii. Press [Enter]
    g. Use the spelling checker to verify that you did not misspell *Conversational Latin*.

    i. On the *Review* tab, in the *Proofing* group, click the **Spelling** button.
    ii. Excel should display an informational alert box asking if you want to continue checking spelling from the beginning of the sheet. Click **Yes**.
    iii. If you didn't make any spelling mistakes, Excel will display a message telling you that the spell check is complete. If you did make a mistake, select the correct spelling in the *Suggestions* list and click the **Change** button. Continue correcting mistakes until Excel tells you the spell check is complete. Click **OK**.
  h. Now return to the *Score Tracker* sheet and see how your change affected the list. The workbook template author used an advanced technique to create the relationship between the list of classes in the Settings sheet and the data entry drop-down list used in the *Score Tracker* sheet. At this stage, you do not need to understand how this was created, but you should understand how the data change on one sheet affects the data in the other sheet.
    i. Click the **Score Tracker** sheet tab. (You could also click the **Score Tracker** button near the top of the *Settings* worksheet.)
    ii. Click cell **C4** again (which still displays *Modern French*).
    iii. Expand the list by clicking the arrow.
    iv. Note the new entry at the top of the list — *Conversational Latin*.
    v. Click **Conversational Latin** to replace the text in the cell.
16. If you think you might like to come back to this workbook later for your personal use, this is a good point to save it. Be sure not to close the file. Use the file name: `[Your Initials]GradesAndGPA`
17. You should still have two workbooks open: the textbooks workbook from the beginning of the project and the grades and GPA workbook based on the template. Arrange the workbooks so you can see both at the same time.
  a. On the *View* tab, in the *Window* group, click the **Arrange All** button.
  b. In the *Arrange Windows* dialog, click the **Vertical** radio button. Click **OK**.
18. The grades and GPA workbook should be active. If not, click the title bar for that window. Review the Your Performance sheet and change the zoom level to 75% so you can see more of the data at once.
  a. Click the *Your Performance* tab.
  b. On the *View* tab, in the *Zoom* group, click the **Zoom** button.
  c. In the *Zoom* dialog, click the **75%** radio button for the zoom option you want. Click **OK**.
  d. Navigate to the *Score Tracker* worksheet again, and note that changing the zoom level of the *Your Performance* sheet did not affect the *Score Tracker* sheet.
19. Close both workbooks. If you made changes to the grades and GPA workbook and you plan to continue using it, be sure to save the changes.

projects

Data files for projects can be found by logging into your SIMnet account and going to the *Library* section.

challenge yourself 1.3

In this project, you will complete a timesheet for David Swinson, similar to the one you worked on in Skill Review 1.1. You will need to enter and format missing dates, correct a data entry mistake, apply number formatting, and enter formulas to calculate the total billable hours per day, the daily total for each day, and the bill total for the week.

Skills needed to complete this project:

- Working in Protected View (Skill 1.3)
- Navigating a Workbook (Skill 1.2)
- Entering and Editing Text and Numbers in Cells (Skill 1.4)
- Inserting Data Using AutoFill (Skill 1.7)
- Entering Dates and Applying Date Formats (Skill 1.6)
- Calculating Totals with the Quick Analysis Tool (Skill 1.12)
- Applying Number Formats (Skill 1.5)
- Understanding Absolute and Relative References (Skill 1.9)
- Entering Simple Formulas (Skill 1.8)
- Previewing and Printing a Worksheet (Skill 1.18)

1. Open the start file **EX2016-ChallengeYourself-1-3** and resave the file as: `[your initials]EX-ChallengeYourself-1-3`
2. If the workbook opens in Protected View, enable editing so you can make changes to the workbook.
3. Verify that the *Swinson Hours* worksheet is active.
4. If necessary, scroll to the bottom of the worksheet so you can see the empty timesheet beginning on row 19.
5. The dates are missing from the timesheet. Enter the date `8/1/2016` in cell **B20**.
6. Use AutoFill to complete the dates in cells **C20:H20**.
7. Change the date format for **B20:H20** to the Short Date format.
8. The hours reported for the Proctor client on Friday (cell F25) are incorrect. Change the number in cell **F25** to: **4**
9. Use the Quick Analysis tool to enter total hours for each day. Use the cell range **B22:H25**. The daily totals should be inserted into the range **B26:H26**.
10. Format the hours billed section (cells **B22:H26**) to use the Comma Style number format. Be sure to include the total row.

11. Enter a formula in cell **B28** to calculate the daily bill for Monday, August 1. The formula should calculate the total billable hours for the day (cell **B26**) times the billable rate (**B4**). Be sure to use an absolute cell reference for the billable rate.
12. Use AutoFill to copy the formula to the remaining days in the timesheet (cells **C28:H28**).
13. Calculate the bill total for the week by summing the daily bill amounts. In cell **B29**, enter a formula using the SUM function. The function argument should be the range of cells representing the daily bill totals (**B28:H28**).
14. Apply the **Currency** number format to cells **B28:H28** and cell **B29**.
15. Preview how the worksheet will look when printed.
16. Save and close the workbook.

projects

Data files for projects can be found by logging into your SIMnet account and going to the *Library* section.

challenge yourself 1.4

In this project you will work with a college budget spreadsheet. You will change a few values in the budget, modify number formats, and calculate totals and the difference between expected income and expenses. You will then create a new budget workbook from a template, and practice changing the zoom level and arranging the workbooks.

Skills needed to complete this project:

- Working in Protected View (Skill 1.3)
- Entering and Editing Text and Numbers in Cells (Skill 1.4)
- Navigating a Workbook (Skill 1.2)
- Using AutoSum to Insert a SUM Function (Skill 1.11)
- Calculating Totals Using the Quick Analysis Tool (Skill 1.12)
- Using the Status Bar (Skill 1.13)
- Applying Number Formats (Skill 1.5)
- Understanding Absolute and Relative References (Skill 1.9)
- Entering Simple Formulas (Skill 1.8)
- Checking Spelling (Skill 1.17)
- Creating a New Workbook Using a Template (Skill 1.15)
- Arranging Workbooks (Skill 1.16)
- Changing the Zoom Level (Skill 1.14)

1. Open the start file **EX2016-ChallengeYourself-1-4** and resave the file as: `[your initials]EX-ChallengeYourself-1-4`
2. If the workbook opens in Protected View, enable editing so you can make changes to the workbook.
3. Make the following changes to the *Budget* worksheet:
   a. Change the *Utilities* item to **Electric** (cell **A12**).
   b. Change the Insurance value from *90* to **75** (cell **B19**).
4. The worksheet is missing formulas to calculate totals. Enter formulas using the **SUM** function to calculate the following totals. Use any of the methods you learned in this chapter.
   a. Enter a formula in cell **B7** to calculate the total monthly income.
   b. Enter a formula in cell **B24** to calculate the total monthly expenses.
   c. Enter a formula in cell **E16** to calculate the total semester expenses.

   d. Use the **status bar** to verify that the formula is calculating the correct total for each cell range.

5. Cell **E18** displays the number of months in the semester. Change the number format in this cell to the **Number** format with no numbers showing after the decimal (so the number appears as **4** instead of **$4.00**).
6. The number format in the *Semester Expenses* section does not match the number format in the other sections of the worksheet. Change the number format for cells **E11:E16** to the **Accounting Number Format**.
7. Review the formulas in the *Discretionary Income* section.
   a. Cells **E4:E6** should contain references to the cells where you just entered the formulas to calculate totals. Add the appropriate formula to cell **E6** to reference the value in cell **E16** (the total semester expenses).
   b. The semester is four months long, so the formulas in cells **E4** and **E5** should multiply the total monthly income and total monthly expenses by four. Correct the formulas in cells **E4** and **E6**. Use an absolute reference to the value in cell **E18** (the number of months in the semester).
8. Use spelling checker to find and correct any spelling errors in the *Budget* worksheet. (*Hint*: There is one spelling error on this worksheet.)
9. Save the workbook. Do not close it or exit Excel.
10. Create a new file from a template called *Personal Expenses Calculator*. If you do not see this template, search for it using the search phrase *personal expenses*.
11. Explore the worksheets in this workbook.
12. If you think you might like to come back to this workbook later for your personal use, this is a good point to save it. Be sure not to close the file. Use the file name: **[Your Initials]PersonalExpenses**
13. You should still have two workbooks open: the college budget workbook from the beginning of the project and the personal expenses workbook based on the template. Arrange the workbooks so you can see both at the same time.
    a. Try different arrangements until you find the one that works best for you.
    b. Practice moving back and forth between the two workbooks.
14. Make the personal budget workbook active and navigate to the Dashboard worksheet. Modify the zoom to **80%**.
15. Close both workbooks. If you made changes to the personal budget workbook and you plan to continue using it, be sure to save the changes.

Data files for projects can be found by logging into your SIMnet account and going to the *Library* section.

on your own 1.5

For Spring Break, you've decided to take a seven-day road trip. Use this Excel workbook to calculate the number of miles you will drive each day and the gas cost for each day. Use the techniques you've learned in this chapter to calculate the total miles and the total gas cost. Don't forget to end the trip at the same location you started! You may want to use the Internet to look up mileage, MPG (miles per gallon), and gas price information.

Skills needed to complete this project:

- Navigating a Workbook (Skill 1.2)
- Working in Protected View (Skill 1.3)
- Entering and Editing Text and Numbers in Cells (Skill 1.4)
- Entering Dates and Applying Date Formats (Skill 1.6)
- Inserting Data Using AutoFill (Skill 1.7)
- Understanding Absolute and Relative References (Skill 1.9)
- Entering Simple Formulas (Skill 1.8)
- Calculating Totals with the Quick Analysis Tool (Skill 1.12)
- Using AutoSum to Insert a SUM Function (Skill 1.11)
- Applying Number Formats (Skill 1.5)
- Checking Spelling (Skill 1.17)

1. Open the start file **EX2016-OnYourOwn-1-5** and resave the file as: `[your initials]EX-OnYourOwn-1-5`
2. If the workbook opens in Protected View, click the **Enable Editing** button in the Message Bar at the top of the workbook so you can modify the workbook.
3. Complete the *Trip Details* section of the *Spring Break* worksheet:
   a. Enter the dates of your road trip. Use a date format that includes the day of the week.
   b. Enter a start and end location for each day. Remember—the starting location for each day should be the same as the end location for the previous day. If you use a formula with a relative reference rather than retyping the location name for each start location, you can use AutoFill to complete the start location column. Consider using a formula to ensure that the final end location is the same as the first start location.

c. Look up and enter the miles between each location. Use an appropriate number format for the *Number of Miles* column. (Hint: Use *mapquest.com* or *maps.google.com* to look up the mileage between locations.)

4. Enter your car information including the MPG (miles per gallon). If you don't know your MPG, the government Web site *www.fueleconomy.gov* has excellent information on average MPG for a variety of car makes, models, and years.
5. Enter the average gas price in your area (or the area of your road trip). Again, the *www.fueleconomy.gov* Web site has links to this type of information.
6. Enter a formula to calculate the gas cost per mile for your car (gas price per gallon/your car's MPG).
7. Now that you have the gas cost per mile for your car, you can figure the cost of the road trip. Enter a formula to figure the gas cost per day (the number of miles * your gas cost per mile) for the first day of the trip. Be sure to use absolute and relative references as appropriate, so you can use AutoFill to copy the formula to the rest of the cells in the *Gas Cost per Day* column.
8. Apply appropriate number formats to all the cells in the workbook that display costs. *Hint:* The Accounting Number Format is best for costs that appear in a column. For costs that appear on their own, you may want to use the Currency Style format.
9. Don't forget to spell check the workbook.
10. Save and close the workbook.

projects

Data files for projects can be found by logging into your SIMnet account and going to the *Library* section.

fix it 1.6

The workbook for this project tracks how many miles you walked each day for the week of October 2, 2016, through October 8, 2016. Your goal for each day is to walk at least four miles. Use the skills learned in this chapter to fix the workbook.

Skills needed to complete this project:

- Navigating a Workbook (Skill 1.2)
- Working in Protected View (Skill 1.3)
- Entering and Editing Text and Numbers in Cells (Skill 1.4)
- Entering Dates and Applying Date Formats (Skill 1.6)
- Inserting Data Using AutoFill (Skill 1.7)
- Applying Number Formats (Skill 1.5)
- Understanding Absolute and Relative References (Skill 1.9)
- Entering Simple Formulas (Skill 1.8)
- Calculating Totals with the Quick Analysis Tool (Skill 1.12)
- Using AutoSum to Insert a SUM Function (Skill 1.11)
- Checking Spelling (Skill 1.17)

1. Open the start file **EX2016-FixIt-1-6** and resave the file as: `[your initials]EX-FixIt-1-6`
2. If the workbook opens in Protected View, click the **Enable Editing** button in the Message Bar at the top of the workbook so you can modify the workbook.
3. The worksheet is missing a title. Type this title in cell A1: `My Exercise Log`
4. The daily goal should be 3, not 30. Correct the value in cell **D2**.
5. The dates are missing from cells **A6:A11**. Use AutoFill to complete the dates for the rest of the week.
6. The exercise log would be more useful if the date showed the day of the week in addition to the date. Change the date format for cells **A5:A11** so the date displays in this format: **Sunday, October 2, 2016**
7. The mileage for each day should use the Comma Style number format. Correct the number format in cells **C5:C11**.
8. Use one of the skills you learned in this chapter to enter formulas using the **SUM** function in cells **C12** and **D12** to calculate the weekly total minutes and miles.
9. The formulas in the *Under/Over Goal* column are not quite right. Fix the formula in cell **D5** to use an absolute reference where appropriate, and then use AutoFill to replace the formulas in cells **D6:D11**.

10. There may be spelling errors. Be sure to use spelling checker before you finish the project.
11. Preview how the worksheet will look when printed.
12. Save and close the workbook.

chapter 2

Formatting Cells

In this chapter, you will learn the following skills:

- Move and copy cell contents using cut, copy, and paste
- Insert, delete, and merge cells
- Work with text and font attributes
- Apply borders and shading
- Format cells using cell styles
- Copy formatting using Format Painter
- Format cells using conditional formatting
- Modify cell data using find and replace
- Work with the print area

introduction

This chapter focuses on skills for working with cells and cell ranges. You will learn to move data and to insert, delete, and merge cells to create a worksheet structure that fits your data. This chapter also covers the essential skills for formatting cells, including in-depth coverage of conditional formatting. Formatting not only enhances a workbook's appearance, but when used properly, it can make the data easier to understand.

Skill 2.1 Cutting, Copying, and Pasting Cell Content

While you may be familiar with cut, copy, and paste functionality from other applications, keep in mind that in Excel you are working with the cell contents – not the cells themselves. **Cut** removes the content from the selected cell, **Copy** duplicates the content from the selected cell, and **Paste** replaces the cell content with whatever was cut or copied.

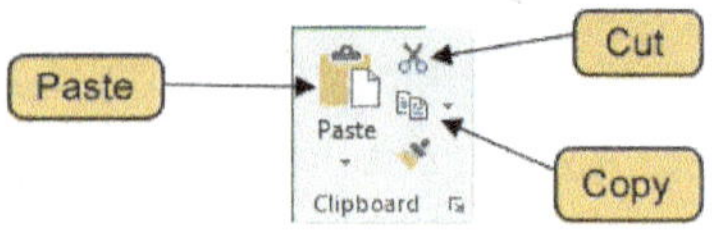

FIGURE EX 2.1

When using *Copy/Paste* or *Cut/Paste* commands in Excel, watch out for cells containing formulas. If you ***copy*** and paste a cell containing a formula with relative references, Excel will update the references to reflect the new position in the workbook. However, if you ***cut*** and paste instead, Excel will treat the formula as if it contained absolute references and will not update the cell references in the formula.

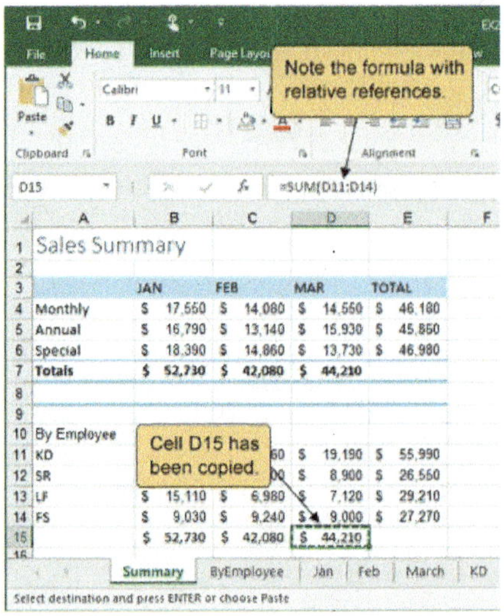

FIGURE EX 2.2

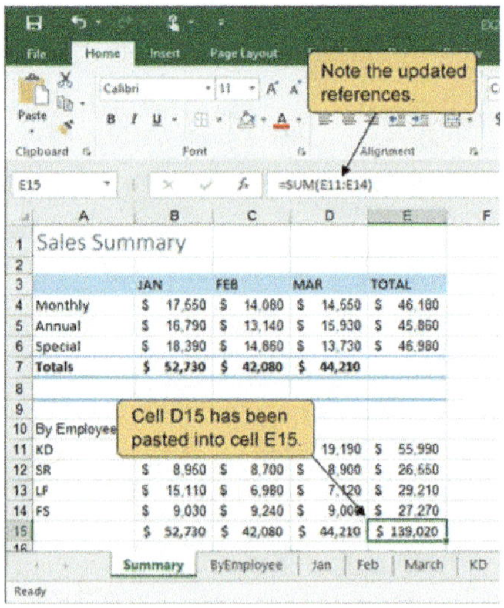

FIGURE EX 2.3

Use the *Cut, Copy,* and *Paste* commands to move or duplicate cell content from one location to another:

1. Select the cell, cell range, row, or column that contains the data you want to move or copy.
2. On the *Home* tab, in the *Clipboard* group, click the **Cut** or **Copy** button.
3. The selection appears with a flashing dotted line around it, and the contents of the cells are stored temporarily in the computer's memory.

4. Click the cell where you want to paste the content. If you selected a range of cells to cut or copy, click the cell in the upper left corner of the area where you want to paste.
5. Click the **Paste** button to paste the cell content and formatting. Notice that if you use the *Cut* command, Excel does not remove the content from its original location until the *Paste* command is used.

tips & tricks

A quick way to move cell content from one location to another is to click and drag with the mouse. Select the cell(s) containing the content you want to move. Place the mouse pointer at the edge of the selection. When the pointer changes to the move pointer, click and drag to the new location, and then release the mouse button.

You can use the same technique to copy cell contents to another location. Press and hold Ctrl to change the move pointer to the copy pointer, drag to the new location, and then release the mouse button.

tell me more

If you paste into a cell that contains data, the original cell data will be overwritten. To paste without overwriting existing cells, use the *Insert Copied Cells* or *Insert Cut Cells* command instead.

1. Copy or cut the cells you want to insert.
2. Select the cell where you want to insert.
3. On the *Home* tab, in the *Cells* group, click the **Insert** button arrow and select **Insert Copied Cells** or **Insert Cut Cells**.

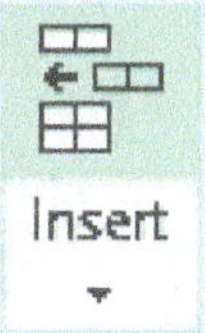

Refer to the skill *Inserting and Deleting Cells* for information about formatting options when using the *Insert* command.

another method

To apply the *Cut*, *Copy*, or *Paste* command, you can also use the following shortcuts:

- **Cut**: Press Ctrl + X, or right-click and select **Cut**.
- **Copy**: Press Ctrl + C, or right-click and select **Copy**.
- **Paste**: Press Ctrl; + V, or right-click and select **Paste**.

let me try *Live!*

Open the student data file **EX2-01-Sales** and try this skill on your own:

1. Copy cell **D15**, and paste to cell **E15**. Note that the formula updated to reflect the new cell range E11:E14.
2. Use the *Cut* and *Paste* commands to move the content in cell **A2** to cell **A10**.
3. If you will be moving on to the next skill in this chapter, leave the workbook open to continue working. If not, save the file as directed by your instructor and close it.

Skill 2.2 Using Paste Options

When you copy and paste data in Excel, you can use the default *Paste* command to paste the copied data (including formulas and formatting) into the selected cell, or you can select from the paste options to control more precisely what is pasted.

	**Paste**—The default paste command that pastes all of the source content and formatting.
	**Formulas**—Pastes the formulas but none of the formatting. The pasted content will use the cell and number formatting of the cell into which it was pasted.
	**Formulas & Number Formatting**—Pastes the formulas and number formatting but none of the cell formatting such as font size, borders, and shading.
	**Keep Source Formatting**—Pastes the content, including formulas, and all formatting from the source.
	**No Borders**—Pastes the content, including formulas, and all formatting except borders.
	**Keep Source Column Widths**—Pastes the copied cell, including formulas and all number and cell formatting. Also adjusts the column width to match the width of the source column.
	**Transpose**—Pastes the rows from the source into columns, and the columns from the source into rows.

When your source includes formulas, you have the option to paste the calculated cell values without pasting the underlying formulas.

	**Values**—Pastes only the values, not the underlying formula or cell formatting.
	**Values & Number Formatting**—Pastes only the values, not the underlying formulas. Includes number formatting but not other cell formatting such as borders and shading.
	**Values & Source Formatting**—Pastes only the values, not the underlying formulas. Includes all formatting from the source.

The final group of paste options provides alternatives to pasting the actual contents of one cell into another.

	**Formatting**—Pastes only the cell and number formatting, not the formula or cell value from the source.
	**Link**—Pastes a formula that references the source cell rather than pasting the contents of the source itself. When the source cell is updated, the linked cell displays the update automatically.
	**Picture**—Pastes an image of the source cell rather than the actual cell contents. The pasted cell looks like any other cell in the worksheet, except it cannot be edited, and when you select the cell, nothing appears in the formula bar.
	**Linked Picture**—Pastes an image, like the Picture paste option, but updates when the source cell is updated.

To use paste options from the *Paste* button on the Ribbon:

1. Copy the content you want to paste and then navigate to the location where you want to paste.
2. On the *Home* tab, in the *Clipboard* group, click the bottom part of the **Paste** button (the **Paste** button arrow to expand the *Paste Options* menu.

3. Move your mouse over the icon for each paste option to see a live preview of how the paste would look, and then click the paste option you want.

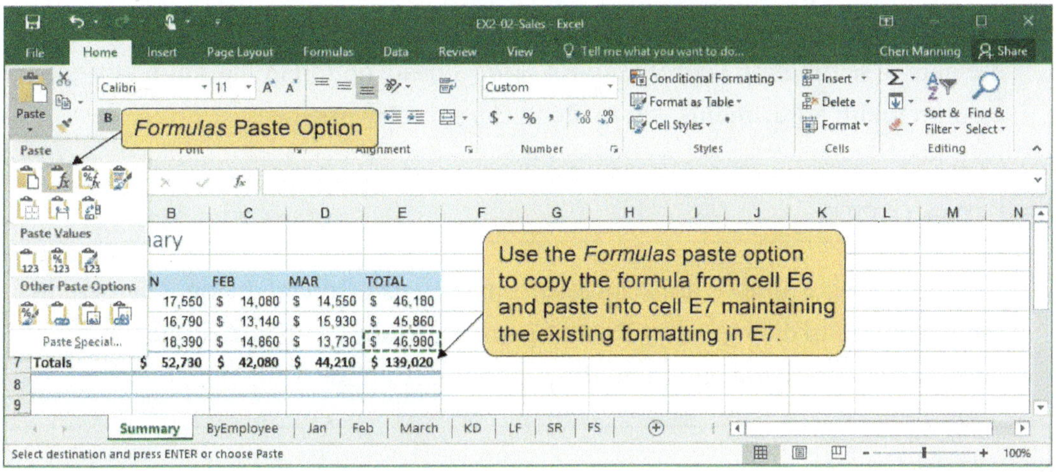

FIGURE EX 2.4

To use the *Paste Options* button:

1. Copy the content you want to paste.
2. Use the standard *Paste* command to paste the content where you want it.
3. The source content is pasted using the default *Paste* option, and the *Paste Options* button appears at the lower right corner of the pasted content.
4. Click the **Paste Options** button or press Ctrl to display the *Paste Options* menu. This is the same menu that is available from the *Paste* button on the Ribbon, but moving your mouse over the icons does not show a preview of how the paste would look.
5. Click the paste option you want.

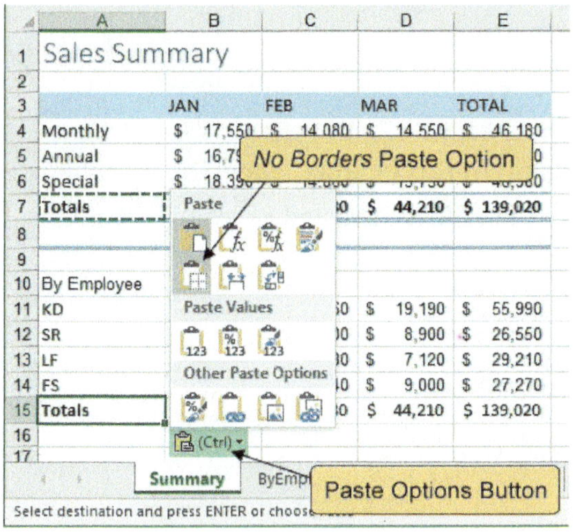

FIGURE EX 2.5

tips & tricks

A useful paste option is *Keep Source Column Widths*. Often, when you paste data into a new worksheet, the default column width is too narrow to display the data. Use the *Keep Source Column Widths* paste option to maintain any column width adjustments you made in the source worksheet.

tell me more

Additional paste options are available from the *Paste Special* dialog. To open the *Paste Special* dialog, select **Paste Special...** from the bottom of the paste options from the *Paste* button on the Ribbon or from the right-click menu.

another method

You can also access the paste options from the right-click menu. Six of the paste options appear on the right-click menu (*Paste*, *Values*, *Formulas*, *Transpose*, *Formatting*, and *Paste Link*). To select an option from the full *Paste Options* menu, point to **Paste Special...**, and then click the paste option you want.

let me try *Live!*

If you do not have the data file from the previous skill open, open the student data file **EX2-02-Sales** and try this skill on your own:

1. On the *Summary* worksheet, copy cell **E6** and paste only the formula to cell **E7**. Do not paste the original cell formatting.
2. Copy cell **A7** and paste the cell value and formatting without borders into cell **A15**.
3. If you will be moving on to the next skill in this chapter, leave the workbook open to continue working. If not, save the file as directed by your instructor and close it.

Skill 2.3 Inserting and Deleting Cells

Use the *Insert* command to insert an empty cell, group of cells, row, or column into your worksheet.

To insert an empty cell range, select the range where you want to insert the new cells.

1. If you have a vertical cell range selected, click the **Insert** button and Excel will automatically shift existing cells to the right to make room for the new cells.
2. If you have a single cell or a horizontal cell range selected, click the **Insert** button and Excel will automatically shift existing cells down to make room for the new cells.

If you want more control over whether cells are shifted to the right or down, use the *Insert* dialog.

1. Select the cell or cell range where you want to insert the new cell(s).
2. On the *Home* tab, in the *Cells* group, click the **Insert** button arrow.
3. Click **Insert Cells...** to open the *Insert* dialog.
4. Select the option you want and then click **OK**.

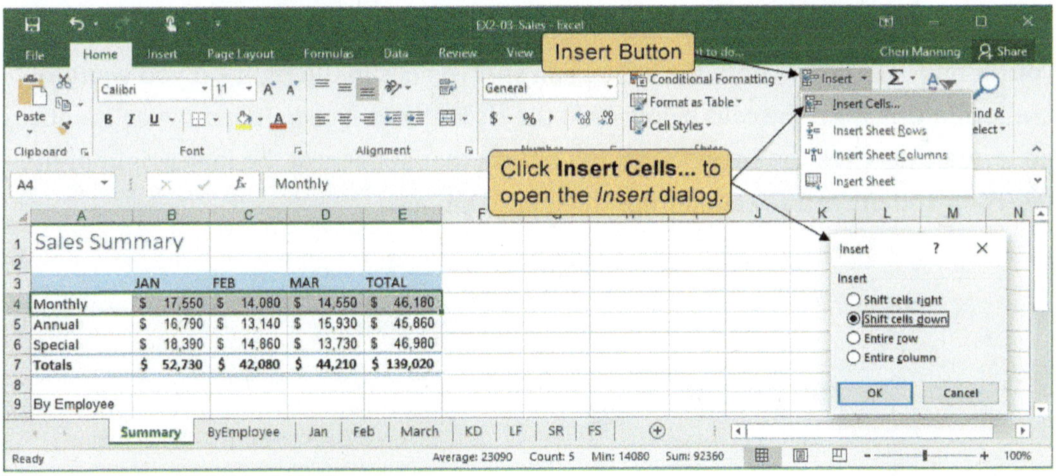

FIGURE EX 2.6

Recall that in Excel, pasting cell content that has been cut or copied will overwrite the content of the cell where it is pasted. If you want to insert the content instead, use the *Insert* command.

1. Cut or copy the cell content and then click the cell where you want to insert the new content.

2. On the *Home* tab, in the *Cells* group, click the **Insert** button arrow.
3. Instead of the *Insert Cells...* option, you now have *Insert Cut Cells* or *Insert Copied Cells*. Select this option to insert new cells with the cut or copied content. These commands are only available immediately after using the *Cut* or *Copy* command.

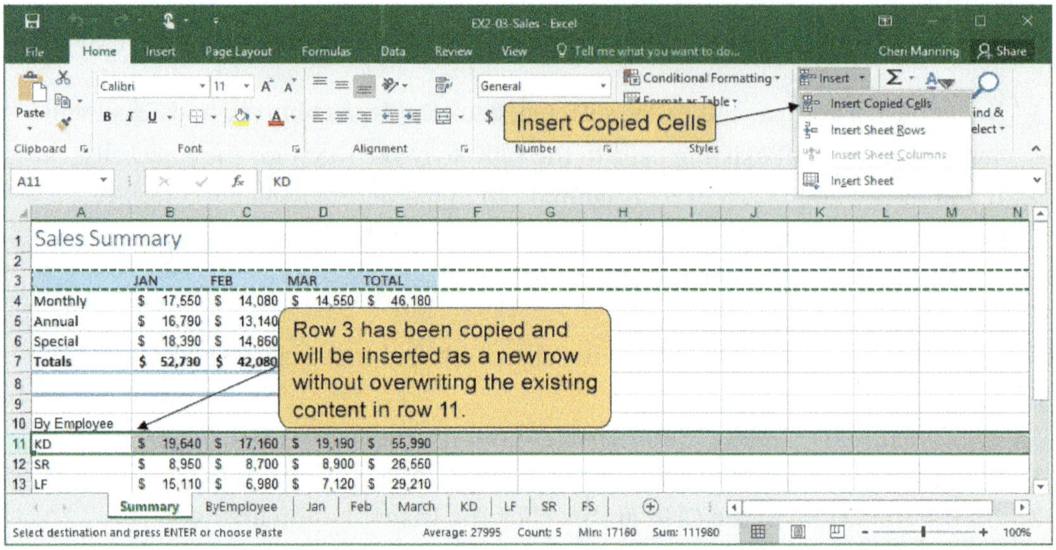

FIGURE EX 2.7

When you insert new cells, the cells will use the same formatting as the cells above (if you shifted cells down) or to the left (if you shifted cells to the right). If you want to use formatting from the cells below or to the right instead, or to insert the cells with no formatting, click the **Insert Options** button that appears at the lower right of the insertion and make a selection from the menu options.

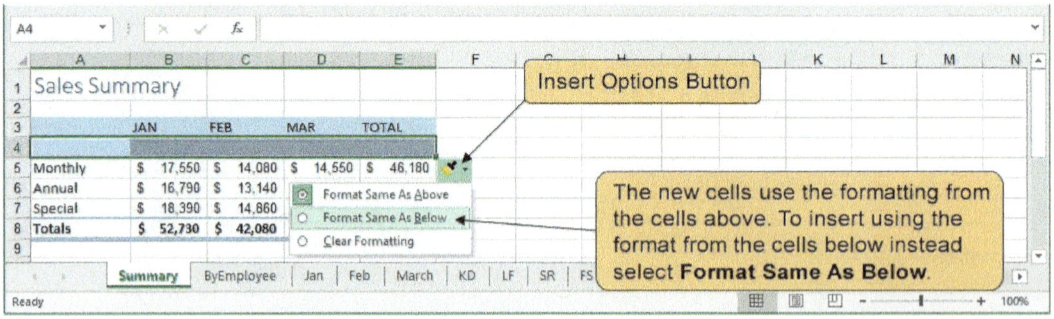

FIGURE EX 2.8

Of course, you can also delete cells. Deleting cells not only deletes the information and formatting in the cell, but also shifts the layout of the worksheet. Even if you delete an empty cell, you shift all the surrounding cells into new positions.

1. If you have a vertical cell range selected, click the **Delete** button and Excel will automatically shift existing cells to the left.

2. If you have a single cell or a horizontal cell range selected, click the **Insert** button and Excel will automatically shift existing cells up.

If you want more control over how the remaining cells are shifted, use the *Delete* dialog.

1. On the *Home* tab, in the *Cells* group, click the **Delete** button arrow.
2. Click **Delete Cells...** to open the *Delete* dialog.
3. Select the option you want and then click **OK**.

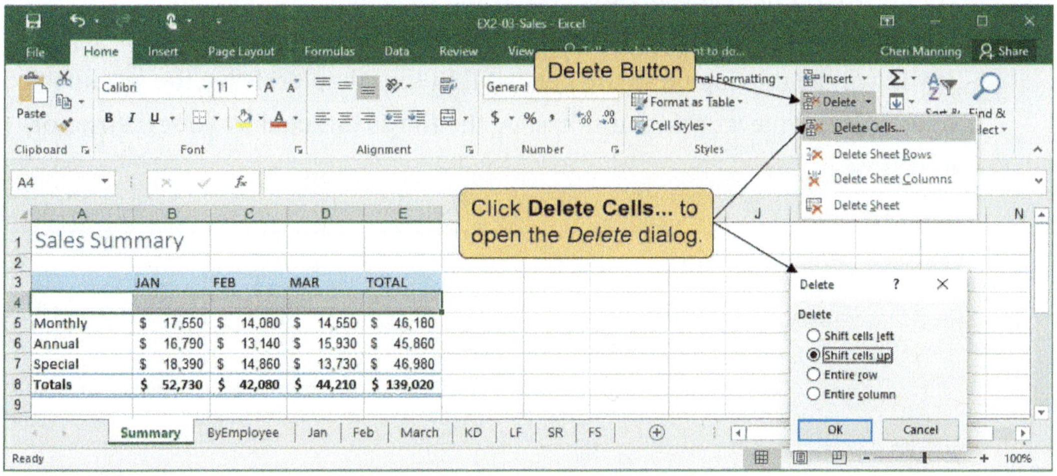

FIGURE EX 2.9

tips & tricks

Be careful not to delete cells that are referenced in formulas. Even though a new value may shift into the original cell's position, the formula will still be looking for the original cell (now deleted), causing an invalid cell reference error.

another method

Both *Insert...* and *Delete...* commands are available from the right-click menu.

Pressing [Delete] will delete the contents of the cell but not the cell itself.

let me try *Live!*

If you do not have the data file from the previous skill open, open the student data file **EX2-03-Sales** and try this skill on your own:

1. On the *Summary* worksheet, select cells **A4:E4**.
2. Insert cells so the remaining cells shift down.
3. Display the *Insert Options* menu and select the option to format the new cells the same as those below.
4. Delete cells **A4:E4**, shifting the remaining cells up.
5. Copy row **3** and insert a copy above row **11**.
6. If you will be moving on to the next skill in this chapter, leave the workbook open to continue working. If not, save the file as directed by your instructor and close it.

Skill 2.4 Wrapping Text in Cells

When you type text in a cell, the text will appear to continue to the right as far as it can until there is another cell that contains data. At that point, the text will appear to be cut off. You could increase the width of the cell to show all the text, but do you really want the entire column to be that wide? If your worksheet includes cells with more text than will comfortably fit in the cell, you should use the wrap text feature. When wrap text is enabled for a cell, the text in the cell will automatically wrap to multiple lines, just as a paragraph would.

To wrap text in a cell:

> On the *Home* tab, in the *Alignment* group, click the **Wrap Text** button. Notice the button appears selected when text wrapping is active for the cell.

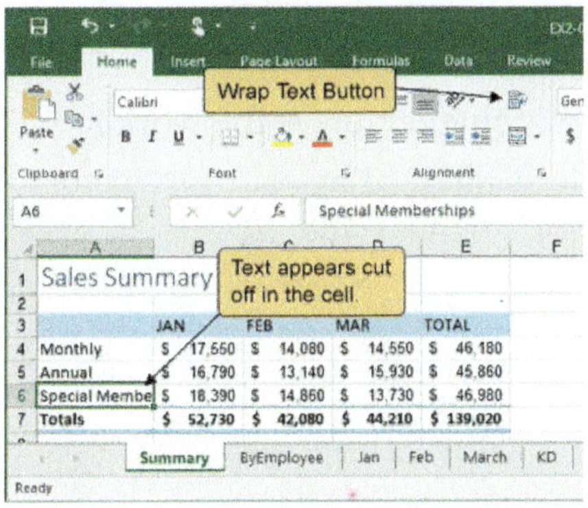

FIGURE EX 2.10

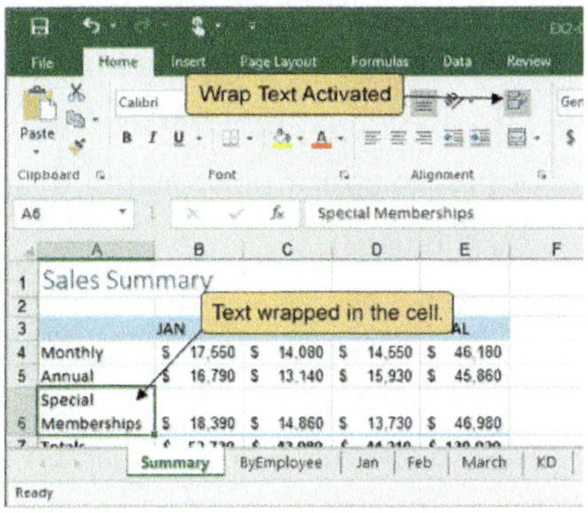

FIGURE EX 2.11

To turn off text wrapping in a cell, click the **Wrap Text** button again to deselect it.

tips & tricks

> The text wrapping feature works only for cells that contain text. If a column is too narrow to display its numerical data, Excel will not wrap it. Instead, the cell will show a series of # symbols, indicating that the cell contains numerical data, but the column is too narrow to display it.

another method

You can also turn on the text wrapping feature from the *Format Cells* dialog.

1. On the *Home* tab, in the *Alignment* group, click the **Alignment Settings dialog launcher** to open the *Format Cells* dialog.
2. In the *Text control* section, click the **Wrap Text** check box.
3. Click **OK**.

let me try *Live!*

If you do not have the data file from the previous skill open, open the student data file **EX2-04-Sales** and try this skill on your own:

1. On the *Summary* worksheet, select cell **A6** and change the text to:
2. Activate text wrapping for cell **A6**.
3. If you will be moving on to the next skill in this chapter, leave the workbook open to continue working. If not, save the file as directed by your instructor and close it.

Skill 2.5 Using Undo and Redo

If you make a mistake when working, the **Undo** command allows you to reverse the last action you performed. The **Redo** command allows you to reverse the *Undo* command and restore the file to its previous state. The Quick Access Toolbar gives you immediate access to both these commands.

To undo the last action taken, click the **Undo** button on the Quick Access Toolbar.

To redo the last action taken, click the **Redo** button on the Quick Access Toolbar.

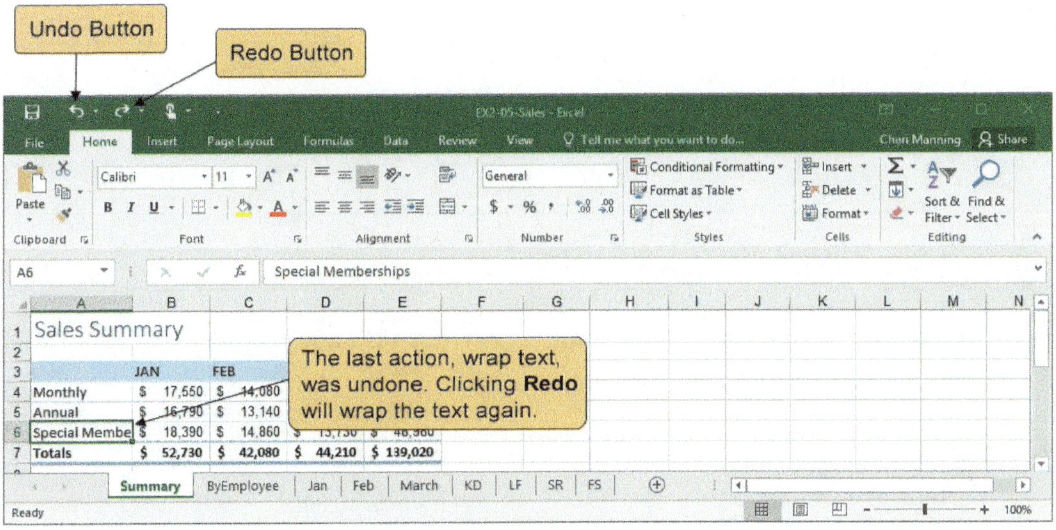

FIGURE EX 2.12

To undo multiple actions at the same time:

1. Click the **Undo** button arrow to expand the list of your most recent actions.
2. Click an action in the list.
3. The action you click will be undone, along with all the actions completed after that. In other words, your workbook will revert to the state it was in before that action.

tips & tricks

Be careful when using the *Undo* and *Redo* commands in Excel. In other Office applications, undo and redo actions are confined to the file you are currently working on–even if you have multiple files open. However, in Excel, the undo-redo list of actions includes all the open workbooks. This means that if you are working on multiple Excel files at the same time, using the *Undo* command can actually undo an action in one of the other open workbooks.

another method

- To undo an action, you can also press Ctrl + Z.
- To redo an action, you can also press Ctrl + Y.

let me try *Live!*

If you do not have the data file from the previous skill open, open the student data file **EX2-05-Sales** and try this skill on your own:

1. Undo the last action.
2. Redo the last action.
3. If you will be moving on to the next skill in this chapter, leave the workbook open to continue working. If not, save the file as directed by your instructor and close it.

Skill 2.6 Aligning Cells

Alignment refers to how text and numbers are positioned within the cell both horizontally and vertically. By default, cells use the **General horizontal alignment**. When cells are formatted using the General horizontal alignment, Excel detects the type of content in the cell. Cells that contain text are aligned to the left, and cells that contain numbers are aligned to the right.

To change the horizontal alignment of a cell, click one of the horizontal alignment buttons located on the *Home* tab, in the *Alignment* group: **Align Left**, **Center**, or **Align Right**.

To change the vertical alignment of a cell, click one of the vertical alignment buttons located on the *Home* tab, in the *Alignment* group: **Top Align**, **Middle Align**, or **Bottom Align**.

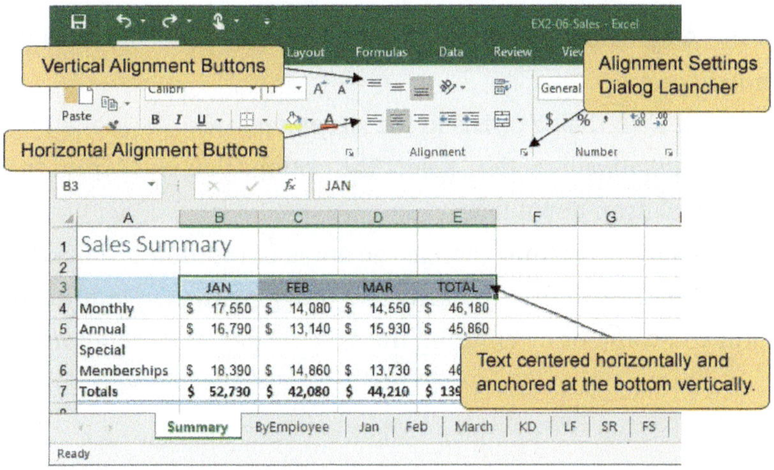

FIGURE EX 2.13

You can also change the angle at which the content displays.

On the *Home* tab, in the *Alignment* group, click the **Orientation** button and select one of the options.

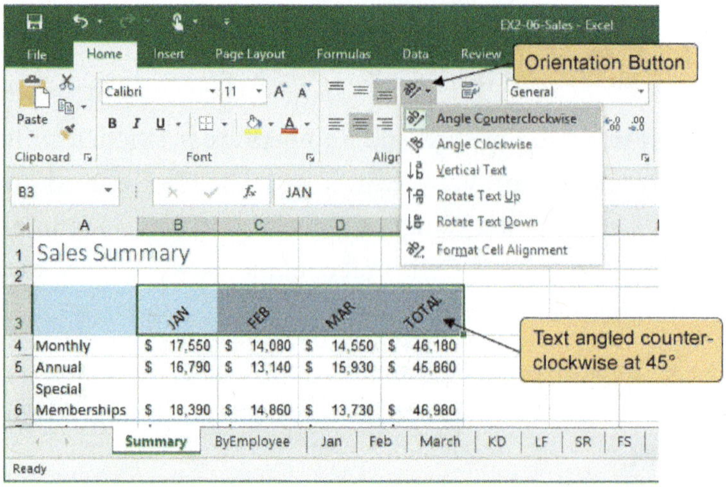

FIGURE EX 2.14

The alignment and orientation options are also available from the *Format Cells* dialog, *Alignment* tab. To change alignment using the *Format Cells* dialog:

1. Click the **Alignment Settings dialog launcher** at the lower right corner of the *Alignment* group.
2. The *Format Cells* dialog opens to the *Alignment* tab.
3. In the *Text alignment* section, select the options you want from the **Horizontal** and **Vertical** drop-down lists.
4. In the *Orientation* section, change the angle of rotation by clicking one of the dots on the *Orientation* dial, by clicking and dragging the *Orientation* dial to the position you want, or by entering the specific degree of rotation in the *Degrees* box.
5. Click **OK**.

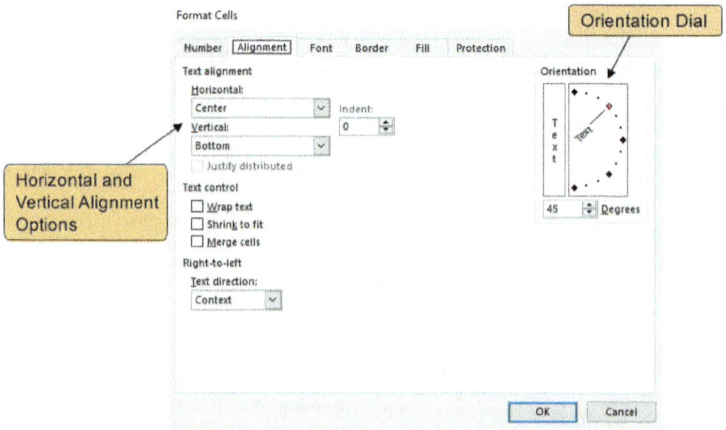

FIGURE EX 2.15

tips & tricks

If you have narrow columns of data with descriptive headers, try using one of the orientation options to angle the cells containing the header text.

let me try *Live!*

If you do not have the data file from the previous skill open, open the student data file **EX2-06-Sales** and try this skill on your own:

1. On the *Summary* worksheet, select cells **B3:E3**.
2. Center the content in each cell horizontally.
3. Change the angle of rotation for these cells to counterclockwise at 45°.
4. If you will be moving on to the next skill in this chapter, leave the workbook open to continue working. If not, save the file as directed by your instructor and close it.

Skill 2.7 Merging Cells and Splitting Merged Cells

Merging cells is one way to control the appearance of your worksheet. You can merge cells to create a header cell across multiple columns of data or center a title across your worksheet. The *Merge & Center* button automatically merges the selected cells and then centers the data from the first cell across the entire merged area. When you merge cells together, Excel will keep only the data in the uppermost left cell. All other data will be lost.

To merge cells and center their content:

1. Select the cells you want to merge, making sure the text you want to keep is in the uppermost left cell.
2. On the *Home* tab, in the *Alignment* group, click the **Merge & Center** button.

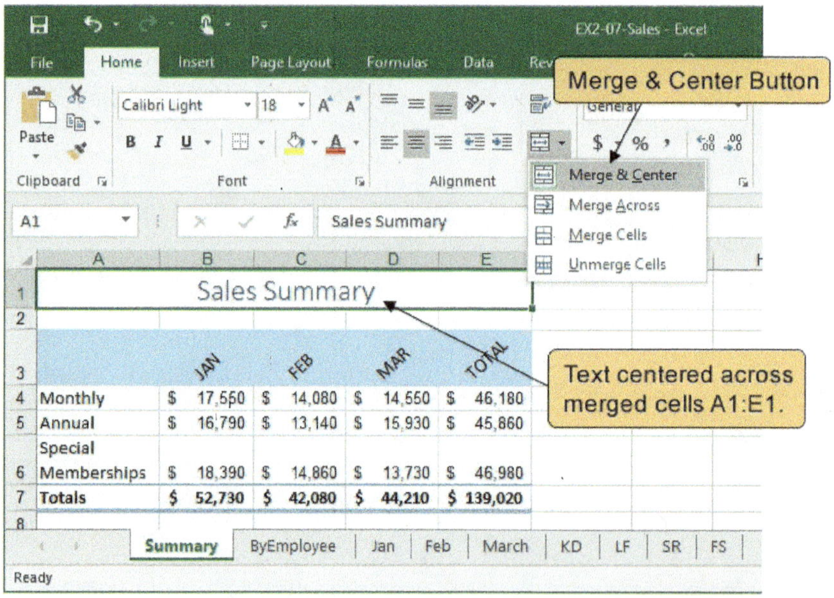

FIGURE EX 2.16

Click the *Merge & Center* button arrow for additional merge commands:

Merge Across—lets you merge cells in multiple rows without merging the rows together. The cells in each row are merged together, keeping the data in the leftmost cell in each row, while still keeping each row separate.

Merge Cells—lets you merge cells together without centering the data. Like the *Merge & Center* command, *Merge Cells* combines all the selected cells into one cell, keeping only the data in the uppermost left cell.

Unmerge Cells—splits a merged cell back into its original cells.

You can also merge and center cells from the *Format Cells* dialog:

1. On the *Home* tab, in the *Alignment* group, click the **Alignment Settings dialog launcher** to open the *Format Cells* dialog.
2. On the *Alignment* tab, in the *Text alignment* section, click the **Horizontal** arrow and select **Center** from the dropdown list. (You can also select **Center Across Selection**. When you merge the cells, it does not matter if the horizontal alignment is *Center* or *Center Across Selection.*)
3. In the *Text control* section, click the **Merge cells** check box.
4. Click **OK**.

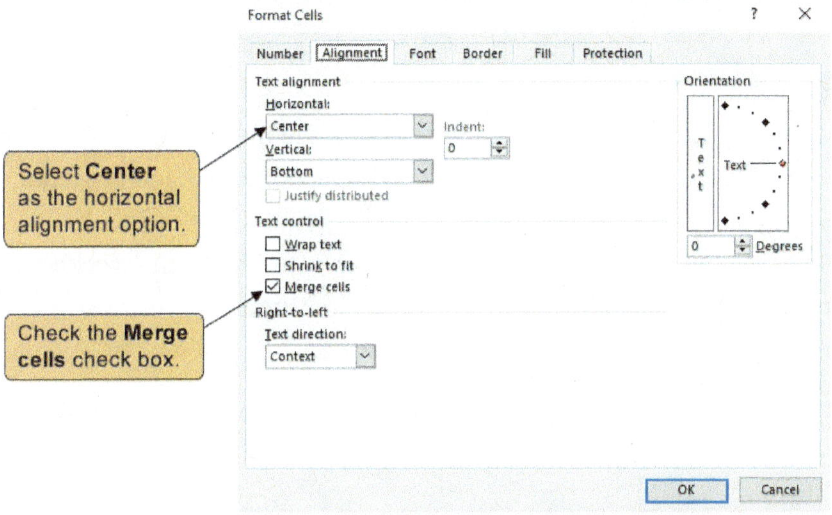

FIGURE EX 2.17

To unmerge a merged cell, use one of these methods:

- On the *Home* tab, in the *Alignment* group, click the **Merge & Center** button. When the selected cell is a merged cell, clicking the *Merge & Center* button will undo the merge and reset the horizontal alignment to *General*.
- On the *Home* tab, in the *Alignment* group, click the **Merge & Center** button arrow and select **Unmerge Cells**.
- In the *Format Cells* dialog, on the *Alignment* tab, in the *Text alignment* section, the *Text control* section, click the **Merge cells** check box to uncheck it.

tips & tricks

You cannot split cells in Excel. You can unmerge a merged cell back into its original cells, but you cannot split a single cell into two new columns or two new rows (like you can with a table in Word or PowerPoint). However, if you have a column of data that you would like to split across multiple cells, you can use the *Text to Columns* command (on the *Data* tab, in the *Data Tools* group).

let me try *Live!*

If you do not have the data file from the previous skill open, open the student data file **EX2-07-Sales** and try this skill on your own:

1. On the *Summary* worksheet, select cells **A1:E1**.
2. Merge the cells so the text appears centered across the merged cells.
3. On the *ByEmployee* worksheet, cells **A1:E1** have been merged and centered. Unmerge them and reset the cell alignment to **General**.
4. If you will be moving on to the next skill in this chapter, leave the workbook open to continue working. If not, save the file as instructed by your instructor and close it.

Skill 2.8 Applying Bold, Italic, and Underline

You may be familiar with using bold, italic, and underline formatting to emphasize text in a Word document or a PowerPoint presentation. You can use these same techniques in Excel to emphasize cells in your workbook.

To apply bold, italic, and underline formatting:

1. Select a cell or cell range to apply the formatting to all the content in the cell(s). To apply formatting to only part of the content in a cell, double-click the cell to enter Edit mode, and then select the text you want to apply the formatting to.
2. On the *Home* tab, in the *Font* group, click the appropriate button to apply formatting to the selected cell(s).

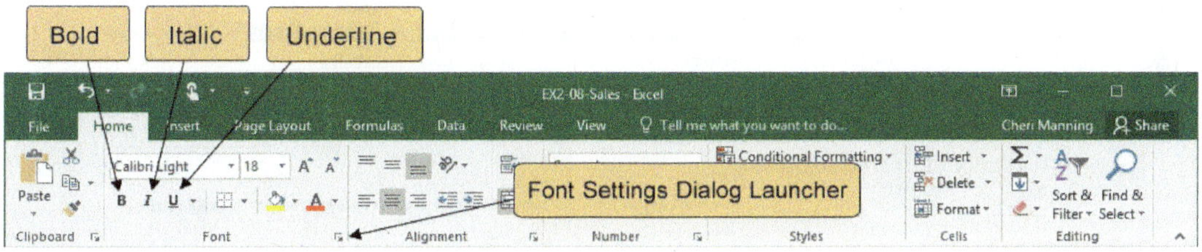

FIGURE EX 2.18

When a cell includes bold, italic, or underline formatting, the applicable buttons appear highlighted on the Ribbon. To remove the formatting, click the highlighted button.

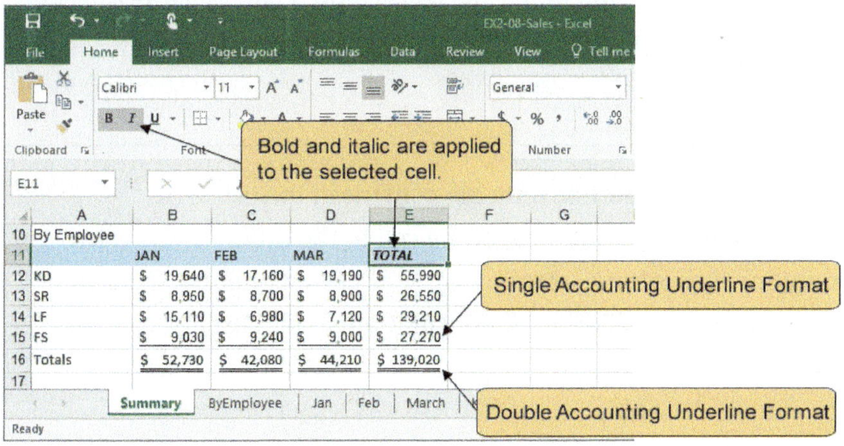

FIGURE EX 2.19

Underline styles used in accounting spreadsheets are slightly different from "regular" underline styles. If you need to apply the accounting style of underline or double underline, do not use the *Underline* button on the Ribbon. Instead, use one of the accounting underline options from the *Format Cells* dialog:

1. On the *Home* tab, in the *Font* group, click the **Font Settings dialog launcher** to open the *Format Cells* dialog.
2. On the *Font* tab, in the *Underline* section, expand the **Underline** list and select **Single Accounting** or **Double Accounting**.
3. Click **OK**.

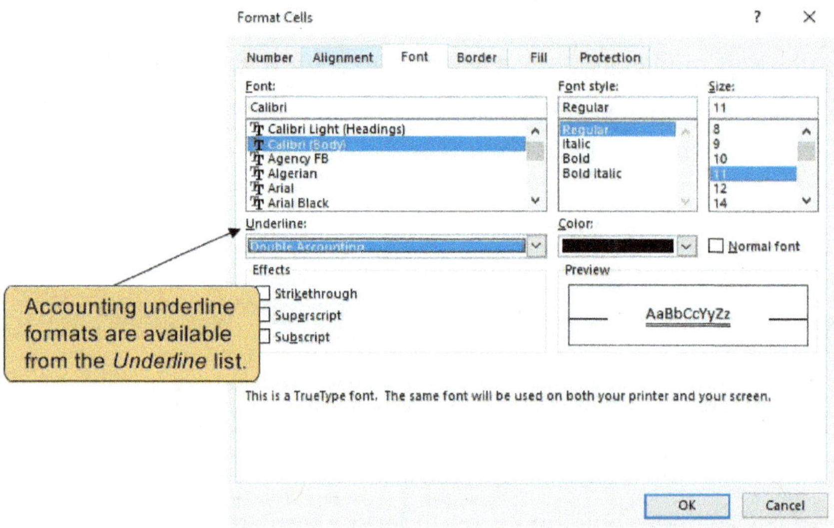

FIGURE EX 2.20

The single and double underline options available when you click the *Underline* button arrow will apply the accounting underline styles only if you recently selected those formats from the *Format Cells* dialog.

tips & tricks

The cell underline formats underline only the content in the cell. The underline does not extend from one edge of the cell to the other. If you want to create an underline that extends across a range of cells without a break in between, use a border instead. (For more information about borders, refer to the skill *Adding Borders*.)

another method

When you right-click a cell, the *Bold* and *Italic* buttons are available on the Mini toolbar.

Bold, italic, and underline font styles are available from the *Format Cells* dialog, *Font* tab. You can also use the keyboard shortcuts:

- Bold: Ctrl + B
- Italic: Ctrl + I
- Underline: Ctrl + U

let me try *Live!*

If you do not have the data file from the previous skill open, open the student data file **EX2-08-Sales** and try this skill on your own:

1. On the *Summary* worksheet, select cell **E11** and apply **bold** and **italic** formatting.
2. Remove just the **bold** formatting.
3. Select cells **B15:E15** and apply the **Single Accounting** underline format.
4. Select cells **B16:E16** and apply the **Double Accounting** underline format.
5. If you will be moving on to the next skill in this chapter, leave the workbook open to continue working. If not, save the file as directed by your instructor and close it.

Skill 2.9 Changing Fonts, Font Size, and Font Color

A **font**, or typeface, refers to a set of characters of a certain design. The font is the shape of a character or number as it appears on-screen or when printed. Use the commands from the *Home* tab, *Font* group to change font attributes such as font family, font size, and font color.

- To change the font, click the **Font** box arrow to expand the list of available fonts, and then select the font you want.
- To change the font size, click the **Font Size** box arrow and select the size you want.
- To change the font color, click the **Font Color** button arrow to expand the color palette, and then select the color you want.

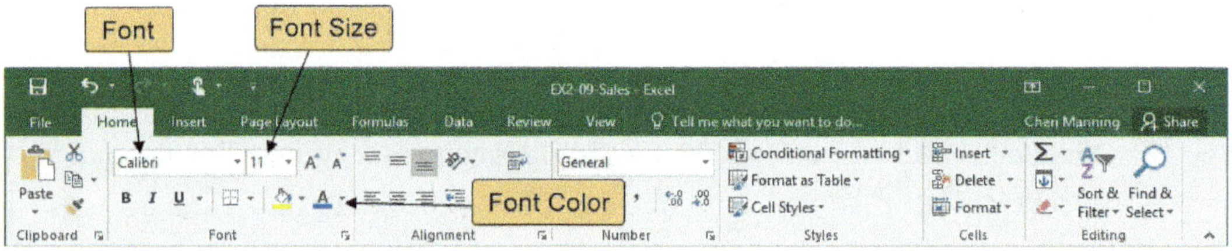

FIGURE EX 2.21

The font color palette is divided into three parts:

1. The top part shows the *Automatic* color choice (black or white, depending on the color of the background).
2. The middle part shows the *Theme Colors* included in the theme that is applied to the workbook. These colors are designed to work together.
3. The bottom part of the palette shows the *Standard Colors* (dark red, red, orange, etc.). These colors are always available, no matter what theme is in use.

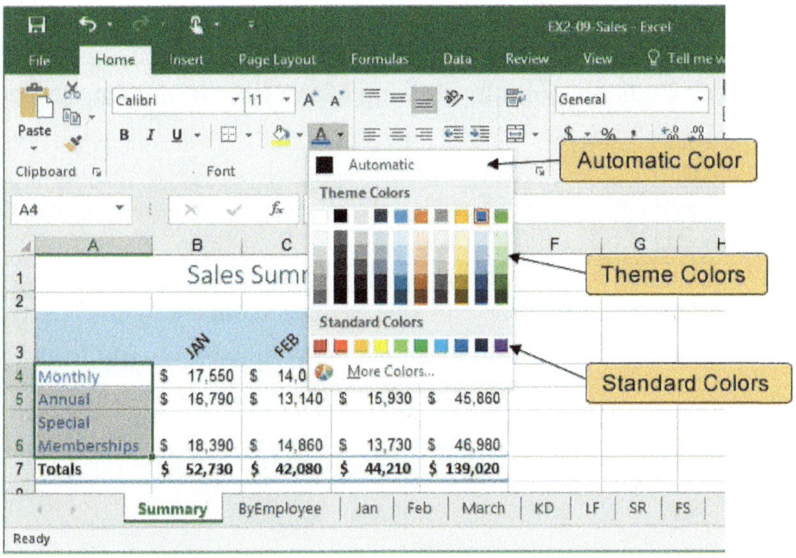

FIGURE EX 2.22

You can also change the font, font size, and font color from the *Format Cells* dialog:

1. On the *Home* tab, in the *Font* group, click the **Font Settings dialog launcher** to open the *Format Cells* dialog.
2. On the *Font* tab, make the font and size selections you want.
3. In the *Color* section, click the arrow to expand the color palette, and then click a color. The color palette from the Ribbon and in the *Format Cells* dialog is the same.
4. Review the sample text in the *Preview* box to see how your choices will look.
5. Click **OK** to apply the changes.

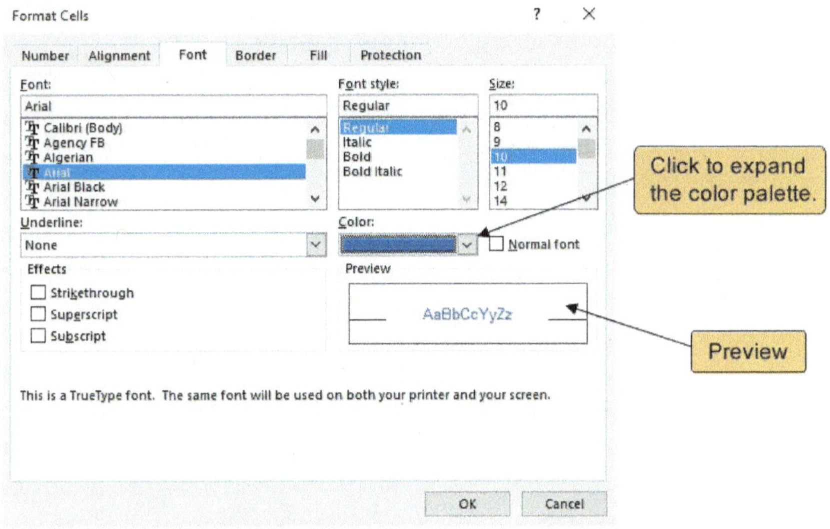

FIGURE EX 2.23

tell me more

You can pick a custom color by clicking **More Colors...** from the bottom of the font color palette.

another method

You can also change the font, font size, or font color by right-clicking and making the font, font size, and font color selections you want from the Mini toolbar.

let me try *Live!*

If you do not have the data file from the previous skill open, open the student data file **EX2-09-Sales** and try this skill on your own:

1. On the *Summary* worksheet, select cells **A4:A6**.
2. Change the font to **Arial**.
3. Change the font size to **10**.
4. Change the font color to **Blue, Accent 5** (in the top row of theme colors, the second color from the right).
5. If you will be moving on to the next skill in this chapter, leave the workbook open to continue working. If not, save the file as directed by your instructor and close it.

Skill 2.10 Adding Borders

Add borders to your workbook to emphasize a cell or group of cells. Use borders to make your workbook look more like a desktop publishing form or to show separation between a column of values and the total row.

To add borders to your workbook:

1. Select the cell(s) you want to add a border to.
2. On the *Home* tab, in the *Font* group, click the **Borders** button arrow and select the border style you want.

To remove borders:

1. Select the cell(s) you want to remove the borders from.
2. On the *Home* tab, in the *Font* group, click the **Borders** button arrow and select **No Border** from the list of border styles.

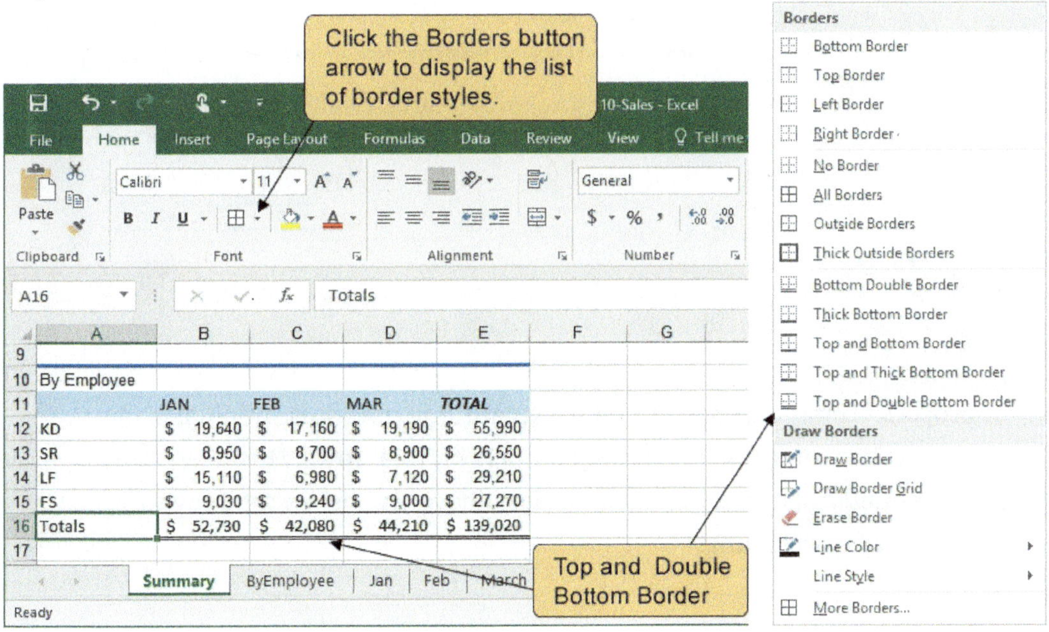

FIGURE EX 2.24

For more control over the look of cell borders, select **More Borders...** from the *Borders* menu to open the *Format Cells* dialog. From the *Border* tab, you can specify the line style and color for the border. You can also see a preview of how the border will look.

1. On the *Home* tab, in the *Font* group, click the **Borders** button arrow and select **More Borders...** from the list of border styles.

2. Select a line style from the *Style* section.
3. Expand the **Color** palette and select a color.
4. To add borders around the outside or inside the selected cells, click the appropriate button(s) in the *Presets* section.
5. In the *Border* section, add a border line by clicking the button representing the location of the border or by clicking directly in the area of the preview image where you want the border to appear.
6. Click **OK**.

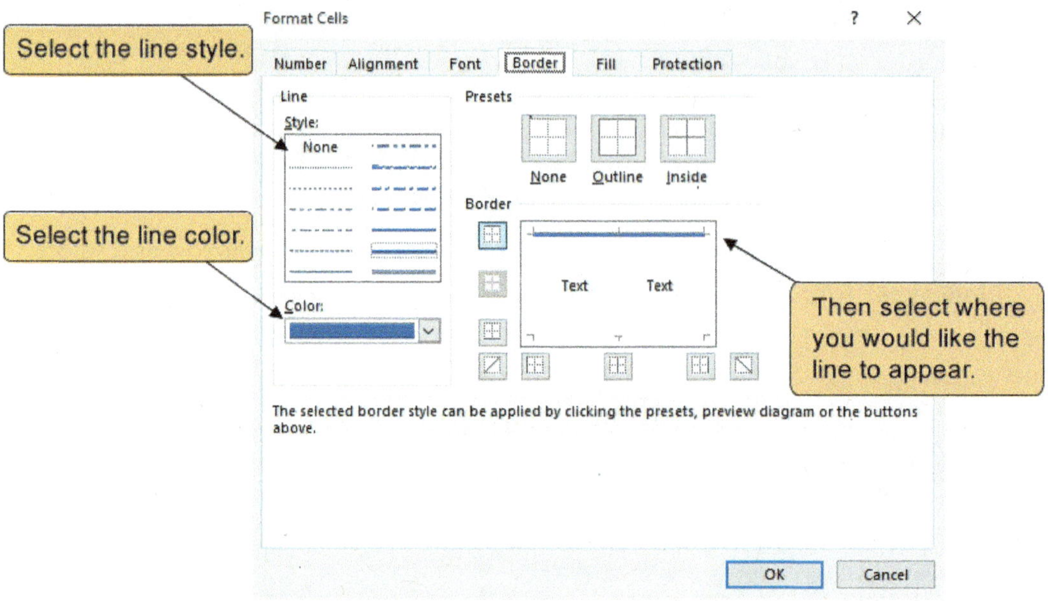

FIGURE EX 2.25

tips & tricks

A properly formatted spreadsheet for accounting purposes should use the cell underline formatting instead of borders on total rows. However, most non-accountant Excel users favor borders above and below total rows instead of using cell underlining.

another method

The *Borders* button displays the most recently used border style. If you want to reuse this style, you can just click the button. You do not need to reselect the border style from the menu again.

The *Borders* button is also available from the Mini toolbar when you right-click a cell.

let me try *Live!*

If you do not have the data file from the previous skill open, open the student data file **EX2-10-Sales** and try this skill on your own:

1. On the *Summary* worksheet, select cells **A9:E9** and remove the borders.
2. Select cells **B15:E16** and remove the underline formatting.
3. Apply the **Top and Double Bottom Border** to cells **A16:E16**.
4. Add a **Blue, Accent 5** (in the top row of theme colors, the second color from the right) top border to cells **A10:E10**. Use the thickest single line style available.
5. If you will be moving on to the next skill in this chapter, leave the workbook open to continue working. If not, save the file as directed by your instructor and close it.

Skill 2.11 Adding Shading with Fill Color

Another way to emphasize cells in your workbook is to use a **fill color** to change the background color of cells. Fill colors are available in a variety of shades to make it easy to read the cell content. Shading is often used to differentiate alternating rows in a large table or to make the heading row stand out. To add shading to your workbook:

1. Select the cell(s) you want to add shading to.
2. On the *Home* tab, in the *Font* group, click the **Fill Color** button arrow to display the color palette. The color palette includes colors from the workbook theme as well as a row of standard colors along the bottom. Notice that as you hold the mouse over each color in the palette, a tool tip appears displaying the color name.
3. Click the color you want.

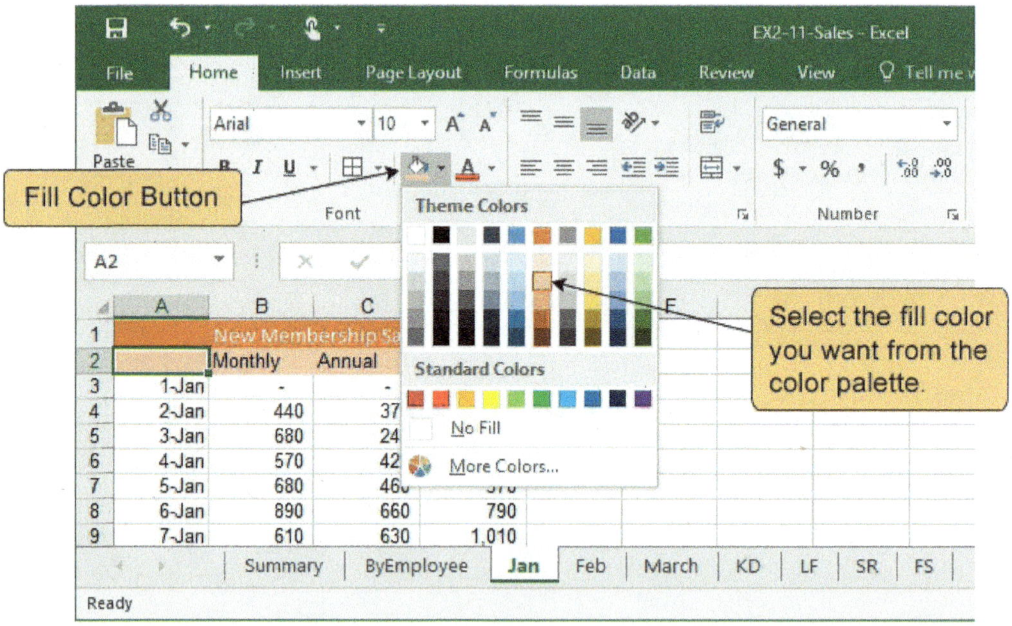

FIGURE EX 2.26

To remove shading:

1. Select the cell(s) you want to remove shading from.
2. On the *Home* tab, in the *Font* group, click the **Fill Color** button arrow to display the color palette.
3. Click **No Fill** to remove the fill color from the selected cells.

tips & tricks

- Avoid overusing shading and using too many colors in your workbook. Shading should be used for emphasis and to make the workbook easier to read, not to make the workbook more colorful.
- If you use a dark color for shading, change the font color to white or another light color.

tell me more

In the *Format Cells* dialog, options for fill effects and pattern styles are available under the *Fill* tab.

another method

Like the *Borders* button, the *Fill Color* button displays the most recently used shading color. If you want to reuse this color, just click the button. You do not need to reselect the color from the Fill Color palette.

The *Fill Color* button is also available from the Mini toolbar when you right-click a cell.

let me try *Live!*

If you do not have the data file from the previous skill open, open the student data file **EX2-11-Sales** and try this skill on your own:

1. On the *Summary* worksheet, select cells **A11:E11** and remove the fill color.
2. On the *Jan* worksheet, select cells **A2:D2** and apply the **Orange, Accent 2, Lighter 60%** fill color (in the third row of theme colors, the fifth color from the right).
3. If you will be moving on to the next skill in this chapter, leave the workbook open to continue working. If not, save the file as directed by your instructor and close it.

from the perspective of . . .

HEALTH CLUB OFFICE MANAGER

I use Excel to prepare financial reports for the club owners and their accountant. Proper formatting makes it easier for the owners to read the reports. I would never submit a report without checking for text that appears cut off or titles that aren't centered across columns. And I always use the accounting underline formats instead of borders in my financial reports. Our accountant insists on it!

Skill 2.12 Applying Cell Styles

A **cell style** is a combination of effects that can be applied at one time. Styles can include formatting such as borders, fill color, font size, and number formatting.

Excel includes an extensive gallery of prebuilt cell styles. You can use these styles to help visualize your data by consistently applying them to your worksheet. Use text styles such as *Title* for the title of your worksheet and *Calculation* and *Input* to highlight cells used in formulas. The *Total* style applies borders and font formatting appropriate for a total row in a table.

To apply a cell style:

1. Select the cell(s) you want to apply the style to.
2. On the *Home* tab, in the *Styles* group, click the **Cell Styles** button.
3. Click the style you want to apply to your cell(s).

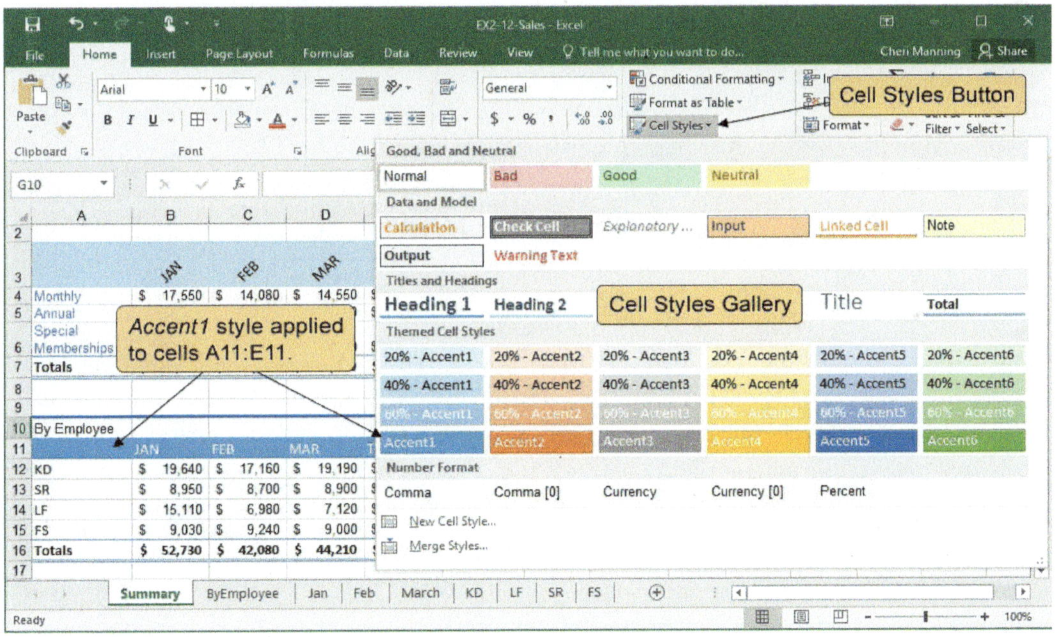

FIGURE EX 2.27

tips & tricks

If you have Live Preview enabled, you can move your mouse over each style in the *Cell Styles* gallery to see a preview of how that style would look applied to your worksheet.

let me try *Live!*

If you do not have the data file from the previous skill open, open the student data file **EX2-12-Sales** and try this skill on your own:

1. On the *Summary* worksheet, select cells **A11:E11** and apply the **Accent1** cell style.
2. Select cells **A16:E16** and apply the **Total** style.
3. If you will be moving on to the next skill in this chapter, leave the workbook open to continue working. If not, save the file as directed by your instructor and close it.

Skill 2.13 Using Format Painter

A professional, well-organized workbook uses consistent formatting. Use the **Format Painter** tool to copy formatting from one part of your worksheet to another, rather than trying to recreate the exact combination of font color and size, number formatting, borders, and shading to reuse.

To use *Format Painter*:

1. Select the cell that has the formatting you want to copy.
2. On the *Home* tab, in the *Clipboard* group, click the **Format Painter** button.
3. Notice that your mouse pointer changes to the Format Painter shape . Click the cell that you want to apply the formatting to or click and drag to apply the formatting to a range of cells.

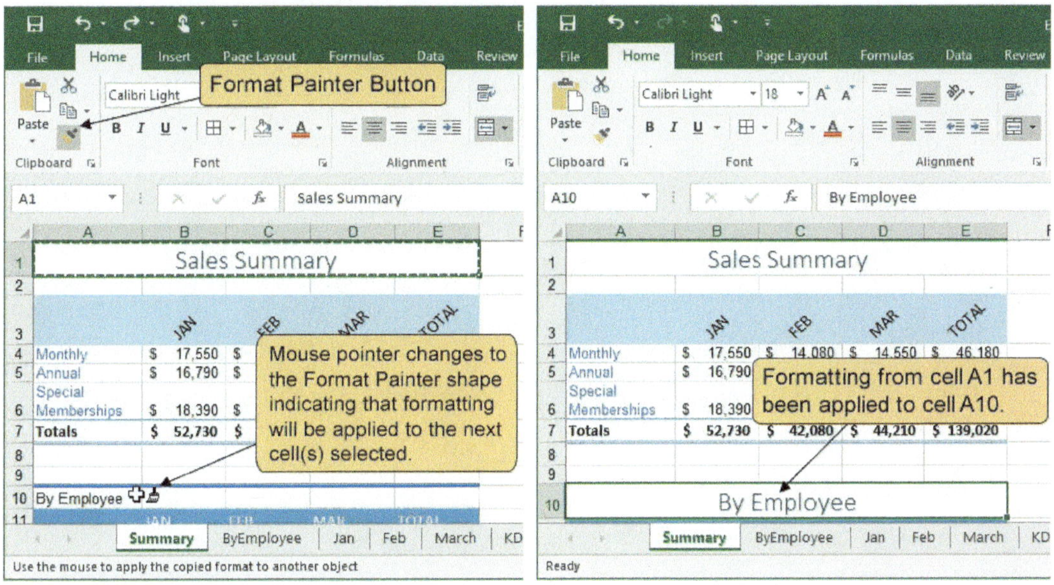

FIGURE EX 2.28

tell me more

If you want to apply the formatting to different parts of a worksheet or workbook, double-click the **Format Painter** button when you select it. It will stay on until you click the **Format Painter** button again or press **Esc** to deselect it.

another method

To activate *Format Painter*, you can also right-click the cell with formatting you want to copy and click the **Format Painter** button on the Mini toolbar.

let me try *Live!*

If you do not have the data file from the previous skill open, open the student data file **EX2-13-Sales** and try this skill on your own:

1. On the *Summary* worksheet, use **Format Painter** to copy the formatting from cell **A1** and apply it to cell **A10**.
2. If you will be moving on to the next skill in this chapter, leave the workbook open to continue working. If not, save the file as directed by your instructor and close it.

Skill 2.14 Applying Conditional Formatting Using the Quick Analysis Tool

Conditional formatting provides a visual analysis of data by applying formatting to cells based on their values. Excel offers a wide variety of conditional formatting options from the *Conditional Formatting* menu (available on the *Home* tab, in the *Styles* group).

- Data bars, color scales, and icon sets display a visual representation comparing all cell values in the selection.
- *Highlight Cells Rules* highlight only cells that meet specific criteria (conditions).
- *Top/Bottom Rules* highlight cells that have the highest or lowest values compared to other cells in the selection.

If you're not sure which conditional formatting option is best for the selected data, use the Quick Analysis tool. The Quick Analysis tool detects whether you've selected numerical or text data and displays only the conditional formatting options appropriate for each type of data. From the Quick Analysis tool, you can also preview conditional formatting before applying it to your data.

To apply conditional formatting with the Quick Analysis tool:

1. Select the cells to which you want to apply conditional formatting.
2. Click the **Quick Analysis** tool button at the lowerright corner of the selection.
3. Notice that Live Preview displays the effect of the conditional formatting on your data as you hover the mouse pointer over each of the formatting options. Review each formatting option before making your selection.
4. Click the button for the type of conditional formatting you want to apply.

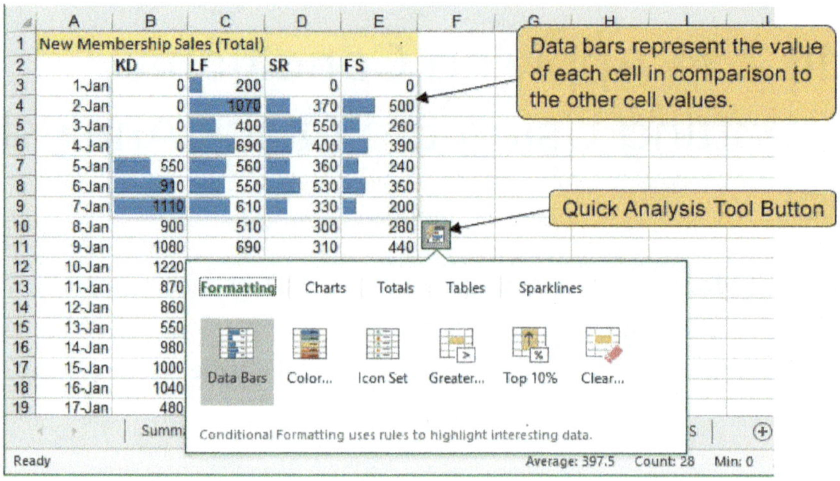

FIGURE EX 2.29

tips & tricks

You should resist the temptation to overuse conditional formatting. Conditional formatting should be used to highlight important data or data trends, not to colorize the entire worksheet.

tell me more

Some types of conditional formatting apply formatting to all the cells in the selection and are applied automatically when you click the button in the Quick Analysis tool. Other types require a comparison value and will open a dialog where you can specify the value for the rule and select formatting options.

another method

You can press Ctrl + Q to open the Quick Analysis tool instead of clicking the *Quick Analysis* tool button.

let me try *Live!*

If you do not have the data file from the previous skill open, open the student data file **EX2-14-Sales** and try this skill on your own:

1. On the *ByEmployee* worksheet, select cells **B3:E9** and apply the **Data Bars** conditional formatting option from the Quick Analysis tool.
2. If you will be moving on to the next skill in this chapter, leave the workbook open to continue working. If not, save the file as directed by your instructor and close it.

from the perspective of . . .

HELP DESK COORDINATOR

I love conditional formatting! Every week, each department sends me a spreadsheet of all the help desk calls for each software package we support. I use color scales to identify the software packages with the highest volume of calls. In my spreadsheet that combines the weekly data, I use icon sets to indicate whether the number of calls went up or down for each software package on a week-by-week basis.

Skill 2.15 Applying Conditional Formatting with Data Bars, Color Scales, and Icon Sets

Data bars, colors scales, and icon sets can be used to visually represent the value of each cell relative to the other cells in the data selection. These types of conditional formatting apply formatting to all the selected cells.

Data Bars—Display a color bar (gradient or solid) representing the cell value in comparison to other values (cells with higher values have longer data bars).

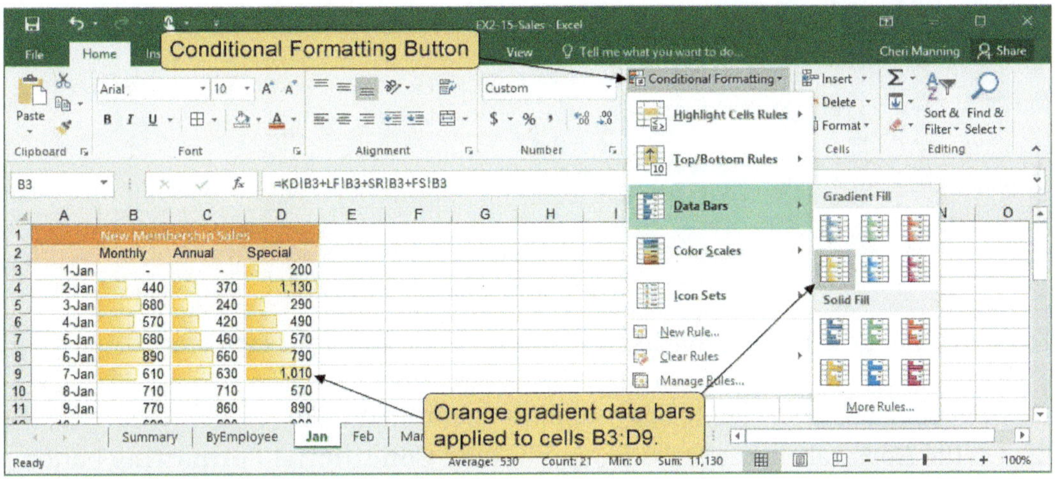

FIGURE EX 2.30

Color Scales—Color the cells according to one of the color scales (e.g., red to green [bad/low to good/high] or blue to red [cold/low to hot/high]).

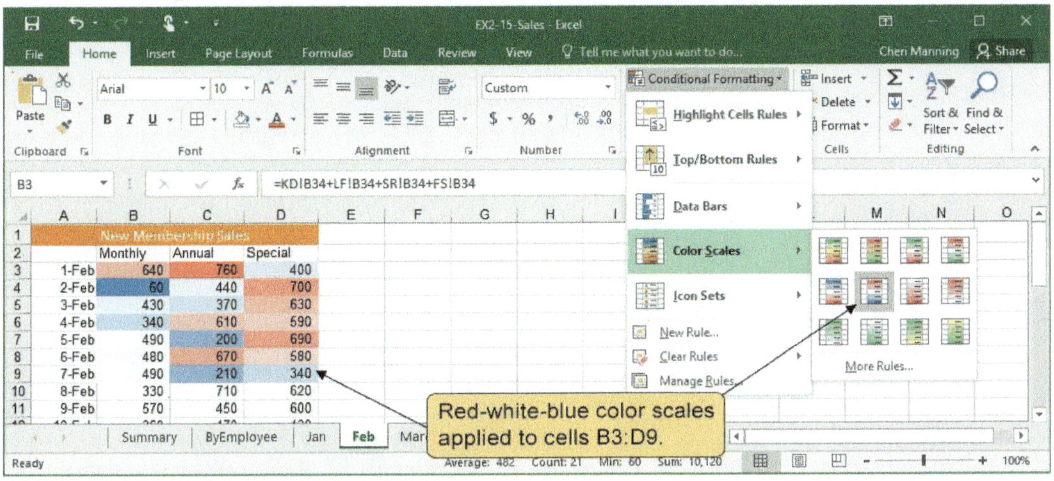

FIGURE EX 2.31

Icon Sets—Display a graphic in the cell representing the cell value in relation to other values.

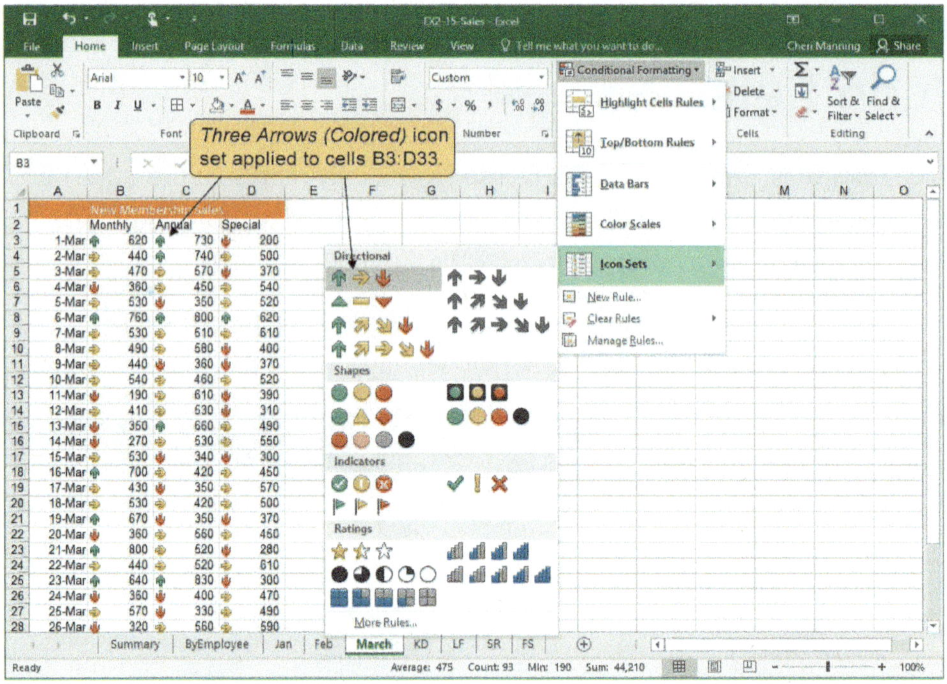

FIGURE EX 2.32

To apply conditional formatting using data bars, color scales, or icon sets:

1. Select the data you want to apply conditional formatting to.
2. On the *Home* tab, in the *Styles* group, click the **Conditional Formatting** button.
3. From the menu, point to **Data Bars**, **Colors Scales**, or **Icon Sets**, and then click the specific style of formatting you want. Notice that Live Preview displays the effect of the conditional formatting on your data as you hover the mouse pointer over each of the formatting options.

let me try *Live!*

If you do not have the data file from the previous skill open, open the student data file **EX2-15-Sales** and try this skill on your own:

1. On the *Jan* worksheet, select cells **B3:D9** and apply conditional formatting using the **orange gradient fill data bar**.
2. On the *Feb* worksheet, select cells **B3:D9** and apply conditional formatting using the **Red-White-Blue color scale**.
3. On the *March* worksheet, select cells **B3:D33** and apply conditional formatting using the **Three Arrows (Colored)** icon set (the first icon set in the *Directional* section).
4. If you will be moving on to the next skill in this chapter, leave the workbook open to continue working. If not, save the file as directed by your instructor and close it.

Skill 2.16 Applying Conditional Formatting with Highlight Cells Rules

Conditional formatting with **Highlight Cells Rules** allows you to define formatting for cells that meet specific numerical or text criteria (e.g., greater than a specific value or containing a specific text string). Use this type of conditional formatting when you want to highlight cells based on criteria you define.

To apply *Highlight Cells Rules*:

1. Select the data you want to apply conditional formatting to.
2. On the *Home* tab, in the *Styles* group, click the **Conditional Formatting** button.
3. From the menu, point to **Highlight Cells Rules**, and click the option you want.
4. Each option opens a dialog where you can enter a value or date to which the value of each cell will be compared. The default formatting is light red fill with dark red text. To change the formatting, expand the dropdown list in the dialog and select another option.
5. Click **OK** to apply the conditional formatting.

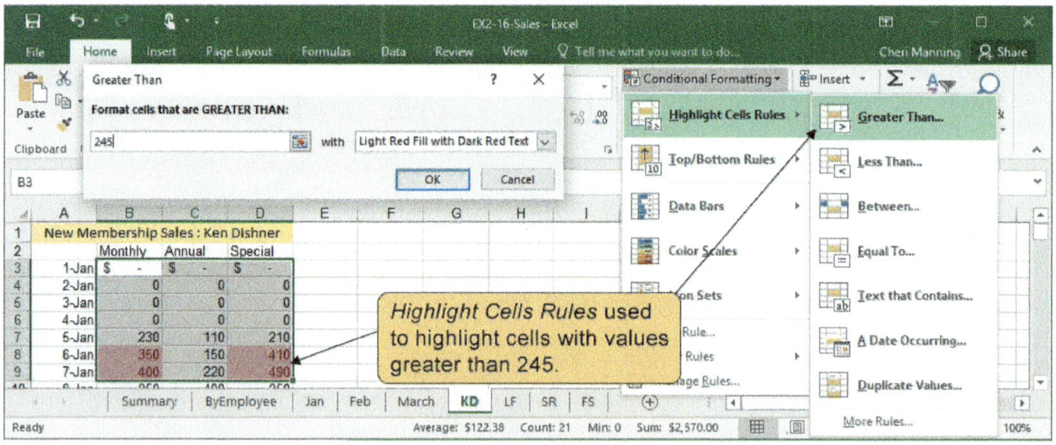

FIGURE EX 2.33

tips & tricks

The *Highlight Cells Rules* menu includes an option to highlight duplicate values. This option can be especially helpful when you are trying to find a potential data entry error in a long list of values.

let me try *Live!*

If you do not have the data file from the previous skill open, open the student data file **EX2-16-Sales** and try this skill on your own:

1. On the *KD* worksheet, select cells **B3:D9** and apply conditional formatting so cells with a value **greater than 245** are formatted using a red fill with dark red text.
2. If you will be moving on to the next skill in this chapter, leave the workbook open to continue working. If not, save the file as directed by your instructor and close it.

Skill 2.17 Applying Conditional Formatting with Top/Bottom Rules

One way to analyze worksheet data is to compare cell values to other cell values. When analyzing a worksheet, you may want to highlight the highest or lowest values or values that are above or below the average. In these cases, use conditional formatting **Top/Bottom Rules**. When you use *Top/Bottom Rules*, Excel automatically finds the highest, lowest, and average values to compare values to, rather than asking you to enter criteria (as you do when using *Highlight Cells Rules*).

To highlight cells with conditional formatting *Top/Bottom Rules*:

1. Select the data you want to apply conditional formatting to.
2. On the *Home* tab, in the *Styles* group, click the **Conditional Formatting** button.
3. From the menu, point to **Top/Bottom Rules**, and click the option you want.
4. Each option opens a dialog where you can select the formatting to apply when cells meet the condition. The top and bottom options allow you to modify the threshold to a value other than 10 (top/bottom 10 items and top/bottom 10%).
5. Click **OK** to apply the conditional formatting.

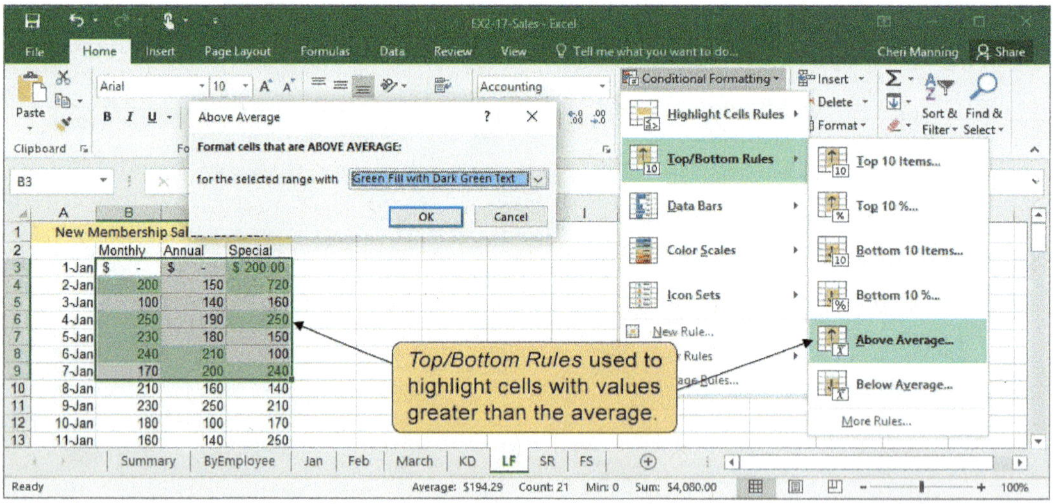

FIGURE EX 2.34

let me try *Live!*

If you do not have the data file from the previous skill open, open the student data file **EX2-17-Sales** and try this skill on your own:

1. On the *LF* worksheet, select cells **B3:D9** and apply conditional formatting so cells with a value **greater than the average** are formatted using a green fill with dark green text.
2. If you will be moving on to the next skill in this chapter, leave the workbook open to continue working. If not, save the file as directed by your instructor and close it.

Skill 2.18 Removing Conditional Formatting

You cannot remove conditional formatting from cells by clearing the data or pressing Delete or Backspace. Instead, you must remove the conditional formatting rule from the cells.

To remove conditional formatting:

1. On the *Home* tab, in the *Styles* group, click the **Conditional Formatting** button.
2. Point to **Clear Rules**, and click the option you want from the menu: **Clear Rules from Selected Cells, Clear Rules from Entire Sheet, Clear Rules from This Table** (available if the selected cells are part of a table), or **Clear Rules from This PivotTable** (available if the selected cells are part of a PivotTable).

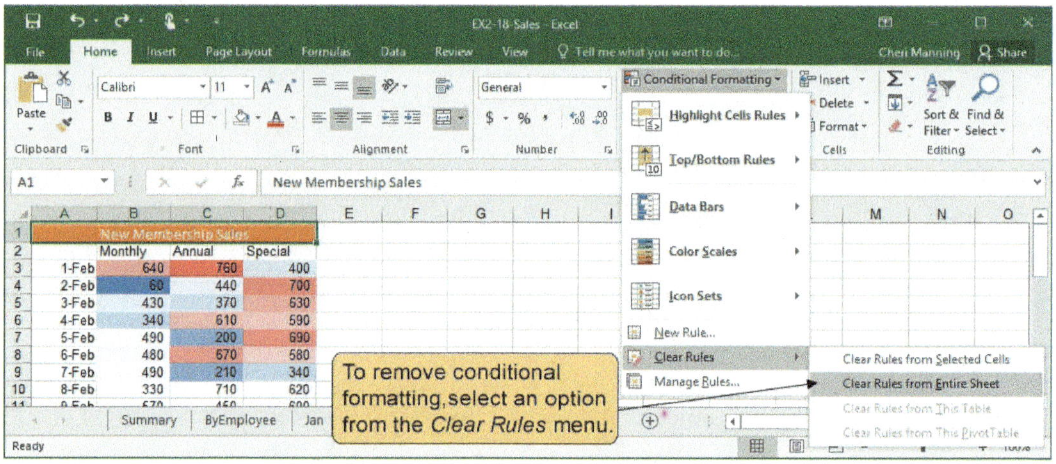

FIGURE EX 2.35

tell me more

Through the Conditional Formatting Rules Manager, you can view all of your conditional formatting rules at one time and add, modify, or delete rules. Open the Conditional Formatting Rules Manager from the *Manage Rules...* option at the bottom of the *Conditional Formatting* menu.

another method

You can also clear conditional formatting from the Quick Analysis tool:

1. Select the cells from which you want to remove conditional formatting.
2. Click the **Quick Analysis** tool button at the lower right corner of the selection, and click the **Clear Format** button.

let me try *Live!*

If you do not have the data file from the previous skill open, open the student data file **EX2-18-Sales** and try this skill on your own:

1. Go to the *Feb* worksheet and clear the conditional formatting rules from this worksheet.
2. If you will be moving on to the next skill in this chapter, leave the workbook open to continue working. If not, save the file as directed by your instructor and close it.

Skill 2.19 Clearing Cell Content

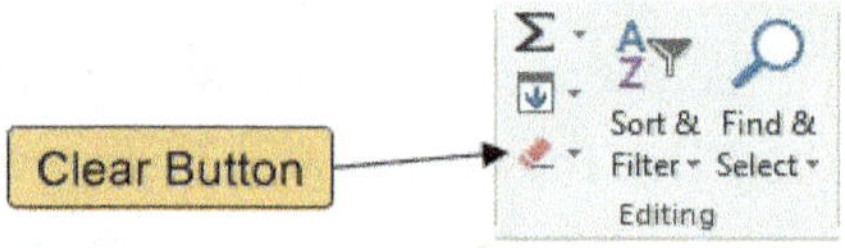

FIGURE EX 2.36

To remove the contents of a cell without removing the cell from the structure of your workbook, on the *Home* tab, in the *Editing* group, click the **Clear** button and select one of the *Clear* menu options. You can remove everything from the cell – contents, formats, comments, and hyperlinks, or remove contents or formatting only.

Figure EX 2.37 shows the original content and formatting in cells A3:E3.

FIGURE EX 2.37

Clear All—clears all cell contents and formatting and deletes any comments or hyperlinks attached to the cell.

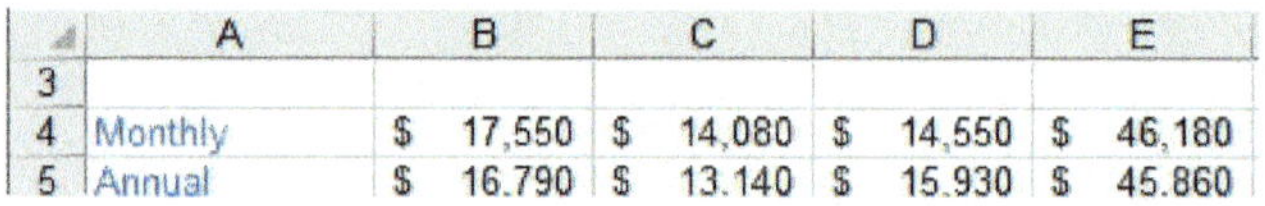

	A	B	C	D	E
3					
4	Monthly	$ 17,550	$ 14,080	$ 14,550	$ 46,180
5	Annual	$ 16,790	$ 13,140	$ 15,930	$ 45,860

FIGURE EX 2.38

Clear Formats—clears only the cell formatting and leaves the cell contents, comments, and hyperlinks. The *Clear Formats command* does not remove conditional formatting.

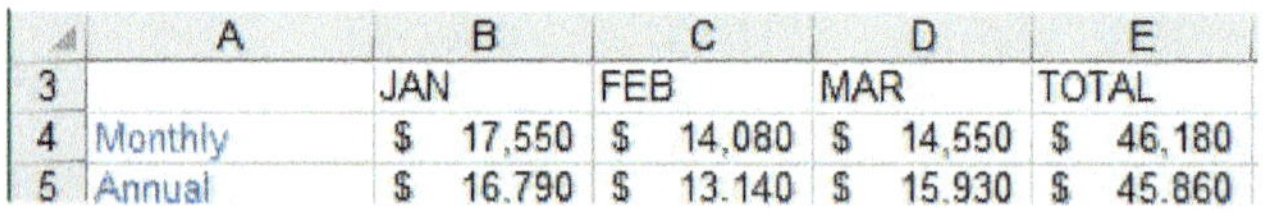

	A	B	C	D	E
3		JAN	FEB	MAR	TOTAL
4	Monthly	$ 17,550	$ 14,080	$ 14,550	$ 46,180
5	Annual	$ 16,790	$ 13,140	$ 15,930	$ 45,860

FIGURE EX 2.39

Clear Contents—clears only the contents (including hyperlinks) and leaves the cell formatting and comments. Figure EX 2.40 has sample text added to cell B3 to illustrate the cell formatting.

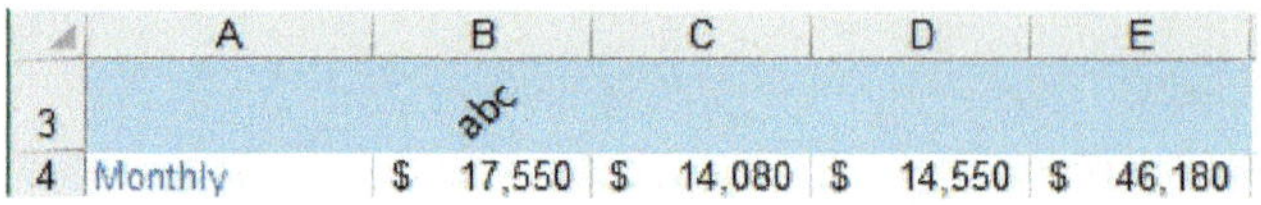

	A	B	C	D	E
3		abc			
4	Monthly	$ 17,550	$ 14,080	$ 14,550	$ 46,180

FIGURE EX 2.40

tell me more

There are two additional options available from the Clear menu:

Clear Comments—deletes any comments attached to the cell while leaving the cell contents, formatting, and hyperlinks intact.

Clear Hyperlinks—removes the hyperlink action from the cell without removing the content or the hyperlink style of formatting.

let me try *Live!*

If you do not have the data file from the previous skill open, open the student data file **EX2-19-Sales** and try this skill on your own:

1. On the *Summary* worksheet, select cells **A3:E3** and clear the formatting only (leaving the content).
2. Select cell **A7** and clear only the content (leaving the formatting).
3. Select cell **A10** and use a single command to clear everything (content and formatting)
4. If you will be moving on to the next skill in this chapter, leave the workbook open to continue working. If not, save the file as directed by your instructor and close it.

Skill 2.20 Using Find and Replace

All of the Microsoft Office applications include **Find** and **Replace** commands that allow you to search for and replace data in your file. In Excel, these commands can be used to find and replace not only text but also numbers in values and formulas in a single worksheet or across an entire workbook.

Before using the *Replace* command, you should use *Find* to make sure the data you are about to replace are what you expect:

1. On the *Home* tab, in the *Editing* group at the far right side of the Ribbon, click the **Find & Select** button.
2. From the *Find & Select* menu, click **Find...**

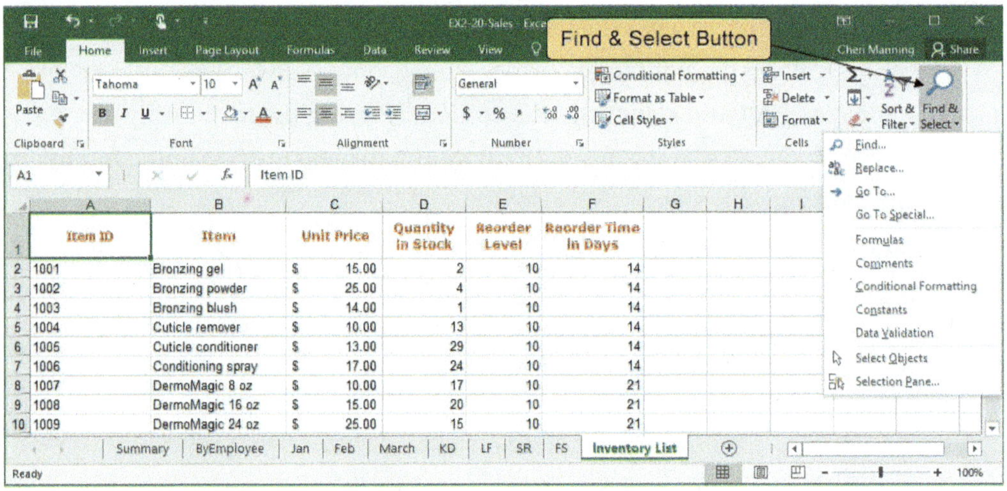

FIGURE EX 2.41

3. The *Find and Replace* dialog opens, with the *Find* tab on top.
4. Type the word, phrase, or number you want to find in the *Find what* box.
   a. To go to just the first instance, click the **Find Next** button.
   b. To find all instances, click the **Find All** button. When you click *Find All*, Excel displays a list detailing every instance of the data—workbook file name, worksheet name, cell name, cell address, the value of the cell, and the formula (if there is one).

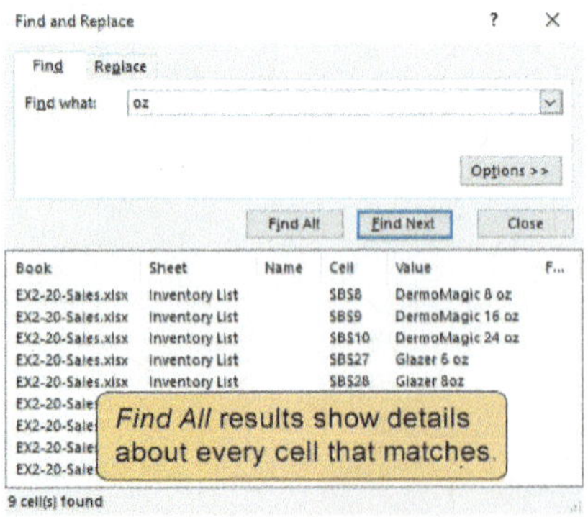

FIGURE EX 2.42

Once you have verified the data you want to replace, switch to the *Replace* tab in the *Find and Replace* dialog:

1. Click the **Replace** tab.
2. Excel keeps the data you typed in the *Find what* box.
3. Now type the replacement text or values in the *Replace with* box.
   a. Click the **Replace** button to replace one instance of the data at a time.
   b. Click the **Replace All** button to replace all instances at once.

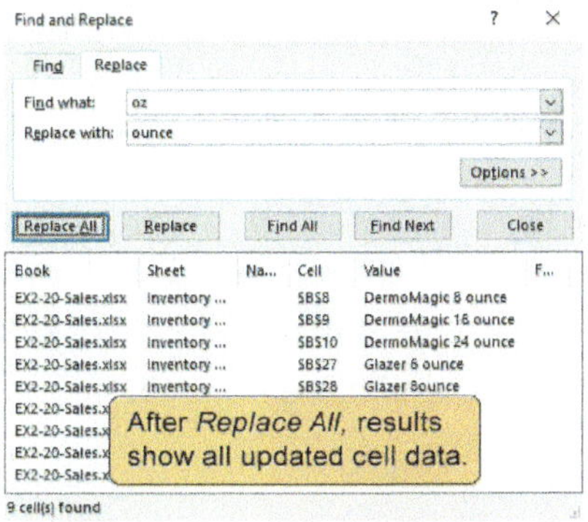

FIGURE EX 2.43

4. If you select *Replace All*, Excel displays a message telling you how many replacements were made. Click **OK** to dismiss the message. The results now display details about every cell that was updated with the *Replace* command.
5. Click **Close** to close the *Find and Replace* dialog.

tell me more

By default, Excel searches for the data both in cell values and within formulas. If you want to limit the search to only cell values, first click the **Options>>** button in the *Find and Replace* dialog to display the find and replace optional settings. Next, expand the *Look in* list by clicking the arrow, and select **Values**.

another method

Use the keyboard shortcut Ctrl + F to open the *Find and Replace* dialog with the *Find* tab on top.

Use the keyboard shortcut Ctrl + H to open the *Find and Replace* dialog with the *Replace* tab on top.

let me try *Live!*

If you do not have the data file from the previous skill open, open the student data file **EX2-20-Sales** and try this skill on your own:

1. On the *Inventory* worksheet, find all instances of the word **oz**.
2. Replace all instances of the word **oz** with **ounce**.
3. If you will be moving on to the next skill in this chapter, leave the workbook open to continue working. If not, save the file as directed by your instructor and close it.

Skill 2.21 Replacing Formatting

The *Find and Replace* commands allow you to find and replace formatting as well as data. This feature is especially helpful when replacing number formats throughout a workbook.

To find and replace formatting:

1. On the *Home* tab, in the *Editing* group, click the **Find & Replace** button and select **Replace...** to open the *Find and Replace* dialog.
2. If necessary, click the **Options >>** button to display the find and replace optional settings. Notice that next to the *Find what* and *Replace with* boxes, the *Preview* box displays *No Format Set.*

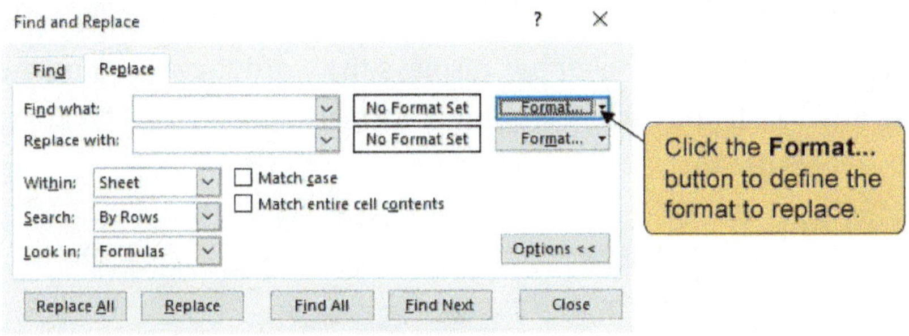

FIGURE EX 2.44

3. If you want to find specific data, enter it in the *Find what* box. If the *Find what* box is empty, Excel will find all cells with the formatting defined in the next step.
4. Click the **Format...** button next to the *Find what* box to open the *Find Format* dialog where you can define the formatting you want to find. The *Find Format* dialog includes all the tabs and formatting options available in the *Format Cells* dialog. Set the formatting to find just as you would set formatting to apply to cells.

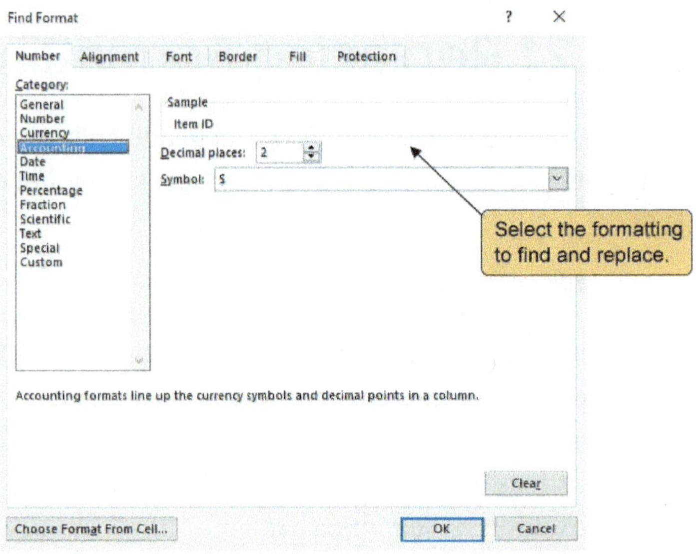

FIGURE EX 2.45

5. The *Preview* box next to the *Find what* box displays the word *Preview* using the formatting you defined. If you included number formatting, *Preview* will appear with an * after it (because the word *Preview* cannot display number formatting).

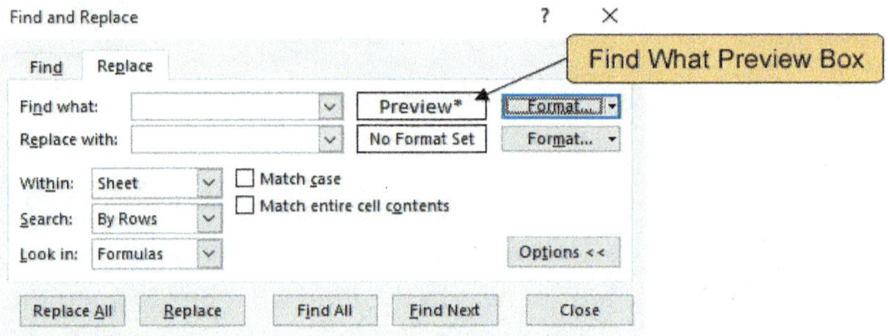

FIGURE EX 2.46

6. Now repeat the same steps to define the replacement formatting.
7. If you want to replace data as well as formatting, enter the replacement data in the *Replace with* box. If you do not enter anything, Excel will modify the formatting and leave the data in each cell unchanged.
8. Click the **Format...** button next to the *Replace with* box and repeat the same process to define the new format you want to use.
9. The *Preview* box next to the *Replaced with* box displays the word *Preview* using the formatting you defined. If you included number formatting, *Preview* will appear with an * after it (because the word *Preview* cannot display number formatting).
10. Click **Replace All**.
11. Click **OK** in the message that appears.
12. Click **Close** to close the *Find and Replace* dialog.

another method

You can also define the formatting styles to find and replace by picking cells that are already formatted with those attributes.

1. In the *Find and Replace* dialog, click the **Format** button arrow next to the *Find what* box and select **Choose Format from Cell...**
2. The cursor changes to a picker shape ✜✎.
3. Click a cell with the formatting attributes you want to find.
4. Click the **Format** button arrow next to the *Replace with* box and select **Choose Format from Cell...**
5. Click a cell with the formatting attributes you want to apply.
6. Click **Replace All.**
7. Click **OK.**
8. Click **Close** to close the *Find & Replace* dialog.

let me try *Live!*

If you do not have the data file from the previous skill open, open the student data file **EX2-21-Sales** and try this skill on your own:

1. On the *Inventory* worksheet, using the *Replace* command, find and replace all cells formatted with the **Accounting Number Format** with the **Currency** format.
2. If you will be moving on to the next skill in this chapter, leave the workbook open to continue working. If not, save the file as directed by your instructor and close it.

Skill 2.22 Setting and Clearing the Print Area

By default, Excel will print the entire active worksheet as shown in Figure EX 2.47.

If you do not want to print your entire worksheet, you can set a print area. The **print area** is a range of cells that you designate as the default print selection. If you have defined a print area for your worksheet, it will be the only part of the worksheet that prints.

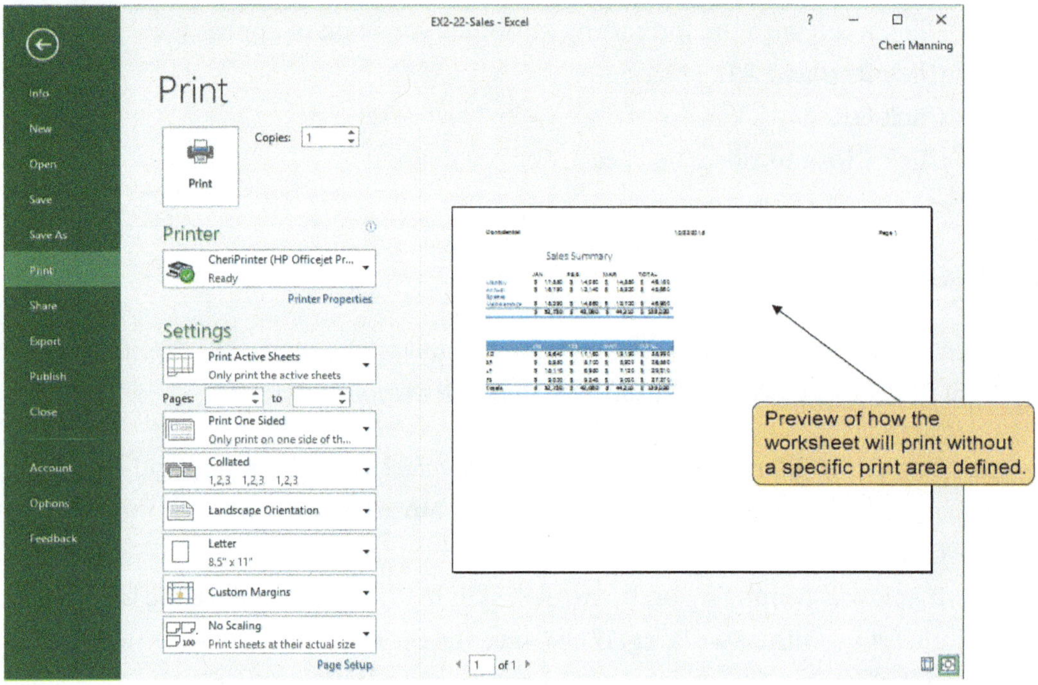

FIGURE EX 2.47

To set a print area:

1. Select the area you want to print.
2. On the *Page Layout* tab, in the *Page Setup* group, click the **Print Area** button.
3. Click **Set Print Area.**

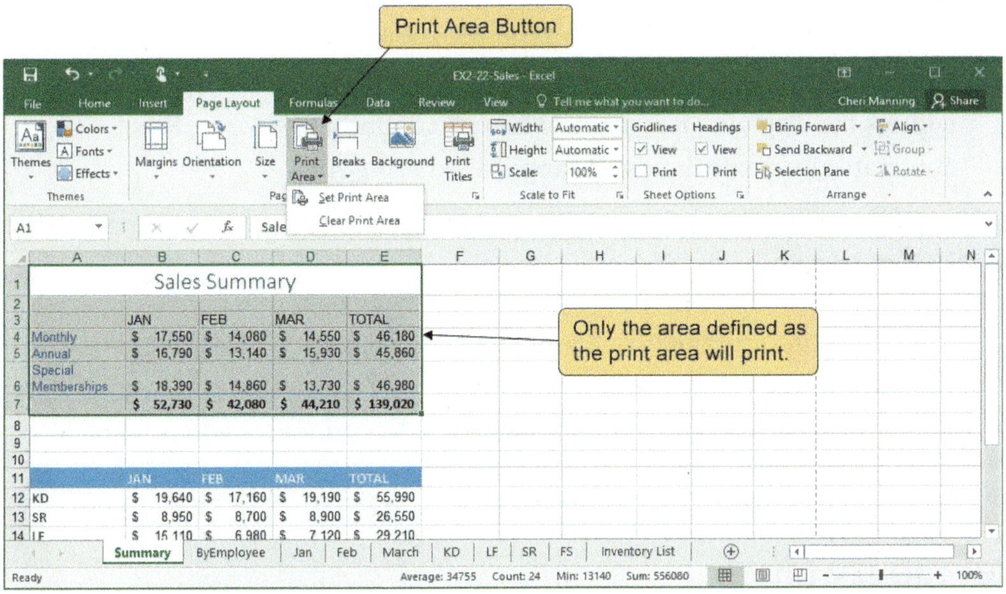

FIGURE EX 2.48

Now only the defined print area will print.

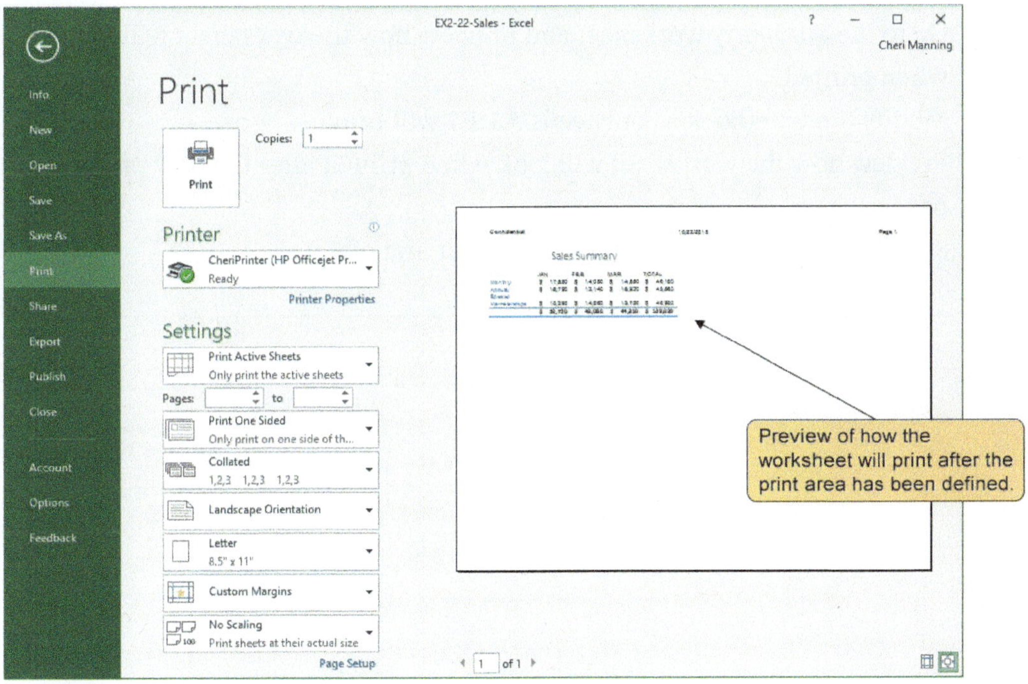

FIGURE EX 2.49

When you save the worksheet, the print area is saved as well. To clear a print area:

1. On the *Page Layout* tab, in the *Page Setup* group, click the **Print Area** button.
2. Click **Clear Print Area**.

tips & tricks

Notice that when the print area is selected, the *Name* box to the left of the address bar displays *Print_Area*. When you define a print area, Excel automatically creates a named range called *Print_Area*.

tell me more

You can define more than one print area per worksheet. Select the cells you want in the first print area, and then press Ctrl and drag the mouse to select the range of cells for the second print area. Each print area will print on a separate page.

let me try *Live!*

If you do not have the data file from the previous skill open, open the student data file **EX2-22-Sales** and try this skill on your own:

1. Go to the *Summary* worksheet and preview how the worksheet will look when printed.
2. Modify the workbook so only cells **A1:E7** will print.
3. Preview how the worksheet will look when printed after the new print area has been set.
4. Save the file as directed by your instructor and close it.

key terms

- Cut
- Copy
- Paste
- Undo
- Redo
- Alignment
- General horizontal alignment
- Font
- Fill color
- Cell style
- Format Painter
- Conditional formatting
- Data bars
- Color scales
- Icon sets
- Highlight Cells Rules
- Top/Bottom Rules
- Find
- Replace
- Print area

concept review

1. When you cut and paste a cell containing a formula with relative references, Excel
   a. updates the cell references to the new location.
   b. does not update the cell references to the new location.
   c. treats the formulas as if it contained absolute references.
   d. b and c
2. Which paste option pastes formulas and number formatting but none of the cell formatting?________________.
   a. Keep Source Formatting
   b. Values
   c. Formulas
   d. Formulas & Number Formatting
3. To split a cell into two cells:
   a. In the *Format Cells* dialog, on the *Alignment* tab, in the *Text Control* section, click the **Merge cells** box to uncheck it.
   b. On the *Home* tab, in the *Alignment* group, click the **Merge & Center** button and select **Unmerge Cells**.
   c. On the *Data* tab, in the *Data Tools* group, click the **Text to Columns** button.
   d. You cannot split a cell into two cells; you can only unmerge merged cells.
4. To apply the Double Underline accounting underline format:
   a. Press Ctrl + U.
   b. In the *Font* dialog, on the *Font* tab, expand the **Underline** list and select **Double Accounting**.
   c. On the *Home* tab, in the *Font* group, click the **Underline** button.
   d. Redo
5. Clicking the Borders button on the Ribbon applies which border style?
   a. None
   b. Outline
   c. Bottom border only
   d. The most recently used border style
6. The keyboard shortcut to open the Quick Analysis tool is
   a. Ctrl + A.
   b. Ctrl + Q.
   c. F7.
   d. F10.

7. To highlight cells with values in the top 10% of the select range, use _______________ conditional formatting.
   a. Highlight Cells Rules
   b. Top/Bottom Rules
   c. Data bars
   d. Icon sets
8. You can remove conditional formatting using the
   a. *Clear All* command.
   b. Ctrl + X keyboard shortcut.
   c. Delete keyboard shortcut.
   d. *Clear Rules from Selected Cells* command.
9. Selecting a cell and pressing Delete clears
   a. cell content only.
   b. cell content and formatting.
   c. cell content, formatting, and formulas.
   d. cell formatting only.
10. Where is the Set Print Area command located?
   a. On the *Page Layout* tab, in the *Page Setup* group
   b. In the *Page Layout* dialog
   c. In the *Print* dialog
   d. On the *Home* tab, in the *Print* group

projects

Data files for projects can be found by logging into your SIMnet account and going to the *Library* section.

skill review 2.1

In this project you will add formatting to a daily vitamin and supplement plan to make the spreadsheet more attractive and easier to read. Throughout the project, use the Undo command (Ctrl + Z) if you make a mistake.

Skills needed to complete this project:

- Using Undo and Redo (Skill 2.5)
- Merging Cells and Splitting Merged Cells (Skill 2.7)
- Applying Cell Styles (Skill 2.12)
- Inserting and Deleting Cells (Skill 2.3)
- Aligning Cells (Skill 2.6)
- Changing Fonts, Font Size, and Font Color (Skill 2.9)
- Using Format Painter (Skill 2.13)
- Adding Borders (Skill 2.10)
- Cutting, Copying, and Pasting Cell Content (Skill 2.1)
- Wrapping Text in Cells (Skill 2.4)
- Applying Conditional Formatting Using the Quick Analysis Tool (Skill 2.14)
- Applying Conditional Formatting with Data Bars, Color Scales, and Icon Sets (Skill 2.15)
- Applying Conditional Formatting with Highlight Cells Rules (Skill 2.16)
- Removing Conditional Formatting (Skill 2.18)
- Applying Conditional Formatting with Top/Bottom Rules (Skill 2.17)
- Replacing Formatting (Skill 2.21)

1. Open the start file **EX2016-SkillReview-2-1**. The file will be renamed automatically to include your name. Change the **project file** name if directed to do so by your instructor, and save it.
2. If the workbook opens in Protected View, click the Enable Editing button in the Message Bar at the top of the workbook so you can modify the workbook.
3. Merge and center the worksheet title across cells A1:H1 and cells A2:H2.
   a. Select cells **A1:H1**.
   b. On the *Home* tab, in the *Alignment* group, click the **Merge & Center** button.
   c. Select cells **A2:H2**.
   d. On the *Home* tab, in the *Alignment* group, click the **Merge & Center** button.
4. Apply the Title style to the main worksheet title.
   a. Select the merged cells **A1:H1**.

b. On the *Home* tab, in the *Styles* group, click the **Cell Styles** button.
c. Click the **Title** style.

5. Apply the Accent1 style to the worksheet subtitle.
   a. Select the merged cells **A2:H2**.
   b. On the *Home* tab, in the *Styles* group, click the **Cell Styles** button.
   c. Click the **Accent1** style.
6. There are extra cells to the left of the patient name and daily cost. Delete them.
   a. Select cells **B3:B4**.
   b. On the *Home* tab, in the *Cells* group, click the **Delete** button.
7. The patient name would look better aligned at the right side of the cell.
   a. Select cell **B3**.
   b. On the *Home* tab, in the *Alignment* group, click the **Align Right** button.
8. Format the *Patient Name* and *Daily Cost* labels with bolding and the Blue, Accent 1 font color.
   a. Select cells A3:A4.
   b. On the *Home* tab, in the *Font* group, click the **Bold** button.
   c. On the *Home* tab, in the *Font* group, click the **Font Color** button arrow, and select the **Blue, Accent 1** color from the first row of the theme colors.
9. Use *Format Painter* to apply the label formatting to the data table header row (cells A6:H6).
   a. If necessary, click cell **A3** or **A4**.
   b. On the *Home* tab, in the *Clipboard* group, click the **Format Painter** button.
   c. Click cell **A6**and drag to cell **H6** to apply the formatting.
10. Add a border beneath the data table header row to separate the titles from the data. The border should be the same color as the font.
    a. If necessary, select cells **A6:H6**.
    b. On the *Home* tab, in the *Font* group, click the **Borders** button arrow, and select **More Borders...**
    c. In the *Format Cells* dialog, on the *Border* tab, expand the **Color** palette, and select the **Blue, Accent 1** color from the first row of the theme colors.
    d. Click the bottom border area of the preview diagram to add the border.
    e. Click **OK**.
11. The data in row 14 are misplaced and belong in the data table. Cut it and insert the cut cells above row 9.
    a. Select cells **A14:H14**.
    b. On the *Home* tab, in the *Clipboard* group, click the **Cut** button.
    c. Click cell **A9**.
    d. On the *Home* tab, in the *Cells* group, click the **Insert** button arrow, and select **Insert Cut Cells**.

12. Apply the Note cell style to the note in cell A13.
    a. Select cell **A13**.
    b. On the *Home* tab, in the *Styles* group, click the **Cell Styles** button.
    c. Click the **Note** style.
13. The note text is much longer than the width of cell A13, and it looks odd with the cell style applied. Apply text wrapping so all the text is visible within the cell formatted with the *Note* style.
    a. If necessary, select cell **A13**.
    b. On the *Home* tab, in the *Alignment* group, click the **Wrap Text** button.
14. Apply conditional formatting using solid blue data bars to cells H7:H11 to represent the relative daily cost of each supplement.
    a. Select cells **H7:H11**.
    b. Click the **Quick Analysis** tool button.
    c. Click the **Data Bars** button.
15. Apply conditional formatting using Highlight Cells Rules to the cost per bottle data (cells F7:F11) to format cells with a value greater than 22 with light red fill with dark red text.
    a. Select cells **F7:F11**.
    b. On the *Home* tab, in the *Styles* group, click the **Conditional Formatting** button.
    c. Point to **Highlight Cells Rules**, and select **Greater Than...**
    d. In the *Greater Than* dialog, type **22** in the **Format cells that are GREATER THAN** box.
    e. Click **OK**.
16. There might be too much conditional formatting in this worksheet. Remove the conditional formatting from cells G7:G11.
    a. Select cells **G7:G11**.
    b. On the *Home* tab, in the *Styles* group, click the **Conditional Formatting** button.
    c. Point to *Clear Rules*, and select **Clear Rules from Selected Cells**.
17. You would still like to highlight the least expensive cost per pill. Apply conditional formatting to cells **G7:G11** using **Top/Bottom Rules** to format only the lowest value with green fill with dark green text.
    a. Select cells **G7:G11**.
    b. On the *Home* tab, in the *Styles* group, click the **Conditional Formatting** button.
    c. Point to **Top/Bottom Rules**, and select **Bottom 10 Items...**
    d. In the *Bottom 10 Items* dialog, type **1** in the **Format cells that rank in the BOTTOM** box.
    e. Expand the formatting list and select **Green Fill with Dark Green Text**.

    f. Click **OK**.
18. Click cell **G12** so the cost per pill data is no longer selected.
19. Find all of the values that use the Accounting Number Format with four digits after the decimal and change the formatting to the Accounting Number Format with two digits after the decimal.
    a. On the *Home* tab, in the *Editing* group, click the **Find & Select** button, and select **Replace...**
    b. In the *Find and Replace* dialog, ensure that there are no values in the *Find what* and *Replace with* boxes.
    c. If necessary, click the **Options>>** button to display the Find and Replace options.
    d. Click the **Format...** button next to the *Find What* box.
    e. In the *Find Format* dialog, on the *Number* tab, click **Accounting** in the *Category* list. If necessary, change the *Decimal places* value to **4**. Verify that the *Symbol* value is $.
    f. Click **OK**.
    g. Click the **Format...** button next to the *Replace with* box.
    h. In the *Replace Format* dialog, on the *Number* tab, click **Accounting** in the *Category* list. If necessary, change the *Decimal* places value to **2**. Verify that the *Symbol* value is $.
    i. Click **OK**.
    j. Click **Replace All**.
    k. Excel should make nine replacements. Click **OK**.
    l. Click **Close**.
20. Save and close the workbook.

skill review 2.2

You want to share your recipe for Greek yogurt with friends, but the spreadsheet is a little rough. Use the formatting skills you learned in this chapter to make the recipe look as good as it tastes.

Throughout the project, use the *Undo* command (Ctrl + Z) if you make a mistake.

Skills needed to complete this project:

- Using Undo and Redo (Skill 2.5)
- Merging Cells and Splitting Merged Cells (Skill 2.7)
- Applying Cell Styles (Skill 2.12)
- Inserting and Deleting Cells (Skill 2.3)
- Using Format Painter (Skill 2.13)
- Changing Fonts, Font Size, and Font Color (Skill 2.9)
- Applying Bold, Italic, and Underline (Skill 2.8)
- Adding Borders (Skill 2.10)
- Using Find and Replace (Skill 2.20)
- Cutting, Copying, and Pasting Cell Content (Skill 2.1)
- Using Paste Options (Skill 2.2)
- Setting and Clearing the Print Area (Skill 2.22)Replacing Formatting (Skill 2.21)

1. Open the start file **EX2016-SkillReview-2-2** and resave the file as: `[your initials]EX-SkillReview-2-2`
2. If the workbook opens in Protected View, click the **Enable Editing** button in the Message Bar at the top of the workbook so you can modify it.
3. Center and merge the recipe title across cells **A1:D1**.
   a. Select cells **A1:D1**.
   b. On the *Home* tab, in the *Alignment* group, click the **Merge & Center** button.
4. Format the title using the *Accent 6* themed cell style.
   a. If necessary, select the merged cells **A1:D1**.
   b. On the *Home* tab, in the *Styles* group, click the **Cell Styles** button.
   c. In the *Themed Cell Styles* section of the gallery, click the **Accent 6** style.
5. Delete cell **B2**, shifting other cells to the left.
   a. Select cell **B2**.
   b. On the *Home* tab, in the *Cells* group, click the **Delete** button arrow and select **Delete Cells...**
   c. Click the **Shift cells left** radio button.
   d. Click **OK**.

6. Use *Format Painter* to copy formatting from the title and apply it to the Ingredients (**A5**) and Directions (**A10**) headers.
   a. Select the merged cells **A1:D1**.
   b. On the *Home* tab, in the *Clipboard* group, double-click the **Format Painter** button.
   c. Click cell **A5**. Notice that *Format Painter* merged cells **A5:D5** and centered the text across the merged cells.
   d. Click cell **A10**. Notice that *Format Painter* merged cells **A10:D10** and centered the text across the merged cells.
   e. On the *Home* tab, in the *Clipboard* group, click the **Format Painter** button again to disable it.
7. The worksheet title should be more prominent than the section headers. Increase the font size to 14 and bold the text.
   a. Select the merged cells **A1:D1**.
   b. On the *Home* tab, in the *Font* group, click the **Font Size** button arrow, and select **14**.
   c. On the *Home* tab, in the *Font* group, click the **Bold** button.
8. Add a bottom border to cells **B6:D6** to separate the headings from the data.
   a. Select cells **B6:D6**.
   b. On the *Home* tab, in the *Font* group, click the **Borders** button arrow and select **Bottom Border**.
9. This recipe is better using organic whole milk. Find and replace all instances of *non fat* with *organic whole.*
   a. On the *Home* tab, in the *Editing* group, click the **Find & Select** button and select **Replace...**
   b. If necessary, display the find and replace options and clear any formats.
      i. Click the **Options >>** button.
      ii. If the button next to the *Find what* box does not display *No Format Set*, click the **Format** button arrow and select **Clear Find Format**.
      iii. If the button next to the *Replace with* box does not display *Not Format Set*, click the **Format** button arrow and select **Clear Replace Format**.
      iv. Click the **Options <<** button to hide the find and replace options.
   c. Type `non fat` in the *Find what* box.
   d. Type `organic whole` in the *Replace with* box.
   e. Click the **Replace All** button.
   f. Excel should make three replacements. Click **OK**.
   g. Click **Close**.
10. Apply thick outside borders around the entire recipe (cells **A1:D20**).
    a. Select cells **A1:D20**.

   b. On the *Home* tab, in the *Font* group, click the **Borders** button arrow and select **Thick Outside Borders**.

11. Now that your recipe is formatted, make a copy of it and change the number of servings to **20**. Be sure to retain formulas and column widths.
    a. If necessary, select cells **A1:D20**.
    b. On the *Home* tab, in the *Clipboard* group, click the **Copy** button.
    c. Click cell **F1**.
    d. On the *Home* tab, in the *Clipboard* group, click the **Paste** button arrow.
    e. Select **Keep Source Column Widths**.
12. Change the value in cell **G2** to **20**.
13. Set the print area so only the original version of the recipe will print. Be sure to preview the printed worksheet.
    a. Select cells **A1:D20**.
    b. On the *Page Layout* tab, it the *Page Setup* group, click the **Print Area** button and select **Set Print Area**.
    c. Click the **File** tab.
    d. Click **Print**.
14. Save and close the workbook.

projects

Data files for projects can be found by logging into your SIMnet account and going to the *Library* section.

challenge yourself 2.3

In this project, you will format a blood pressure report to make it look less like a spreadsheet and more like a form. You will use conditional formatting to highlight important data.

Skills needed to complete this project:

- Using Undo and Redo (Skill 2.5)
- Adding Shading with Fill Color (Skill 2.11)
- Merging Cells and Splitting Merged Cells (Skill 2.7)
- Applying Cell Styles (Skill 2.12)
- Changing Fonts, Font Size, and Font Color (Skill 2.9)
- Aligning Cells (Skill 2.6)
- Adding Borders (Skill 2.10)
- Using Format Painter (Skill 2.13)
- Applying Bold, Italic, and Underline (Skill 2.8)
- Applying Conditional Formatting with Data Bars, Color Scales, and Icon Sets (Skill 2.15)
- Applying Conditional Formatting with Top/Bottom Rules (Skill 2.17)
- Setting and Clearing the Print Area (Skill 2.22)

1. Open the start file **EX2013-ChallengeYourself-2-3** and resave the file as: `[your initials]EX-ChallengeYourself-2-3`
2. If the workbook opens in Protected View, click the **Enable Editing** button in the Message Bar at the top of the workbook so you can modify it.
3. Select cells **A1:F26** and apply the white fill color.
4. Merge and center the title across cells **A1:F1**.
5. Apply the **Title** cell style to the merged cells.
6. Apply the **Gold, Accent 2, Lighter 80%** fill color to the merged cells.
7. Change the font color to **Brown, Accent 5**.
8. Merge cells **C2:D2** and right-align the content in the cell.
9. Apply the default **Outside Borders** border style to the merged cells **C2:D2**.
10. Apply the **40% - Accent4** cell style to cells **C4:D4**.
11. Apply the same formatting to cells **C7:D7**.
12. Apply the default **Outside Borders** border style to cells **C4:D5** and cells **C7:D8**.
13. Bold cells **B2**, **B5**, **B8**, and **B10**.
14. Merge cells **C10:D10** and right-align the content in the cell.

15. Apply the default **Outside Borders** border style to the merged cells.
16. Apply the **Green, Accent 4, Lighter 40%** fill color to cells **A12:F12**.
17. Left-align the content in cells **A13:A26**.
18. Apply the default **All Borders** border style to cells **A13:F26**.
19. Add conditional formatting to cells **E13:E26** using the **3 Arrows (Gray)** icon set.
20. Add conditional formatting to cells **C13:C26** to format values **greater than 139** with **light red fill with dark red text.**
21. Add conditional formatting to cells **C13:C26** to format values **between 120 and 139** with **yellow fill with dark yellow text**.
22. Add conditional formatting to cells **D13:D26** to format values **greater than 89** with **light red fill with dark red text**.
23. Add conditional formatting to cells **D13:D26** to format values **between 80 and 89** with **yellow fill with dark yellow text**.
24. Apply the default **Thick Outside Borders** border style around cells **A1:F26**.
25. .Set cells **A1:F26** as the print area.
26. Preview how the worksheet will look when printed.
27. Save and close the workbook.

projects

Data files for projects can be found by logging into your SIMnet account and going to the *Library* section.

challenge yourself 2.4

In this project you will add formatting to a college budget spreadsheet and rearrange items that are in the wrong categories.

Skills needed to complete this project:

- Using Undo and Redo (Skill 2.5)
- Merging Cells and Splitting Merged Cells (Skill 2.7)
- Applying Cell Styles (Skill 2.12)
- Adding Shading with Fill Color (Skill 2.11)
- Applying Bold, Italic, and Underline (Skill 2.8)
- Cutting, Copying, and Pasting Cell Content (Skill 2.1)
- Using Paste Options (Skill 2.2)
- Inserting and Deleting Cells (Skill 2.3)
- Using Format Painter (Skill 2.13)
- Applying Conditional Formatting with Data Bars, Color Scales, and Icon Sets (Skill 2.15)
- Wrapping Text in Cells (Skill 2.4)
- Adding Borders (Skill 2.10)

1. Open the start file **EX2013-ChallengeYourself-2-4** and resave the file as: `[your initials]EX-ChallengeYourself-2-4`
2. If the workbook opens in Protected View, click the **Enable Editing** button in the Message Bar at the top of the workbook so you can modify it.
3. Center and merge the title across cells **A1:E1**.
4. Apply the **Heading 1** cell style to the merged cells.
5. Merge and center the four section titles across the appropriate cells (**Monthly Income**, **Discretionary Income**, **Monthly Expenses**, and **Semester Expenses**).
6. Apply cell styles to the section titles as follows:
    a. Monthly Income—**20% - Accent1**
    b. Discretionary Income—**20% - Accent4**
    c. Monthly Expenses—**20% - Accent6**
    d. Semester Expenses—**20% - Accent5**
7. Add the **White, Background 1, Darker 25%** fill color to cells **A3:B3**.
8. Bold cells **A3:B3**.

9. Copy only the formatting of cells **A3:B3** to the headers in the other sections (cells **A10:B10**, **D3:E3**, and **D10:E10**).
10. The line item for lab fees (cells **A21:B21**) is in the wrong category. Cut the cells and insert them into cells **D12:E12**, shifting the other cells down. Do not overwrite the existing data.
11. Delete the empty cells **A21:B21**, shifting the other cells up.
12. Cell E6 has the wrong number format applied. Copy the formatting from cell **E5** and apply it to cell **E6**.
13. Apply conditional formatting to cells **B11:B23** to display an orange gradient data bar in each cell.
14. The text in cell **A21** appears cutoff. Apply text wrapping to the cell.
15. Apply the default **All Borders** border style to the following cell ranges: **A3:B7**, **D3:E7**, **A10:B24**, and **D10:E16**.
16. Save and close the workbook.

projects

Data files for projects can be found by logging into your SIMnet account and going to the *Library* section.

on your own 2.5

In this project, you will add your own data to a worksheet that tracks the original cost and current resell value for textbooks. As you format the worksheet, keep in mind that you want the worksheet to be visually appealing, but you don't want it to look like a circus! Try a variety of formatting options and keep using the *Undo* command until you find the formats you like best.

Skills needed to complete this project:

- Using Undo and Redo (Skill 2.5)
- Adding Shading with Fill Color (Skill 2.11)
- Merging Cells and Splitting Merged Cells (Skill 2.7)
- Applying Cell Styles (Skill 2.12)
- Inserting and Deleting Cells (Skill 2.3)
- Aligning Cells (Skill 2.6)
- Changing Fonts, Font Size, and Font Color (Skill 2.9)
- Using Format Painter (Skill 2.13)
- Adding Borders (Skill 2.10)
- Cutting, Copying, and Pasting Cell Content (Skill 2.1)
- Applying Conditional Formatting Using the Quick Analysis Tool (Skill 2.14)
- Applying Conditional Formatting with Data Bars, Color Scales, and Icon Sets (Skill 2.15)
- Replacing Formatting (Skill 2.21)
- Wrapping Text in Cells (Skill 2.4)
- Applying Bold, Italic, and Underline (Skill 2.8)
- Applying Conditional Formatting with Highlight Cells Rules (Skill 2.16)
- Applying Conditional Formatting with Top/Bottom Rules (Skill 2.17)

1. Open the start file **EX2013-OnYourOwn-2-5** and resave the file as: `[your initials]EX-OnYourOwn-2-5`
2. If the workbook opens in Protected View, click the **Enable Editing** button in the Message Bar at the top of the workbook so you can modify it.
3. Update the data in the workbook with an inventory of textbooks you own. Include the purchase price and estimated resell value for each title.
4. Add and delete cells as necessary.
5. Wrap text if any of your book titles are too long to fit in the cell.

6. Format the worksheet title and data table using cell styles, borders, and fill color. Change fonts, font color, and font size as appropriate.
7. Remember to use *Format Painter* to copy formatting from one part of the worksheet to another.
8. You can also use the *Replace* command if you want to change formatting from one style to another in multiple cells at the same time.
9. Apply conditional formatting to identify the most expensive books and the ones with the highest resell values. Use any type of conditional formatting you'd like.
10. When you are satisfied with the appearance of the worksheet, save and close the workbook.

projects

Data files for projects can be found by logging into your SIMnet account and going to the *Library* section.

fix it 2.6

In this project, you will fix a rather unattractive worksheet that was intended for recording walking/running miles and times.

Skills needed to complete this project:

- Using Undo and Redo (Skill 2.5)
- Adding Shading with Fill Color (Skill 2.11)
- Merging Cells and Splitting Merged Cells (Skill 2.7)
- Applying Cell Styles (Skill 2.12)
- Inserting and Deleting Cells (Skill 2.3)
- Changing Fonts, Font Size, and Font Color (Skill 2.9)
- Using Format Painter (Skill 2.13)
- Adding Borders (Skill 2.10)
- Wrapping Text in Cells (Skill 2.4)
- Applying Conditional Formatting Using the Quick Analysis Tool (Skill 2.14)
- Applying Conditional Formatting with Data Bars, Color Scales, and Icon Sets (Skill 2.15)
- Using Find and Replace (Skill 2.20)
- Applying Bold, Italic, and Underline (Skill 2.8)

1. Open the start file **EX2013-FixIt-2-6** and resave the file as: **[your initials]EX-FixIt-2-6**
2. If the workbook opens in Protected View, click the **Enable Editing** button in the Message Bar at the top of the workbook so you can modify it.
3. Begin by removing all the fill color, font colors, and borders from the worksheet. This worksheet has so many different formats; it is probably easier to start from a clean slate.

   Hint: Do not use the *Clear Formats* command. Using this command will remove all numbering formats to the General number format.
4. All fonts in the worksheet should be set to **Calibri**, **12** point size.
5. Merge cells **A1:D1** and center the title across the merged cells.
6. Apply appropriate formatting for the title. Use the **Title** cell style.

7. Apply the **White, Background 1, Darker 25%** fill color to cells **B4:D9** to make the data table stand out.
8. Apply a dotted border to the inside of cells **A4:D9**. *Hint:* Use the *Format Cells* dialog, and select the second border style in the list after *None*. In the *Presets* section, apply the **Inside** option.
9. Apply a border around cells **A3:D9** using the **Thick Outside Borders** option.
10. Apply a border to cells **A3:D3** using the **Bottom Double Border** option.
11. Apply bold to cells **B3:D3** and **A4:A9** to make row and column headers stand out from the data.
12. Apply text wrapping in cell **D3**.
13. An entry for June 9 is missing. You walked for 40 minutes that day, and went 3 miles. Insert the data in the appropriate place. (You can copy the formula to calculate miles per hour from one of the other cells).

    NOTE: You must complete step 13 correctly in order to be able to receive points for completing the next steps. Check your work carefully.
14. Apply conditional formatting using data bars to visually compare the distance jogged each day.
15. Ensure that all entries for miles and miles per hour display using the Number format with two digits after the decimal.
16. Ensure that all average calculations display using the Number format with two digits after the decimal.
17. Find all instances of *walk* and replace with *jog*.

    NOTE: If you receive the warning message "We couldn't find anything to replace. Click options for more ways to search," clear replace format options.
18. Save and close the workbook.

chapter 3

Using Formulas and Functions

In this chapter, you will learn the following skills:

- Use a variety of methods to enter functions
- Use statistical functions
- Use date and time functions
- Use text functions
- Work with named ranges
- Use the IF logical function
- Use the PMT financial function
- Use lookup functions
- Troubleshoot formulas
- Display and print formulas

Skill 3.15 Using the Logical Function IF

Skill 3.16 Calculating Loan Payments Using the PMT Function

Skill 3.17 Finding Data Using the VLOOKUP Function

Skill 3.18 Checking Formulas for Errors

Skill 3.19 Finding Errors Using Trace Precedents and Trace Dependents

Skill 3.20 Displaying and Printing Formulas

introduction

It is time to go beyond simple formulas. In this chapter you will learn to use the functions built into Excel to compute statistics, insert dates, modify text, work with logical expressions, compute loan payments, and perform table lookups. Also, you will create formulas that reference named ranges and other worksheets for fast replication. Finally, you will learn skills necessary for troubleshooting formulas.

Skill 3.1 Using the Function Arguments Dialog to Enter Functions

In Chapter 1, you learned to enter functions three ways:

1. **Typing the formula directly in the cell or the formula bar.** This method is easiest for simple functions.
2. **Using the *AutoSum* button.** This method works well when your spreadsheet includes numerical data organized in rows or columns. Functions available via AutoSum are limited to simple math and statistical functions (SUM, AVERAGE, COUNT, MIN, and MAX).
3. **Using the Quick Analysis tool.** This method is the easiest way to enter totals for multiple rows or columns of data at once. Like AutoSum, the Quick Analysis tool offers a limited number of functions (SUM, AVERAGE, and COUNT). It has the advantage of including options not available from AutoSum (calculating running totals and calculating the percentage of the overall total for each row or column) and showing a live preview of the totals before you make a selection.

Every function can be entered using its *Function Arguments* dialog. This dialog is different for each function. There are two primary methods for opening the *Function Arguments* dialog.

1. **Select the function from the *Formulas* tab, *Function Library* group.** Each button in this Ribbon group represents a category of functions. Clicking a button displays a menu of functions in that category. Selecting a function opens its *Insert Function* dialog.

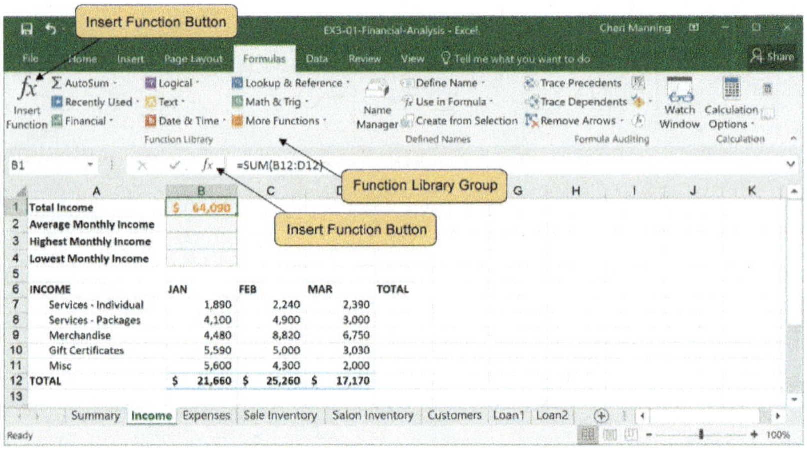

FIGURE EX 3.1

2. **Select the function from the *Insert Function* dialog.** To open the *Insert Function* dialog, on the *Formulas* tab, in the *Function Library* group, click the **Insert Function** button. You can also click the **Insert Function** button to the left of the formula bar.

To use the *Insert Function* dialog:

1. Functions in the *Insert Function* dialog are organized in the same categories as the *Function Library* group. By default, the category list will default to the category you last used or it will show the *Most Recently Used* list. To select another category, expand the **Or select a category** list and select the function category you want.
2. Click a function in the *Select a function* box to see a brief description of what it does and the arguments it takes.
3. Click **OK** to open the *Function Arguments* dialog for the selected function.

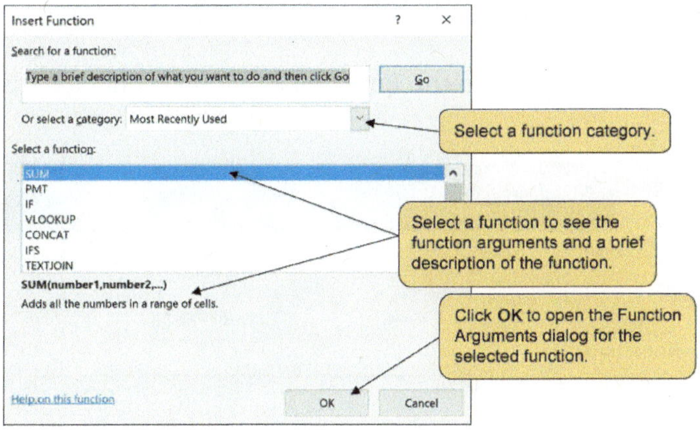

FIGURE EX 3.2

To use the *Function Arguments* dialog:

1. Enter values or cell references in each of the argument boxes as needed by typing or by clicking the cell or cell range in the worksheet. As you click each argument box, a brief description of the argument appears near the bottom of the dialog. The *Function Arguments* dialog also displays a preview of the result of the calculation. This value updates as you add arguments.

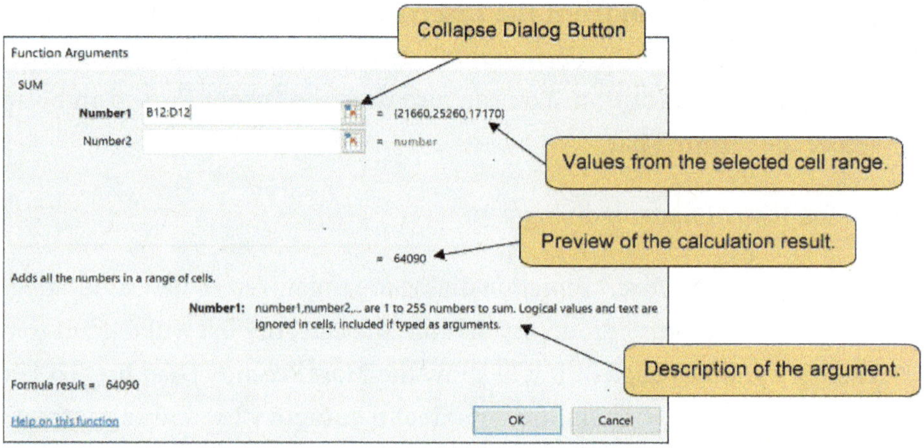

FIGURE EX 3.3

2. If the position of the *Function Arguments* dialog makes it difficult to click the cell you want, click the **Collapse Dialog** button next to the argument box. As shown in Figure EX 3.4, the *Function Arguments* dialog collapses to show only the function argument box you are working with. Click the cell(s) to add the reference to the dialog.
3. Click the **Expand Dialog** button to return the *Function Arguments* dialog to its full size.

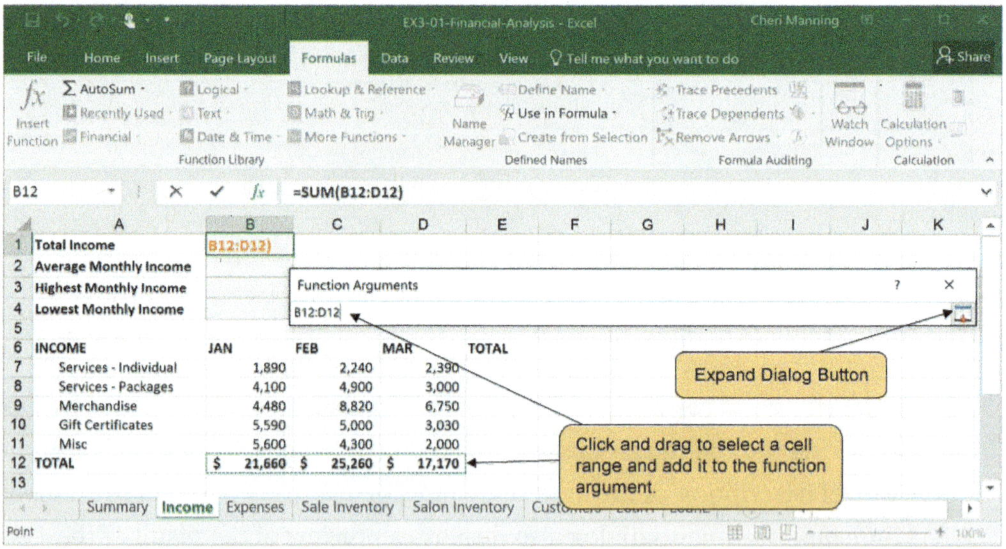

FIGURE EX 3.4

4. When you are finished entering arguments, click **OK**.

tips & tricks

The *SUM Function Arguments* dialog shown in Figure EX 3.3 includes an extra argument box. For functions that calculate a value based on a series of cells, Excel adds a blank argument box each time you enter an argument (up to 256 arguments). Enter values or cell references only in the argument boxes you need.

tell me more

If you're not sure of the name of the function you want, open the *Insert Function* dialog and type keywords describing the function in the *Search for a function* box, and then click the **Go** button. The *Or select a category* box changes to *Recommended*, and the *Select a function* box now displays a list of functions that match the keywords you typed.

let me try *Live!*

Open the student data file **EX3-01-Financial-Analysis** and try this skill on your own:

1. On the **Income** worksheet, enter a SUM function in cell **B1** to calculate the total of cells **B12:D12.** Open the *Function Arguments* dialog from the *Formulas* tab, *Function Library* group, **Math & Trig** button. You will have to scroll down the list to find SUM.
2. Enter a SUM function in cell **E7** to calculate the total of cells **B7:D7.** Use the *Insert Function* dialog. If the SUM function is not listed in the *Select a Function* box, expand the **Or select a category list,** and select either **Math & Trig** or **Most Recently Used.** Again, Excel enters the adjacent cell range as the function arguments for you.
3. If you will be moving on to the next skill in this chapter, leave the workbook open to continue working. If not, save the file as directed by your instructor and close it.

Skill 3.2 Using Formula AutoComplete to Enter Functions

Formula AutoComplete is a shortcut for entering functions. When you type = and then a letter, Formula AutoComplete displays a list of potential matches (functions and other valid reference names). This is a good method to use if you prefer typing the function arguments, but you need a reminder of what the arguments are or the order in which they should be entered.

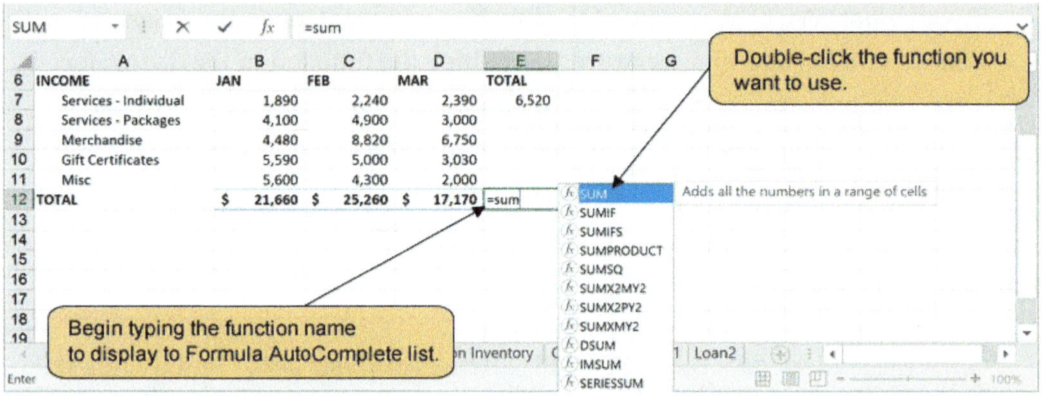

FIGURE EX 3.5

1. Type = in the cell or the formula bar to begin the formula. Formula AutoComplete displays the list of potential matches.
2. Type more letters to shorten the Formula AutoComplete list.
3. Double-click a function name to enter it in your formula.
4. Enter the expected arguments by typing values or selecting a cell or cell range.
5. Press Enter to complete the formula. Excel enters the closing) for you.

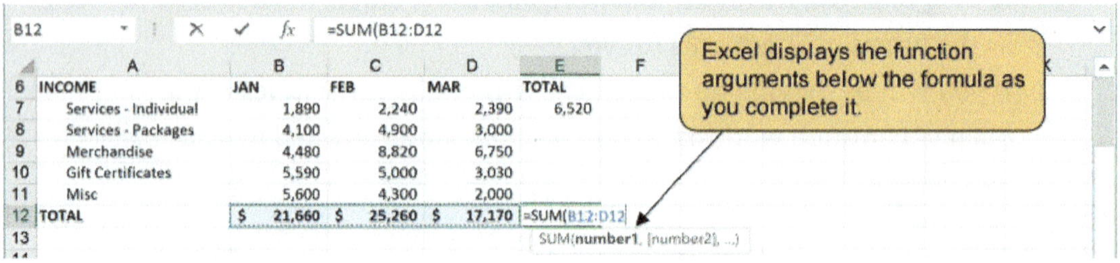

FIGURE EX 3.6

tips & tricks

When you use Formula AutoComplete, you can click the function name in the ScreenTip to open the Excel help topic for that function.

let me try *Live!*

If you do not have the data file from the previous skill open, open the student data file **EX3-02-Financial-Analysis** and try this skill on your own:

1. On the **Income** worksheet, use Formula AutoComplete to enter a SUM function in cell **E12** to calculate the total of cells **B12:D12.**
2. If you will be moving on to the next skill in this chapter, leave the workbook open to continue working. If not, save the file as directed by your instructor and close it.

Skill 3.3 Calculating Averages

The **AVERAGE** statistical function is used to calculate the average value of a group of values. Average is calculated by adding the values, and then dividing the sum by the number of values.

A formula using the AVERAGE function looks like this: **=AVERAGE(B12:D12)**

The result of this formula is the sum of the values in cells B12:D12 divided by the number of values in that cell range.

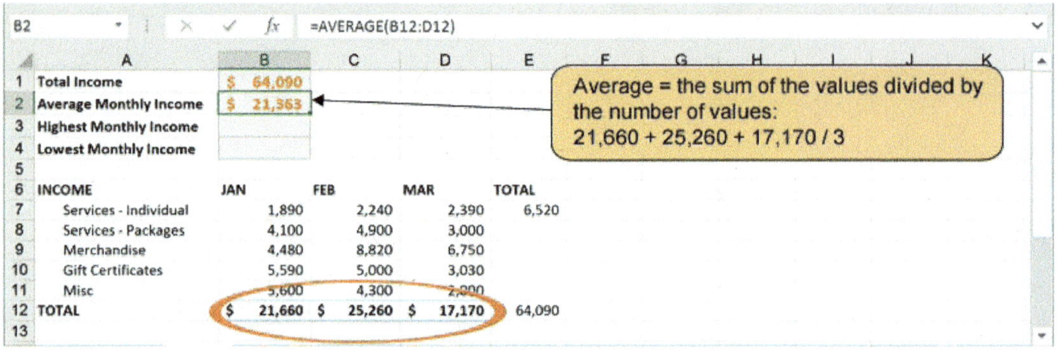

FIGURE EX 3.7

To create a formula with the AVERAGE function, use any of these methods:

- If you prefer typing in the cell or the formula bar, try using Formula AutoComplete.
- If the data are organized in rows or columns, you can use AutoSum. On the *Home* tab, *Editing* group or on the *Formula* tab, *Function Library* group, click the **AutoSum** button arrow and select **Average.**
- If you want to calculate the average for multiple rows or columns at once, use one of the average options in the Quick Analysis tool, *Totals* tab.
- If you prefer using the *Function Arguments* dialog, on the *Formulas* tab, in the *Function Library* group, click the **More Functions** button, point to **Statistical,** and click **AVERAGE.**

tips & tricks

When calculating an average, Excel will ignore empty cells. If you want to include those cells in your average calculations, make sure they have a value of zero.

tell me **more**

What you might think of as the "average" is actually the statistical mean. *Average* is a general term in statistics that includes **mean** (the sum of a group of values divided by the number of values in the group), **median** (the middle value of a set of values) and **mode** (the value that appears most often in a group of values). In Excel, the AVERAGE function calculates the mean value. Most people say *average* when they really want to calculate the mean value.

let me **try** *Live!*

If you do not have the data file from the previous skill open, open the student data file **EX3-03-Financial-Analysis** and try this skill on your own:

1. On the **Income** worksheet, enter a formula in cell **B2** to calculate the average value of cells **B12:D12.** Use any method you like.
2. If you will be moving on to the next skill in this chapter, leave the workbook open to continue working. If not, save the file as directed by your instructor and close it.

Skill 3.4 Finding Minimum and Maximum Values

In addition to AVERAGE, there are a few other statistical functions you may find useful in working with day-to-day spreadsheets.

The **MAX** (maximum) statistical function will give you the largest value in a range of values. A formula using the MAX function looks like this: **=MAX(A3:A6)**

The **MIN** (minimum) statistical function will give you the smallest value in a range of values. A formula using the MIN function looks like this: **=MIN(A3:A6)**

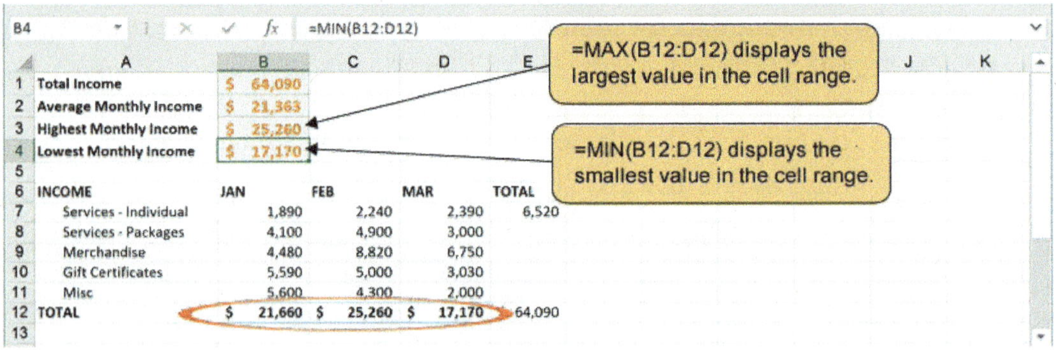

FIGURE EX 3.8

To create a formula with the MAX or MIN function, use any of these methods:

- If you prefer typing in the cell or the formula bar, try using Formula AutoComplete.
- If the data are organized in rows or columns, you can use AutoSum. On the *Home* tab, *Editing* group or on the *Formula* tab, *Function Library* group, click the **AutoSum** button arrow and select **Max** or **Min.**
- If you prefer using the *Function Arguments* dialog, on the *Formulas* tab, in the *Function Library* group, click the **More Functions** button, point to **Statistical,** and click **MAX** or **MIN.**

let me try *Live!*

If you do not have the data file from the previous skill open, open the student data file **EX3-04-Financial-Analysis** and try this skill on your own:

1. On the **Income** worksheet, in cell **B3,** enter a formula to find the highest (maximum) monthly income total (cells **B12:D12**).
2. On the **Income** worksheet, in cell **B4,** enter a formula to find the lowest (minimum) monthly income total (cells **B12:D12**).
3. If you will be moving on to the next skill in this chapter, leave the workbook open to continue working. If not, save the file as directed by your instructor and close it.

Skill 3.5 Using Date and Time Functions

Excel includes two functions that insert the current date or date and time. The **NOW** function inserts the current date and time. The **TODAY** function inserts only the current date. Both of these functions are **volatile**—that is, they are not constant. They update with the current date or date and time each time the workbook is opened.

A formula using the NOW function looks like this: **=NOW()**

A formula using the TODAY function looks like this: **=TODAY()**

Notice that both of these functions include parentheses, but there are no arguments inside them. These functions do not require arguments.

To create a formula with NOW or TODAY, use either of these methods:

- If you prefer typing in the cell or the formula bar, try using Formula AutoComplete.
- If you prefer using the *Function Arguments* dialog, on the *Formulas* tab, in the *Function Library* group, click the **Date & Time** button and click **NOW** or **TODAY.**

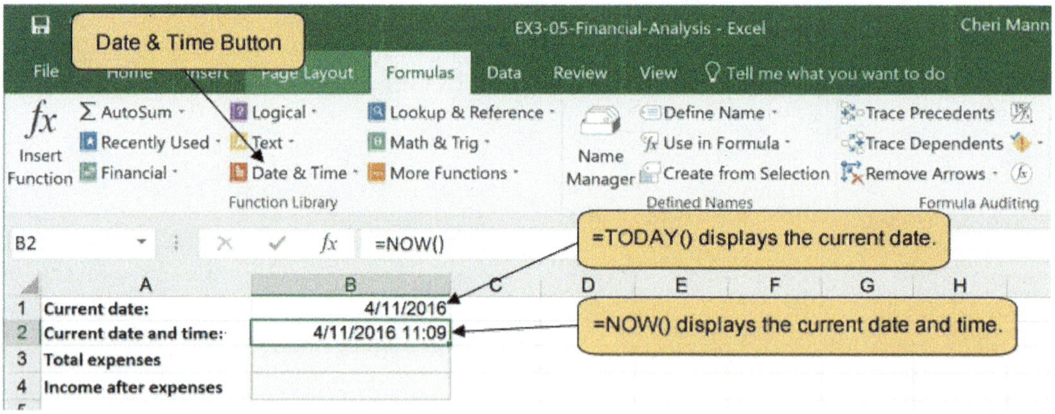

FIGURE EX 3.9

tips & tricks

Both NOW and TODAY use the date and time from your computer's clock. If your computer's clock is wrong, the date and time displayed in your workbook will be wrong as well.

tell me **more**

If the cell is formatted to use a date format that does not display the time, the result of the NOW and TODAY functions will appear the same. However, the underlying value will be different. If you change the formatting of the cell to display the time, a cell using the TODAY function will always display a time of 12:00 AM, whereas a cell using the NOW function will display the correct time.

let me **try** *Live!*

If you do not have the data file from the previous skill open, open the student data file **EX3-05-Financial-Analysis** and try this skill on your own:

1. On the **Summary** worksheet, enter a formula in cell **B1** to display only the current date.
2. On the **Summary** worksheet, enter a formula in cell **B2** to display the current date and time.
3. If you will be moving on to the next skill in this chapter, leave the workbook open to continue working. If not, save the file as directed by your instructor and close it.

Skill 3.6 Creating Formulas Using Counting Functions

The counting functions are useful when you need to know how many numbers or items are in a list or how many rows are missing data for a particular column.

COUNT—Counts the number of cells that contain numbers within a specified range of cells. A formula using the COUNT function looks like this: **=COUNT(A7:A20)**

The result of this formula is the number of cells in **A7** through **A20** that contain numerical values. If you want to include cells that contain text, use COUNTA instead.

To count numbers, you have two additional options:

- If the data are organized in rows or columns, you can use AutoSum to enter the COUNT function. On the *Home* tab, *Editing* group or on the *Formula* tab, *Function Library* group, click the **AutoSum** button arrow and select **Count Numbers.**
- If you want to count the numbers in multiple rows or columns at once, use one of the *Count* options from the Quick Analysis tool, *Totals* tab.

COUNTA—Counts the number of cells that are not blank within a specified range of cells. Use COUNTA if your cell range includes text data or a mix of text and numbers. A formula using the COUNTA function looks like this: **=COUNTA(B7:B20)**

The result of this formula is the number of cells in **B7** through **B20** that contain any data (numerical or text).

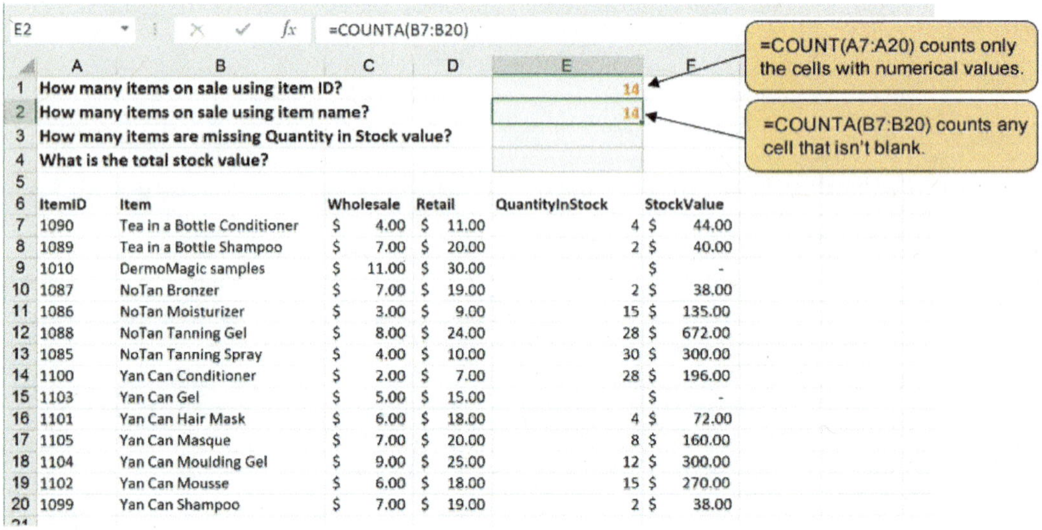

FIGURE EX 3.10

COUNTBLANK—Counts the number of empty (blank) cells within a specified range of cells. Cells that contain a zero (0) or a formula that results in zero are not considered blank. Use COUNTBLANK to find the number of rows missing values in a column. A formula using the COUNTBLANK function looks like this:

=COUNTBLANK(E7:E20)

The result of this formula is the number of cells in **E7** through **E20** that are empty.

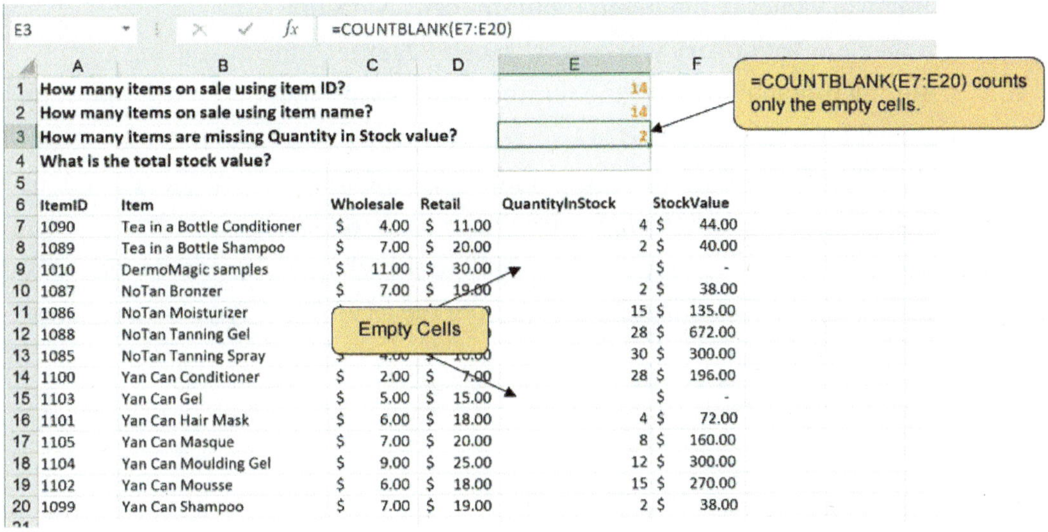

	A	B	C	D	E	F
1	How many items on sale using item ID?				14	
2	How many items on sale using item name?				14	
3	How many items are missing Quantity in Stock value?				2	
4	What is the total stock value?					
5						
6	ItemID	Item	Wholesale	Retail	QuantityInStock	StockValue
7	1090	Tea in a Bottle Conditioner	$ 4.00	$ 11.00	4	$ 44.00
8	1089	Tea in a Bottle Shampoo	$ 7.00	$ 20.00	2	$ 40.00
9	1010	DermoMagic samples	$ 11.00	$ 30.00		$ -
10	1087	NoTan Bronzer	$ 7.00	$ 19.00	2	$ 38.00
11	1086	NoTan Moisturizer	[illegible]	[illegible]	15	$ 135.00
12	1088	NoTan Tanning Gel	[illegible]	[illegible]	28	$ 672.00
13	1085	NoTan Tanning Spray	[illegible]	[illegible]	30	$ 300.00
14	1100	Yan Can Conditioner	$ 2.00	$ 7.00	28	$ 196.00
15	1103	Yan Can Gel	$ 5.00	$ 15.00		$ -
16	1101	Yan Can Hair Mask	$ 6.00	$ 18.00	4	$ 72.00
17	1105	Yan Can Masque	$ 7.00	$ 20.00	8	$ 160.00
18	1104	Yan Can Moulding Gel	$ 9.00	$ 25.00	12	$ 300.00
19	1102	Yan Can Mousse	$ 6.00	$ 18.00	15	$ 270.00
20	1099	Yan Can Shampoo	$ 7.00	$ 19.00	2	$ 38.00

FIGURE EX 3.11

To create a formula with COUNT, COUNTA, or COUNTBLANK, use either of these methods:

- If you prefer typing in the cell or the formula bar, try using Formula AutoComplete.
- If you prefer using the *Function Arguments* dialog, on the *Formulas* tab, in the *Function Library* group, click the **More Functions** button, point to **Statistical,** and click **COUNT, COUNTA,** or **COUNTBLANK.**

tips & tricks

The COUNT and COUNTA functions can take multiple arguments.

COUNTBLANK accepts only a single argument. If you want to count blanks across a non-contiguous range of cells, you will need to create a formula adding together the results of multiple functions.

=COUNTBLANK(A1:C1)+COUNTBLANK(B10:C15)

let me try *Live!*

If you do not have the data file from the previous skill open, open the student data file **EX3-06-Financial-Analysis** and try this skill on your own:

1. On the **Sale Inventory** worksheet, in cell **E1,** enter a formula using a counting function to count the number of items on sale. Count the numerical values in the *ItemID* column (cells **A7:A20**).
2. On the **Sale Inventory** worksheet, in cell **E2,** enter a formula using a counting function to count the number of items on sale. Count the values in the *Item* column (cells **B7:B20**).
3. In cell **E3,** enter a formula using a counting function to count the number of blank cells in the *QuantityInStock* column (cells **E7:E20**).
4. If you will be moving on to the next skill in this chapter, leave the workbook open to continue working. If not, save the file as directed by your instructor and close it.

Skill 3.7 Formatting Text Using Functions

Functions can do more than perform calculations. Excel includes a special group of functions to modify text. These text functions are useful for ensuring that text data have a consistent appearance. In functions, text is referred to as a **string** or **text string**.

Commonly used text functions are:

PROPER—Converts the text string to proper case (the first letter in each word is capitalized). A formula using the PROPER function looks like this: **=PROPER(D2)**

UPPER—Converts the text string to all uppercase letters. A formula using the UPPER function looks like this: **=UPPER(F2)**

LOWER—Converts the text string to all lowercase letters. A formula using the LOWER function looks like this: **=LOWER(H2)**

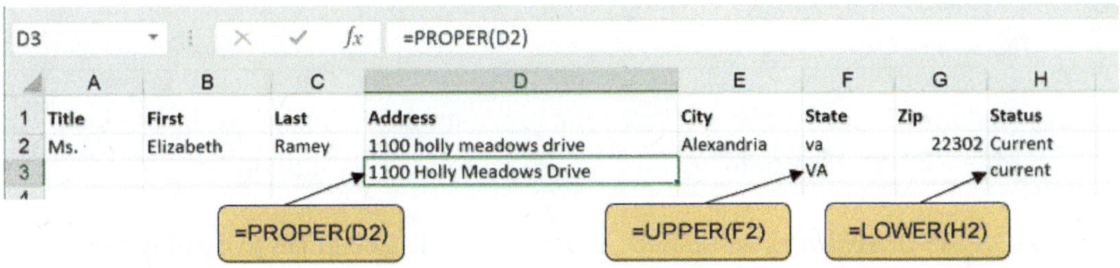

FIGURE EX 3.12

To create a formula with PROPER, UPPER, or LOWER, use either of these methods:

- If you prefer typing in the cell or the formula bar, try using Formula AutoComplete.
- If you prefer using the *Function Arguments* dialog, on the *Formulas* tab, in the *Function Library* group, click the **Text** button and click **PROPER, UPPER,** or **LOWER.**

tips & tricks

Typically, when you use one of the text functions, you are left with two groups of cells containing the same data: One group has the original incorrectly formatted text; the second group contains the formulas and displays correctly formatted text. There are two options for managing this:

- Hide the columns or rows that contain the original text. For information on hiding rows and columns, refer to the skill *Hiding and Unhiding Rows and Columns*.
- Copy the cells containing the text formulas; use one of the *Paste Values* options to paste just the values of the text formulas over the original cells, then delete the cells containing the text formulas. For information on using the *Paste Values* commands, refer to the skill *Using Paste Options*.

let me try *Live!*

If you do not have the data file from the previous skill open, open the student data file **EX3-07-Financial-Analysis** and try this skill on your own:

1. On the **Customers** worksheet, enter a formula in cell **D3** to display the text from cell **D2** so the first letter in each word is capitalized.
2. On the **Customers** worksheet, enter a formula in cell **F3** to display the text from cel **F2** so all the letters display in uppercase.
3. On the **Customers** worksheet, enter a formula in cell **H3** to display the text from cell **H2** so all the letters display in lowercase.
4. If you will be moving on to the next skill in this chapter, leave the workbook open to continue working. If not, save the file as directed by your instructor and close it.

Skill 3.8 Using CONCAT to Combine Text

To **concatenate** means to link items together. You can use the **CONCAT** function to combine the text values of cells or cell ranges. In Figure EX 3.13, the customer name in cell B3 is created by concatenating the values in column B (first name) and column C (last name). The formula looks like this: **=CONCAT(B2 ," ", C2)**

The argument in the middle (" ") places a one-space text string between the values of cells B2 and C2.

If you are building a long string from multiple cells, you may want to use the *Function Arguments* dialog until you become familiar with this function. Of course, you can always type directly in the cell or formula bar and use Formula AutoComplete.

1. On the *Formulas* tab, in the *Function Library* group, click the **Text** button.

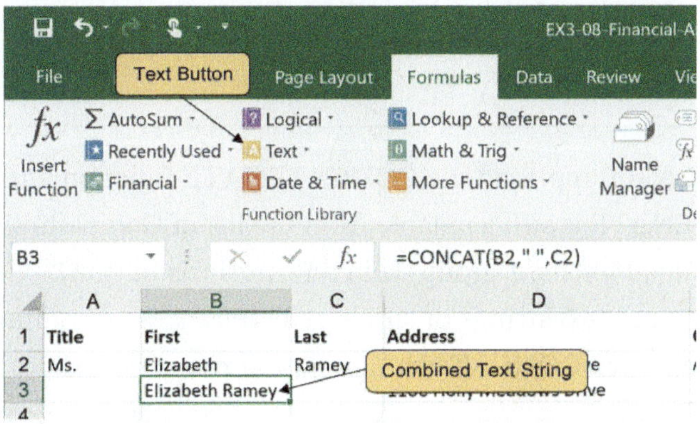

FIGURE EX 3.13

2. Click **CONCAT**.
3. In the *Function Arguments* dialog, enter each cell reference or text string you want to combine in its own argument. If one of the arguments is a blank space, enter ;" " in the argument box.

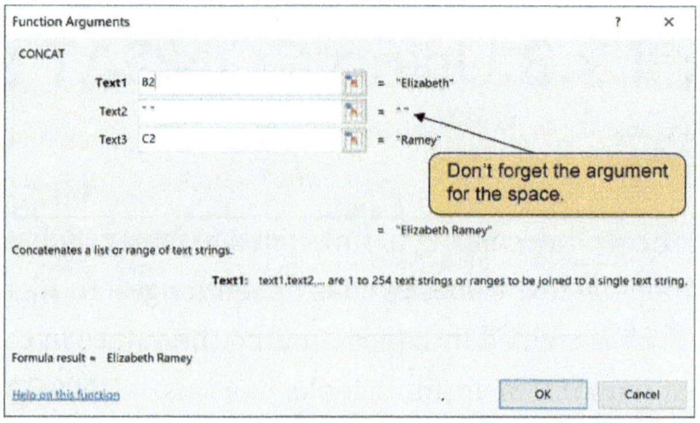

FIGURE EX 3.14

4. Click **OK.**

tips & tricks

For sorting purposes, you may want to keep the cells that you concatenate. If you do not want them to display in your worksheet, hide the columns or rows that contain the original text. For information on hiding rows and columns, refer to the skill *Hiding and Unhiding Rows and Columns.*

tell me more

In February 2016, Microsoft replaced the CONCATENATE function with CONCAT. CONCATENATE is still available from the list of Compatibility functions (*Formulas* tab, *Functions* group, **More Functions** button). CONCATENATE required text strings or single cell references as arguments while the new and improved CONCAT can handle cell range references.

let me try *Live!*

If you do not have the data file from the previous skill open, open the student data file **EX3-08-Financial-Analysis** and try this skill on your own:

1. On the **Customers** worksheet, enter a formula in cell **B3** to combine the text from cells **B2** and **C2** to display the customer name in the format *Elizabeth Ramey.* Don't forget the argument for the space.
2. If you will be moving on to the next skill in this chapter, leave the workbook open to continue working. If not, save the file as directed by your instructor and close it.

Skill 3.9 Using TEXTJOIN to Combine Text

Another way to combine text is to use the **TEXTJOIN** function. TEXTJOIN concatenates cells using a **delimiter** character to separate values in the new text string. In Figure EX 3.15, the customer name in cell B4 is created by combining the values in A2 (title), B2 (first name), and C2 (last name) and separating each text value with a space. The formula looks like this:

=TEXTJOIN(" ", TRUE,A2:C2)

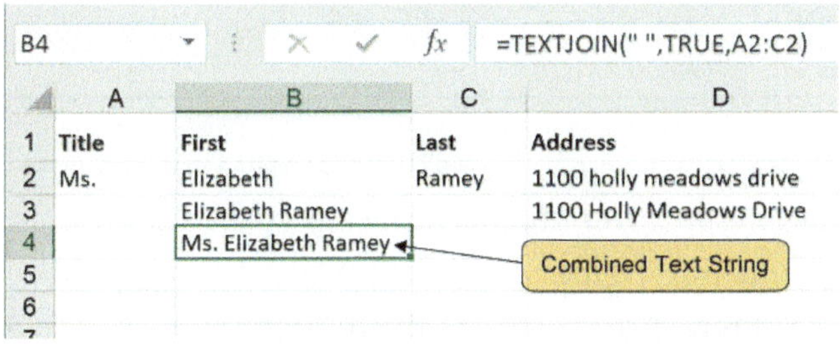

FIGURE EX 3.15

To combine text using TEXTJOIN:

1. On the *Formulas* tab, in the *Function Library* group, click the **Text** button.
2. Click **TEXTJOIN.**
3. Enter the **Delimiter** argument. This argument defines the character to use between each text item.
4. Enter the **Ignore_empty** argument. If set to TRUE, the function will skip blank cells. If set to FALSE, the function will include the blank cells, resulting in two of the delimiter characters together.
5. Enter the **Text1** argument. This argument is first text string, cell, or cell range to combine. If you use a cell range, the delimiter character will be added between the values from each cell in the range.
6. Continue adding **Text** arguments as necessary.
7. Click **OK.**

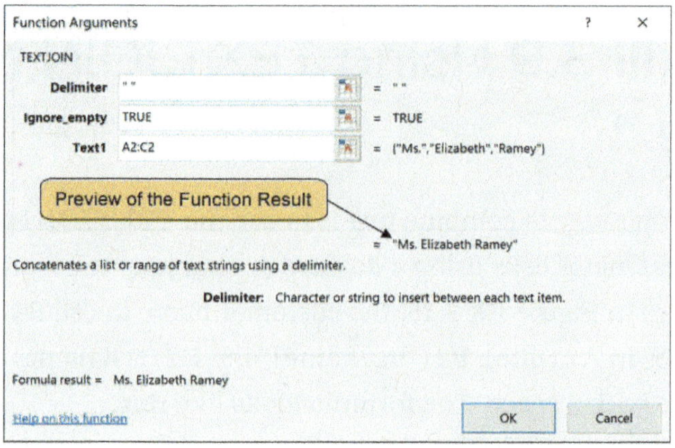

FIGURE EX 3.16

tips & tricks

When using a space as the delimiter in a TEXTJOIN formula, if you type the formula directly in the cell or address bar, you must enclose the space in quotation marks. If you use the *Function Arguments* dialog, you can just type the space in the *Delimiter* argument box. Excel will add the quotation marks for you.

tell me more

Microsoft added the TEXTJOIN function to Excel in February 2016. If you have an Office 365 subscription, your version of Excel should update automatically to include this new function.

let me try *Live!*

If you do not have the data file from the previous skill open, open the student data file **EX3-09-Financial-Analysis** and try this skill on your own:

1. On the **Customers** worksheet, enter a formula in cell **B4** to combine the text from cells **A2:C2** to display the customer name in the format *Ms. Elizabeth Ramey*. Use a space as the delimiter. Ignore blank cells.
2. If you will be moving on to the next skill in this chapter, leave the workbook open to continue working. If not, save the file as directed by your instructor and close it.

Skill 3.10 Creating Formulas Referencing Data from Other Worksheets

Cell references are not limited to cells within the same worksheet. To specify a cell location in another worksheet, begin the reference with the name of the worksheet followed by an exclamation point ! and then the cell reference. This feature is useful when you want to create summary sheets or perform analysis on data from multiple sheets at once.

The formula shown in Figure EX 3.17 displays the value of cell E8 from the *Expenses* worksheet:

= Expenses!E8

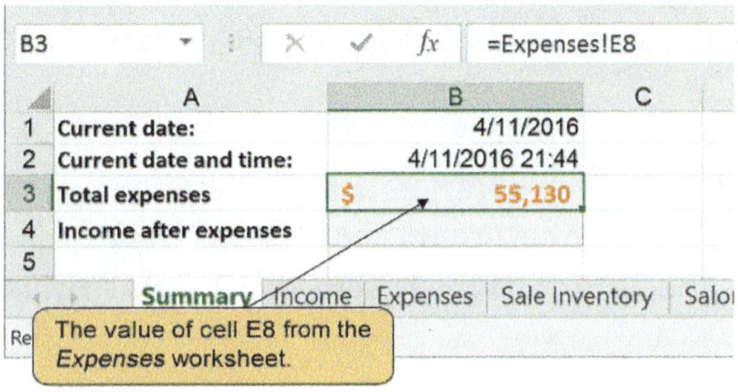

FIGURE EX 3.17

To include a reference to a cell from another sheet in your workbook:

1. Click the cell where you want the formula.
2. Type: =
3. Navigate to the cell you want to reference by clicking the sheet tab and then clicking the cell. Notice Excel adds the worksheet name to the cell reference for you.
4. Press Enter to complete the formula.

You can also refer to cells in other worksheets within formulas as shown in Figure EX 3.18.

=Income!B1-Expenses!E8

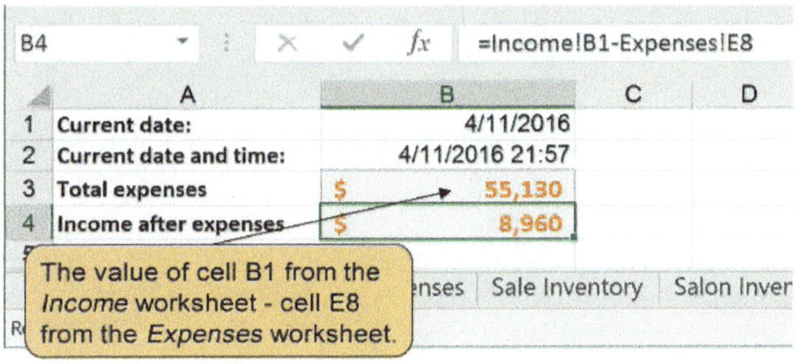

FIGURE EX 3.18

To include a reference to another worksheet in a formula:

1. Begin entering the formula as normal.
2. When you want to add a reference to a cell in another sheet, click the sheet tab, then click the cell(s) you want to add to the formula or click and drag to select a cell range.
3. When you are finished with the formula, Press Enter.

let me try *Live!*

If you do not have the data file from the previous skill open, open the student data file **EX3-10-Financial-Analysis** and try this skill on your own:

1. On the **Summary** sheet, in cell **B3,** enter a formula to display the value of cell **E8** from the **Expenses** worksheet.
2. On the **Summary** sheet, in cell **B4,** enter a formula to calculate the value of cell **B1** from the **Income** worksheet **minus** cell **E8** from the **Expenses** worksheet.
3. If you will be moving on to the next skill in this chapter, leave the workbook open to continue working. If not, save the file as directed by your instructor and close it.

Skill 3.11 Naming Ranges of Cells

Cell references like A4 and F7:F20 do not provide much information about what data the cells contain—they just tell you where the cells are located in the worksheet. However, you can assign names to cells or ranges of cells to give your cell references names that are more user-friendly. These **names** (also called **range names** or **named ranges**) act as a list of shortcuts to the cell locations.

To create a named range:

1. Select the cell or range of cells to which you want to assign a name.
2. Type the name in the *Name* box to the left of the formula bar.
3. Press Enter to apply the name to the cell(s).

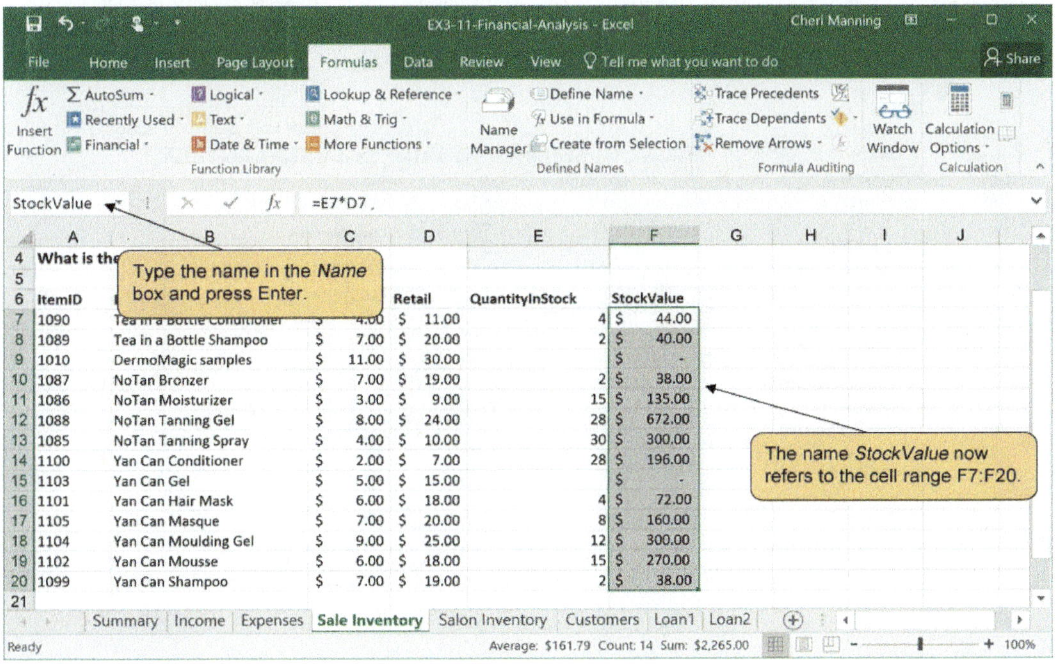

FIGURE EX 3.19

If your worksheet is organized in a table format, with column or row labels, you can automatically create named ranges for each column or row using the labels as names:

1. Select the range of cells you want to name including the labels.
2. On the *Formulas* tab, in the *Defined Names* group, click the **Create from Selection** button.
3. In the *Create Names from Selection* dialog, click the check box to indicate where the names are (*Top row, Left column, Bottom row,* or *Right column*).
4. Click **OK.**

Excel automatically creates named ranges for the cell range associated with each label. The named ranges will not include the labels. The *Create Names from Selection* command in Figure EX 3.20 will create the following named ranges:

Name:	ItemID	Item	Wholesale	QuantityInStock	ReorderLevel
Refers to cell range:	A5:A20	B5:B20	C5:C20	D5:D20	E5:E20

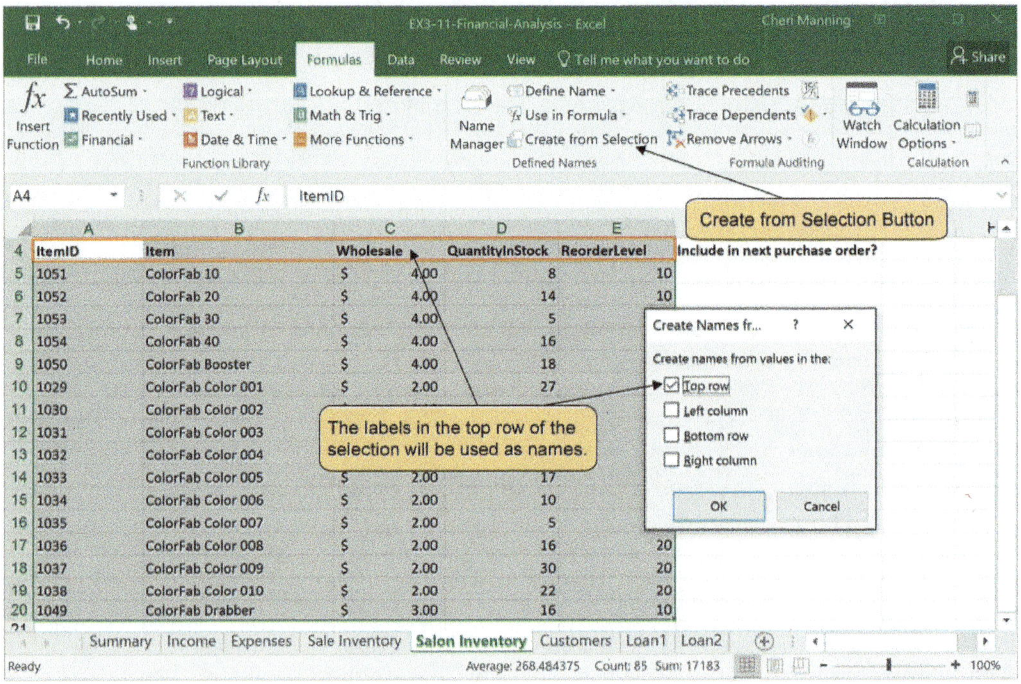

FIGURE EX 3.20

tips & tricks

Remember, names may not include spaces. If you use the *Create Names from Selection* command and the values for your names include spaces, Excel will replace the spaces with underscore _ characters.

another method

You can also create new names through the *New Name* dialog.

1. On the *Formulas* tab, in the *Defined Names* group, click the **Define Name** button.
2. The selected cell(s) is (are) entered in the *Refers to* box.
3. Type the name you want in the *Name* box. If the cell to the immediate left or immediately above the selected cell appears to include a label, Excel will prepopulate the *Name* box with that text.
4. Click **OK**

let me try *Live!*

If you do not have the data file from the previous skill open, open the student data file **EX3-11-Financial-Analysis** and try this skill on your own:

1. On the **Sale Inventory** worksheet, select cells **F7:F20,** and name them as follows: **StockValue**
2. On the **Salon Inventory** worksheet, select cells **A4:E20** and use the *Create from Selection* command to create named ranges for the data table **A5:E20** using the labels in row **4** as the basis for the names.
3. If you will be moving on to the next skill in this chapter, leave the workbook open to continue working. If not, save the file as directed by your instructor and close it.

Skill 3.12 Working with Named Ranges

Rather than using a range of cells in your formulas, you can use a named range. The name will always refer to the cells, even if their position in the worksheet changes. Using named ranges in your formulas also makes it easier for others to use your workbook. Which formula is easier to understand: **=SUM(F7:F20)** or **=SUM(StockValue)**?

Formula AutoComplete lists named ranges as well as functions. Named ranges are identified by the label icon next to the name. Using the AutoComplete list is a good way to avoid typographical errors and ensure that you enter the name correctly.

To use a named range in a formula:

1. Click the cell where you want to enter the new formula.
2. Type the formula, substituting the range name for the cell references.
3. As you type alphabetical characters, Formula AutoComplete will offer name suggestions. If you see the name you want, double-click it and Excel will insert the name into the formula.
4. Press Enter to accept the formula.

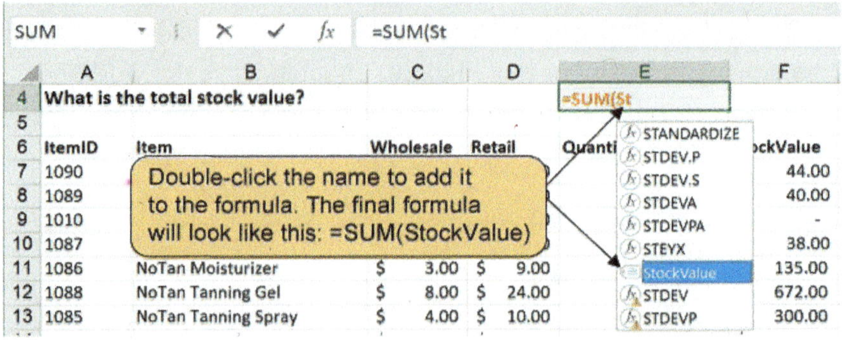

FIGURE EX 3.21

tips & tricks

- When you copy and paste a formula containing a named range, the name does not change with the new position in the workbook (similar to using an absolute reference).
- If you move a named cell, the name updates with the new cell location automatically.

another method

- On the *Formulas* tab, in the *Defined Names* group, click the **Use in Formula** button to display a list of names in your workbook, and then click one of the names to insert it into your formula.
- You can also click **Paste Names...** from the bottom of the *Use in Formula* list. The *Paste Names* dialog opens and lists all of the names in your workbook. Click a name and then click **OK** to add it to your formula.

let me try *Live!*

If you do not have the data file from the previous skill open, open the student data file **EX3-12-Financial-Analysis** and try this skill on your own:

1. On the **Sale Inventory** worksheet, in cell **E4**, enter a formula to calculate the total stock value. Use the **SUM** function and use the range name **StockValue** as the function argument.
2. If you will be moving on to the next skill in this chapter, leave the workbook open to continue working. If not, save the file as directed by your instructor and close it.

Skill 3.13 Updating Named Ranges with the Name Manager

The **Name Manager** lists all the named ranges used in your workbook, the current value for each, the cells to which the name refers (including the sheet name), the scope of the name (whether it is limited to a specific worksheet or applies to the entire workbook), and comments (if there are any).

To open the Name Manager, on the *Formulas* tab, in the *Defined Names* group, click the **Name Manager** button.

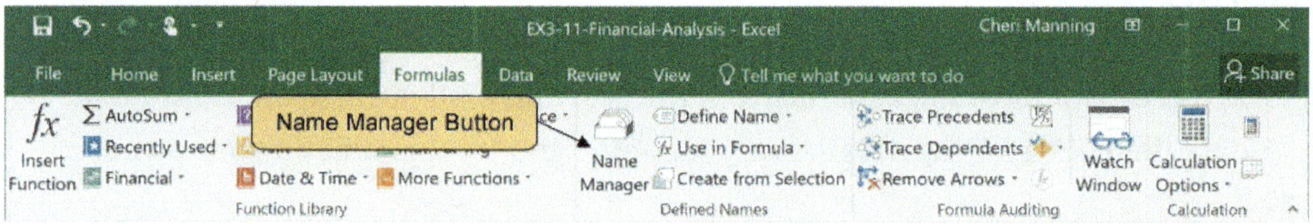

FIGURE EX 3.22

To change the cell or range of cells to which a name refers:

1. Open the Name Manager and select the name you want to modify.
2. Edit the cell references in the *Refers to* box. You can also click the **Collapse Dialog** button to hide the Name Manager, and then click and drag to select the new cell range. When you are finished, click the **Expand Dialog** button to display the Name Manager again.

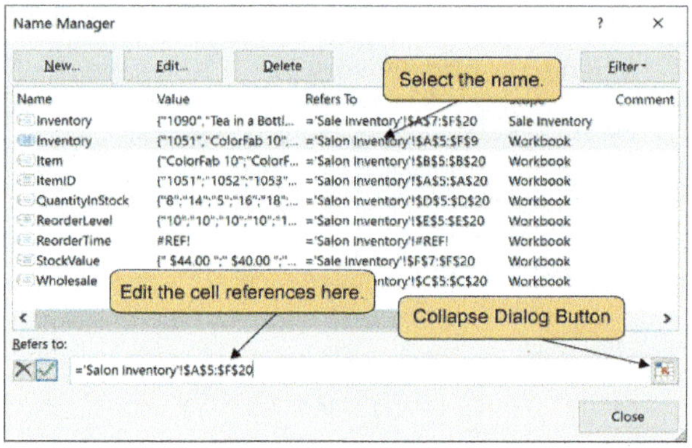

FIGURE EX 3.23

3. Click the checkmark icon to the left of the *Refers to* box to accept the change.
4. Click **Close** to close the Name Manager. If you forgot to save your change, Excel will ask if you want to save the change you made to the cell reference. Click **Yes**.

let me try *Live!*

If you do not have the data file from the previous skill open, open the student data file **EX3-13-Financial-Analysis** and try this skill on your own:

1. Open the Name Manager.
2. Edit the workbook **Inventory** name so it refers to cells **A5:F20** on the **Salon Inventory** worksheet. Be sure to modify the second Inventory name, not the one that is limited in scope to just the **Sale Inventory** worksheet.
3. Close the Name Manager.
4. If you will be moving on to the next skill in this chapter, leave the workbook open to continue working. If not, save the file as directed by your instructor and close it.

Skill 3.14 Editing and Deleting Names with the Name Manager

When you copy data, you may find that some of the names in your workbook are repeated. Remember that names must be unique—but only within their scopes. You can have more than one named range with the same name, but only one can belong to the entire workbook. The others are specific to the worksheet in which they are defined.

In Figure EX 3.24, there are two *Inventory* names. The first is limited in scope to the *Sale Inventory* worksheet. If you refer to the name *Inventory* in a formula in any other sheet in the workbook, it will refer to the second *Inventory* named range.

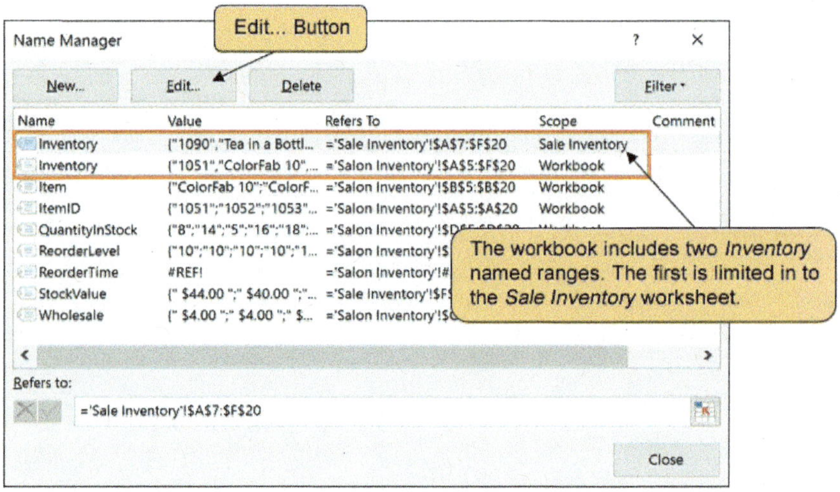

FIGURE EX 3.24

Duplicate names can be confusing. A good practice is to rename duplicates to make them easier to identify and use.

To change a name:

1. Open the Name Manager.
2. Click the name you want to modify, and then click the **Edit...** button.
3. The *Edit Name* dialog opens.
4. Type the new name in the *Name* box.
5. Click **OK** to save your changes.
6. Click the **Close** button to close the Name Manager.

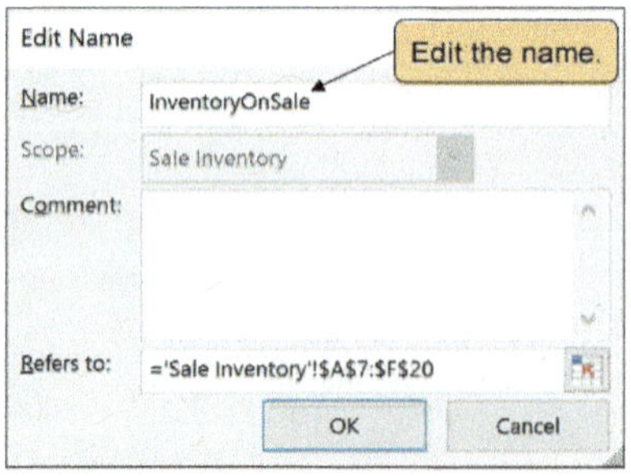

FIGURE EX 3.25

When you change a name, Excel updates the name in any formulas that reference that name.

If your workbook includes names you no longer need, you should delete them.

To delete a name:

1. On the *Formulas* tab, in the *Defined Names* group, click the **Name Manager** button.
2. Click the name you want to delete, and then click the **Delete** button.
3. Excel displays a message asking if you are sure you want to delete the name. Click **OK.**

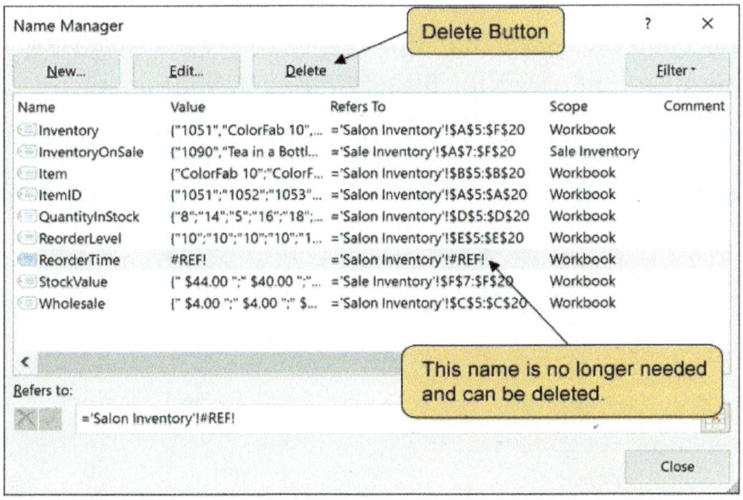

FIGURE EX 3.26

tips & tricks

- There are two types of names identified in the Name Manager. **Defined names** are the names you created and names that Excel creates automatically when you define a print area or print titles. Table names are names created automatically when you define a data range as a table. By default, tables are named Table1, Table2, Table3, and so on. To make table names easier to use, consider renaming them through the Name Manager.
- If your workbook includes many named ranges, you may find it useful to filter the list of names in the Name Manager. Click the **Filter** button in the upper right corner of the Name Manager and filter the list to show only names with errors or only names limited in scope to a worksheet.

let me **try** *Live!*

If you do not have the data file from the previous skill open, open the student data file **EX3-14-Financial-Analysis** and try this skill on your own:

1. Open the Name Manager.
2. There are two *Inventory* names. Rename the one that is limited in scope to the *Sale Inventory* worksheet to: **InventoryOnSale**
3. In the Name Manager, review the information about the *ReorderTime* name. The name results in an error—probably because the data to which it referred were deleted. Delete the **ReorderTime** name.
4. Close the Name Manager.
5. If you will be moving on to the next skill in this chapter, leave the workbook open to continue working. If not, save the file as directed by your instructor and close it

Skill 3.15 Using the Logical Function IF

The **IF** logical function returns one value if a condition is true and another value if the condition is false. The IF function can return a numerical value or display a text string.

The formula in Figure 3.27 uses the IF function to determine whether or not an item should be ordered. If the value of cell D2 (the quantity in stock) is greater than the value of cell E2 (the reorder level), the formula will return "do not order". If the value of cell D2 is not greater than the value of cell E2, the formula will return "order". The formula looks like this:

=IF(D5>E5,"do not order","order")

In Figure EX 3.27, the value of cell D5 is ***not*** greater than the value of cell E5, so the IF function returns the *Value_if_false* argument displaying the word *order.* In the next row in the worksheet, the value of cell D6 ***is*** greater than the value of cell E6, so the IF function returns the *Value_if_true* argument displaying the phrase *do not order.*

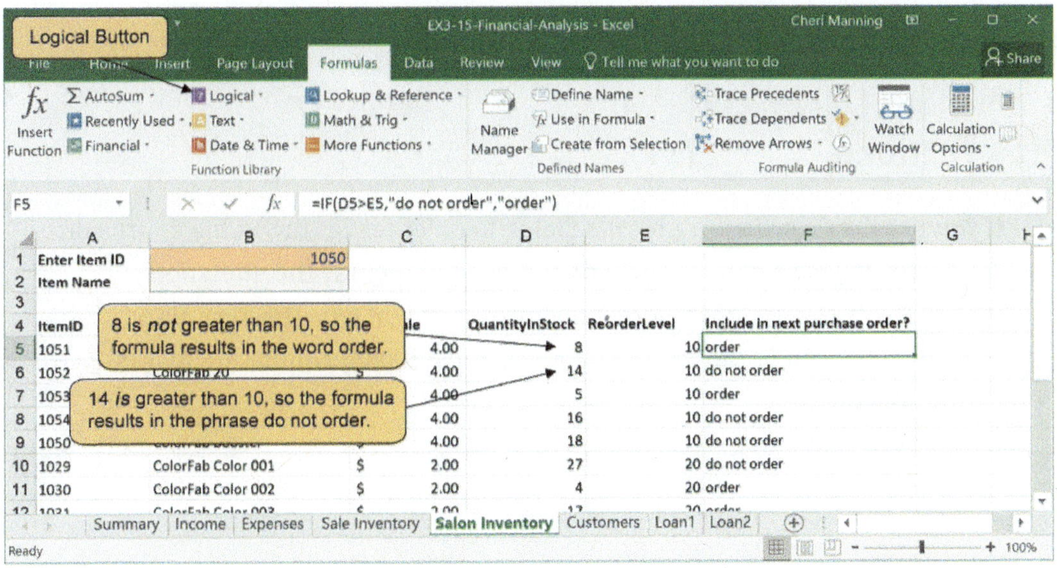

FIGURE EX 3.27

To create a formula using the IF function:

1. Select the cell where you want to enter the formula.
2. On the *Formulas* tab, in the *Function Library* group, click the **Logical** button.
3. Select **IF** to open the *Function Arguments* dialog. IF functions take three arguments as shown in the *Function Arguments* dialog in Figure EX 3.28.

4. Enter the **Logical_test** argument. This argument states the condition you want to test for. The *Logical_test* always includes a comparison operator (=, >, <, etc.).
5. Enter the **Value_if_true** argument. This argument is the text string or value that will be displayed or the formula that will be calculated if the *Logical_test* argument is true.
6. Enter the **Value_if_false** argument. This argument is the text string or value that will be displayed or the formula that will be calculated if the *Logical_test* argument is false.
7. Click **OK.**

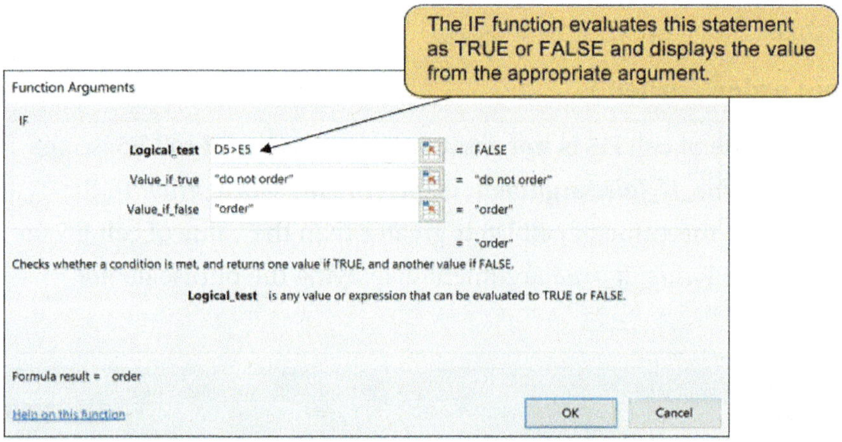

FIGURE EX 3.28

tips & tricks

If you use the *Function Arguments* dialog to enter text as the *Value_if_true* or the *Value_if_false* argument, you do not need to include the quotation marks. Excel will add them for you. However, if you type the formula directly in the cell or the formula bar, you must include quotation marks around the text.

let me try *Live!*

If you do not have the data file from the previous skill open, open the student data file **EX3-15-Financial-Analysis** and try this skill on your own:

1. On the **Salon Inventory** worksheet, enter a formula in cell **F5** using the logical function IF to display **do not order** if the quantity in stock (cell **D5**) is greater than the reorder level (cell **E5**) and **order** if it is not.
2. Copy the formula to cells **F6:F20** and review the results for each row.
3. If you will be moving on to the next skill in this chapter, leave the workbook open to continue working. If not, save the file as directed by your instructor and close it.

from the perspective of . . .

INSTRUCTOR

I use a spreadsheet to keep a grid of class attendance by student and by day. Using formulas and functions for grading gives me the flexibility to add scores, calculate averages, and provide feedback to my students.

Skill 3.16 Calculating Loan Payments Using the PMT Function

One of the most useful financial functions in Excel is **PMT** (payment), which you can use to calculate loan payments. The PMT function is based on constant payments and a constant interest rate. To calculate a payment using PMT, you need three pieces of information: the interest rate (the *Rate* argument), the number of payments (the *Nper* argument), and the amount of the loan (the *Pv* argument).

=PMT(Rate,Nper,Pv)

Because the result of the formula is a payment (money going out), it is expressed as a negative number. If you want the result expressed as a positive number instead, add a negative symbol before the loan amount (the *Pv* argument).

When working with complex functions like PMT, use cell references as arguments rather than entering values directly. This way you can change values in your spreadsheet and see the results instantly without opening the *Function Arguments* dialog again.

Using cell references, the PMT function in Figure EX 3.29 looks like this:
=PMT(B4/12,B5,-B3)

In this example, the ***annual*** interest rate in cell B4 is 4%. To calculate ***monthly*** payments, the interest rate must be divided by the number of payments per year (12).

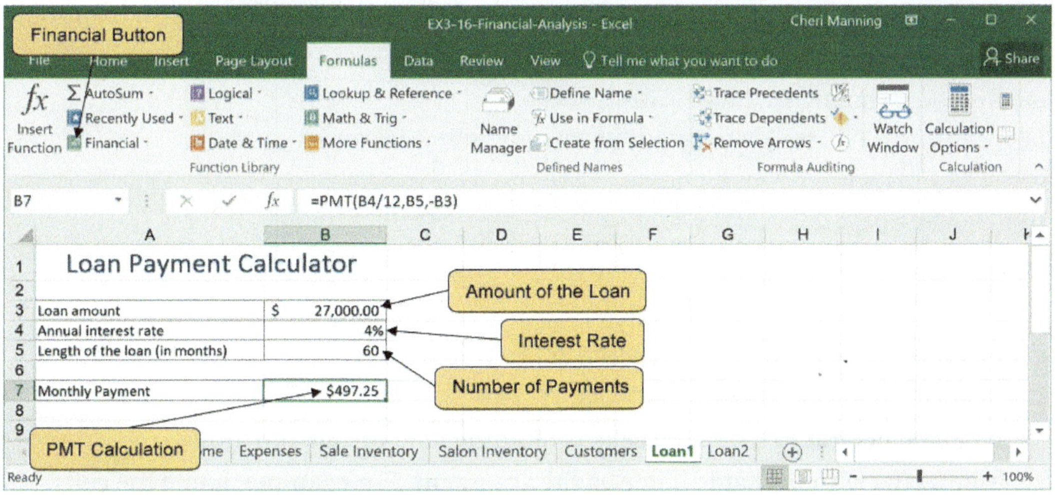

FIGURE EX 3.29

To use the PMT function:

1. Select the cell where you want to enter the formula.

2. On the *Formulas* tab, in the *Function Library* group, click the **Financial** button.
3. Select **PMT** from the list to open the *Function Arguments* dialog. PMT takes three required arguments and two optional arguments as shown in Figure EX 3.30.
4. Enter the **Rate** argument. This argument is the interest rate. Usually, interest rate is expressed as an annual rate. If the loan requires a monthly payment, the annual percentage rate (APR) should be divided by 12.
5. Enter the **Nper** argument. This argument is the total number of payments over the life of the loan.
6. Enter the **Pv** argument. This argument is the present value of the loan—how much you owe now (the loan principal).
7. (Optional) The **Fv** argument is future value of the loan. Excel assumes a value of 0 unless you include the argument and specify a different value. If you will make payments on the loan until it is completely paid off, you can leave this argument blank or enter 0.
8. (Optional) The **Type** argument represents when payments will be made during each loan period. Enter 1 if the payment is at the beginning of the period. If you omit this argument, Excel assumes a value of 0 (meaning each payment is at the end of the period).
9. Click **OK.**

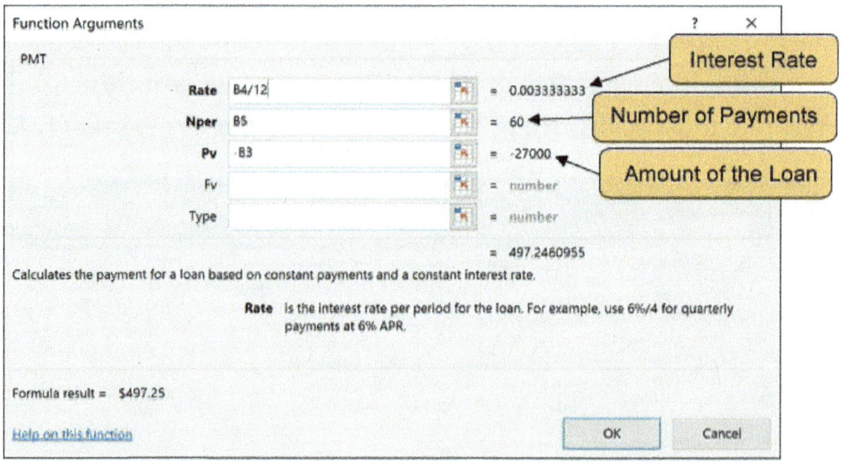

FIGURE EX 3.30

tips & tricks

It can be helpful to name the cells containing data for the function arguments with the same name as the argument. For example, name the cell with the interest rate **Rate**. Then when you build the PMT function, the cell names match the argument names. It makes creating the function easy.

let me try *Live!*

If you do not have the data file from the previous skill open, open the student data file

EX3-16-Financial-Analysis and try this skill on your own:

1. On the **Loan1** worksheet, enter a formula in cell **B7** using the PMT function to calculate the monthly loan payment. Use cell references as the function arguments. Remember, payments will be monthly, so divide the annual interest rate by 12. Use a negative number for the **Pv** argument. Do not include the optional arguments.
2. If you will be moving on to the next skill in this chapter, leave the workbook open to continue working. If not, save the file as directed by your instructor and close it.

Skill 3.17 Finding Data Using the VLOOKUP Function

Excel includes a group of functions that can be used to look up matching values in a cell range. The **VLOOKUP** function finds a value or cell reference in a cell range and returns another value from the same row. VLOOKUP requires you to specify the value you want to find, the cell range that contains the data, and the column that contains the value you want the function to return.

=VLOOKUP(Lookup_value,Table_array,Col_index_num,Range_lookup)

The formula in Figure 3.31 finds the value from cell **B2** in the cell range named **Inventory** and then returns the value from the second column of the range. In other words, VLOOKUP finds the item ID and returns the item name.

=VLOOKUP(B2,Inventory,2,FALSE)

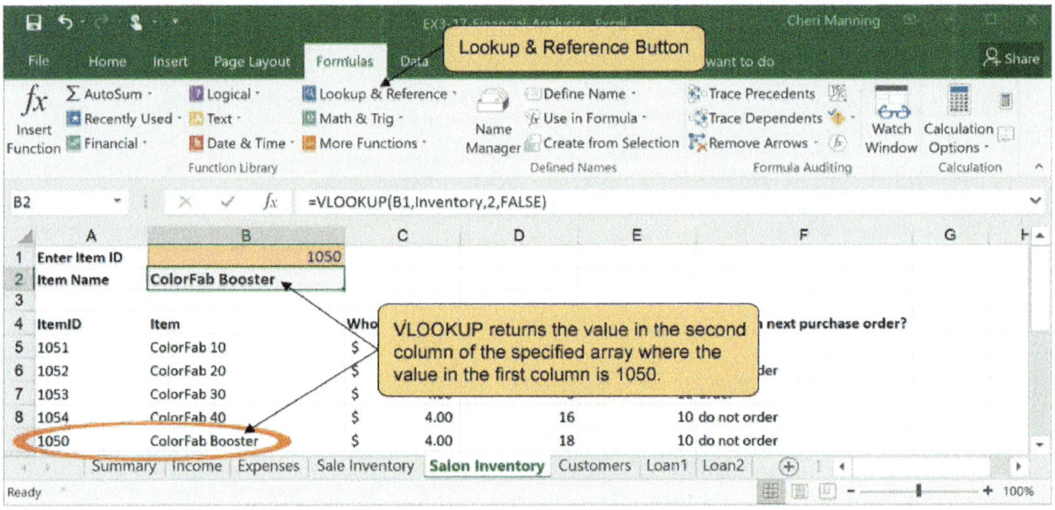

FIGURE EX 3.31

To use the VLOOKUP function:

1. Select the cell where you want to enter the formula.
2. On the *Formulas* tab, in the *Function Library* group, click the **Lookup & Reference** button.
3. Select **VLOOKUP** from the list to open the *Function Arguments* dialog. VLOOKUP takes three required arguments and one optional argument as shown in Figure EX 3.32.

4. Enter the **Lookup_value** argument. Enter the cell reference for which you want to find a corresponding value. In other words, the value you want to look up. The *Lookup_value* must be located in the first column of the cell range defined in the *Table_array* argument.
5. Enter the **Table_array** argument. Enter the range of cells (or the range name) that contains the lookup data. If your data include a header row, do not include it in the range used for the *Table_array* argument.
6. Enter the **Col_index_num** argument. This argument is the position of the column in the *Table_array* from which the function should return a matching value. Enter the column number, not the letter or the column heading.
7. (optional) Enter the **Range_lookup** argument. Type FALSE if you want to find only an exact match for the value entered in the *Lookup_value* box. If you omit this argument, Excel assumes a value of **TRUE** and will return the value for the closest match in the first column.
8. Click **OK.**

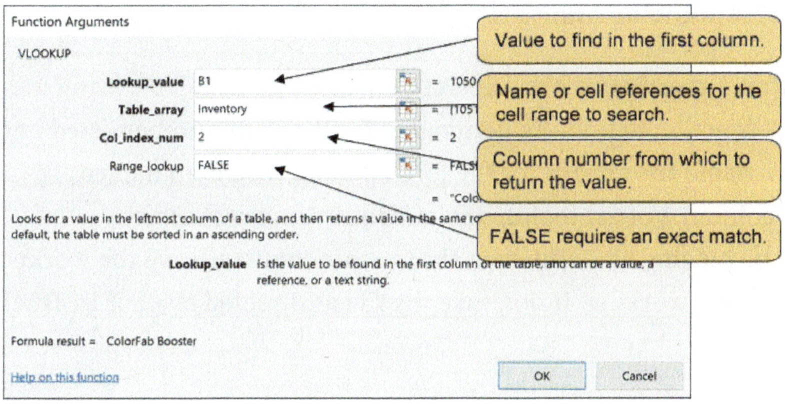

FIGURE EX 3.32

tips & tricks

If you do not specify *False* for the *Range_lookup* argument, be aware that the formula will return the first close match it finds. You may see unexpected results.

tell me **more**

The examples here all use the VLOOKUP function to find corresponding values in different columns within the same row (a *vertical* lookup). The **HLOOKUP** function works similarly, except you use it to find corresponding values in different rows within the same column (a *horizontal* lookup).

Use HLOOKUP when your worksheet uses a horizontal layout—few rows with many columns.

Use VLOOKUP when your worksheet uses a vertical layout—few columns with many rows.

let me **try** *Live!*

If you do not have the data file from the previous skill open, open the student data file **EX3-17-Financial-Analysis** and try this skill on your own:

1. On the **Salon Inventory** worksheet, enter a formula in cell **B2** using the VLOOKUP function to find the item name for the item number listed in cell **B1.** Use the name **Inventory** for the lookup table. The item names are located in column **2** of the lookup table. Require an exact match.
2. If you will be moving on to the next skill in this chapter, leave the workbook open to continue working. If not, save the file as directed by your instructor and close it.

Skill 3.18 Checking Formulas for Errors

Some worksheet errors are easily identifiable—such as divide by zero errors, which look like this in your worksheet: **#DIV/0!** (because Excel cannot calculate a value to display). Other potential errors, like formulas that leave out part of a cell range, are harder to find yourself. You can use Excel's error checking features to review your worksheet for errors.

Cells that include potential errors are marked with a green triangle in the upper-left corner of the cell. When you click the cell, Excel displays a **Smart Tag** to help you resolve the error.

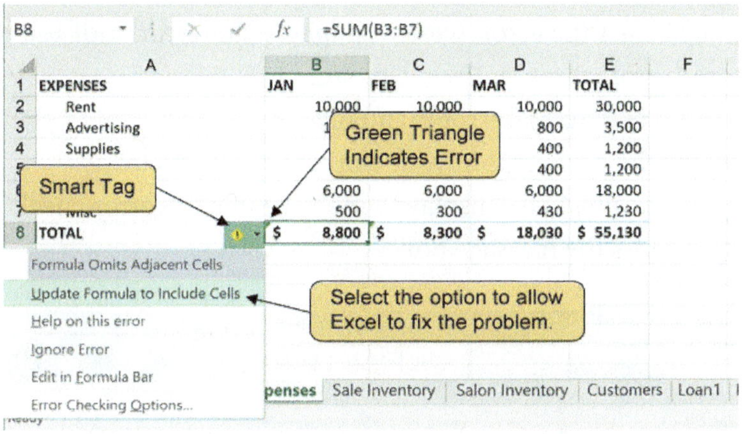

FIGURE EX 3.33

To use Smart Tags to resolve errors in formulas:

1. When a Smart Tag appears, move your mouse over the icon to display a tool tip describing the possible error.
2. Click the **Smart Tag** to display the possible error resolutions.
3. If you want to keep the formula as it is, select **Ignore Error.**
4. If you want to resolve the error, select one of the options:
   - The first option is usually a suggestion of how to resolve the error. Click it to accept Excel's suggestion.
   - Select **Help on this error** to open Microsoft Office Help.
   - Select **Ignore Error** to leave the cell unchanged.
   - Select **Edit in Formula Bar** to manually edit the formula.
   - Select **Error Checking Options...** to open the *Options* dialog and modify the way that Excel checks for errors.
5. Once you have made a selection from the Smart Tag options, the Smart Tag is dismissed.

Error checking is also available from the *Formulas* tab, *Formula Auditing* group. The *Error Checking* dialog displays each error it finds, allowing you to resolve or ignore each error in turn.

To use error checking to find errors in your worksheet:

1. On the *Formulas* tab in the *Formula Auditing* group, click the **Error Checking** button.
2. The *Error Checking* dialog displays information about the first error. The buttons available in the dialog will differ, depending on the type of error found.
   - If Excel is able to offer a solution to the error, the dialog will include a button to accept the suggested fix.
   - Click the **Help on this error** button to open Microsoft Office Help.
   - Click **Ignore Error** to dismiss the error. Excel will ignore this error until you manually reset ignored errors through Excel *Options*.
   - Click **Edit in Formula Bar** to fix the error manually.
3. Click the **Next** button to see the next error in your worksheet.
4. When you have reviewed all errors, Excel displays a message that the error check is complete. Click **OK** to dismiss the message box.

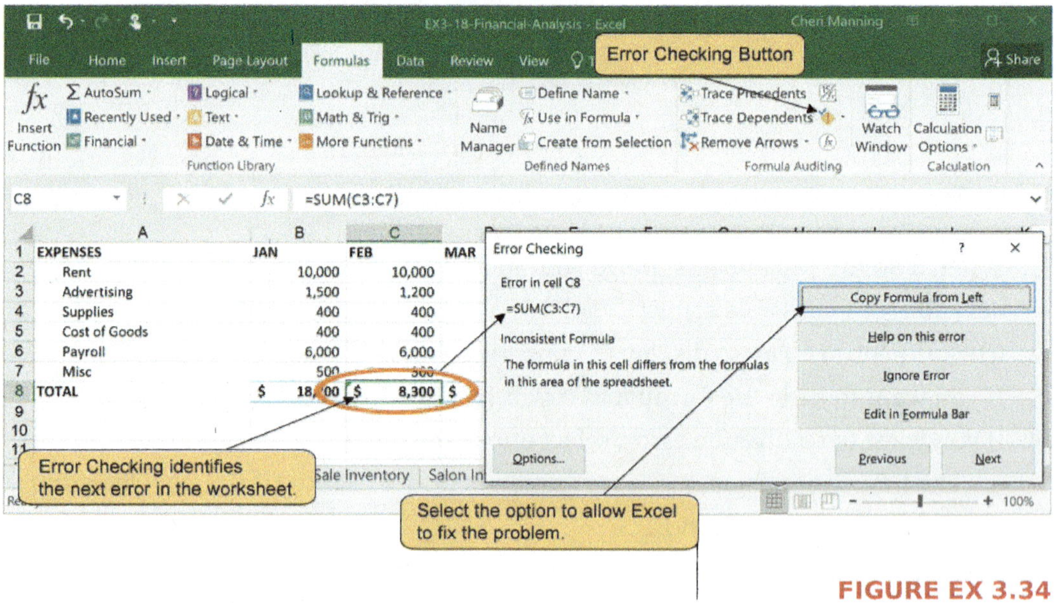

FIGURE EX 3.34

tips & tricks

You can make changes to your worksheet without closing the *Error Checking* dialog. When you click away from the dialog, one of the buttons changes to a *Resume* button and none of the other buttons in the dialog are available. When you are ready to return to error checking, click the **Resume** button.

tell me **more**

If the error is part of a complex formula, Excel may include a *Show Calculation Steps...* button in the *Error Checking* dialog. This button launches the *Evaluate Formula* dialog where you can walk through the formula step by step to try to find the cause of the error.

If the error is related to a reference to another cell, Excel will offer a *Trace Error* button to display precedent and dependent arrows showing dependencies between formulas in your worksheet.

another method

You can also start the Error Checking feature by clicking the **Error Checking** button arrow and selecting **Error Checking...**

let me **try** *Live!*

If you do not have the data file from the previous skill open, open the student data file **EX3-18-Financial-Analysis** and try this skill on your own:

1. On the **Expenses** worksheet, cell **B8** has an error. Display the **Smart Tag** and accept Excel's suggestion for fixing the error.
2. On the *Formulas* tab, in the *Formula Auditing* group, open the *Error Checking* dialog and check the rest of the worksheet for errors.
3. Review the information about the next error and select the option to edit the error in the formula bar.
4. Correct the error and resume error checking until Excel reports that the error check is complete.
5. If you will be moving on to the next skill in this chapter, leave the workbook open to continue working. If not, save the file as directed by your instructor and close it.

Skill 3.19 Finding Errors Using Trace Precedents and Trace Dependents

In a complex worksheet where formulas often reference each other, an error in one formula can cause a ripple effect of errors throughout the entire workbook. However, finding and fixing the formula that is the root cause of the errors can be difficult. One way to review your workbook for errors is to display the dependencies between formulas.

There are two types of dependencies: precedents and dependents. A **precedent** is the cell containing the formula or value the selected cell refers to. A **dependent** is the cell containing a formula that references the value or formula in the selected cell. On the *Formulas* tab, the *Formula Auditing* group includes commands for displaying and hiding arrows tracing dependencies.

Tracer arrows normally appear blue. If the tracer arrow points to a cell that contains an error, the tracer arrow will appear red. If the tracer arrow points to a cell that references a cell in another worksheet or workbook, the arrow will appear black and include a small worksheet icon. Double-click the tracer arrow to open the *Go To* dialog to navigate to the worksheet or workbook that contains the referenced cell.

Figure EX 3.35 shows both precedent tracer arrows for cell B8. You can see that the precedent arrow changes from blue to red at cell B6. The formula in that cell is the first error. (However, the error itself is not necessarily in that cell. It could be in another cell that B6 refers to.)

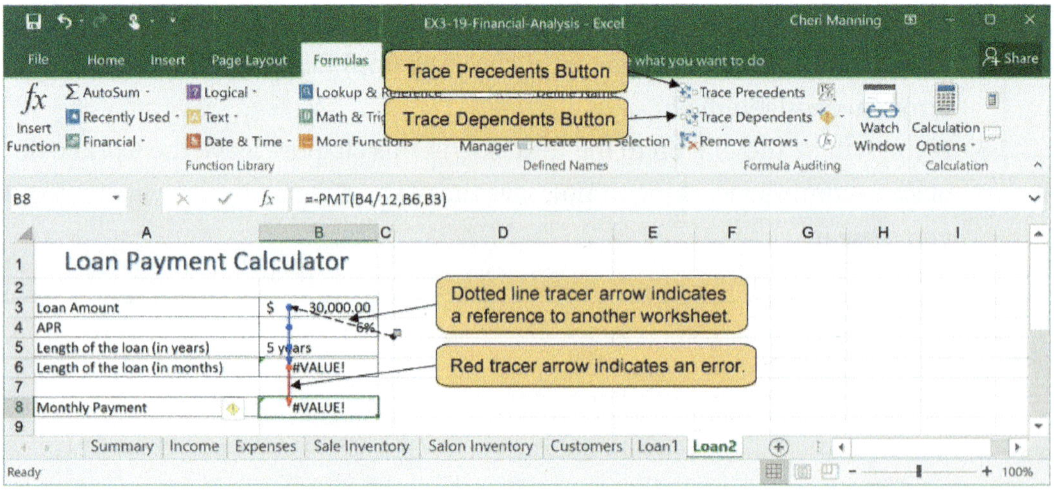

FIGURE EX 3.35

To trace precedents:

1. Select the cell containing the formula for which you want to trace precedents.
2. On the *Formulas* tab, in the *Formula Auditing* group, click the **Trace Precedents** button.
3. Tracer arrows appear pointing to the selected cell from precedent cells.

To trace dependents:

1. Select the cell containing the formula for which you want to trace dependents.
2. On the *Formulas* tab, in the *Formula Auditing* group, click the **Trace Dependents** button.
3. Tracer arrows appear pointing from the selected cell to dependent cells.

To remove the tracer arrows from your worksheet, on the *Formulas* tab, in the *Formula Auditing* group, click the **Remove Arrows** button arrow and select the option you want:

- To remove the precedent tracer arrows, select **Remove Precedent Arrows.**
- To remove the dependent tracer arrows, select **Remove Dependent Arrows.**
- To remove all tracer arrows at once, select **Remove Arrows.** Clicking the *Remove Arrows* button instead of the button arrow will also remove all the tracer arrows.

tips & tricks

Tracer arrows cannot identify cells with incorrect values or values of the wrong type (for example, a text value where a number is expected). However, using the tracer arrows may help you find those errors yourself.

tell me more

There may be multiple layers of dependencies in your workbook. Clicking the **Trace Precedents** button or the **Trace Dependents** button once only displays the immediate dependencies. To display tracer arrows from the precedent and dependent cells to their precedents and dependents, click the appropriate button again. Continue clicking the **Trace Precedents** button or the **Trace Dependents** button until you reach the end of the trail.

Selecting **Remove Precedent Arrows** and **Remove Dependent Arrows** removes the tracer arrows one level at a time.

another method

If the selected cell contains an error, you can display tracer arrows by clicking the **Error Checking** button arrow and selecting **Trace Error**.

let me try *Live!*

If you do not have the data file from the previous skill open, open the student data file **EX3-19-Financial-Analysis** and try this skill on your own:

1. On the **Loan2** worksheet, show the dependent arrows for cell **B6.**
2. Show the precedent arrows for cell **B8.**
3. Show the next level of precedent arrows. Note that cell B3 refers to a cell in another worksheet.
4. Change the value in cell **B5** to: 5. Note that the arrows change color from red to blue.
5. Hide all of the arrows at once.
6. If you will be moving on to the next skill in this chapter, leave the workbook open to continue working. If not, save the file as directed by your instructor and close it.

Skill 3.20 Displaying and Printing Formulas

How do you troubleshoot a worksheet that is displaying unexpected values? When you look at a worksheet, you see only the results of formulas—cells display the values, not the formulas themselves. When you click a cell, the formula is displayed in the formula bar. But what if you want to view all of the formulas in your worksheet at once?

To display the formulas in the current worksheet instead of values:

On the *Formulas* tab in the *Formula Auditing* group, click the **Show Formulas** button.

To hide the formulas and display calculated values:

Click the **Show Formulas** button again.

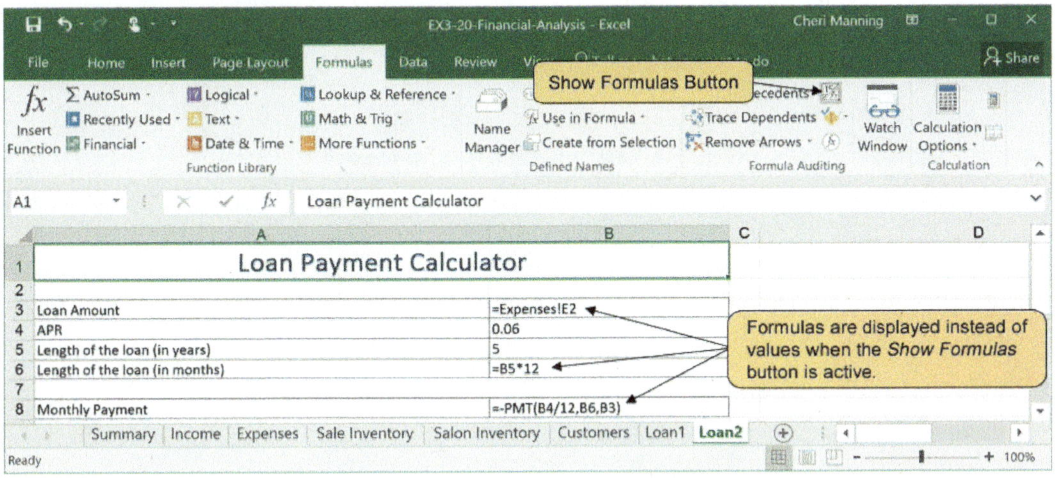

FIGURE EX 3.36

tips & tricks

When you show formulas in your worksheet, Excel automatically adjusts the column sizes so the formulas are visible.

another method

The keyboard shortcut to display (or hide) formulas is Ctrl + ` (the ` key is directly to the left of 1 at the top of the keyboard).

let me try *Live!*

If you do not have the data file from the previous skill open, open the student data file **EX3-20-Financial-Analysis** and try this skill on your own:

1. On the **Loan2** worksheet, display the formulas in this worksheet.
2. Preview how the worksheet will look when printed.
3. Save the file as directed by your instructor and close it.

key terms

- Formula AutoComplete
- AVERAGE
- Mean
- Median
- Mode
- MAX
- MIN
- NOW
- TODAY
- Volatile
- COUNT
- COUNTA
- COUNTBLANK
- String
- Text String
- PROPER
- UPPER
- LOWER
- Concatenate
- CONCAT
- TEXTJOIN
- Delimiter (TEXTJOIN)
- Name
- Range name
- Named range
- Name Manager
- Defined name
- IF
- PMT
- VLOOKUP
- HLOOKUP
- Smart Tag
- Precedent
- Dependent

concept review

1. Which of these methods can you use to enter a formula using the AVERAGE function?
   a. Formula AutoComplete
   b. AutoSum
   c. *Function Arguments* dialog
   d. all of the above
2. Which of these functions returns the current date and time?
   a. TIME
   b. DATE
   c. NOW
   d. TODAY
3. To count the number of cells that contain text or numerical values, but not blanks, use which function?
   a. COUNT
   b. COUNTA
   c. COUNTALL
   d. COUNTBLANK
4. What is the definition of *concatenate*?
   a. to link items together
   b. to look up a value
   c. a logical comparison
   d. to convert text to proper case
5. A formula to display the value of cell A5 on the *Inventory* worksheet looks like this:
   a. =Inventory!A5
   b. =A5,Inventory!
   c. =Inventory,A5
   d. =Inventory(A5)
6. Which of these is **not** an acceptable name for a named range?
   a. CurrentInventory
   b. CURRENTINVENTORY
   c. Current_Inventory
   d. Current Inventory

7. Identify the *Value_if_true* argument in this formula: =IF(A2>100,"sell","buy")
   a. A2
   b. 100
   c. sell
   d. buy
8. Identify the *Pv* argument in this formula: =PMT(B1/12,B2,-B3)
   a. B1
   b. B1/12
   c. B2
   d. -B3
9. In a PMT function, what is the *Pv* argument?
   a. the number of payments
   b. the interest rate
   c. the present value of the loan
   d. the value of the loan at the end of the loan period
10. A(n) ________________ is the cell containing a formula that references the value or formula in the selected cell.
    a. argument
    b. 3-D reference
    c. precedent
    d. dependent

projects

Data files for projects can be found by logging into your SIMnet account and going to the *Library* section.

skill review 3.1

In this project you will complete a staff billing workbook similar to the one you worked on in Chapter 1. This worksheet is more complicated and uses a variety of formulas to calculate information about each staff member's weekly billing and to generate client bills from the staff hours. As you work on the *Marshall Hours* worksheet, you can use the *Lutz Hours* or *Stevens Hours* worksheet as a guide. This is a long project. Be sure to save your work often!

Skills needed to complete this project:

- Naming Ranges of Cells (Skill 3.11)
- Using CONCAT to Combine Text (Skill 3.8)
- Creating Formulas Referencing Data from Other Worksheets (Skill 3.10)
- Finding Data Using the VLOOKUP Function (Skill 3.17)
- Working with Named Ranges (Skill 3.12)
- Using the Function Arguments Dialog to Enter Functions (Skill 3.1)
- Creating Formulas Using Counting Functions (Skill 3.6)
- Using Formula AutoComplete to Enter Functions (Skill 3.2)
- Calculating Averages (Skill 3.3)
- Finding Minimum and Maximum Values (Skill 3.4)
- Using the Logical Function IF (Skill 3.15)
- Displaying and Printing Formulas (Skill 3.20)
- Using Date and Time Functions (Skill 3.5)
- Checking Formulas for Errors (Skill 3.18)
- Finding Errors Using Trace Precedents and Trace Dependents (Skill 3.19)
- Updating Named Ranges with the Name Manager (Skill 3.13)
- Editing and Deleting Names with the Name Manager (Skill 3.14)
- Calculating Loan Payments Using the PMT Function (Skill 3.16)

1. Open the start file **EX2016-SkillReview-3-1** and resave the file as: `[your initials]EX-SkillReview-3-1`
2. If the workbook opens in Protected View, click the **Enable Editing** button in the Message Bar at the top of the workbook so you can modify it.
3. The *Lutz Hours*%nbsp∧nbsp%*Stevens Hours* worksheets are completed, but they contain errors. You'll need to fix the errors before working on the *Marshall Hours* worksheet.
   a. Click the **Lutz Hours** sheet tab.

b. Click cell **C4.**

c. Notice the #NAME? error. Move your mouse over the **Smart Tag** icon to display a tool tip describing the possible error—*The formula contains unrecognized text.*

d. The formula =VLOOKUP(C3,BillableRates,4,FALSE) references the named range BillableRates. That name has not yet been defined. That's what is causing the error.

4. Billable rates are kept in the *Rates* worksheet. Create the name **BillableRates** to use in formulas throughout the workbook.

a. Click the **Rates** sheet tab.

b. Select cells **A3:D5.**

c. Type `BillableRates` in the *Name* box.

d. Press [Enter].

e. Return to the *Lutz Hours* worksheet. Notice all the errors have been fixed. Now you can move on to completing the *Marshall Hours* sheet.

5. Use a formula to display Marshall's full name in the format *Bob Smith.* Staff names are kept in the *Rates* worksheet.

a. Click the **Marshall Hours** sheet tab, and click cell **C2.**

b. On the *Formulas* tab, in the *Function Library* group, click the **Text** button, and select **CONCAT.**

c. Click the **Rates** sheet tab. If necessary, position the *Function Arguments* dialog so you can click the sheet tabs.

d. Click cell **C4** to enter the cell reference in the *Text1* argument box.

e. Press [Tab] to move to the *Text2* argument box.

f. Type **" "** to place a space between the first and last names.

g. Press [Tab] to move to the *Text3* argument box.

h. Click the **Rates** tab again.

i. Click cell **B4** to enter the text reference in the *Text3* argument box.

j. Click **OK.** The completed formula should look like this: **=CONCAT(Rates!C4," ",Rates!B4)**

6. Use a formula to look up Marshall's current billable rate. Use the employee number as the lookup value.

a. Click cell **C4.**

b. On the *Formulas* tab, in the *Function Library* group, click the **Lookup & Reference** button, and select **VLOOKUP.**

c. Click cell **C3** to enter it in the *Lookup_value* argument box.

d. Type `BillableRates` in the *Table_array* argument box.

e. The rates are located in the fourth column of the lookup table. Type `4` in the *Col_index_num* argument box.

f. Ensure that the function will return only an exact match. Type `false` in the *Range_lookup* argument box.

g. Click **OK.** The completed formula should look like this: **=VLOOKUP(C3,BillableRates,4,FALSE)**

7. Enter formulas to calculate the number of clients served each day.

   a. Click cell **B16.**

   b. Type `=COU`

   c. Double-click **COUNT** in the Formula AutoComplete list.

   d. Click cell **B8** and drag to cell **B11.**

   e. Press Enter. The completed formula should look like this: **=COUNT(B8:B11)**

   f. Copy the formula in cell **B16** to cells **C16:H16.** Use any method you want.

8. Use a formula to calculate the average daily billable hours.

   a. Click cell **H18.**

   b. Type `=AV` and then double-click **AVERAGE** in the Formula AutoComplete list.

   c. Click cell **B12** and drag to cell **H12.**

   d. Press Enter. The completed formula should look like this: **=AVERAGE(B12:H12)**

9. Use a formula to calculate the total billable hours for the week.

   a. Click cell **H19.**

   b. Type `=SU` and then double-click **SUM** in the Formula AutoComplete list.

   c. Click cell **B12** and drag to cell **H12.**

   d. Press Enter. The completed formula should look like this: **=SUM(B12:H12)**

10. Use a formula to calculate the lowest daily bill for the week.

    a. Click cell **H21.**

    b. Type `=MIN(` and then click cell **B14** and drag to cell **H14.**

    c. Press Enter. The completed formula should look like this: **=MIN(B14:H14)**

11. Use a formula to calculate the highest daily bill for the week.

    a. Click cell **H22.**

    b. Type `=MAX(` and then click cell **B14** and drag to cell **H14.**

    c. Press Enter. The completed formula should look like this: **=MAX(B14:H14)**

12. Each staff member is required to log a minimum number of billable hours per week. Enter a formula using an IF statement to display "yes" if the total billable hours for the week is greater than or equal to the required hours and "no" if they are not.

    a. Click cell **H3.**

    b. On the *Formulas* tab, in the *Function Library* group, click **Logical.**

    c. Click **IF.**

    d. If necessary, move the *Function Arguments* dialog to the side so you can see the worksheet data.

    e. In the *Logical_test* argument box, type: `H19>=H2`

    f. In the *Value_if_true* argument box, type: `yes`

    g. In the *Value_if_false* argument box, type: `no`

    h. Click **OK.** The completed formula should look like this: **=IF(H19>=H2,"yes","no")**

13. Display your formulas temporarily to check for accuracy.

    a. On the *Formulas* tab, in the *Formula Auditing* group, click the **Show Formulas** button.

    b. When you are ready to continue, hide the formulas and display formula values by clicking the **Show Formulas** button again.

14. Now that the worksheet for Marshall is complete, you can generate a bill for the Smith client for the week. All bills are due 60 days from the date the bill was created. Calculate the bill due date using the TODAY function.

    a. Click the **Smith Bill** sheet tab.

    b. Double-click cell **C2.**

    c. Type the formula: `=TODAY()+60`

    d. Press Enter.

15. Enter formulas to reference the number of hours each staff member billed for Smith.

    a. Click cell **B5** and type = to begin the formula.

    b. Click the **Lutz Hours** sheet, and click cell **J11.**

    c. Press Enter. The completed formula should look like this: **='Lutz Hours'!J11**

    d. Type = to begin the next formula in cell B6.

    e. Click the **Marshall Hours** sheet, and click cell **J11.**

    f. Press Enter. The completed formula should look like this: **='Marshall Hours'!J11**

    g. Type = to begin the next formula in cell B7.

h. Click the **Stevens Hours** sheet, and click cell **J11.**

i. Press Enter. The completed formula should look like this: **='Stevens Hours'!J11**

16. There are errors in the *Rate* and *Bill Amount* columns in the *Smith Bill* worksheet. Use your error checking skills to track down the cause of the error.

    a. On the *Formulas* tab, in the *Formula Auditing* group, click the **Error Checking** button to open the *Error Checking* dialog.

    b. After you've reviewed the first error, click the **Next** button to go to the next error. Continue reviewing each error and clicking **Next** until you receive the message that the error check is complete for the entire sheet. Click **OK.**

17. Did you notice that every error in the worksheet is a "value not available" error? You probably need to dig deeper to find the root cause of the problem.

    a. Click cell **D5** and look at the formula in the formula bar: =B5*C5

    b. Display the Trace Precedent and Trace Dependent arrows for this cell. On the *Formulas* tab, in the *Formula Auditing* group, click both the **Trace Precedents** button and the **Trace Dependents** button.

    c. You can see that the problem appears to start in the precedent cell C5. Hide the arrows for cell **D5** by clicking the **Remove Arrows** button, and then click cell **C5** and click the **Trace Precedents** button.

    d. Notice that one of the precedent arrows for cell C5 refers to another worksheet. Double-click the dashed precedent arrow line.

    e. In the *Go To* dialog, click the worksheet reference and then click the **OK** button.

18. The link takes you to the *Rates* sheet where cells A2:D5 are selected. Notice that the *Name* box displays the name *ClientRates.* (Depending on your screen resolution, the name may be slightly cut off.) The formula in cell C5 is a lookup formula that uses the named range *ClientRates* as the *Table_array* argument. There are two problems with the definition of the named range: It includes the label row (A2:D2), and it includes the employee number data (A2:A5).

    a. On the *Formulas* tab, in the *Defined Names* group, click the **Name Manager** button.

    b. Click the **ClientRates** name and review the cell range in the *Refers to* box. The range is incorrect. The ClientRates name should refer to cells **B3:D5** on the *Rates* sheet.

    c. Click in the *Refers to* box and then click and drag to select the cell range **B3:D5.** The reference in the *Refers to* box should update to: **`=Rates!$B$3:$D$5`**

    d. Click the **Close** button to close the Name Manager.

    e. When Excel asks if you want to save the changes to the name reference, click **Yes.**

19. Now that the total bill amount is computing correctly, you can create a formula

to give the client the option of a monthly payment plan. You are authorized to offer a 9-month payment plan at a 4% annual percentage rate. Use cell references in the formula.

a. If necessary, click the **Smith Bill** sheet.

b. Click cell **D12.**

c. On the *Formulas* tab, in the *Function Library* group, click the **Financial** button.

d. Scroll down the list, and click **PMT.**

e. In the *Function Arguments* dialog, enter the *Rate* argument: `D11/12`

f. Click in the **Nper** argument box, and then click cell **D10** (the number of payments).

g. Click in the **Pv** argument box, type - and then click cell **D8** (the present value of the loan). You want to use a negative value for the *Pv* argument so the result of the formula will appear as a positive number.

h. In the *Function Arguments* dialog, click **OK.** The completed formula should look like this:
=PMT(D11/12,D10,-D8)

20. Save and close the workbook.

projects

Data files for projects can be found by logging into your SIMnet account and going to the *Library* section.

skill review 3.2

In this project you will edit a worksheet to compute student grades and grade statistics. Be sure to save your work often!

Skills needed to complete this project:

- Using Date and Time Functions (Skill 3.5)
- Using CONCAT to Combine Text (Skill 3.8)
- Formatting Text Using Functions (Skill 3.7)
- Creating Formulas Using Counting Functions (Skill 3.6)
- Using Formula AutoComplete to Enter Functions (Skill 3.2)
- Displaying and Printing Formulas (Skill 3.20)
- Naming Ranges of Cells (Skill 3.11)
- Using the Logical Function IF (Skill 3.15)
- Using the Function Arguments Dialog to Enter Functions (Skill 3.1)
- Working with Named Ranges (Skill 3.12)
- Finding Minimum and Maximum Values (Skill 3.4)
- Calculating Averages (Skill 3.3)
- Finding Data Using the VLOOKUP Function (Skill 3.17)
- Checking Formulas for Errors (Skill 3.18)

1. Open the start file **EX2016-SkillReview-3-2** and resave the file as: `[your initials]EX-SkillReview-3-2`
2. If the workbook opens in Protected View, click the **Enable Editing** button in the Message Bar at the top of the workbook so you can modify it.
3. Take a look at the two sheets. The first sheet contains the students' names and their scores. The second sheet will be used to look up the letter grade for each student.
4. On the *Scores* worksheet, enter a function in cell **B3** to display the current date and time.
    a. If necessary, click the **Scores** worksheet tab. Click cell **B3.**
    b. On the *Formulas* tab, in the *Function Library* group, click the **Date &Time** button.
    c. Click **NOW.**
    d. Click **OK.**

5. The first column should display the full student name. Use CONCAT to combine the values from the *First Name* and *Last Name* columns.
   a. Click cell **A10.**
   b. On the *Formulas* tab, in the *Function Library* group, click the **Text** button, and select **CONCAT.**
   c. Click cell **C10** to enter the cell reference in the *Text1* argument box.
   d. Press Tab to move to the *Text2* argument box.
   e. Type " " to place a space between the first and last names.
   f. Press Tab to move to the *Text3* argument box.
   g. Click cell **B10** to enter the text reference in the *Text3* argument box.
   h. Click **OK.** The completed formula should look like this: **=CONCAT(C10," ",B10)**
6. Add the PROPER function to the formula so student names do not appear in all uppercase.
   a. Double-click cell **A10** to edit the formula.
   b. Create a nested formula by typing **PROPER(** between the = symbol and CONCAT.
   c. Type another) at the end of the formula.
   d. Press Enter. The completed formula should look like this: **=PROPER(CONCAT(C10," ",B10))**
   e. Copy the formula from cell **A10** to **A11:A26** to fill the list of student names. Use any method you want.
7. Count the number of students to calculate the class size.
   a. Click cell **B2.**
   b. Type **=COU**
   c. Double-click **COUNTA** in the Formula AutoComplete list.
   d. Click cell **A10** and drag to cell **A26.**
   e. Press Enter. The completed formula should look like this: **=COUNTA(A10:A26)**
8. Display your formulas to check for accuracy.
   a. On the *Formulas* tab, in the *Formula Auditing* group, click the **Show Formulas** button.

   b. When you are ready to continue, hide the formulas and display formula values by clicking the **Show Formulas** button again.

9. Define a named range for the total possible points up to the class drop cut-off point.
   a. Select cells **D7:R7.**
   b. In the **Name** box, type: `PossiblePtsMid`
   c. Press Enter.

10. Find out which students have a grade below C at the cut-off point for dropping the class. Enter an IF function in cell **S10** to check if the student's total points divided by the total possible points through the midterm is less than 70% (the lowest percentage for a C grade). Use SUM functions within the IF function. Be sure to use the range name you just defined for possible points. If the student is below a C grade, display **Warning!** in the cell; otherwise leave the cell blank.
    a. Click cell **S10.**
    b. On the *Formulas* tab, in the *Function Library* group, click **Logical.**
    c. Click **IF.**
    d. If necessary, move the *Function Arguments* dialog so you can see the worksheet data.
    e. In the *Logical_test* argument box, type: `SUM(D10:R10)/SUM(PossiblePtsMid)<70%`
    f. In the *Value_if_true* argument box, type: `Warning!`
    g. In the *Value_if_false* argument box, type: `""`
    h. Click **OK.** The completed formula should look like this: **=IF(SUM(D10:R10)/SUM(PossiblePtsMid)<70%,"Warning!"," ")**
    i. Fill the IF function in cell **S10** down for all students. Use any method you want. There should be three students with **Warning!** in the *Class Drop Cut-Off Point* column.

11. Find the highest score for each assignment.
    a. Click cell **D4.**
    b. Type `=MAX(` and then click cell **D10** and drag to cell **D26.**
    c. Press Enter. The completed formula should look like this: **=MAX(D10:D26)**

d. Copy the formula across the row to cell **AB4**. Use any method you want. Be sure to leave cell S4 blank.

12. Find the lowest score for each assignment.

    a. Click cell **D5.**

    b. Type `=MIN(` and then click cell **D10** and drag to cell **D26.**

    c. Press [Enter]. The completed formula should look like this: **=MIN(D10:D26)**

    d. Copy the formula across the row to cell **AB5.** Use any method you want. Be sure to leave cell S5 blank.

13. Calculate the average score for each assignment.

    a. Click cell **D6.**

    b. Type `=AV` and then double-click **AVERAGE** in the Formula AutoComplete list.

    c. Click cell **D10** and drag to cell **D26.**

    d. Press [Enter]. The completed formula should look like this: **=AVERAGE(D10:D26)**

    e. Copy the formula across the row to cell **AB6.** Use any method you want. Be sure to leave cell S6 blank.

14. Compute the students' total points. Enter a SUM function in cell **AC10** to add all the points across for the first student.

    a. Click cell **AC10.**

    b. Type `=SU` and then double-click **SUM** in the Formula AutoComplete list.

    c. Click cell **D10** and drag to cell **AB10.**

    d. Press [Enter]. The completed formula should look like this: **=SUM(D10:AB10)**

    e. Copy the formula from **AC10** through cell **AC26.** Use any method you want.

15. Enter a formula to compute the percentage for the first student. Divide the student's total points by the total possible points. You will be copying this formula, so make sure the reference to the total possible points uses an absolute reference.

    a. In cell **AD10,** enter the following formula to calculate the percentage: **=AC10/$AC$7**

    b. Copy the formula from **AD10** through **AD26.** Use any method you want.

16. The grade scale is stored in the *Grades* worksheet. Before calculating students' final grades, create a named range to use in the formula.

    a. Click the **Grades** sheet tab.

    b. Select cells **B4:C8.**

    c. Type `GradeScale` in the *Name* box.

    d. Press Enter.

17. Now you are ready to create a lookup formula to display each student's final letter grade.

    a. Return to the **Scores** sheet, and click cell **AE10.**

    b. On the *Formulas* tab, in the *Function Library* group, click the **Lookup & Reference** button, and select **VLOOKUP.**

    c. Click cell **AD10** to enter it in the *Lookup_value* argument box.

    d. Type `GradeScale` in the *Table_array* argument box.

    e. The rates are located in the second column of the lookup table. Type `2` in the *Col_index_num* argument box.

    f. In this case, you do not want to specify an exact match, as the percentage grades do not match the grade scale percentages exactly. An approximate match will return the correct letter grade.

    g. Click **OK.** The completed formula should look like this: **=VLOOKUP(AD10,GradeScale,2)**

    h. Fill down for all students. Use any method you want.

18. Before closing the project, check your workbook for errors.

    a. On the *Formulas* tab, in the *Formula Auditing* group, click the **Error Checking** button.

    b. If errors are found, use the error checking skills learned in this chapter to find and fix the errors.

    c. When Excel displays a message that the error check is complete, click **OK.**

19. Save and close the workbook.

projects

Data files for projects can be found by logging into your SIMnet account and going to the *Library* section.

challenge yourself **3.3**

In this project you will complete a vehicle shopping workbook to compare the purchase of several vehicles. After completing the project, you can make a copy of the file and use it to compare vehicle purchases you are considering for yourself. Be sure to save your work often!

Skills needed to complete this project:

- Naming Ranges of Cells (Skill 3.11)
- Calculating Averages (Skill 3.3)
- Finding Data Using the VLOOKUP Function (Skill 3.17)
- Working with Named Ranges (Skill 3.12)
- Using the Function Arguments Dialog to Enter Functions (Skill 3.1)
- Using the Logical Function IF (Skill 3.15)
- Calculating Loan Payments Using the PMT Function (Skill 3.16)
- Creating Formulas Referencing Data from Other Worksheets (Skill 3.10)
- Displaying and Printing Formulas (Skill 3.20)
- Finding Errors Using Trace Precedents and Trace Dependents (Skill 3.19)
- Finding Minimum and Maximum Values (Skill 3.4)
- Using Formula AutoComplete to Enter Functions (Skill 3.2)
- Updating Named Ranges with the Name Manager (Skill 3.13)
- Editing and Deleting Names with the Name Manager (Skill 3.14)
- Checking Formulas for Errors (Skill 3.18)

1. Open the start file **EX2016-ChallengeYourself-3-3** and resave the file as: `[your initials]EX-ChallengeYourself-3-3`
2. If the workbook opens in Protected View, click the **Enable Editing** button in the Message Bar at the top of the workbook so you can modify it.
3. The registration fee information in cells **B11:C17** on the **Data** sheet will be used in lookup formulas later in this project. Name the range `RegistrationFees` to make it easier to use later.
4. Return to the **Purchase** worksheet.
5. Calculate the average MPG for each vehicle.
    a. Enter a formula in cell **C10** using the AVERAGE function to calculate the average value of **C8:C9.** Use only one argument.
    b. Copy the formula to the appropriate cells for the other vehicles.

c. Excel will detect a possible error with these formulas. Use the **SmartTag** to ignore the error. *Hint:* Use the **SmartTag** while cells **C10:F10** are selected and the error will be ignored for all the selected cells.

6. Calculate the registration fee for each vehicle.

   a. Enter a formula in cell **C13** to look up the registration fee for the first vehicle. Use the vehicle type in cell **C4** as the *Lookup_value* argument. Use the **RegistrationFees** named range as the *Table_array* argument. The registration fees are located in column **2** of the data table. Require an exact match.

   b. Copy the formula to the appropriate cells for the other vehicles.

7. Determine whether or not you will need a loan for each potential purchase.

   a. In cell **C15,** enter a formula using an IF function to determine if you need a loan. Your available cash is located on the *Data* sheet in cell **A3.** If the price of the car is less than or equal to your available cash, display **"no".** If the price of the car is more than your available, cash, display **"yes".** Use absolute references where appropriate—you will be copying this formula across the row.

   b. Copy the formula to the appropriate cells for the other vehicles.

8. Calculate how much you would need to borrow for each purchase.

   a. In cell **C16,** enter a formula to calculate the price of the vehicle minus your available cash (from cell **A3** in the **Data** worksheet). Use absolute references where appropriate—you will be copying this formula across the row.

   b. Copy the formula to the appropriate cells for the other vehicles.

9. Calculate the monthly payment amount for each loan.

   a. In cell **C20,** enter a formula using the PMT function to calculate the monthly loan payment for the first vehicle.

      - *Hint:* Divide the interest rate by 12 in the *Rate* argument to reflect monthly payments.
      - *Hint:* Multiply the number of years by 12 in the *Nper* argument to reflect the number of monthly payments during the life of the loan.
      - *Hint:* Use a negative value for the loan amount in the *Pv* argument so the payment amount is expressed as a positive number.

   b. Copy the formula to the appropriate cells for the other vehicles.

10. Compute the monthly cost of gas.

a. In cell **C21,** enter a formula to calculate the number of miles you expect to drive each month. Divide the value of number of miles (cell **A5** from the **Data** sheet) by the average MPG for the vehicle multiplied by the price of a gallon of gas (cell **A6** from the **Data** sheet).

b. Copy the formula to the appropriate cells for the other vehicles.

c. If cells **D21:F21** display an error or a value of 0, display formulas and check for errors.

d. If you still can't find the error, try displaying the precedent arrows.

e. *Hint:* The references to the cells on the *Data* sheet should use absolute references. If they do not, the formula will update incorrectly when you copy it across the row.

11. Compute the monthly cost of maintenance.

    a. In cell **C22,** enter a formula to calculate the monthly maintenance cost: Divide cell **C12** by 12.

    b. Copy the formula to the appropriate cells for the other vehicles.

12. Compute the monthly cost of insurance.

    a. In cell **C23,** enter a formula to calculate the monthly insurance cost: Divide cell **C14** by 12.

    b. Copy the formula to the appropriate cells for the other vehicles.

13. In cells **C24:F24,** compute the total the monthly cost for each vehicle.

14. Determine which vehicles are affordable.

    a. In cell **C26,** enter a formula using the IF function to display **"yes"** if the total monthly cost (cell **C24**) is less than or equal to the total monthly amount available for vehicle expenses (*Data* sheet, cell **A4**). Display **"no"** if the total monthly cost is not less than or equal to the total monthly amount available.

    b. Copy the formula to the appropriate cells for the other vehicles.

    c. Display formulas and use the error checking skills learned in this lesson to track down and fix any errors.

15. Complete the Analysis section using formulas with statistical functions. Use named ranges instead of cell references in the formulas.

    a. *Hint:* Select cells **B7:F24** and use Excel's **Create from Selection** command to create named ranges for each row using the labels at the left side of the range as the names.

b. *Hint:* Open the **Name Manager** and review the names Excel created. Notice that any spaces or special characters in the label names are converted to _ characters in the names.

c. *Hint:* To avoid typos as you create each formula, try using Formula AutoComplete to select the correct range name.

16. Before finishing the project, check the worksheet for errors.
17. Save and close the workbook.

projects

Data files for projects can be found by logging into your SIMnet account and going to the *Library* section.

challenge yourself 3.4

In this project, you will record data about your completed and planned college courses. You will compute your GPA, college course costs, and various statistics. You will compute your expected college loan payment and count down the days to graduation and paying off the loan. Be sure to save your work often!

Skills needed to complete this project:

- Finding Errors Using Trace Precedents and Trace Dependents (Skill 3.19)
- Finding Data Using the VLOOKUP Function (Skill 3.17)
- Using the Function Arguments Dialog to Enter Functions (Skill 3.1)
- Checking Formulas for Errors (Skill 3.18)
- Creating Formulas Referencing Data from Other Worksheets (Skill 3.10)
- Calculating Loan Payments Using the PMT Function (Skill 3.16)
- Using Date and Time Functions (Skill 3.5)
- Finding Minimum and Maximum Values (Skill 3.4)
- Using Formula AutoComplete to Enter Functions (Skill 3.2)
- Calculating Averages (Skill 3.3)
- Using the Logical Function IF (Skill 3.15)

1. Open the start file **EX2016-ChallengeYourself-3-4** and resave the file as: `[your initials]EX-ChallengeYourself-3-4`
2. If the workbook opens in Protected View, click the **Enable Editing** button in the Message Bar at the top of the workbook so you can modify it.
3. There are three sheets. Start with the *GPA* sheet.
4. There is at least one error on this sheet. Click the cell that displays an error and use the precedent arrows to find the cause of the error. If the error is caused by missing values in other cells in the worksheet, you will probably fix the error by the end of this project. Hide the arrows before continuing.
5. Enter the formulas for the GPA worksheet as follows.
    a. In cell **B14** compute the cost for the first course by multiplying the unit cost (cell **C11**) by the number of units for the course (cell **G14**). Use absolute references where appropriate.
    b. Fill and copy to compute the cost for each course, both semesters (cells **B15:B16** and **B19:B22**).
6. Look up the grade points for each letter grade as follows:

a. In cell **I14,** enter a formula using the VLOOKUP function. Use the cell range **J3:K7** as the *Table_array* argument. The grade points are located in column **2** of this table. Use absolute references where appropriate.

b. Fill and copy to look up the grade points for each courses, both semesters (cells **I15:I16** and **I19:I22**).

7. Multiply the grade points by the units to calculate the quality points for each course, for both semesters.

   a. In cell **J14,** enter a formula to multiply **I14** (the grade points) * cell **G14** (the units).

   b. Copy the formula to cells **J15:J16** and **J19:J22.**

8. Use AutoSum to calculate totals for cost (cells **B17** and **B23**), units (cells **G17** and **G23**), and quality points (cells **J17** and **J23**) for each semester.

9. In cell **K17,** compute the GPA for the first semester by dividing the total quality points by the total units (**J17/G17**).

10. In cell **K23,** compute the GPA for the second semester using the same formula.

11. Check the worksheet for errors. Is the error you found in step 4 fixed now? (It should be!)

12. Next go to the *Loan* worksheet.

13. In cell **B3,** enter a formula to display the total cost shown in cell **B9** on the *GPA* sheet.

14. Enter a formula in cell **B7** to look up the number of years to pay based on the loan amount show in cell **B3.** Use the data table in cells **G6:H11** as the *Table_array* argument. Do not require an exact match.

15. Now that you have the loan amount and the number of payments, enter a formula using the PMT function in cell **B8** to calculate the payment amount. Allow the payment to display as a negative number.

16. In cell **B10,** enter a formula to display the current date (just the date, not the date and time).

17. Enter a formula in cell **B16** to estimate the date of the last loan payment. Take the number of years to pay (cell **B7**) times **365.3** and add that to the date of the first loan payment (cell **B15**).

18. Enter a formula in cell **B17** to estimate the number of days until the loan is paid off.

19. Complete the *Summary* sheet information.

20. On the *Summary* sheet, in cell **B5,** enter a simple formula to reference the *Cumulative GPA* number from the *GPA* worksheet (***GPA*****worksheet, cell B5**).
21. Do the same for Total Units (cell **B6**), Total Cost (cell **B8**), and Total Debt (cell **B9**). For Total Debt, reference the Amount Owed number from the *Loan* sheet.
22. Compute the Average Cost Per Unit by dividing the Total Cost (cell **B8**) by the Total Units (cell **B6**).
23. Compute Average Debt Per Unit in the same way.
24. In cell **B14,** enter a formula using a statistical function to calculate the most paid for any semester. Reference cells **B17** and **B23** in the *GPA* sheet. *Hint:* You will need two arguments.
25. In cell **B16,** enter a formula to calculate the average semester cost. Reference cells **B17** and **B23** in the *GPA* sheet. *Hint:* You will need two arguments.
26. In cell **F1,** enter a formula using the IF function to determine if the student met her GPA goal. Display **"yes"** if the goal was met and **"no"** if it was not.
27. In cell **F2,** enter a formula using the IF function to determine if the student met her unit goal. Display **"yes"** if the goal was met and **"no"** if it was not.
28. Before finishing the project, check each worksheet for errors.
29. Save and close the workbook.

projects

Data files for projects can be found by logging into your SIMnet account and going to the *Library* section.

on your own 3.5

In this project you will complete a dental plan workbook. Be sure to save your work often!

Skills needed to complete this project:

- Updating Named Ranges with the Name Manager (Skill 3.13)
- Editing and Deleting Names with the Name Manager (Skill 3.14)
- Naming Ranges of Cells (Skill 3.11)
- Working with Named Ranges (Skill 3.12)
- Finding Data Using the VLOOKUP Function (Skill 3.17)
- Using the Function Arguments Dialog to Enter Functions (Skill 3.1)
- Calculating Averages (Skill 3.3)
- Finding Minimum and Maximum Values (Skill 3.4)
- Using Formula AutoComplete to Enter Functions (Skill 3.2)
- Creating Formulas Using Counting Functions (Skill 3.6)
- Using CONCAT to Combine Text (Skill 3.8)
- Creating Formulas Referencing Data from Other Worksheets (Skill 3.10)
- Formatting Text Using Functions (Skill 3.7)
- Using Date and Time Functions (Skill 3.5)
- Using the Logical Function IF (Skill 3.15)
- Calculating Loan Payments Using the PMT Function (Skill 3.16)
- Checking Formulas for Errors (Skill 3.18)
- Finding Errors Using Trace Precedents and Trace Dependents (Skill 3.19)
- Displaying and Printing Formulas (Skill 3.20)

1. Open the start file **EX2016-OnYourOwn-3-5** and resave the file as: `[your initials]EX-OnYourOwn-3-5`
2. If the workbook opens in Protected View, click the **Enable Editing** button in the Message Bar at the top of the workbook so you can modify it.
3. Start with the *Pocket Chart* worksheet. This dental chart is designed to be used to record measurements of the depth of gum pockets around the teeth. Each tooth is identified by number and name. The teeth of the upper and lower jaws are arranged across the worksheet from the patient's right side to the left. Pocket depth measurements have been entered.

4. Enter your name as the patient's name and enter the date of the examination. Do not use a function for the date. (You don't want the value to update every time you open the workbook.)
5. Review the information in the *Look Up* worksheet and assign names as necessary to each of the lookup tables to use in formulas in other worksheets. One of the lookup tables already has a name assigned.
6. Return to the *Pocket Chart* worksheet and complete the patient data.
   a. Use VLOOKUP functions to determine the severity level for each tooth.
   b. Use statistical functions to calculate the smallest pocket depth, the largest pocket depth, and the average pocket depth for the upper and lower teeth sections. Use similar formulas in **O2:O4** to calculate the overall statistical information for the patient (the average, minimum, and maximum pocket depths for both upper and lower teeth).
   c. Count the number of cells missing pocket depth information (blank cells). *Hint:* Remember, the COUNTBLANK function accepts only one argument, so you will need to count the blank cells for the upper teeth and the lower teeth and then add those values together.
7. Now switch to the *Treatment Plan* worksheet and fix any errors. ***Hint:*** Display formulas and then use the **Name Manager** to review names and create missing names as needed. Delete any duplicate names you may have accidentally created.
8. Create a formula to display the patient name in the format Bob Smith. Reference the patient name cells from the *Pocket Chart* sheet. Be sure to include a space between the first and last names.
9. Modify the formula that displays the patient name so the name appears in all uppercase.
10. Enter a formula to display today's date in cell **I1.**
11. Cells B7:C9 summarize the number of teeth with each severity level. Use this data table to complete the treatment plan. For each treatment, display **"yes"** if the patient meets the requirement below and **"no"** if he does not.
    a. Sonic Toothbrush: Recommend only if the patient has more than five mild pockets.
    b. Scaling & Planing: Recommend only if the patient has more than seven moderate pockets.
    c. Surgery: Recommend only if the patient has more than three severe pockets.
12. Complete the billing information.
    a. Look up the cost of each treatment.
    b. Compute the amount the insurance company will cover for each treatment. Multiply the treatment cost by the insurance company rate. *Hint:* Use the HLOOKUP function to find the insurance company rate.

c. Compute the billable amount for each treatment. If the treatment is recommended, compute the billable amount by subtracting the amount insurance will cover from the cost of the treatment. If the treatment is not recommended, display **"N/A"** instead.

d. Enter a formula to calculate the total bill for the patient.

13. Enter a formula to compute the monthly payment for the payment plan option. Be sure to display the number as a positive value.
14. Display your formulas and check for errors. Use the error checking skills you learned in this chapter as needed.
15. Save and close the workbook.

projects

Data files for projects can be found by logging into your SIMnet account and going to the *Library* section.

fix it 3.6

In this project, you will correct function mistakes and other formula errors in a workbook designed for planning a large party or event. Be sure to save your work often!

Skills needed to complete this project:

- Checking Formulas for Errors (Skill 3.18)
- Finding Errors Using Trace Precedents and Trace Dependents (Skill 3.19)
- Displaying and Printing Formulas (Skill 3.20)
- Creating Formulas Using Counting Functions (Skill 3.6)
- Finding Minimum and Maximum Values (Skill 3.4)
- Formatting Text Using Functions (Skill 3.7)
- Using CONCAT to Combine Text (Skill 3.8)
- Finding Data Using the VLOOKUP Function (Skill 3.17)
- Using the Function Arguments Dialog to Enter Functions (Skill 3.1)
- Using Formula AutoComplete to Enter Functions (Skill 3.2)
- Calculating Averages (Skill 3.3)
- Naming Ranges of Cells (Skill 3.11)
- Working with Named Ranges (Skill 3.12)
- Updating Named Ranges with the Name Manager (Skill 3.13)
- Editing and Deleting Names with the Name Manager (Skill 3.14)
- Using Date and Time Functions (Skill 3.5)
- Using the Logical Function IF (Skill 3.15)
- Creating Formulas Referencing Data from Other Worksheets (Skill 3.10)
- Calculating Loan Payments Using the PMT Function (Skill 3.16)

1. Open the start file **EX2016-FixIt-3-6** and resave the file as: `[your initials]EX-FixIt-3-6`
2. If the workbook opens in Protected View, click the **Enable Editing** button in the Message Bar at the top of the workbook so you can modify the workbook.
3. On the *GuestList* sheet, check all the formulas. Cells to check are filled with the light orange color. Most of them need to be corrected. Use error checking as needed and/or display the formulas on-screen for easy viewing.
   a. In the *Name Tag* column, modify the formula to display the guest name in this format: **BILL SMITH** *Hint:* There are multiple errors in this formula. Fix the formula in cell **D10** and then copy it to the other cells in the column.

b. Correct the function used in cell **A3** to calculate the sum of the values in the *NumAttending* column.
c. Correct the function used in cell **A4** to count the number of values in the *Street* column.
d. Correct the function used in cell **A5** to count the number of blank cells in the *NumAttending* column.
e. Correct the function used in cell **A6** to display the largest value in the *NumAttending* column.
f. Correct the function used in cell **A7** to display the average value in the *NumAttending* column.

4. On the *Shopping List* sheet, check all the formulas. Cells to check are filled with the light orange color. Most of them need to be corrected. Many of the problems on this worksheet can be solved by creating named ranges or using a name that already exists.
   a. The formula in cell **B2** uses the wrong function.
   b. The formulas in cells **A9:A23** reference a named range that doesn't exist. There is more than one correct way to fix this problem using the cell range **A5:H18** on the *Places to Shop* worksheet. You can create the named range referenced in the formulas, or you can change the function arguments to reference the cell range instead.
   c. The formula in cell **H9** results in the correct value. However, the workbook author copied this formula to the remaining cells in the column and those values are definitely not correct! Fix the formula in cell **H9** and copy it to cells **H10:H23**. *Hint*: Notice that cell **H8** is named *Tax*.
5. If you've fixed the formulas in cells **H9:H23** correctly, the formulas in cells I9:I23 and G5 should be calculate properly now. However, the formulas in cells **G2:G4** still have errors that need to be fixed. *Hint:* Use error checking as needed and/or display the formulas on-screen for easy viewing.
   a. Correct the function used in cell **G2** to average value of the *Cost* column.
   b. Correct the function used in cell **G3** to display the largest value in the *Cost* column.
   c. Correct the function used in cell **G4** to display the smallest value in the *Cost* column.
6. On the *Summary* sheet, you will be entering all the formulas. Cells to complete are filled with the light orange color. *Hint:* Use error checking as needed and/or display the formulas on-screen for easy viewing.
   a. Cell **B2** should use a function that will update the date to the current date every time the workbook is opened.

b. Cell **B4** references a named range that doesn't exist. It should reference cell **A4** on the *Guest List* sheet. You can create the named range or edit the formula to reference the cell instead.

c. Cell **B5** references a named range that doesn't exist. It should reference cell **A3** on the *Guest List* sheet. You can create the named range or edit the formula to reference the cell instead.

d. Cell **B8** is missing the formula to calculate whether or not the total *Cost* with tax on the *Shopping List* sheet + the total *Cost* for purchasing and mailing invitations on the *Guest List* sheet is greater than the available cash. The cell should display *yes* or *no*.

e. Add a formula to cell **B9** to calculate the amount to borrow (total *Cost* with tax on the *Shopping List* sheet + the total *Cost* for purchasing and mailing invitations on the *Guest List* sheet – the cash available) if the value in cell **B8** is *yes*. If the value in cell **B8** is not *yes*, the cell should display 0.

f. Add a formula to cell **B12** to calculate the monthly loan payment based on the information in cells **B9:B11**. Use a negative number for the *Pv* argument.

7. Save and close the workbook.

chapter 4

Formatting Worksheets and Managing the Workbook

In this chapter, you will learn the following skills:

- Insert, delete, and format worksheets
- Apply themes
- Insert, delete, and modify rows and columns
- Modify the worksheet view
- Manage how the worksheet prints

Skill 4.17 Changing Worksheet Orientation

Skill 4.18 Setting Up Margins for Printing

Skill 4.19 Scaling Worksheets for Printing

Skill 4.20 Printing Titles

Skill 4.21 Printing Selections, Worksheets, and Workbooks

introduction

As Excel projects get bigger and more complicated, more formatting skills are required. In this chapter, you will learn how to manage the organization and appearance of worksheets for the optimal display of data both on-screen and when printed.

Skill 4.1 Inserting Worksheets

When you create a new workbook, it contains a single worksheet named *Sheet1*. If you need more than one worksheet, you can add more. It is a good practice to keep all related information in the same workbook by adding more worksheets, rather than starting a new workbook.

- To add a new worksheet to the right of the active worksheet, click the **New sheet** button to the right of the last worksheet tab .
- To add a worksheet to the left of the active worksheet, on the *Home* tab, in the *Cells* group, click the **Insert** button arrow, and select **Insert Sheet.**

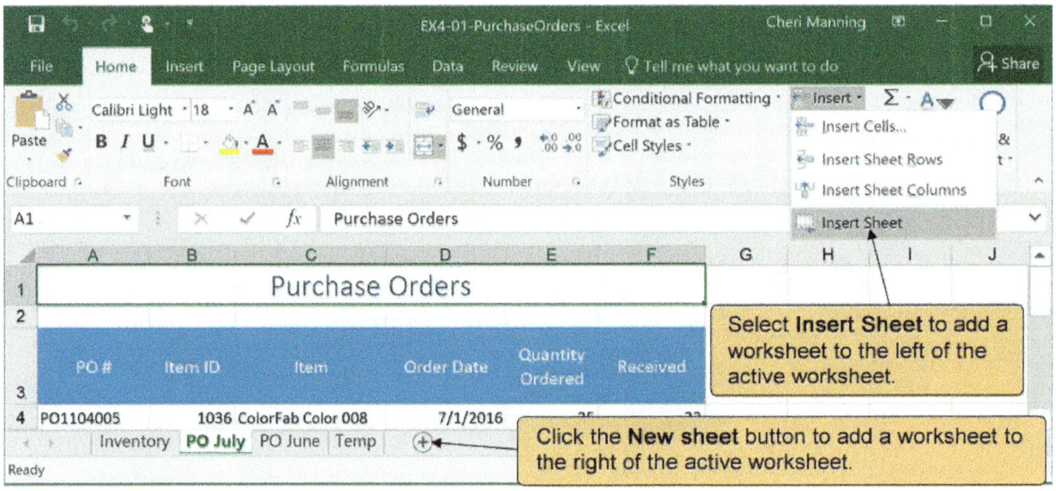

FIGURE EX 4.1

The new sheet is given the name Sheet# (where # is the next number available—for example, if your workbook contains *Sheet1* and *Sheet2*, the next sheet inserted will be named *Sheet3*).

another method

To add a worksheet, you can also:

1. Right-click on a sheet tab and select **Insert...** on the shortcut menu.
   - To insert a blank worksheet, click the **Worksheet** icon in the dialog.
   - To insert a formatted worksheet, click the **Spreadsheet Solutions** tab, and click any of the template icons.
2. Click **OK**.

let me try *Live!*

Open the student data file **EX4-01-PurchaseOrders** and try this skill on your own:

1. Add a new worksheet to the right of the *PO July* sheet.
2. Add another new worksheet to the left of the new *PO July* worksheet.
3. If you will be moving on to the next skill in this chapter, leave the workbook open to continue working. If not, save the file as directed by your instructor and close it.

Skill 4.2 Naming Worksheets

When you create a new workbook, Excel automatically includes a worksheet named *Sheet1*. Additional worksheets that you insert are automatically named *Sheet2, Sheet3,* and so forth. It is a good idea to rename your worksheets to something more descriptive. Giving your worksheets descriptive names can help organize multiple worksheets, making it easier for you to find and use information.

To rename a worksheet:

1. Double-click the sheet tab or right-click the worksheet tab and select **Rename**.
2. Excel highlights the sheet name, allowing you to replace it as you type.
3. Type the new sheet name, and press Enter.

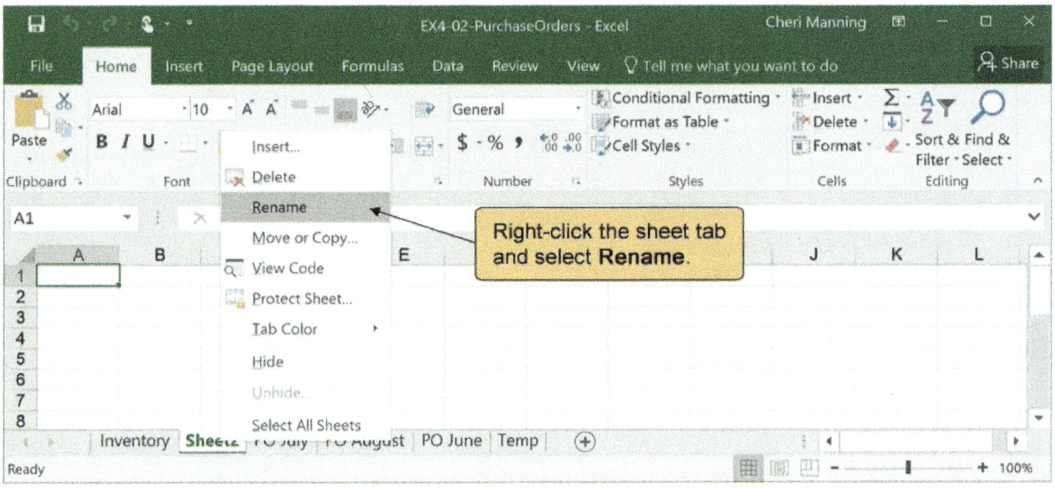

FIGURE EX 4.2

another method

You can also use the Ribbon to rename a worksheet.

1. Click the sheet tab you want to rename.
2. On the *Home* tab, in the *Cells* group, click the **Format** button.
3. Select **Rename Sheet**.
4. Type the new sheet name, and press Enter.

let me try *Live!*

If you do not have the data file from the previous skill open, open the student data file **EX4-02-PurchaseOrders** and try this skill on your own:

1. Rename *Sheet1*: `PO August`
2. Rename *Sheet2*: `Orders`
3. If you will be moving on to the next skill in this chapter, leave the workbook open to continue working. If not, save the file as directed by your instructor and close it.

Skill 4.3 Changing the Color of Sheet Tabs

By default, all the worksheet tabs in Excel are white. If you have many sheets in your workbook, changing the tab colors can help you organize your data.

To change a worksheet tab color:

1. Right-click the sheet tab and point to **Tab Color** to display the color palette.
2. Hover the mouse pointer over each color to preview how the color will look when the worksheet is active.
3. Click the color you want.

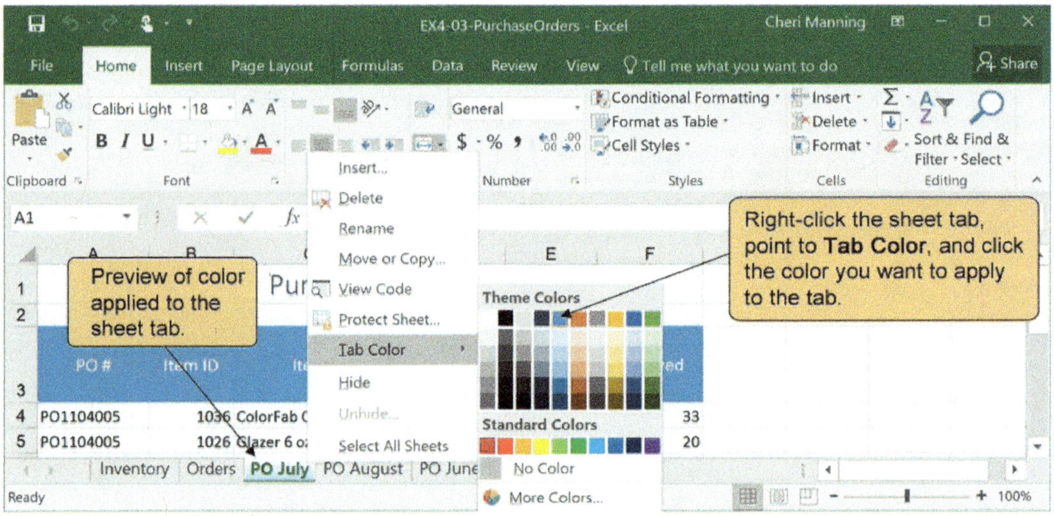

FIGURE EX 4.3

tips & tricks

- The color palette used for worksheet tab color is the same color palette used for font color, fill color, and border color. The colors available change depending on the theme applied to the workbook.
- If you have sheets that contain related data, color them using different shades of the same color.

another method

1. Click the sheet tab you want to color.
2. On the *Home* tab, in the *Cells* group, click the **Format** button.
3. Point to **Tab Color** to display the color palette.
4. Click the color you want.

let me try *Live!*

If you do not have the data file from the previous skill open, open the student data file **EX4-03-PurchaseOrders** and try this skill on your own:

1. Change the color of the sheet tab for the *PO July* worksheet to **Blue, Accent 1** (the fifth color from the left in the top row of theme colors).
2. If you will be moving on to the next skill in this chapter, leave the workbook open to continue working. If not, save the file as directed by your instructor and close it.

Skill 4.4 Moving and Copying Worksheets

You can move worksheets around in a workbook, rearranging them into the most logical order.

To move a worksheet within a workbook:

1. Click the worksheet tab and hold down the mouse button.
2. Notice that the mouse pointer changes to the shape.
3. Drag the mouse cursor to the position where you want to move the sheet, and release the mouse button. Excel places a small black triangle ▼ to let you know where the sheet will be placed.

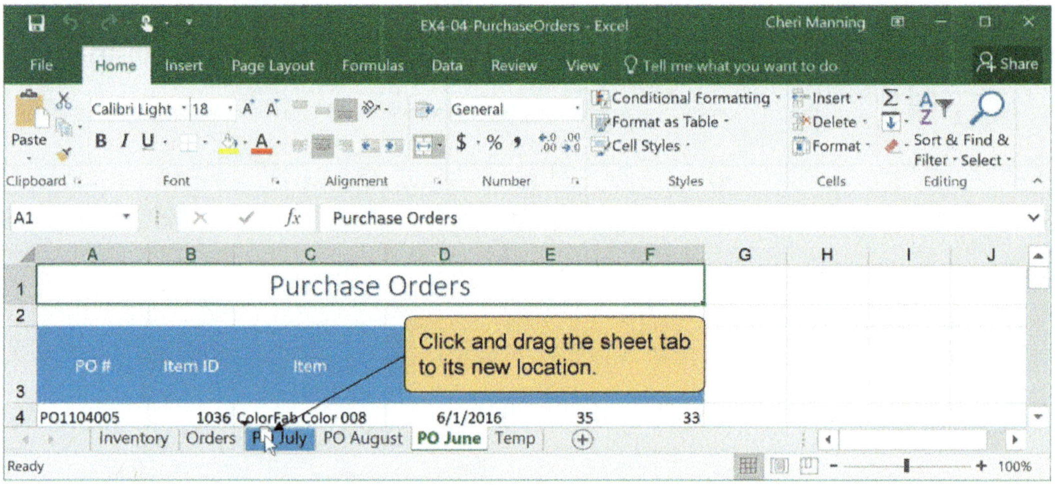

FIGURE EX 4.4

If you want to experiment with worksheet layouts or formulas, you can create a copy of the worksheet in case you want to go back to the original version.

To create a copy of a worksheet:

1. Click the worksheet tab, hold down the mouse button, and press and hold Ctrl.
2. Notice that the mouse pointer changes to the shape.
3. Drag the mouse cursor to the position where you want to insert a copy of the selected sheet, and release the mouse button.

To move or copy a worksheet to another workbook or to a new workbook:

1. Right-click the sheet tab, and select **Move or Copy...** to open the *Move or Copy* dialog.
2. In the *Move or Copy* dialog, expand the **To book** list at the top of the dialog. The *To book* list shows all the Excel workbooks you have open. Click the workbook you want. To move or copy the sheet to a new blank workbook, select **(new book).**
3. The list of sheets in the *Before sheet* box will update to show the sheets available in the workbook you selected. Click the name of the sheet you want to move the selected sheet before. If you want to move the sheet to the end of the workbook, select **(move to end)** in the *Before sheet* box.
4. If you want to create a copy of the selected sheet, instead of moving the original, click the **Create a copy** check box.
5. Click **OK.**

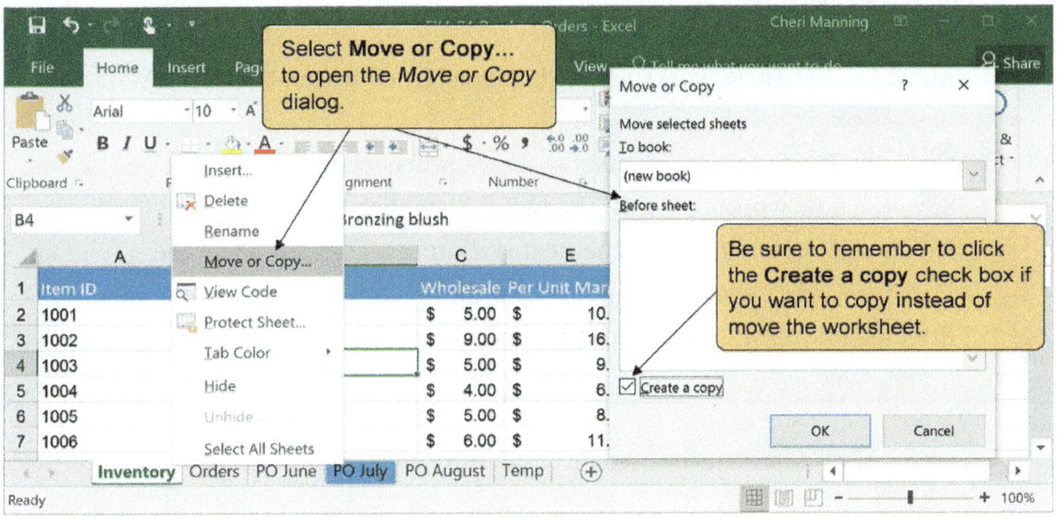

FIGURE EX 4.5

You can use this same method to move or copy worksheets within a workbook by not changing the workbook listed in the *To book* list in the *Move or Copy* dialog.

tips & tricks

Moving a worksheet from one workbook to another deletes the worksheet from the original workbook. Consider copying the worksheet to the second workbook first, and then, once you are confident that formulas work as you intend, delete the worksheet from the original workbook.

tell me **more**

To move or copy more than one worksheet, press Shift and click the worksheets you want to move or copy. If the worksheets are not consecutive, then press Ctrl instead.

another method

You can also open the *Move or Copy* dialog from the Ribbon. On the *Home* tab, in the *Cells* group, click the **Format** button, and select **Move or Copy Sheet...**

let me **try** *Live!*

If you do not have the data file from the previous skill open, open the student data file **EX4-04-PurchaseOrders** and try this skill on your own:

1. Move the **PO June** worksheet so it is positioned before the *PO July* worksheet.
2. Copy the **Inventory** worksheet to a new workbook.
3. Save the new workbook with the name `InventoryCopy` and close it.
4. If you will be moving on to the next skill in this chapter, leave the *PurchaseOrders* workbook open to continue working. If not, save the file as directed by your instructor and close it.

Skill 4.5 Deleting Worksheets

It is always a good practice to delete any unnecessary worksheets in your workbook.

To delete a worksheet:

1. Select the sheet you want to delete by clicking the worksheet tab.
2. On the *Home* tab, in the *Cells* group, click the **Delete** button arrow, and select **Delete Sheet.**
3. If you try to delete a sheet that contains data, Excel will display a warning that the sheet may contain data and ask if you are sure you want to permanently remove it from your workbook. Click the **Delete** button to continue and delete the worksheet.

Be careful—you cannot undo the *Delete Sheet* command.

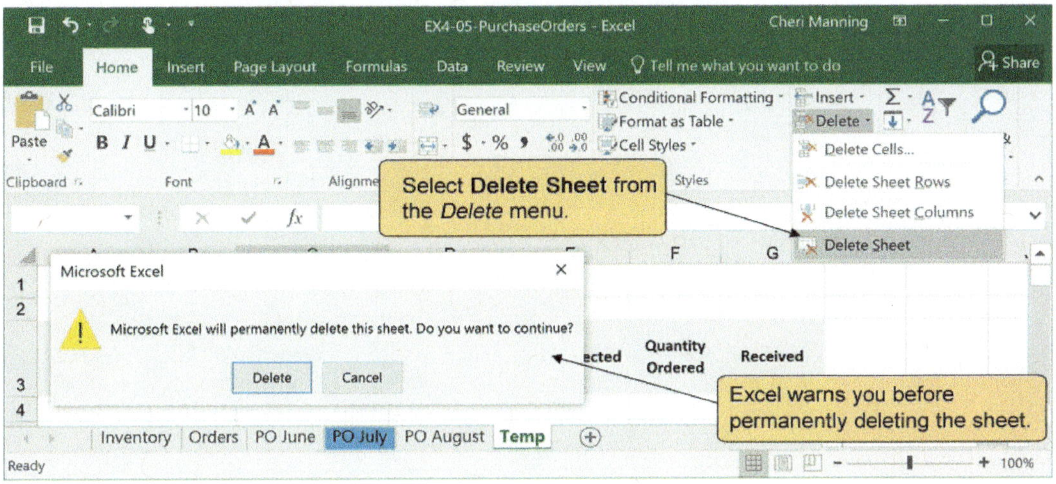

FIGURE EX 4.6

tips & tricks

If you have multiple copies of the same worksheet in a workbook, be sure to delete the versions you no longer need.

tell me more

You can delete multiple worksheets at the same time. First, select all the sheet tabs you want to remove, and then invoke the *Delete Sheet* command.

another method

To delete a worksheet, right-click on a sheet tab and then select **Delete** from the shortcut menu.

let me try *Live!*

If you do not have the data file from the previous skill open, open the student data file **EX4-05-PurchaseOrders** and try this skill on your own:

1. Delete the **Temp** worksheet.
2. If you will be moving on to the next skill in this chapter, leave the workbook open to continue working. If not, save the file as directed by your instructor and close it.

Skill 4.6 Grouping Worksheets

If you have multiple worksheets with the same structure, you can make changes to all of the worksheets at the same time by **grouping** them. This is convenient when you are setting up a series of worksheets with the same row or column headings. When sheets are grouped together, you can also change column widths and formatting, add formulas such as totals, or add headers and footers. Using grouping saves time and ensures that the sheets share a consistent format.

To group worksheets:

1. Click the first worksheet tab.
2. Hold down Shift and click the tab for the last worksheet you want included in the group. If you want to select noncontiguous worksheets (sheets that are not next to each other), press Ctrl instead, and then click each sheet tab.
3. Notice that the title bar now includes [Group] after the file name.
4. Make the change you want to the sheet. This same change will be made to all sheets in the group.
5. To ungroup, click any sheet tab that is not part of the group.

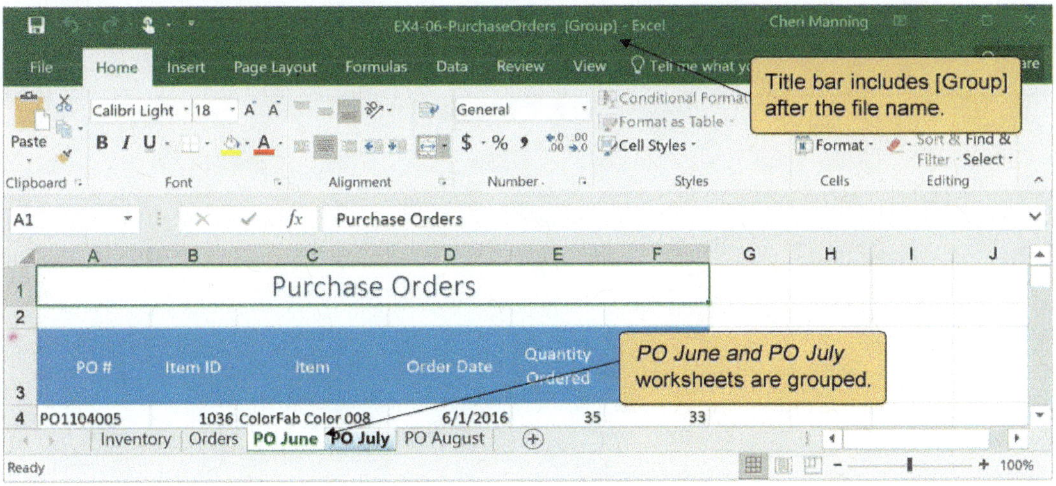

FIGURE EX 4.7

tell me **more**

To group together all the sheets in your workbook, right-click any sheet tab and then click **Select All Sheets**.

To ungroup sheets, right-click one of the grouped sheet tabs and then click **Ungroup**. If all of the sheets in your workbook are grouped together, clicking any sheet will ungroup them all.

let me **try** *Live!*

If you do not have the data file from the previous skill open, open the student data file **EX4-06-PurchaseOrders** and try this skill on your own:

1. Group sheets **PO June** and **PO July**.
2. Change the text in cell **E3** to: `Ordered`
3. Review cell **E3** in sheets *PO June* and *PO July* to ensure that the change was made to both sheets. Notice that the sheets remain grouped as you click back and forth between them.
4. If you will be moving on to the next skill in this chapter, leave the workbook open to continue working. Keep the sheets grouped. If not, save the file as directed by your instructor and close it.

Skill 4.7 Inserting and Deleting Rows and Columns

You may find you need to add rows or columns of new information into the middle of your workbook. Adding a new row will shift down other rows; adding a new column will shift other columns to the right.

To insert a column:

1. Place your cursor in a cell in the column to the right of where you want the new column.
2. On the *Home* tab, in the *Cells* group, click the **Insert** button arrow and select **Insert Sheet Columns**.
3. The new column will appear to the left of the selected cell.

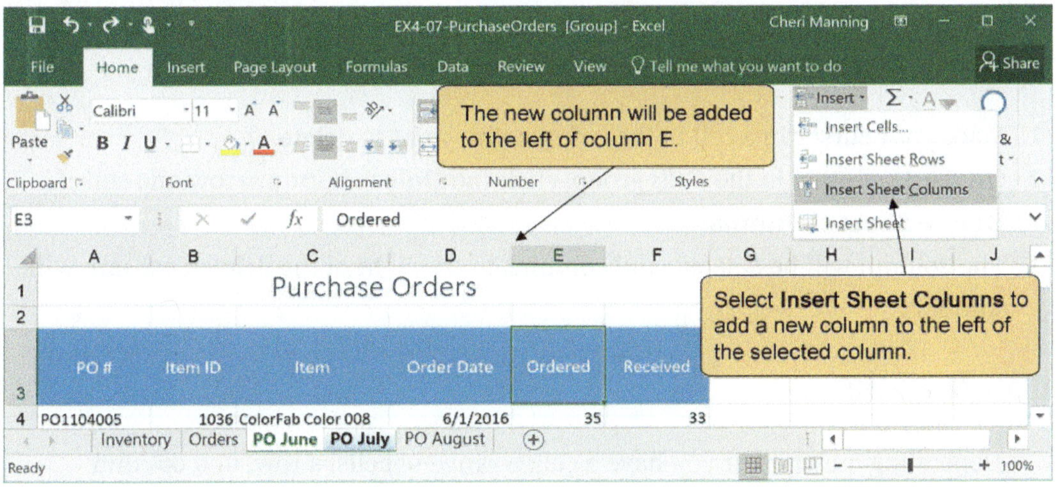

FIGURE EX 4.8

To insert a row:

1. Place your cursor in a cell in the row below where you want the new row.
2. On the *Home* tab, in the *Cells* group, click the **Insert** button arrow and select **Insert Sheet Rows**.
3. The new row will appear above the selected cell.

Of course, you can also delete rows and columns. Deleting a row will shift other rows up; deleting a column will shift the remaining columns to the left.

To delete a row:

1. Place your cursor in a cell in the row you want to delete.

2. On the *Home* tab, in the *Cells* group, click the **Delete** button arrow and select **Delete Sheet Rows.**
3. The row will be deleted and the rows below it will shift up.

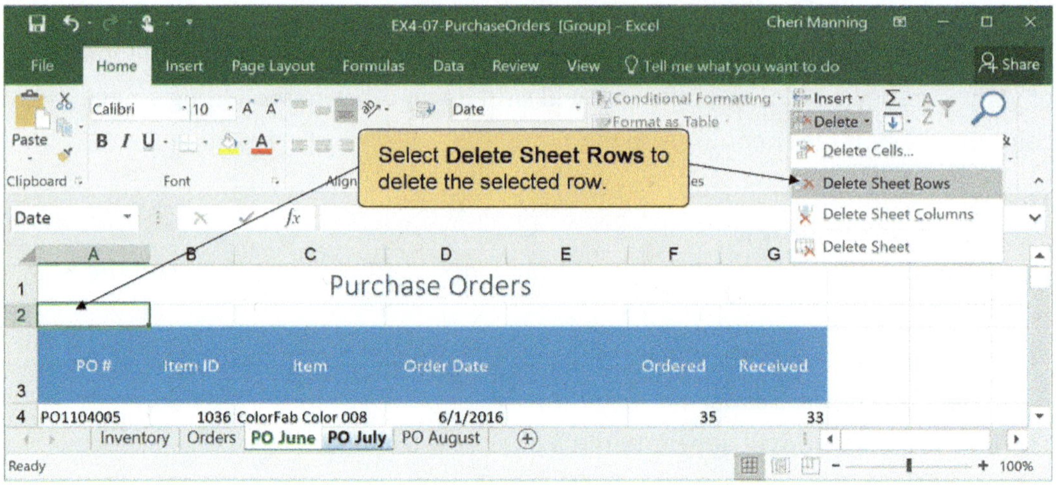

FIGURE EX 4.9

To delete a column:

1. Place your cursor in a cell in the column you want to delete.
2. On the *Home* tab, in the *Cells* group, click the **Delete** button arrow and select **Delete Sheet Columns.**
3. The column will be deleted, and columns to the right of the deleted column will shift left.

tips & tricks

Depending on whether you have a cell, a range of cells, a row, or a column selected, the behavior of the *Insert* and *Delete* commands will change. If you have a single cell selected and click the **Insert** button instead of the button arrow, Excel will insert a single cell, automatically moving cells down. However, if you select the entire column first, and then click the **Insert** button, Excel will automatically insert a column.

tell me **more**

When you insert a row or column, a Smart Tag will appear. Click the **Smart Tag** to choose formatting options for the new row or column—**Format Same as Above**, **Format Same as Below**, or **Clear Formatting** for rows and **Format Same as Left**, **Format Same as Right**, or **Clear Formatting** for columns. The Smart Tag formatting options are not available if you are inserting a row or column in two or more grouped worksheets.

another method

To insert or delete rows and columns:

1. Right-click in a cell, then select **Insert...** or **Delete...**
2. In the dialog, select **Entire row** or **Entire column**.
3. Click **OK**.

You can also insert or delete an entire row or column by right-clicking the row or column selector and selecting **Insert** or **Delete** from the menu. Because you have already selected an entire row or column, Excel will not ask you to specify what you want to insert or delete.

let me try *Live!*

If you do not have the data file from the previous skill open, open the student data file **EX4-07-PurchaseOrders** and try this skill on your own:

1. If necessary, group sheets **PO June** and **PO July**.
2. Insert a new column to the left of column **E**.
3. Delete row **2**.
4. Verify that the changes were made to both worksheets.
5. If you will be moving on to the next skill in this chapter, leave the workbook open to continue working. If not, save the file as directed by your instructor and close it.

Skill 4.8 Applying Themes

A **theme** is a unified color, font, and effects scheme. When you apply a theme to the workbook, you ensure that all visual elements work well together, giving the workbook a polished, professional look. When you create a new blank workbook in Excel 2016, the Office theme is applied by default.

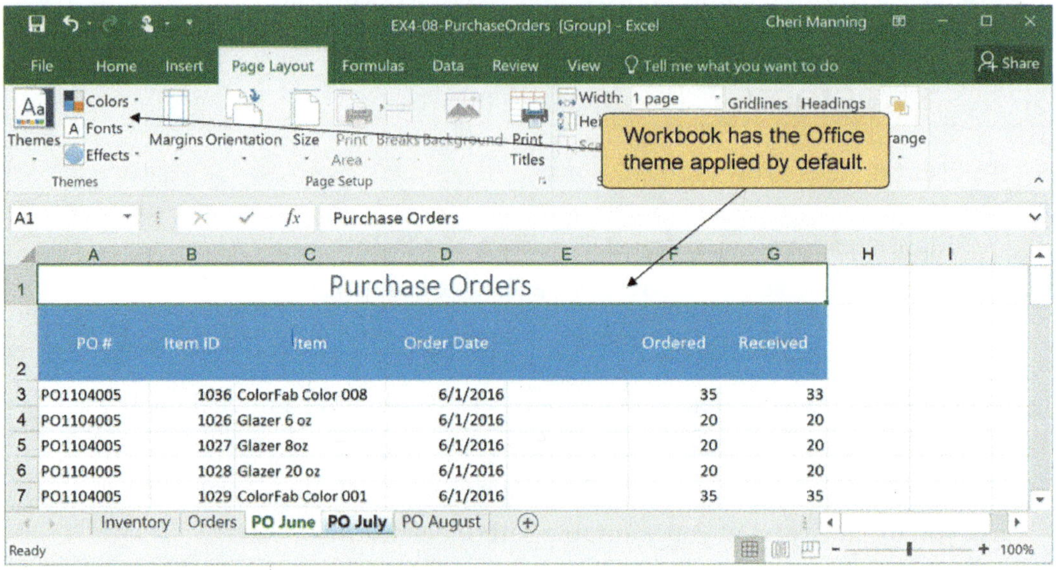

FIGURE EX 4.10

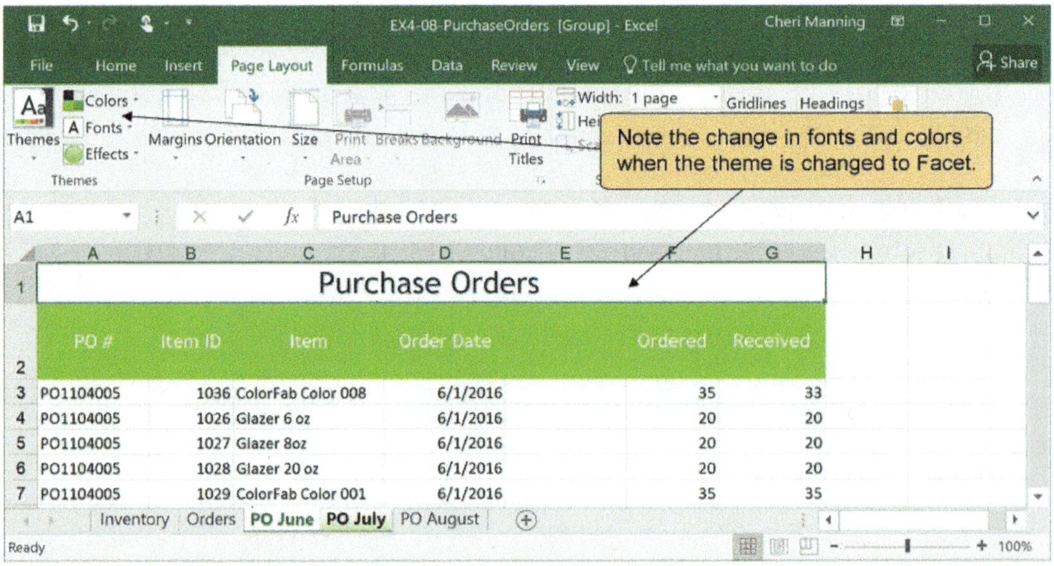

FIGURE EX 4.11

To apply a theme to a workbook:

1. On the *Page Layout* tab, in the *Themes* group, click the **Themes** button to expand the gallery.

2. Roll your mouse over each theme in the gallery to preview the formatting changes.
3. Click one of the themes to apply it to your workbook.

FIGURE EX 4.12

From the *Themes* group, you can apply specific aspects of a theme by making a selection from the *Theme Colors, Theme Fonts,* or *Theme Effects* gallery. Applying one aspect of a theme (for example, colors) will not change the other aspects (fonts and effects).

Theme Colors—Limits the colors available from the color palette for fonts, borders, and cell shading. Notice that when you change themes, the colors in the color palette change.

Theme Fonts—Affects the fonts used for cell styles (including titles and headings). Changing the theme fonts does not limit the fonts available to you from the *Font* group on the Ribbon.

Theme Effects—Controls the way graphic elements in your worksheet appear. Chart styles change according to the theme color and effects.

tips & tricks

Changing the theme affects all the worksheets in the workbook.

When you change the workbook theme, the look of the built-in cell styles changes. Be careful, as the change in style may increase the font size, causing some of your data to be too wide for the columns. If you change themes, you may need to adjust some of your column widths or row heights.

let me try *Live!*

If you do not have the data file from the previous skill open, open the student data file **EX4-08-PurchaseOrders** and try this skill on your own:

1. If necessary, click the **PO June** sheet tab. If the *PO June* and *PO July* worksheets are still grouped, you do not need to ungroup them.
2. Expand the *Themes* gallery and preview how each theme would affect the workbook.
3. Apply the **Facet** theme and note the changes to the workbook.
4. Reapply the **Office** theme.
5. If you will be moving on to the next skill in this chapter, leave the workbook open to continue working. If not, save the file as directed by your instructor and close it.

Skill 4.9 Modifying Column Widths and Row Heights

Some columns in your spreadsheet may be too narrow to display the data properly. If a cell contains text data, the text appears cut off. (If the cell to the right is empty, however, the text appears to extend into the empty cell.) If the cell contains numerical data, Excel displays a series of pound signs (#) when the cell is too narrow to display the entire number. You should adjust the column widths so the spreadsheet is easy to read.

Excel offers an easy way to automatically set columns to the width to best fit the data in the column:

To make the column automatically fit the contents:

1. Move your mouse over the right column boundary.
2. The cursor will change to a ✛ shape.
3. Double-click the right column border.

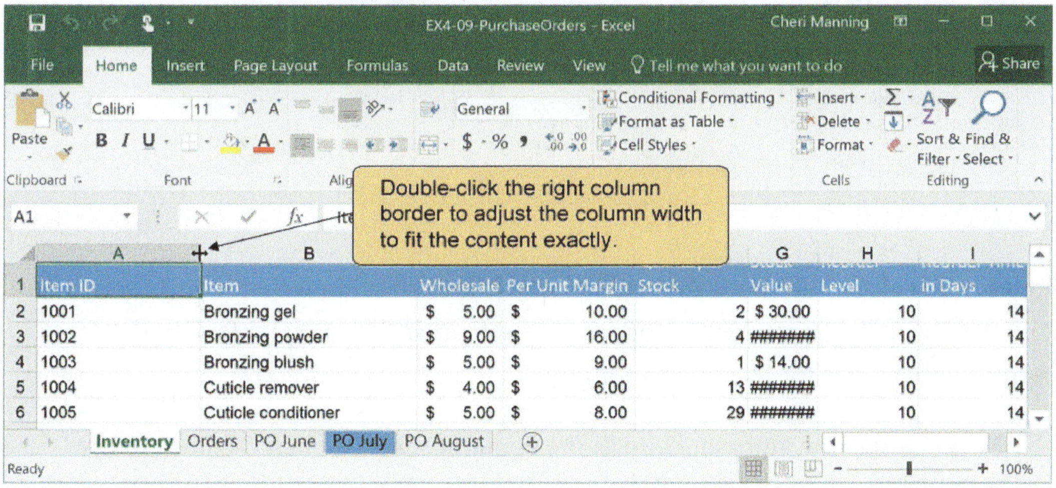

FIGURE EX 4.13

You can also modify column widths manually:

1. Move your mouse over the right column boundary.
2. The cursor will change to a ✛ shape.
3. Click and drag until the column is the size you want, and then release the mouse button.

To specify an exact column width for multiple columns:

1. Select the columns you want to modify. Click the column selector for the first column, press and hold Shift, and click the column selector for the last column.
2. On the *Home* tab, in the *Cells* group, click the **Format** button.
3. Select **Column Width...**
4. Enter the value you want in the *Column Width* dialog.
5. Click **OK.**

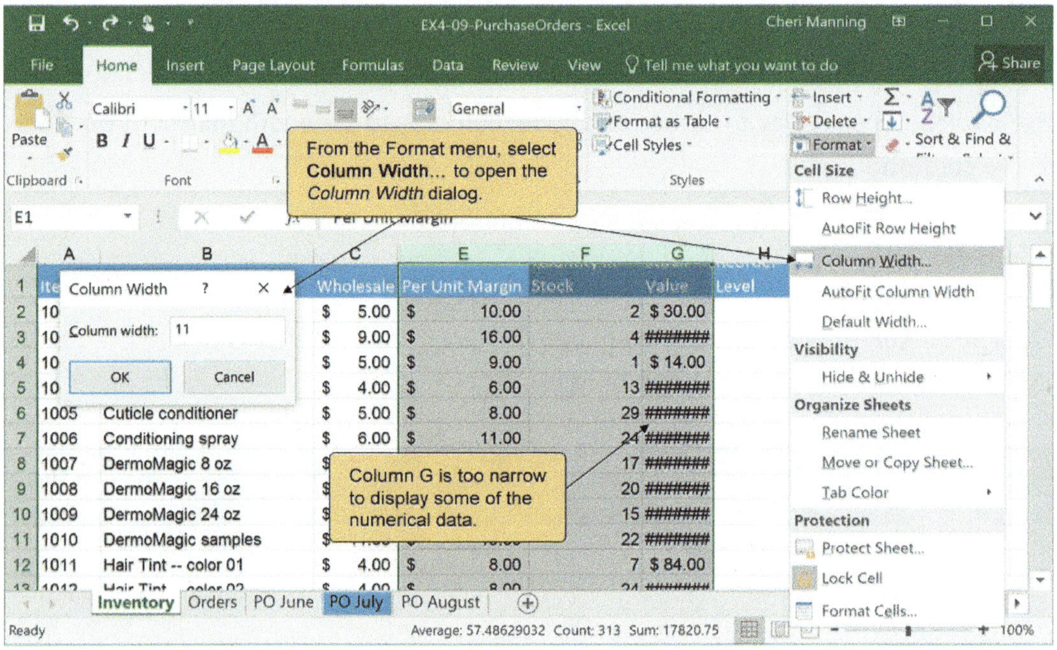

FIGURE EX 4.14

Rows in Excel are automatically sized to fit the font size. However, if you change the font size or apply a new theme, you may need to modify row heights. Use the same techniques you use for resizing columns:

- To make the row automatically fit the contents, double-click the bottom row boundary.
- To modify row heights manually, click and drag until the bottom row boundary up or down.
- Select the row(s) you want to modify and then from the *Format* button menu, select **Row Height...** to enter the row height value in the *Row Height* dialog.

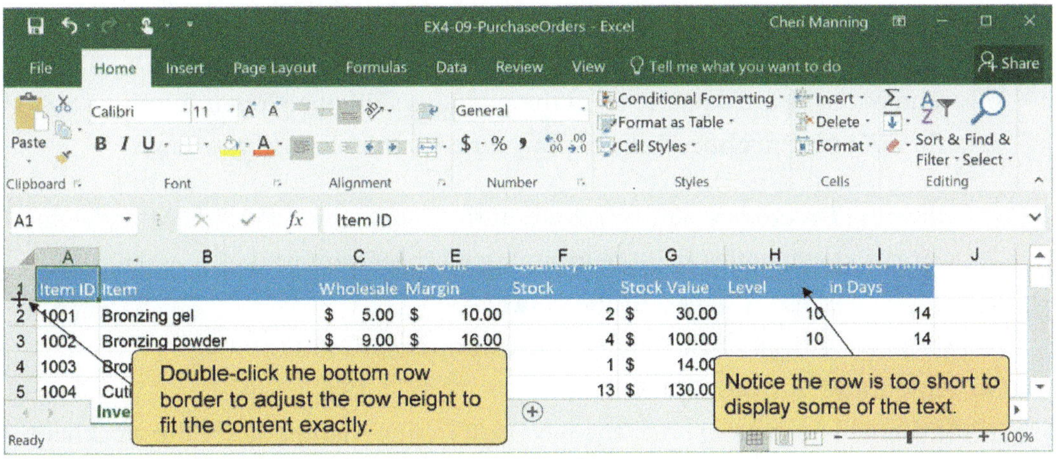

FIGURE EX 4.15

another method

You can also apply the *AutoFit* command from the Ribbon:

To autofit a column:

1. Click the column selector for the column you want to resize.
2. On the *Home* tab, in the *Cells* group, click the **Format** button.
3. Click **AutoFit Column Width**.

To autofit a row:

1. Click the row selector for the row you want to resize.
2. On the *Home* tab, in the *Cells* group, click the **Format** button.
3. Click **AutoFit Row Height**.

let me try *Live!*

If you do not have the data file from the previous skill open, open the student data file **EX4-09-PurchaseOrders** and try this skill on your own:

1. Click the **Inventory** worksheet tab. If the *PO June* and *PO July* worksheets were grouped, notice that the grouping has been removed.
2. Autofit column **A** to best fit the data.
3. Select columns **E:G** and change the column width to **11**.
4. Autofit row **1** to best fit the data.
5. If you will be moving on to the next skill in this chapter, leave the workbook open to continue working. If not, save the file as directed by your instructor and close it.

Skill 4.10 Freezing and Unfreezing Rows and Columns

If you have a large spreadsheet, you may want to **freeze** part of the worksheet so it is always visible. By doing this, you can keep column headings and row labels visible as you scroll through your data.

To freeze part of the worksheet:

1. Arrange the worksheet so the row you want to be visible is the top row or the column you want is the first column visible at the left.
2. On the *View* tab, in the *Window* group, click the **Freeze Panes** button.
   - If you want the first row to always be visible, click **Freeze Top Row.**
   - If you want the first column to always be visible, click **Freeze First Column.**

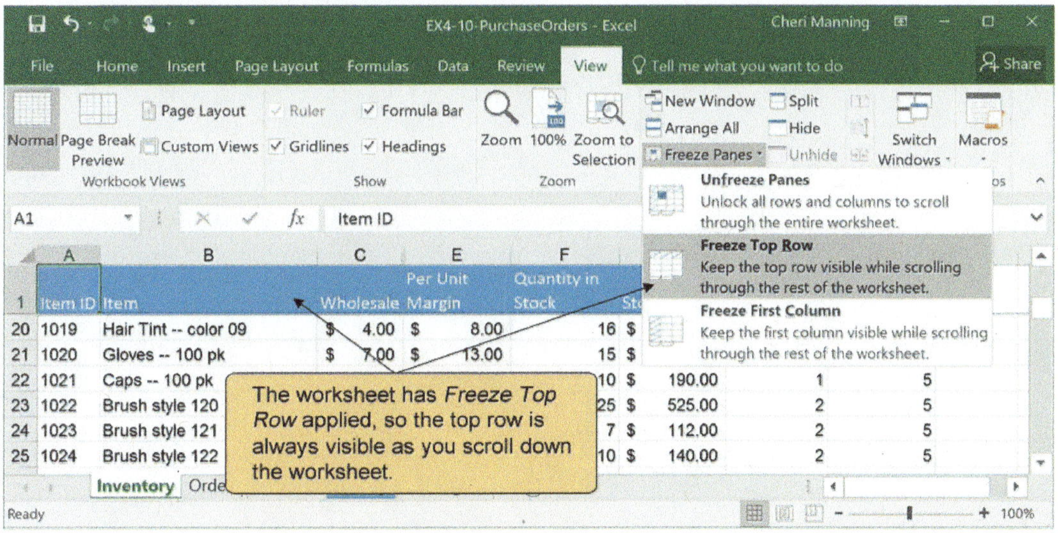

FIGURE EX 4.16

If your worksheet has both a header row and a column of labels in the first column, use the *Freeze Panes* option to freeze the worksheet at the selected cell, so the rows above the cell and the columns to the left of the cell are always visible.

1. Select the cell immediately below the header row and immediately to the right of the label column (usually cell B2).
2. On the *View* tab, in the *Window* group, click the **Freeze Panes** button, and select **Freeze Panes.**

To return your worksheet to normal, click the **Freeze Panes** button and select **Unfreeze Panes.**

let me try *Live!*

If you do not have the data file from the previous skill open, open the student data file **EX4-10-PurchaseOrders** and try this skill on your own:

1. Verify that the *Inventory* sheet is selected and the header row (row 1) is visible at the top of the worksheet.
2. Apply the **Freeze Panes** command so the top row will remain visible as you scroll down the worksheet.
3. If you will be moving on to the next skill in this chapter, leave the workbook open to continue working. If not, save the file as directed by your instructor and close it.

Skill 4.11 Hiding and Unhiding Rows and Columns

When you hide a row or column, the data still remain in your workbook, but they are no longer displayed on-screen and are not part of the printed workbook. Hiding rows can be helpful when you want to print a copy of your workbook for others but do not want to share all the information contained in your workbook.

To hide a row or column:

1. Select any cell in the row or column you want to hide.
2. On the *Home* tab, in the *Cells* group, click the **Format** button.
3. Point to **Hide & Unhide,** and click **Hide Rows** or **Hide Columns.**

To unhide a row or column:

1. Select the rows or columns on either side of the row or column you want to unhide.
2. On the *Home* tab, in the *Cells* group, click the **Format** button.
3. Point to **Hide & Unhide,** and click **Unhide Rows** or **Unhide Columns.**

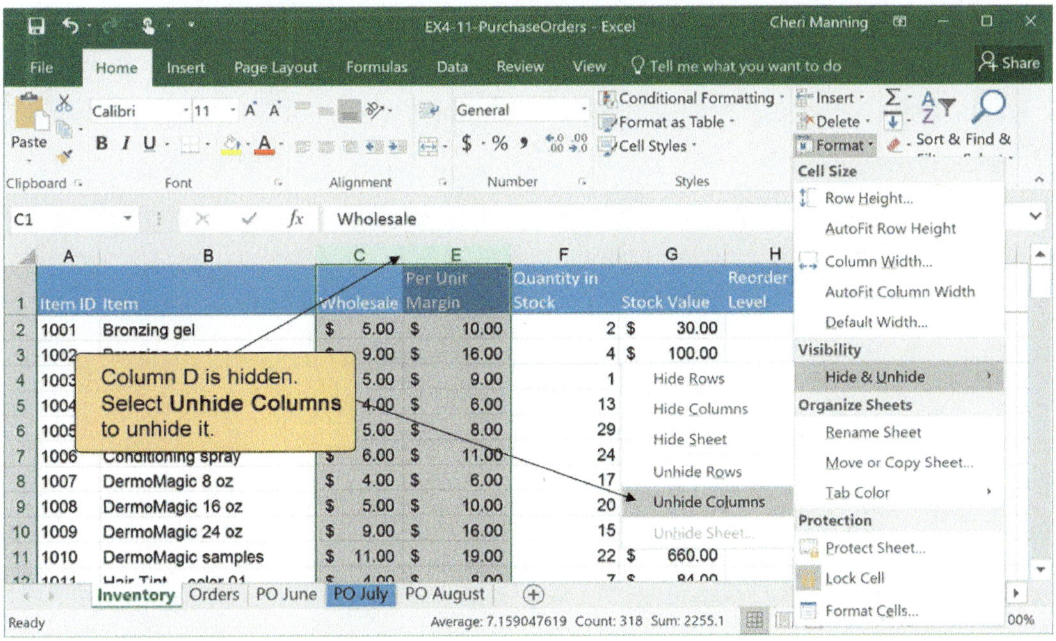

FIGURE EX 4.17

another method

The *Hide* and *Unhide* commands are also available from the right-click menu when columns or rows are selected.

let me try *Live!*

If you do not have the data file from the previous skill open, open the student data file **EX4-11-PurchaseOrders** and try this skill on your own:

1. Verify that the *Inventory* sheet is selected.
2. Unhide column **D**.
3. Hide column **G** (Stock Value).
4. If you will be moving on to the next skill in this chapter, leave the workbook open to continue working. If not, save the file as directed by your instructor and close it.

Skill 4.12 Splitting Workbooks

In Excel, you can split the worksheet view into two or four panes. Each pane scrolls independently of the other(s), so you can see two (or four) different areas of the worksheet at the same time. This can be especially helpful if you want to compare data in multiple parts of the worksheet at the same time.

To split the worksheet view:

1. Click the cell in the worksheet where you would like to split the view. You can select an entire row or column as the split point.
   - If you want to split the worksheet into two horizontal panes, click a cell in column **A**.
   - If you want to split the worksheet into two vertical panes, click a cell in row **1**.
   - If you want to split the worksheet into four panes, click any cell in the worksheet. The cell you selected will be the top left cell in the pane in the lower-right quadrant.
2. On the *View* tab, in the *Window* group, click the **Split** button.

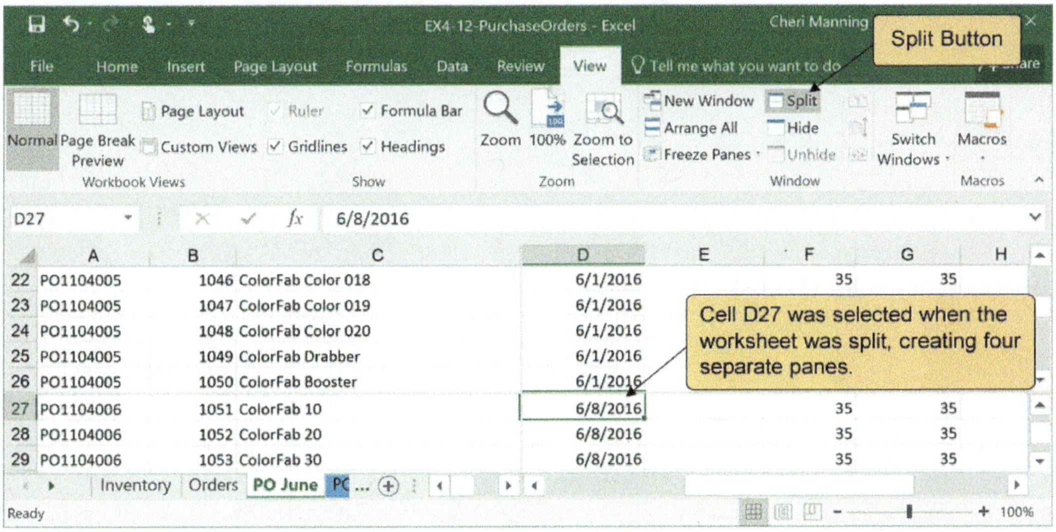

FIGURE EX 4.18

To undo the split and return the worksheet to a single view, click the **Split** button again.

tips & tricks

Splitting your worksheet will undo the *Freeze Panes* command.

tell me **more**

To adjust the size of a pane, click and drag the pane border.

let me **try** *Live!*

If you do not have the data file from the previous skill open, open the student data file **EX4-12-PurchaseOrders** and try this skill on your own:

1. Select the **PO June** worksheet.
2. Select cell **D27**, and then split the worksheet into four panes. Observe how using the scroll bars affects the view in each of the panes.
3. Remove the split and return the worksheet to a single view. *Hint:* The *Undo* command will not undo the *Split* command.
4. If you will be moving on to the next skill in this chapter, leave the workbook open to continue working. If not, save the file as directed by your instructor and close it.

Skill 4.13 Changing the Worksheet View

Excel offers three ways to view a worksheet.

Just as the name implies, **Normal view** is the typical working view. In Normal view, Excel shows the aspects of the worksheet that are visible only on-screen. Elements that are visible only when printed (like headers and footers) are hidden.

Page Layout view shows all the worksheet elements as they will print, including page margins and headers and footers as shown in Figure EX 4.19. You will work with Page Layout view when you learn about headers and footers.

Page Break Preview view allows you to manipulate where page breaks occur when the worksheet is printed. You will work with Page Break Preview view when you learn about inserting page breaks.

To switch between worksheet views, click the appropriate button in the status bar at the bottom of the Excel window, or on the *View* tab, in the *Workbook Views* group, click the button for the view you want.

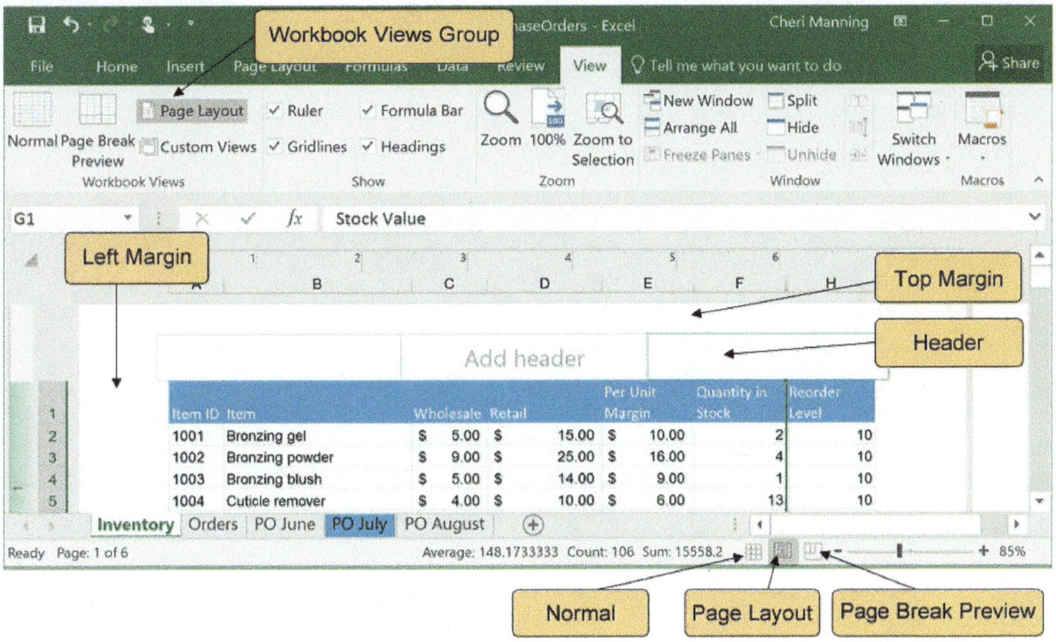

FIGURE EX 4.19

tips & tricks

Page Layout view is not compatible with *Freeze Panes*. If you have *Freeze Panes* applied to your worksheet, Excel will warn you before switching to Page Layout view. Click **OK** in the message box to continue to *Page Layout* view and undo *Freeze Panes*.

let me try *Live!*

If you do not have the data file from the previous skill open, open the student data file **EX4-13-PurchaseOrders** and try this skill on your own:

1. Select the **Inventory** worksheet.
2. Switch to **Page Break Preview** view.
3. Switch to **Page Layout** view. If Excel warns you that Page Layout view is not compatible with *Freeze Panes*, click **OK**.
4. If you will be moving on to the next skill in this chapter, leave the workbook open in Page Layout view to continue working. If not, save the file as directed by your instructor and close it.

Skill 4.14 Adding Headers and Footers

A **header** is text that appears at the top of every page, just below the top margin; a **footer** is text that appears at the bottom of every page, just above the bottom margin. Typically, headers and footers display information such as dates, page numbers, sheet names, file names, and authors' names.

To add a header or footer to a worksheet from Page Layout view:

1. Switch to Page Layout view by clicking the **Page Layout** button on the status bar.
2. The header area has three sections with the text *Add header* in the center section. If you do not see the *Add header* text, move the mouse pointer to the area just above row 1 to make the header area visible. Click the header section where you want to add information (left, center, or right).
3. The *Header & Footer Tools Design* tab appears.
4. In the *Header & Footer* group, click the **Header** button and select one of the predefined headers, or click a button in the *Header & Footer Elements* group to add a specific header element such as the sheet name or the current date. Excel inserts the code for the header element as show in Figure EX 4.20. Once you click away from the header, you will see the actual header text as shown in Figure EX 4.21.

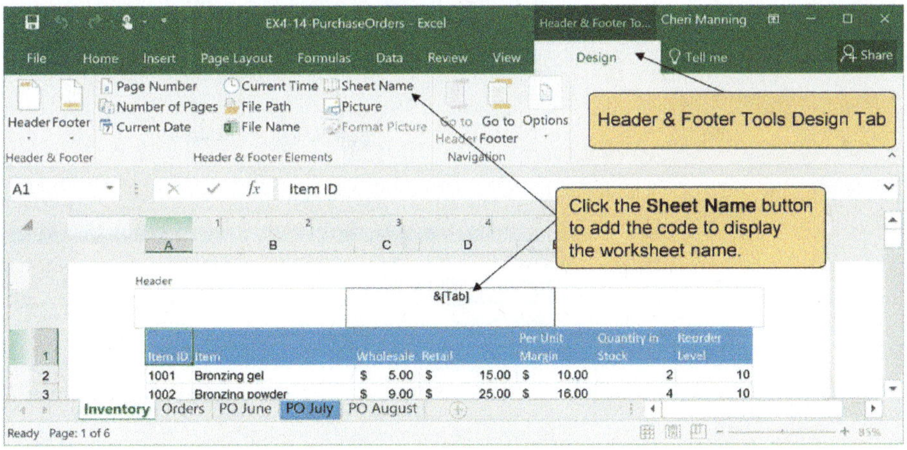

FIGURE EX 4.20

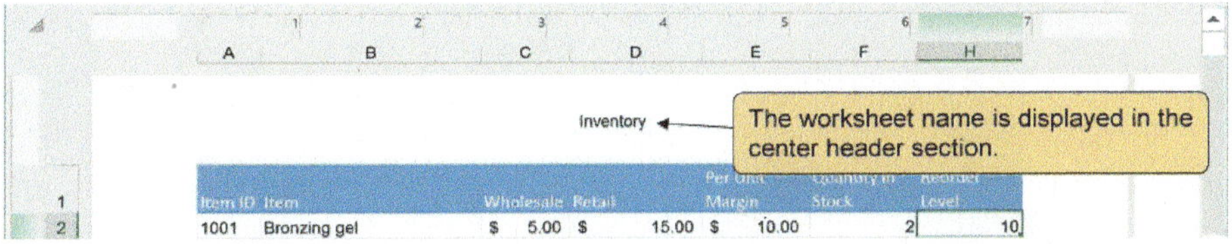

FIGURE EX 4.21

5. In the *Navigation* group, click the **Go to Footer** button to switch to the footer. Add footer elements the same way you add header elements.
6. When you are finished adding your header and footer elements, click anywhere in the worksheet and then switch back to Normal view to continue working.

Another method for adding headers and footers uses the *Page Setup* dialog. This method will be familiar to users who have worked with older versions of Excel.

To add a header or footer to a worksheet using the *Page Setup* dialog:

1. On the *Page Layout* tab, in the *Page Setup* group, click the **Page Setup Dialog Launcher** to open the *Page Setup* dialog.

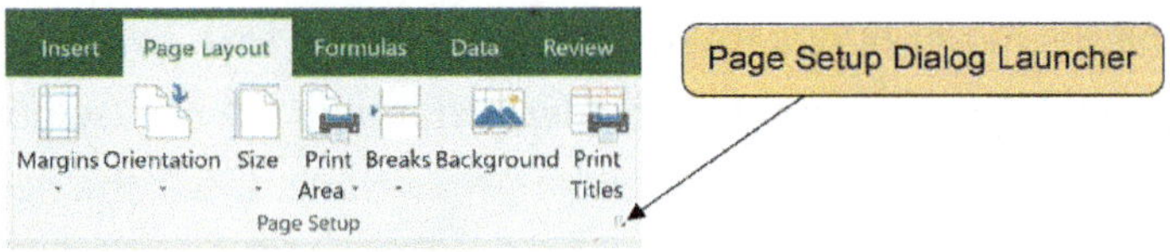

FIGURE EX 4.22

2. Click the **Header/Footer** tab.
3. Click the arrow beneath the *Header* or *Footer* area to expand the list of predefined header/footer options. Click the option you want to use.
4. Click **OK**.

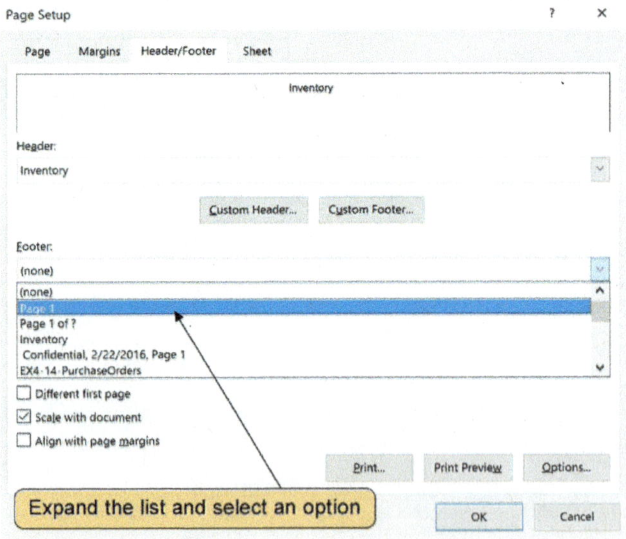

FIGURE EX 4.23

tell me **more**

If the predefined header/footer options in the *Page Setup* dialog do not meet your needs, you can customize the header or footer by clicking the **Custom Header...** or **Custom Footer...** button and adding elements through the *Header* or *Footer* dialog. In the *Header* or *Footer* dialog, click the section you want, and then click one of the header/footer element buttons.

another method

Another way to add a header or footer to your worksheet is to click the *Insert* tab. In the *Text* group, click the **Header & Footer** button. The worksheet will automatically switch to Page Layout view when you click the **Header & Footer** button.

let me try *Live!*

If you do not have the data file from the previous skill open, open the student data file **EX4-14-PurchaseOrders** and try this skill on your own:

1. Verify that the *Inventory* sheet is open in Page Layout view.
2. From the *Header & Footer Tools Design* tab, add a header that displays the sheet name in the center section.
3. Add a footer that displays the word *Page* and then the page number in the center section. *Hint:* Use one of the predefined footer options from the *Page Setup* dialog.
4. Click anywhere in the worksheet grid, and then switch back to Normal view.
5. Preview how the worksheet will look when printed and note the header and footer.
6. If you will be moving on to the next skill in this chapter, leave the workbook open to continue working. If not, save the file as directed by your instructor and close it.

Skill 4.15 Inserting Page Breaks

Excel automatically inserts page breaks so columns and rows are not split across pages when you print. However, you may want to control where page breaks happen so your worksheet prints in a more logical order. When the worksheet is in Normal view, page breaks appear as faint dotted lines. To view the page breaks more clearly, switch to Page Break Preview view.

To manually insert a new page break:

1. From Normal view or Page Break Preview view, begin by selecting the cell below and to the right of where you want the new page break.
2. On the *Page Layout* tab, in the *Page Setup* group, click the **Breaks** button.
3. Click **Insert Page Break.**
4. A new page break is inserted to the left of the selected column or above the selected row.

When the worksheet is in Page Break Preview view, automatic page breaks appear as blue dotted lines and manually inserted page breaks appear as solid blue lines. You can manually move a page break by clicking the page break line, and then dragging to the right or left or up or down. Release the mouse button when the line appears where you want the break. Notice that if you move an automatic page break, the line changes from dotted to solid.

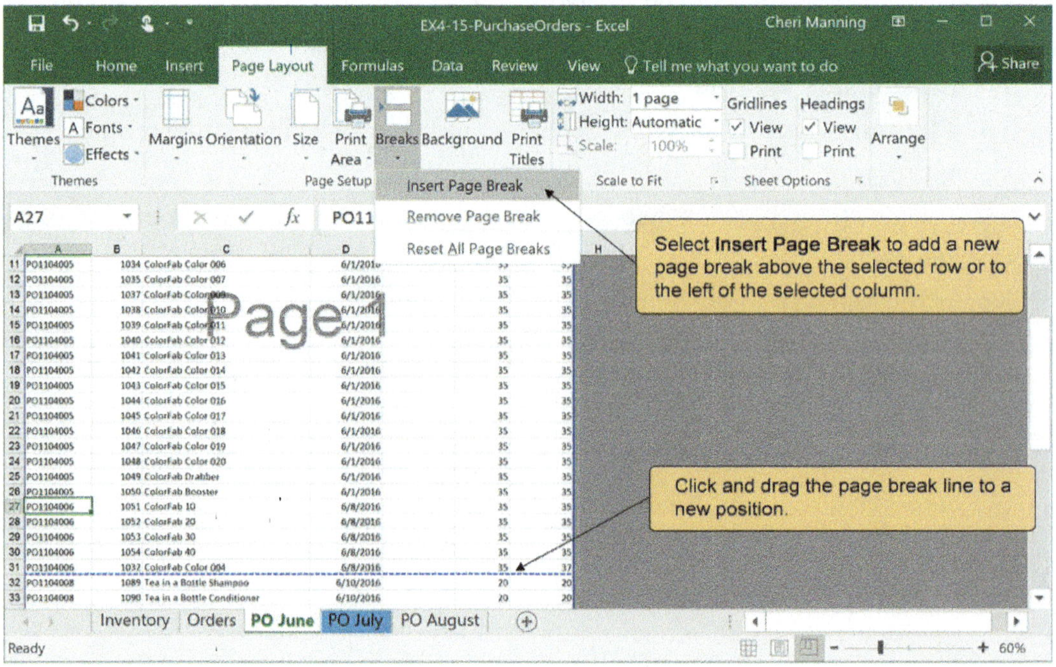

FIGURE EX 4.24

To remove a manual page break, select any cell adjacent to (to the right of or below) the break, then on the *Page Layout* tab, in the *Page Setup* group, click the **Breaks** button, and click **Remove Page Break**.

tips & tricks

If you insert a page break but nothing seems to happen, check to see if you have the scaling option set for printing. For example, if you have the worksheet set to print all columns on a single page, inserting a new page break between columns will not appear to have any effect on the worksheet. However, if you remove the scaling option, the new manual page break will appear.

tell me more

To remove all the manual page breaks at once, on the *Page Layout* tab, in the *Page Setup* group, click the **Breaks** button, and click **Reset All Page Breaks**.

let me try *Live!*

If you do not have the data file from the previous skill open, open the student data file **EX4-15-PurchaseOrders** and try this skill on your own:

1. Select the **PO June** worksheet.
2. Switch to Page Break Preview view and observe the page breaks.
3. Move the page break between pages 1 and 2 to just below **row 26**. Do not insert a new page break.
4. If you will be moving on to the next skill in this chapter, leave the workbook open to continue working. If not, save the file as directed by your instructor and close it.

from the perspective of . . .

WAREHOUSE LOGISTICS SUPERVISOR

Part of our company's "green" initiative is to minimize paper usage for printing. Using Excel's page break controls and layout controls like scaling, page orientation, and margins, we make sure that the reports we *have* to print use as little paper as possible.

Skill 4.16 Showing and Hiding Worksheet Elements

Gridlines are the lines that appear on the worksheet defining the rows and columns. Gridlines make it easy to see the individual cells in your worksheet. By default, gridlines are visible on-screen when you are working in Excel, but they do not print.

Headings are the numbers at the left of rows and the letters at the top of columns. By default, Excel displays the row and column headings on-screen to make it easy to identify cell references but they do not print.

To hide gridlines or headings on-screen:

On the *Page Layout* tab, in the *Sheet Options* group, click the **View** check box under **Gridlines** or **Headings** to remove the checkmark.

To print the gridlines and headings when you print the worksheet:

On the *Page Layout* tab, in the *Sheet Options* group, click the **Print** check box under **Gridlines** or **Headings.**

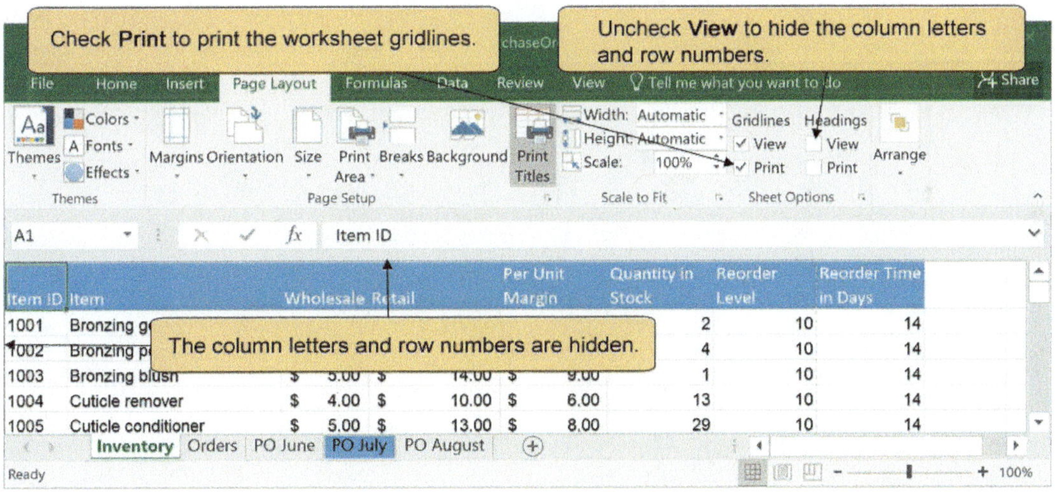

FIGURE EX 4.25

another method

- Set gridlines to print from the *Page Setup* dialog. On the *Page Layout* tab, in the *Page Setup* group, click the **Page Setup Dialog Launcher**. In the *Page Setup* dialog, click the **Sheet** tab. In the *Print* section, click the **Gridlines** check box. Click **OK**.
- To show or hide gridlines and headings on-screen, you can also check or uncheck the appropriate boxes on the *View* tab, in the *Show* group.

let me try *Live!*

If you do not have the data file from the previous skill open, open the student data file **EX4-16-PurchaseOrders** and try this skill on your own:

1. Modify the **Inventory** worksheet so gridlines will print.
2. Modify the **Inventory** worksheet so headings are hidden on-screen.
3. If you will be moving on to the next skill in this chapter, leave the workbook open to continue working. If not, save the file as directed by your instructor and close it.

Skill 4.17 Changing Worksheet Orientation

Orientation refers to the direction the worksheet prints. It doesn't affect the way the worksheet looks on your computer screen. The default print setting is for **portrait orientation**—when the height of the page is greater than the width (like a portrait hanging on a wall). If your workbook is wide, you may want to use **landscape orientation** instead, where the width of the page is greater than the height.

You can set the worksheet orientation from the *Page Layout* tab on the Ribbon:

1. On the *Page Layout* tab, in the *Page Setup* group, click the **Orientation** button.
2. Click the **Portrait** or **Landscape** option.

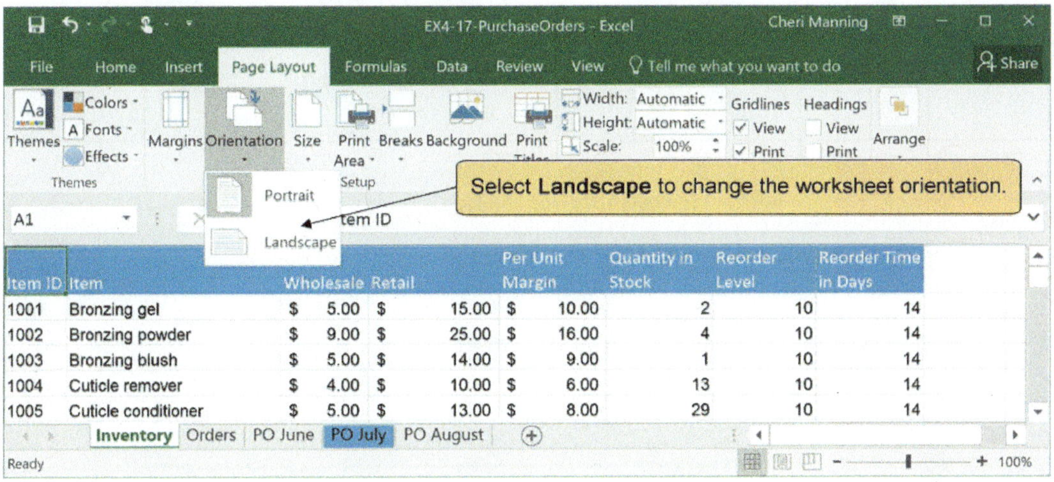

FIGURE EX 4.26

You can also change the worksheet orientation when you print:

1. Click the **File** tab to open Backstage view.
2. Click **Print**.
3. In the *Settings* section, click the button displaying the current orientation setting, and then click the orientation setting you want.

tips & tricks

Changing the *Orientation* setting affects only the active worksheet.

another method

On the *Page Layout* tab, in the *Page Setup* group, click the **Page Setup Dialog Launcher**. In the *Page Setup* dialog, click the **Page** tab. Click the **Portrait** or **Landscape** radio button. Click **OK**.

let me try *Live!*

If you do not have the data file from the previous skill open, open the student data file **EX4-17-PurchaseOrders** and try this skill on your own:

1. Verify that the **Inventory** worksheet is active. Note the page break line between the *Reorder Level* and *Reorder Time in Days* columns.
2. Change the worksheet orientation to **Landscape**.
3. Note that the page is wider now and all the columns fit on one page.
4. If you will be moving on to the next skill in this chapter switch back to **Portrait** orientation, leave the workbook open to continue working. If not, save the file as directed by your instructor and close it.

Skill 4.18 Setting Up Margins for Printing

Margins are the blank spaces at the top, bottom, left, and right of a printed page. You may need to adjust the margins individually for each worksheet in your workbook to ensure they print exactly as you intend. Excel provides three margin settings:

- **Normal**—Uses Excel's default margins: 0.75 inch for the top and bottom and 0.7 inch for the left and right.
- **Wide**—Adds more space at the top, bottom, left, and right sides.
- **Narrow**—Reduces the amount of space at the top, bottom, left, and right sides, so more of your worksheet fits on each printed page.

If none of the automatic margins options is exactly what you want, the *Custom Margins...* option opens the *Page Setup* dialog where you can specify exact margins.

To change the margins, on the *Page Layout* tab, in the *Page Setup* group, click the **Margins** button, and click one of the preset margins options: **Normal, Wide,** or **Narrow,** or click **Custom Margins...** to specify your own values.

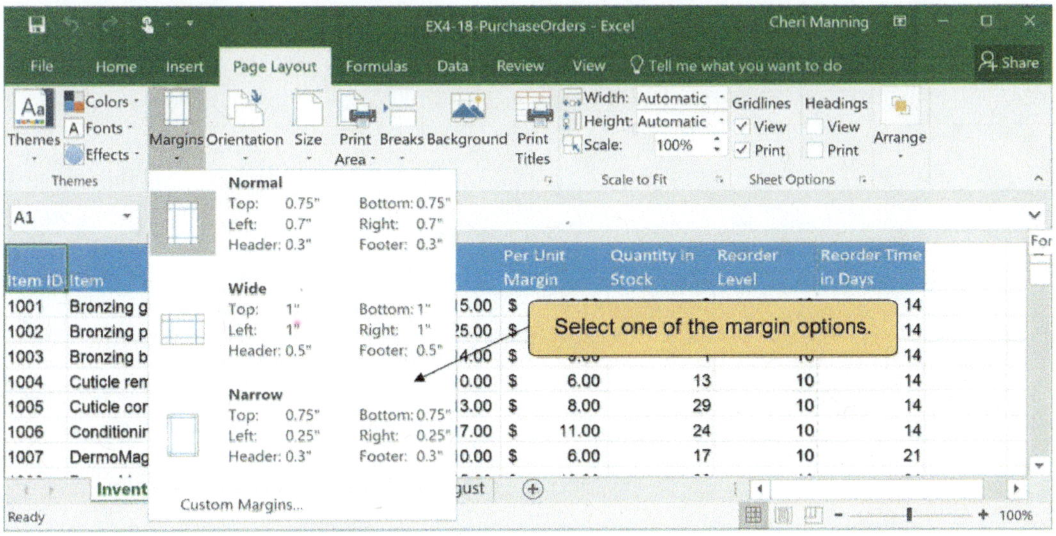

FIGURE EX 4.27

Because you will often want to adjust margins once you are ready to print, Excel allows you to adjust the margins directly from Backstage view.

1. Click the **File** tab to open Backstage view.
2. Click **Print**.
3. In the *Settings* section, click the button displaying the current margins setting, and then select the option you want.

let me try *Live!*

If you do not have the data file from the previous skill open, open the student data file **EX4-18-PurchaseOrders** and try this skill on your own:

1. Verify that the **Inventory** worksheet is active. If necessary, set the orientation back to **portrait**. Note the page break line between the *Reorder Level* and *Reorder Time in Days* columns.
2. Change the worksheet margins to the **Narrow** option.
3. Note the printable area has become larger and all the columns fit on one page now.
4. If you will be moving on to the next skill in this chapter, switch back to **Normal** margins and leave the workbook open to continue working. If not, save the file as directed by your instructor and close it.

Skill 4.19 Scaling Worksheets for Printing

When printing your worksheet, you can set the **scale** and specify that the worksheet prints at a percentage of the original size or at a maximum number of pages wide and/or tall. Each worksheet in the workbook has its own scale settings.

On the *Page Layout* tab, in the *Scale to Fit* group, select the option(s) you want.

- Click the **Width** arrow and select the maximum number of pages you want the worksheet to print across.
- Click the **Height** arrow and select the maximum number of pages you want the worksheet to print vertically.
- Click the **Scale** box and enter a percentage to grow or shrink the worksheet when printed.

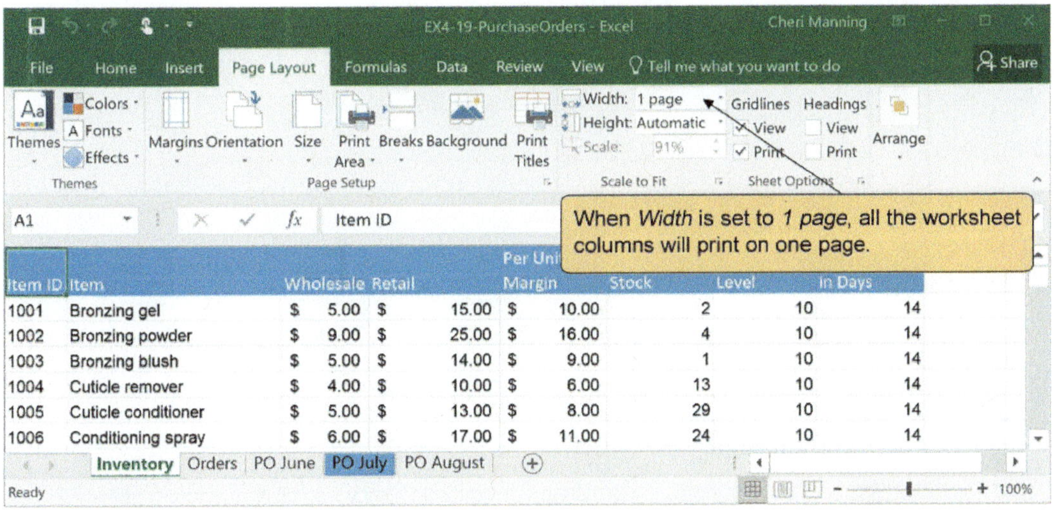

FIGURE EX 4.28

Because you often need to adjust scaling once you are ready to print, Excel has included scaling options on the Print page in Backstage view:

1. Click the **File** tab to open Backstage view.
2. Click **Print**.
3. In the *Settings* section, click the button displaying the current scaling setting and select the setting you want to use.

tips & tricks

When scaling your worksheet, be careful not to make the worksheet too small to read.

let me try *Live!*

If you do not have the data file from the previous skill open, open the student data file **EX4-19-PurchaseOrders** and try this skill on your own:

1. Verify that the **Inventory** worksheet is active. If necessary, switch the orientation back to **portrait** and the margins to **Normal**.
2. Set the scaling options so all the columns will print on one page across.
3. If you will be moving on to the next skill in this chapter, leave the workbook open to continue working. If not, save the file as directed by your instructor and close it.

Skill 4.20 Printing Titles

If your worksheet includes a large table of data that prints on more than one page, you should ensure that the column or row labels print on every page.

To repeat rows and columns on every printed page:

1. On the *Page Layout* tab, in the *Page Setup* group, click the **Print Titles** button.
2. In the *Page Setup* dialog, on the *Sheet* tab, click in the **Rows to repeat at top** box, and then click and drag to select the rows to repeat. You can also type the row reference(s) using the format $1:$1. This example would repeat the first row only.
3. Click in the **Columns to repeat at left** box, and then click and drag to select the columns to repeat. You can also type the column reference(s) using the format $A:$A. This example would repeat the first column only. $A:$B would repeat columns A and B on every printed page.
4. Click **OK**.

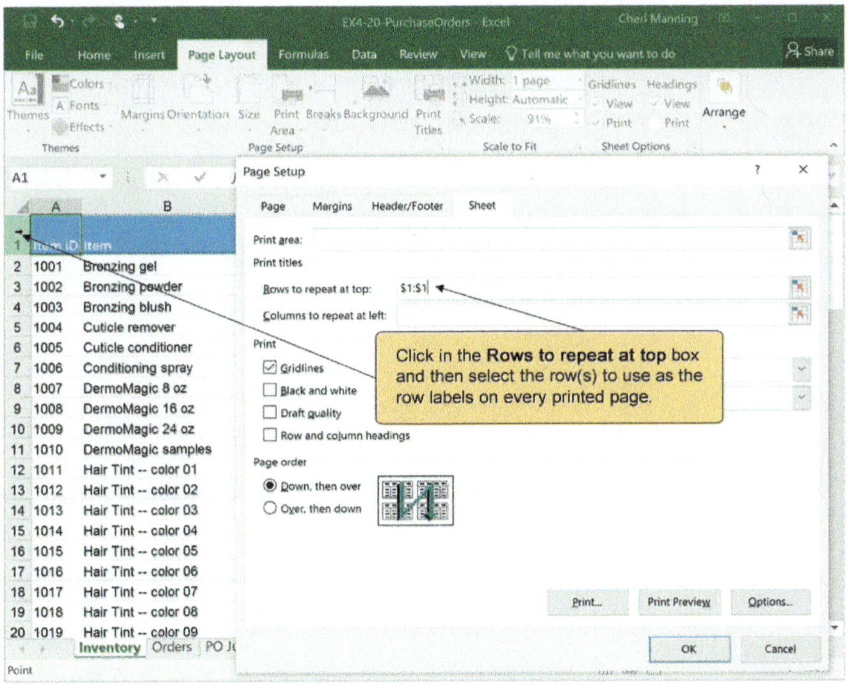

FIGURE EX 4.29

let me try *Live!*

If you do not have the data file from the previous skill open, open the student data file **EX4-20-PurchaseOrders** and try this skill on your own:

1. Verify that the **Inventory** worksheet is active. If necessary, check the worksheet *Headings* **View** option so the column letters and row numbers are visible. This will make it easier to understand which row is set to print on every page.
2. Set row **1** to print on every page.
3. Go to Backstage view and preview how the worksheet will look when printed. Verify that the titles from row 1 are included at the top of every page.
4. If you will be moving on to the next skill in this chapter, leave the workbook open to continue working. If not, save the file as directed by your instructor and close it.

Skill 4.21 Printing Selections, Worksheets, and Workbooks

By default, Excel will print the current, active worksheet. You can change the printing options, however, to print only part of a worksheet or the entire workbook at once.

1. Click the **File** tab to open Backstage view.
2. Click **Print.**
3. In the *Settings* section, the first button displays which part of the workbook will print. By default, **Print Active Sheets** is selected. To change the print selection, click the button, and then click one of the other options:
   - **Print Entire Workbook**—Prints all the sheets in the workbook.
   - **Print Selection**—Prints only the selected cells in the active worksheet, overriding any print area definitions in the active worksheet.
   - **Print Selected Table**—Prints the table only (available only if the current selection is within a defined table).
4. If you want to ignore the defined print area, click **Ignore Print Area** at the bottom of the list.
5. Click the **Print** button to print.

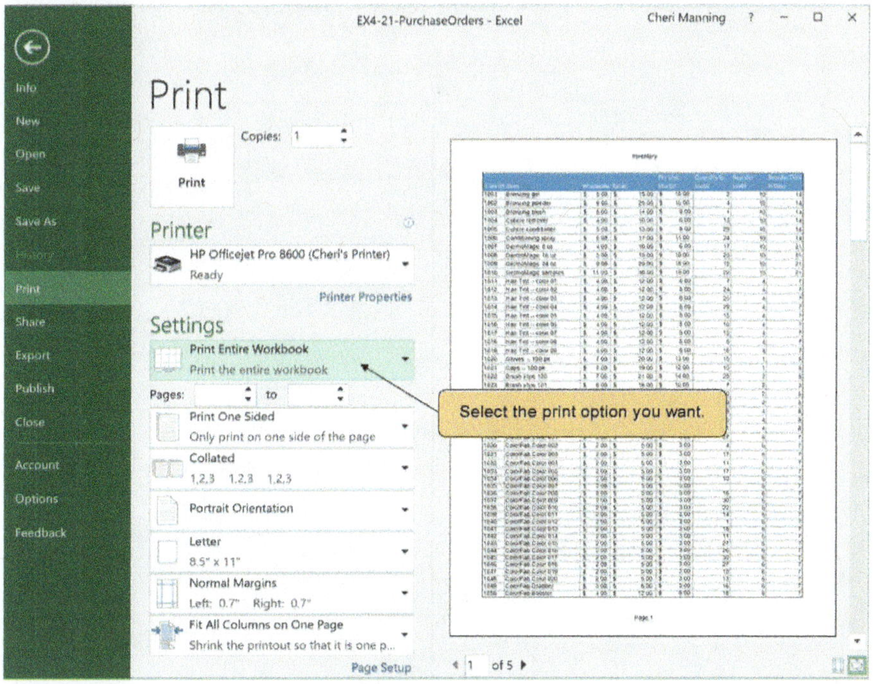

FIGURE EX 4.30

let me try *Live!*

If you do not have the data file from the previous skill open, open the student data file **EX4-21-PurchaseOrders** and try this skill on your own:

1. Change the print option to print the entire workbook.
2. Verify that all the worksheets in the workbook are included in the print preview.
3. Save the file as directed by your instructor and close it.

key terms

- **Group**
- **Theme**
- **Theme Colors**
- **Theme Fonts**
- **Theme Effects**
- **Freeze**
- **Normal view**
- **Page Layout view**
- **Page Break Preview view**
- **Header**
- **Footer**
- **Gridlines**
- **Headings**
- **Orientation**
- **Portrait orientation**
- **Landscape orientation**
- **Margins**
- **Scale**

concept review

1. If you delete a worksheet, you can undo the action.
   a. true
   b. false
2. To group worksheets that are not next to each other, select the first worksheet and press the ________ key, and then click the other sheet tabs you want included in the group.
   a. Shift
   b. Alt
   c. Ctrl
   d. None of the above
3. A ________ is a unified color, font, and effects scheme you apply to a workbook.
   a. style
   b. theme
   c. cell format
   d. conditional format
4. To keep column headings as you scroll through a large spreadsheet you should use the ________ command.
   a. *Freeze Top Row*
   b. *Freeze First Column*
   c. *Split*
   d. *View Headings*
5. When you hide a row or column, the data remain in your workbook. They are no longer displayed on-screen but will be part of the printed workbook.
   a. true
   b. false
6. To display a worksheet in two or four panes, you should ________ the worksheet.
   a. merge
   b. freeze
   c. split
   d. group

7. A ________________ is text that appears at the bottom of every page just above the margin.
   a. header
   b. footer
   c. headings
   d. sheet tab
8. ________________ are the numbers at the left of rows and the letters at the top of columns.
   a. Headings
   b. Headers
   c. Footers
   d. Gridlines
9. If your worksheet is wide, you may want to use portrait orientation where the height of the page is greater than the width.
   a. true
   b. false
10. If you want more or less white space around your worksheet area when printing, you should adjust the ________________.
    a. margins
    b. scaling
    c. orientation
    d. page size

projects

Data files for projects can be found by logging into your SIMnet account and going to the *Library* section.

skill review 4.1

In this project, you will work on an attendance log for a 16-week college course. For one section of the course, you will set up the sheet to print as an attendance sign-in sheet. For another section, you will set up the sheet to print as an attendance report for the administration office. This is a long project. Be sure to save often!

Skills needed to complete this project:

- Naming Worksheets (Skill 4.2)
- Changing the Color of Sheet Tabs (Skill 4.3)
- Moving and Copying Worksheets (Skill 4.4)
- Grouping Worksheets (Skill 4.6)
- Modifying Column Widths and Row Heights (Skill 4.9)
- Changing the Worksheet View (Skill 4.13)
- Adding Headers and Footers (Skill 4.14)
- Applying Themes (Skill 4.8)
- Splitting Workbooks (Skill 4.12)
- Inserting and Deleting Rows and Columns (Skill 4.7)
- Deleting Worksheets (Skill 4.5)
- Freezing and Unfreezing Rows and Columns (Skill 4.10)
- Hiding and Unhiding Rows and Columns (Skill 4.11)
- Changing Worksheet Orientation (Skill 4.17)
- Setting Up Margins for Printing (Skill 4.18)
- Scaling Worksheets for Printing (Skill 4.19)
- Showing and Hiding Worksheet Elements (Skill 4.16)
- Printing Selections, Worksheets, and Workbooks (Skill 4.21)
- Printing Titles (Skill 4.20)
- Inserting Page Breaks (Skill 4.15)

1. Open the start file **EX2016-SkillReview-4-1** and resave the file as: `[your initials]EX-SkillReview-4-1`
2. If the workbook opens in Protected View, click the **Enable Editing** button in the Message Bar at the top of the workbook so you can modify the workbook.
3. Rename *Sheet1* and change the color of the sheet tab.
   a. Right-click on the *Sheet1* tab, choose **Rename,** and type: `TTh300`
   b. Press Enter.

c. Right-click the sheet tab again, point to **Tab Color,** and select **Green, Accent 6** (the last color in the first row of theme colors).

4. Make a copy of the *TTh300* sheet.
   a. Right-click the sheet tab and select **Move or Copy...** to open the *Move or Copy* dialog.
   b. In the *Before sheet* box, select **Sheet2.**
   c. Check the **Create a copy** check box.
   d. Click **OK.**
5. Name the new sheet **TTh301** and change the tab color.
   a. Right-click the new *TTh300 (2)* sheet tab, choose **Rename,** and type: `TTh301`
   b. Press Enter.
   c. Right-click the sheet tab again, point to **Tab Color,** and select **Blue, Accent 5** (the second color from the right in the first row of theme colors).
6. Group sheets *TTh300* and *TTh301* so you can apply formatting changes to both sheets at once.
   a. Click the **TTh300** sheet tab, press and hold Ctrl, and click the **TTh301** sheet tab. Now any changes made to one of the sheets will be made to both sheets.
   b. Verify that [Group] appears in the title bar, indicating that the selected sheets are grouped.
7. Resize **column A** in both worksheets at once to best fit the data by double-clicking the right border of the column heading.
8. Add a header and footer to both worksheets at once.
   a. Switch to Page Layout view by clicking the **Page Layout** button on the status bar.
   b. Click in the center section of the header.
   c. On the *Header & Footer Tools Design* tab, in the *Header & Footer Elements* group, click the **File Name** button. The code **&[File]** will be entered in the center section of the header. Once you click somewhere else, this will display the name of your file.
   d. Click in the right section of the header and type your own name.
   e. On the *Header & Footer Tools Design* tab, in the *Navigation* group, click the **Go to Footer** button.
   f. Click in the center section of the footer.
   g. On the *Header & Footer Tools Design* tab, in the *Header & Footer Elements* group, click the **Sheet Name** button. The code **&[Tab]** will be entered. Once you click somewhere else, this will display the name of the sheet.
   h. Click in the right section of the footer.
   i. On the *Header & Footer Tools Design* tab, in the *Header & Footer Elements* group, click the **Current Date** button. Once you click somewhere else, this will display the current date.

j. Click in any cell of the worksheet and click the **Normal** button on the status bar.

9. Ungroup the sheets by clicking *Sheet2.* Verify that the same formatting was applied to both sheets and that they are now ungrouped.
10. Apply the **Integral** theme to the workbook.
    a. On the *Page Layout* tab, in the *Themes* group, click the **Themes** button to display the *Themes* gallery.
    b. Notice that as you hover the mouse pointer over each option in the *Themes* gallery, Excel updates the worksheet to display a live preview of how the theme would affect the worksheet.
    c. Click the **Integral** option.
11. Select the **TTh300** sheet. It can be difficult to work with such a wide worksheet. Scroll to the right to see the end of the semester, and you can no longer see the student names. Split the screen into two views of different parts of this worksheet.
    a. Click cell **D1.** On the *View* tab, in the *Window* group, click the **Split** button. Now you can scroll each pane separately, but it is all still the same worksheet. You can drag the split bar to the right or left as needed.
    b. Scroll to show the student names and the last few weeks of the semester on your screen.
    c. Click the **Split** button again to return to normal.
12. Insert a new row to add a new student to the list.
    a. Right-click on the row heading for row number **9** and select **Insert**.
    b. Click the **Insert Options** button that appears immediately below where you right-clicked, and select **Format Same As Below**.
    c. Enter the new student name: **`Aaron, Kayla`**
    d. Enter her student ID #: **`1350679`**
13. Select the **TTh301** sheet. Because this sheet was copied from the TTh300 class worksheet, the student names and ID numbers are not those of the students in TTh301 class. Copy the student data from *Sheet2,* and then delete *Sheet2* when it is no longer needed.
    a. On sheet *TTh301*, select cells **A9:B29**. Press [Delete] to delete the content.
    b. Go to **Sheet2** and copy the student names and ID numbers from cells **A2:B20**.
    c. Paste the copied names and ID numbers to cell **A9** in the *TTh301* sheet.
    d. Delete *Sheet2* by right-clicking on the sheet name and selecting **Delete**.
    e. When Excel displays the message telling you that you can't undo deleting sheets, click the **Delete** button to complete the action.
14. Jay Parson has decided to drop the class. Remove him from the TTh301 class roster.

   a. On worksheet *TTh301*, delete the entire row for Jay by right-clicking on the row heading for row number **21** and selecting **Delete**.
15. Use the *Freeze Panes* option to keep rows 1:8 and columns A:B visible at all times.
   a. Verify that the *TTh301* sheet is selected, and click cell **C9**.
   b. On the *View* tab, in the *Window* group, click the **Freeze Panes** button, then click the **Freeze Panes** option.
   c. Verify that you selected the correct point at which to freeze panes. Scroll down and to the right. Are rows 1:8 and columns A:B visible regardless of where you scroll?
16. Modify sheet *TTh301* to print as an attendance sign-in sheet.
17. First, hide the student ID numbers by right-clicking on the **column B** heading and selecting **Hide**.
18. Set the page layout options.
   a. On the *Page Layout* tab, in the *Page Setup* group, click the **Orientation** button, and select **Landscape**.
   b. On the *Page Layout* tab, in the *Page Setup* group, click the **Margins** button, and select **Narrow**.
   c. On the *Page Layout* tab, in the *Scale to Fit* group, expand the **Width** list and select **1 page,** and expand the **Height** list and select **1 page**.
   d. On the *Page Layout* tab, in the *Sheet Options* group, click the **Print** check box under **Gridlines**.
19. Print only the part of the worksheet to use as the attendance sign-in sheet.
   a. Select the appropriate cells to print as an attendance sign-in by selecting cells **A1:C26**.
   b. Click the **File** tab to open Backstage view, and then click **Print** to display the Print page.
   c. Under *Settings,* click the **Print Active Sheets** button to expand the options, and select **Print Selection**.
   d. If your instructor has directed you to print the attendance sign-in list, click the **Print** button.
   e. Click the **Back** arrow to exit Backstage view.
20. At the end of the semester you will need to print all the attendance records to turn in to the administration office. Let's set this up for the *TTh300* class worksheet.
21. Select the **TTh300** worksheet, and hide the attendance sign-in column by right-clicking the **column C** heading and selecting **Hide**.
22. Modify the worksheet so column A and rows 1 through 8 will print on every page.
   a. On the *Page Layout* tab, in the *Page Setup* group, click the **Print Titles** button.

b. Click in the **Rows to repeat at top** box, and then click and drag with the mouse to select rows **1:8**. When you release the mouse button, you should see $1:$8 in the box.
c. Click in the **Columns to repeat at left** box, and then click with the mouse to select column **A**. When you release the mouse button, you should see $A:$A in the box.
d. Click **OK**.

23. Preview how the worksheet will look when printed and make adjustments from the Print page to keep the report to four or fewer pages.
    a. Click the **File** tab to open Backstage view, and then click **Print**.
    b. Verify **Print Active Sheets** is selected under *Settings*.
    c. Note that the current settings will cause the worksheet to print on five pages.
    d. Under *Settings*, click the **Portrait Orientation** button and switch to **Landscape Orientation** instead.
    e. Under *Settings*, click the **Normal Margins** button, and select **Custom Margins...** to set your own margins.
    f. In the *Page Setup* dialog, on the *Margins* tab, change the **Top, Bottom, Left,** and **Right** values to **0.5**. Click **OK**.
    g. Under *Settings*, click the **No Scaling** button, and select **Fit All Rows on One Page**.
24. Modify the worksheet page breaks so weeks 1-8 print on the first page and weeks 9-16 print on the second page.
    a. Click the **Back** arrow to exit Backstage.
    b. If necessary, scroll to the right so columns T:V are visible. Note that the current page break occurs between columns U and V (after week 9).
    c. Click cell **T1**.
    d. On the *Page Layout* tab, in the *Page Setup* group, click the **Breaks** button, and select **Insert Page Break**. This inserts a page break to the left of the selected cell (after week 8).
    e. Click the **File** tab to open Backstage view, and then click **Print** to preview how the change will affect the printed pages.
    f. If your instructor has directed you to print the worksheet, click the **Print** button.
    g. Click the **Back** arrow to exit Backstage view.
25. Save and close the workbook.

projects

Data files for projects can be found by logging into your SIMnet account and going to the *Library* section.

skill review 4.2

In this project, you will be working with a workbook designed to plan employees' or volunteers' work schedules.

Skills needed to complete this project:

- Naming Worksheets (Skill 4.2)
- Changing the Color of Sheet Tabs (Skill 4.3)
- Deleting Worksheets (Skill 4.5)
- Applying Themes (Skill 4.8)
- Grouping Worksheets (Skill 4.6)
- Modifying Column Widths and Row Heights (Skill 4.9)
- Splitting Workbooks (Skill 4.12)
- Freezing and Unfreezing Rows and Columns (Skill 4.10)
- Moving and Copying Worksheets (Skill 4.4)
- Hiding and Unhiding Rows and Columns (Skill 4.11)
- Showing and Hiding Worksheet Elements (Skill 4.16)
- Changing the Worksheet View (Skill 4.13)
- Adding Headers and Footers (Skill 4.14)
- Changing Worksheet Orientation (Skill 4.17)
- Setting Up Margins for Printing (Skill 4.18)
- Scaling Worksheets for Printing (Skill 4.19)
- Inserting Page Breaks (Skill 4.15)
- Printing Titles (Skill 4.20)
- Printing Selections, Worksheets, and Workbooks (Skill 4.21)

1. Open the start file **EX2016-SkillReview-4-2** and resave the file as:
   `[your initials]EX-SkillReview-4-2`
2. If the workbook opens in Protected View, click the **Enable Editing** button in the Message Bar at the top of the workbook so you can modify the workbook.
3. Look at the various worksheets. The monthly schedule worksheets need to be named and color coded.
   a. Double-click the tab for **Sheet 1,** type January and press Enter.
   b. Right-click the tab, point to **Tab Color,** and select **Orange, Accent 2** (the fifth color from the right in the top row of theme colors).
   c. Double-click the tab for **Sheet 2,** type February and press Enter.
   d. Right-click the tab, point to **Tab Color,** and select **Gold, Accent 4** (the third

color from the right in the top row of theme colors).

e. Double-click the tab for **Sheet 3,** type March and press Enter.

f. Right-click the tab, point to **Tab Color,** and select **Blue, Accent 5** (the second color from the right in the top row of theme colors).

4. The *Sheet 4* worksheet is unnecessary. Delete it.

   a. Click the **Sheet 4** tab.

   b. On the *Home* tab, in the *Cells* group, click the **Delete** button arrow and select **Delete Sheet.**

   c. Click the **Delete** button when prompted.

5. Apply a new theme to the workbook.

   a. On the *Page Layout* tab, in the *Themes* group, click the **Themes** button. Slide the mouse over different themes and notice the preview of the theme appearance on the worksheet.

   b. Choose the **Ion** theme.

6. The monthly schedule sheets all need formatting. Group them and then format them all at once.

   a. Click the **January** sheet tab, hold down Shift, click the **March** sheet tab, and then release Shift. Notice the three sheet tabs' appearance has changed to indicate that the three are selected. The *Regular Schedule* tab is not selected.

   b. Verify that the title bar displays [Group]. Any changes you make to the current sheet will be made to all three of the selected sheets, so be very careful.

7. Adjust column widths and row heights to fit the contents and to make the worksheet more readable.

   a. Look in column **A**. If you see ########### it means that the cell content is too wide for the column. Double-click the right column border to autofit the column to the data.

   b. Select all the time columns (**B:U**). Locate the columns that are too narrow to display both the *From* time and the *To* time. Double-click the right column border to best fit the column width to the content. All the selected columns will size to match.

   c. Select all the rows (**5:35**).

   d. On the *Home* tab, in the *Cells* group click the **Format** button, and select **Row Height**. In the *Row Height* dialog, change the height value to **18** to make each row a little roomier.

   e. Click **OK.**

8. Ungroup the sheets by clicking the *Regular Schedule* sheet.

   a. Look at the *January, February,* and *March* sheets; they should all have been formatted.

b. Verify that the sheets are now ungrouped.

9. Select just the **Regular Schedule** sheet. It is hard to work with such a wide worksheet. Scroll to the right to see the night shift and you can no longer see the dates. Split the screen into two views of different parts of this worksheet.
   a. Click cell **G1**. On the *View* tab, in the *Window* group, click the **Split** button. Now you can scroll each pane separately, but it is all still the same worksheet. You can drag the split bar to the right or left as needed.
   b. Scroll to show the morning and night shifts on your screen.
   c. Click the **Split** button again to return to normal.
10. Another way to deal with large worksheets is to freeze panes.
   a. Select any one of the month worksheets.
   b. Select cell **B5**. On the *View* tab, in the *Window* group, click **Freeze Panes,** and select **Freeze Panes**.
   c. Now you can scroll up or down and everything above and to the left of B5 remains visibly frozen on the screen.
   d. Freeze panes must be set on each of the month sheets separately. Grouping does not work for freeze panes. Repeat the freeze panes process for each of the month worksheets.
11. Drag the sheet tab for **Regular Schedule** before the sheet tab for **January** so that *Regular Schedule* is the first worksheet in the workbook.
12. Look closely at the *Regular Schedule* sheet. There are two row numbers missing.
   a. Select the rows before and after the missing rows. Select the entire rows by dragging over the row heading numbers at the far left.
   b. With both rows selected, right-click on the selection, and select **Unhide** to reveal the rows for Tuesdays and Wednesdays.
13. Ensure that the worksheet gridlines will print with the worksheet.
   a. On the *Page Layout* tab, in the *Sheet Options* group, click the **Print** check box under *Gridlines.*
   b. Repeat this process for the *January, February,* and *March* worksheets. (If you group the sheets first, be sure to ungroup them when you are finished.)
14. Prepare to print your worksheets by adding headers and footers. You will need to use the *Page Setup* dialog instead of Page Layout view because your worksheets have *Freeze Panes* applied.
   a. Group all the worksheets to save time. This way the headers and footers may be added to all the sheets at once. Verify that all the sheets are selected.
   b. On the *Page Layout* tab, in the *Page Setup* group, click the **Page Setup dialog launcher** button.
   c. In the *Page Setup* dialog, click the **Header/Footer** tab.
   d. Click the **Custom Header...** button.
   e. Click in the **Center section** and then click the **Insert File Name** button.

   f. Click **OK**.
   g. Click the **Custom Footer**... button.
   h. Click in the **Center section** and then click the **Insert Sheet Name** button.
   i. Click **OK**.
   j. Click **OK** again to close the *Page Setup* dialog.
   k. Ungroup the sheets. Right-click on any sheet tab and choose **Ungroup Sheets**.
15. Set up printing options for the *Regular Schedule* sheet.
   a. Select the **Regular Schedule** sheet. Click the **File** tab, and then click **Print**.
   b. Scroll down to see all the pages for your worksheet. Scroll back up to the first page.
   c. Click the **Portrait Orientation** button and select **Landscape**.
   d. Click the **Normal Margins** button and select **Narrow**.
   e. Click the **No Scaling** button, and select **Fit Sheet on One Page**.
16. The monthly schedules would be easier to read if the morning, afternoon, and night shifts each printed on a separate page in a reasonably large font size.
   a. Click the **Back** arrow to return to the worksheet.
   b. Group sheets **January:March**.
   c. On the *Page Layout* tab, in the *Page Setup* group, click the **Orientation** button, and select **Landscape**.
   d. On the *Page Layout* tab, in the *Page Setup* group, click the **Margins** button, and select **Narrow**.
   e. Review the current page break. Switch to Page Break Preview view if you want by clicking the **Page Break Preview** button at the lower right corner of the status bar.
   f. Notice that the schedule just barely requires two pages vertically. On the *Page Layout* tab, in the *Scale to Fit* group, click the **Height** box arrow and select **1 Page**.
   g. Click cell **I1**. On the *Page Layout* tab, in the *Page Setup* group, click the **Breaks** button. Select **Insert Page Break**. (Note that you cannot drag the page break lines when the worksheets are grouped. You must use the Ribbon method to insert manual page breaks.)
   h. Click in cell **N1**. On the *Page Layout* tab, in the *Page Setup* group, click the **Breaks** button. Select **Insert Page Break**.
   i. Click the **Normal** button to return to Normal view.
17. The days will show only on the first sheet, so the second and third sheets will make no sense. Set the worksheets so column A will print on every page. You must ungroup the sheets first.
   a. Click the **Regular Schedule** sheet to ungroup the sheets, and then click the **January** sheet tab again.

b. On the *Page Layout* tab, in the *Page Setup* group, click **Print Titles** button.
c. In the *Columns to repeat at left* box enter $A:$A or click in the box and then click anywhere in column **A**.
d. Click **OK** in the *Page Setup* dialog.
e. Repeat this process with the **February** and **March** worksheets.

18. Preview how the entire workbook will print. Be sure to verify that column A will print at the left side of the *January, February,* and *March* worksheets.
    a. Click the **File** tab to open Backstage view.
    b. Click **Print**.
    c. Click the **Print Active Sheets** button and select **Print Entire Workbook**.
    d. Use the **Next Page** button below the print preview to review how every printed page will look. There should be 10 pages. Note the worksheet name in the footer area at the bottom of each page.
19. Save and close the workbook.

projects

Data files for projects can be found by logging into your SIMnet account and going to the *Library* section.

challenge yourself 4.3

In this project, you will be working with a workbook used to analyze loan payments.

Skills needed to complete this project:

- Naming Worksheets (Skill 4.2)
- Applying Themes (Skill 4.8)
- Changing the Color of Sheet Tabs (Skill 4.3)
- Changing the Worksheet View (Skill 4.13)
- Adding Headers and Footers (Skill 4.14)
- Freezing and Unfreezing Rows and Columns (Skill 4.10)
- Moving and Copying Worksheets (Skill 4.4)
- Inserting and Deleting Rows and Columns (Skill 4.7)
- Grouping Worksheets (Skill 4.6)
- Modifying Column Widths and Row Heights (Skill 4.9)
- Hiding and Unhiding Rows and Columns (Skill 4.11)
- Showing and Hiding Worksheet Elements (Skill 4.16)
- Deleting Worksheets (Skill 4.5)
- Changing Worksheet Orientation (Skill 4.17)
- Printing Titles (Skill 4.20)
- Scaling Worksheets for Printing (Skill 4.19)
- Printing Selections, Worksheets, and Workbooks (Skill 4.21)

1. Open the start file **EX2016-ChallengeYourself-4-3** and resave the file as: `[your initials]EX-ChallengeYourself-4-3`
2. If the workbook opens in Protected View, click the **Enable Editing** button in the Message Bar at the top of the workbook so you can modify the workbook.
3. Change the name of *Sheet1* to: `NewTruck`
4. Apply the **Organic** theme.
5. Change the *NewTruck* sheet tab color to **Red, Accent 4** (the third color from the right in the top row of theme colors).
6. Add header and footer information to the *NewTruck* worksheet.
   a. Set the left header section to display the sheet name.
   b. Add the page number to the center footer section.
   c. Set the right footer section to display the current date.
7. Freeze panes so rows **1:8** and columns **A:B** remain in place when you scroll through the worksheets.

8. Make a copy of the *NewTruck* sheet, placing before the *Temp* worksheet.
9. Change the name of the new sheet to: **`Option2`**
10. Change the *Option2* sheet tab color to **Gold, Accent 6** (the first color at the right in the top row of theme colors).
11. Change the values in the *Option2* worksheet.
    a. Change the amount borrowed (cell **B3**) to: **`12,000`**
    b. Change the APR (cell **B5**) to: **`3.5%`**
12. Delete any extra rows at the bottom of the worksheet where the payment due is 0 (rows **40:41**).
13. Group the *NewTruck* and *Option2* worksheets. Make the following changes to both sheets at once.
14. Change the width of the *Payment Date* column (column **C**) to exactly **19**.
15. Delete the extra column (column **H**).
16. Unhide column **G**.
17. Hide the gridlines so they do not appear on-screen.
18. Ungroup the worksheets.
19. Delete the *Temp* worksheet.
20. Change the page orientation for the *NewTruck* sheet to **Landscape**.
21. Modify the *NewTruck* sheet so row **8** will repeat at the top of every printed page.
22. Scale the *Option2* sheet so all columns will fit on one page and all rows will fit on one page.
23. Print preview the entire workbook.
24. Save and close the workbook.

projects

Data files for projects can be found by logging into your SIMnet account and going to the *Library* section.

challenge yourself 4.4

In this project, you will be working with data about automobile emissions and fuel economy. These green car data were downloaded from the Web site fueleconomy.gov. The SmartWay scores range from 0 to 10, where 10 is best. The vehicles with the best scores on both air pollution and greenhouse gas receive the Elite designation. More information about the SmartWay program can be found at http://www3.epa.gov/greenvehicles/you/smartway.htm.

Skills needed to complete this project:

- Naming Worksheets (Skill 4.2)
- Applying Themes (Skill 4.8)
- Changing the Color of Sheet Tabs (Skill 4.3)
- Changing the Worksheet View (Skill 4.13)
- Adding Headers and Footers (Skill 4.14)
- Moving and Copying Worksheets (Skill 4.4)
- Inserting and Deleting Rows and Columns (Skill 4.7)
- Grouping Worksheets (Skill 4.6)
- Modifying Column Widths and Row Heights (Skill 4.9)
- Hiding and Unhiding Rows and Columns (Skill 4.11)
- Showing and Hiding Worksheet Elements (Skill 4.16)
- Setting Up Margins for Printing (Skill 4.18)
- Changing Worksheet Orientation (Skill 4.17)
- Scaling Worksheets for Printing (Skill 4.19)
- Printing Titles (Skill 4.20)
- Freezing and Unfreezing Rows and Columns (Skill 4.10)
- Inserting Page Breaks (Skill 4.15)
- Printing Selections, Worksheets, and Workbooks (Skill 4.21)

1. Open the start file **EX2016-ChallengeYourself-4-4** and resave the file as: `[your initials]EX-ChallengeYourself-4-4`
2. If the workbook opens in Protected View, click the **Enable Editing** button in the Message Bar at the top of the workbook so you can modify the workbook.
3. Rename the *all_alpha_10* worksheet: `Raw Data`
4. Apply the **Facet** workbook theme.
5. Color the *Raw Data* worksheet tab **Dark Green, Accent 2** (the fifth color from the right in the first row of theme colors).

6. Review the worksheet header and footer.
   a. Delete the text in the left footer section and replace it with: **`Source: fueleconomy.gov`**
   b. Add the sheet name to the footer center section. *Hint:* Do not type the sheet name in the footer. Insert a code so Excel will display the name of the current worksheet.
7. Copy the *Raw Data* worksheet. Place the new worksheet at the end of the workbook.
8. Rename the new worksheet: **`Tesla`**
9. Color the *Tesla* worksheet tab **Green, Accent 1** (the sixth color from the right in the first row of theme colors).
10. In the *Tesla* worksheet, delete rows **2:383** and then delete rows **14:92** so only the 12 Tesla models remain.
11. Group the *Raw Data* and *Tesla* worksheets.
12. Autofit column **K** to best fit the data.
13. Set the column width for columns **L:Q** to: **`5`**
14. Set the row height for row **1** to: **`65`**
15. Hide the **Underhood ID** and **Stnd Description** columns.
16. Set the worksheet gridlines to print.
17. Set **Wide** margins.
18. Set the worksheet orientation to **Landscape**.
19. Scale the worksheets so all columns will print on one page.
20. Ungroup the sheets.
21. Set the worksheet options so row **1** will print on every page. You will need to do this individually for each worksheet.
22. Review the page breaks in the *Raw Data* worksheet. Move the page break between pages 3 and 4 to after row **106** so the fourth page begins with the first Fiat model.
23. Apply **Freeze Panes** to the *Raw Data* worksheet so the first row is always visible as you scroll down the worksheet.
24. Preview how the entire workbook will print.
25. Save and close the workbook.

projects

Data files for projects can be found by logging into your SIMnet account and going to the *Library* section.

on your own 4.5

In this project you will work with data from the United States Census Bureau. The data were downloaded from http://www.census.gov/popest/data/state/totals/2015/index.html.

Skills needed to complete this project:

- Moving and Copying Worksheets (Skill 4.4)
- Naming Worksheets (Skill 4.2)
- Applying Themes (Skill 4.8)
- Changing the Color of Sheet Tabs (Skill 4.3)
- Inserting and Deleting Rows and Columns (Skill 4.7)
- Modifying Column Widths and Row Heights (Skill 4.9)
- Changing the Worksheet View (Skill 4.13)
- Adding Headers and Footers (Skill 4.14)
- Freezing and Unfreezing Rows and Columns (Skill 4.10)
- Changing Worksheet Orientation (Skill 4.17)
- Setting Up Margins for Printing (Skill 4.18)
- Scaling Worksheets for Printing (Skill 4.19)
- Showing and Hiding Worksheet Elements (Skill 4.16)
- Inserting Page Breaks (Skill 4.15)
- Printing Selections, Worksheets, and Workbooks (Skill 4.21)

1. Open the start file **EX2016-OnYourOwn-4-5** and resave the file as: `[your initials]EX-OnYourOwn-4-5`
2. If the workbook opens in Protected View, click the **Enable Editing** button in the Message Bar at the top of the workbook so you can modify the workbook.
3. The workbook includes one worksheet with census data for regions and individual states. Create one or more copies of the original worksheet and modify the data in each so each worksheet has a unique set of data.
4. Delete any rows you do not want to include in each worksheet. *Hint:* The Note near the bottom of the original worksheet is very long and will print across multiple pages. You may want to delete it or move it to a cell with *Wrap Text* applied.
5. Rename each worksheet.
6. Apply a theme of your choice to the workbook.
7. Apply a color to the tab of each worksheet.

8. Add a row at the top of each sheet and enter an appropriate title.
9. Adjust column widths to best fit the data (all worksheets individually).
10. Add header and footer elements of your choice to all the worksheets at once. *Hint:* You may want to move the suggested citation from the last rows in the worksheet into the worksheet footer.
11. As appropriate, apply *Freeze Panes* to make it easier to work with each worksheet.
12. Apply cell styles and cell formatting to make the data easier to read.
13. Make an attractive readable printout of each worksheet. Each should fit neatly on one page or have logical page breaks and print titles when more than one page is required. Print the worksheets only if directed to do so by your instructor.
    a. Set the worksheets' orientation appropriately.
    b. Set appropriate margins.
    c. Scale the worksheets appropriately.
    d. Add manual page breaks if necessary.
    e. Set at least one of the sheets to print with gridlines and at least one to print without gridlines.
    f. For worksheets that print on more than one page, ensure that the label row will be included on every page.
    g. For one worksheet, adjust the print settings to print a useful selection of just some cells that will fit all on one page.
14. Save and close the workbook.

projects

Data files for projects can be found by logging into your SIMnet account and going to the *Library* section.

fix it 4.6

In this project, you will correct errors in a party planning workbook.

Skills needed to complete this project:

- Changing the Worksheet View (Skill 4.13)
- Applying Themes (Skill 4.8)
- Deleting Worksheets (Skill 4.5)
- Adding Headers and Footers (Skill 4.14)
- Showing and Hiding Worksheet Elements (Skill 4.16)
- Naming Worksheets (Skill 4.2)
- Moving and Copying Worksheets (Skill 4.4)
- Modifying Column Widths and Row Heights (Skill 4.9)
- Inserting and Deleting Rows and Columns (Skill 4.7)
- Hiding and Unhiding Rows and Columns (Skill 4.11)
- Changing Worksheet Orientation (Skill 4.17)
- Setting Up Margins for Printing (Skill 4.18)
- Scaling Worksheets for Printing (Skill 4.19)
- Freezing and Unfreezing Rows and Columns (Skill 4.10)
- Printing Titles (Skill 4.20)
- Inserting Page Breaks (Skill 4.15)

1. Open the start file **EX2016-FixIt-4-6** and resave the file as:
   `[your initials]EX-FixIt-4-6`
2. If the workbook opens in Protected View, click the **Enable Editing** button in the Message Bar at the top of the workbook so you can modify the workbook.
3. The workbook was last saved in Page Break Preview view. Switch it back to Normal view.
4. The workbook uses a very unattractive theme. Change the theme to **Office**.
5. The copy of the *Shopping List* worksheet is incomplete. Delete it. Be careful to delete the copy, not the original.
6. Both worksheets should include the sheet name in the header center section.
7. Both worksheets should include the gridlines when printed.
8. Correct the following errors in the *Shopping List* worksheet:
   a. The worksheet tab is misspelled. Correct the spelling of *Shopping*.
   b. The *Shoping List* worksheet should be first in the workbook.

c. One of the columns is not wide enough to display the data. Autofit that column.
d. There is an extra row between the label row and the shopping data. Delete the extra row.

9. Correct the following errors in the *Guest List* worksheet:
   a. Column **D** should not be visible.
   b. Row **3** is too tall. Autofit the row to fit the content.
   c. Page orientation should be **Portrait**.
   d. Margins should be set to the **Narrow** option.
   e. All columns should fit on one page when printed.
   f. The footer center section should include the page number.
   g. Rows **1:3** should always be visible as you scroll down the worksheet. *Hint:* Select the entire row where you want to apply the *Freeze Panes* command.
   h. Rows **1:3** should also print on every page.
   i. The page break should be between rows **53** and **54** so the guests who have not yet RSVP'd are grouped together on the second page.
   j. If you were working in Page Layout view or Page Break Preview view, be sure to switch back to **Normal** view.
10. Review your work by previewing how each worksheet will print and then save and close the workbook.

chapter

5

Adding Charts and Analyzing Data

In this chapter, you will learn the following skills:

- Create and format charts
- Create and format tables
- Sort and filter data
- Create PivotTables and PivotCharts
- Conduct what-if analysis using Goal Seek and data tables

Skill 5.17	Filtering Data
Skill 5.18	Filtering Table Data with Slicers
Skill 5.19	Converting Tables to Ranges
Skill 5.20	Creating PivotTables Using Recommended PivotTables
Skill 5.21	Creating a PivotChart from a PivotTable
Skill 5.22	Analyzing Data with Data Tables
Skill 5.23	Analyzing Data with Goal Seek

introduction

This chapter introduces data analysis. You will learn to use charts to visualize data; to use tables and PivotTables to quickly sort, filter, and summarize data; and to conduct what-if analyses using data tables and Goal Seek.

Skill 5.1 Exploring Charts

A **chart** is a graphic that represents numeric data visually. In a chart, the values selected in the worksheet, the **data points**, are transformed into graphic **data markers**. Data markers can be columns, bars, pie pieces, lines, or other visual elements. Related data points, usually in the same row or column, are grouped into a **data series**. Some chart types allow you to plot multiple data series.

Figure EX 5.1 shows a column chart with a single data series—*Services - Individual*. You can tell at a glance that the FEB column is the shortest and, therefore, that February has the fewest sales for individual services.

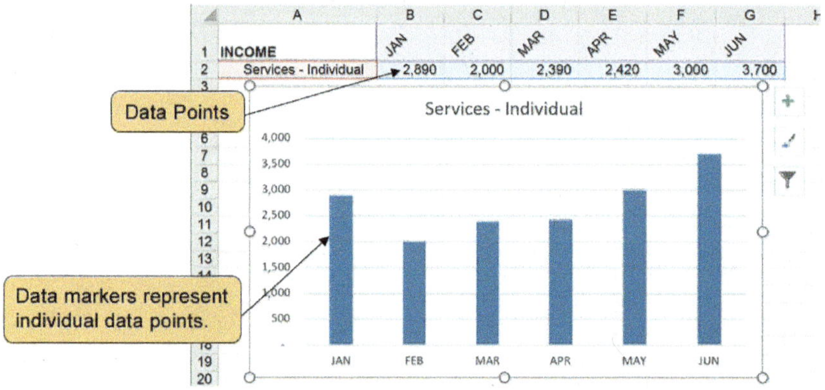

FIGURE EX 5.1

Figure 5.2 is a pie chart using the same data as Figure 5.1. Each individual data point is represented by a piece of the pie. In this chart, it is not as obvious that FEB is the smallest data point.

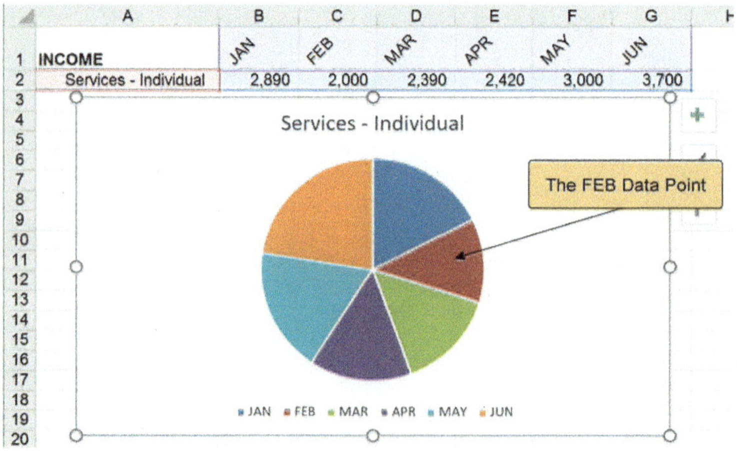

FIGURE EX 5.2

Most charts plot data along two axes. The **y axis** goes from bottom to top. It is the vertical axis. The **x axis** goes from left to right. It is the horizontal axis. Typically, but not always, values are plotted against the y axis and categories are listed along the x axis.

When working with charts, there are a few other common chart elements you should be familiar with:

- The **plot area** is the area where the data series are plotted.
- The **chart area** is the area that encompasses the entire chart including the plot area and optional layout elements, such as title and legend.
- The **chart title** is a text box above or overlaying the chart.
- The **legend** tells you which data point or data series is represented by each color in the chart.

When a chart is selected, two contextual tabs are available: the *Chart Tools Design* tab and the *Chart Tools Format* tab. On the *Chart Tools Format* tab, in the *Current Selection* group, the *Chart Elements* box displays the name of the chart element that is currently selected. This can be helpful if you need to ensure that you have selected the chart area, the plot area, or another chart element. To select a specific chart element, expand the **Chart Elements** list and select the chart element you want to select.

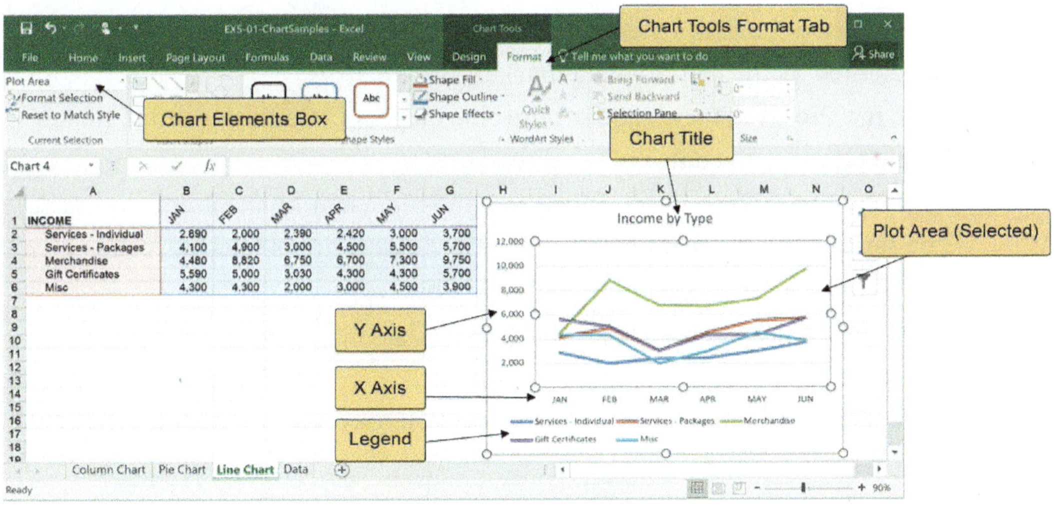

FIGURE EX 5.3

tips & tricks

Because charts make it easier to see trends and relationships, they are an important tool for analyzing data. However, the chart type and formatting can influence how others perceive the data. Be careful that the chart does not present the data in a way that may be misleading.

tell me more

If the chart is located on the same worksheet as its data, Excel will highlight that data when you select certain chart elements. For example, select the chart area or the plot area, and Excel highlights the cells containing the data point values in blue, the data series labels in red, and the category labels in purple. If you select a single data series, only those data will be highlighted.

let me try *Live!*

Open the student data file **EX5-01-ChartSamples** and try this skill on your own:

1. Begin with the **Column Chart** sheet. Click any of the data markers to select the entire data series. Use the *Chart Elements* box to verify that you have selected the data series. Observe how the worksheet data are represented by the column data markers.
2. Go to the **Pie Chart** sheet. Select the chart legend. Use the legend to match the pie pieces to the data point values.
3. Go to the **Line Chart** sheet. Select the line representing the *Merchandise* data series. Observe that when the *Merchandise* series is selected, cells B4:G4 (the data points) are highlighted in blue.
4. Select the x axis, and then select the y axis. Use the *Chart Elements* list if necessary.
5. Close the file without saving any changes you may have made accidentally.

from the perspective of . . .

COLLEGE STUDENT

I use Excel to track my monthly budget. Before I started using charts, the spreadsheets were just numbers. I knew how much money was going out each month, but I didn't really understand how much of my money I was spending on unnecessary expenses. Once I starting using pie charts, it was obvious that I was spending more on lattes than on transportation! I bought a coffee maker, and now I have a little extra cash each month to put away for a rainy day.

Skill 5.2 Using the Recommended Charts Feature

One trick to working with charts is to select the correct chart type. Excel 2016 makes this easier by recommending specific chart types based on the data you have selected in the worksheet. The recommended charts are available from both the Quick Analysis tool and the *Chart Options* dialog.

To add a recommended chart to a worksheet using the Quick Analysis tool:

1. Select the data you want to visualize as a chart.
2. The *Quick Analysis Tool* button appears near the lower right corner of the selected range. Click the **Quick Analysis Tool** button, and then click the **Charts** tab.
3. Hover the mouse cursor over each chart type to see a live preview of the chart. Click the button for the chart type you want. Recommended charts may include multiple versions of the same chart type. Check the live preview carefully to ensure that the data display exactly as you want.

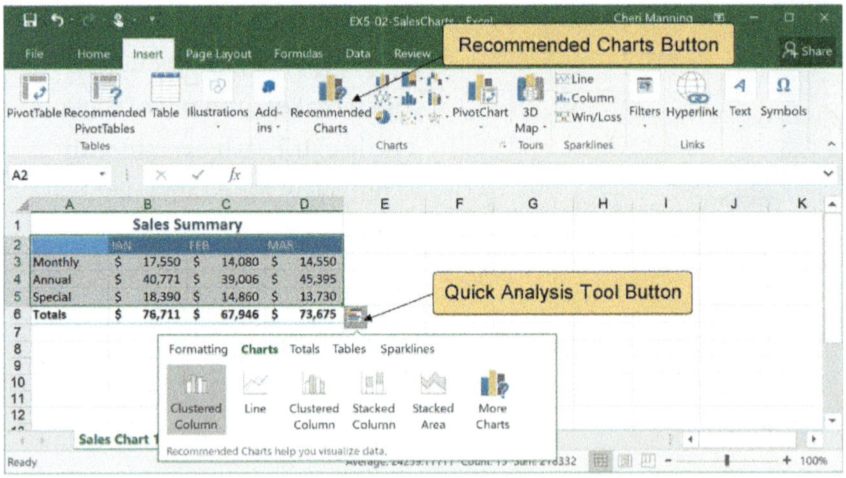

FIGURE EX 5.4

If none of the recommended charts presented in the Quick Analysis tool are precisely what you want, use the *Insert Chart* dialog instead:

1. Select the data for the chart.
2. Click the **Quick Analysis Tool** button.
3. Click the **Charts** tab, and then click the **More Charts** button to open the *Insert Chart* dialog. You can also open the *Insert Chart* dialog from the *Insert* tab, *Charts* group, by clicking the **Recommended Charts** button.

4. The first tab in the *Insert Chart* dialog, *Recommended Charts,* displays the same chart options as the *Charts* tab in the Quick Analysis tool, plus a few more. When you select a chart type, a preview of the chart appears in the right pane of the dialog.
5. Click **OK** to insert the selected chart into the worksheet.

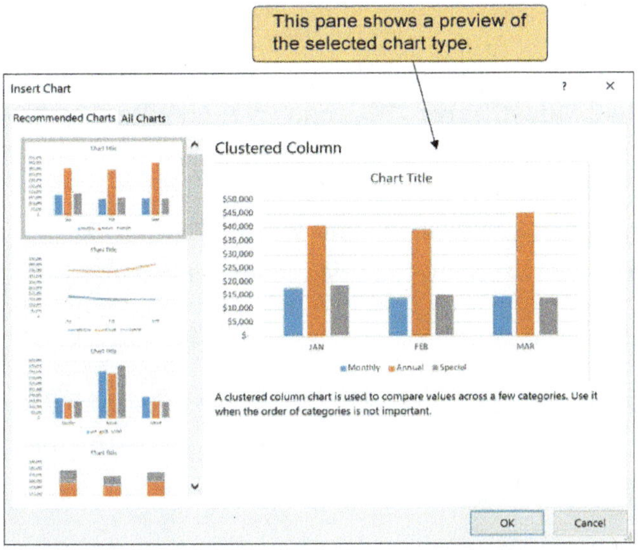

FIGURE EX 5.5

To change the title text, click the box to select it and edit the text directly in the text box. You can also type new text in the formula bar and then press Enter.

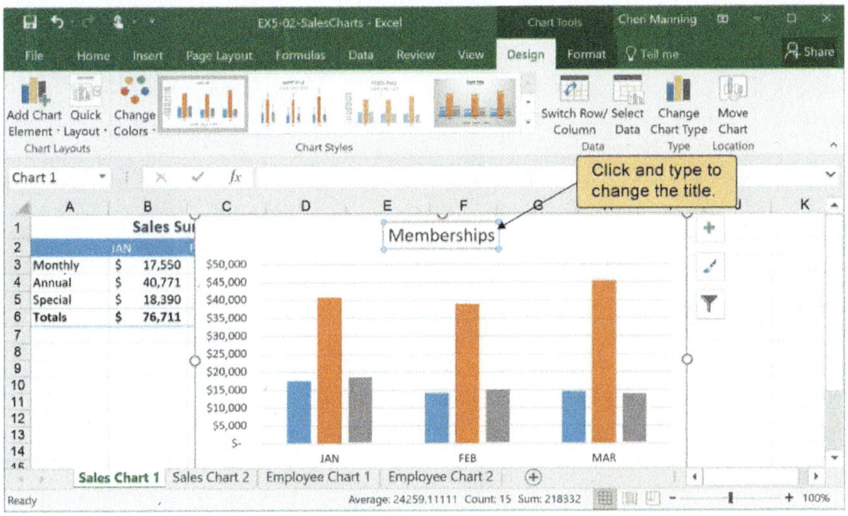

FIGURE EX 5.6

tips & tricks

The Quick Analysis tool is available only if the data selected for the chart are in contiguous cells—a group of cells that are all next to one another without any cells left out of the group.

let me try *Live!*

Open the student data file **EX5-02-SalesCharts** and try this skill on your own:

1. If necessary, go to the **Sales Chart 1** worksheet, and select cells **A2:D5.**
2. Insert a **Clustered Column** chart based on the first recommended chart type.
3. Change the title to: `Memberships`
4. If you will be moving on to the next skill in this chapter, leave the workbook open to continue working. If not, save the file as directed by your instructor and close it.

Skill 5.3 Inserting a Column Chart or a Bar Chart

Column charts work best with data that are organized into rows and columns like a table. Data point values are transformed into columns, with the values plotted along the vertical (y) axis. Each row in the table is grouped as a data series. Excel uses the column labels as the categories along the horizontal (x) axis.

In the clustered column chart shown in Figure EX 5.7, each column represents a single data point. The data points are grouped (clustered) together by category. Each data series is represented by a single color as shown in the legend below the chart.

To insert a column chart:

1. Select the data you want to include in the column chart.
2. On the *Insert* tab, in the *Charts* group, click the **Insert Column or Bar Chart** button.
3. Click the chart type you want to insert the chart into the worksheet.

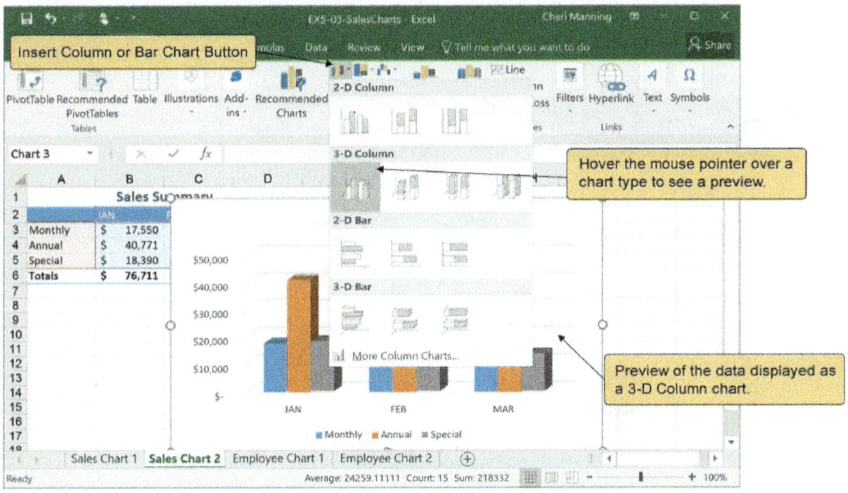

FIGURE EX 5.7

Bar charts are like column charts turned on their side. The categories are displayed on the vertical axis, and the data point values are plotted along the horizontal axis.

The clustered bar chart in Figure EX 5.8 displays the same data as Figure EX 5.7. Each bar represents a single data point. However, in this bar chart, the sales values are plotted along the horizontal axis, grouped into data series by membership type, and the months are displayed along the vertical axis.

To insert a bar chart:

1. Select the data you want to include in the bar chart.
2. On the *Insert* tab, in the *Charts* group, click the **Insert Column or Bar Chart** button.
3. Click the chart type you want to insert the chart into the worksheet.

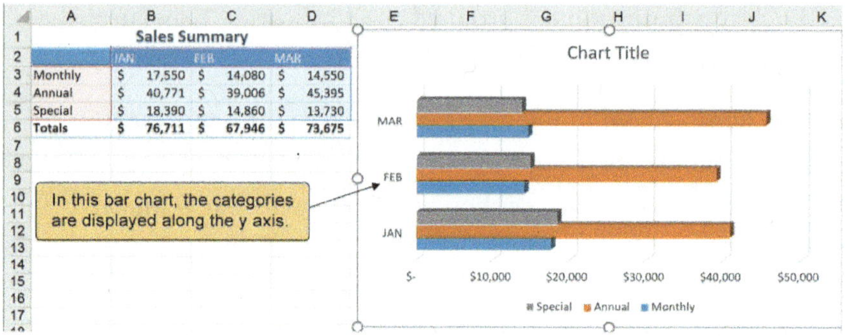

FIGURE EX 5.8

If you don't like the way Excel grouped the data series, you can switch them, making the categories the data series and the data series the categories. On the *Chart Tools Design* tab, in the *Data* group, click the **Switch Row/Column** button. Figure EX 5.9 charts the same data as Figure 5.8 with the rows and columns switched, so the data points are organized into data series by column instead of by row.

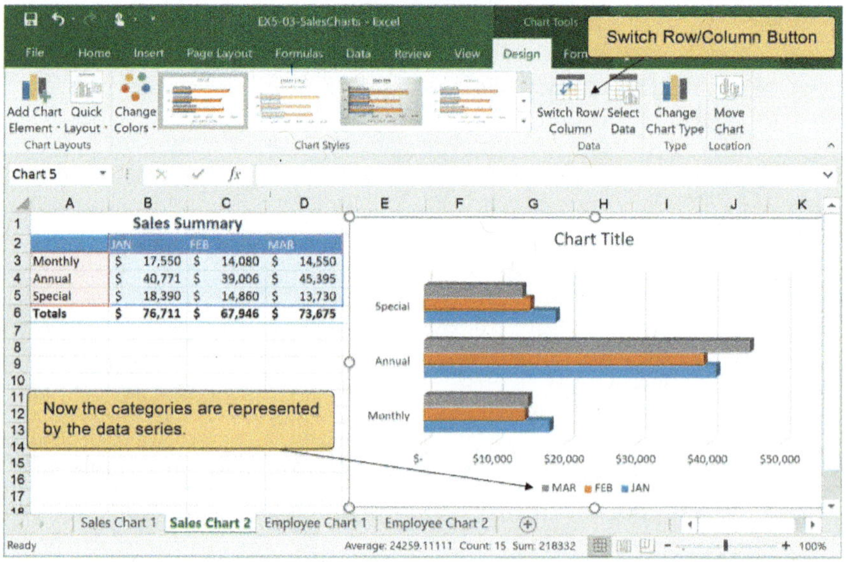

FIGURE EX 5.9

tips & tricks

In previous versions of Excel, column charts and bar charts had separate buttons on the *Insert* tab, *Charts* group.

another method

You can also insert a column chart or a bar chart from the *Insert Chart* dialog, *All Charts* tab.

let me try *Live!*

If you do not have the data file from the previous skill open, open the student data file
EX5-03-SalesCharts and try this skill on your own:

1. If necessary, go to the **Sales Chart 2** worksheet, and select cells **A2:D5.**
2. Insert a **3-D Clustered Bar** chart (the first chart type in the *3-D Bar* section of the *Insert Column or Bar Chart* menu).
3. Switch the rows and columns in the chart, so the data points are grouped into data series by column.
4. If you will be moving on to the next skill in this chapter, leave the workbook open to continue working. If not, save the file as directed by your instructor and close it.

Skill 5.4 Inserting a Pie Chart

Pie charts represent data as parts of a whole. They do not have x and y axes like column charts. Instead, each value is a visual "slice" of the pie. Pie charts work best when you want to evaluate values as they relate to a total value—for example, departmental budgets in relation to the entire budget, or each employee's bonus in relation to the entire bonus pool.

In Figure EX 5.10, the total sales for each salesperson is represented by a slice of the pie.

To add a pie chart:

1. Select the data you want to include in the pie chart.
2. On the *Insert* tab, in the *Charts* group, click the **Insert Pie Chart** button.
3. Click the chart type you want to insert the chart into the worksheet.

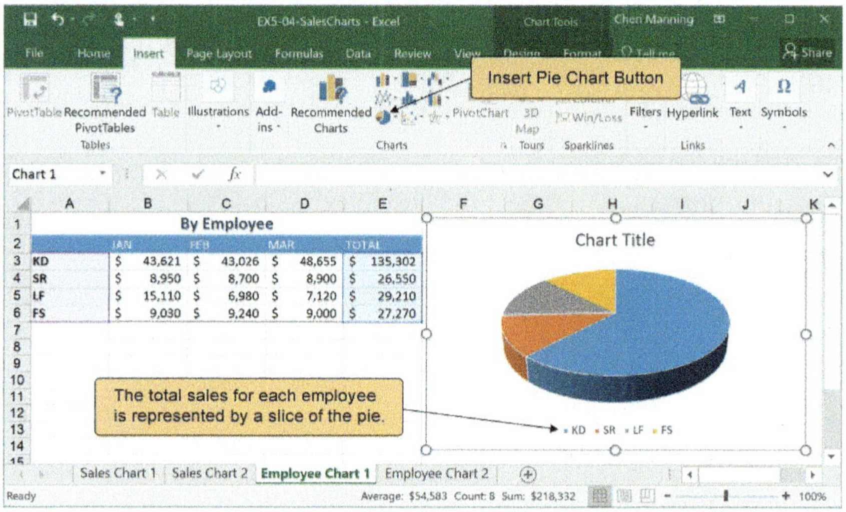

FIGURE EX 5.10

tips & tricks

In an "exploded" pie chart, each slice is slightly separated from the whole. You can explode a single slice by clicking it and dragging it away from the rest of the slices. Exploding a single slice of data gives it emphasis.

tell me **more**

Doughnut charts are similar to pie charts, but they can display more than one series. Each series is represented by a ring around the doughnut. Each data point in the series is represented by a piece of the ring proportional to the total. Doughnut charts can be confusing and are not commonly used.

another method

You can also insert a pie chart from the *Insert Chart* dialog, *All Charts* tab.

let me try *Live!*

If you do not have the data file from the previous skill open, open the student data file
EX5-04-SalesCharts and try this skill on your own:

1. If necessary, go to the **Employee Chart 1** worksheet, and select cells **A3:A6** (the row labels) and cells **E3:E6** (the row totals). *Hint:* Remember to press Ctrl to select noncontiguous cells.
2. Insert a **3-D Pie** chart.
3. If you will be moving on to the next skill in this chapter, leave the workbook open to continue working. If not, save the file as directed by your instructor and close it.

Skill 5.5 Inserting a Line Chart

Line charts feature a line connecting each data point—showing the movement of values over time. Line charts work best when data trends over time are important.

The line chart in Figure EX 5.11 shows sales over a three-month period. Each data series represents sales for a specific employee. This type of line chart, called a **line with markers**, includes dots along the line for each data point.

To add a line chart:

1. Select the data you want to include in the line chart. Be sure to include both values and the related cells that represent time segments (dates, calendar quarters, etc.).
2. On the *Insert* tab, in the *Charts* group, click the **Insert Line Chart** button.
3. Click the chart type you want to insert the chart into the worksheet.
4. If Excel does not display the time categories along the x axis, switch the data series and the categories. On the *Chart Tools Design* tab, in the *Data* group, click the **Switch Row/Column** button.

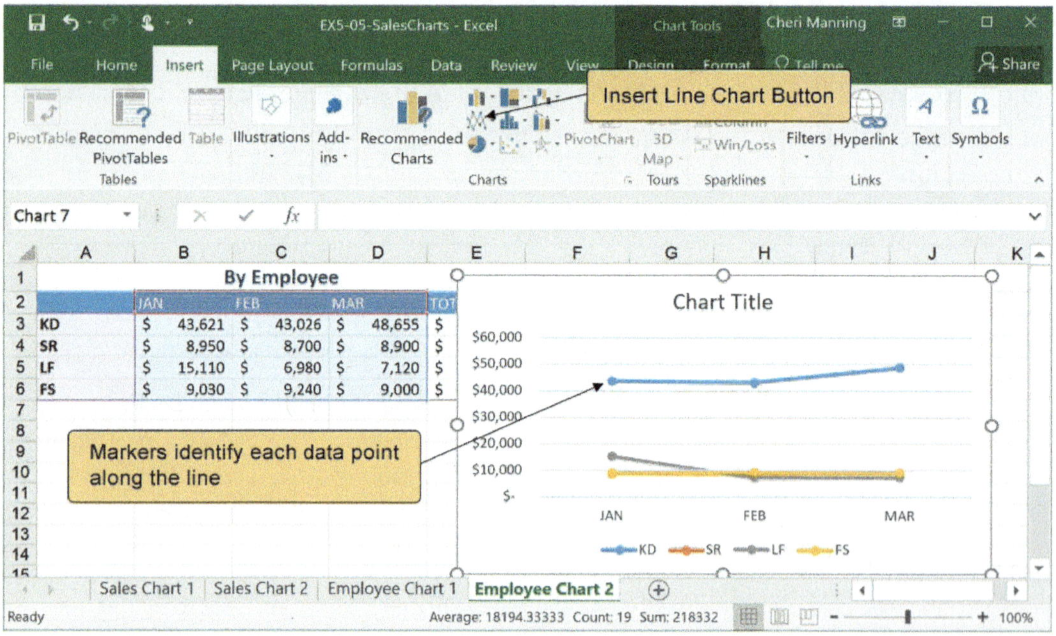

FIGURE EX 5.11

tips & tricks

While line charts are a good choice if the data set has many data points, use a line chart with markers only if there are relatively few data points.

another method

You can also insert a line chart from the *Insert Chart* dialog, *All Charts* tab.

let me try *Live!*

If you do not have the data file from the previous skill open, open the student data file
EX5-05-SalesCharts and try this skill on your own:

1. If necessary, go to the **Employee Chart 2** worksheet, and select cells **A2:D6.**
2. Insert a **Line with Markers** chart (the fourth chart type in the *Insert Line Chart* menu).
3. If necessary, switch the rows and columns in the chart to list the months along the x axis.
4. If you will be moving on to the next skill in this chapter, leave the workbook open to continue working. If not, save the file as directed by your instructor and close it.

Skill 5.6 Resizing and Moving Charts

When you first create a chart, Excel places the chart in the middle of the worksheet. Often, you will need to resize and move the chart so it doesn't cover the worksheet data.

With the chart selected, resize the chart using the resize handles located at the four corners and the middle of each side of the chart area. Click and drag toward the center of the chart to make it smaller or outward to make it larger.

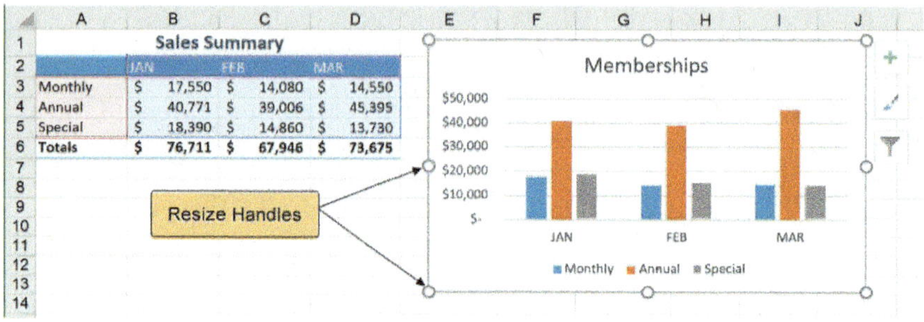

FIGURE EX 5.12

To move a chart to a new position on the worksheet:

1. Select the chart. Be careful not to click in the plot area or you will move just the plot area instead of the entire chart. Your mouse cursor will change to the move cursor.
2. With your left mouse button depressed, drag the chart to the new location on the worksheet, and then release the mouse button to "drop" the chart at the new location.

If your chart is large or complex, you may want the chart to appear on its own worksheet. To move a chart to a new sheet:

1. If necessary, select the chart. If you just created the chart, it will still be selected.
2. On the *Chart Tools Design* tab, in the *Location* group, click the **Move Chart** button.
3. In the *Move Chart* dialog, click the **New sheet** radio button to move the chart to its own worksheet. If you want to specify a name for the new sheet, type it in the *New sheet* box. To move the chart to an existing worksheet, click the **Object in** radio button, and then select the name of the sheet you want to move the chart to.
4. Click **OK.**

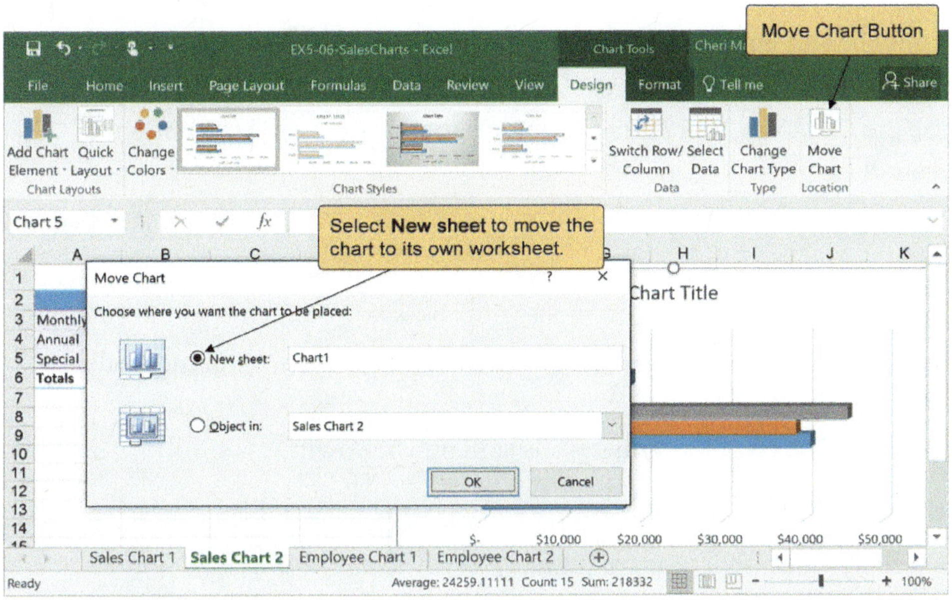

FIGURE EX 5.13

When you use the *Move Chart* dialog to move a chart to its own sheet, Excel creates a special type of worksheet called a **chart sheet**. The chart sheet does not include the columns, rows, and cells you are used to seeing in Excel; it contains only the chart object. The new chart sheet automatically changes the zoom level so the entire chart is visible.

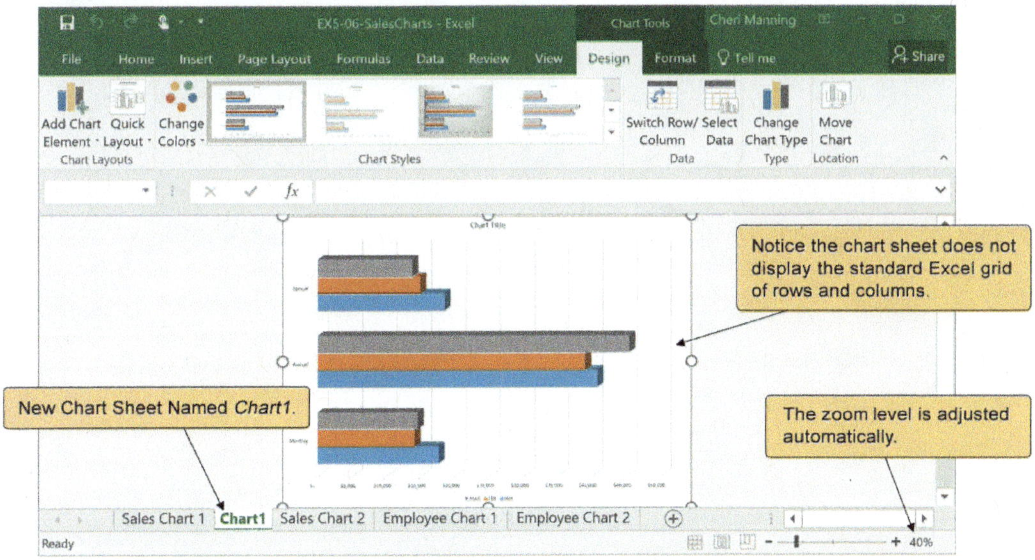

FIGURE EX 5.14

tips & tricks

You cannot resize a chart in a chart sheet.

another method

- Right-click an empty area of the chart and select **Move Chart...** to open the *Move Chart* dialog.
- Use the *Cut, Copy*, and *Paste* commands to move a chart from one sheet to another.

let me try *Live!*

If you do not have the data file from the previous skill open, open the student data file
EX5-06-SalesCharts and try this skill on your own:

1. If necessary, go to the **Sales Chart 1** worksheet and select the chart.
2. Resize the chart so it is approximately 13 rows tall.
3. Move the chart to the empty area of the worksheet to the right of the data.
4. Go to the **Sales Chart 2** worksheet and move the chart to a new worksheet.
5. If you will be moving on to the next skill in this chapter, leave the workbook open to continue working. If not, save the file as directed by your instructor and close it.

Skill 5.7 Showing and Hiding Chart Elements

Showing and hiding chart elements such as the chart title, axes, and gridlines can make a chart easier to read. Other common chart elements include:

Data labels—Display data values for each data marker.

Data table—Displays a table of the data point values below the chart.

To hide or show chart elements:

1. Click any empty area of the chart area to select the chart.
2. Click the **Chart Elements** button that appears near the upper right corner of the chart.
3. Click the check boxes to show or hide chart elements.
4. To select a specific option for a chart element, click the arrow that appears at the right side of the element name, and then click an option.

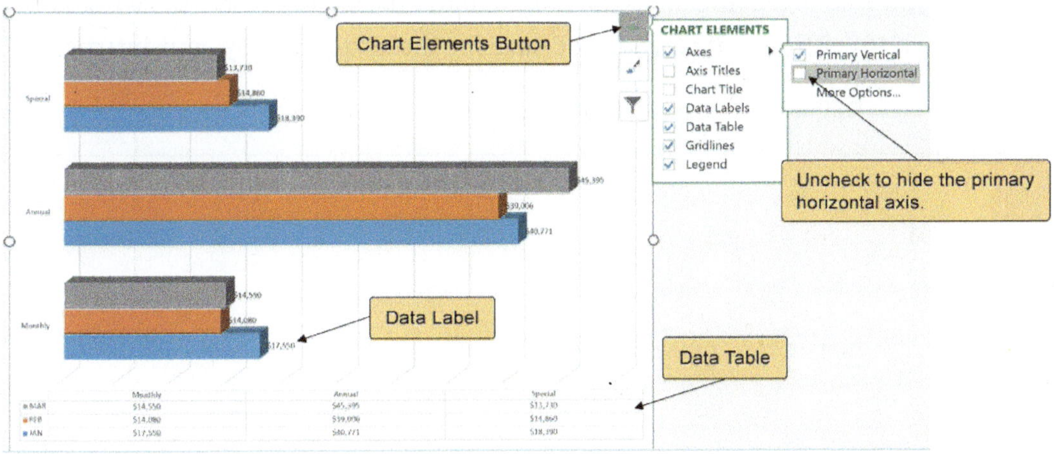

FIGURE EX 5.15

tell me **more**

You can apply a combination of chart elements at once by selecting one of the Quick Layout options from the *Chart Tools Design* tab, *Chart Layouts* group.

another method

You can hide or show chart elements and control their appearance and position from the *Chart Tools Design* tab, *Chart Layouts* group. Click the **Add Chart Elements** button, point to the chart element you want, and click an option.

let me try *Live!*

If you do not have the data file from the previous skill open, open the student data file
EX5-07-SalesCharts and try this skill on your own:

1. If necessary, select the chart on the **Chart1** worksheet.
2. Hide the chart title.
3. Hide the primary horizontal axis.
4. Display the data table, including the legend keys.
5. Display the data labels.
6. If you will be moving on to the next skill in this chapter, leave the workbook open to continue working. If not, save the file as directed by your instructor and close it.

Skill 5.8 Applying Quick Styles and Colors to Charts

You can change the style of a chart using the predefined **Quick Styles**. Quick Styles apply combinations of fonts, line styles, fills, and shape effects. You can also change the color scheme from a preset list of colors that coordinate with the workbook theme.

To change the chart style:

1. Select the chart.
2. On the *Chart Tools Design* tab, in the *Chart Styles* group, click the style you want to use, or click the **More** button to see all of the Quick Styles available.
3. To change the color scheme, on the *Chart Tools Design* tab, in the *Chart Styles* group, click the **Change Colors** button and select the color scheme you want.

FIGURE EX 5.16

another method

Quick Styles and color schemes are also available from the *Chart Styles* button that appears near the upper right corner of the chart when it is selected.

let me try *Live!*

If you do not have the data file from the previous skill open, open the student data file
EX5-08-SalesCharts and try this skill on your own:

1. If necessary, select the chart on the **Sales Chart 1** worksheet.
2. Apply the **Style 3** Quick Style.
3. Apply the **Color 3** color scheme from the *Colorful* section.
4. If you will be moving on to the next skill in this chapter, leave the workbook open to continue working. If not, save the file as directed by your instructor and close it.

Skill 5.9 Changing the Chart Type

If you find that your initial chart selection wasn't quite right, you can change the chart type from the *Change Chart Type* dialog without having to delete and recreate the chart.

To change the chart type:

1. On the *Chart Tools Design* tab, in the *Type* group, click the **Change Chart Type** button.

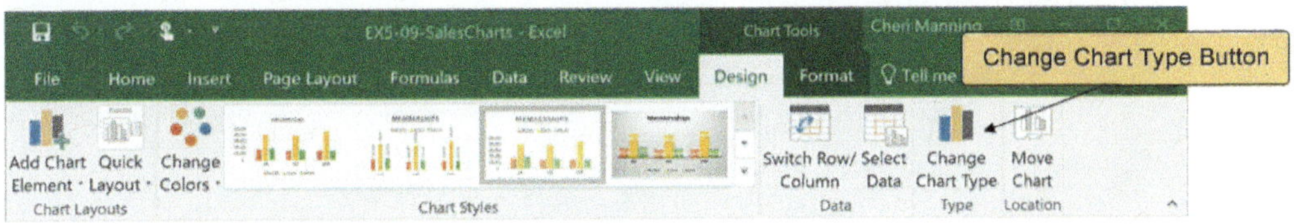

FIGURE EX 5.17

2. In the *Change Chart Type* dialog, click a chart type category to display that category in the right pane.
3. Click one of the chart types along the top of the right pane to see previews of the options available, and then click the chart type you want.
4. Click **OK.**

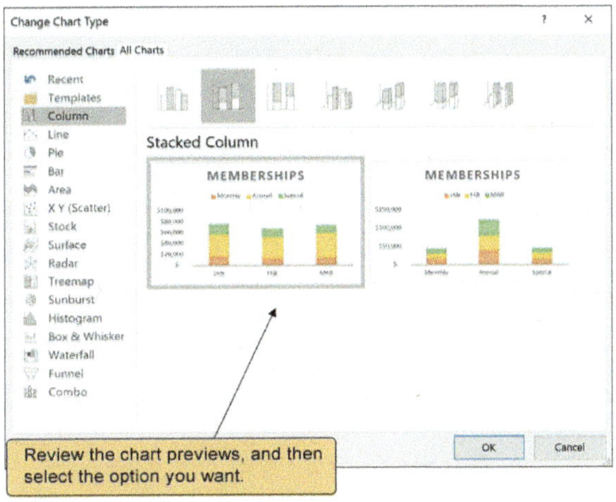

FIGURE EX 5.18

The chart type you select affects the story your chart tells. A **clustered column chart** would show a separate column for sales of each membership type per month, but it doesn't depict the total sales for all memberships. By changing the chart type to a **stacked column chart** as shown in the preview in Figure EX 5.18, each column will represent the total sales for the month, and individual sales for each membership type are represented by a piece of that column. Using this chart type makes it easier to compare total sales as well as sales for each individual type of membership.

another method

To change the chart type, you can also right-click in the chart area and select **Change Chart Type...**

let me try *Live!*

If you do not have the data file from the previous skill open, open the student data file
EX5-09-SalesCharts and try this skill on your own:

1. If necessary, select the chart on the **Sales Chart 1** worksheet.
2. Change the chart type to the first stacked column option.
3. If you will be moving on to the next skill in this chapter, leave the workbook open to continue working. If not, save the file as directed by your instructor and close it.

Skill 5.10 Filtering Chart Data

Excel includes a feature that allows you to hide and show data in a chart without having to modify the chart data source. The chart in Figure EX 5.19 shows the category options filtered to show just the *JAN* and *FEB* categories along the x axis with a preview of what the chart would look like if the *Special* series were the only series option selected.

To filter chart data:

1. Select the chart.
2. Click the **Chart Filters** button that appears near the upper right corner of the chart.
3. Notice that when you hover the mouse pointer over the chart filter options, the live preview does not take into account the options that are checked or unchecked. The preview shows what the chart would look like if the highlighted option were the only one checked by dimming all the other series or categories.
4. Click the check boxes to add or remove data series or categories from the chart.
5. Click the **Apply** button to apply the changes.

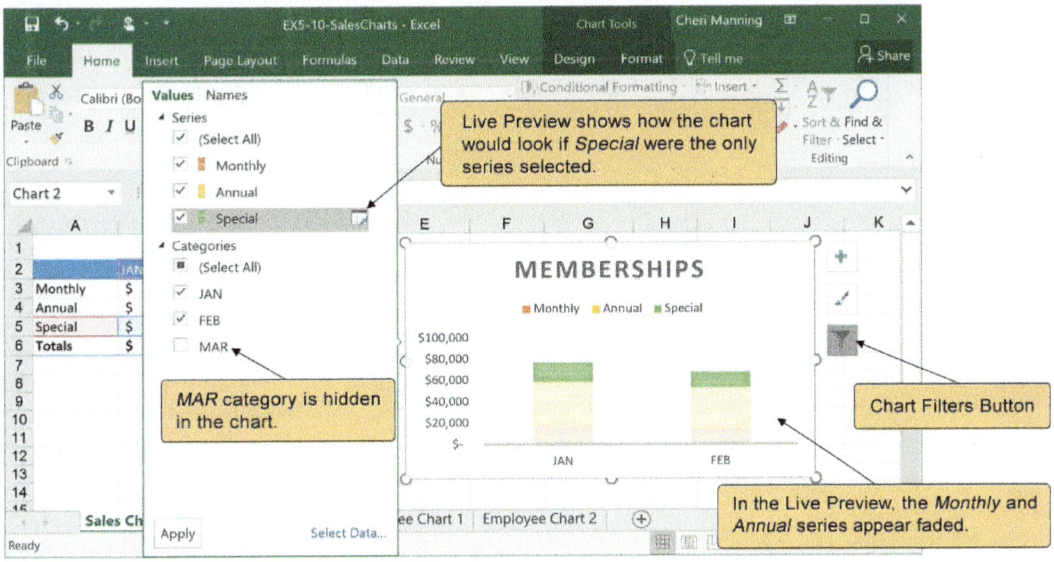

FIGURE EX 5.19

let me try *Live!*

If you do not have the data file from the previous skill open, open the student data file
EX5-10-SalesCharts and try this skill on your own:

1. If necessary, select the chart on the **Sales Chart 1** worksheet.
2. Without changing the data source, filter the chart so the **MAR** series is hidden.
3. If you will be moving on to the next skill in this chapter, leave the workbook open to continue working. If not, save the file as directed by your instructor and close it.

Skill 5.11 Inserting Sparklines

Sparklines represent a series of data values as an individual graphic within a single cell. As you update the underlying data series, the Sparklines update immediately.

To add Sparklines to your worksheet using the Quick Analysis tool:

1. Select the data you want to visualize as Sparklines. If you want the Sparklines to appear in empty cells, ensure that there are empty cells to the right of your selection.
2. The Quick Analysis Tool button appears near the lower right corner of the selected range. Click the **Quick Analysis Tool** button, and then click the **Sparklines** tab.
3. Click the button for the Sparkline type you want.

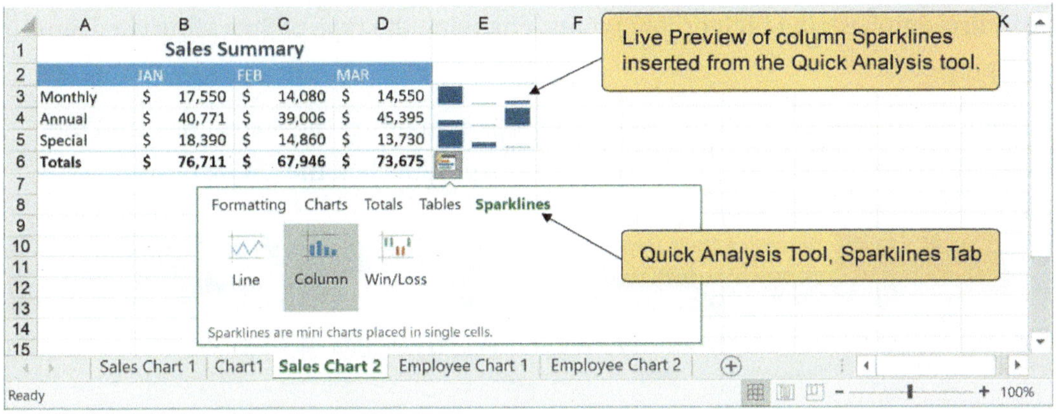

FIGURE EX 5.20

If you do not want Excel to place the Sparklines automatically, or if you are adding Sparklines in a situation where the Quick Analysis tool is not available, use the *Create Sparklines* dialog to specify their location:

1. Select the data range with the data points for the Sparklines.
2. On the *Insert* tab, in the *Sparklines* group, click the button for the type of Sparkline you want to insert: **Line, Column,** or **Win/Loss.**
3. The *Create Sparklines* dialog opens with the selected range added to the *Data Range* box.
4. In the *Location Range* box, enter the cell range where you want the Sparklines to appear. You can type the cell range or click and drag in the worksheet to select the cells.
5. Click **OK** to insert the Sparklines.

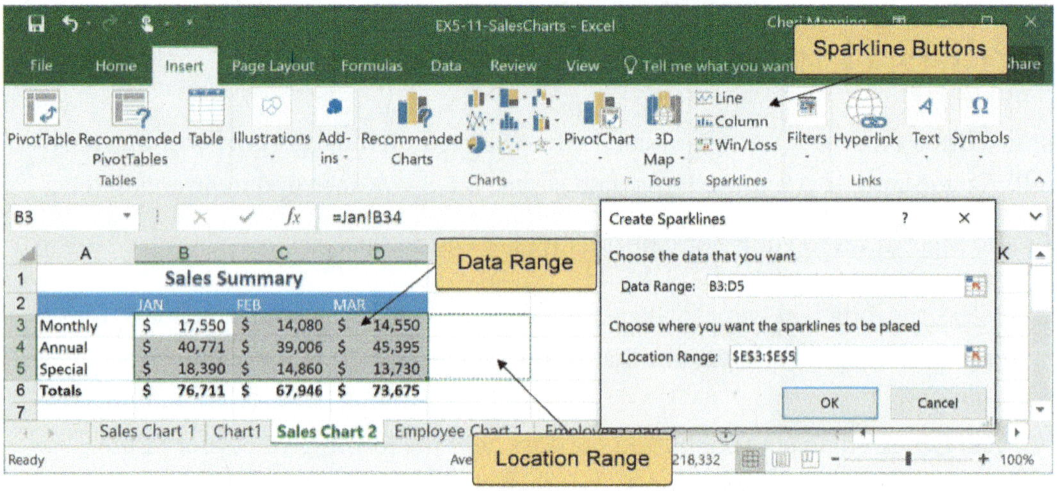

FIGURE EX 5.21

When cells containing Sparklines are selected, the *Sparkline Tools Design* contextual tab becomes active. From this tab you can customize the look of the Sparklines including emphasizing high or low points, changing the type of Sparkline used, and changing colors.

To remove Sparklines, you must select the cells containing the Sparklines, and then on the *Sparkline Tools Design* tab, in the *Group* group, click the **Clear** button.

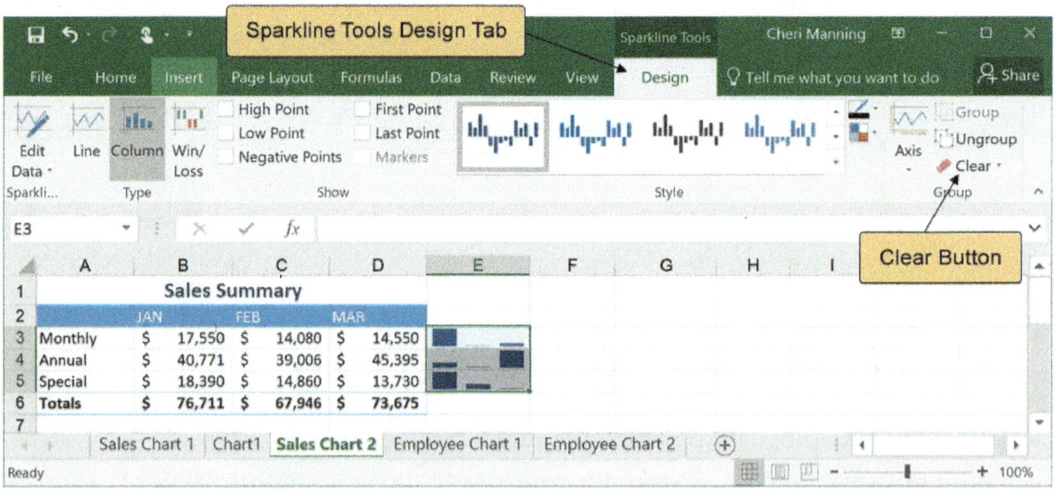

FIGURE EX 5.22

tips & tricks

Sparklines are not actually chart objects—they are charts in the background of the cells. You can add text and other data to the cells that contain Sparklines. You can also extend the Sparklines over multiple cells using the *Merge & Center* commands.

let me try *Live!*

If you do not have the data file from the previous skill open, open the student data file
EX5-11-SalesCharts and try this skill on your own:

1. Go to the **Sales Chart 2** worksheet and select cells **B3:D5** as the data range for the Sparklines.
2. Insert column Sparklines in cells **E3:E5**.
3. Save the file as directed by your instructor and close it.

Skill 5.12 Converting Data into Tables

In Excel, you can define a series of adjacent cells as a **table**. When you define data as a table, Excel provides a robust tool set for formatting and analyzing the data. In the table, the header row automatically includes filtering and sorting. When you add data to the right of the table, Excel includes the new column in the table automatically.

To define data as a table:

1. Click any cell in the data range. You do not need to select the entire range.
2. On the *Home* tab, in the *Styles* group, click the **Format as Table** button to display the *Table Styles* gallery.
3. Click the style you want to use for your table.

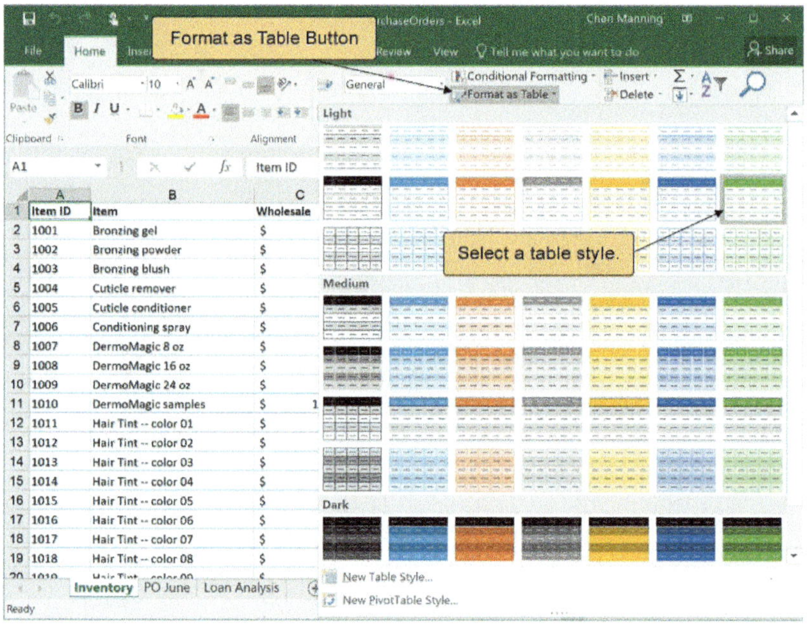

FIGURE EX 5.23

4. Excel will automatically populate the *Format As Table* dialog with the entire data range. If the data range is not correct, you can manually enter the cell range in the dialog.
5. Be sure to check the **My table has headers** check box if appropriate.
6. Click **OK** to create the table.

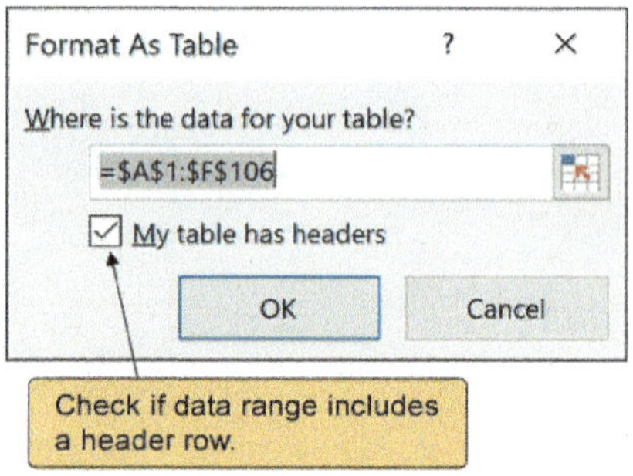

FIGURE EX 5.24

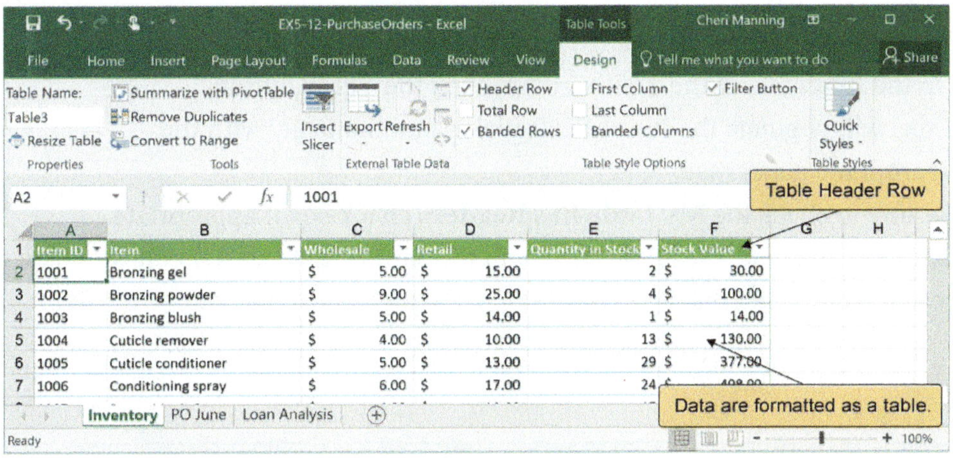

FIGURE EX 5.25

tips & tricks

You cannot create a table in a shared workbook. If your workbook contains a table, you will need to convert the table back to a normal cell range before sharing the workbook.

tell me more

One of the most useful features of tables is the ability to reference table column names in formulas. When you enter a formula in a table, you can reference column names by enclosing the column header text in brackets. For example, to add a new column to the table in Figure EX 5.25 to calculate the cost of each inventory record, you would enter the formula **`[Wholesale]*[Quantity in Stock]`** in the first row of the new column. Excel will copy the formula to the remaining cells in the table column automatically.

another method

To insert a table without specifying the table formatting:

1. Select any cell in the data range for the table.
2. On the *Insert* tab, in the *Tables* group, click the **Table** button.
3. Excel will populate the *Insert Table* dialog automatically with the appropriate data range.
4. Be sure to check the **My table has headers** check box if appropriate.
5. Click **OK** to create the table. Excel will format the table with the most recent table style used.

let me try *Live!*

Open the student data file **EX5-12-PurchaseOrders** and try this skill on your own:

1. On the **Inventory** worksheet, click any cell in the range **A1:F106**.
2. Convert the cell range to a table using table style **Table Style Light 14**. The data range contains a header row.
3. If you will be moving on to the next skill in this chapter, leave the workbook open to continue working. If not, save the file as directed by your instructor and close it.

Skill 5.13 Applying Quick Styles to Tables

When you are working with a table, use the *Table Tools Design* tab to apply formatting. This contextual tab is available when you select any cell in the table. From the *Table Styles* gallery, you can select a Quick Style to apply a combination of font colors, fill colors, and banding options. **Banding** applies a fill color to alternating rows or columns, making the table easier to read.

To apply a table Quick Style:

1. Click anywhere in the table.
2. On the *Table Tools Design* tab, in the *Table Styles* group, click the **Quick Styles** button to display the full *Table Styles* gallery. Depending on the width of your Excel window, you may see part of the *Quick Styles* gallery displayed in the Ribbon. In this case, click the **More** button to expand the entire gallery.
3. Click a style to apply it to the table.

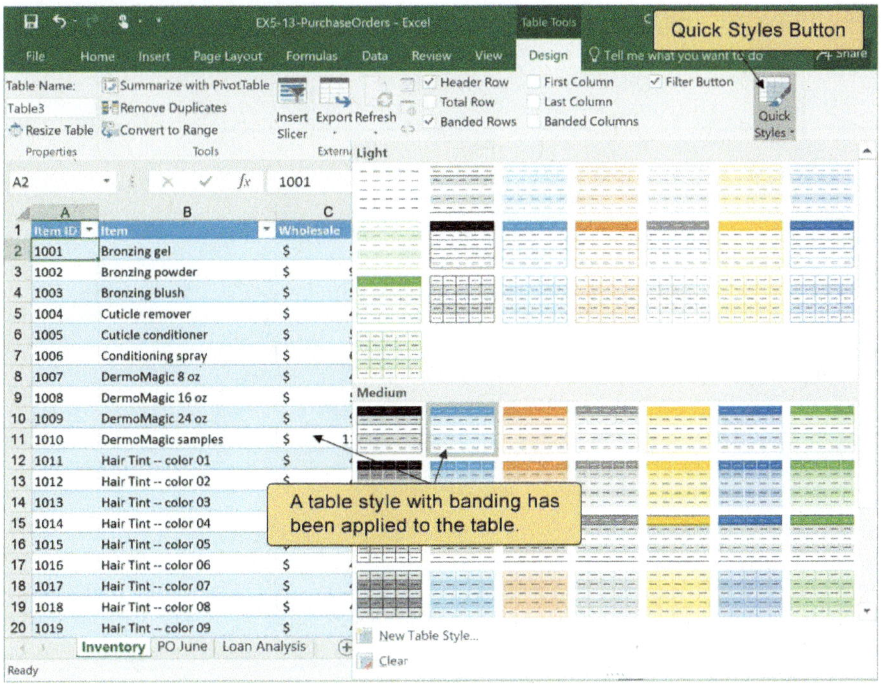

FIGURE EX 5.26

tips & tricks

If your table includes a header row like the one in Figure EX 5.26, select a style that includes formatting for the first row to help it stand out from the rest of the table.

tell me more

Use the check boxes in the *Table Style Options* group to customize the table formatting by adding or removing banding for rows or columns.

let me try *Live!*

Open the student data file **EX5-13-PurchaseOrders** and try this skill on your own:

1. On the **Inventory** worksheet, if necessary, click any cell in the table.
2. Apply the **Table Style Medium 2** Quick Style.
3. If you will be moving on to the next skill in this chapter, leave the workbook open to continue working. If not, save the file as directed by your instructor and close it.

Skill 5.14 Adding Total Rows to Tables

If you have data formatted as a table, you can add a **Total row** to quickly calculate an aggregate function such as the sum, average, minimum, or maximum of all the values in the column.

To add a Total row to a table:

1. On the *Table Tools Design* tab, in the *Table Style Options* group, click the **Total Row** check box.
2. In the Total row at the bottom of the table, click the cell where you want to add the calculation.
3. Click the arrow, and select a function. Excel inserts the formula for you.

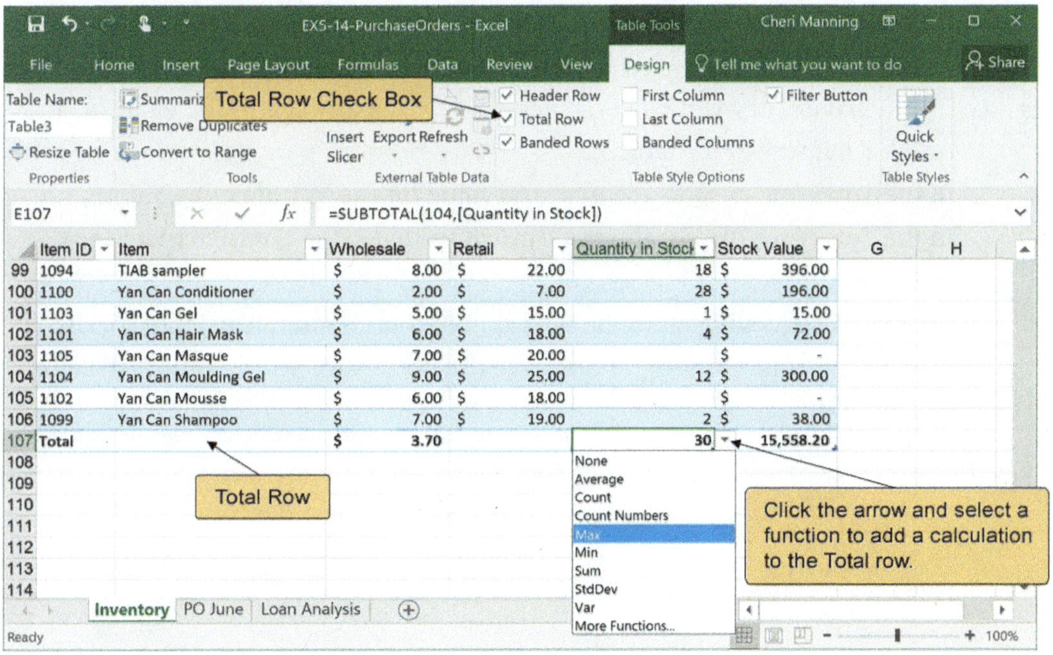

FIGURE EX 5.27

tips & tricks

The **Count** option can be useful when filtering records in a table. Count tells you how many records are included in the filtered table. The Count option from the Total row uses the COUNTA function.

tell me **more**

When you enable the Total row, the first cell in the Total row displays the word "Total" automatically and the last cell in the Total row calculates the sum of the values in that column (if the column contains numbers).

another method

To add the Total row to the table, right-click any cell in the table, point to **Table**, and click **Total Row**.

let me try *Live!*

Open the student data file **EX5-14-PurchaseOrders** and try this skill on your own:

1. On the **Inventory** worksheet, if necessary, click any cell in the table.
2. Add a Total row to the table.
3. In the Total row, display the **average** value for the **Wholesale** column.
4. In the Total row, display the **maximum** value for the **Quantity in Stock** column.
5. If you will be moving on to the next skill in this chapter, leave the workbook open to continue working. If not, save the file as directed by your instructor and close it.

Skill 5.15 Removing Duplicate Rows from Tables

If you have a large table, it may be difficult to identify rows with duplicate data. Excel includes a tool to find and remove duplicate rows. A "duplicate" can be an exact match, where every cell in the row contains the same data, or you can specify matching data for certain columns only.

To remove duplicate rows from a table:

1. Select any cell in the table.
2. On *Table Tools Design* tab, in the *Tools* group, click the **Remove Duplicates** button.
3. By default, all the columns are selected in the *Remove Duplicates* dialog and Excel will remove duplicates only where the data in the rows are 100 percent identical. To identify duplicate rows where only some of the columns have duplicate data, click the check boxes to uncheck column names. Now Excel will identify rows as duplicates only when the checked columns have the same data.
4. Click **OK** to remove duplicate rows from the table.
5. Excel displays a message box, telling you how many duplicate rows were found and removed and how many unique values remain in the table. Click **OK** to dismiss the message box.

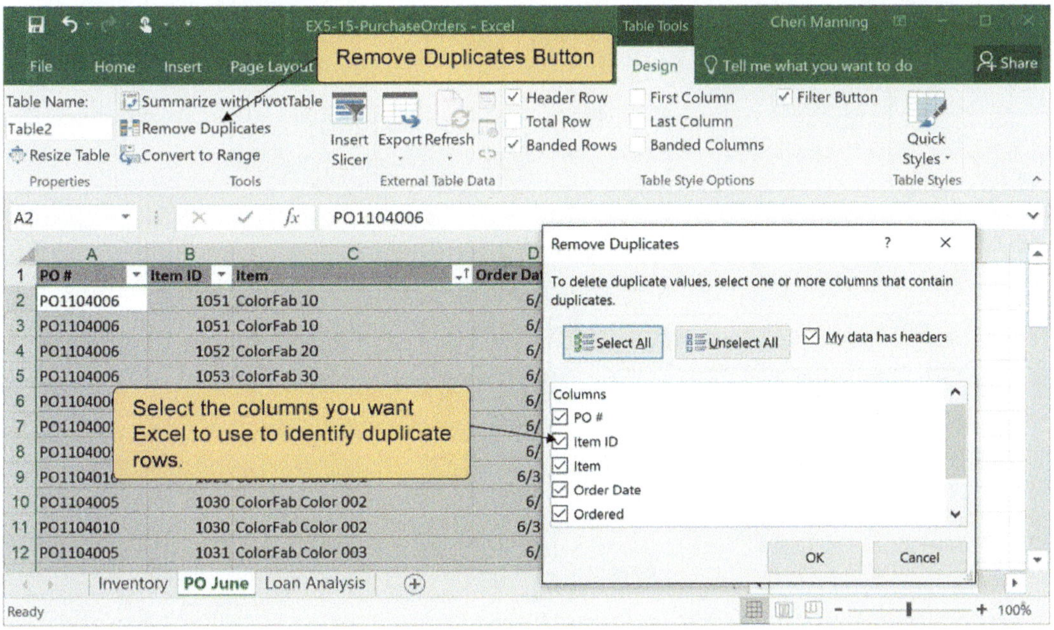

FIGURE EX 5.28

another method

If the data are not formatted as an Excel table, you can access the *Remove Duplicates* command from the *Data* tab, *Data Tools* group.

let me try *Live!*

Open the student data file **EX5-15-PurchaseOrders** and try this skill on your own:

1. If necessary, click any cell in the table on the **PO June** worksheet.
2. Remove duplicate rows where data in all the columns are identical. Excel should remove two duplicate rows, leaving 59 unique values.
3. If you will be moving on to the next skill in this chapter, leave the workbook open to continue working. If not, save the file as directed by your instructor and close it.

Skill 5.16 Sorting Data

Sorting rearranges the rows in your worksheet by the data in a column or columns. You can sort alphabetically by text, by date, or by values. Sorting works the same whether or not the data have been formatted as a table.

To sort data:

1. Click any cell in the column you want to sort by.
2. On the *Data* tab, in the *Sort & Filter* group, click the button for the sort order you want:

- 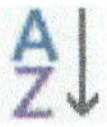 sorts text in alphabetical order from A to Z, numbers from smallest to largest, and dates from oldest to newest.
- 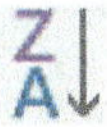 sorts text in reverse alphabetical order from Z to A, numbers from largest to smallest, and dates from newest to oldest.

If the data are formatted as a table, you can click the arrow at the top of any column and select the sort order you want from the options available.

When a table column has been sorted, the column header displays an arrow indicating which way the column has been sorted. An arrow pointing up indicates an A-Z sort order; an arrow pointing down indicates a Z-A sort order.

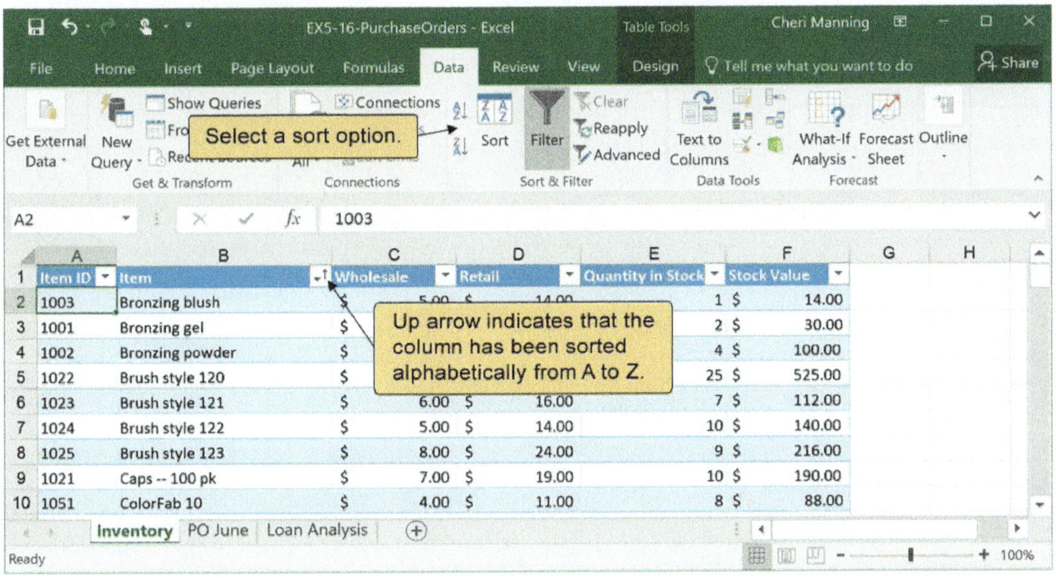

FIGURE EX 5.29

another method

Sort options are also available from the *Home* tab, *Editing* group. Click the **Sort & Filter** button and then select the option you want.

You can also right-click any cell in the column you want to sort by. Point to **Sort**, and select the option you want.

let me try *Live!*

Open the student data file **EX5-16-PurchaseOrders** and try this skill on your own:

1. Verify that the **Inventory** worksheet is active.
2. Sort the **Item** column in alphabetical order from A to Z.
3. Go to the **PO June** worksheet, and sort the **Order Cost** column so the largest numbers are listed first.
4. If you will be moving on to the next skill in this chapter, leave the workbook open to continue working. If not, save the file as directed by your instructor and close it.

Skill 5.17 Filtering Data

If your worksheet has many rows of data, you may want to **filter** the data to show only rows that meet criteria you specify. If your data are formatted as a table, filtering is enabled automatically. If your data are not formatted as a table, you must first enable filtering:

1. On the *Home* tab, in the *Editing* group, click the **Sort & Filter** button.
2. Click the **Filter** button to enable filtering. An arrow will appear in each cell of the heading row just as if the data were formatted as a table.

Once filtering is enabled, it works the same whether or not the data have been formatted as a table.

To filter data:

1. Click the arrow at the top of the column that contains the data you want to filter for.
2. At first, all the filter options are checked. Click the **(Select All)** check box to remove all the checkmarks.
3. Click the check box or check boxes in front of the values you want to filter by.
4. Click **OK.** Excel displays only the rows that include the values you specified.

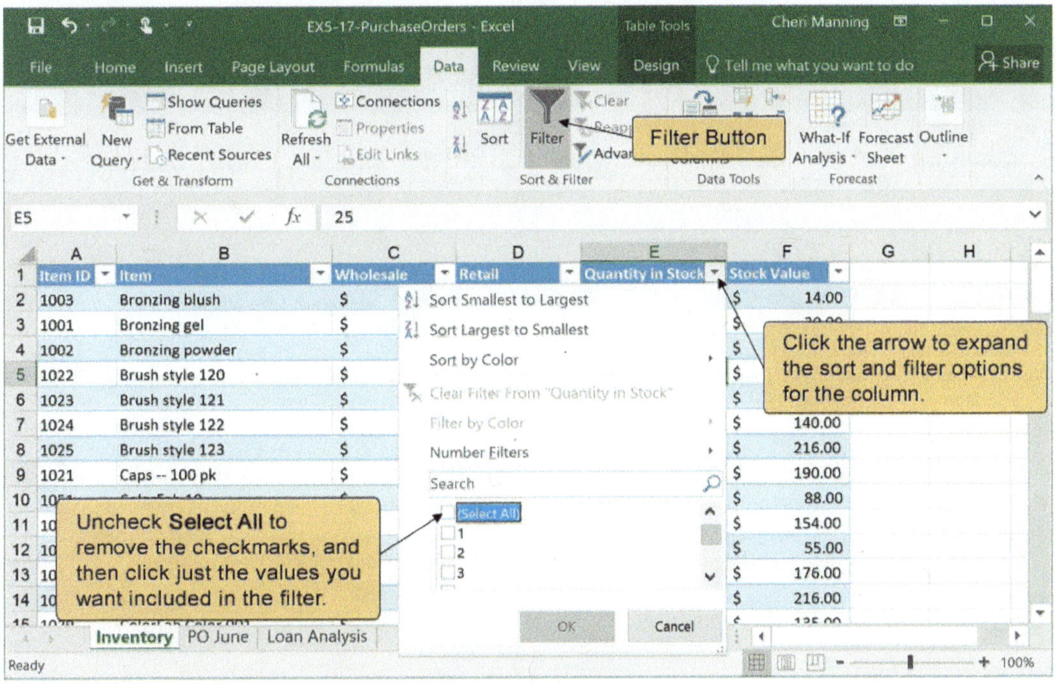

FIGURE EX 5.30

When a filter has been applied to a column, the column header will display a funnel icon.

To clear the filter, on the *Data* tab, in the *Sort & Filter* group, click the **Clear** button. You can also click the funnel icon at the top of the filtered column and select **Clear Filter From "Name of Column"**.

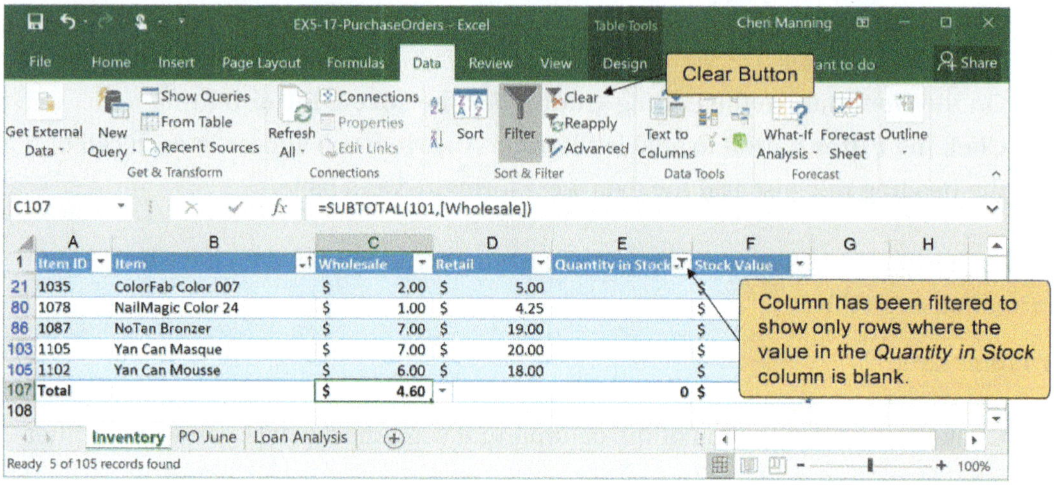

FIGURE EX 5.31

If the column values are dates, Excel will group the dates in the filter list if possible. You can filter for an entire grouping such as a year or month or for a specific date. Use the + and – buttons in front of each date grouping to expand or collapse the group.

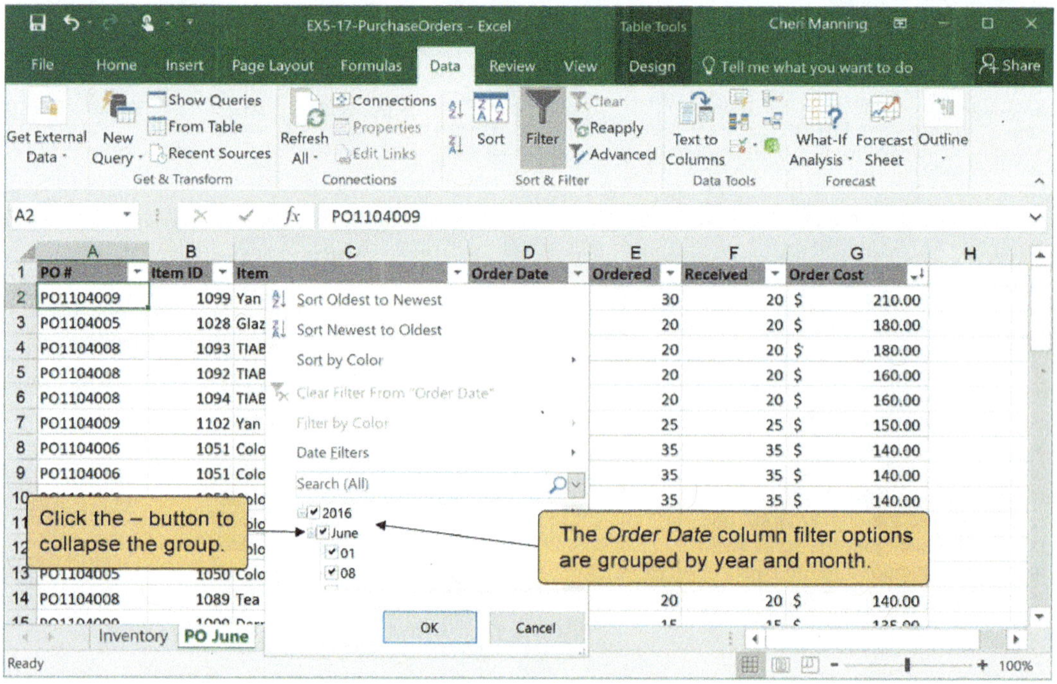

FIGURE EX 5.32

another method

- When filtering is enabled, you can clear the filter and disable filtering from the *Data* tab, *Sort & Filter* group, by clicking the **Filter** button again.
- You can also enable or clear filtering from the *Home* tab, *Editing* group, by clicking the **Sort & Filter** button and then making the appropriate choice from the menu.

let me try *Live!*

Open the student data file **EX5-17-PurchaseOrders** and try this skill on your own:

1. If necessary, go to the **Inventory** worksheet.
2. If the data in this worksheet are no longer formatted as a table, enable filtering.
3. Filter the **Quantity in Stock** column so only rows with the blanks are shown. *Hint:* Scroll to the bottom of the filter list to find the *(Blanks)* option.
4. If you will be moving on to the next skill in this chapter, leave the workbook open to continue working. If not, save the file as directed by your instructor and close it.

Skill 5.18 Filtering Table Data with Slicers

A **slicer** is a visual representation of filtering options. You can display multiple slicers and filter the table by multiple values from each. Slicers are available only when the data have been formatted as a table.

To add a slicer:

1. Click anywhere in the table to activate the *Table Tools Design* tab.
2. On the *Table Tools Design* tab, in the *Tools* group, click the **Insert Slicer** button.
3. In the *Insert Slicers* dialog, click the check boxes for the column(s) you want in the slicers.
4. Click **OK.**

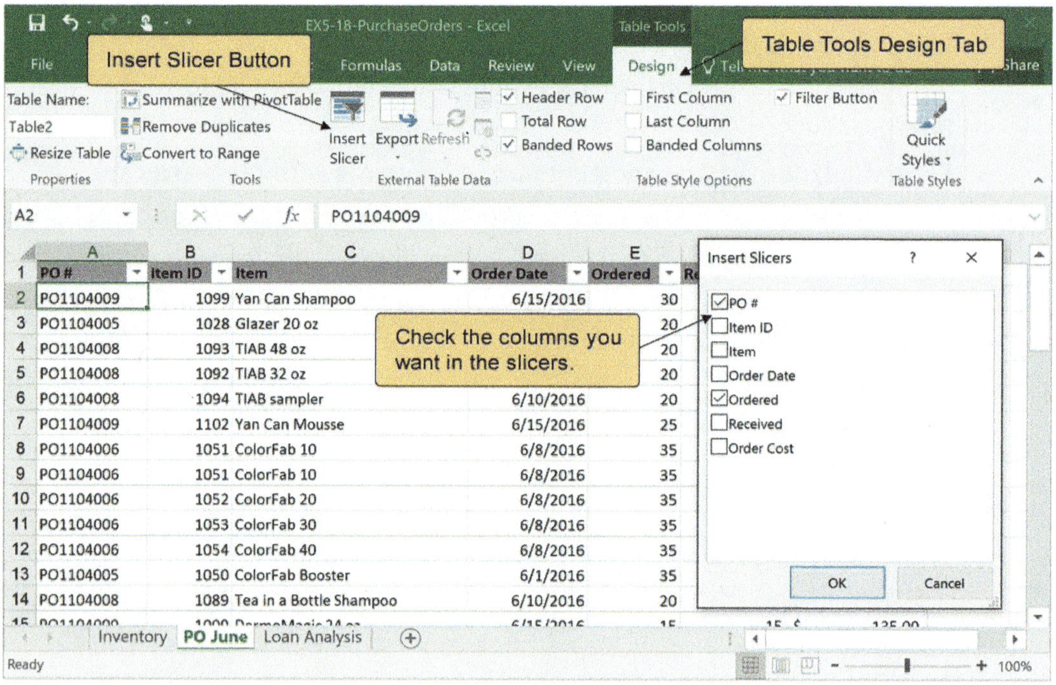

FIGURE EX 5.33

- In the slicer, click the option you want to use as the data filter. If you click another option in the slicer, the first option you selected will toggle off and the new selection will be used as the filter.
- To use more than one filtering option in a slicer, click the **Multi-Select** button at the upper right corner of the slicer box. When you enabled multi-select, all the slicer options remain ***on*** by default. Click the options you do ***not*** want included in the filter to turn them off.

› Notice that as you make selections in one slicer, options in the other slicer may become unavailable—indicating that there are no data available for that option under the current filtering conditions.

The table in Figure EX 5.34 has been filtered to show only rows with **PO1104009** in the *PO #* column and **20** and **25** in the *Ordered* column. Notice that the PO1104008 and PO1104011 options in the PO # slicer are disabled—indicating that they do not include rows with 20 or 25 in the *Ordered* column. Also, in the Ordered slicer, the 35 option is disabled—indicating that PO1104009 does not include any rows with the value 35 in the *Ordered* column.

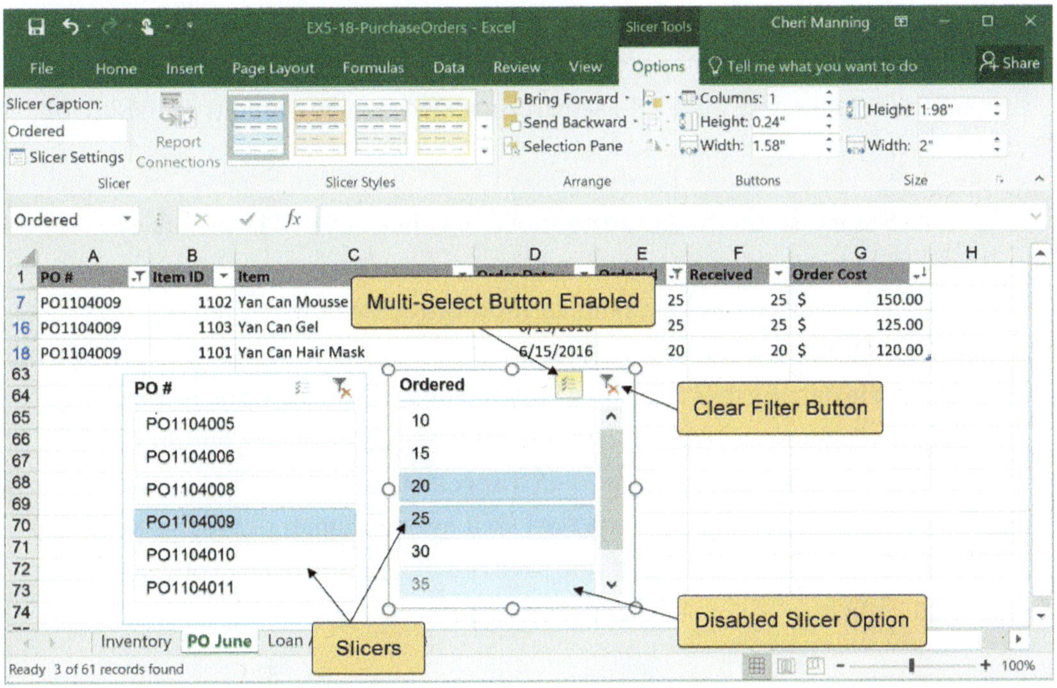

FIGURE EX 5.34

To remove filtering, click the **Clear Filter** button in the upper right corner of the slicer.

To remove a slicer from the table, click the slicer and then press Delete. Removing a slicer does not clear the filtering from the table.

tell me **more**

- To move a slicer, move your mouse pointer over the slicer. When the cursor changes to the move cursor, click and drag the slicer to a new position on the worksheet.
- When a slicer is selected, the *Slicer Tools Options* tab becomes available. From this tab, you can apply a style to the slicer and control slicer settings.

let me **try** *Live!*

Open the student data file **EX5-18-PurchaseOrders** and try this skill on your own:

1. If necessary, select the **PO June** sheet and click any cell in the table.
2. Add slicers for **PO #** and **Ordered**.
3. Using the slicers, filter the table to show only rows where the PO # is **PO1104009.**
4. Filter the data further to display only records where the value in the *Ordered* column is **20** or **25**. *Hint:* Enable the **Multi-Select** button to apply more than one filter option in the **Ordered** slicer.
5. If you will be moving on to the next skill in this chapter, leave the workbook open to continue working. If not, save the file as directed by your instructor and close it.

Skill 5.19 Converting Tables to Ranges

Although Excel tables are extremely useful, there are times when you do not want your data formatted as a table. Certain data analysis tools, including creating subtotals and grouping outlines, are not available if data are formatted as a table.

To convert a table to a normal range:

1. On the *Table Tools Design* tab, in the *Tools* group, click the **Convert to Range** button.
2. Excel displays a message box asking if you want to convert the table to a normal range. Click **Yes.**

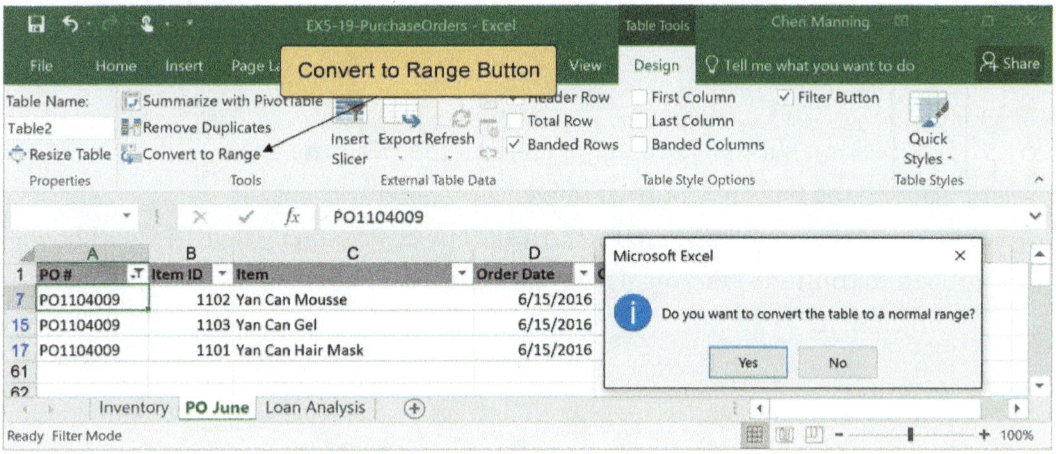

FIGURE EX 5.35

As shown in Figure EX 5.36, when you convert from a table to a normal range, Excel removes any filtering that may have been applied. Any table formatting such as banding and the Total row are still applied to the range.

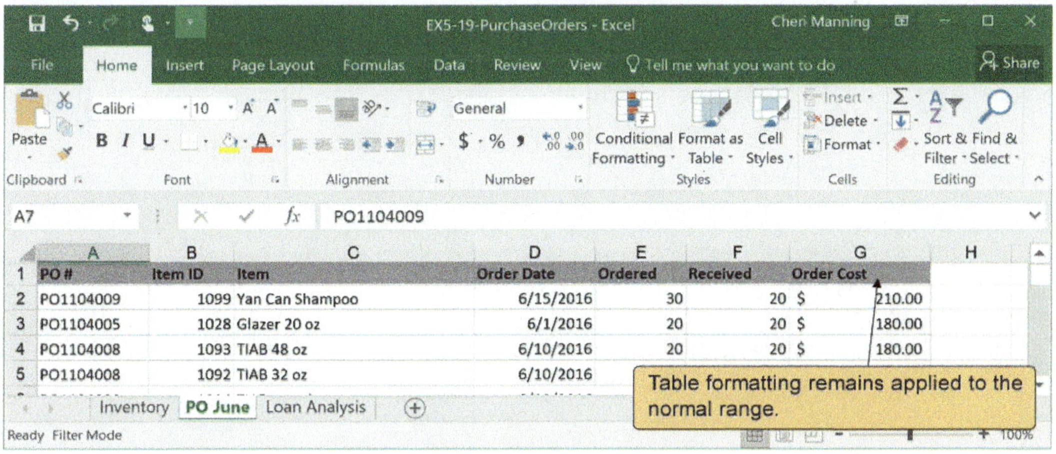

FIGURE EX 5.36

tips & tricks

If you want to use one of the table styles but do not want the data formatted as a table, begin by formatting the range as a table, applying the table style you want, and then convert the table back to a normal range.

another method

You can also right-click anywhere in the table, point to **Table**, and select **Convert to Range.**

let me try *Live!*

Open the student data file **EX5-19-PurchaseOrders** and try this skill on your own:

1. If necessary, click any cell in the table on the **PO June** sheet.
2. Convert the table to a normal range.
3. If you will be moving on to the next skill in this chapter, leave the workbook open to continue working. If not, save the file as directed by your instructor and close it.

Skill 5.20 Creating PivotTables Using Recommended PivotTables

A **PivotTable** is a special report view that summarizes data and calculates the intersecting totals. PivotTables do not contain any data themselves—they summarize data from a cell range or a table in another part of your workbook.

The easiest way to begin a new PivotTable is to use one of the recommended PivotTables:

1. Select any cell within the table or cell range you want to use for your PivotTable.
2. On the *Insert* tab, in the *Tables* group, click the **Recommended PivotTables** button.
3. Preview each of the options in the *Recommended PivotTables* dialog. Click the one that is closest to how you want your final PivotTable to look.
4. Click **OK** to create the PivotTable in a new worksheet.

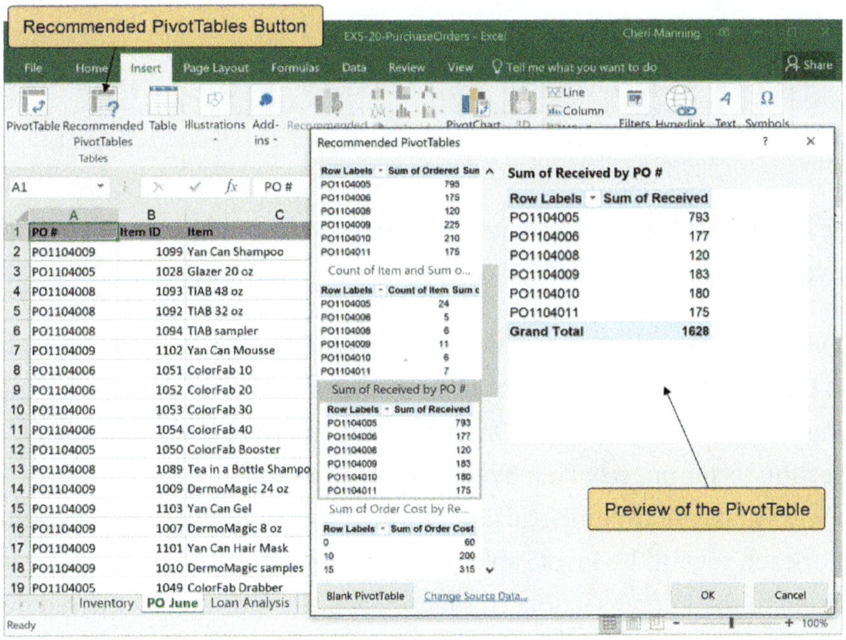

FIGURE EX 5.37

Use the *PivotTable Fields* pane to review and modify the structure of the PivotTable. The top part of the *PivotTable Fields* pane shows you the list of available fields—the columns from the PivotTable's data source. The bottom part of the *PivotTable Fields* pane allows you to build or modify the PivotTable by adding field data to one of four areas: *Filters, Columns, Rows,* or *Values.* In Figure EX 5.38, the recommended PivotTable added the *PO #* field to the *Rows* section and the *Received* field to the *Values* section. The PivotTable summarizes values in the *Received* field for each value in the *PO #* field.

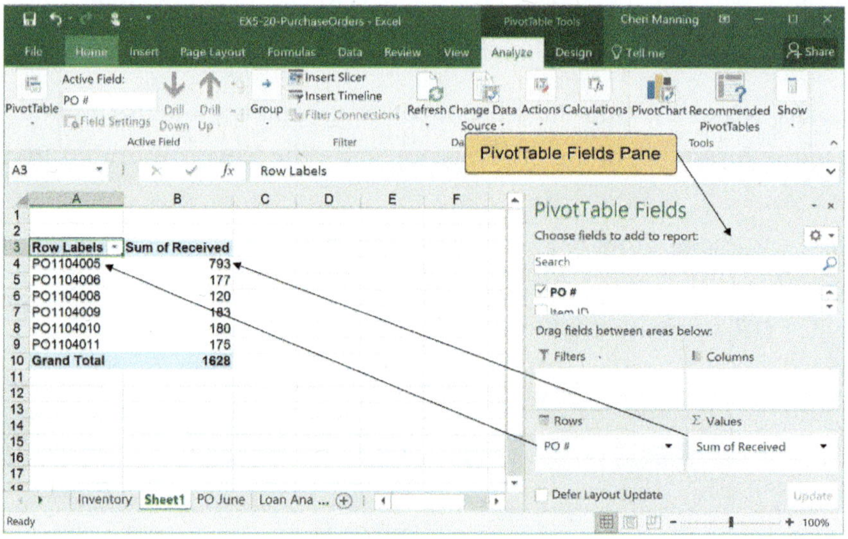

FIGURE EX 5.38

In the *PivotTable Fields* pane, check the boxes in from of each column name to add or remove fields from the PivotTable.

- Fields that contain text or date data are added to the *Rows* section automatically. If there are multiple rows, Excel will attempt to group them in a logical way. In Figure EX 5.39, adding the *Order Date* field to the PivotTable adds it to the *Rows* section to summarize data by date for each PO #.
- Fields that contain numeric data are added to the *Values* section automatically. For each row in the PivotTable, Excel summarizes the values in each of the fields listed in the *Values* section. In Figure EX 5.39, adding the *Ordered* field to the PivotTable adds it to the *Values* section and calculates the total value ordered for each PO # and date ordered.

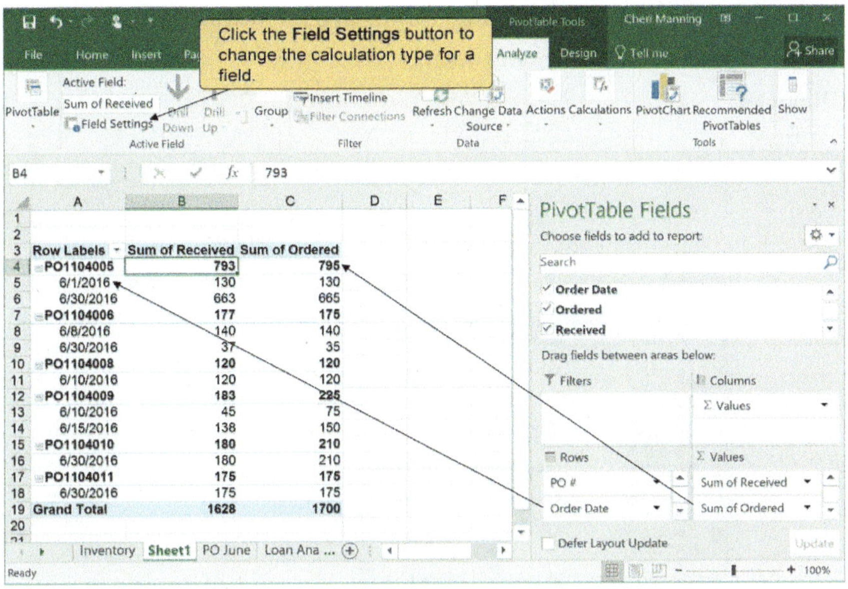

FIGURE EX 5.39

Excel summarizes numerical data in the PivotTable using the SUM function by default. You can choose another calculation type such as count or average.

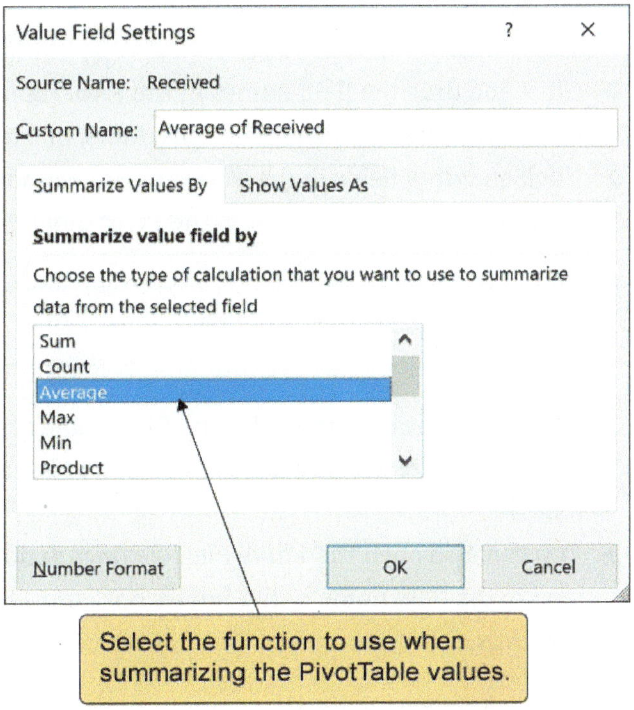

FIGURE EX 5.40

To change the calculation type for a field:

1. Click anywhere in the field you want to change.
2. On the *PivotTable Tools Analyze* tab, in the *Active Field* group, click the **Field Settings** button.

3. In the *Value Field Settings* dialog, *Summarize Values By* tab, select the function for the type of calculation you want.
4. Click **OK.**

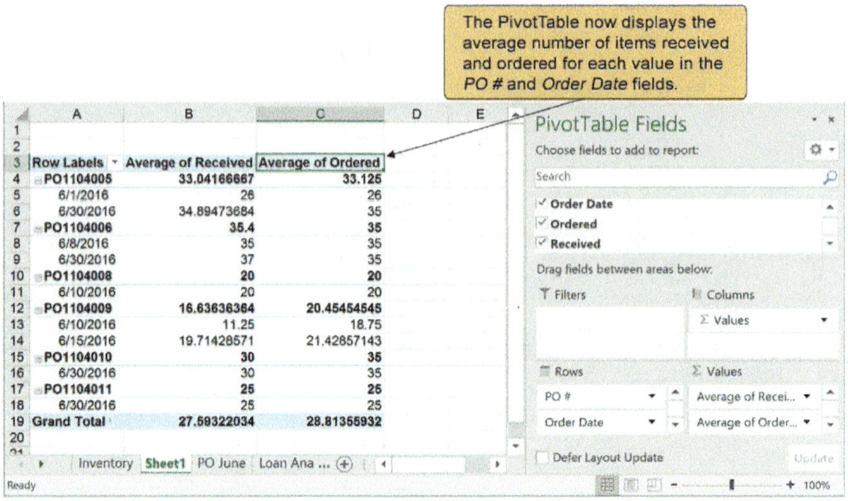

FIGURE EX 5.41

tips & tricks

- Click and drag the field names in the *PivotTable Fields* pane to move them between the *Filters, Columns, Rows,* or *Values* boxes.
- Click and drag fields in the *Rows* and *Values* boxes in the *PivotTable Fields* pane to reorder them in the PivotTable.

another method

- If you have the data range for the PivotTable selected, the recommended PivotTables are also available from the *Tables* tab in the Quick Analysis tool.
- You can also open the *Value Field Settings* dialog by clicking the arrow next to the field name in the *Values* box, and then selecting **Value Field Settings...**

let me try *Live!*

Open the student data file **EX5-20-PurchaseOrders** and try this skill on your own:

1. Verify that the **PO June** sheet is active and one of the cells in the data range is selected.
2. Insert a recommended PivotTable using the **Sum of Received by PO #** option. *Hint:* You many need to scroll down the list of recommended PivotTables to find this option.
3. Add the **Order Date** field to the PivotTable.
4. Add the **Ordered** field to the PivotTable.
5. Modify the **Received** and **Ordered** fields to use the **AVERAGE** function instead of the SUM function.
6. If you will be moving on to the next skill in this chapter, leave the workbook open to continue working. If not, save the file as directed by your instructor and close it.

Skill 5.21 Creating a PivotChart from a PivotTable

A **PivotChart** is a graphic representation of a PivotTable. In a column chart, the category fields are represented along the x (horizontal) axis while the data values are represented along the y (vertical) axis.

To create a PivotChart from a PivotTable:

1. Select any cell in the PivotTable.
2. On the *PivotTable Tools Analyze* tab, in the *Tools* group, click the **PivotChart** button.

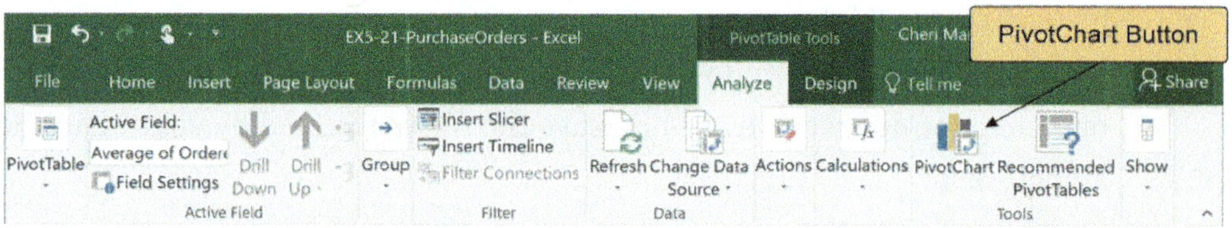

FIGURE EX 5.42

3. Select a chart type from the *Insert Chart* dialog.
4. Click **OK.**

The *Insert Chart* dialog used when creating a PivotChart is very similar to the one used when creating regular charts. Click a chart type at the left side of the dialog, and then click an option from the examples along the top of the right hand pane. Excel displays a preview of the chart. There are no recommended charts for PivotCharts.

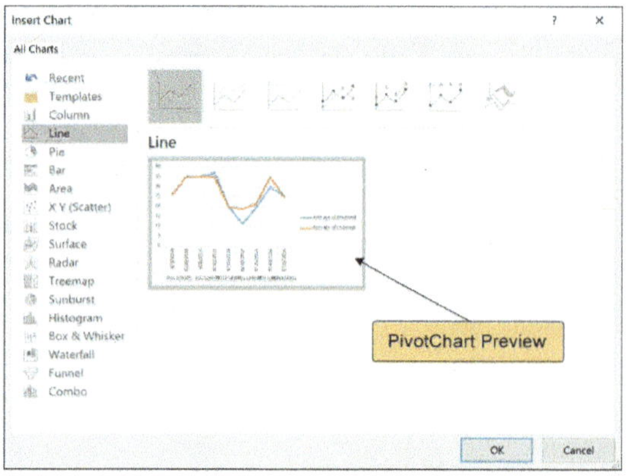

FIGURE EX 5.43

If you need more room to display the PivotChart, you may want to hide the *PivotTable Fields* pane. On the *PivotChart Tools Analyze* tab, in the *Show/Hide* group, click the **Field List** button to hide or display the *PivotTable Fields* pane.

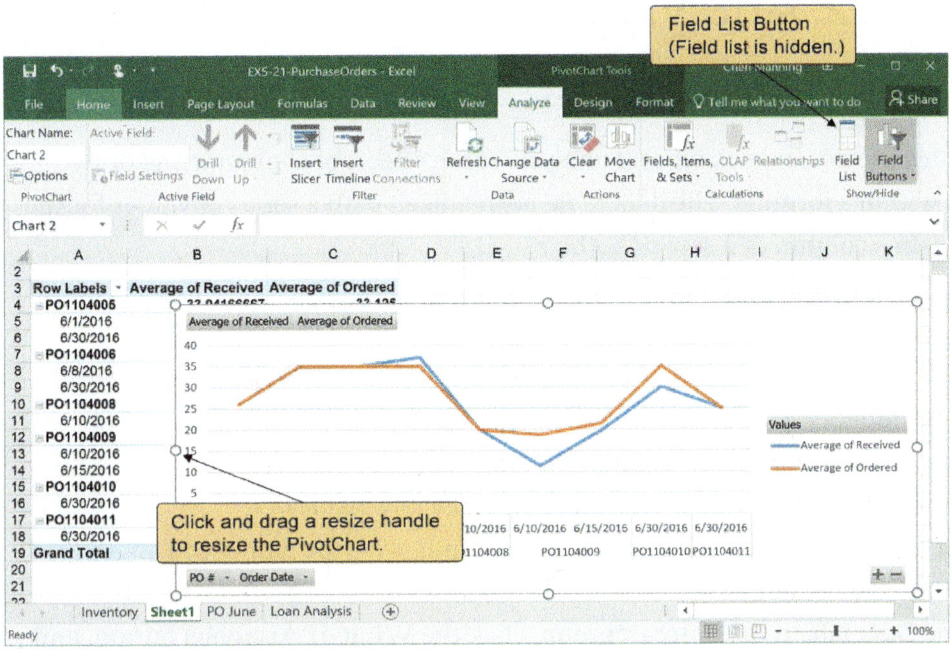

FIGURE EX 5.44

PivotCharts include all the formatting options that regular charts do. You can apply Quick Styles and hide or show chart elements from the *PivotChart Tools Design* tab. You can also resize the PivotChart or move it to its own sheet.

tell me **more**

To sort or filter the category data in the PivotChart, click the button in the lower left corner of the PivotChart with the name of the field you want to sort or filter. If your PivotTable used multiple row labels, you will see a button for each.

let me **try** *Live!*

Open the student data file **EX5-21-PurchaseOrders** and try this skill on your own:

1. If necessary, click anywhere in the PivotTable.
2. Insert a PivotChart using the first line chart type.
3. If you will be moving on to the next skill in this chapter, leave the workbook open to continue working. If not, save the file as directed by your instructor and close it.

Skill 5.22 Analyzing Data with Data Tables

Data tables provide a quick what-if analysis of the effects of changing one or two variables within a formula. The data table is organized with a series of values for the variable(s) in a column or a row or both.

To create a one-variable data table with a column input format:

1. In a column, type the series of values you want to substitute for the variable in your formula.
2. In the cell above and to the right of the first value, type the formula that references the cell you want to replace with the new values.
3. Select the cell range for the data table, beginning with the empty cell above the first value you entered.
4. On the *Data* tab, in the *Forecast* group, click the **What-If Analysis** button, and click **Data Table...**
5. In the *Data Table* dialog, the input cell is the cell that contains the original value for which you want to substitute the data table values. In this data table, the output values will be listed in a column, so enter the cell reference in the *Column input cell* box.
6. Click **OK.**

In the one-variable data table in Figure EX 5.45, the formula in cell **B9** references the loan amount in cell **B2**—the *pv* argument for the PMT function. This is the **column input cell** for the data table. The substitute values for cell B2 are listed in cells **A5:A14.**

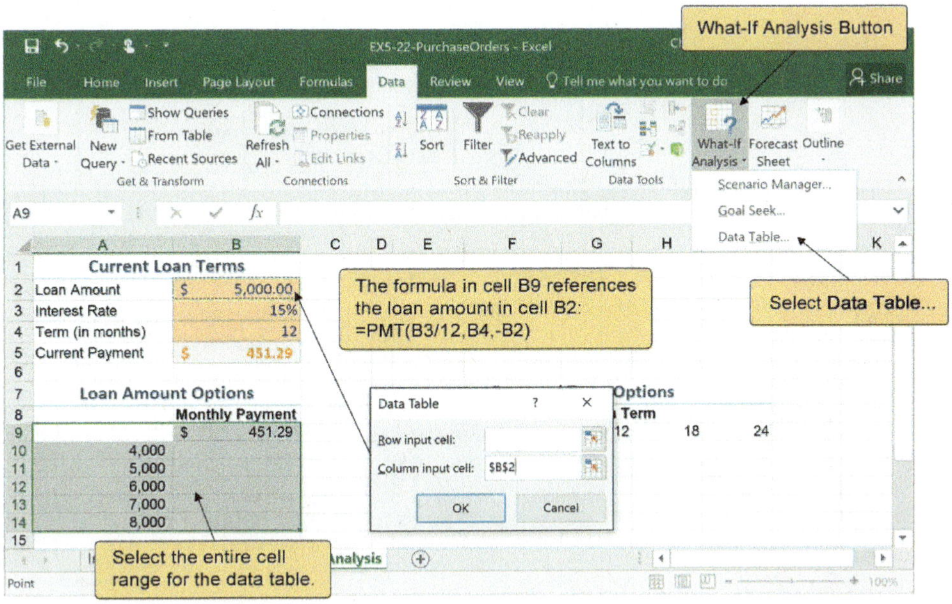

FIGURE EX 5.45

Excel completes the values in the table, using the substitute values in the formula:

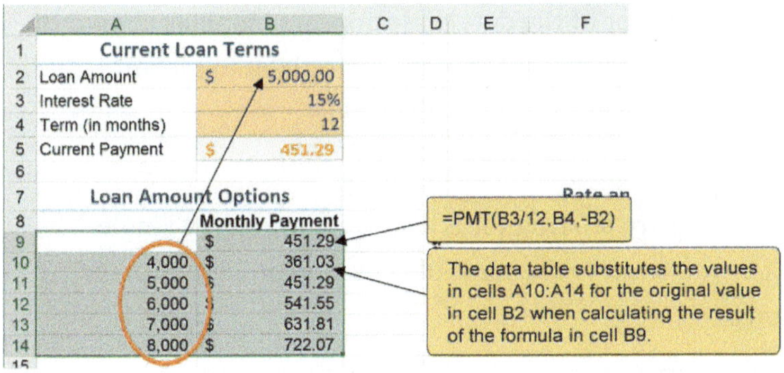

FIGURE EX 5.46

A **two-variable data table** works the same way as a one-variable data table, using inputs for both a column and a row variable. In a two-variable data table, the formula is located in the cell above the column input values and to the left of the row input values.

In the two-variable data table in Figure EX 5.47, the formula in cell E9 references the loan term in cell **B4**—the *nper* argument for the PMT function. This is the **row input cell** for the data table. The substitute values for cell **B4** are listed in cells **F8:I8.** The formula also references the second variable used in the data table, the interest rate in cell **B3**—the *rate* argument for the PMT function. This is the column input cell for the data table. The substitute values for cell B3 are listed in cells **E9:E14.**

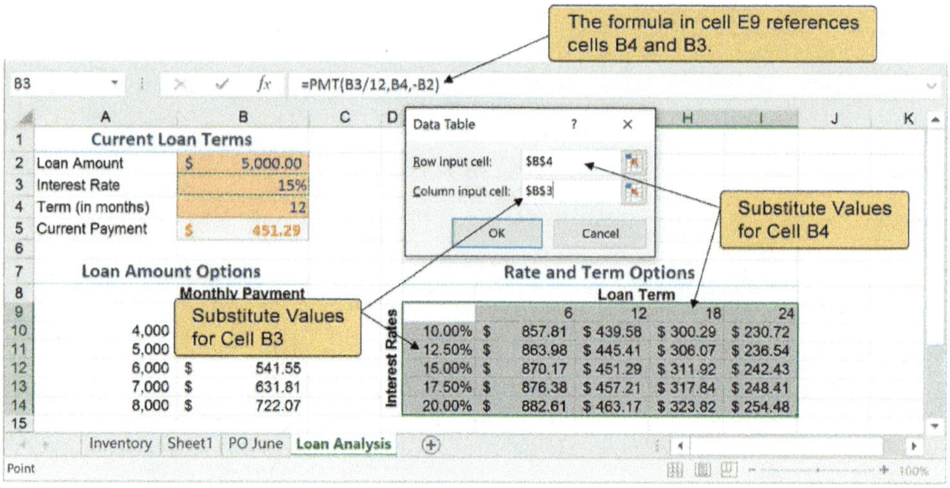

FIGURE EX 5.47

In a two-variable data table, you may want to hide the data table formula by changing the cell font color to match the worksheet background. The data table is easier to follow if the cell in the upper left corner of the data table appears blank as shown in cell E9 in Figure EX 5.47. Of course, you can still see the formula in the formula bar.

tips & tricks

> Use Goal Seek if the result you are looking for is a specific value in a single cell. Use data tables when you want to see multiple possible outcomes based on multiple input options.

let me try *Live!*

Open the student data file **EX5-22-PurchaseOrders** and try this skill on your own:

1. Go to the **Loan Analysis** worksheet.
2. Insert a one-variable data table in cells **A9:D14** to calculate the monthly loan payment for the loan amounts listed in cells A10:A14. The formula has been entered for you in cell B9. It references the original loan amount in cell **B2**.
3. Insert a two-variable data table in cells **E9:I14** to calculate the monthly loan payments for various interest rates and loan terms. The formula in cell E9 has been formatted using the white font color so it appears hidden. It references the original interest rate in cell **B3** and the loan term in cell **B4**.
4. If you will be moving on to the next skill in this chapter, leave the workbook open to continue working. If not, save the file as directed by your instructor and close it.

Skill 5.23 Analyzing Data with Goal Seek

Excel's **Goal Seek** function lets you enter a desired value (outcome) for a formula and specify an input cell that can be modified in order to reach that goal. Goal Seek changes the value of the input cell incrementally until the target outcome is reached. In Figure EX 5.48, the outcome cell is cell **B5,** the loan payment; the desired outcome value is 750; and the input cell is cell **B2,** the loan amount.

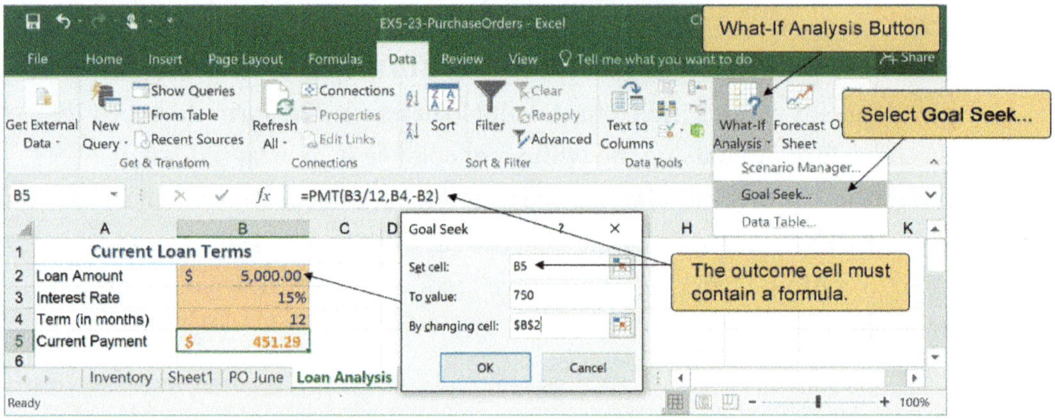

FIGURE EX 5.48

To find a value using Goal Seek:

1. On the *Data* tab, in the *Forecast* group, click the **What-If Analysis** button, and then click **Goal Seek...**
2. Enter the outcome cell in the *Set cell* box. This cell must contain a formula.
3. Enter the outcome value you want in the *To value* box.
4. Enter the input cell (the cell that contains the value to be changed) in the *By changing cell* box. This cell must be referenced in the formula in the outcome cell either directly or indirectly and must contain a value, not a formula.
5. Click **OK.**

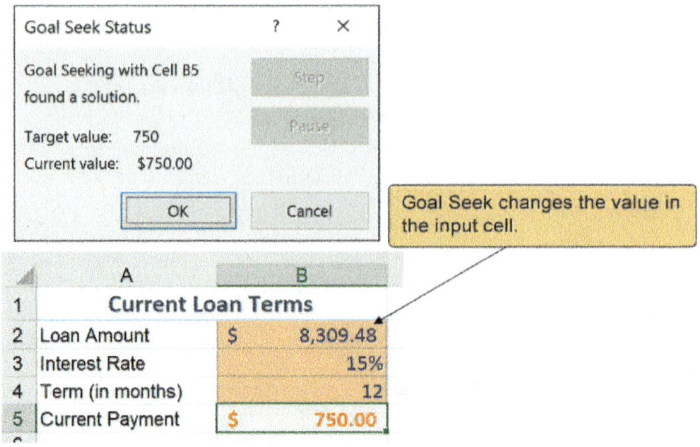

FIGURE EX 5.49

6. The *Goal Seek Status* box appears, letting you know if Goal Seek was able to find a solution. Click **OK** to accept the solution and change the value in the input cell or click **Cancel** to return the input cell to its original value.

tips & tricks

Goal Seek works best in situations where there is only one variable, such as:

- Finding the loan amount to result in a specific loan payment when the loan rate and terms are inflexible.
- Finding the required number of units to sell to reach a sales goal when the price is inflexible.

let me try *Live!*

Open the student data file **EX5-23-PurchaseOrders** and try this skill on your own:

1. Use Goal Seek to find the amount of loan you can afford (cell **B2**) that will result in a payment of **750** in cell **B5**.
2. If Goal Seek is able to find a solution, accept it.
3. Save the file as directed by your instructor and close it.

key terms

- Chart
- Data points
- Data markers
- Data series (chart)
- Y axis
- X axis
- Plot area
- Chart area
- Chart title
- Legend
- Column charts
- Bar charts
- Pie charts
- Doughnut charts
- Line charts
- Line with markers
- Chart sheet
- Data labels
- Data table (chart)
- Quick Styles
- Clustered column chart
- Stacked column chart
- Sparklines
- Table
- Banding
- Total row
- Sort
- Filter
- Slicer
- PivotTable
- PivotChart
- Data table (what-if analysis)
- Column input cell
- Two-variable data table
- Row input cell
- Goal Seek

concept review

1. Data markers are graphic representations of the values of data points in a chart.
   a. true
   b. false
2. ________________ charts represent data as parts of a whole.
   a. Column
   b. Line
   c. Pie
   d. Bar
3. ________________ apply combinations of fonts, line styles, fills, and shape effects to charts.
   a. Quick Styles
   b. Quick Layouts
   c. Chart Effects
   d. Chart Templates
4. ________________ represent each data series as an individual graphic within a single cell.
   a. Sparklines
   b. Charts
   c. Tables
   d. PivotCharts
5. A Total row can be used to quickly calculate the ________________ of all the values in a column.
   a. sum
   b. average
   c. both a and b
   d. neither a nor b
6. When you format data as a table, the header row automatically includes filtering and sorting.
   a. true
   b. false
7. ________________ rearranges the rows in your worksheet by the data in a column or columns.
   a. Sorting
   b. Filtering
   c. Formatting
   d. Grouping

8. ________________ is a special report view that summarizes data and calculates the intersecting totals.
   a. PivotTable
   b. table
   c. chart
   d. scenario
9. The ________________ command provides a quick what-if analysis of the effects of changing one or two variables within a formula.
   a. *Scenario*
   b. *Data Table*
   c. *Consolidate*
   d. *Goal Seek*
10. The ________________ command lets you enter a designated value for a formula and specify an input cell that can be modified in order to reach that goal.
   a. *Scenario*
   b. *Data Table*
   c. *Consolidate*
   d. *Goal Seek*

projects

Data files for projects can be found by logging into your SIMnet account and going to the *Library* section.

skill review 5.1

In this project, you will analyze data for an event planning company

Skills needed to complete this project:

- Converting Data into Tables (Skill 5.12)
- Adding Total Rows to Tables (Skill 5.14)
- Sorting Data (Skill 5.16)
- Filtering Data (Skill 5.17)
- Analyzing Data with Data Tables (Skill 5.22)
- Using the Recommended Charts Feature (Skill 5.2)
- Changing the Chart Type (Skill 5.9)
- Applying Quick Styles and Colors to Charts (Skill 5.8)
- Showing and Hiding Chart Elements (Skill 5.7)
- Resizing and Moving Charts (Skill 5.6)
- Analyzing Data with Goal Seek (Skill 5.23)
- Inserting a Pie Chart (Skill 5.4)
- Exploring Charts (Skill 5.1)
- Creating PivotTables Using Recommended PivotTables (Skill 5.20)
- Creating a PivotChart from a PivotTable (Skill 5.21)

1. Open the start file **EX2016-SkillReview-5-1** and resave the file as:
   `[your initials]EX-SkillReview-5-1`
2. If the workbook opens in Protected View, click the **Enable Editing** button in the Message Bar at the top of the workbook so you can modify the workbook.
3. Format the data on the *Table* worksheet into a table using one of the table Quick Styles.
   a. Select all the data including the headings, being careful not to select any blank rows or columns.
   b. On the *Home* tab, in the *Styles* group, click the **Format as Table** button to display the *Table Styles* gallery.
   c. Click the **Table Style Light 9** Quick Style.
   d. Verify that the correct cells will be used. Check the **My table has headers** check box. Click **OK.**
4. Add a Total row to the table to count the number of invitations sent.
   a. On the *Table Tools Design* tab, in the *Table Style Options* group, click the **Total Row** check box.

    b. In the Total row at the bottom of the table, note the total count of guests attending.
    c. In the Total row at the bottom of the table, click in the **City** column, click the arrow, and select the **Count** function to count the invitations sent.
5. Sort the table by city in alphabetical order:
    a. Click anywhere in the **City** column.
    b. On the *Data* tab, in the *Sort & Filter* group, click the **A-Z** button.
6. Filter the data in the table to show only guests from the city of Auburn.
    a. Click the arrow in the **City** column header.
    b. Click the **(Select All)** check box to remove all of the checkmarks.
    c. Click the check box in front of **Auburn** to filter for only guests from Auburn.
    d. Click **OK.** Excel displays only the rows for invitations sent to Auburn.
7. Switch to work with the *Data Table* worksheet and use a data table to estimate costs for different numbers of attendees. Cell C18 contains a formula that sums the costs in cells **C3:C15.** The formulas in those cells all refer to the number of guests in cell **C1.**
    a. Select cells **B18:C25** to use as the data table.
    b. On the *Data* tab, in the *Forecast* group, click the **What-If Analysis** button, and click **Data Table...**
    c. In the *Column input cell* box, type C1 and then click **OK.**
    d. Review the data table results computing the party costs for the various numbers of guests.
8. Use the recommended charts feature to create a column chart to compare the cost of various size parties.
    a. Select cells **B17:C25.**
    b. Click the **Quick Analysis Tool** button at the lower right corner of the selected range.
    c. Click the **Charts** tab.
    d. Click the **Clustered Column** option.
9. Change the chart to a line chart.
    a. If necessary, click to select the chart.
    b. On the *Chart Tools Design* tab, in the *Type* group, click the **Change Chart Type** button.
    c. In the *Change Chart Type* dialog, click **Line,** and click the first line chart type.
    d. Click **OK.**
10. Format the chart using a Quick Style. On the *Chart Tools Design* tab, in the *Chart Styles* group, click **Style 3.**
11. Display the chart gridlines and hide the data labels.

a. Click the **Chart Elements** button that appears near the upper right corner of the chart.
b. Click the **Gridlines** check box to add a checkmark.
c. Click the **Data Labels** check box to add a checkmark.

12. Move the chart to its own sheet in the workbook.
    a. On the *Chart Tools Design* tab, in the *Location* group, click the **Move Chart** button.
    b. In the *Move Chart* dialog, click the **New sheet** radio button.
    c. In the *New sheet* box, type: `Data Table Chart`
    d. Click **OK.**
13. Use Goal Seek to determine the most you can afford for dinner per person on a total $9,000 budget for 100 guests assuming all other per guest costs remain the same.
    a. Switch to the *Goal Seek* sheet.
    b. Select the outcome cell **C18** and review the formula.
    c. On the *Data* tab, in the *Forecast* group, click the **What-If Analysis** button and click **Goal Seek...**
    d. Verify that the outcome cell **C18** is referenced in the *Set cell* box.
    e. Enter the outcome value of `9000` in the *To value* box.
    f. Enter the input cell `A4` in the *By changing cell* box.
    g. Click **OK** to run Goal Seek.
    h. Click **OK** again to accept the Goal Seek solution.
14. Insert a 3-D pie chart to show the breakdown of the per guest costs.
    a. Select cells **B3:C11.**
    b. On the *Insert* tab, in the *Charts* group, click the **Pie** button, and click the **3-D Pie** option.
    c. Move the chart to the right so it does not cover the worksheet data.
    d. Change the chart title to: `Per Guest Costs`
15. Create a PivotTable listing the number attending from each city
    a. Return to the *Table* worksheet.
    b. Click anywhere in the table.
    c. On the *Insert* tab, in the *Tables* group, click the **Recommended PivotTables** button.
    d. Select the option **Sum of NumAttending by City.**
    e. Click **OK.**
16. Modify the PivotTable to calculate the average number of attendees per city instead of the total.
    a. Click anywhere in the **Sum of NumAttending** field.
    b. On the *PivotTable Tools Analyze* tab, in the *Active Field* group, click the **Field Settings** button.

c. In the *Value Field Settings* dialog, *Summarize Values By* tab, select **Average** to change the calculation from SUM to AVERAGE.

d. Click **OK.**

17. Create a PivotChart from the PivotTable.

a. Select any cell in the PivotTable.

b. On the *PivotTable Tools Analyze* tab, in the *Tools* group, click the **PivotChart** button.

c. Verify that the Clustered Column chart type is selected in the *Insert Chart* dialog.

d. Click **OK.**

e. Click the title and change it to read: `Number of Guests Attending from Each City`

f. Hide the legend by clicking the **Chart Elements** button that appears near the upper right corner of the PivotChart and clicking the **Legend** check box to remove the checkmark.

g. If necessary, move the PivotChart to the right so it does not cover the PivotTable.

18. Save and close the workbook.

projects

Data files for projects can be found by logging into your SIMnet account and going to the *Library* section.

skill review 5.2

In this project you will analyze real estate data.

Skills needed to complete this project:

- Converting Data into Tables (Skill 5.12)
- Adding Total Rows to Tables (Skill 5.14)
- Sorting Data (Skill 5.16)
- Filtering Data (Skill 5.17)
- Inserting a Line Chart (Skill 5.5)
- Resizing and Moving Charts (Skill 5.6)
- Showing and Hiding Chart Elements (Skill 5.7)
- Exploring Charts (Skill 5.1)
- Applying Quick Styles and Colors to Charts (Skill 5.8)
- Creating PivotTables Using Recommended PivotTables (Skill 5.20)
- Inserting Sparklines (Skill 5.11)
- Creating a PivotChart from a PivotTable (Skill 5.21)
- Analyzing Data with Data Tables (Skill 5.22)
- Analyzing Data with Goal Seek (Skill 5.23)

1. Open the start file **EX2016-SkillReview-5-2** and resave the file as: `[your initials]EX-SkillReview-5-2`
2. If the workbook opens in Protected View, click the **Enable Editing** button in the Message Bar at the top of the workbook so you can modify the workbook.
3. Format the data on the *Sales Data* worksheet as a table using the **Table Style Light 14** table style:
   a. Select any cell in the data.
   b. On the *Home* tab, in the *Styles* group, click the **Format as Table** button to display the *Table Styles* gallery.
   c. Click the **Table Style Light 14** style.
   d. Verify that the **My table has headers** check box is checked and that the correct data range is selected.
   e. Click **OK.**
4. Add a Total row to the table to display the number of buyers; the average number of bedrooms and bathrooms for each sale; and the average purchase price, interest rate, and mortgage length.

a. On the *Table Tools Design* tab, in the *Table Style Options* group, click the **Total Row** check box.
b. In the Total row at the bottom of the table, click in the **Buyers** column, click the arrow, and select the **Count** function.
c. In the Total row at the bottom of the table, click in the **Bedrooms** column, click the arrow, and select the **Average** function.
d. In the Total row at the bottom of the table, click in the **Bathrooms** column, click the arrow, and select the **Average** function.
e. In the Total row at the bottom of the table, click in the **Purchase Price** column, click the arrow, and select the **Average** function.
f. In the Total row at the bottom of the table, click in the **Rate** column, click the arrow, and select the **Average** function.
g. In the Total row at the bottom of the table, click in the **Mortgage Years** column, click the arrow, and select the **Average** function.

5. Sort the data so the newest purchases appear at the top.
    a. Click anywhere in the **Date of Purchase** column.
    b. On the *Data* tab, in the *Sort & Filter* group, click the **Z-A** button.
6. Filter the data to show only houses sold by owner with four or five bedrooms.
    a. Click the arrow at the top of the **Agent** column.
    b. Click the **(Select All)** check box to remove all of the checkmarks.
    c. Click the check box in front of **By Owner.**
    d. Click **OK.**
    e. Click the arrow at the top of the **Bedrooms** column.
    f. Click the **(Select All)** check box to remove all of the checkmarks.
    g. Click the check boxes in front of **4** and **5.**
    h. Click **OK.**
7. Create a line chart showing the purchase prices for houses by date.
    a. Select the **Date of Purchase** data cells. Be careful not to include the column heading. Press and hold Ctrl and click and drag to select the **Purchase Price** data cells, again being careful not to include the column heading.
    b. On the *Insert* tab, in the *Charts* group, click the **Insert Line Chart** button.
    c. Select the first line chart type shown.
    d. Click **OK.**
8. Move the chart to its own sheet named *Purchase Prices.*
    a. If necessary, select the chart. On the *Chart Tools Design* tab, in the *Locations* group, click the **Move Chart** button.
    b. In the *Move Chart* dialog, click the **New sheet** radio button.
    c. In the box type: `Purchase Prices`
    d. Click **OK.**
9. Update the chart title and display the data labels as callouts.

a. Change the chart title to: `For Sale By Owner`
b. Click the **Chart Elements** button near the upper right corner of the chart.
c. Click the **Data Labels** check box to add a checkmark.
d. Point to **Data Labels,** click the arrow that appears at the right side, and click **Data Callout.**

10. Apply the **Style 2** Quick Style to the chart.
    a. Click the **Chart Styles** button that appears near the upper right corner of the chart.
    b. Click **Style 2.**
11. Create a PivotTable to summarize the average purchase price of different house types for each agent.
    a. Return to the *Sales Data* worksheet and click anywhere in the table.
    b. Click the **Insert** tab. In the *Tables* group, click the **Recommended PivotTables** button.
    c. Verify that the first recommended PivotTable is **Sum of Purchase Price by Agent.**
    d. Click **OK.**
    e. Select any cell in the **Sum of Purchase Price** column.
    f. On the *PivotTable Tools Analyze* tab, in the *Active Field* group, click the **Field Settings** button.
    g. In the *Summarize value field by* box, select **Average.**
    h. Click **OK.**
    i. Add the **House Type** field to the PivotTable by clicking the check box in the *Fields List* pane. Excel automatically places the *House Type* field in the Rows box and displays the house type data as a subgroup of rows below each agent.
    j. To summarize the house type data for each agent, use the *House Type* field as columns in the PivotTable. Click and drag the **House Type** field from the Rows box to the Columns box in the *PivotTable Fields* pane.
12. Add column Sparklines to the right of the PivotTable.
    a. Select cells **B5:E9** to use as the data for the Sparklines. You do not want to include the grand total column or row.
    b. On the *Insert* tab, in the *Sparklines* group, click the **Column** button.
    c. In the *Create Sparklines* dialog, verify that the cell range **B5:E9** is listed in the *Data Range* box.
    d. Add the range **G5:G9** to the *Location Range* box either by typing the cells range or by clicking and dragging to select it in the worksheet.
    e. Click **OK.**
13. Create a PivotChart from the PivotTable.
    a. Select any cell in the PivotTable.
    b. On the *PivotTable Tools Analyze* tab, in the *Tools* group, click the **PivotChart**

button.

c. Select the first bar chart type from the *Insert Chart* dialog. Click **OK.**
d. If necessary, move the PivotChart to another part of the worksheet so it does not cover the PivotTable data.

14. Use the data in the *Loan Worksheet* sheet to run a what-if scenario for a client to show loan payments for a variety of interest rates and loan lengths. This what-if scenario requires a two-variable data table.
    a. Go to the **Loan Worksheet** sheet and familiarize yourself with the formula in cell **B5.** Pay close attention to the cell references.
    b. Select cells **B5:E25** to use the payment formula in B5 and the various years and rates as the data table.
    c. On the *Data* tab, in the *Forecast* group, click the **What-If Analysis** button, and click **Data Table.**
    d. In the *Row input cell* box, enter the cell reference for the length of the loan—the *nper* argument from the formula in cell B5: `C2`
    e. In the *Column input cell* box, enter the cell reference for the loan interest rate—the *interest* argument from the formula in cell B5: `A2`
    f. Click **OK.**
15. Use Goal Seek to determine the most you can afford to borrow, on a $950 per month budget:
    a. On the *Loan Worksheet* sheet, select the outcome formula cell, **H4.**
    b. On the *Data* tab, in the *Forecast* group, click the **What-If Analysis** button and click **Goal Seek...**
    c. Verify that the outcome cell **H4** is referenced in the *Set cell* box.
    d. Enter the outcome value of `950` in the *To value* box.
    e. Enter the input cell `H9` in the *By changing cell* box.
    f. Click **OK.**
    g. Click **OK** again to accept the Goal Seek solution.
    h. Notice the loan payment changed to $950 and the amount to borrow was computed to be $198,988.
16. Save and close the workbook.

projects

Data files for projects can be found by logging into your SIMnet account and going to the *Library* section.

challenge yourself 5.3

In this project, you will analyze shoe sales data and use what-if analysis to determine your commission potential and your sales goal.

Skills needed to complete this project:

- Converting Data into Tables (Skill 5.12)
- Adding Total Rows to Tables (Skill 5.14)
- Removing Duplicate Rows from Tables (Skill 5.15)
- Filtering Data (Skill 5.17)
- Sorting Data (Skill 5.16)
- Inserting a Line Chart (Skill 5.5)
- Filtering Chart Data (Skill 5.10)
- Resizing and Moving Charts (Skill 5.6)
- Filtering Table Data with Slicers (Skill 5.18)
- Creating PivotTables Using Recommended PivotTables (Skill 5.20)
- Creating a PivotChart from a PivotTable (Skill 5.21)
- Showing and Hiding Chart Elements (Skill 5.7)
- Inserting Sparklines (Skill 5.11)
- Analyzing Data with Data Tables (Skill 5.22)
- Analyzing Data with Goal Seek (Skill 5.23)

1. Open the start file **EX2016-ChallengeYourself-5-3** and resave the file as: `[your initials]EX-ChallengeYourself-5-3`
2. If the workbook opens in Protected View, click the **Enable Editing** button in the Message Bar at the top of the workbook so you can modify the workbook.
3. Convert the shoe sales data in the *Sales* worksheet into a table.
    a. Use the **Table Style Medium 3** table style.
    b. Add a Total row to the table to display the total for the *Total Sale* column.
    c. In the Total row, display the average for the *# of Pairs* and the *Price Per Pair* columns.
    d. Delete any rows in the table that have duplicate data in all the columns. There are four.
4. Filter to show just the sales for the **Oregon** region.
5. Sort the table by order date with the newest orders first.
6. Insert a line chart to show the total sale amount for each order by order date.

a. Create the line chart using just the data from the *Order Date* and *Total Sale* columns. Be sure to include the header row when selecting the data for the chart.
b. There was an ordering glitch on September 8 that caused a spike in sales. Apply a filter to the chart to hide orders from that date.
c. If necessary, move the chart so it does not cover the table data.

7. Add a slicer to the table so you can filter by shoe name. Use the slicer to display data for the **Sperry** shoe only. Notice the effect on the chart.
8. Create a PivotTable from the data in the *Sales* worksheet. Use the **Sum of Price Per Pair by Region** recommended PivotTable.
   a. Modify the PivotTable so the *Price Per Pair* data are averaged, not totaled.
   b. Add the **Shoe** field to the PivotTable. It should appear in the *Rows* section below the *Region* field.
   c. Format all the values in the PivotTable using the **Accounting Number Format.**
9. Create a clustered column PivotChart based on the PivotTable data. Use the first recommended column chart type.
   a. Hide the chart title and legend.
   b. If necessary, move the PivotChart on the worksheet so it does not cover the PivotChart data.
10. Go to the *By Region* worksheet and add Column Sparklines in **F3:F7** for data in columns **B3:E7.**
11. On the *By Region* worksheet, create a pie chart to display the sales by region for the Sperry shoe.
    a. Display the data labels as data callouts.
    b. Hide the chart legend.
    c. If necessary, move the chart so it does not cover the table data.
12. You have been told that you will receive a commission between 5 and 10 percent. On the *Commission* sheet, make a one-variable data table using cells **A4:B14** to determine how much that commission may be based on $15,000 in sales. The column input cell is **A4.**
13. You owe $8,000 in student loans and would like to pay it all off with your commissions. Use Goal Seek to determine the amount you must sell (cell **G5**) in order for cell **G3** (your commission) to equal $8,000 so you can fully pay off your student loans. Accept the Goal Seek solution.
14. Save and close the workbook.

Data files for projects can be found by logging into your SIMnet account and going to the *Library* section.

challenge yourself 5.4

In this project, the local library has received a significant collection of DVDs as a donation and has asked you to provide an analysis of the titles. It needs to decide whether it should keep the collection or sell it to raise money for a new computer.

Skills needed to complete this project:

- Converting Data into Tables (Skill 5.12)
- Adding Total Rows to Tables (Skill 5.14)
- Removing Duplicate Rows from Tables (Skill 5.15)
- Applying Quick Styles to Tables (Skill 5.13)
- Sorting Data (Skill 5.16)
- Filtering Data (Skill 5.17)
- Filtering Table Data with Slicers (Skill 5.18)
- Creating PivotTables Using Recommended PivotTables (Skill 5.20)
- Creating a PivotChart from a PivotTable (Skill 5.21)
- Showing and Hiding Chart Elements (Skill 5.7)
- Analyzing Data with Data Tables (Skill 5.22)
- Analyzing Data with Goal Seek (Skill 5.23)

1. Open the start file **EX2016-ChallengeYourself-5-4** and resave the file as: `[your initials]EX-ChallengeYourself-5-4`
2. If the workbook opens in Protected View, click the **Enable Editing** button in the Message Bar at the top of the workbook so you can modify the workbook.
3. Convert the data on the *Videos* sheet into a table using the style **Table Style Light 13.**
   a. Add a Total row to the table and count the number of movie titles and the average price.
   b. Delete all the duplicate rows. Be careful, there may be duplicate rows with the same movie title, but different data in the other columns. When you are finished, there should be 294 unique titles in the collection.
   c. Change the table style to use the **Table Style Medium 16** Quick Style.
4. Sort the data in the table alphabetically by category.
5. Filter the table to show only Disney and family movies that are rated G.
6. Create a PivotTable from the table data using the **Sum of Price by Rating** recommended PivotTable.
7. Create a pie PivotChart from the PivotTable.

a. Display the data labels using the **Inside End** option.
b. Hide the chart title.

8. On the *Data Table* worksheet, create a one-variable data table to determine the amount of money that would be raised if 150 DVDs were sold at the various prices listed. Review the formula in cell **C7** to identify the appropriate cell to use as the input cell for the data table.
9. How many DVDs would the library need to sell at $1.50 each to raise $500? Use Goal Seek to find a value for cell **F9** that will result in a value of 500 for cell **F7.**
10. Save and close the workbook.

projects

Data files for projects can be found by logging into your SIMnet account and going to the *Library* section.

on your own 5.5

In this project, you will be working with data about automobile emissions and fuel economy. These green car data were downloaded from the Web site fueleconomy.gov. The SmartWay scores range from 0 to 10, where 10 is best. The vehicles with the best scores on both air pollution and greenhouse gas receive the Elite designation. More information about the SmartWay program can be found at http://www3.epa.gov/greenvehicles/you/smartway.htm.

Skills needed to complete this project:

- Converting Data into Tables (Skill 5.12)
- Filtering Data (Skill 5.17)
- Filtering Table Data with Slicers (Skill 5.18)
- Sorting Data (Skill 5.16)
- Inserting a Column Chart or a Bar Chart (Skill 5.3)
- Showing and Hiding Chart Elements (Skill 5.7)
- Applying Quick Styles and Colors to Charts (Skill 5.8)
- Changing the Chart Type (Skill 5.9)
- Creating PivotTables Using Recommended PivotTables (Skill 5.20)
- Creating a PivotChart from a PivotTable (Skill 5.21)
- Analyzing Data with Data Tables (Skill 5.22)
- Analyzing Data with Goal Seek (Skill 5.23)

1. Open the start file **EX2016-OnYourOwn-5-5** and resave the file as:
   `[your initials]EX-OnYourOwn-5-5`
2. If the workbook opens in Protected View, click the **Enable Editing** button in the Message Bar at the top of the workbook so you can modify the workbook.
3. The *Green Cars* worksheet contains almost 500 rows. That's a lot of data! Use filtering techniques to find the subset of cars that meet the following criteria:
   a. Display only cars with the **Elite** Smartway designation. *Hint:* The *Smartway* column is at the far right side of the data. You may need to scroll to find it.
   b. Include only cars in the **midsize car** class (use the *Veh Class* column).
   c. Include only cars with **Electricity** as the only fuel (use the *Fuel* column).
   d. You should end up with six records visible.
4. Sort the data so the cars with the best combination MPG (*Cmb MPG* column) appear at the top.

5. Create a chart comparing the **City MPG, Hwy MPG,** and **Cmb MPG** for the cars shown.
   a. Add and remove chart elements as necessary to make the chart clear and easy to read.
   b. Apply one of the chart Quick Styles.
   c. Try changing the chart to another chart type. Is there another chart type available that's appropriate for the data?
6. Create a PivotTable from the car data. Use one of the recommended PivotTables or create one from scratch. Add at least two fields to the *Values* section. Change the function used for at least one of the value fields. Name the worksheet: `Pivot`
7. Create a PivotChart from the PivotTable data.
8. On the *Commuting Costs* worksheet, create a two-variable data table to calculate the daily cost of gas for a variety of gas prices and a variety of miles driven per day. If you have a daily commute to school or work, use variations on your actual commuting miles in the data table.
   a. The formula to calculate the cost of your daily commute is: Commuting miles/your car's MPG*price of gas per gallon
   b. In the data table formula, you can use the MPG in cell B3 or change the value to your car's estimated MPG.
   c. Find a way to hide the data table formula.
   d. Add formatting as appropriate.
9. You're in the market for a new car, and you'd like to reduce your monthly gas costs to around $30. What's the minimum gas mileage you should look for in your new car? Can you use Goal Seek with the data on this worksheet to find an answer?
10. Save and close the workbook.

Data files for projects can be found by logging into your SIMnet account and going to the *Library* section.

fix it 5.6

The staff members of a private college preparatory school have been trying to analyze student data and create what-if scenarios regarding investment decisions. Unfortunately, they've made a mess of this workbook. Can you help them fix it?

Skills needed to complete this project:

- Sorting Data (Skill 5.16)
- Converting Data into Tables (Skill 5.12)
- Filtering Table Data with Slicers (Skill 5.18)
- Removing Duplicate Rows from Tables (Skill 5.15)
- Adding Total Rows to Tables (Skill 5.14)
- Creating PivotTables Using Recommended PivotTables (Skill 5.20)
- Inserting a Pie Chart (Skill 5.4)
- Changing the Chart Type (Skill 5.9)
- Analyzing Data with Data Tables (Skill 5.22)

1. Open the start file **EX2016-FixIt-5-6** and resave the file as:
   `[your initials]EX-FixIt-5-6`
2. If the workbook opens in Protected View, click the **Enable Editing** button in the Message Bar at the top of the workbook so you can modify the workbook.
3. The data in the *Student Test Data* worksheet has a couple of problems to fix:
   a. The data should be organized alphabetically by student.
   b. Format the data so the school faculty can use slicers to filter data. Use any style you want.
   c. Display slicers so data can be filtered by month, by subject, or by student or by any combination of the three. Go ahead and display the slicers, but you don't need to apply any filtering.
   d. Find and delete the duplicate records. There should be 90 unique records.
   e. The data should include a Total row to calculate the average score.
4. The PivotTable on the *Student Pivot* sheet should summarize the average scores for each subject for each student by month. However, the *Score* field data have been added to the wrong section of the PivotTable.
   a. Move the *Score* field to the correct section of the PivotTable.
   b. Modify the calculation to display the average score instead of the total score.
5. The PivotChart on the *Faculty Pivot* sheet should show the size of each department as a proportional part of a whole. A line chart was the wrong choice.

a. Change the chart type to a better choice.

b. Display Data Labels using the **Data Callout** format.

6. The school finance committee has determined that a $28,000 facilities upgrade will be needed in 12 years. An alumnus has donated $20,000. If invested, will it grow to be enough? That depends on the rate of return. On the *Data Table* worksheet, an attempt has been made to use Excel's data table feature to determine the value of the investment after ten years at different rates of return. The formula in cell D6 is correct, but something went wrong with the data table. Delete the zeros in cells **D7:D30** and try again. Even if you're not familiar with the FV formula used in cell D6, you should be able to figure this out.
7. Save and close the workbook.

chapter 6

Exploring Advanced Functions

In this chapter, you will learn the following skills:

- Round numbers using functions
- Use advanced math functions to calculate totals
- Analyze data using statistical functions to calculate averages, count values, find middle values, and calculate standard deviation
- Create formulas with the logical functions AND, OR, and IFS
- Work with financial functions to calculate future value, present value, number of payments, and depreciation
- Analyze data using the lookup functions MATCH and INDEX and database functions
- Manage formula errors using the IFERROR function
- Troubleshoot formulas

Skill 6.13 Calculating Future Value with the FV Function

Skill 6.14 Using PV to Calculate Present Value When Payments Are Constant

Skill 6.15 Using NPV to Calculate Present Value When Payments Are Variable

Skill 6.16 Calculating the Number of Payments with NPER

Skill 6.17 Creating a Depreciation Schedule

Skill 6.18 Finding Data with MATCH and INDEX

Skill 6.19 Using Database Functions

Skill 6.20 Managing Errors with the IFERROR Function

Skill 6.21 Analyzing Complex Formulas Using Evaluate Formula

introduction

This chapter expands on Chapter 3's introduction to formulas and functions. You will learn to use advanced mathematical, statistical, financial, logical, lookup, and database functions to find the answers to complex data questions. You will also learn to use the Evaluate Formula feature to troubleshoot formula errors.

Skill 6.1 Rounding with Functions

Rounding refers to adjusting a number up or down to make it more appropriate to the context in which it is being used. Numbers can be rounded up or down to the nearest whole number or the nearest factor of ten, hundred, thousand, or any limit. The rounding functions in Excel are used specifically to control the number of digits to the right of the decimal point.

In Figure EX 6.1, the average unit price is 16.9387755102041. Excel stores the value up to fifteen decimal places. However, when the cell is formatted using the General format, Excel displays only 16.93877551 as shown in cell B3. In cell B4, the same formula displays 16.94 when formatted using the *Accounting Number Format*. The number stored in the workbook remains 16.9387755102041 even if you modify the number format to display fewer digits after the decimal. Excel uses the stored value, not the displayed value, in calculations.

By adding one of the rounding functions to the formula, you can ensure that the stored value matches the displayed value.

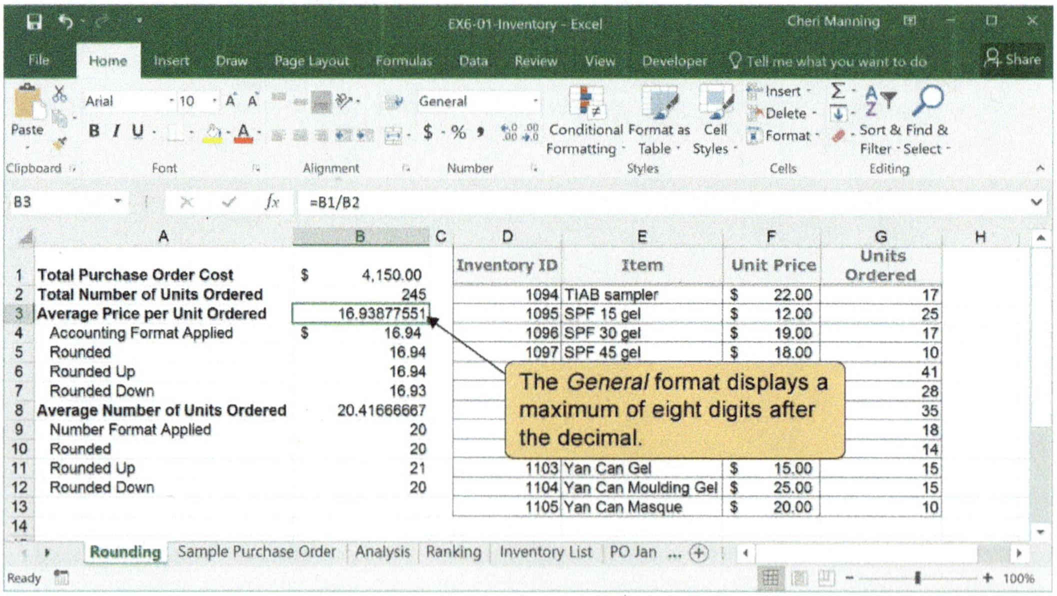

FIGURE EX 6.1

There are three main rounding functions. Each of these functions takes two arguments:

Number—the number or formula to round.

Num_digits—the number of digits to the right of the decimal to round to.

ROUND—Rounds the number up or down to the number of decimal places specified in the *Num_digits* argument. The rules of rounding state that if the number immediately to the right of the rounding point is 0, 1, 2, 3, or 4, the trailing digits are cut off. If the number immediately to the right of the rounding point is 5, 6, 7, 8, or 9, the number is rounded up. A formula using the ROUND function looks like this:

- =ROUND(*Number,Num_digits*)
- =ROUND(B1/B2,2)

The result of this formula is 16.94. The number 16.9387755102041 is rounded up to 16.94 because the *num_digits* argument is 2 and the third digit after the decimal is 8.

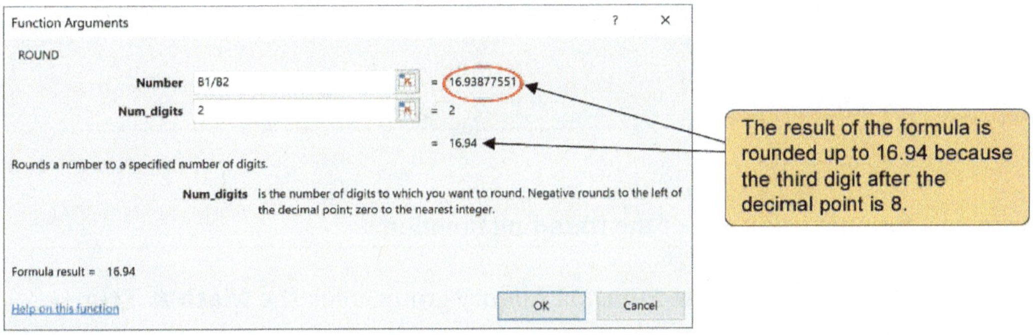

FIGURE EX 6.2

ROUNDUP—Ignores the rules of rounding and automatically rounds up to the next number, regardless of the value to the right of the rounding point. A formula using the ROUNDUP function looks like this:

- =ROUNDUP(*Number,Num_digits*)
- =ROUNDUP(B1/B2,2)

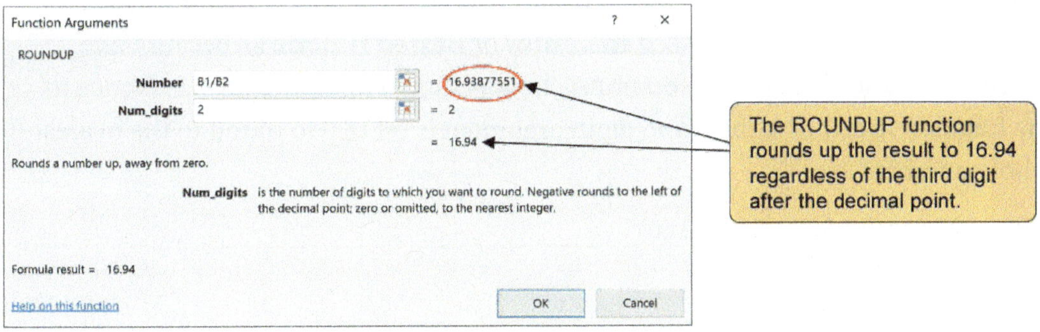

FIGURE EX 6.3

ROUNDDOWN—Ignores the rules of rounding and automatically rounds down, regardless of the value to the right of the rounding point. A formula using the ROUNDDOWN function looks like this:

- =ROUNDDOWN(*Number,Num_digits*)
- =ROUNDDOWN(B1/B2,2)

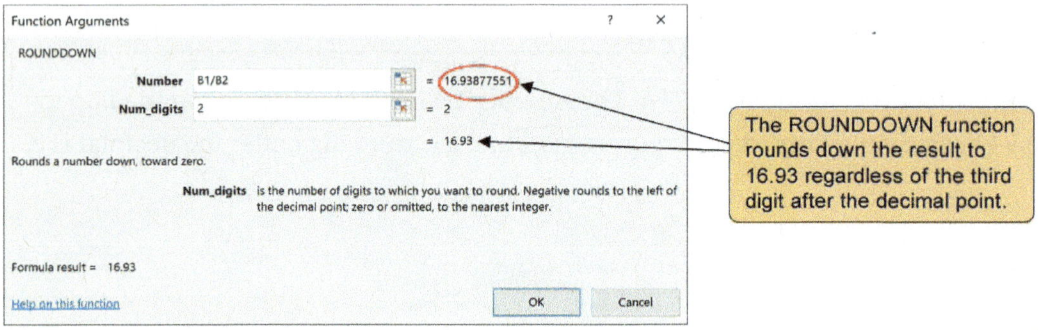

FIGURE EX 6.4

To create a formula using one of the rounding functions:

1. On the *Formulas* tab, in the *Function Library* group, click the **Math & Trig** button.
2. Select the rounding function you want to open the *Function Arguments* dialog.
3. In the *Number* argument box, enter the number, cell reference, or formula you want rounded.
4. In the *Num_digits* argument box, enter the number of digits you want to the right of the decimal.
5. Click **OK**.

Rounding functions are often used in conjunction with another function. These formulas are referred to as **nested formulas** or **nested functions** because one function is "nested" within the other function as shown in Figure EX 6.5. Notice in the function in cell B10, the *Num_digits* argument is set to *0* to round to the nearest whole number.

=ROUND(AVERAGE(G1:G13),0)

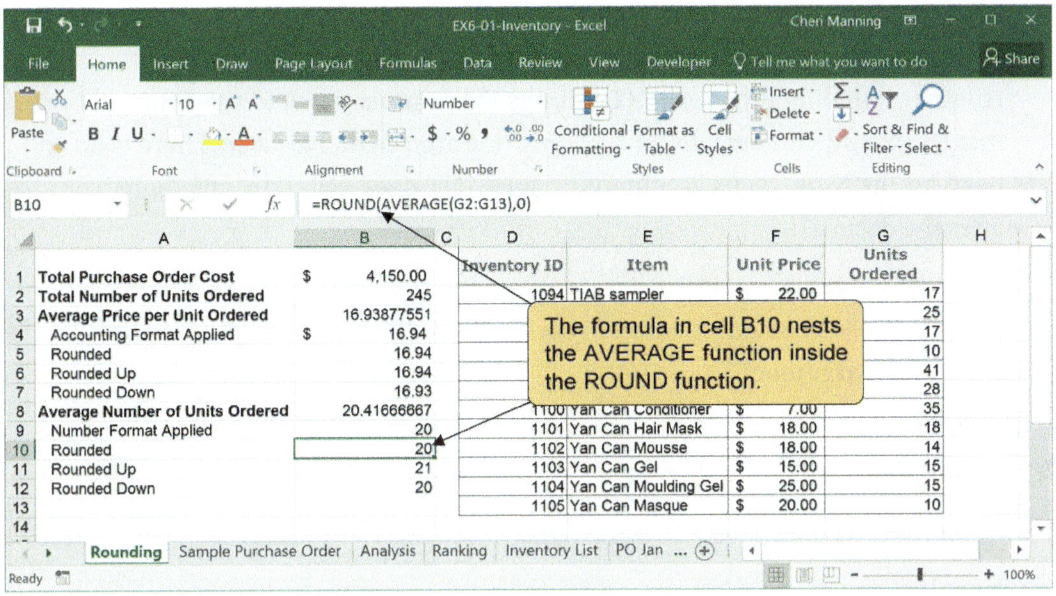

FIGURE EX 6.5

When ROUND is used in a nested formula, the *Number* argument contains the formula you want to calculate.

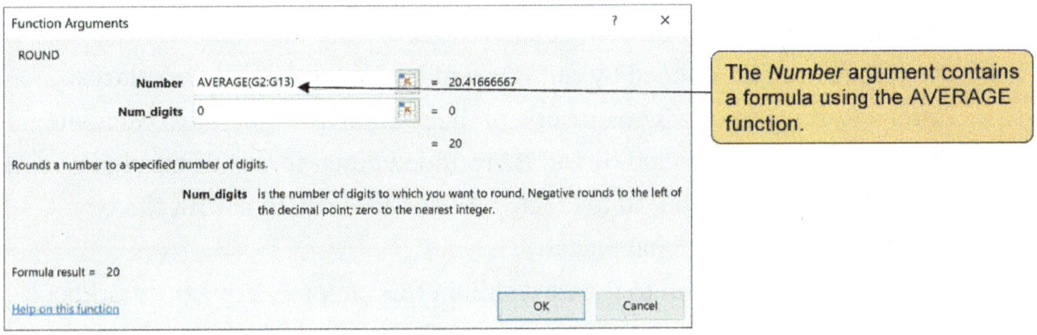

FIGURE EX 6.6

The easiest way to add ROUND to an existing formula is to edit the formula directly in the formula bar or the cell, adding ROUND and the *Num_digits* argument without going through the *Function Arguments* dialog.

1. Click in the formula bar or double-click the cell to enter Edit mode.
2. Move the cursor to the beginning of the formula after the = and type: **ROUND(**
3. The existing formula is the *Number* argument. Move the cursor to the end of the formula, type a comma, and then type the number to use as the *Num_digits* argument.
4. Type the closing parenthesis **)** and press **[Enter]**.

tell me **more**

Another rounding function, INT, rounds the number *down* to the nearest integer (whole number). INT takes only one argument, *Number*. There is no need for the *Num_digits* argument because INT does not allow any digits after the decimal.

INT always rounds up. If you want to round to the nearest whole number using the rule of rounding instead, use the ROUND function with 0 as the *Num_digits* argument.

let me **try** *Live!*

Open the student data file **EX6-01-Inventory** and try this skill on your own:

1. On the **Rounding** worksheet, enter a formula in cell **B5** using one of the rounding functions to calculate the value of cell **B1** divided by cell **B2** rounded to two decimal places.
2. Enter a formula in cell **B6** using one of the rounding functions to calculate the value of cell **B1** divided by cell **B2** rounded up to two decimal places.
3. Enter a formula in cell **B7** using one of the rounding functions to calculate the value of cell **B1** divided by cell **B2** rounded down to two decimal places.
4. Edit the formula in cell **B10** to create a nested formula to **round** the result of the formula to 0 decimal places.
5. If you will be moving on to the next skill in this chapter, leave the workbook open to continue working. If not, save the file as directed by your instructor and close it.

Skill 6.2 Calculating Totals with SUMPRODUCT

In mathematics, a **product** is the result of multiplying two or more numbers. The **SUMPRODUCT** function allows you to multiply the corresponding cells in two or more ranges and then sum (add together) the products. This function is very useful when totaling columns of data such as hours worked and hourly rates or unit prices and number of units ordered. To use SUMPRODUCT, arrays do not need to be next to each other, but they must have the same number of rows or columns. If the arrays are different sizes, the formula will return an error.

The formula in Figure EX 6.7 first multiplies each value in the range C4:C15 by its corresponding value in the range D4:D15 and then sums the products:

- =SUMPRODUCT(*Array1,[Array2],[Array3]...*)
- =SUMPRODUCT(C4:C15,D4:D15)

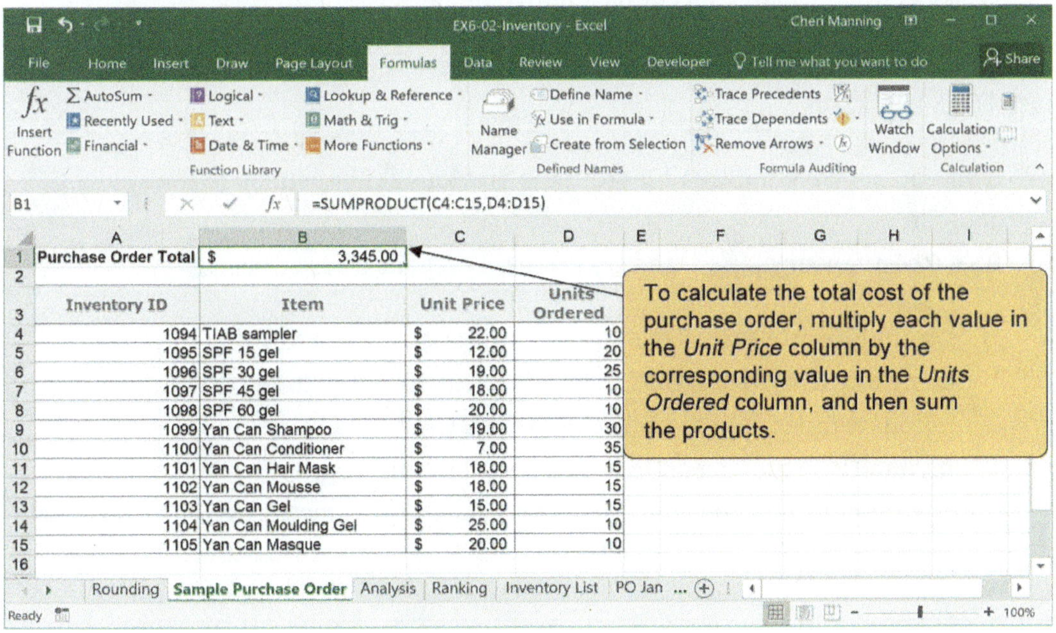

FIGURE EX 6.7

To create a formula using SUMPRODUCT:

1. On the *Formulas* tab, in the *Function Library* group, click the **Math & Trig** button. Select **SUMPRODUCT** to open the *Function Arguments* dialog.
2. In the *Array1* argument box, enter the first cell range or named range.
3. In the *Array2* argument box, enter the cell range or named range you want to multiply the values in *Array1* by.

4. Continue entering *arrays* as necessary.
5. Click **OK**.

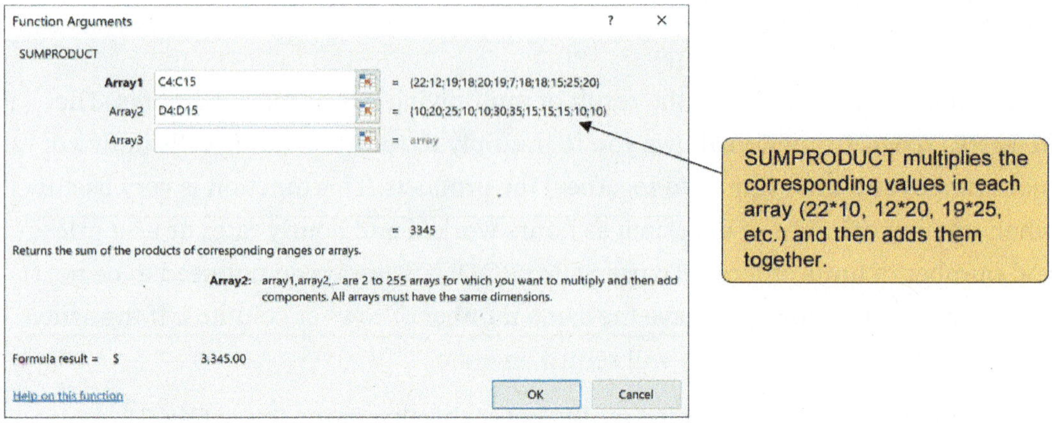

FIGURE EX 6.8

tips & tricks

While the example shown in Figure EX 6.7 uses data arranged in columns, SUMPRODUCT works just as well with data in rows.

let me try *Live!*

If you do not have the data file from the previous skill open, open the student data file **EX6-02-Inventory** and try this skill on your own:

1. On the **Sample Purchase Order** worksheet, enter a formula in cell **B1** using the **SUMPRODUCT** function to calculate the total cost of the purchase order. Use the cell ranges **C4:C15** and **D4:D15**.
2. If you will be moving on to the next skill in this chapter, leave the workbook open to continue working. If not, save the file as directed by your instructor and close it.

from the perspective of . . .

BRAND MANAGER

Every week I receive sales data from all our retail stores. To calculate totals quickly, I apply range names to the columns of units sold and prices and then use SUMPRODUCT to calculate the grand total. Now all I have to do each week is replace the data in my spreadsheet with the updated sales figures and I'm finished. What a time saver!

Skill 6.3 Using SUMIF and SUMIFS

At this point, you should be able to use SUM to total a range of cells and use SUMPRODUCT to total the product of two cell ranges, but what if you want to sum together only cells that meet specific criteria? You could filter the data and then use SUM, but it is more efficient to use the SUMIF function. The **SUMIF** function totals the values only where cells meet the specified criteria.

SUMIF takes two required arguments and one optional argument:

- **Range**—the range of cells to evaluate against the criteria
- **Criteria**—the conditions (the criteria) the cell must meet in order to be included in the total, and optionally
- **Sum_range**—(optional) the range of cells containing the values to be summed. *Sum_range* must be the same size as *Range*. This argument is necessary only when the values to be summed are not the same as the values to be evaluated against the criteria.

The formula in Figure EX 6.9 uses SUMIF to calculate the total number of items ordered for the Item ID specified in cell B1. SUMIF evaluates the values in the *JuneItems* range (the *Item ID* column). If the value matches the criteria specified in cell *B1*, then the corresponding value in the *JuneOrdered* range (the *Ordered* column) is included in the total.

- =SUMIF(*Range,Criteria,*[*Sum_range*])
- =SUMIF(JuneItems,B1,JuneOrdered)

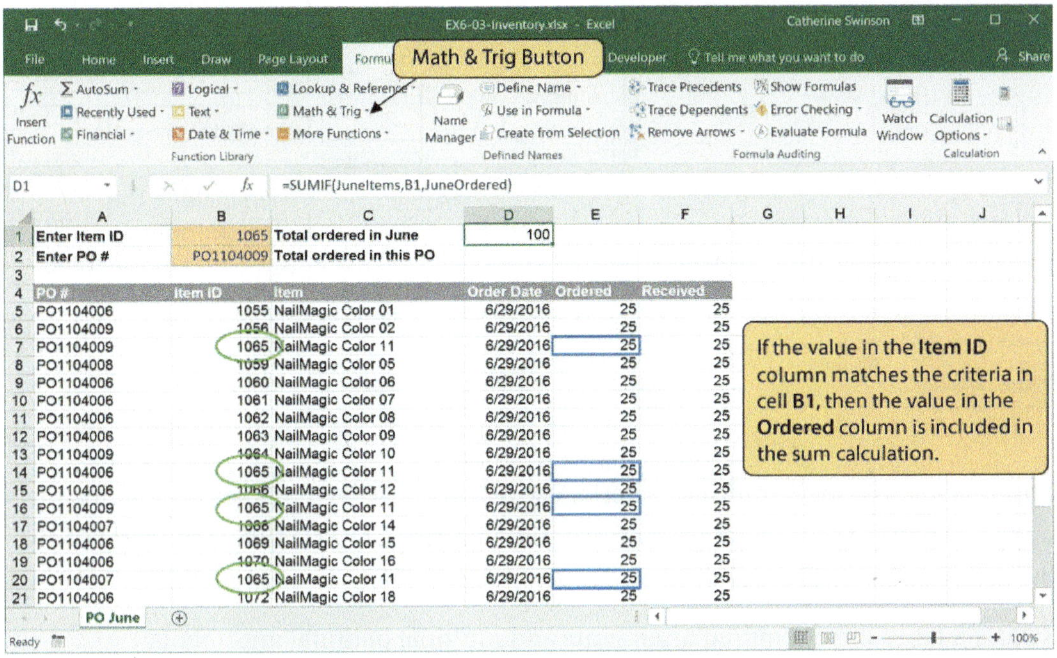

FIGURE EX 6.9

To create a formula using SUMIFS:

1. Select the cell where you want to enter the formula.
2. On the *Formulas* tab, in the *Function Library* group, click the **Math & Trig** button, and select **SUMIF** to open the *Function Arguments* dialog.
3. In the *Range* argument box, enter the cell range or named range to evaluate against the criteria.
4. In the *Criteria* argument box, enter the criteria. The criteria can be a text string, numerical value, expression, or cell reference. Text strings and expressions must be enclosed in quotation marks.
5. In the *Sum_range* argument box, enter the cell range or named range containing the values you want to add together. If you omit this argument, SUMIF will total the values in the *Range* argument instead.
6. Click **OK**.

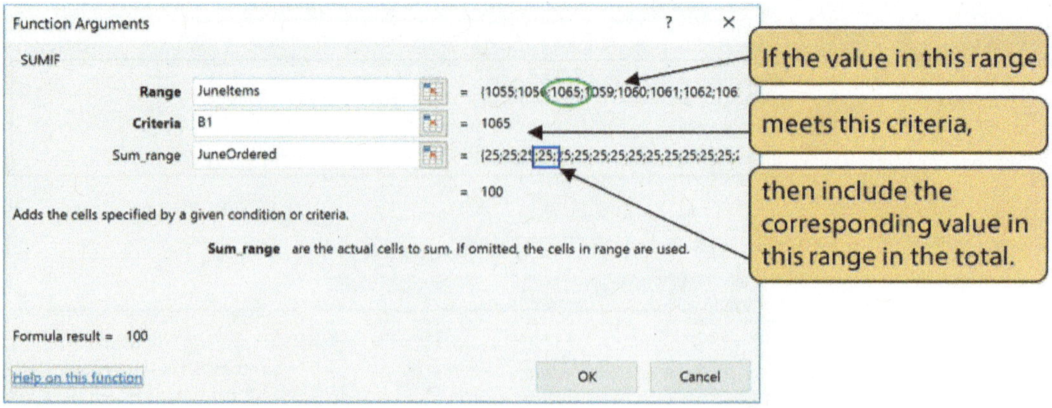

FIGURE EX 6.10

To sum data that meet multiple criteria, use SUMIFS. **SUMIFS** takes arguments for up to 127 pairs of criteria ranges and criteria. The result of SUMIFS is the total of all the cells that meet all criteria.

SUMIFS takes three required arguments and multiple optional arguments:

- **Sum_range**—the range of cells to sum where criteria are met
- **Criteria_range1**—the range of cells containing the values to be evaluated against the first criteria
- **Criteria1**—the first criteria
- **Criteria_range2**—(optional) the range of cells containing the values to be evaluated against the second criteria
- **Criteria2**—(optional) the second criteria (continuing up to *Criteria_range127* and *Criteria127*)

The formula in Figure EX 6.11 uses SUMIFS to calculate the sum of the values in the *Ordered* column (the range *JuneOrdered*) where the Item ID (the range *JuneItems*) meets the criteria specified in cell B1 and the PO # (the range *JunePOs*) meets the criteria specified in cell B2.

=SUMIFS(*Sum_range,Criteria_range1,Criteria1,[Criteria_range2],[Criteria2]...*)
=SUMIFS(JuneOrdered,JuneItems,B1,JunePOs,B2)

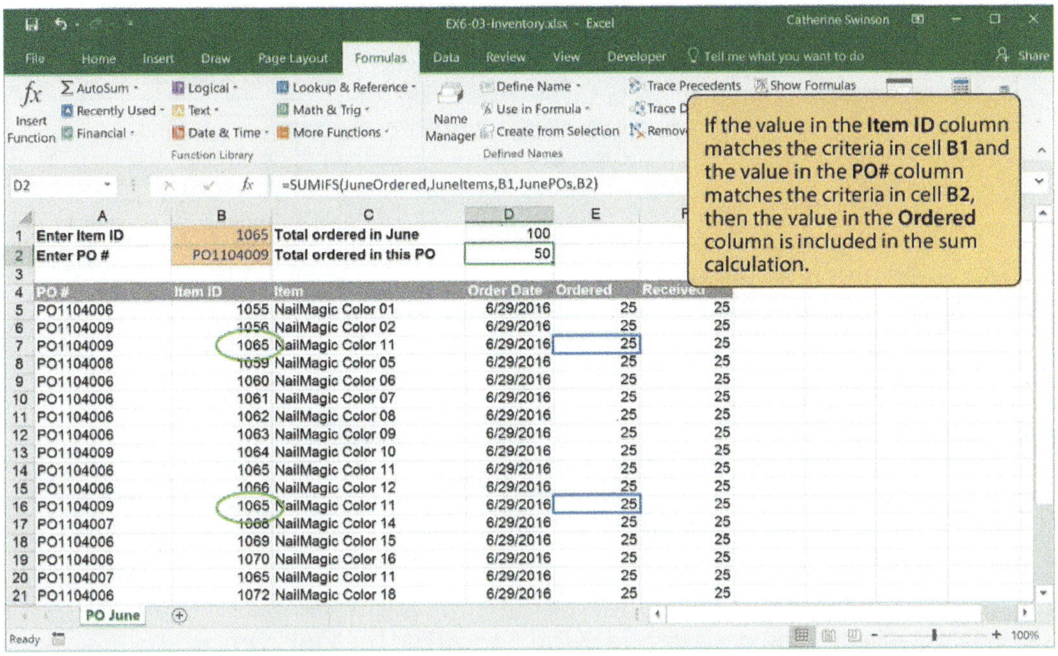

FIGURE EX 6.11

To create a formula using SUMIFS:

1. Select the cell where you want to enter the formula.
2. On the *Formulas* tab, in the *Function Library* group, click the **Math & Trig** button and select **SUMIFS** to open the *Function Arguments* dialog.
3. In the *Sum_range* argument box, enter the cell range or range name containing the values to be summed if all the criteria are met.
4. In the *Criteria_range1* box, enter the cell range or range name containing the values to be evaluated against the first criteria. Text strings and expressions must be enclosed in quotation marks.
5. In the *Criteria1* argument box, enter the text string, number, expression, or cell reference for the first criteria.
6. In the *Criteria_range2* box, enter the cell range or range name containing the values to be evaluated against the second criteria.
7. In the *Criteria2* argument box, enter the text string, number, expression, or cell reference for the second criteria. Text strings and expressions must be enclosed in quotation marks.
8. Continue entering the criteria range and criteria pairs until you are finished.
9. Click **OK**.

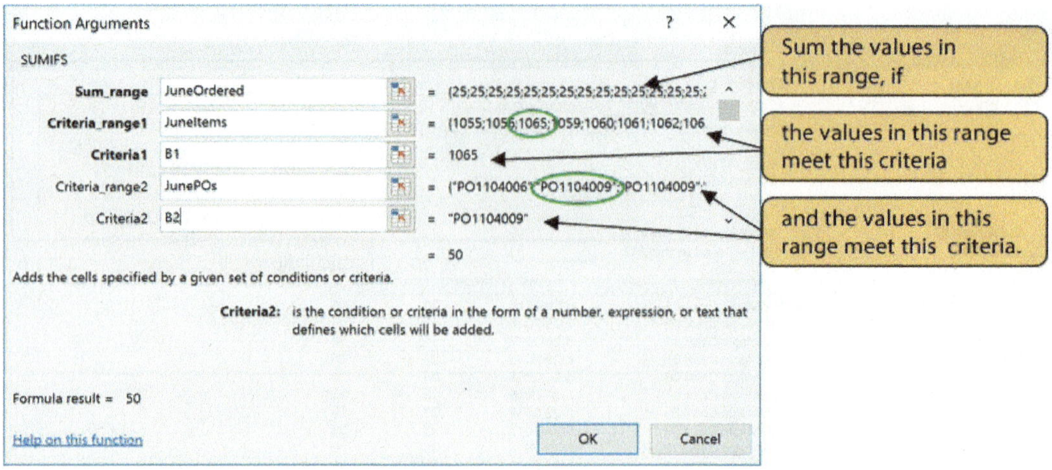

FIGURE EX 6.12

tips & tricks

It is important to note that while SUMIF and SUMIFS look similar, the arguments are in a different order. SUMIF begins with the cell range to be evaluated against the criteria, while SUMIFS begins with the cell range to be summed. If you find it difficult to remember the difference, stick with SUMIFS. You can use SUMIFS to evaluate against a single criteria range. If the range you are summing is the same as the range you are evaluating, SUMIFS will allow you to use the same cell range in both arguments.

tell me more

When entering a numerical expression such as "<10" as the *Criteria* argument, you must enclose the expression in quotation marks. Text criteria must also be enclosed in quotation marks, but cell references or single numerical values do not.

let me try *Live!*

If you do not have the data file from the previous skill open, open the student data file
EX6-03-Inventory and try this skill on your own:

1. On the *June PO* worksheet, enter a formula in cell **D1** using **SUMIF** to calculate the total number of items ordered for the item number specified in cell **B1**. Use the range name **JuneItems** for the *Range* argument and **JuneOrdered** for the *Sum_range* argument.
2. Now enter a formula in cell **D2** using **SUMIFS** to calculate the number of items ordered (use the named range **JuneOrdered**) where the value in the **JuneItems** named range is equal to the value in cell **B1** and the value in the **JunePOs** named range is equal to **B2**.
3. If you will be moving on to the next skill in this chapter, leave the workbook open to continue working. If not, save the file as directed by your instructor and close it.

Skill 6.4 Using AVERAGEIF and AVERAGEIFS

The statistical functions AVERAGEIF and AVERAGEIFS are similar to SUMIF and SUMIFS. They calculate the average value where cells meet specified criteria.

The **AVERAGEIF** takes two required arguments and one optional argument:

Range—the range of cells to evaluate against the criteria

Criteria—the conditions (the criteria) the cell must meet in order to be included in the total, and optionally

Average_range—(optional) the range of cells containing the values to be averaged. *Average_range* must be the same size as *Range*. This argument is necessary only when the values to be averaged are not the same as the values to be evaluated against the criteria.

The formula in Figure EX 6.13 uses AVERAGEIF to calculate the average delivery time for items currently on order. AVERAGEIF evaluates the values in the *ReorderStatus* range (the *On Order?* column). If the value matches the criteria specified (*yes*), then the corresponding value in the *DeliveryTime* range (the *Delivery Time in Days* column) is included in the range of values to be averaged. Note that the text criteria *yes* must be enclosed in quotation marks.

=AVERAGEIF(*Range*,*Criteria*,[*Average_range*])
=AVERAGEIF(ReorderStatus,"yes",DeliveryTime)

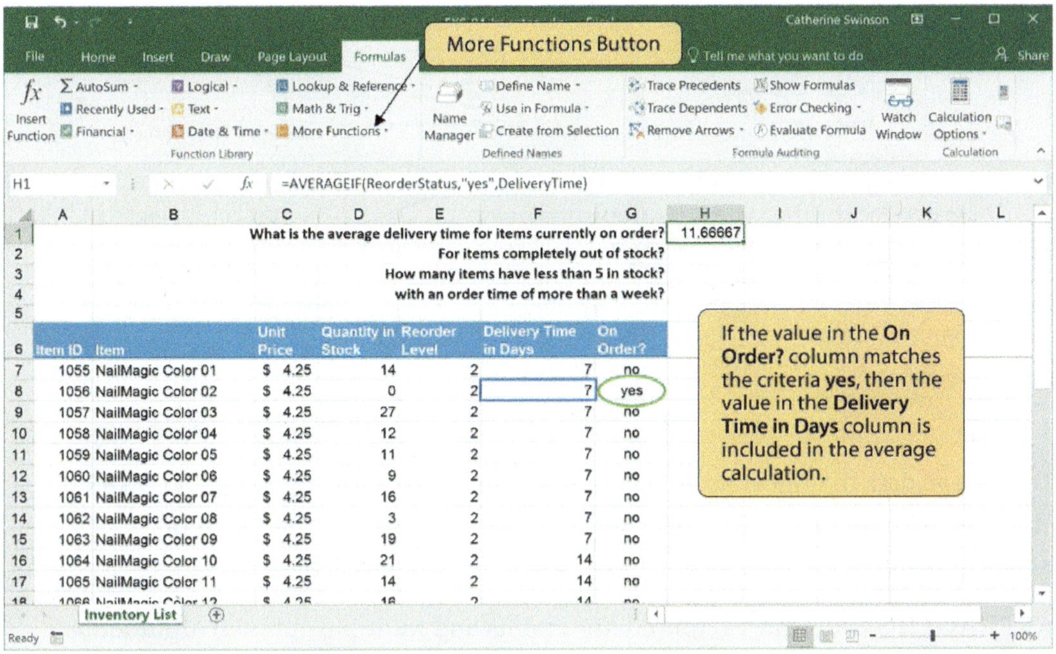

FIGURE EX 6.13

To create a formula using AVERAGEIF:

1. Select the cell where you want to enter the formula.
2. On the *Formulas* tab, in the *Function Library* group, click the **More Functions** button, point to **Statistical,** and select **AVERAGEIF** to open the *Function Arguments* dialog.
3. In the *Range* argument box, enter the cell range or named range to evaluate against the criteria.
4. In the *Criteria* argument box, enter the criteria. The criteria can be a text string, numerical value, expression, or cell reference. Remember, text strings and expressions must be enclosed in quotation marks.
5. In the *Average_range* argument box, enter the cell range or named range containing the values you want to average. If you omit this argument, AVERAGEIF will average the values in the *Range* argument instead.
6. Click **OK.**

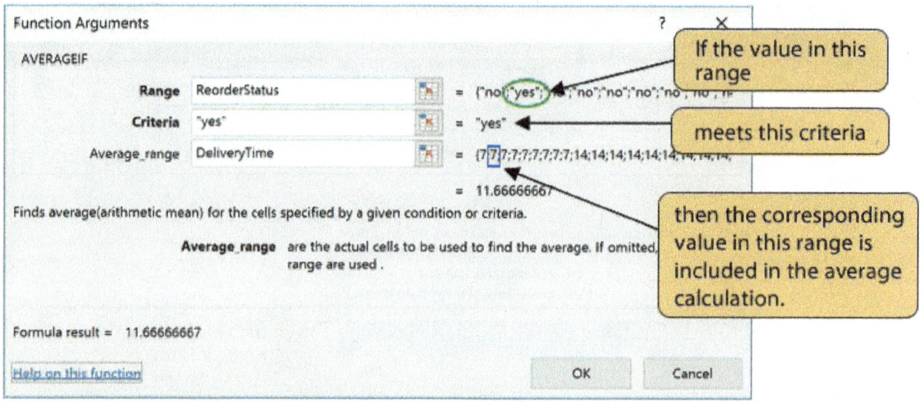

FIGURE EX 6.14

To average data that meet multiple criteria, use AVERAGEIFS. **AVERAGEIFS** takes arguments for up to 127 pairs of criteria ranges and criteria. The result of AVERAGEIFS is the average of all the cells that meet all criteria.

AVERAGEIFS takes three required arguments and multiple optional arguments:

Average_range—the range of cells to average where criteria are met

Criteria_range1—the range of cells containing the values to be evaluated against the first criteria

Criteria1—the first criteria

Criteria_range2—(optional) the range of cells containing the values to be evaluated against the second criteria

Criteria2—(optional) the second criteria continuing up to *Criteria_range127* and *Criteria127*)

The formula in Figure EX 6.15 uses AVERAGEIFS to calculate the average delivery time for items currently on order that are out of stock. The values in the *DeliveryTime* range (the *Delivery Time in Days* column) are included in the range of values to be averaged only where the corresponding value in the *ReorderStatus* range (the *On Order?* column) match the criteria specified (*yes*) and the corresponding value in the *InStock* range (the *Quantity in Stock* column) match the criteria specified (*0*).

=AVERAGEIFS(*Sum_range*,*Criteria_range1*,*Criteria1*,[*Criteria_range2*],
[*Criteria2*]...)
=AVERAGEIFS(DeliveryTime,ReorderStatus,"yes",InStock,0)

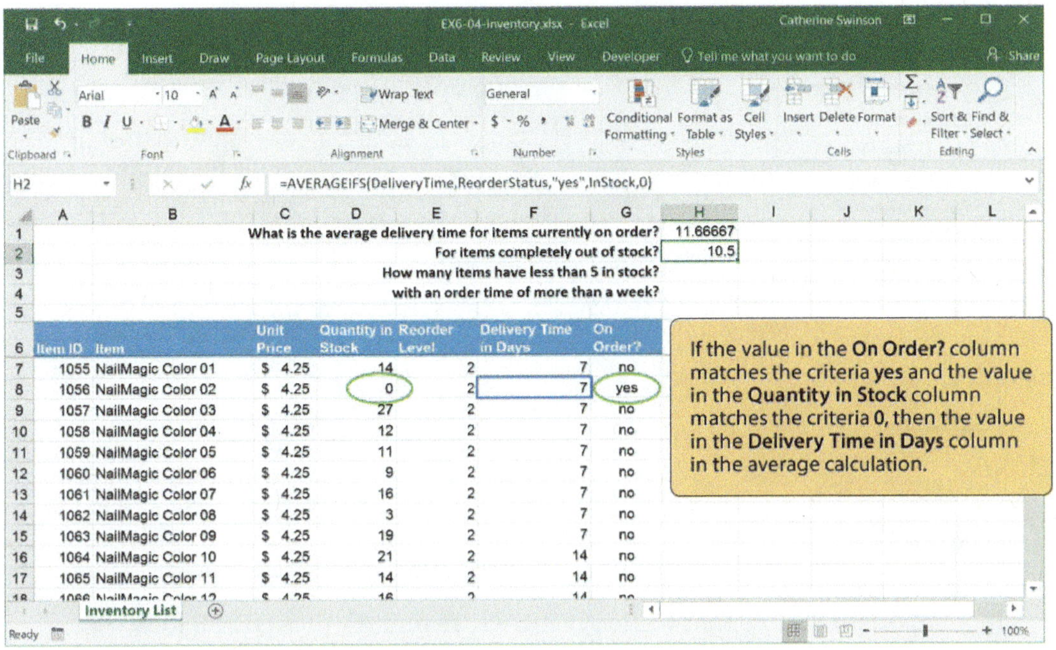

FIGURE EX 6.15

To create a formula using AVERAGEIFS:

1. Select the cell where you want to enter the formula.
2. On the *Formulas* tab, in the *Function Library* group, click the **More Functions** button, point to **Statistical,** and select **AVERAGEIFS** to open the *Function Arguments* dialog.
3. In the *Average_range* argument box, enter the cell range or range name containing the values to be averaged if all the criteria are met.
4. In the *Criteria_range1* box, enter the cell range or range name containing the values to be evaluated against the first criteria.
5. In the *Criteria1* argument box, enter the text string, number, expression, or cell reference for the first criteria. Remember, text strings and expressions must be enclosed in quotation marks.
6. In the *Criteria_range2* box, enter the cell range or range name containing the values to be evaluated against the second criteria.
7. In the *Criteria2* argument box, enter the text string, number, expression, or cell reference for the second criteria. Remember, text strings and expressions must be enclosed in quotation marks.
8. Continue entering the criteria range and criteria pairs until you are finished.
9. Click **OK.**

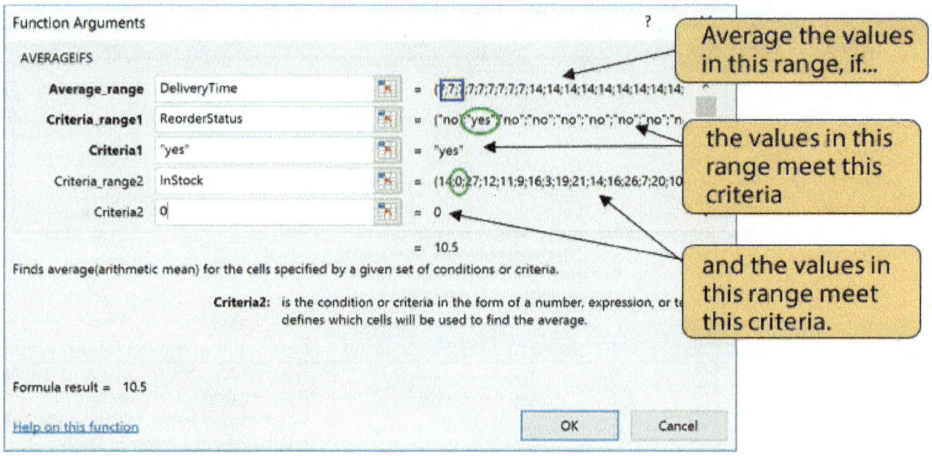

FIGURE EX 6.16

tips & tricks

It is important to note that while AVERAGEIF and AVERAGEIFS look similar, the arguments are in a different order. AVERAGEIF begins with the cell range to be evaluated against the criteria, while AVERAGEIFS begins with the cell range to be averaged. If you find it difficult to remember the difference, stick with AVERAGEIFS. You can use AVERAGEIFS to evaluate against a single criteria range. If the range you are summing is the same as the range you are evaluating, AVERAGEIFS will allow you to use the same cell range in both arguments.

let me try *Live!*

If you do not have the data file from the previous skill open, open the student data file **EX6-04-Inventory** and try this skill on your own:

1. On the *Inventory List* worksheet, enter a formula in cell **H1** using **AVERAGEIF** to calculate the average delivery time for items currently on order. Use the range name **ReorderStatus** for the *Range* argument, **yes** for the *Criteria* argument, and **DeliveryTime** for the *Average_range* argument.
2. Now enter a formula in cell **H2** using **AVERAGEIFS** to calculate the average delivery time. Use the named range **DeliveryTime** where the value in the **ReorderStatus** named range is equal to **yes** and the value in the **InStock** named range is equal to **0**.
3. If you will be moving on to the next skill in this chapter, leave the workbook open to continue working. If not, save the file as directed by your instructor and close it.

Skill 6.5 Using COUNTIF and COUNTIFS

You should be familiar with the basic counting functions COUNT, COUNTA, and COUNTBLANK that allow you to count the numbers, values, and blank cells in a cell range. Similar to SUMIF/SUMIFS and AVERAGEIF/AVERAGEIFS, there are also counting functions that allow you to count only data that meet specific criteria: **COUNTIF** and **COUNTIFS**.

COUNTIF takes two arguments:

Range—the range of cells to count

Criteria—the conditions (the criteria) the cell must meet in order to be counted. The criteria can be a text string or numerical value or expression

The formula in Figure EX 6.17 uses COUNTIF to count the number of cells where there are less than five items in stock. COUNTIF evaluates the values in the *InStock* range (the *Quantity in Stock* column). If the value matches the criteria specified (<5), then the cell is included in the count. Note that the expression criteria <5 must be enclosed in quotation marks.

=COUNTIF(*Range*,*Criteria*)
=COUNTIF(Instock,"<5")

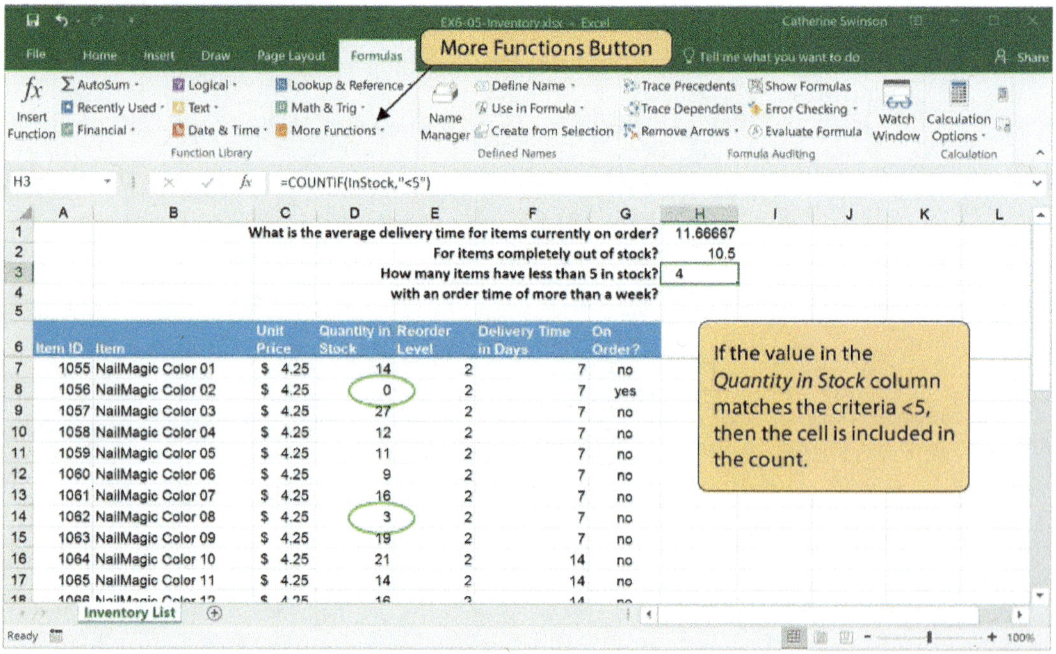

FIGURE EX 6.17

To create a formula using COUNTIF:

1. Select the cell where you want to enter the formula.
2. On the *Formulas* tab, in the *Function Library* group, click the **More Functions** button, point to **Statistical,** and select **COUNTIF** to open the *Function Arguments* dialog.
3. In the *Range* argument box, enter the cell range or named range to evaluate against the criteria.
4. In the *Criteria* argument box, enter the criteria. The criteria can be a text string, numerical value, expression, or cell reference. Remember, text strings and expressions must be enclosed in quotation marks.
5. Click **OK**.

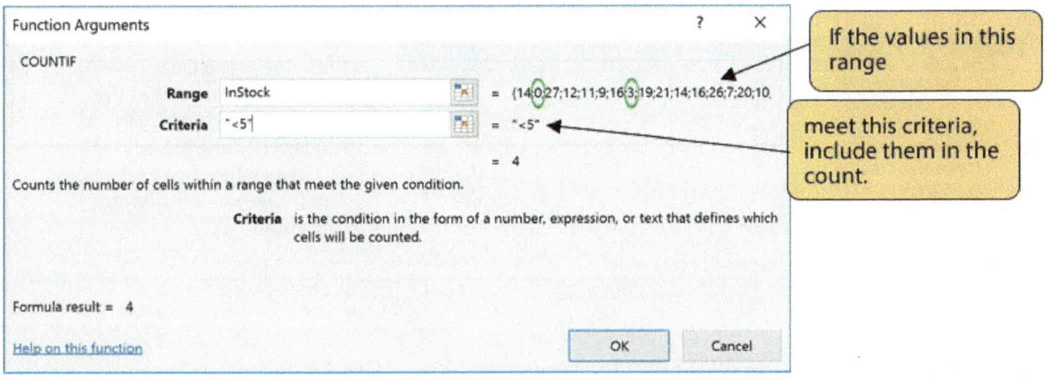

FIGURE EX 6.18

To count data that meet multiple criteria, use **COUNTIFS**. COUNTIFS takes arguments for up to 127 pairs of criteria ranges and criteria. The result of COUNTIFS is the average of all the cells that meet all criteria.

COUNTIFS takes two required arguments and multiple optional arguments:

Criteria_range1—the range of cells containing the values to be evaluated against the first criteria

Criteria1—the first criteria

Criteria_range2—(optional) the range of cells containing the values to be evaluated against the second criteria

Criteria2—(optional) the second criteria (continuing up to *Criteria_range127*and *Criteria127*)

The formula in Figure EX 6.19 uses COUNTIFS to count the number of rows with less than five items in stock and a delivery time of greater than seven days. COUNTIFS evaluates the values in the *InStock* range (the *Quantity in Stock* column) against the criteria <5 and the values in the *DeliveryTime* range (the *Delivery Time in*

Days column) against the criteria >7. Where both criteria are met, the row is included in the count. Note that the criteria expressions <5 and >7 must be enclosed in quotation marks.

=COUNTIFS(*Criteria_range1*,*Criteria1*,[*Criteria_range2*],[*Criteria2*]...)
=COUNTIFS(InStock,"<5",DeliveryTime,">7")

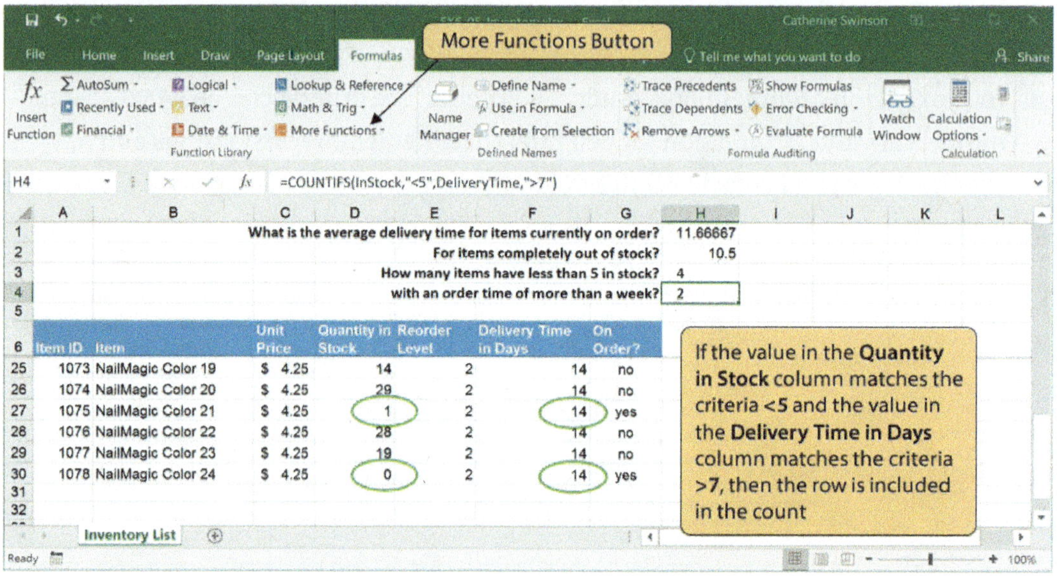

FIGURE EX 6.19

To create a formula using COUNTIFS:

1. Select the cell where you want to enter the formula.
2. On the *Formulas* tab, in the *Function Library* group, click the **More Functions** button, point to **Statistical,** and select **COUNTIFS** to open the *Function Arguments* dialog.
3. In the *Criteria_range1* box, enter the cell range or range name containing the values to be evaluated against the first criteria.
4. In the *Criteria1* argument box, enter the text string, number, expression, or cell reference for the first criteria.
5. In the *Criteria_range2* box, enter the cell range or range name containing the values to be evaluated against the second criteria.
6. In the *Criteria2* argument box, enter the text string, number, expression, or cell reference for the second criteria.
7. Continue entering the criteria range and criteria pairs until you are finished.
8. Click **OK.**

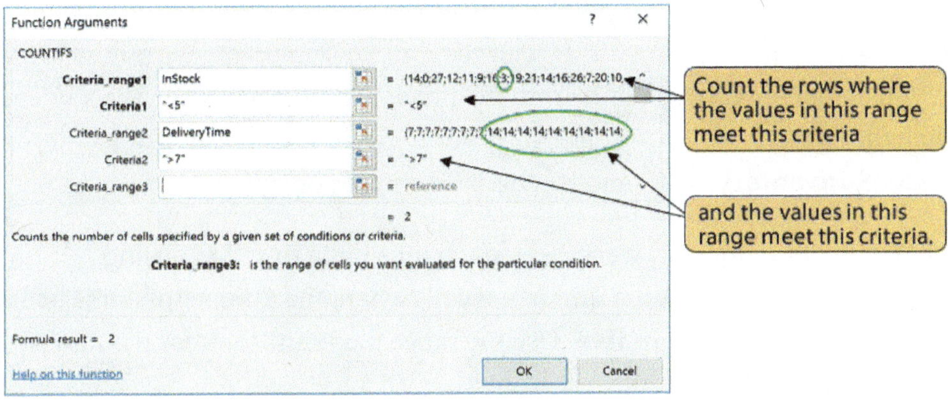

FIGURE EX 6.20

tips & tricks

The COUNTIFS function is compatible only with Excel 2007 and later.

tell me more

When working with text criteria, you can use the wildcard characters * and ? to find inexact text matches. The * wildcard replaces any string of characters. The ? wildcard replaces a single character.

- Enter the criteria argument "spa * " to return data that begin with the letters *spa*.
- Enter the criteria argument " * a" to return data that end with the letter *a*
- Enter the criteria argument " * spa * " to return data that include the letters *spa* anywhere in the string.
- Enter the criteria argument "sp?" to return data that end with any single character after *sp* (e.g., *spa* or *spy*).
- Enter the criteria argument "sp??" to return data that end with any two characters after *sp* (e.g., *spar* or *spin*).

let me try *Live!*

If you do not have the data file from the previous skill open, open the student data file
EX6-05-Inventory and try this skill on your own:

1. On the *Inventory List* worksheet, enter a formula in cell **H3** using **COUNTIF** to count the number of cells where the number of items in inventory is **less than five**. Use the range name **InStock** for the *Range* argument.
2. Now enter a formula in cell **H4** using **COUNTIFS** to calculate the number of rows where the value in the **InStock** named range **less than five** and the value in the **DeliveryTime** named range is **greater than 7**.
3. If you will be moving on to the next skill in this chapter, leave the workbook open to continue working. If not, save the file as directed by your instructor and close it.

Skill 6.6 Finding the Middle Value with MEDIAN

When analyzing a list of values, calculating the statistical average may not always provide the information you need. For example, in the purchase order in Figure EX 6.21, the average number of items received is 24.0952381. Of course you cannot actually receive 24.0952381 items. How do you find the actual number of items received in the middle of the range?

The statistical **median** is the middle value of a set of values. If you were to sort the list of values from highest to lowest, you would find that $25 is right in the middle. The formula in Figure EX 6.21 uses **MEDIAN** to find the middle value for the range C2:C22.

=MEDIAN(*Number1,[Number2]...*)
=MEDIAN(C2:C22)

MEDIAN is a simple function to use. Most of the time you may find it easiest to type the formula directly in the cell or the formula bar. Type **`=MEDIAN`** (and then enter the cell range or named range for the*Number1* argument. Type **`)`** and press **[Enter]**. If you prefer using the *Function Arguments* dialog, on the *Formulas* tab, in the *Function Library* group, click the **More Functions** button, point to **Statistical**, and then click **MEDIAN** to open the *Function Arguments* dialog. MEDIAN takes up to 255*Number* arguments.

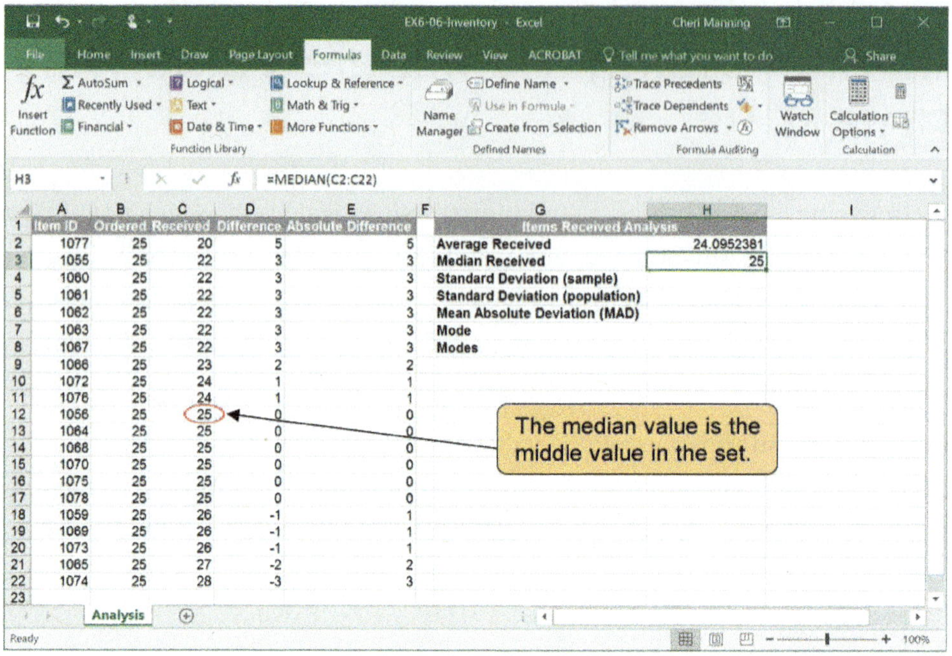

FIGURE EX 6.21

tips & tricks

- MEDIAN ignores empty cells and cells that contain text.
- If there is an even number of values in the range, MEDIAN will return the average (mean) of the two middle values.

let me try *Live!*

If you do not have the data file from the previous skill open, open the student data file

EX6-06-Inventory and try this skill on your own:

1. On the **Analysis** worksheet, enter a formula in cell **H3** to find the middle value (the median) for values in the *Received* column. Use the cell range **C2:C22**.
2. If you will be moving on to the next skill in this chapter, leave the workbook open to continue working. If not, save the file as directed by your instructor and close it.

Skill 6.7 Calculating the Standard Deviation

Standard deviation measures how far values in a data set (or "**population**") are spread out from the mean (average).

Excel offers two functions to calculate standard deviation. **STDEV.S** calculates standard deviation for a set of values based on a sample from the population and **STDEV.P** calculates standard deviation using the entire set of values as the argument. In Figure EX 6.22, the calculation in cell H4 uses the STDEV.S function while the calculation in cell H5 uses the STDEV.P function. Observe the difference in the two results. When calculating standard deviation, be sure to select the correct function for your data set. Is the function argument the entire population or is it only a sample of a larger dataset?

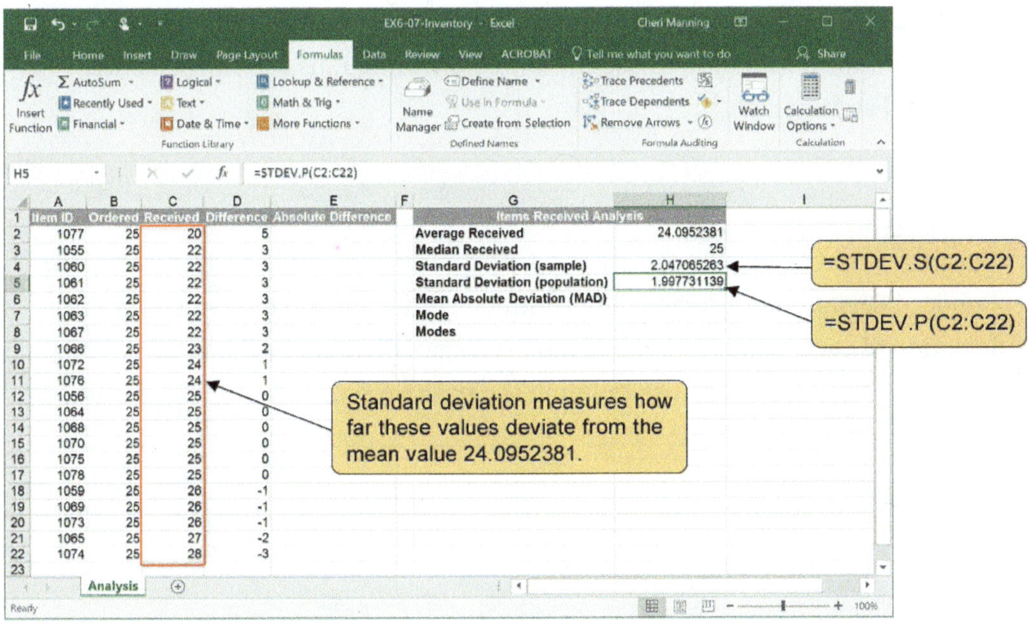

FIGURE EX 6.22

To calculate standard deviation when only a sample of the data is available:

1. On the *Formulas* tab, in the *Function Library* group, click the **More Functions** button, point to **Statistical**, and select **STDEV.S**.
2. In the *Number1* argument box, enter the cell range or named range for the sample data.
3. If you want the calculation to use multiple noncontiguous cell ranges, enter additional arguments.
4. Click **OK**.

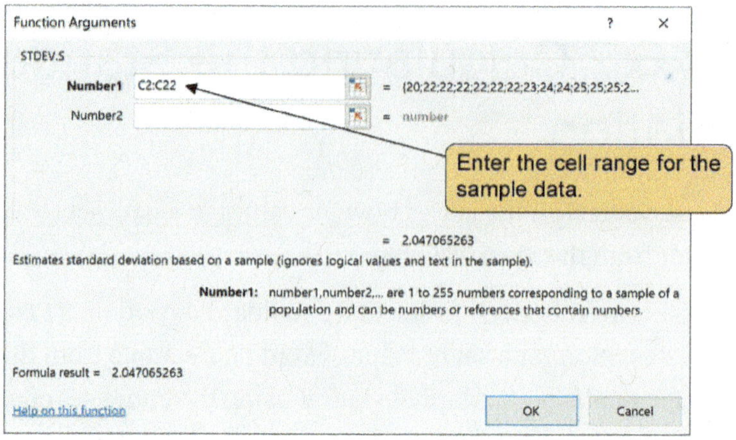

FIGURE EX 6.23

To calculate standard deviation using the entire data population:

1. On the *Formulas* tab, in the *Function Library* group, click the **More Functions** button, point to **Statistical**, and select **STDEV.P**.
2. In the *Number1* argument box, enter the cell range or named range for the data.
3. If you want the calculation to use multiple noncontiguous cell ranges, enter additional arguments.
4. Click **OK**.

tell me more

Standard deviation is calculated by adding together the squared values of the deviation of each value from the mean (average), dividing by the total number of values, and then calculating the positive square root of the result.

let me try *Live!*

If you do not have the data file from the previous skill open, open the student data file **EX6-07-Inventory** and try this skill on your own:

1. On the **Analysis** worksheet, enter a formula in cell **H4** to calculate the standard deviation of the values in cells **C2:C22**. Assume this array is a sample of a larger set of values.
2. Enter a formula in cell **H5** to calculate the standard deviation of the values in cells **C2:C22**. This array of values is the entire data set.
3. If you will be moving on to the next skill in this chapter, leave the workbook open to continue working. If not, save the file as directed by your instructor and close it.

Skill 6.8 Calculating the Mean Absolute Deviation (MAD)

An alternative way to calculate how far values in a population deviate from the average is to calculate the **mean absolute deviation** (**MAD**). The mean absolute deviation is the average of the absolute differences between each value and the overall mean.

The **absolute value of a number** measures how far the number is from 0. The absolute value of a positive number is the same as the number. The absolute value of a negative number is the number without the negative sign.

- The absolute value of 1 is 1.
- The absolute value of -1 is 1.

The function to calculate absolute value, ABS, takes a single argument *Number*. Number is a value or reference to a cell with a value for which you want to calculate the absolute value.

To calculate the mean absolute deviation:

1. First calculate the absolute value for each item in the data set. Type `=ABS(` and then enter the cell reference or formula for the *Number* argument. Type `)` and press **[Enter]**.
2. Copy the formula as necessary to generate all the absolute values.
3. Once you have a list of absolute values for the data set, create a formula using the AVERAGE function. Use the list of absolute values as the *Number1* argument.

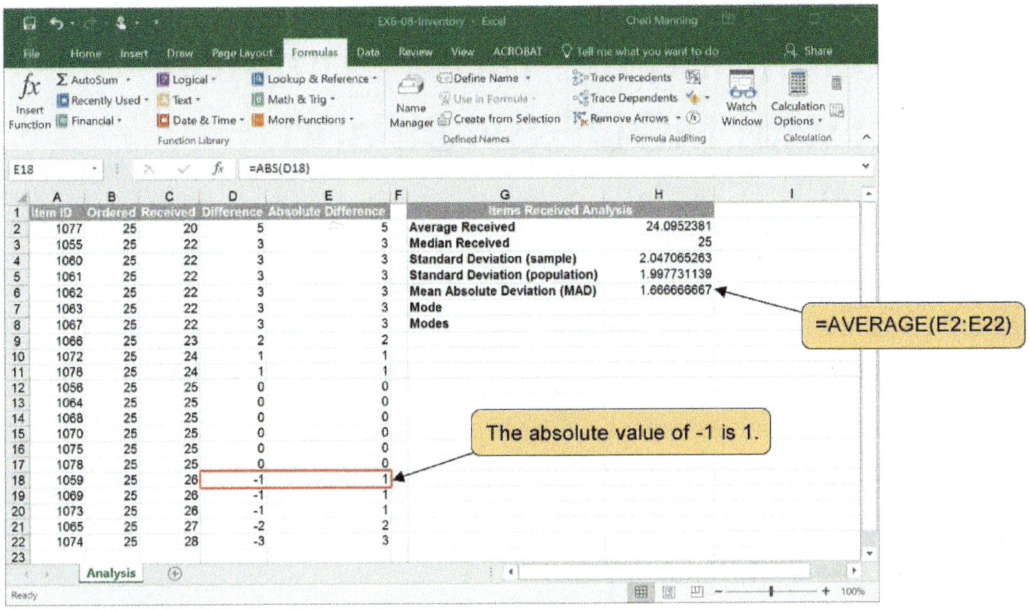

FIGURE EX 6.24

let me try *Live!*

If you do not have the data file from the previous skill open, open the student data file **EX6-08-Inventory** and try this skill on your own:

1. On the **Analysis** worksheet, enter a formula in cell **E2** to calculate the absolute value of the value in cell **D2**. You will be copying this formula, so be sure to use a relative reference.
2. Copy the formula in cell **E2** to cells **E3:E22**.
3. Enter a formula in cell **H6** to calculate the mean absolute deviation of the values in cells **E2:E22**.
4. If you will be moving on to the next skill in this chapter, leave the workbook open to continue working. If not, save the file as directed by your instructor and close it.

Skill 6.9 Finding the Most Common Value(s) with MODE.SNGL and MODE.MULT

By now you should know how to find the average (mean) value or the middle (median) value in a list of values, but what if you want to find the most common value? The statistical **mode** is the value that appears most often in a group of values.

In Figure EX 6.25, two values appear six times in the cell range C2:C22: 22 and 25. The **MODE.SNGL** function returns a single mode value (the first mode value it finds). If there are no duplicate values, MODE.SNGL will return the error #N/A.

=MODE.SNGL(*Number1*,*[Number2]*...)
=MODE.SNGL(C2:C22)

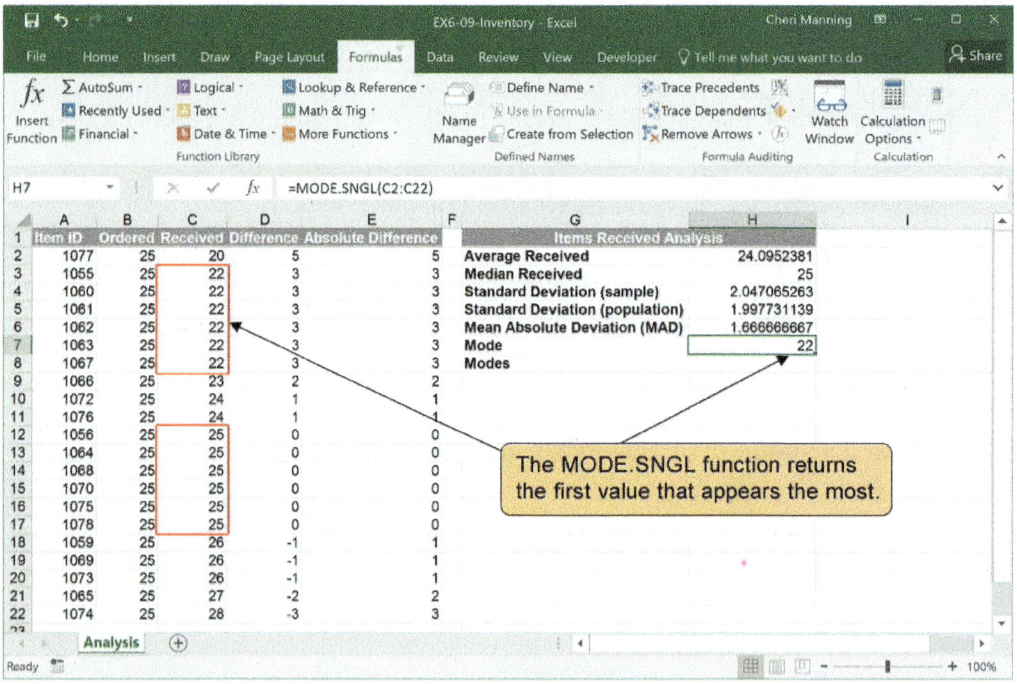

FIGURE EX 6.25

MODE.SNGL is a simple function to use. Most of the time you may find it easiest to type the formula directly in the cell or the formula bar. If you prefer using the *Function Arguments* dialog, on the *Formulas* tab, in the *Function Library* group, click the **More Functions** button, point to **Statistical**, and then click **MODE.SNGL** to open the *Function Arguments* dialog. You may enter up to 255 cell ranges or range names as arguments.

If your dataset includes more than one mode, you can use the **MODE.MULT** function in an array formula to return multiple values. An **array** formula is capable of conducting multiple calculations, in this case, producing multiple results.

The MODE.MULT function used in Figure EX 6.26 populates cells H8:H9 (the results array) with the two mode values: 22 and 25.

=MODE.MULT(*Number1,[Number2]...*)
=MODE.MULT(C2:C22)

Notice that the formula using MODE.MULT is the same as the formula for MODE.SNGL except the formula in Figure EX 6.26 is surrounded by braces. The braces tell Excel that this is an array formula and that the selected cells should be populated with multiple values.

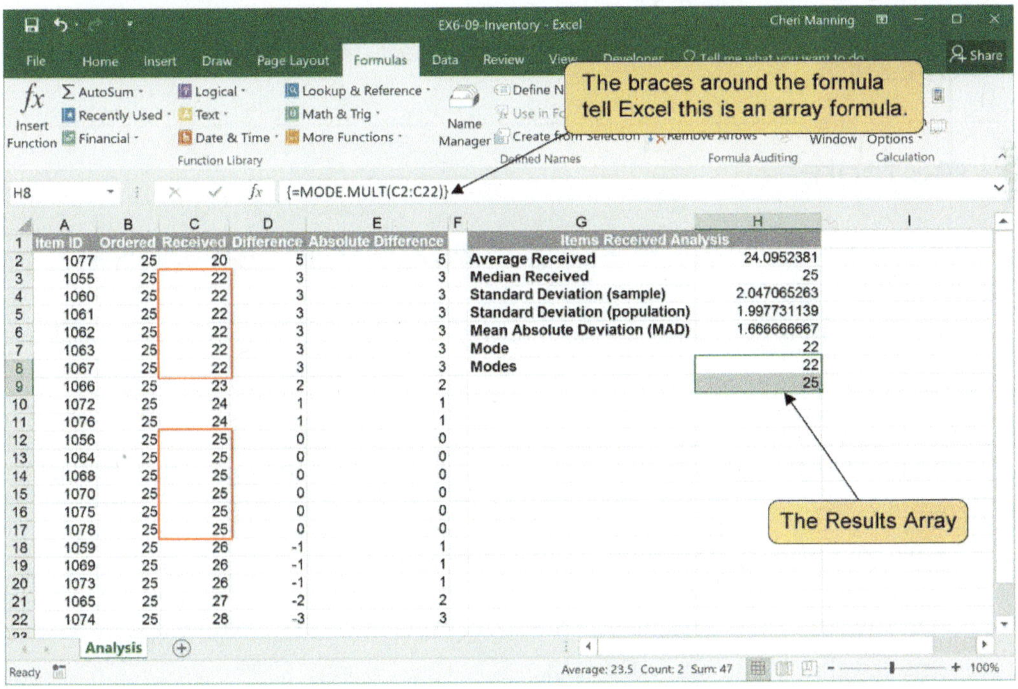

FIGURE EX 6.26

To use MODE.MULT, instead of selecting a single cell, select the range of cells in which you want the results to display. This defines the results array. You do not need to know the exact number of cells to select; if the results array has more cells than there are modes, the extra cells display #N/A.

Use one of these methods to enter the formula:

1. Enter the formula by typing it directly in the formula bar. After typing the formula, press **[Ctrl]+[Shift]+[Enter]**. Using this keystroke combination instructs Excel to enter an array formula. Notice that Excel places braces around the formula. You cannot type the braces. You must use **[Ctrl]+[Shift]+[Enter]**

after typing the formula.

2. Enter the formula using the *Function Arguments* dialog.
   a. On the *Formulas* tab, in the *Function Library* group, click the **More Functions** button, point to **Statistical**, and then click **MODE.MULT**.
   b. Enter the cell range or range name to evaluate in the argument box.
   c. Click **OK**.
   d. Place the cursor in the formula bar and press **[Ctrl]+[Shift]+[Enter]** before clicking another cell or pressing any other keyboard key.

tips & tricks

Both MODE.SNGL and MODE.MULT are compatible only with Excel 2010 and later. If you are sharing your workbook with someone using Excel 2007 or earlier, you can use the older function MODE. It returns the same value as MODE.SNGL.

tell me more

MODE.SNGL and MODE.MULT ignore empty cells and cells that contain text.

let me try *Live!*

If you do not have the data file from the previous skill open, open the student data file
EX6-09-Inventory and try this skill on your own:

1. On the **Analysis** worksheet, enter a formula in cell **H7** to display the first mode value in the range **C2:C22**.
2. Enter an array formula in cells **H8:H9** to display the two mode values from the range **C2:C22**. Remember to select the results array before entering the formula.
3. If you will be moving on to the next skill in this chapter, leave the workbook open to continue working. If not, save the file as directed by your instructor and close it.

Skill 6.10 Ranking Values in a Dataset with RANK.EQ and RANK.AVG

Ranking refers to the sort order of a value relative to all the other values in the data set. Excel includes two functions to calculate rank. If the data set includes duplicate values, and you want the lowest ranking for that value, use the function **RANK.EQ**. If you want the average ranking for that value, use **RANK.AVG** instead.

RANK.EQ and RANK.AVG both take two required arguments and one optional argument.

Number—the number, cell reference, or formula for which you want to find the ranking.

Ref—the cell range of the list within which the *Number* argument should be ranked.

Order (optional)—tells Excel which way to sort the list to determine ranking. By default, the values are sorted in descending order so the largest value has a ranking of 1. If this is the ranking order you want, you can omit this argument. If you want to sort the ranking the other way, so the smallest value has a ranking of 1, enter any non-zero value in the *Order* argument.

The formula in cell E1 in Figure EX 6.27 uses RANK.EQ to find the ranking for the price of item 1101 ($18.00). $18.00 appears three times in the list. The first time it appears, it is the seventh highest price in the list, so using RANK.EQ, it has a rank of 7.

=RANK.EQ(*Number*,*Ref*,[*Order*])
=RANK.EQ(C12,C5:C16)

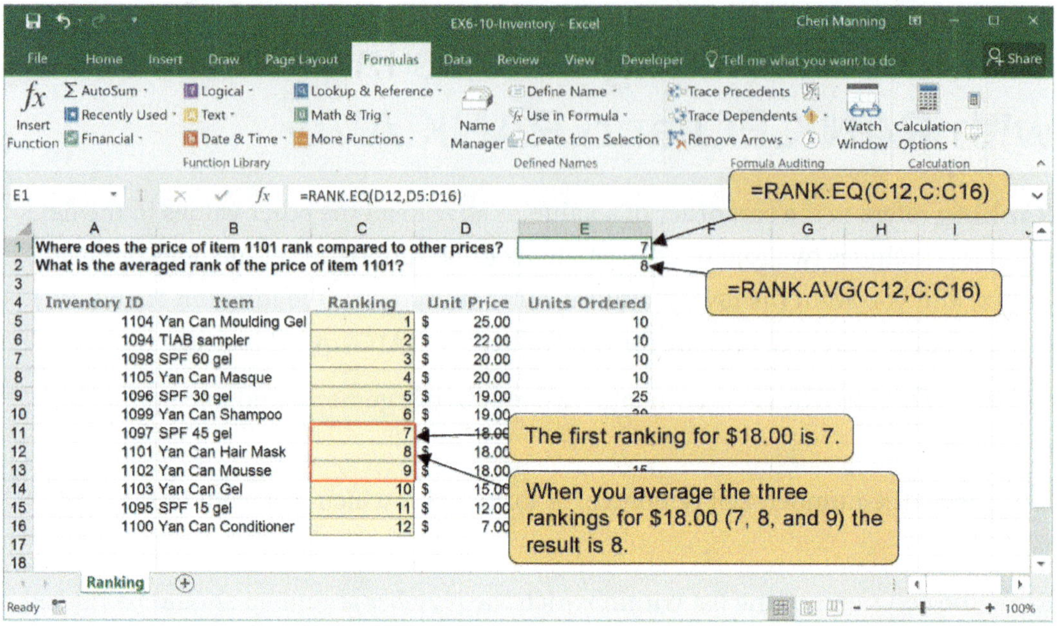

FIGURE EX 6.27

Because the value $18.00 appears more than once in the list, you might want to find the average ranking value instead. In Figure EX 6.27, the formula in cell E2 uses RANK.AVG to find the average of the rankings for the price of item 1101 ($18.00). The three rankings for $18.00 are 7, 8, and 9. The average of these values is 8-(7+8+9)/3.

=RANK.AVG(*Number*,*Ref*,[*Order*])
=RANK.AVG(C12,C5:C16)

To calculate the rank of a value in a list of values:

1. On the *Formulas* tab, in the *Function Library* group, click the **More Functions** button, point to **Statistical**, and select **RANK.EQ** or **RANK.AVG**.
2. In the *Number* argument box, enter the cell reference or number for which you want to find the ranking.
3. In the *Ref* argument box, enter the cell range or named range for the array of values.
4. The *Order* argument is optional. By default, Excel will calculate the ranking based on sorting all the values in descending order (so the highest value = 1). If you want to find the rank in the opposite order, enter **1** in the *Order* argument.
5. Click **OK**.

tell me **more**

Excel includes the previous function RANK for compatibility with Excel 2007 and earlier.

let me **try** *Live!*

If you do not have the data file from the previous skill open, open the student data file
EX6-10-Inventory and try this skill on your own:

1. On the **Analysis** worksheet, enter a formula in cell **E1** to calculate the rank of the value in cell **C12** compared to the values in the range **C5:C16**.
2. Enter a formula in cell **E2** to calculate the **averaged** rank of the value in cell **C12** compared to the values in the range **C5:C16**.
3. If you will be moving on to the next skill in this chapter, leave the workbook open to continue working. If not, save the file as directed by your instructor and close it.

Skill 6.11 Exploring More Logical Functions: AND and OR

You should already be familiar with the logical function IF. While you could use the IF function to return text strings "true" and "false", it is easier to use one of the other logical functions designed specifically to return a TRUE or FALSE response—AND and OR. As you will see from the examples in this skill, there are multiple correct approaches to asking questions about your data. How you pose the question determines which function you should use to answer it—AND or OR?

- If you are looking for a true value to multiple conditions, use AND.
- If you are looking for a true value to any one of multiple conditions, use OR.

The logical function **AND** returns TRUE if all the arguments are true, and FALSE if at least one of the arguments is false.

In Figure EX 6.28, the formula used to evaluate whether or not the purchase order line item can be closed will return TRUE only if the value in the *Ordered* column is equal to the value in the *Received* column AND the value in the *Invoice Pd* column is *Yes*. In this case, the AND function requires two *Logical* arguments. Both arguments must be true in order for the function to return TRUE.

=AND(*Logical1*, [*Logical2*]...)
=AND(C2=D2,E2="yes")

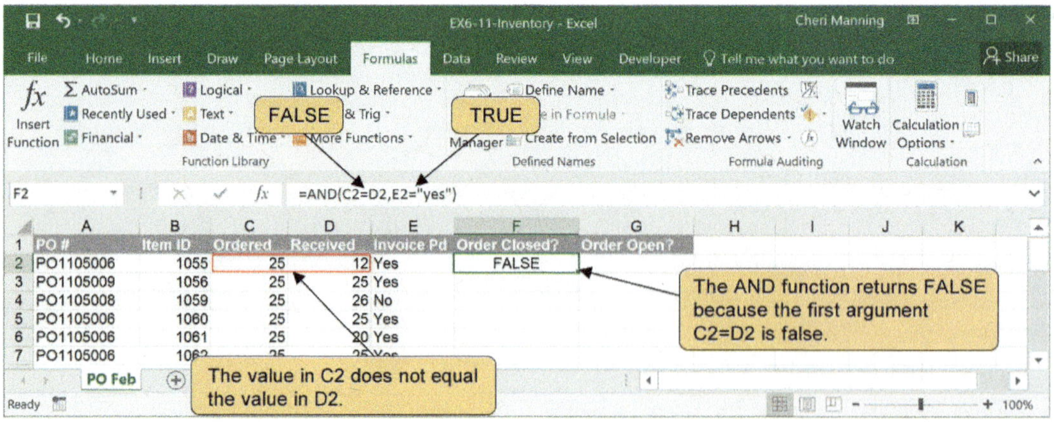

FIGURE EX 6.28

To create a formula using the AND function:

1. Select the cell where you want to enter the formula.
2. On the *Formulas* tab, in the *Function Library* group, click the **Logical** button. Select **AND** to open the *Function Arguments* dialog.

3. Enter the first comparison expression in the *Logical1* box. Enter additional arguments as necessary. The AND function can take up to 255 arguments. Remember, *all* the arguments must be true in order for the AND function to return TRUE.
4. Click **OK**.

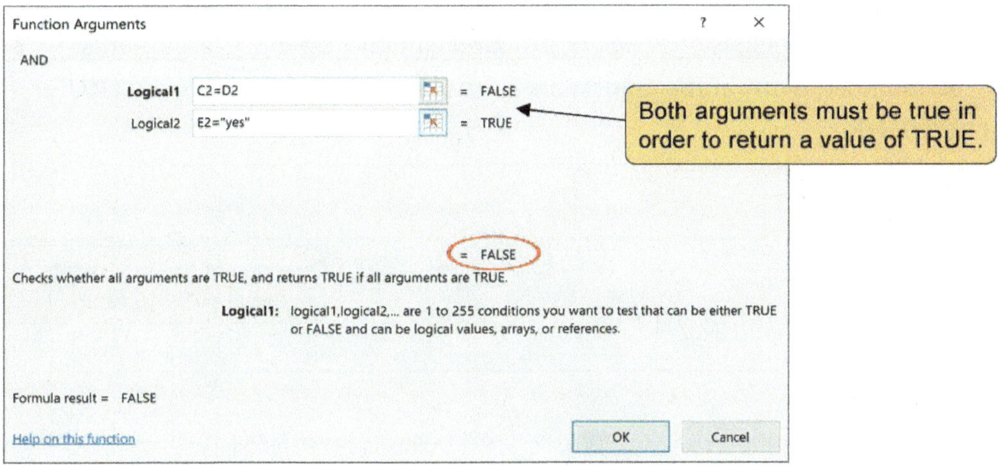

FIGURE EX 6.29

The logical function **OR** returns TRUE if at least one of the arguments is true, and FALSE if all the arguments are false.

In Figure EX 6.30, we turn the purchase order question on its head. Now we want to know if the PO item is still open instead of closed. The PO item is considered open if the value in the *Ordered* column does not equal the value in the *Received* column OR the value in the *Invoice Pd* column is *No*. The OR function returns TRUE if *either* argument is true.

=OR(*Logical1*,[*Logical2*]...)

=OR(C2<>D2,E2="no")

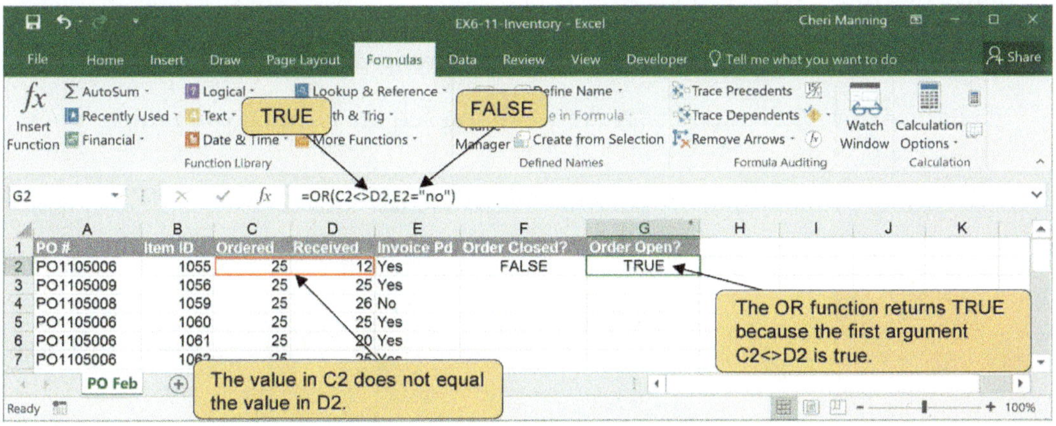

FIGURE EX 6.30

To create a formula using the OR function:

1. Select the cell where you want to enter the formula.
2. On the *Formulas* tab, in the *Function Library* group, click the **Logical** button. Select **OR** to open the *Function Arguments* dialog.
3. Enter the first comparison expression in the *Logical1* box. Enter additional arguments as necessary. The OR function can take up to 255 arguments. Remember, if *any* of the arguments is true, the OR function returns TRUE.
4. Click **OK**

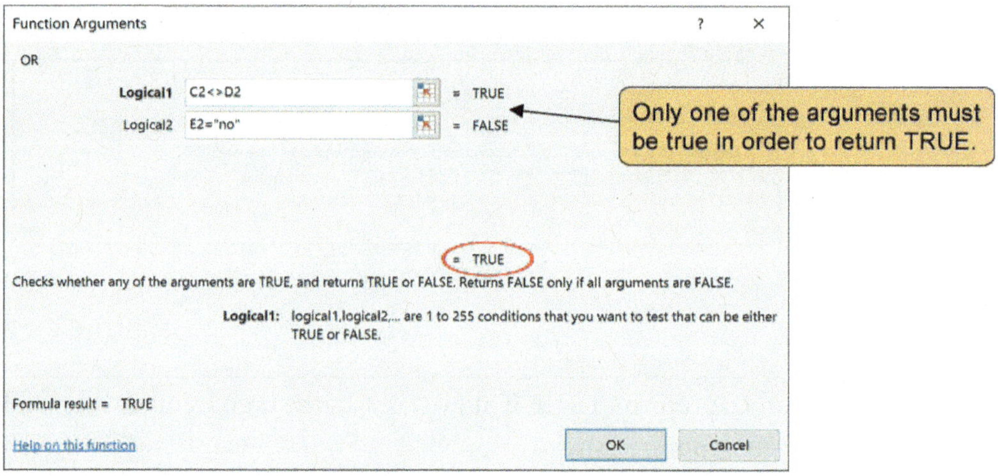

FIGURE EX 6.31

tips & tricks

AND and OR statements are often used as *Logical test* arguments within IF functions when the formula needs to evaluate more than one condition or display a result other than TRUE or FALSE. For example, a formula using an IF function to return a value of green if cell A2 is blue and cell A3 is yellow looks like this:

=IF(AND(A2="blue",A3="yellow"),"green","wrong color")

If either A2 or A3 does not meet the condition set, the formula will return "wrong color."

tell me **more**

If you are looking for a true value to a question posed in the negative, use NOT. The logical function **NOT** returns TRUE if the argument is false, and FALSE if the argument is true. NOT evaluates only one logical test.

To create a formula using the NOT function:

1. Select the cell where you want to enter the formula.
2. On the *Formulas* tab, in the *Function Library* group, click the **Logical** button. Select **NOT** to open the *Function Arguments* dialog.
3. Enter the expression to evaluate in the *Logical1* box. Remember, if the expression is false, the NOT function returns TRUE.
4. Click **OK.**

let me try *Live!*

If you do not have the data file from the previous skill open, open the student data file
EX6-11-Inventory and try this skill on your own:

1. On the **PO Feb** worksheet, enter a formula in cell **F2** using the **AND** function to return TRUE if **C2** (the value in the *Ordered* column) is **equal to D2** (the value in the *Received* column) **and** the value in cell **E2** is **yes**. *Hint:* Remember to enclose text strings in quotation marks.
2. Copy the formula to cells **F3:F24**.
3. Enter a formula in cell **G2** using the **OR** function to return TRUE if **C2** (the value in the *Ordered* column) is **not equal to D2** (the value in the *Received* column) **or** the value in cell **E2** is **no.** *Hint:* Use <> for the not equal to operator.
4. Copy the formula to cells **G3:G24**.
5. If you will be moving on to the next skill in this chapter, leave the workbook open to continue working. If not, save the file as directed by your instructor and close it.

Skill 6.12 Using the IFS Function

In previous versions of Excel, to evaluate a series of logical tests, you needed to create complex formulas using nested IF functions. In 2016, Excel introduced the **IFS** function which allows you to evaluate multiple logical tests in a single function.

In Figure EX 6.32, the IFS function used in cell H2 has three logical tests. If the first logical test is true, the cell will display *Order Closed*. If not, then the second logical test will be evaluated. If true, then the cell will display *Order Short*. If not, then the third logical test will be evaluated. If true, the cell will display *Invoice Due*.

=IFS(F2=TRUE,"Order Closed",D2<C2,"Order Short",E2="no","Invoice Due")

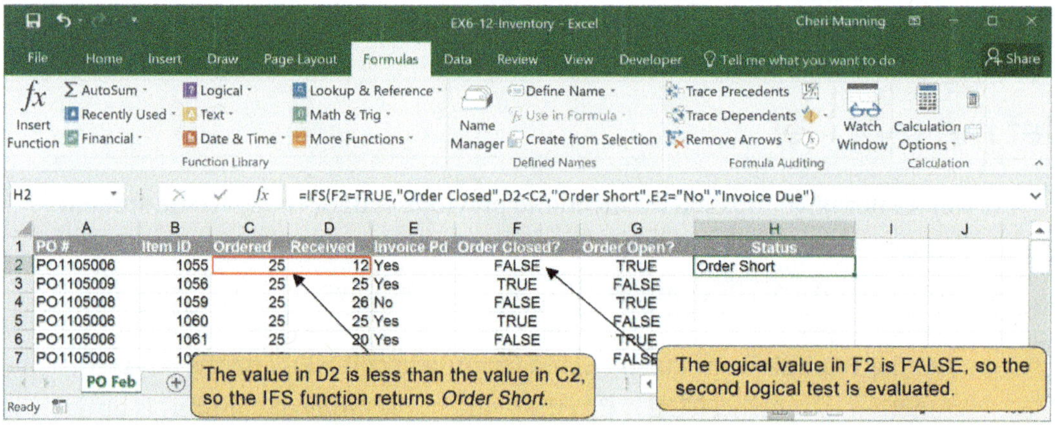

FIGURE EX 6.32

To create a formula using IFS:

1. On the *Formulas* tab, in the *Function Library* group, click the **Logical** button and select **IFS**.
2. In the *Logical_test1* argument box, enter the first condition for which you want to test.
3. In the *Value_if_true1* argument box, enter the text string or value that will be displayed or the formula that will be calculated if the *Logical_test1* argument is true.
4. In the *Logical_test2* argument box, enter the condition to evaluate if the *Logical_test1* argument is false.
5. In the *Value_if_true2* argument box, enter the text string or value that will be displayed or the formula that will be calculated if the *Logical_test2* argument is true.
6. Repeat steps 4–5 until you have covered all the conditions for which you want to test.
7. Click **OK** to complete the formula.

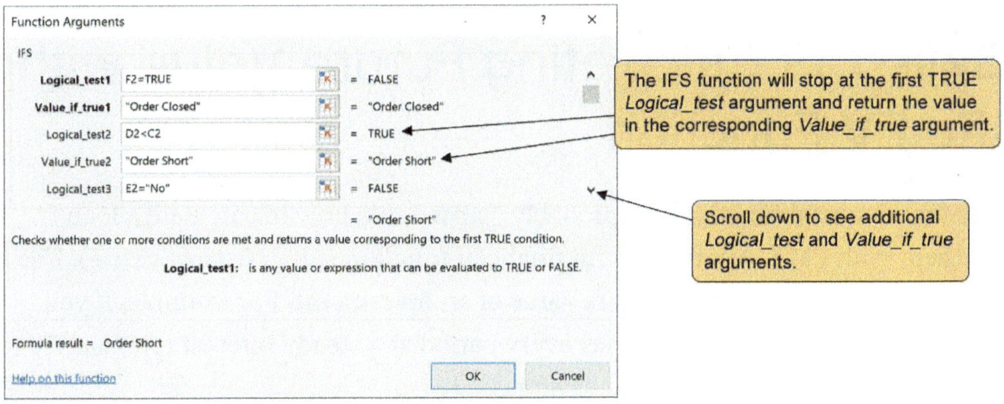

FIGURE EX 6.33

tips & tricks

If you are testing only for one logical condition, use the IF function instead of IFS.

let me try *Live!*

If you do not have the data file from the previous skill open, open the student data file **EX6-12-Inventory** and try this skill on your own:

1. On the **PO Feb** worksheet, enter a formula in cell **H2** using the IFS function to display **Order Closed** if the value in cell **F2** is **true**, **Order Short** if the value in cell **D2** is **less than** the value in cell **C2**, and **Invoice Due** if the value in cell **E2** is **No**. *Hint:* When evaluating against a logical value, do not enclose it in quotation marks like you would with a text string.
2. Copy the formula to cells **H3:H24**.
3. Save the file as directed by your instructor and close it.

Skill 6.13 Calculating Future Value with the FV Function

The first financial function you probably learned was how to calculate a loan payment with PMT. Another useful financial function is FV (**future value**). Use the **FV** function to calculate the future value of an investment. For example, if you deposit the same amount of money every period at a steady interest rate, use FV to calculate the future value of your savings.

The FV function has three required arguments and two optional arguments:

Rate—the interest rate. If the interest rate is an annual interest rate, it must be divided by the number of payment periods per year.

Nper—the total number of payments.

Pmt—the amount of each payment. As the payment is money going *out*, it is usually expressed as a negative number.

Pv—(optional) the present value or how much the investment is worth today. If there is no money in the investment vehicle prior to the first payment, you can omit this argument. When the *Pv* argument is empty, Excel assumes a value of 0.

Type—(optional) when the *Type* argument is empty, Excel assumes a value of 0 and calculates the result based on payments at the end of each period. Enter **1** for this argument if funds are added to the investment the beginning of each period.

Figure EX 6.34 shows a formula using the FV function to calculate the future value of an investment where cell B4 is the annual interest rate (the *Rate* argument), cell B5 is the number of payments made once a year (the *Nper* argument), and cell B3 is the amount contributed every year (the *Pmt* argument). There is no money in the account at the beginning, so the *Pv* argument is omitted, and new funds are added at the end of every year, so the *Type* argument is also omitted. Notice that the *Pmt* argument is negative.

=FV(*Rate*,*Nper*,*Pmt*,[*Pv*],[*Type*])
=FV(B4,B5,-B3)

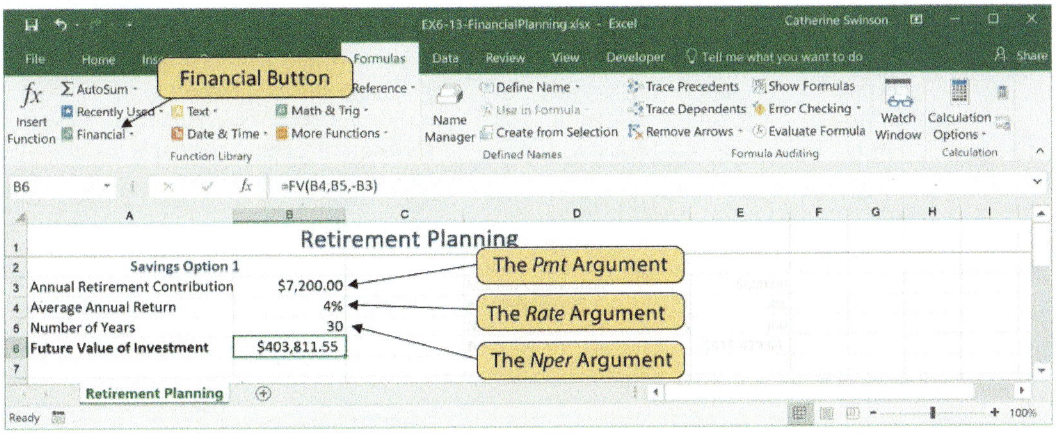

FIGURE EX 6.34

Let's look at another example in Figure EX 6.35 where the annual interest rate is also 4%, but the contributions are made monthly and funds are added at the end of every month. In this example, you must divide the *annual* interest rate by 12 because contributions are made monthly (twelve times a year).

=FV(E4/12,E5,-E3)

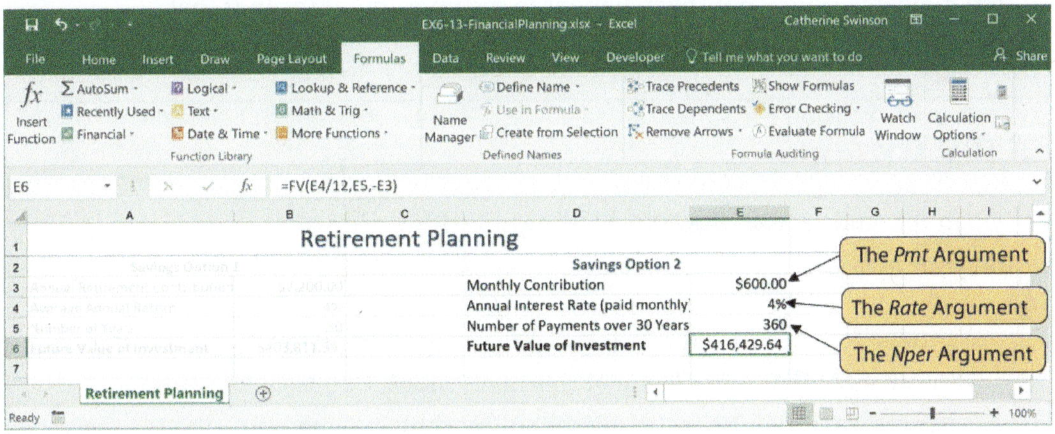

FIGURE EX 6.35

To create a formula using FV:

1. Select the cell where you want to enter the formula.
2. On the *Formulas* tab, in the *Function Library* group, click the **Financial** button. Click **FV** to open the *Function Arguments* dialog.
3. Enter the arguments. In Figure EX 6.36, the interest rate is annual and the payments are monthly, so the interest rate must be divided by 12. Notice that the *Pmt* argument includes a hyphen before the cell reference to make it negative. The *Pv* and *Type* arguments are optional and not necessary in this example.
4. Click **OK**.

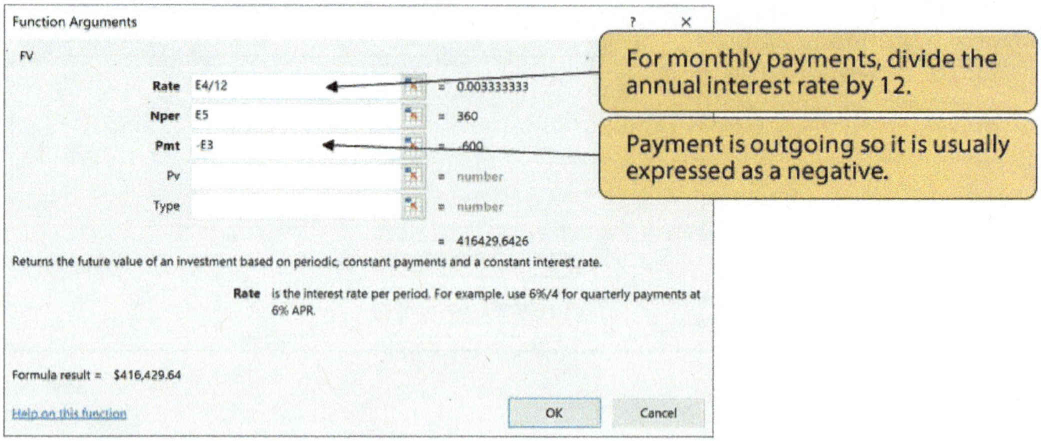

FIGURE EX 6.36

tips & tricks

When working with the financial functions, keep in mind that the *Pmt* argument (the payment) is negative if you are paying out the money, and positive if the money is coming in. This may seem counterintuitive, but you are really making a monthly payment *to* the investment (even if that "investment" is your own savings account).

let me try *Live!*

Open the student data file **EX6-13-FinancialPlanning** and try this skill on your own:

1. Enter a formula in cell **E6** on the *Retirement Planning* worksheet using **FV** to calculate the future value of this investment. Cell **E4** is the annual interest rate. Cell **E5** is the number of monthly payments. Cell **E3** is the amount of payment each month. Remember to express the *Pmt* argument as a negative and divide the annual interest rate by the number of payments per year. Omit the optional argument.
2. If you will be moving on to the next skill in this chapter, leave the workbook open to continue working. If not, save the file as directed by your instructor and close it.

Skill 6.14 Using PV to Calculate Present Value When Payments Are Constant

In financial terms, **present value** is the value today of a series of future payments. For example, at today's interest rates, what is the lump sum you would need to fund a retirement account to pay an annuity (a series of constant payments) to yourself? Present value can be calculated using the **PV** function when the payments are constant.

The PV function has three required arguments and two optional arguments:

Rate—the interest rate. If the interest rate is an annual interest rate, it must be divided by the number of payment periods per year.

Nper—the total number of payments.

Pmt—the amount of each payment. As the payment is money going *out*, it is usually expressed as a negative number.

Fv—(optional) the amount of money left after the last payment is made (the future value of the investment). If the final balance in the account is expected to be zero, you can omit this argument. When the *Fv* argument is empty, Excel assumes a value of 0.

Type—(optional) enter **1** for this argument if the payment is made at the beginning of each period. When the *Type* argument is empty, Excel assumes a value of 0 and calculates the result based on payments at the end of each period. When using PV to calculate the amount needed for annuity payments, the payment would generally be at the beginning of the period, so *Type* must be set to *1*.

The example in Figure EX 6.37 uses the PV function to calculate the required starting balance to fund a retirement account to pay $3,000 monthly for 20 years assuming a steady annual rate of return of 4%. Notice the two commas after the *Pmt* argument. The *Fv* argument is omitted because the value of the account is expected to be zero after the final payment, but the placeholder comma for that argument is still required because the formula includes the next argument, *Type*. Because the annuity would be paid at the beginning of every month, the *Type* argument is necessary and is set to *1*.

=PV(*Rate*,*Nper*,*Pmt*,[*Fv*],[*Type*])
=PV(B10/12,B11*12,-B9,,1)

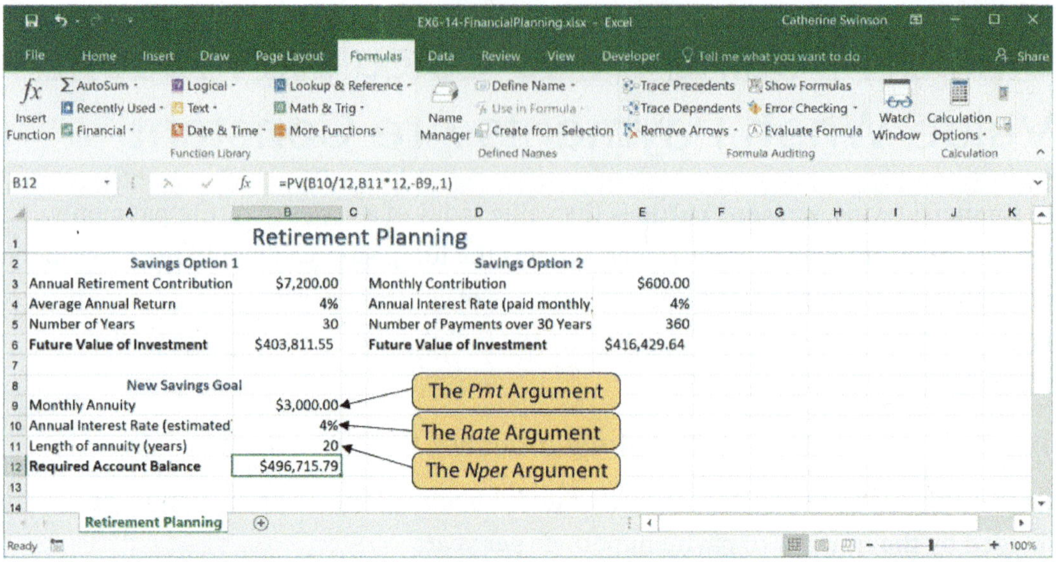

FIGURE EX 6.37

To create a formula using PV:

1. Select the cell where you want to enter the formula.
2. On the *Formulas* tab, in the *Function Library* group, click the **Financial** button. Click **PV** to open the *Function Arguments* dialog.
3. Enter the arguments. In our example, the payments will be monthly, so the annual interest rate (*Rate*) must be divided by 12 and the number of payout years (*Nper*) must be multiplied by twelve as shown in Figure EX 6.38. The *Pmt* argument includes a hyphen before the cell reference to make it negative. The *Fv* argument is omitted, but payments will be made at the beginning of every period, so the *Type* argument must be set to *1*. If this argument is omitted, Excel assumes a value of 0.
4. Click **OK**.

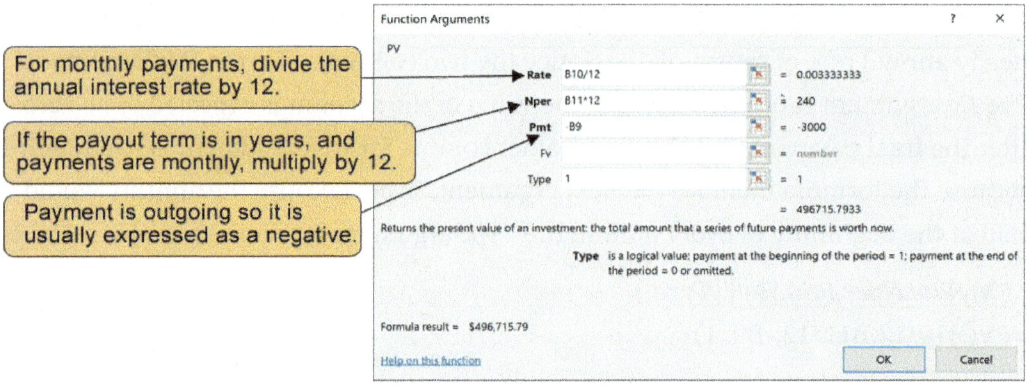

FIGURE EX 6.38

tell me **more**

The concept of the **Time Value of Money (TVM)** is essential to finance. It is the principle that a dollar in hand today is worth more than a promise of a dollar tomorrow because you have the opportunity to invest that dollar today and thus make even more money by tomorrow. The present value (the value today) of a series of future payments is actually less than the sum of those payments. This works *for* you when saving money for future payments to yourself. It can sometimes work *against* you when investing capital today in exchange for a series of future payments. Calculating present value is essential to making good financial decisions.

let me **try** *Live!*

If you do not have the data file from the previous skill open, open the student data file
EX6-14-FinancialPlanning and try this skill on your own:

1. Enter a formula using **PV** in cell **B12** on the *Retirement Planning* worksheet to calculate the present value needed to pay a monthly annuity over the next twenty years. Cell **B10** is the expected annual interest rate. Cell **B11** is the number of years over which the monthly payments will be made. Cell **B9** is the amount of each monthly payment. Omit the *Fv* argument. Payment will be at the beginning of each period, so set the *Type* argument to the appropriate value. Pay attention to the time periods for the interest rate, payout period, and payment schedule. Remember to express the *Pmt* argument as a negative.
2. If you will be moving on to the next skill in this chapter, leave the workbook open to continue working. If not, save the file as directed by your instructor and close it.

Skill 6.15 Using NPV to Calculate Present Value When Payments Are Variable

The **NPV** function is similar to PV, but it allows for variable payment amounts when calculating the present value of future payments. NPV can be especially useful for comparing two investment or payment options.

The NPV function has two required arguments:

Rate—the **discount rate**—the interest rate that would be reasonably expected if the money were invested elsewhere.

Value—the payment amount both incoming (positive) and outgoing (negative). NPV takes up to 254 *Value* arguments (*Value1*, *Value2*, etc.).

NPV assumes payments are made over consistent periods of time and each payment comes at the end of the period. NPV ignores cells containing text and blank cells. If your argument range includes periods with no values, be sure to enter **0** instead of leaving the cells blank.

In Figure EX 6.39, a project with a total budget of $250,000 has two payment options. The first option pays $50,000 every year for five years. Using PV, you find that the true value of those payments is $222,591.12. Option 2 payments are variable—paid at the beginning, middle, and end of the project. Using an NPV formula, you find the true value of Option 2 payments is $224,473.11.

=NPV(*Rate*,*Value1*,[*Value2*] . . .)
=NPV(B9,C2:C6)

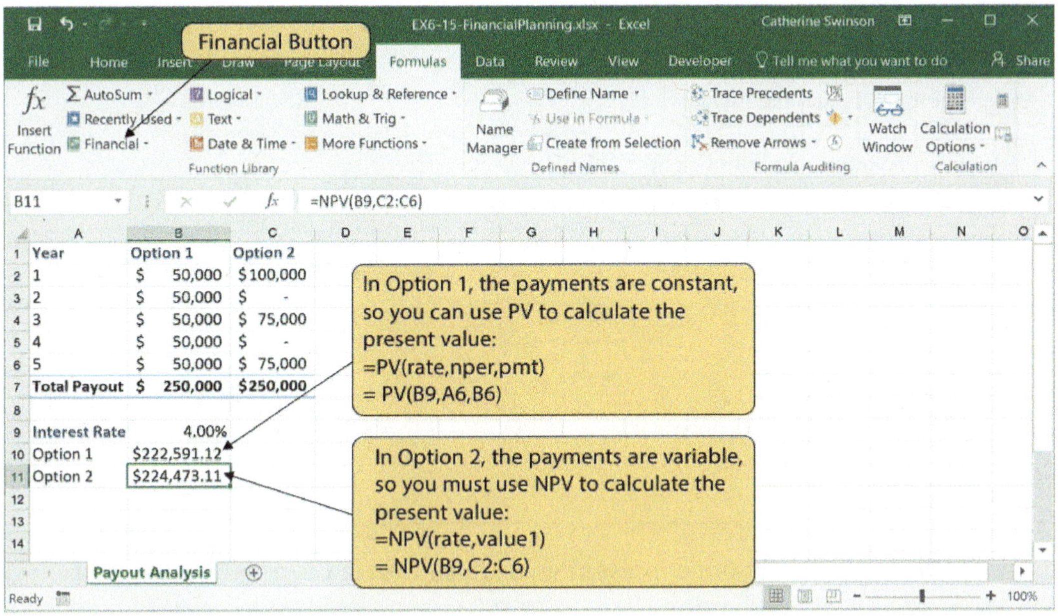

FIGURE EX 6.39

If you are the party paying out the money, Option 1 is the better choice. If you are receiving the payments, however, Option 2 would be better.

To use the NPV function:

1. Select the cell where you want to enter the formula.
2. On the *Formulas* tab, in the *Function Library* group, click the **Financial** button. Click **NPV** to open the *Function Arguments* dialog.
3. In the *Rate* box, enter the interest rate. The NPV *Function Arguments* dialog calls this the discount rate. When working with NPV, the discount rate is the same as the interest rate—just different terminology.
4. The remaining arguments are the payments (negative values) and income (positive values). NPV accepts up to 254 *Value* arguments. You can use cell ranges, named ranges, or individual cell references. If you use a cell range or named range, verify that they do not include blank cells—they will be ignored and the NPV calculation will be wrong.
5. Click **OK**.

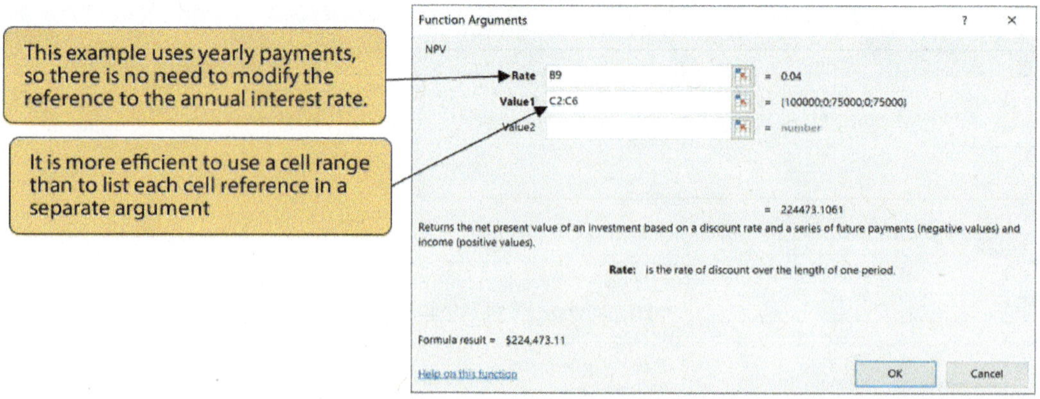

FIGURE EX 6.40

tips & tricks

The financial concept of net present value (also referred to as NPV) does not correspond to Excel's NPV function exactly. Net present value is the value today of future payments minus the cost of the investment—in other words, how much is the investment worth? The Excel function NPV actually calculates present value—the same as the PV function—except it allows for variable value inputs.

tell me more

As with all financial functions that use a *Rate* argument, *Rate* must be expressed in terms of the same time period as the payments. In other words, if you are using an annual interest rate and payments are made monthly, you will need to divide the interest rate by 12 for the *Rate* argument.

let me try *Live!*

If you do not have the data file from the previous skill open, open the student data file **EX6-15-FinancialPlanning** and try this skill on your own:

1. In cell **B11** on the *Payout Analysis* worksheet, enter a formula using the NPV function to calculate the present value of the series of yearly payments in the cell range **C2:C6**. The annual interest rate is in cell **B9**. Use a cell range as a single *Value* argument.
2. If you will be moving on to the next skill in this chapter, leave the workbook open to continue working. If not, save the file as directed by your instructor and close it.

Skill 6.16 Calculating the Number of Payments with NPER

Most of the financial functions we've worked with use *Nper* as an argument—the number of payments in the calculation. But what if you know all the variables except the number of payments? You can use the **NPER** function to calculate the number of payments available from a retirement account or due on a loan given a constant interest rate and payment amount.

The NPER function has three required arguments and two optional arguments:

Rate—the interest rate. If the interest rate is an annual interest rate, it must be divided by the number of payment periods per year.

Pmt—the amount of each payment. As the payment is money going *out*, it is usually expressed as a negative number.

Pv—the value of the investment or loan today.

Fv—(optional) the amount of money left after the last payment is made (the future value). If the final balance in the account is expected to be zero, you can omit this argument. When the *Fv* argument is empty, Excel assumes a value of 0.

Type—(optional) enter **1** for this argument if the payment is made at the beginning of each period. When the *Type* argument is empty, Excel assumes a value of 0 and calculates the result based on payments at the end of each period. When paying yourself from a retirement account, the payment is usually made at the beginning of each period, so set *Type* to *1*.

The example in Figure EX 6.41 uses the NPER function to calculate the number of payments a retirement account can provide given an annual interest rate of 4%, a monthly payment of $3,000, and a starting balance of $400,000. Notice the two commas after the *Pv* argument. The *Fv* argument is omitted because the value of the account is expected to be zero after the final payment, but the placeholder comma for that argument is still required because the formula includes the next argument, *Type*. Payments would be paid at the beginning of every month, so the *Type* argument is necessary and is set to *1*.

=NPER(*Rate*,*Pmt*,*Pv*,[*Fv*],[*Type*])
=NPER(B4 / 12,-B3,B2,,1)

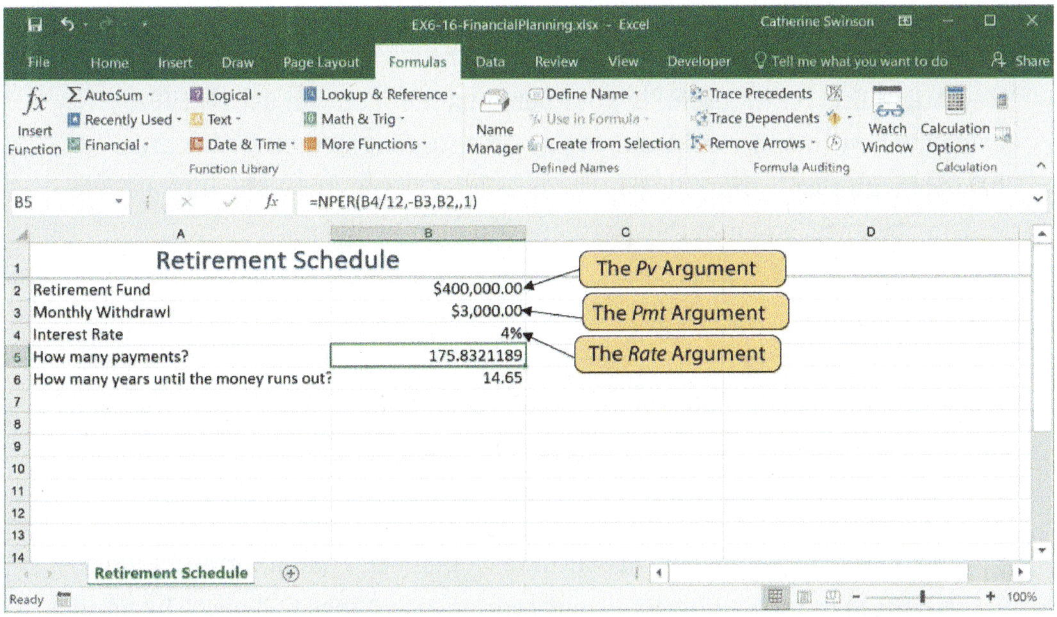

FIGURE EX 6.41

To create a formula using NPER:

1. Select the cell where you want to enter the formula.
2. On the *Formulas* tab, in the *Function Library* group, click the **Financial** button. Click **NPER** to open the *Function Arguments* dialog.
3. Enter the arguments. In our example, the payments will be monthly, so the annual interest rate (*Rate*) must be divided by 12. The *Pmt* argument includes a hyphen before the cell reference to make it negative. The *Fv* argument is omitted, but the *Type* argument is set to *1* because payments will be made at the beginning of every period.
4. Click **OK**.

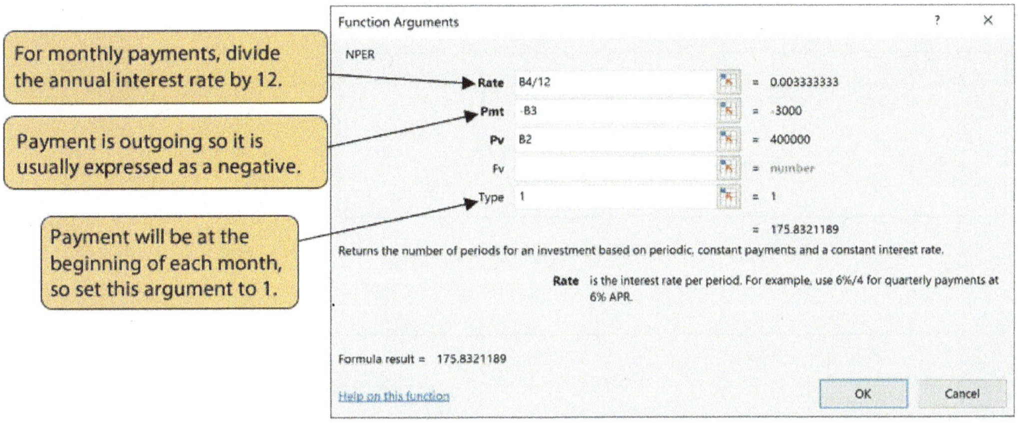

FIGURE EX 6.42

tips & tricks

You might find NPER useful in your personal life. You can use NPER to calculate how long it would take to pay off a student loan or credit card balance with steady monthly payments as long as you know the interest rate, starting balance, and monthly payment you plan to make.

let me try *Live!*

If you do not have the data file from the previous skill open, open the student data file
EX6-16-FinancialPlanning and try this skill on your own:

1. In cell **B5** on the *Retirement Schedule* worksheet, enter a formula using **NPER** to calculate how long your retirement savings will last. The annual interest rate is in cell **B4**. The current value of the account is in cell **B2**. The monthly payment is in cell **B3**. Payments will be made at the beginning of every period. Remember to adjust the interest rate to reflect the same time period as the payments and to express the *Pmt* argument as a negative.
2. Save the file as directed by your instructor and close it.

Skill 6.17 Creating a Depreciation Schedule

When a business purchases a significant asset such as equipment or computer software, generally accepted accounting principles (GAAP) state that the expense must be spread over the asset's useful lifetime. This is referred to as **depreciation**. Depreciation over the life of an asset is figured in a **depreciation schedule**. Depreciation is important because the value of the asset must be stated accurately on financial statements like the business's balance sheet. At the end of each accounting period, the asset's **book value** is recalculated using the initial cost minus the accumulated depreciation.

There are multiple ways to calculate depreciation, but most depreciation functions use the same arguments:

Cost—the initial cost of the asset—usually the purchase price.

Salvage—the fair market value of the asset at the end of its useful life.

Life—the number of years the asset will be used.

Per or **Period**—the number of the accounting period, where each accounting period is one year of the asset's life.

Cost, *Salvage*, and *Life* are constant values in the depreciation schedule and require an absolute cell reference or name reference. *Period* is usually a relative reference to the column in the depreciation schedule that displays the period number. As the depreciation formula is copied, this reference updates automatically.

Figure EX 6.43 shows a five-year depreciation schedule comparing four different depreciation functions available in Excel. Cell B3 is named *Cost*, cell B4 is named *Salvage*, and cell B2 is named *Life*.

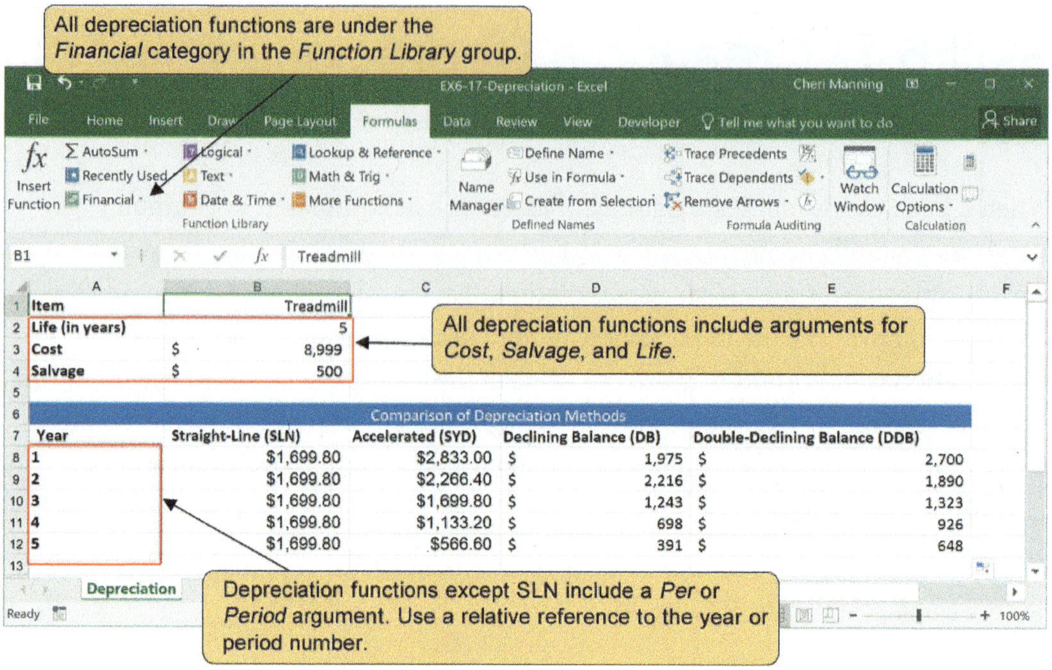

FIGURE EX 6.43

Straight Line

Straight-line depreciation is the simplest depreciation to figure: (the cost of the asset minus the salvage value) divided by the life of the asset (in years). Because straight-line depreciation is the same for every period in the depreciation schedule, there is no need for a period argument. To calculate straight-line depreciation, use the **SLN** function.

=SLN(*Cost*,*Salvage*,*Life*)

=SLN(Cost,Salvage,Life)

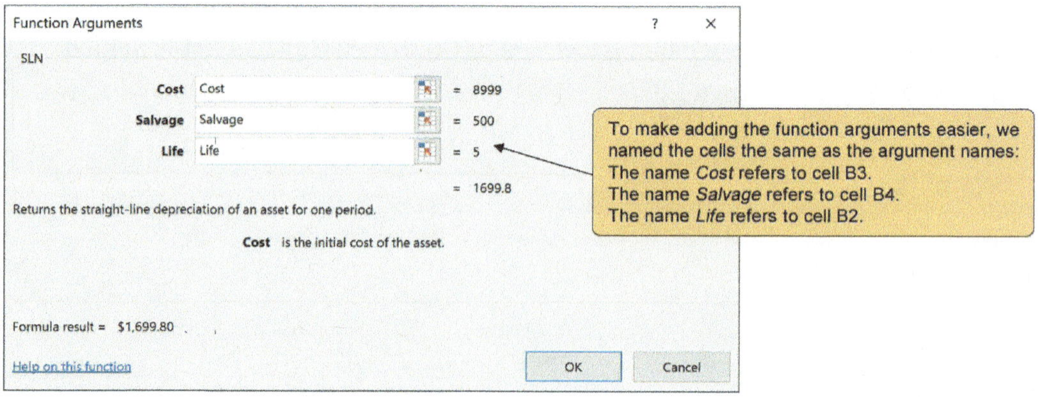

FIGURE EX 6.44

Accelerated

Accelerated depreciation assumes that the asset is worth more at the beginning of its lifespan and uses a higher rate of depreciation for early years in the depreciation schedule. In accounting, this is called **sum-of-the-years' digits (SOYD) depreciation**. Use the **SYD** function to calculate SOYD depreciation.

=SYD(*Cost*,*Salvage*,*Life*,*Per*)
=SYD(Cost,Salvage,Life,A5)

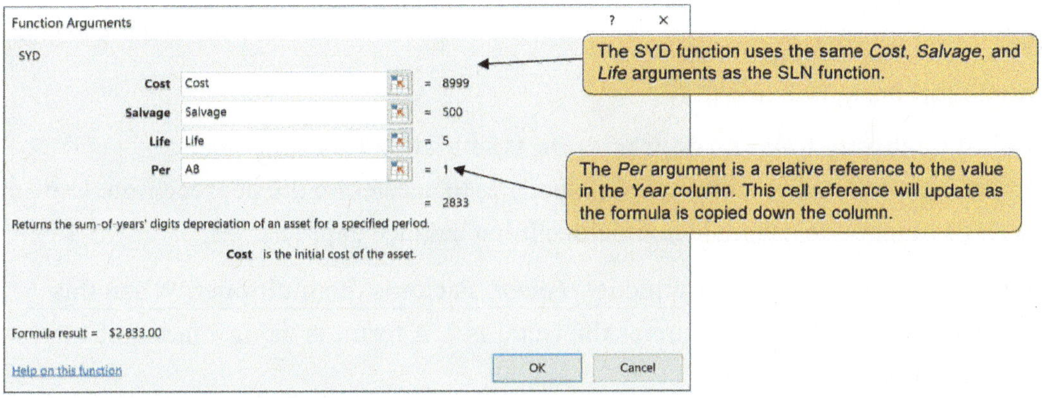

FIGURE EX 6.45

Declining Balance (DB)

Declining balance depreciation takes into account the declining book value of the asset. Use the **DB** function to calculate declining balance depreciation.

DB includes one optional argument—*Month*. This is used when the asset was in use for only part of the first accounting period. Its value is the number of months the asset was in service. When using this argument in a depreciation schedule, be careful to use it in the cell for period 1 only. Do not copy it to the remaining cells in the column. The formula for period 1 for an asset in use for 6 months in the first year looks like this:

=DB(*Cost*,*Salvage*,*Life*,*Period*,[*Month*])
=DB(Cost,Salvage,Life,A5,6)

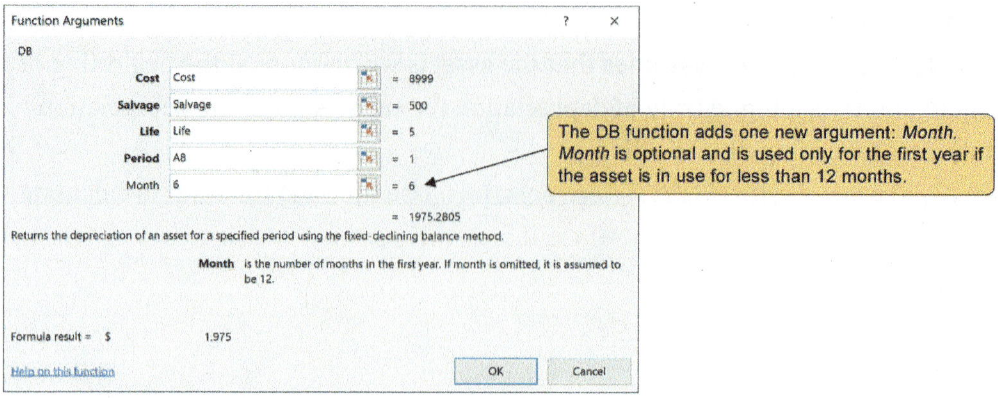

FIGURE EX 6.46

Double-Declining Balance (DDB)

Double-declining balance depreciation is similar to declining balance depreciation, but it uses a multiplier (usually 2) to accelerate the depreciation. Use the **DDB** function to calculate double-declining balance depreciation.

DDB includes one optional argument—*Factor*. Factor is the multiplier. When this argument is omitted, Excel assumes the factor is 2. A formula using a factor of 1.5 looks like this:

=DDB(*Cost*,*Salvage*,*Life*,*Period*,[*Factor*])
=DDB(Cost,Salvage,Life,A5,1.5)

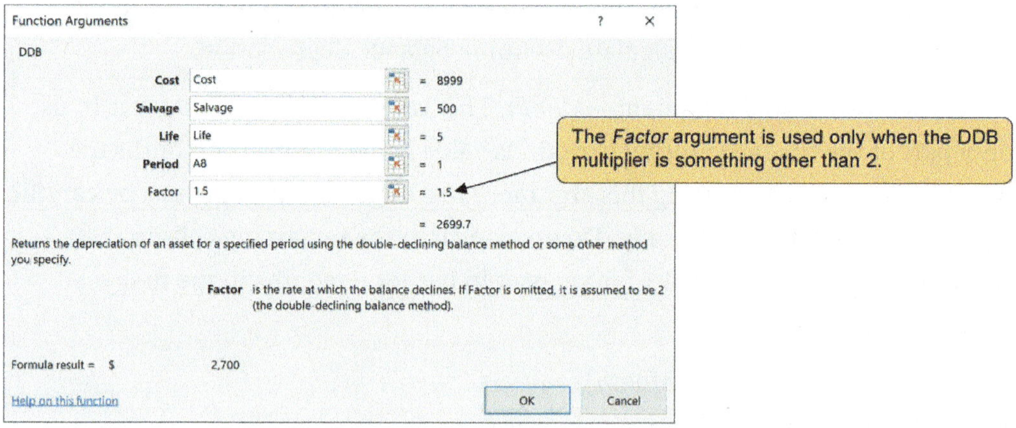

FIGURE EX 6.47

To create a depreciation schedule using one of the depreciation functions:

1. First, set up the values for the arguments. Create cells containing the cost, salvage, and life values. Ideally, name the cells the same as the arguments—**Cost**, **Salvage**, and **Life**. This will make it easier to copy the formulas to the remaining cells in the schedule.
2. List the periods (year numbers) in a column. The depreciation formula will be entered in the column to the right of the period column.

3. Click the cell immediately to the right of the period 1 cell. On the *Formulas* tab, in the *Function Library* group, click the **Financial** button, and then click the depreciation function you want to use.
4. Enter absolute cell references or names for the *Cost*, *Salvage*, and *Life* arguments. If you selected SLN as the depreciation function, skip to step 9.
5. Enter a relative cell reference for the *Per* or *Period* argument. Use the first cell in the list of period numbers.
6. If you selected the DB function, and period 1 is a partial period, enter the number of months the item was in use during period 1 in the *Month* argument.
7. If you are using DDB, and the multiplier is something other than 2, enter the multiplier in the *Factor* argument.
8. Click **OK**.
9. Copy the formula to the remaining cells in the depreciation schedule.

> If you are using DB, copy the formula to the cell for period 2, remove the *Month* argument, and then copy the formula to the remaining cells in the schedule.
> If you are using SLN, the depreciation schedule will have the same value for every period.

tips & tricks

When calculating the value of assets, the book value of the asset may not be the same as its taxable value. For tax purposes (in the United States), the IRS uses the modified accelerated cost recovery system (MACRS) depreciation schedule. The IRS groups assets in classes and specifies the length of time over which each class can be depreciated.

tell me more

If you format the data as a table, Excel will automatically copy the formula to the remaining cells in the column. If you are using the DB function and you have a value in the *Month* argument for year 1, it is best to not format the data as a table since you will need to modify the formula for the remaining years in the schedule.

let me try *Live!*

Open the student data file **EX6-17-Depreciation** and try this skill on your own:

1. In cell **B8**, enter a formula using the function for the **Straight-line** depreciation method. Use the cell names **Cost**, **Salvage**, and **Life** as the function arguments. Copy the formula to cells **B9:B12**.
2. In cell **C8**, enter a formula using the function for the **Accelerated** depreciation method. Use the cell names **Cost**, **Salvage**, and **Life** as the function arguments. Use a relative reference to cell **A8** for the *Per* argument. Copy the formula to cells **C9:C12**.
3. In cell **D8**, enter a formula using the function for the **Declining balance** depreciation method. Use the cell names **Cost**, **Salvage**, and **Life** as the function arguments. Use a relative reference to cell **A8** for the *Period* argument. The asset will be in use for only **six** months in the **first** period. Modify the function as necessary and copy it to cells **D9:D12**.
4. In cell **E8**, enter a formula using the function for the **Double-declining balance** depreciation method. Use the cell names **Cost**, **Salvage**, and **Life** as the function arguments. Use a relative reference to cell **A8** for the *Per* argument. Use **1.5** as the multiplier. Copy the formula to cells **E6:E9**.
5. Save the file as directed by your instructor and close it.

Skill 6.18 Finding Data with MATCH and INDEX

The skill *Finding Data Using the VLOOKUP Function* introduced lookup and reference functions with VLOOKUP. Recall that with VLOOKUP, the value you "look up" must match a value in the first column of the data array. But what if the value you want to look up is in a column other than the first? Instead of using VLOOKUP, you can use a combination of two functions: MATCH and INDEX.

MATCH returns the position of a specific value in a single row or column array. INDEX returns the value at the intersection of a specified row and column in an array. First use MATCH to find the row or column position of the value you want, and then use the results of MATCH as the row number or column number argument in INDEX.

The MATCH function has two required arguments and one optional argument:

Lookup_value—the text, number, or logical value you want to match.

Lookup_array—the range of cells grouped in a single row or column that contains the value you want to look up. If your data are organized as a table, be careful not to include the header row or label column in the *Lookup_array* range.

Match_type—(optional) If you want to return only an exact match, you must enter `0` as the argument value. If the lookup array is sorted from smallest to largest, enter `1` (or omit the argument) to find the first position where the value is less than or equal to the lookup value. If the array is sorted from largest to smallest, enter `-1` to find the first position where the value is greater than or equal to the lookup value.

The formula shown in Figure EX 6.48 uses MATCH to find the row position in the *InventoryItems* named range for the item entered in cell B1. *Match_type* is set to *0* to ensure an exact match only.

=MATCH(*Lookup_value*, *Lookup_array*,[*Match_type*])
=MATCH(B1,ItemNames,0)

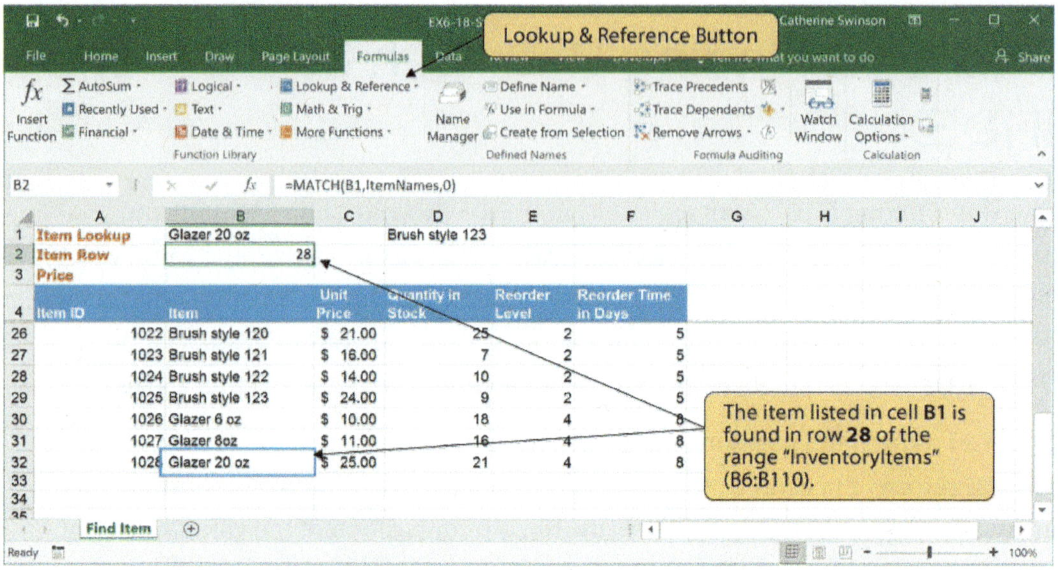

FIGURE EX 6.48

To create a formula using MATCH:

1. Select the cell where you want to enter the formula.
2. On the *Formulas* tab, in the *Function Library* group, click the **Lookup & Reference** button, and select **MATCH** to open the *Function Arguments* dialog.
3. Enter the **Lookup_value** argument. The example in Figure EX 6.48 allows the workbook user to enter an item name in cell B1. The *Lookup_value* argument then references that cell as shown in Figure EX 6.49.
4. Enter the **Lookup_array** argument. In Figure EX 6.49, this argument uses a named range that refers to a vertical range of cells.
5. If necessary, enter the **Match_type** argument box. In this example, we want to ensure an exact match, so *0* is entered as the *Match_type* argument.
6. Click **OK**.

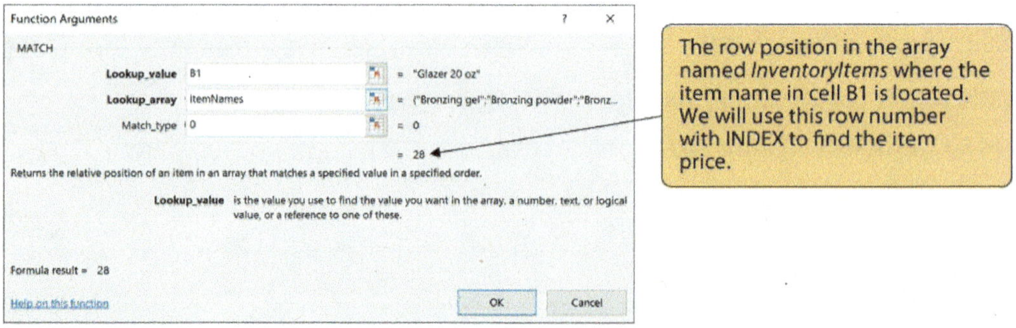

FIGURE EX 6.49

Now that you have identified the row position, you can use INDEX to find the value at the intersection of the row and column.

The INDEX function in this example has three required arguments:

Array—the range of cells containing the entire data array. If your data include a header row, do not include it in the cell range or named range used for the *Array* argument.

Row_num—the row position in the array for the value you want to look up.

Column_num—the column position in the array for the value you want to look up.

=INDEX(*Array, Row_num,Column_num*)
=INDEX(UpdatedStock,B2,3)

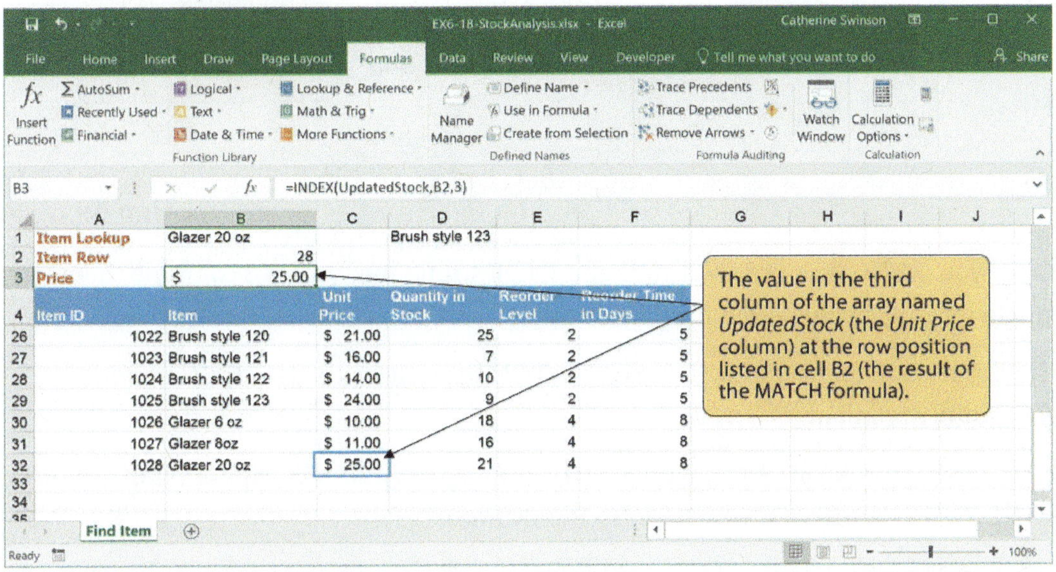

FIGURE EX 6.50

To create a formula using INDEX:

1. Select the cell where you want to enter the formula.
2. On the *Formulas* tab, in the *Function Library* group, click the **Lookup & Reference** button, and select **INDEX** to open the *Function Arguments* dialog.
3. There are two possible arguments lists for the INDEX function. Select the **array,row_num,column_num** option. Click **OK**.

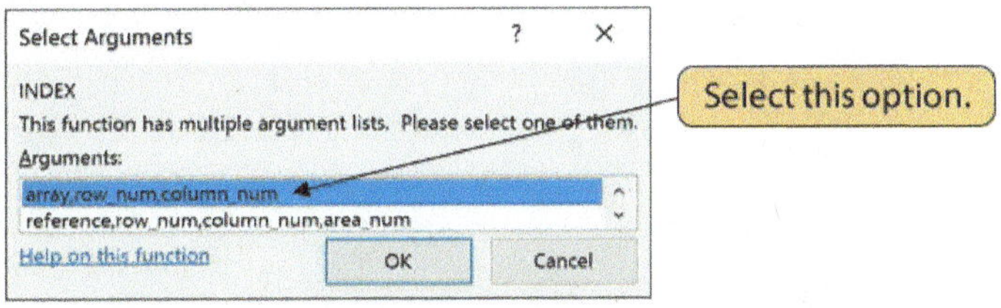

FIGURE EX 6.51

4. In the **Array** box, enter the range of cells or the name for the entire data array.

5. In the **Row_num** box, enter the reference to the cell that contains the row position you want to look up in the array. In this example, that is the cell containing the MATCH formula.
6. In the **Column_num** box, enter the number of the column that contains the data you want displayed in the formula results.
7. Click **OK**.

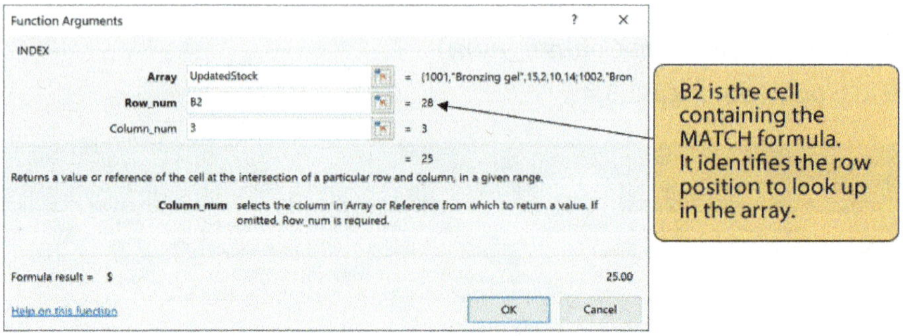

FIGURE EX 6.52

Once you understand how MATCH and INDEX function, you can combine them in a single formula using nested functions.

The formula in Figure EX 6.53 uses a MATCH formula as the INDEX function *Row_num* argument.

=INDEX(*Array*, MATCH(*Lookup_value*, *Lookup_array*, *Match_type*),*Column_num*)
=INDEX(UpdatedStock, MATCH(D1,ItemNames,0),3)

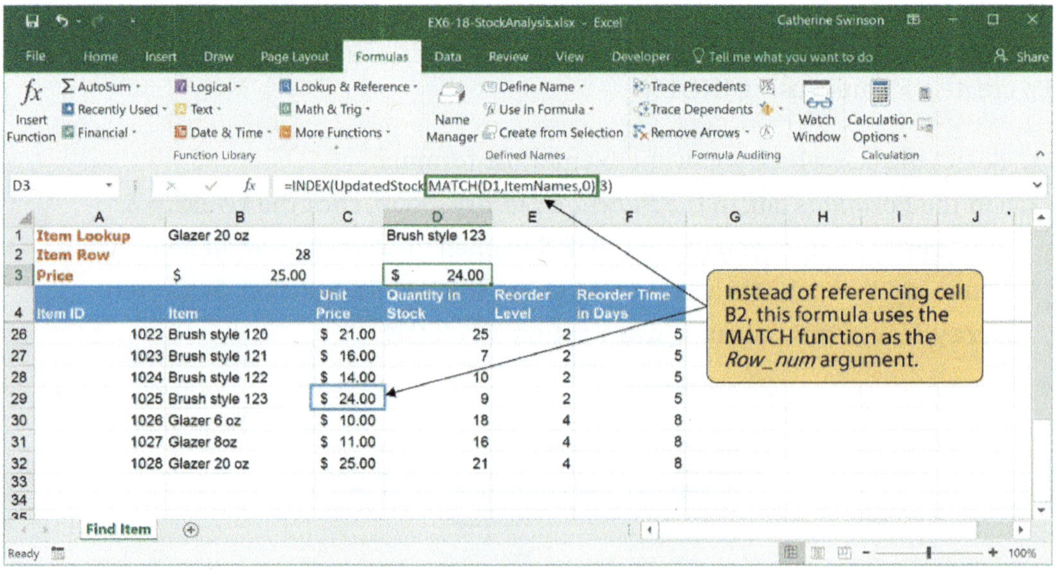

FIGURE EX 6.53

1. Begin the formula with the INDEX function.

2. Add the *Array* and *Column_num* arguments and then click in the *Row_num* argument box.
3. Expand the list of recently used functions in the *Name* box to the left of the formula bar. Select **MATCH** as shown in Figure EX 6.54.

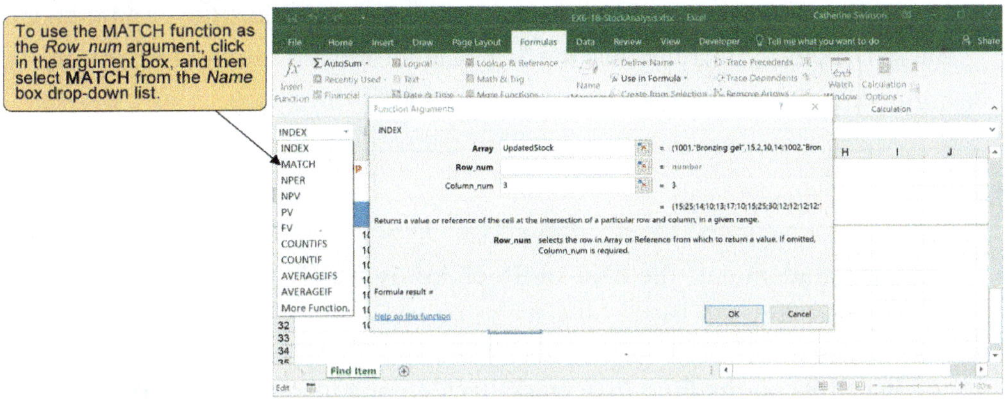

FIGURE EX 6.54

4. The *Function Arguments* dialog for MATCH opens.
5. Enter the arguments for the MATCH function.
6. Click **OK**.

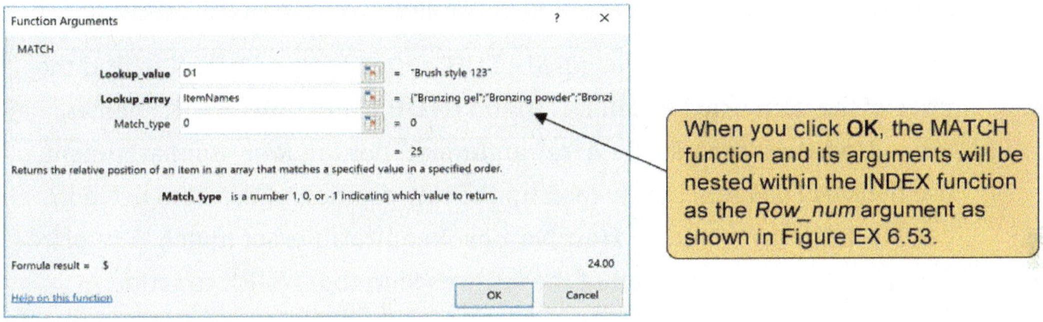

FIGURE EX 6.55

tips & tricks

If you are trying to match or look up a text string, and you're not sure of the exact text, you can use the * and ? wildcard characters. For more information about using wildcards and text strings, refer to the tell me more box in the skill Using COUNTIF and COUNTIFS.

tell me **more**

The example here uses a data array with a vertical layout—few columns and many rows. You can apply the same technique to a horizontal layout. Use MATCH to find the column position instead of the row position, and then in the INDEX formula, reference the MATCH formula in the Column_num argument instead of the Row_num argument.

let me try *Live!*

Open the student data file **EX6-18-StockAnalysis** and try this skill on your own:

1. In cell **B2** on the *Find Item* worksheet, enter a formula using **MATCH** to look up the row position of the item listed in cell **B1** in the array named **ItemNames**. Require an exact match.
2. In cell **B3**, enter a formula using **INDEX** to look up the price of the item at the row position in cell **B2**. Use the named range **UpdatedStock** as the *Array* argument. The price is found in the third column of the array.
3. In cell **D3**, enter a formula using MATCH nested within INDEX to find the price of the item listed in cell D1. In the **INDEX** function, use the named range **UpdatedStock** as the *Array* argument. For the *Row_num* argument, use the **MATCH** function to look up the row position of the item listed in cell **D1** in the array named **ItemNames**. Require an exact match. The price is found in the third column of the array used in the INDEX function.
4. If you will be moving on to the next skill in this chapter, leave the workbook open to continue working. If not, save the file as directed by your instructor and close it.

Skill 6.19 Using Database Functions

Database functions allow you to perform statistical analysis on data that meet specific criteria by building queries similar to those used when working with a database. You could perform the same analysis by first filtering the data to meet the criteria, and then using the regular statistical functions, but using the database versions of the functions is more efficient.

Excel includes database versions of many statistical functions you are already familiar with. They have the same names, with a *D* added to indicate *database*: DSUM, DAVERAGE, DMIN, DMAX, DCOUNT, DCOUNTA, and a few more. All the database functions require the same arguments:

Database—the data arranged in rows and columns with column labels.

Field—the column to use in the calculation. The column can be identified by the column number in the database array or by the column label enclosed in quotation marks.

Criteria—the cell range defining the conditions the data must meet in order to be included in the calculation. The criteria range must have at least two rows. The first row includes labels that match the column labels in the database range. You need to include only the columns for which you will enter criteria. The second row is where you enter the criteria. Criteria can be numeric values, expressions, or text.

The formula in Figure EX 6.56 uses the DSUM function to calculate the total quantity in stock for items with a price greater than 15 in the cell range named *Inventory1*. (The *Inventory1* range includes the column labels in row 8.) The *Criteria* argument includes the entire criteria range A4:F5. It would also work with a smaller cell range C4:C5 since that is the only column with criteria entered.

=DSUM(*Database*,*Field*,*Criteria*)
=DSUM(Inventory1,"Qty in Stock",A4:F5)

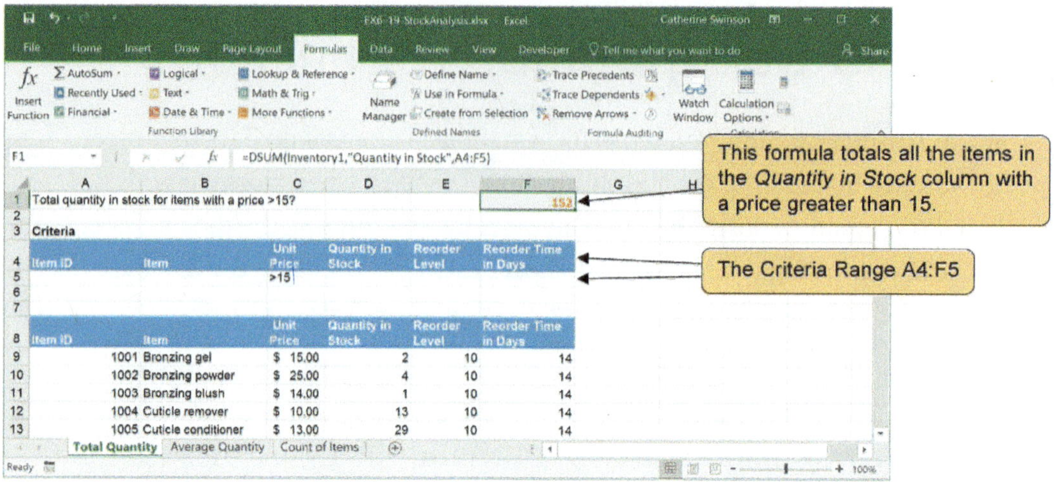

FIGURE EX 6.56

The formula in Figure EX 6.57 uses the DAVERAGE function to calculate the average quantity in stock for items with a price less than 20 and a reorder time greater than 10 in the cell range named *Inventory2*. (The *Inventory2* range include the column labels in row 8.) The *Criteria* argument includes the entire criteria range A4:F5. It would also work with a smaller cell range C4:E5 since columns C and E are the only columns with criteria entered.

=DAVERAGE(*Database,Field,Criteria*)
=DAVERAGE(Inventory2,"Qty in Stock",A4:F5)

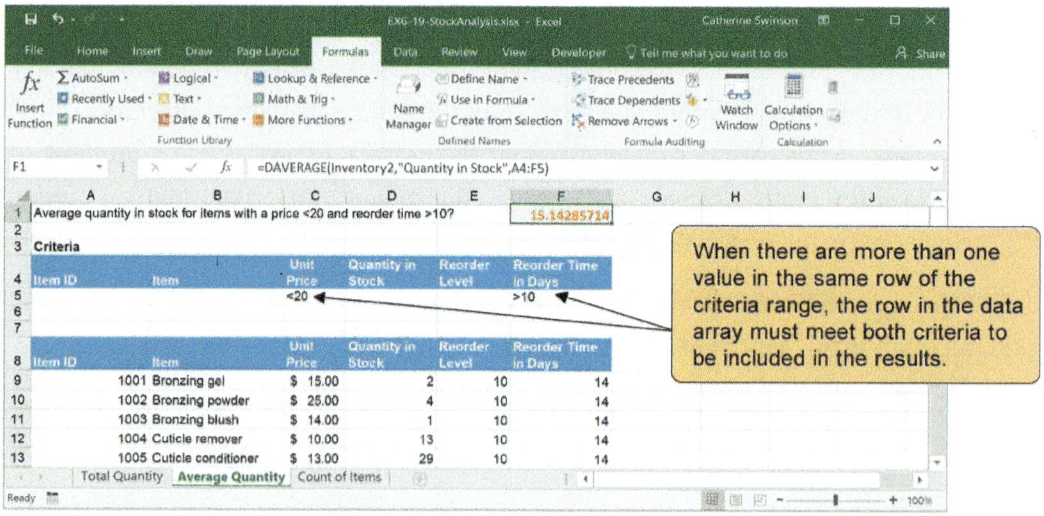

FIGURE EX 6.57

To create a formula using one of the database functions:

1. First, set up the criteria range. If you place the criteria range above the database range, include a blank row between the two ranges.
2. Enter the criteria in the blank row below the appropriate column heading.

3. After setting up the criteria range, select the cell where you want to enter the formula. On the *Formulas* tab, in the *Function Library* group, click the **Insert Function** button to open the *Insert Function* dialog. (Database functions are not accessible from any of the Ribbon buttons.)
4. If necessary, expand the **Or select a category** list and select **Database**.

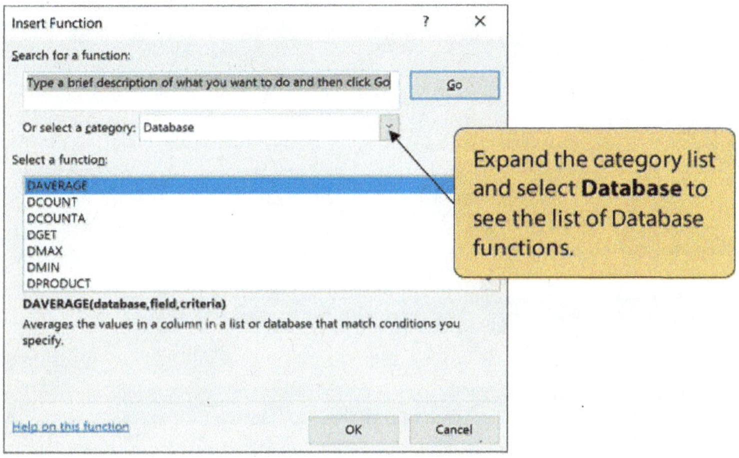

FIGURE EX 6.58

5. Select the function you want, and then click **OK** to open the *Function Arguments* dialog.
6. In the **Database** box, enter the range of cells or the name for the data array. Include the heading row.
7. In the **Field** box, enter the column number or the column label of the column containing the data to use in the calculation.
8. In the **Criteria** box, enter the range of cells or the name for the criteria range.
9. Click **OK**.

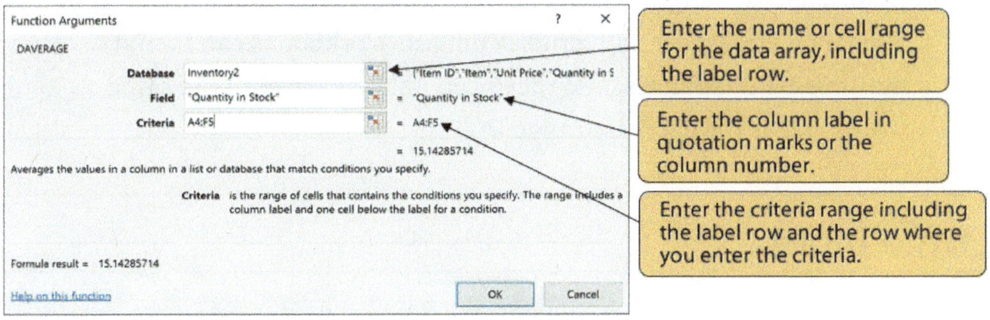

FIGURE EX 6.59

You can include multiple criteria in the criteria range. If you are familiar with creating a query in Access, this process is similar to entering multiple criteria for a query. To include only data that meet all the criteria, enter multiple criteria on the same row. To include data that meet any one of multiple criteria, add more rows to the criteria range, and enter each condition in a separate row.

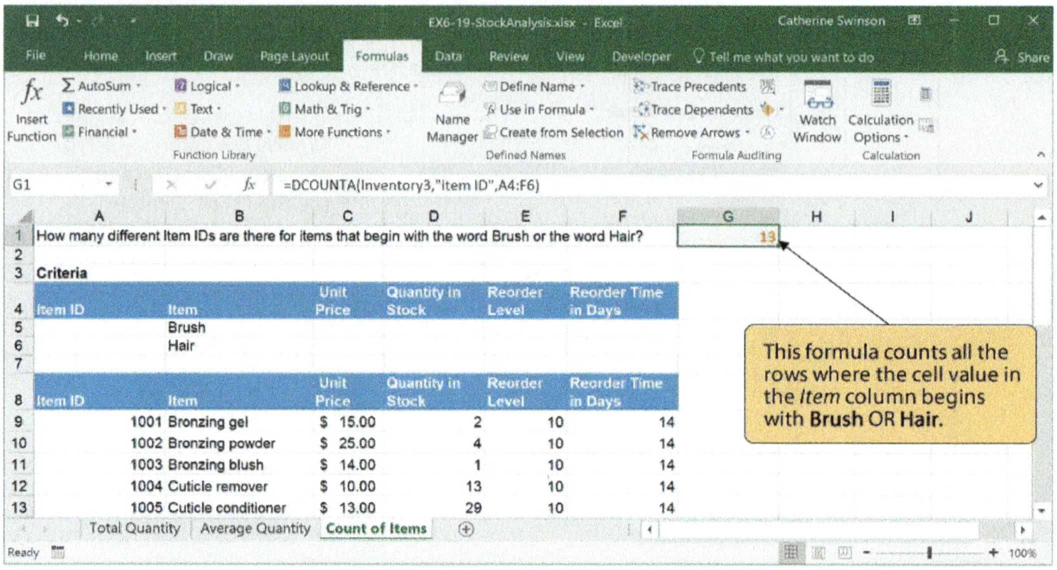

FIGURE EX 6.60

tips & tricks

- When using Lookup & Reference functions like VLOOKUP, MATCH, and INDEX, the data array should not include the label row. However, Database functions expect the array to be organized like a database, so the array must include the label row.
- If the database range includes a large amount of data, consider setting up a separate worksheet with criteria ranges. Workbooks can include multiple criteria ranges, and they need not be located in the same worksheet as the database range.

tell me more

Text criteria need not be enclosed in quotation marks unless you are including wildcard characters. Text criteria that include wildcard characters must begin with ="= followed by the text criteria and ending with a closing quotation mark " (for example, type ="=*gel" to include any text values ending with the letters gel).

let me try *Live!*

If you do not have the data file from the previous skill open, open the student data file **EX6-19-StockAnalysis** and try this skill on your own:

1. On the *Total Quantity* worksheet, use **DSUM** to calculate the total of values in the **Quantity in Stock** column for items with a **price greater than 15** in the data array named **Inventory1**. Use the criteria range in cells **A4:F5**. Enter the appropriate criteria in the criteria range and then enter the formula in cell **F1**.
2. In the *Average Quantity* worksheet, use **DAVERAGE** to calculate the average of the values in the **Quantity in Stock** column for items with a **price less than 20** and a **recorder time greater than 10** in the data array named **Inventory2**. Use the criteria range in cells **A4:F5**. Enter the appropriate criteria in the criteria range and then enter the formula in cell **F1**.
3. In the *Count of Items* worksheet, use **DCOUNTA** to count the cells in the **Item ID** column in the data array named **Inventory3** where the **Item** value **begins with Brush** or **Hair**. Use the criteria range in cells **A4:F6**. Enter the appropriate criteria in the criteria range and then enter the formula in cell **G1**.
4. If you will be moving on to the next skill in this chapter, leave the workbook open to continue working. If not, save the file as directed by your instructor and close it.

Skill 6.20 Managing Errors with the IFERROR Function

Most of Excel's functions return an error when a value cannot be found or when the formula cannot be calculated. Rather than displaying an error message to users, it may be more useful to display a text message or a specific value that you define. The **IFERROR** function performs this task.

The VLOOKUP formula in Figure EX6-61 cannot find a match for the lookup value in cell B1, and so it displays the error #N/A. (If you need a refresher on the VLOOKUP function, refer to the skill *Finding Data Using the VLOOKUP Function.*)

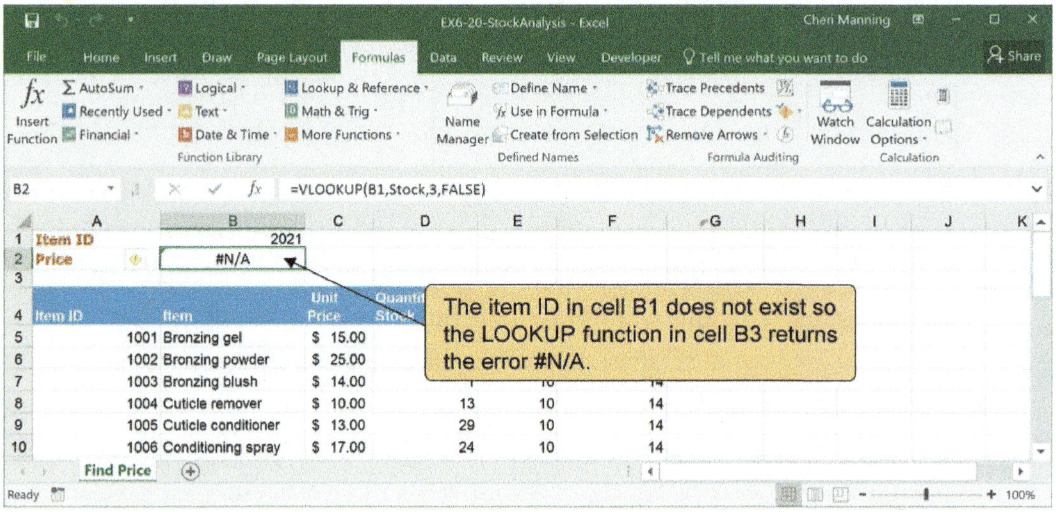

FIGURE EX 6.61

By adding the IFERROR function around the existing VLOOKUP function, we can make the error message more user-friendly, as shown in Figure EX6-62. The IFERROR function takes two arguments.

Value—the formula to calculate.

Value_if_error—the value, text string, or formula to use if the formula in the *Value* argument results in an error. If you use a text string, enclose it in quotation marks.

=IFERROR(*Value*,*Value_if_error*)
=IFERROR(VLOOKUP(B1,Stock,3,FALSE),"item not found")

Notice that IFERROR is used in a nested formula. The first argument contains the formula you want to calculate. The second argument is the text string, value, or formula to display if there is an error.

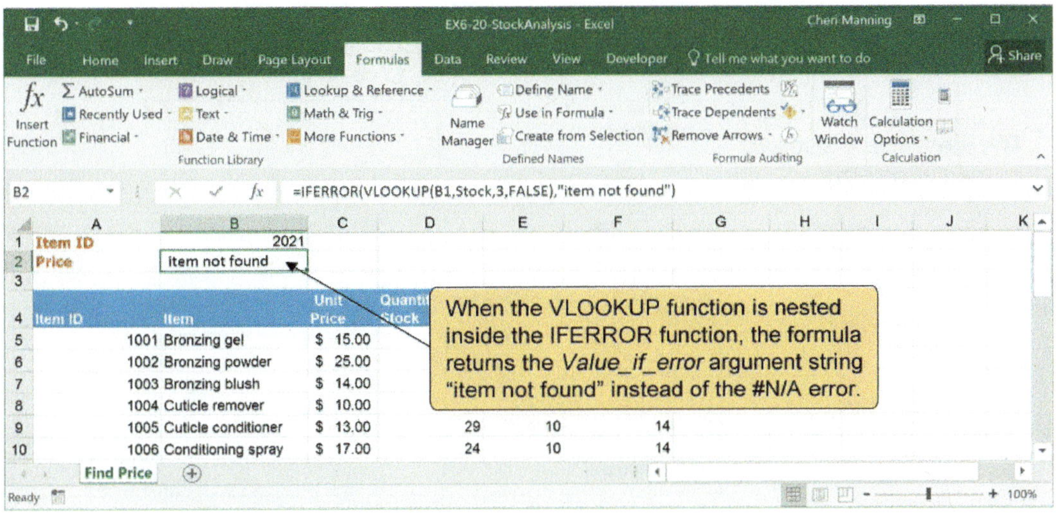

FIGURE EX 6.62

Often, you will think to add IFERROR only after you notice that the initial formula results in errors. In these cases, it is easier to edit the formula directly in the formula bar or the cell, adding IFERROR and the *Value_if_error* argument without going through the *Function Arguments* dialog.

1. Click in the formula bar or double-click the cell to enter Edit mode.
2. Move the cursor to the beginning of the formula after the = and type: `IFERROR(`
3. The existing formula is the *Value* argument. Move the cursor to the end of the formula, type a comma, and then type the text string, value, or formula to use as the *Value_if_error* argument. If the*Value_if_error* argument is a text string, remember to enclose it in quotation marks.
4. Type the closing parenthesis `)` and press **Enter**.

To use the *Function Arguments* dialog to create a formula using IFERROR:

1. On the *Formulas* tab, in the *Function Library* group, click the **Logical** button, and select **IFERROR**.
2. In the **Value** argument box, enter the formula you want to calculate.
3. In the **Value_if_error** argument box, enter the text string, value, or formula the IFERROR formula should use if Excel is unable to compute a value for the formula in the *Value* argument.
4. Click **OK**.

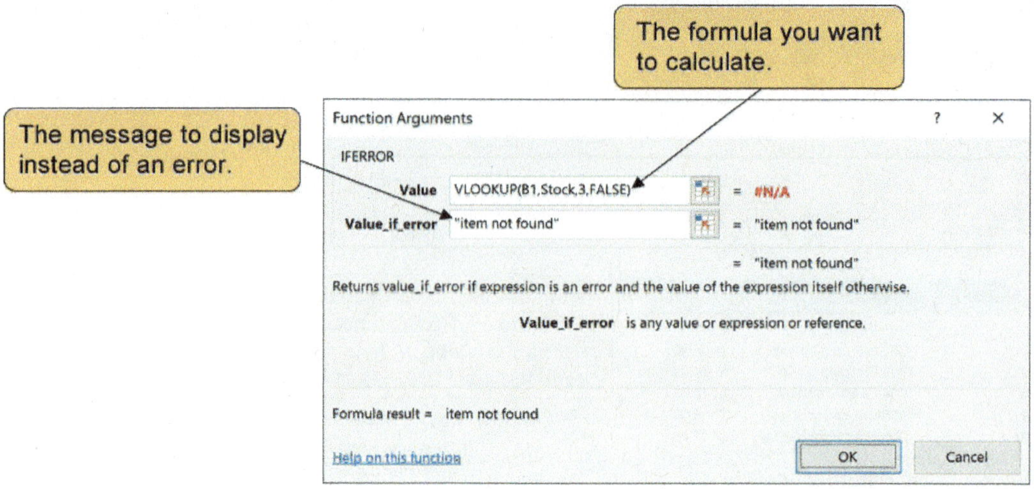

FIGURE EX 6.63

tips & tricks

IFERROR is compatible only with Excel 2010 and later.

tell me more

The *Value_if_error* argument may contain an alternative formula rather than a specific value or cell reference. You can also nest multiple IFERROR functions within each other.

let me try *Live!*

If you do not have the data file from the previous skill open, open the student data file
EX6-20-StockAnalysis and try this skill on your own:

1. On the *Find Price* worksheet, modify the VLOOKUP formula in cell **B2** using IFERROR so if the VLOOKUP formula results in an error, the message **item not found** will display instead of the #N/A error.
2. If you will be moving on to the next skill in this chapter, leave the workbook open to continue working. If not, save the file as directed by your instructor and close it.

Skill 6.21 Analyzing Complex Formulas Using Evaluate Formula

When working with a workbook that contains complex formulas, it can be very helpful to evaluate the formulas step by step before attempting to make any changes. The *Evaluate Formula* feature allows you to view and analyze the current value of each part of a formula.

To use the Evaluate Formula feature:

1. To evaluate a specific formula, click the cell that contains the formula you want to review.
2. On the *Formulas* tab, in the *Formula Auditing* group, click the **Evaluate Formula** button to open the *Evaluate Formula* dialog for the selected cell. In the *Evaluate Formula* dialog, the current cell is identified at the left side of the dialog under *Reference* and the formula is listed in the *Evaluation* box. In the *Evaluation* box, the first element to evaluate is underlined. This may be a cell reference, a named range, or a nested function.

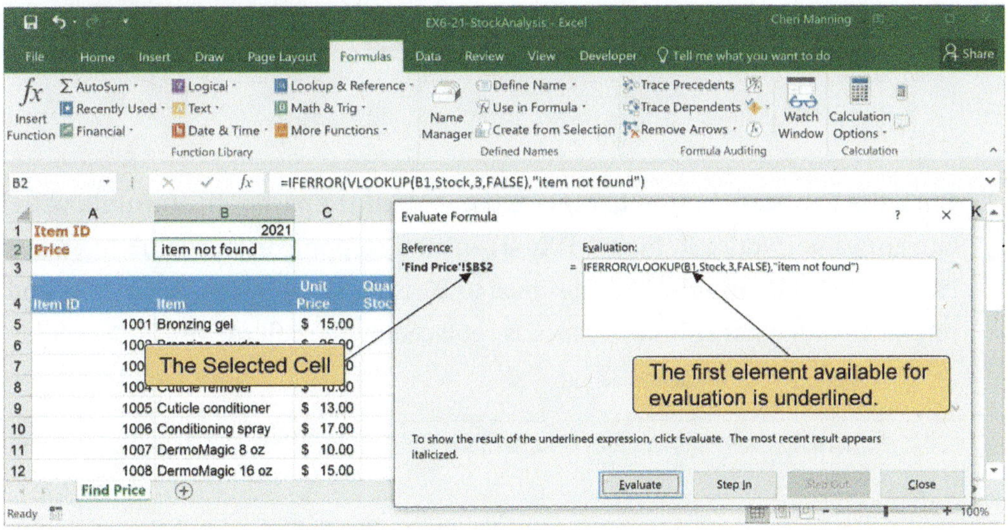

FIGURE EX 6.64

3. If the underlined part of the formula references a cell, named range, or another formula, click the **Step In** button to review the details.

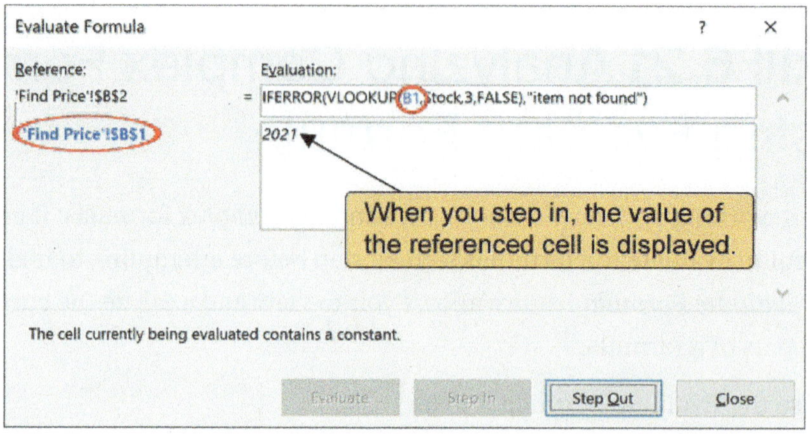

FIGURE EX 6.65

4. Click the **Step Out** button to return to the original formula. Notice that when you click **Step Out**, Evaluate Formula moves on to the next part of the formula for which you can click **Evaluate** or **Step In**

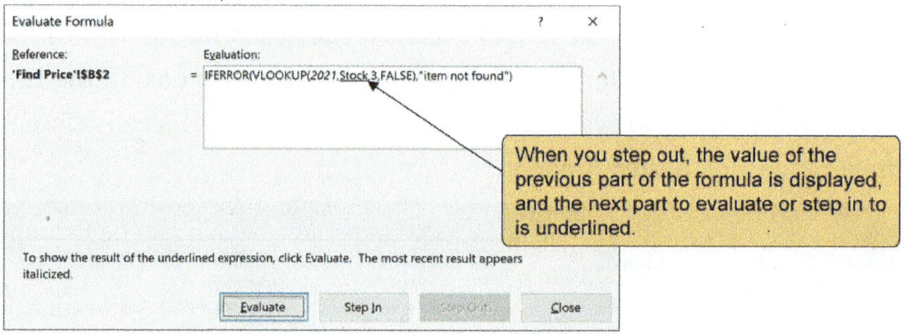

FIGURE EX 6.66

5. Click the **Evaluate** button to replace the underlined part of the formula with its current value. Notice in Figure EX6-21-4, after stepping in or evaluating the first two parts of the formula, the reference to B1 is replaced by the value 2021 and the reference to the named range *Stock* is replaced by the cell range.

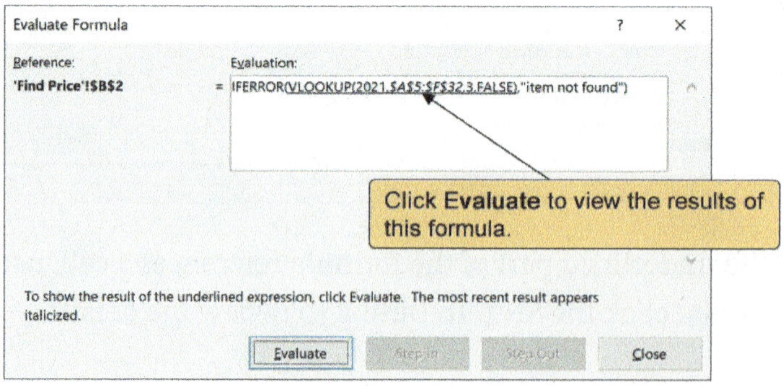

FIGURE EX 6.67

- If you reach a part of the formula that Excel cannot compute, the *Evaluation* box will display an error message instead of a value.

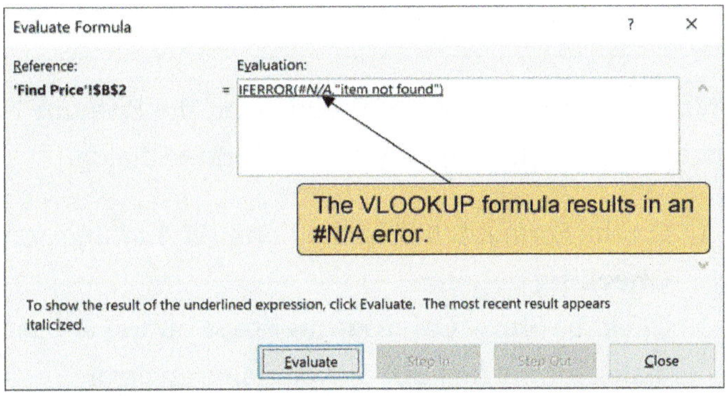

FIGURE EX 6.68

- Once you click the **Evaluate** button, you cannot go back to review the previous part of the formula. If you find that you wanted to "step in" instead of evaluating that part of the formula, you'll need to click the **Close** button and reopen the *Evaluate Formula* dialog to start over.

6. Continue clicking **Step Out** and **Evaluate** until you have examined all parts of the formula, at which point you can click the **Start Over** button to begin the evaluation process from the beginning.

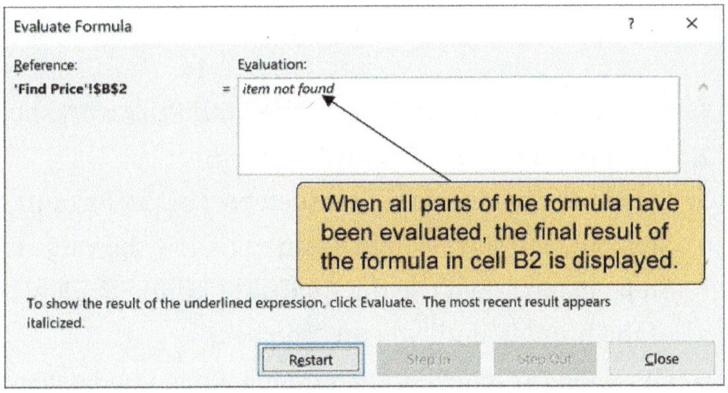

FIGURE EX 6.69

7. Click the **Close** button to dismiss the *Evaluate Formula* dialog.

tips & tricks

In complex formulas, you may need to click **Step In** multiple times to identify all the precedents. The previous formula is still shown in the dialog to help you follow the trail that leads back to the formula in the cell you originally selected.

tell me **more**

When the worksheet contains an error, the *Evaluate Formula* dialog can be launched directly from the *Error Checking* dialog.

1. On the *Formulas* tab, in the *Formula Auditing* group, click the **Error Checking** button.
2. Click the **Show Calculation Steps** button to open the *Evaluate Formula* dialog for the first cell that contains an error.
3. When you are finished evaluating the formula, click the **Close** button in the *Evaluate Formula* dialog to return to the *Error Checking* dialog.
4. Click the **Resume** button to continue checking the worksheet for errors.

let me try *Live!*

If you do not have the data file from the previous skill open, open the student data file
EX6-21-StockAnalysis and try this skill on your own:

1. If necessary, select cell **B2** on the *Find Price* worksheet.
2. Open the **Evaluate Formula** dialog.
3. Step in to review first underlined part of the formula.
4. Step out, and then step in again to review the value of the named range.
5. Step out, and then use the **Evaluate** button to view the results for each part of the formula until you are finished.
6. Close the *Evaluate Formula* dialog when you have evaluated all parts of the formula.
7. Save the file as directed by your instructor and close it.

key terms

- Rounding
- ROUND
- ROUNDUP
- ROUNDDOWN
- Nested formula
- Nested function
- Product
- SUMPRODUCT
- SUMIF
- SUMIFS
- AVERAGEIF
- AVERAGEIFS
- COUNTIF
- COUNTIFS
- Median
- MEDIAN
- Standard deviation
- Population
- STDEV.S
- STDEV.P
- mean absolute deviation (MAD)
- absolute value of a number
- mode
- MODE.SNGL
- MODE.MULT
- Array
- Ranking
- RANK.EQ
- RANK.AVG
- AND
- OR
- NOT
- IFS
- Future value
- FV
- Present Value

- **PV**
- **Time Value of Money (TVM)**
- **NPV**
- **Discount rate**
- **NPER**
- **Depreciation**
- **Depreciation schedule**
- **Book value**
- **Straight-line depreciation**
- **SLN**
- **Accelerated Depreciation**
- **Sum-of-the-years' digits (SOYD) depreciation**
- **SYD**
- **Declining balance depreciation**
- **DB**
- **Double-declining balance depreciation**
- **DDB**
- **MATCH**
- **INDEX**
- **Database functions**
- **IFERROR**

concept review

1. Identify the result of this formula: =ROUND(4.9446021,2).
   a. 4
   b. 4.93
   c. 4.94
   d. 4.95
2. Identify the *criteria_range1* argument in this formula: =SUMIFS(JuneOrdered,JuneItems,B1,JunePOs,B2)
   a. JuneOrdered
   b. JuneItems
   c. B1
   d. B2
3. To find the middle value in a list of values, use the ________________ function.
   a. AVERAGE
   b. MEDIAN
   c. MODE
   d. DAVERAGE
4. Which function would you use to measure how far values in a data set are spread out from the average based on a sample of the entire population?
   a. STDEV
   b. STDEV.S
   c. STDEV.P
   d. MEDIAN
5. To create an array formula, press ________________ after entering the formula in the formula bar.
   a. Ctrl + Shift
   b. Shift + Alt
   c. Ctrl + Shift + Enter
   d. Ctrl + Alt + Del
6. Identify the correct formula to calculate how much money you will have in an investment account where $1200 is invested every month for five years at 3.5% annual interest.
   a. =PV(3.5%/12,60,-100)
   b. =FV(3.5%/12,60,-100)
   c. =FV(3.5%,5,-100)
   d. =FV(3.5%/12,5,-100)

7. To calculate the present value of a future investment with variable inflows and outflows of capital, use the ________________ function.
   a. PV
   b. FV
   c. NPV
   d. NPER
8. Identify the *Salvage* argument in this function: =SLN(B1,B2,B3)
   a. B1
   b. B2
   c. B3
   d. It's a trick question; the SLN function does not have a Salvage argument.
9. When naming a range of cells to be used as the Array argument with the INDEX function, should you include the label row?
   a. yes
   b. no
10. The IFERROR function displays TRUE if the formula results in an error and FALSE if it does not.
   a. true
   b. false

projects

Data files for projects can be found by logging into your SIMnet account and going to the *Library* section.

skill review 6.1

In this project, you will finalize a gradebook by entering formulas to compute final grades and class statistics. You will also create a worksheet to look up specific assignment grades for one student at a time and answer specific questions about overall class performance.

Skills needed to complete this project:

- Using COUNTIF and COUNTIFS (Skill 6.5)
- Rounding with Functions (Skill 6.1)
- Using the IFS Function (Skill 6.12)
- Analyzing Complex Formulas Using Evaluate Formula (Skill 6.21)
- Finding the Middle Value with MEDIAN (Skill 6.6)
- Calculating the Standard Deviation (Skill 6.7)
- Finding the Most Common Value(s) with MODE.SNGL and MODE.MULT (Skill 6.9)
- Managing Errors with the IFERROR Function (Skill 6.20)
- Finding Data with MATCH and INDEX (Skill 6.18)
- Using Database Functions (Skill 6.19)

1. Open the start file **EX2016-SkillReview-6-1** and resave the file as: `[your initials]EX-SkillReview-6-1`
2. If the workbook opens in Protected View, click the **Enable Editing** button in the Message Bar at the top of the workbook so you can modify the workbook.
3. Use COUNTIF to compute the number of absences for each student using the criteria *Absent*.
   a. In cell **L2**, enter the following formula: `=COUNTIF(B2:K2,"Absent")`
   b. Use the fill handle to fill the same formula from **L3:L8**.
4. Compute the raw average for each student. Omit absences from the average calculation.
   a. In cell **N2**, enter the following formula: `=SUM(B2:K2)/(10-L2)`
   b. Use the fill handle to fill this formula from **N3:N8**.
5. Compute the rounded average for each student, rounding the value in the *Raw Average* column to zero decimal place.
   a. In cell **O2**, enter the following formula: `=ROUND(N2,0)`
   b. Use the fill handle to fill this formula from **O3:O8**.
6. Use a nested IF statement to determine the final grade for each student.
   a. In cell **P2**, enter the following formula:`=IF(O2>93,"A",IF(O2>85,"B",IF(O2>74,"C",IF(O2>69,"D","F"))))`

   b. Fill this formula from **P3:P8.**
7. Use the *Evaluate Formula* feature to review the results of the nested formulas.
   a. Select cell **P2.**
   b. On the *Formulas* tab, in the *Formula Auditing* group, click the **Evaluate Formula** button.
   c. Click the **Step In** button twice to view the formula in cell **N2.**
   d. Click the **Evaluate** button until you see the final value *93.9*. Observe the values in the *Evaluation* box each time you click the *Evaluate* button.
   e. Click the **Step Out** button, and then click the **Evaluate** button to view the value for cell **O2.**
   f. Click the **Step Out** button again. Observe the formula updated with the value for cell **O2** resulting in the comparison *94>89*.
   g. Click the **Evaluate** button to view the result of TRUE. When the IFS function encounters a *TRUE* result, it returns the next argument—in this case, *A*.
   h. Click the **Close** button to close the *Evaluate Formula* dialog.
   i. Repeat the same process for cells **N3:N8,** using the **Step In**, **Evaluate**, and **Step Out** buttons as necessary until you have a clear understanding of how the IFS function arrived at the grade result for each student.
8. Determine the middle score (the median) for each assignment.
   a. In cell **B10**, enter the following formula: `=MEDIAN(B2:B8)`
   b. Use the fill handle to fill the cells **C10:K10** with the formula.
9. Determine the average for each assignment.
   a. In cell **B11**, enter the following formula: `=AVERAGE(B2:B8)`
   b. Use the fill handle to fill the cells **C11:K11.**
10. Determine the standard deviation for each assignment.
   a. In cell **B12**, enter the following formula: `=STDEV.P(B2:B8)`
   b. Use the fill handle to fill the cells **C12:K12.**
11. Determine the two most common scores for each assignment (the modes). Remember that the MODE.MULT function is an array function. You will select multiple cells before entering the formula, and then press Ctrl+Shift+Enter to complete it.
   a. Select cells **B13:B14.**
   b. In the formula bar, type the formula =MODE.MULT(B2:B8) and then press Ctrl+Shift+Enter.
   c. Use the fill handle to fill the cells **C13:K14.**
12. Determine the median and average scores, standard deviation, and the mode for both the *Raw Average* and *Rounded Average* columns.
   a. In cell **N10**, enter the formula to find the middle score: `=MEDIAN(N2:N8)`
   b. In cell **N11**, enter the formula to compute the average score: `=AVERAGE(N2:N8)`
   c. In cell **N12**, enter the formula to compute the standard deviation: `=STDEV.P(N2:N8)`
   d. In cell **N13**, enter the formula to compute a single mode value as follows: `=MODE.SNGL(N2:N8)`

13. Use the IFERROR function to display the message "no mode" instead of an error if no mode value is found.
    a. If necessary, select cell **N13** again.
    b. In the formula bar, edit the MODE.SNGL formula, placing the IFERROR function and the *Value_if_error* argument as follows: `=IFERROR(MODE.SNGL(N2:N8),"no mode")`
14. Copy cells **N10:N13** to cells **O10:O13**.
15. Switch to the **student lookup** worksheet.
16. Enter a nested formula in cell B3 using MATCH and INDEX to find the specific assignment grade for the student listed in cell B1 and the assignment week listed in cell B2. Notice the student name in cell B1 uses a wildcard.
    a. Click cell **B3**.
    b. On the *Formulas* tab, in the *Function Library* group, click the **Lookup & Reference** button and select **INDEX**.
    c. Click **OK** in the *Select Arguments* dialog to select the first set of arguments.
    d. Type the name `WeeklyGrades` in the *Array* argument box. This named range has already been defined in the workbook for you. It references B2:K8 in the *gradebook* worksheet.
    e. Click in the **Column_num** argument box. You want to enter the *Column_num* argument before the *Row_num* argument because you are going to use a nested function for the *Row_num*.
    f. Enter `B2` as the *Column_num* argument. The value in cell B2 corresponds to the column position for that week's assignment in the *WeeklyGrades* named range.
    g. Now click in the **Row_num** argument box where you are going to enter a MATCH function.
    h. Click the arrow in the *Name* box to the left of the formula bar. If **MATCH** is listed, select it.
        i. If not, click **More Functions...** at the bottom of the list to open the *Insert Function* dialog.
        ii. If necessary, expand the **Or select a category** list and select **Lookup & Reference**.
        iii. Click **MATCH**, and then click **OK**.
    i. Enter the arguments in the MATCH *Function Arguments* dialog:
        i. Enter **B1** as the *Lookup_value* argument.
        ii. Use the named range **Students** as the *Lookup_array* argument. This named range has already been defined for you. It references A2:A8 in the *gradebook* worksheet.
        iii. Enter `0` as the *Match_type* argument. You want to ensure an exact match.
        iv. Click **OK**.
    j. The final formula in cell B3 should look like this and should result in a value of 89: `=INDEX(WeeklyGrades,MATCH(B1,Students,0),B2)`
17. Use database functions to answer the questions posed on the *semester analysis* worksheet. Begin by setting up the empty criteria ranges for each of the questions. We'll use the same criteria range for both questions.

a. Go to the **gradebook** worksheet.
b. Copy cells **L1:P1**. These are the column labels for the criteria ranges.
c. Go to the **semester analysis** worksheet.
d. Paste the copied cells to **D1:H1** and **D4:H4**. Notice the empty column (*E*) that was part of the *gradebook* worksheet structure and must be included in the criteria ranges. You may hide the column if you want.
e. Now enter the criteria for the first question "How many students had a final rounded average of >79%?" Type `>79%` in cell **G2** below the *Rounded Average* column label.
f. Click cell **B1**.
g. On the *Formulas* tab, in the *Function Library* group, click the **Insert Function** button. Expand the **Or select a category** list and select **Database**. Click **DCOUNT** and click **OK**.
h. In the *Function Arguments* dialog, enter `gradebook` as the *Database* argument. This named range has already been defined in the workbook for you. It references B2:K8 in the *gradebook* worksheet.
i. Enter `Rounded Average` as the *Field* argument. When you use the *Function Arguments* dialog, Excel will enclose the column label in quotation marks for you.
j. Enter `D1:H2` as the *Criteria* argument. Using the larger criteria range now will make it easier if you want to change the question and the criteria in the future.
k. Click **OK**. The final formula should look like this:
`=DCOUNT(gradebook,"Rounded Average",D1:H2)`
l. Click cell **B4** and repeat steps g–k to create a formula using **DAVERAGE** to calculate the average number of missed assignments for students who received a **C** grade. Use **gradebook** as the *Database* argument; use the column label "number of assignments missed" as the *Field* argument; and use **D4:H5** as the *Criteria* argument. Remember to enter the criteria `C` in cell **H5**. The final formula should look like this:
`=DAVERAGE(gradebook,"number of assignments missed",D4:H5)`

18. Save and close the workbook.

projects

Data files for projects can be found by logging into your SIMnet account and going to the *Library* section.

skill review 6.2

In this project, you will create a worksheet to analyze inventory and financial data for a sporting goods store.

Skills needed to complete this project:

- Calculating Totals with SUMPRODUCT (Skill 6.2)
- Finding the Middle Value with MEDIAN (Skill 6.6)
- Finding the Most Common Value(s) with MODE.SNGL and MODE.MULT (Skill 6.9)
- Using SUMIF and SUMIFS (Skill 6.3)
- Using AVERAGEIF and AVERAGEIFS (Skill 6.4)
- Using COUNTIF and COUNTIFS (Skill 6.5)
- Using Database Functions (Skill 6.19)
- Finding Data with MATCH and INDEX (Skill 6.18)
- Managing Errors with the IFERROR Function (Skill 6.20)
- Analyzing Complex Formulas Using Evaluate Formula (Skill 6.21)
- Calculating Future Value with the FV Function (Skill 6.13)
- Calculating the Number of Payments with NPER (Skill 6.16)
- Rounding with Functions (Skill 6.1)
- Using NPV to Calculate Present Value When Payments Are Variable (Skill 6.15)
- Creating a Depreciation Schedule (Skill 6.17)

1. Open the start file **EX2016-SkillReview-6-2** and resave the file as:
   `[your initials]EX-SkillReview-6-2`
2. If the workbook opens in Protected View, click the **Enable Editing** button in the Message Bar at the top of the workbook so you can modify the workbook.
3. Start with the *Analysis* worksheet. Use the SUMPRODUCT function to calculate the total value of the inventory. Use the values in the *Selling Price* column and the corresponding values in the *Stock* column as the *Array* arguments.
   a. Click cell **B2**.
   b. Type: `=SUMPRODUCT(`
   c. Click the **Inventory** sheet tab, and then click and drag to select cells **G4:G26**.
   d. Type `,` and then click and drag to select cells **H4:H26**.
   e. Type `)` and press Enter.
   f. The formula should look like this:
   `=SUMPRODUCT(Inventory!G3:G25,Inventory!H3:H25)`

4. Enter a formula to calculate the average selling price.
   a. Click cell **D2**.
   b. Type: `=AVERAGE(`
   c. Click the **Inventory** sheet tab, and then click and drag to select cells **G4:G26**.
   d. Press Enter. The formula should look like this:
      `=AVERAGE(Inventory!G3:G25)`
5. Enter a formula to find the middle selling price.
   a. Click cell **E2**.
   b. Type: `=MEDIAN(`
   c. Click the **Inventory** sheet tab, and then click and drag to select cells **G4:G26**.
   d. Press Enter. The formula should look like this:
      `=MEDIAN(Inventory!G3:G25)`
6. Enter a formula to find the most common selling price.
   a. Click cell **F2**.
   b. Type: `=MODE.SNGL(`
   c. Click the **Inventory** sheet tab, and then click and drag to select cells **G4:G26**.
   d. Press Enter. The formula should look like this:
      `=MODE.SNGL(Inventory!G3:G25)`
7. What if there are multiple selling prices that are the most common? Enter an array
   formula in cells G2:G5 to find up to four most common selling prices.
   a. Select cells **G2:G5**.
   b. Type: `=MODE.MULT(`
   c. Click the **Inventory** sheet tab, and then click and drag to select cells **G4:G26**.
   d. Press Ctrl + Shift + Enter. The formula should look like this:
      `{=MODE.MULT(Inventory!G3:G25)}`
8. Use the SUMIFS function to calculate the total number of blue shoes in inventory. Use the values in the *Cost* column as the *Sum_range* argument. Use the values in the *Item Description* column as the *Criteria_range1* argument and use the criteria **shoes* to find all items that end in the word *shoes*. Use the values in the *Color* column as the *Criteria_range2* argument and use the criteria *blue*.
   a. Click cell **B3**.
   b. On the *Formulas* tab, in the *Function Library* group, click the **Math & Trig** button and select **SUMIFS**.
   c. In the *Function Arguments* dialog, verify that the cursor is in the *Sum_range* argument box. Click the **Inventory** sheet tab, and click and drag to select cells **H3:H25**.
   d. In the *Function Arguments* dialog, press Tab to move to the *Criteria_range1* argument box.
   e. Click the **Inventory** sheet tab, and click and drag to select cells **A3:A25**.

f. In the *Function Arguments* dialog, press Tab to move to the *Criteria1* argument box.
g. Type `"*shoes"` to find any text string that ends with the word *shoes*.
h. Press Tab. Verify that the cursor is in the *Criteria_range2* argument box.
i. Click the **Inventory** sheet tab, and click and drag to select cells **C3:C25**.
j. In the *Function Arguments* dialog, press Tab to move to the *Criteria2* argument box.
k. Type: `"blue"`
l. Click **OK**.
m. The formula should look like this:
`=SUMIFS(Inventory!H3:H25,Inventory!A3:A25,"*shoes",Inventory!C3:C25,"blue")`

9. Use the AVERAGEIFS function to find the average selling price of blue shoes in inventory. Use the values in the *Selling Price* column as the *Average_range* argument. Use the values in the *Item Description* column as the *Criteria_range1* argument and use the criteria **shoes* to find all items that end in the word *shoes*. Use the values in the *Color* column as the *Criteria_range2* argument and use the criteria *blue*.
a. Click cell **B4**.
b. On the *Formulas* tab, in the *Function Library* group, click the **More Functions** button, point to **Statistical**, and select **AVERAGEIFS**.
c. In the *Function Arguments* dialog, verify that the cursor is in the *Average_range* argument box. Click the **Inventory** sheet tab, and click and drag to select cells **G3:G25**.
d. In the *Function Arguments* dialog, press Tab to move to the *Criteria_range1* argument box.
e. Click the **Inventory** sheet tab, and click and drag to select cells **A3:A25**.
f. In the *Function Arguments* dialog, press Tab to move to the *Criteria1* argument box.
g. Type `"*shoes"` to find any text string that ends with the word *shoes*.
h. Press Tab. Verify that the cursor is in the *Criteria_range2* argument box.
i. Click the **Inventory** sheet tab, and click and drag to select cells **C3:C25**.
j. In the *Function Arguments* dialog, press Tab to move to the *Criteria2* argument box.
k. Type: `"blue"`
l. Click **OK**.
m. The formula should look like this:
`=AVERAGEIFS(Inventory!G3:G25,Inventory!A3:A25,"*shoes",Inventory!C3:C25,"blue`

10. Use the COUNTIFS function to find the number of blue shoe inventory items. Use the values in the *Item Description* column as the *Criteria_range1* argument and use the criteria **shoes* to find all items that end in the word *shoes*. Use the

values in the *Color* column as the *Criteria_range2* argument and use the criteria *blue*.

a. Click cell **B5**.
b. On the *Formulas* tab, in the *Function Library* group, click the **More Functions** button, point to **Statistical**, and select **COUNTIFS**.
c. In the *Function Arguments* dialog, verify that the cursor is in the *Criteria_range1* argument box.
d. Click the **Inventory** sheet tab, and click and drag to select cells **A3:A25**.
e. In the *Function Arguments* dialog, press Tab to move to the *Criteria1* argument box.
f. Type `"*shoes"` to find any text string that ends with the word shoes.
g. Press Tab. Verify that the cursor is in the *Criteria_range2* argument box.
h. Click the **Inventory** sheet tab, and click and drag to select cells **C3:C25**.
i. In the *Function Arguments* dialog, press Tab to move to the Criteria2 argument box.
j. Type: `"blue"`
k. Click **OK**.
l. The formula should look like this:
`=COUNTIFS(Inventory!A3:A25,"*shoes",Inventory!C3:C25,"blue")`

11. Now use database functions to analyze inventory data. This method gives you more flexibility in your analysis. Once you set up the formulas, you can change the criteria in the worksheet without changing the formulas. The *InventoryDB* named range has been created for you to use as the *Database* argument. It references A2:H25 on the *Inventory* worksheet. Notice this named range ***includes*** the label row.

Use the DAVERAGE database function to calculate the average selling price for all items with the word *Football* in the item description. Use the wildcard character * before and after the word *Football* to find all item descriptions with *Football* anywhere in the text. Use the column label *Selling Price* as the *Field* argument. Remember to enclose the column label in quotation marks. Set up the criteria range. In cell **D8**, type: Item Description

a. In cell **D9**, type: `*Football*`
b. Click cell **B9** where you will enter the formula.
c. On the *Formulas* tab, in the *Function Library* group, click the **Insert Function** button.
d. If necessary, expand the **Or select a category** list, and select **Database**.
e. Double-click **DAVERAGE** to open the *Function Arguments* dialog.
f. In the *Database* argument box, type the range name: `InventoryDB`
g. In the *Field* argument box, type the column label: `"Selling Price"`

h. Click in the *Criteria* argument box and then click and drag to select cells **D8:D9**.
i. Click **OK**.
j. The formula should look like this: `=DAVERAGE(InventoryDB,"Selling Price",D8:D9)`

12. Use the DCOUNT database function to calculate the number of items in stock where the item description includes the word *Football* and the selling price is less than $20. Use the wildcard character * before and after the word *Football* to find all item descriptions with *Football* anywhere in the text. Use the column label *Stock* as the *Field* argument. Remember to enclose the column label in quotation marks.
    a. Set up the criteria range.
        i. In cell **D11**, type: `Item Description`
        ii. In cell **D12**, type: `*Football*`
        iii. In cell **E11**, type: `Selling Price`
        iv. In cell **E12**, type: `<20`
    b. Click cell **B12** where you will enter the formula.
    c. On the *Formulas* tab, in the *Function Library* group, click the **Insert Function** button.
    d. If necessary, expand the **Or select a category** list, and select **Database**.
    e. Double-click **DCOUNT** to open the *Function Arguments* dialog.
    f. In the *Database* argument box, type the range name: `InventoryDB`
    g. In the *Field* argument box, type the column label: `"Stock"`
    h. Click in the *Criteria* argument box and then click and drag to select cells **D11:E12**.
    i. Click **OK**.
    j. The formula should look like this: `=DCOUNT(InventoryDB,"Stock",D11:E12)`

13. Now use MATCH and INDEX to look up the item description, quantity in stock, and selling price of an item based on the inventory number. The *Inventory* named range has been created for you to use in these formulas. It references A3:H25 on the *Inventory* worksheet. Notice this named range does ***not*** include the label row.

    First, use MATCH to find the row position for the item listed in cell **B15**. Remember, the *Lookup_array* argument must be a single column. Require an exact match. Use absolute references so you can copy the formula.
    a. Click cell **B16**.
    b. On the *Formulas* tab, in the *Function Library* group, click the **Lookup & Reference** button, and select **MATCH**.

c. Use an absolute reference to cell **B15** for the *Lookup_value* argument. Type $B$15 and then press [Tab].
d. Verify that the cursor is in the *Lookup_array* argument box. Click the **Inventory** sheet tab and click and drag to select cells **B3:B25**. Edit the cell references to be absolute.
e. In the *Match_type* argument box, type: `0`
f. Click **OK.**
g. The formula should look like this: `=MATCH($B$15,Inventory!$B$3:$B$25,0)`

14. Now add an INDEX function around the MATCH function to find the item description (column **1**) for the row position identified by the MATCH function. Use the named range **Inventory** as the *Array* argument.
   a. If necessary, select cell **B16** again, and then click in the formula bar so you can edit the formula.
   b. After the =, type: `INDEX(Inventory,`
   c. Move the cursor to the end of the formula and type: `,1)`
   d. Press [Enter].
   e. The formula should now look like this:
   `=INDEX(Inventory,MATCH($B$15,Inventory!$B$3:$B$25,0),1)`
15. Add an IFERROR function around the INDEX function to hide any error messages by displaying an empty text string ("").
   a. If necessary, select cell **B16** again, and then click in the formula bar so you can edit the formula.
   b. After the =, type: `IFERROR(`
   c. Move the cursor to the end of the formula and type: `,"")`
   d. Press [Enter].
   e. The formula should now look like this:
   `=IFERROR(INDEX(Inventory,MATCH($B$15,Inventory!$B$3:$B$25,0),1),"")`
16. Copy the formula from cell **B16** to cells **B17:B18**.
17. Modify the formula in cell **B17** to use **8** as the *Column_num* argument for the INDEX function. The formula should look like this:
   `=IFERROR(INDEX(Inventory,MATCH($B$15,Inventory!$B$3:$B$25,0),8),"")`
18. Modify the formula in cell **B18** to use **6** as the *Column_num* argument for the INDEX function. The formula should look like this:
   `=IFERROR(INDEX(Inventory,MATCH($B$15,Inventory!$B$3:$B$25,0),6),"")`
19. If necessary, apply the **Accounting Number Format** to cell **B18**.
20. Enter a formula using RANK.EQ to calculate the ranking of this item's price.
   a. Click cell **B19**.
   b. On the *Formulas* tab, in the *Function Library* group, click the **More Functions** button, point to **Statistical**, and select **RANK.EQ**.
   c. In the *Number* argument box, type `1.15` and then press [Tab].

d. Verify that the cursor is in the *Ref* argument box. Click the **Inventory** sheet tab and click and drag to select cells **F3:F25**. Edit the cell references to be absolute.
e. Click **OK**.
f. Save the file.

21. If you are having trouble with these formulas, use the **Evaluate Formula** feature to review the results of the nested formulas.
    a. Select the cell containing the formula you want to evaluate.
    b. On the *Formulas* tab, in the *Formula Auditing* group, click the **Evaluate Formula** button.
    c. Use the *Step In, Evaluate*, and *Step Out* buttons as necessary until you have a clear understanding of how the nested INDEX and MATCH formulas work together.
22. Hank's Sporting Goods is considering taking out a $20,000 loan to pay for inventory. The details of that loan are shown on the *Financials* worksheet in cells C2:D6. You will help Hank calculate how much money he would make if he invested those same monthly payments in a money market account instead. Calculate the theoretical future value of the same amount deposited monthly in a money market account.
    a. Switch to the **Financials** worksheet.
    b. Click cell **D9**.
    c. On the *Formulas* tab, in the *Function Library* group, click the **Financial** button, and select **FV**.
    d. Enter the *Rate* argument, referring to the money market interest rate in cell **B4**. The rate is expressed as an annual interest rate, and payments will be monthly, so divide the interest rate by 12: `B4/12`
    e. Enter the *Nper* argument, referring to cell **D5**. There will be monthly payments, so multiple the number of years by 12: `D5*12`
    f. Enter the *Pmt* argument referring to the cell showing the monthly payment amount for the loan: **D4**
       Notice that the loan payment is already expressed as a negative number so there is no need to alter the *Pmt* argument.
    g. There is no value in the investment prior to the first investment period, so you can skip the *Pv* argument.
    h. Deposits would be scheduled for the beginning of each payment period. Enter the appropriate *Type* argument: `1`
    i. Click **OK**. The formula in cell D10 should look like this:
       `=FV(B4/12,D5*12,D4,,1)`
    j. Save the file.

23. Hank would like to consider another loan option with the same loan amount and the same interest rate. How many months would it take to pay off the loan if he paid a flat $900 every month?
    a. Click cell **D13**. On the *Formulas* tab, in the *Function Library* group, click the **Financial** button, and select **NPER**.
    b. Enter the *Rate* argument, referring to the loan interest rate in cell **B3**. The rate is expressed as an annual interest rate, and payments will be monthly, so divide the interest rate by 12: **B3/12**
    c. Enter the *Pmt* argument referring to the cell showing the new monthly payment amount for the loan: **D12**
    Notice that the loan payment is already expressed as a negative number so there is no need to alter the *Pmt* argument.
    d. Enter the *Pv* argument referring to the original loan amount in cell **D3**.
    e. The loan will be completely paid off, so you can skip the *Fv* argument.
    f. Payments would be applied at the end of each payment period, so you can skip the *Type* argument.
    g. Click **OK**. The formula in cell D14 should look like this:
    `=NPER(B3/12,D12,D3)`
24. Hank is easily confused by too many digits after the decimal point, so add a ROUND function to round the number of months to zero decimal places.
    a. If necessary, click cell **D13** again.
    b. In the formula bar, add the ROUND function using the existing FV function as the *Number* argument and **0** as the *Num_digits* argument. The formula should now look like this: **`=ROUND(NPER(B3/12,D12,D3),0)`**
25. Hank has another financial question for you. He needs to decide between three equipment purchase options. **Option 1** is the least expensive and will require minimal repairs. It will generate the lowest increase in revenue. **Option 2** is $10,000 more than Option 1 and will generate a higher increase in revenue, but it will require significant repairs in year 5 and will begin declining in productivity in year 7. **Option 3** is the most expensive. It will also generate the highest increase in revenue. However, it will require more frequent and expensive repairs than the other two options.
26. Enter the formula to calculate net present value for Option 1 using the revenue schedule in cells **B9:B18**. Use a discount rate of **1.5%**.
    a. Click the **Equipment Decision** worksheet.
    b. Click cell **B5**.
    c. Type: **`=NPV(`**
    d. Type: **`1.5%,`**
    e. Click and drag to select cells **B9:B18**.
    f. Type **`)`** and then press Enter to complete the formula: **`=NPV(1.5%,B9:B18)`**

27. Copy the formula in cell **B5** to cells **C5** and **D5** to calculate the NPV for Option 2 and Option 3.
28. Format cells **B5:D5** with the **Accounting Number Format**.
29. Calculate the true cost of the investment by adding the initial investment (the purchase cost) to the calculated NPV amount:
    a. In cell **B6** enter the formula as follows: **`=B4 + B5`**
    b. Copy the formula in cell **B6** to cells **C6** and **D6**.
30. Use the **Thick Outside Borders** option to place a border around cells **D3:D6** to highlight the best investment option.
31. Now calculate two alternative depreciation schedules for the selected equipment option. First, set up the values that will be used for the common arguments *Cost*, *Life*, and *Salvage*.
    a. In cell **G3**, enter a reference to cell **D4**. For the depreciation schedule, the cost value should be a positive number, so precede the cell reference with a - character: **`=-D4`**
    b. In cell **G4**, enter the useful life of the equipment: **`10`**
    c. In cell **G5**, enter the salvage value of the equipment. Calculate this as 20% of the cost: **`=G3*0.2`**
32. In cell **J4**, enter the formula to calculate depreciation for year 1 using the declining balance method.
    a. On the *Formulas* tab, in the *Function Library* group, click the **Financial** button, and then select **DB**.
    b. Enter the *Cost* argument as an absolute cell reference so the reference will not update when you copy the formula: **`$G$3`**
    c. Enter the *Salvage* argument as an absolute cell reference so the reference will not update when you copy the formula: **`$G$5`**
    d. Enter the *Life* argument as an absolute cell reference so the reference will not update when you copy the formula: **`$G$4`**
    e. Enter the *Period* argument as a relative cell reference so the reference will update when you copy the formula: **`I4`**
    f. The equipment will be in use for 12 months during the first year, so you can skip the *Month* argument.
    g. Click **OK**. The formula in cell J4 should look like this: **`=DB($G$3,$G$5,$G$4,I4)`**
    h. Copy the formula to **J5:J13**.
33. In cell **K4**, enter the formula to calculate depreciation for year 1 using the straight-line method.
    a. On the *Formulas* tab, in the *Function Library* group, click the **Financial** button, and then select **SLN**.

b. Enter the *Cost* argument as an absolute cell reference so the reference will not update when you copy the formula: **`$G$3`**

c. Enter the *Salvage* argument as an absolute cell reference so the reference will not update when you copy the formula: **`$G$5`**

d. Enter the *Life* argument as an absolute cell reference so the reference will not update when you copy the formula: **`$G$4`**

e. Click OK. The formula in cell K4 should look like this: **`=SLN($G$3,$G$5,$G$4)`**

f. Copy the formula to **K5:K13**. Notice that the straight-line method returns the same depreciation value for each period in the schedule.

34. Save and close the workbook.

projects

Data files for projects can be found by logging into your SIMnet account and going to the *Library* section.

challenge yourself 6.3

In this project, you are an accountant for National Pharmaceutical Sales. You want to make a spreadsheet that contains each sales associate's statistics. Because the company has over 100 sales associates, only a partial spreadsheet will be provided. Please follow the steps below to complete the partial spreadsheet.

Skills needed to complete this project:

- Using the IFS Function (Skill 6.12)
- Rounding with Functions (Skill 6.1)
- Finding the Middle Value with MEDIAN (Skill 6.6)
- Calculating the Standard Deviation (Skill 6.7)
- Using SUMIF and SUMIFS (Skill 6.3)
- Using AVERAGEIF and AVERAGEIFS (Skill 6.4)
- Using Database Functions (Skill 6.19)
- Managing Errors with the IFERROR Function (Skill 6.20)
- Analyzing Complex Formulas Using Evaluate Formula (Skill 6.21)

1. Open the start file **EX2016-ChallengeYourself-6-3** and resave the file as: `[your initials]EX-ChallengeYourself-6-3`
2. If the workbook opens in Protected View, click the **Enable Editing** button in the Message Bar at the top of the workbook so you can modify the workbook.
3. On the *Sales Data* worksheet, calculate the commission rate and commission paid for each sales associate.
    a. Beginning in cell **F4**, enter a formula using the IFS function to calculate the commission rate based on the following table.

IF ANNUAL SALES ARE:	THEN THE COMMISSION RATE IS:
>=225,000	6%
>=175,000	4%
>=100,000	2%
<100,000	0%

b. Fill the formula down through cell **F64**. If necessary, format the range as a percentage, and center the values in the cells.
c. In cell **G4**, calculate the commission earned by multiplying the annual sales by the commission rate (**E4*F4**).
d. Add a rounding function to the formula in cell **G4** to round the result to **two** decimal places.
e. Fill the formula down through cell **G64**. If necessary, format the range using the default **Comma Style** number format.

4. In the *Summary* sheet, calculate average and median sales and commissions. Use the named ranges shown in cells **A23:B26**.
   a. In cell **B5**, enter a formula to calculate the average annual sales for all sales associates. Use the named range **AnnualSales**.
   b. In cell **C5**, enter a formula to calculate the median annual sales for all sales associates. Use the named range **AnnualSales**.
   c. In cell **D5**, enter a formula to calculate the standard deviation for sales. This dataset is a sample of the larger population. Use the named range **AnnualSales**.
   d. Add a rounding function to the formula in cell **D5** to round the result to two decimal places.
   e. In cell **B6**, enter a formula to calculate the average commission. Use the named range **CommissionEarned**.
   f. In cell **C6**, enter a formula to calculate the median commission. Use the named range **CommissionEarned**.
   g. In cell **D6**, enter a formula to calculate the standard deviation for commissions. This dataset is a sample of the larger population. Use the named range **CommissionEarned**.
   h. Add a rounding function to the formula in cell **D6** to round the result to two decimal places.
   i. If necessary, format cells **B5:D6** with the default **Accounting Number Format**.
5. Calculate the total and average sales by region.
   a. In cell **B10**, use a **SUMIF** formula to calculate the sum of **AnnualSales** where the value in the **Regions** named range is equal to the region listed in cell **B9**.
   b. Copy the formula to cells **C10:I10**.
   c. In cell **B11**, use an **AVERAGEIF** formula to calculate the average of **AnnualSales** where the value in the **Regions** named range is equal to the region listed in cell **B9**.
   d. Add a rounding function to the formula in cell **B11** to round the result to two decimal places.

e. Copy the formula to cells **C11:I11**.
f. If necessary, format cells **B10:I11** with the default **Accounting Number Format**.

6. The second part of the *Summary* sheet contains a sales associate lookup form, but the appropriate formulas have not been entered yet.
   a. In cell **B18**, enter a formula to calculate the average commission earned for the sales associate last name entered in cell **A16**. (*Hint:* Use a database function. Use the named range **Earnings** as the *Database* argument and the column label **Commission Earned** as the *Field* argument. The criteria range should be **A15:B16**.)
   b. In cell **B19**, enter a formula to calculate the total commission earned for that same sales associate. (*Hint:* Use a different database function. The function arguments are the same as those you used in step 6a.)
   c. If necessary, apply the **Accounting Number Format** to cells **B18:B19**.
   d. In cell **B20**, enter a formula to calculate the number of clients the sales associate had with annual sales reaching the target set in cell **B16**. (*Hint:* This time, use the column label **Client** as the *Field* argument. The criteria range should be **A15:B16**.) Remember, the values in the *Client* field are text values. Use the appropriate function.
   e. If necessary, apply the **General** number format to cell **B20**.
   f. Test your formulas by entering `Schmidt` as the sales associate's last name (cell **A16**) and **>175000** as the sales target (cell **B16**).
   g. Add an **IFERROR** function to the formula in cell **B18** to display the error text **Associate not found**.
   h. If you receive errors, use **Evaluate Formula** to troubleshoot your formulas.
7. Save and close the workbook.

projects

Data files for projects can be found by logging into your SIMnet account and going to the *Library* section.

challenge yourself 6.4

In this project, you will complete a series of budget worksheets, including a home loan analysis, rental comparison, and savings and retirement planning. The fair market rent information in the *Final FY2017 Virginia FMR* worksheet was copied from the U.S. Department of Housing and Urban Development Web site at http://www.huduser.org.

Skills needed to complete this project:

- Calculating the Number of Payments with NPER (Skill 6.16)
- Rounding with Functions (Skill 6.1)
- Finding Data with MATCH and INDEX (Skill 6.18)
- Calculating Future Value with the FV Function (Skill 6.13)
- Using PV to Calculate Present Value When Payments Are Constant (Skill 6.14)
- Using NPV to Calculate Present Value When Payments Are Variable (Skill 6.15)

1. Open the start file **EX2016-ChallengeYourself-6-4** and resave the file as: `[your initials]EX-ChallengeYourself-6-4`
2. If the workbook opens in Protected View, click the **Enable Editing** button in the Message Bar at the top of the workbook so you can modify the workbook.
3. On the *Loan Terms* worksheet, calculate how quickly you could pay off the loan if you increased the monthly payment.
   a. In cell **D11**, use **NPER** to calculate the number of months to pay off the loan using the new monthly loan payment amount in cell **D10**. Remember to use a negative value for the *Pmt* argument and be careful to reference the loan amount, not the home price. You can omit both the *Fv* and *Type* arguments —home loans are usually set up so the payment is applied at the end of each period.
   b. In cell **D12**, calculate the approximate number of years to pay off the loan by dividing the value in cell **D11** by **12** and then rounding to zero decimal places.
4. Look up the equivalent fair market rents in the same area. These data can be found in the *Final FY2017 Virginia FMR* worksheet.
   a. In cell **D16**, enter a nested formula using MATCH and INDEX to find the fair market rent for a one-bedroom rental unit in the county listed in cell **D15**. We've already defined two named ranges for you to use. **FMR_2017** is the named range to use for the INDEX function *Array* argument. This range

includes all the data in cells **A3:H137** in the *Final FY2017 Virginia FMR* worksheet. The one-bedroom rent data is in column **4**. The second named range, **Counties**, can be used as the MATCH *Lookup_array* argument. This range is the column of county names, cells **G3:G137**, in the *Final FY2017 Virginia FMR* worksheet. Require an exact match for the MATCH function.

b. In cell **D17**, enter a nested formula using **MATCH** and **INDEX** to find the fair market rent for a two-bedroom rental unit in the county listed in cell **D15**. You can use the same formula as in D16, but substitute column **5** for the INDEX *Column_num* argument.

5. Now that you've calculated mortgage and rental options, let's look at savings. Go to the **Savings** worksheet.

    a. You want to save at least $10,000 for a down payment on a new car. In cell **B6**, enter a formula to calculate how much you will have saved by putting away $400 per month for 24 months at a 1.75% annual interest rate. Use the appropriate cell references. Remember to use a negative value for the *Pmt* argument. There is no money in the account yet and payments are applied at the end of every month, so omit both the *Pv* and *Type* arguments. (*Hint:* Use the **FV** function.)

    b. You also want to save for retirement. In cell **B12**, enter a formula to calculate how much you will have saved by putting away that same $400 per month for 25 years at 4%. Use the appropriate cell references. Remember to use a negative value for the *Pmt* argument and to adjust the *Rate* and *Nper* arguments to reflect monthly payments. There is no money in the account yet and payments are applied at the end of every month, so omit both the *Pv* and *Type* arguments. (*Hint:* Use the **FV** function.)

    c. Once you've saved 25 years for retirement, how much can you draw from the retirement account over the next 30 years? In cell **B14**, enter a formula to calculate how much you can pay yourself from the retirement account every month. Assume that the account will continue to earn the same interest rate. At the end of the **30 years**, the account balance will be zero. Payments to you will be made at the **beginning** of every month. Use the appropriate cell references. (*Hint:* Use the **PMT** function to calculate the payments to yourself. Enter a negative sign before the formula so the result appears as a positive number.)

6. You have two options for additional guaranteed monthly payments in retirement (annuities). Go to the **Annuities** worksheet to calculate the value of each of these options.

    a. The first annuity costs $20,000 and pays you $200 per month for 120 months (10 years). In cell **B5**, enter a formula to calculate the present value of this investment. Remember to express the *Pmt* argument as a negative number and set the *Type* argument to **1** as the payment will be made at the beginning of each month. (*Hint:* Use the **PV** function.)

b. The second annuity also costs $20,000 but it pays a variable annual payment. In cell **B13**, enter a formula to calculate the present value of this investment using the annual interest rate in cell **B8** and the payment schedule in cells **B14:B23**. (*Hint:* Use the **NPV** function.)

7. Save and close the workbook.

projects

Data files for projects can be found by logging into your SIMnet account and going to the *Library* section.

on your own 6.5

In this project, you will complete a personal budget workbook.

Skills needed to complete this project:

- Rounding with Functions (Skill 6.1)
- Finding the Middle Value with MEDIAN (Skill 6.6)
- Finding the Most Common Value(s) with MODE.SNGL and MODE.MULT (Skill 6.9)
- Managing Errors with the IFERROR Function (Skill 6.20)
- Using the IFS Function (Skill 6.12)
- Calculating the Number of Payments with NPER (Skill 6.16)
- Calculating Future Value with the FV Function (Skill 6.13)

1. Open the start file **EX2016-OnYourOwn-6-5** and resave the file as: `[your initials]EX-OnYourOwn-6-5`
2. If the workbook opens in Protected View, click the **Enable Editing** button in the Message Bar at the top of the workbook so you can modify the workbook.
3. Begin with the *Budget* worksheet. We have set up a budget with rows for common personal budget income and expense categories and sample data. You may choose to use the sample data or modify the budget to use your own income and expense categories and data.
    a. In cell **O8**, enter a formula using AVERAGE to calculate the average monthly expense for this category. Be careful not to include the total column (column N). Add the ROUND function to the formula to round the formula result to zero decimal places. Copy the formula to the other cells in the column.
    b. In cell **P8**, enter a formula using MEDIAN to calculate the median monthly expense for this category. Be careful not to include the total column (column N). Copy the formula to the other cells in the column.
    c. In cell **Q8**, enter a formula using MODE.SNGL to find the most common value for each category. Be careful not to include the total column (column N). Copy the formula to the other cells in the column.
    d. Add the IFERROR function to the formula in cell **Q8** to display nothing if there is no mode. (*Hint:* Use "" as the *Value_if_error* argument.) Copy the formula to the other cells in the column.
4. In cell **B22**, we've set a target goal for monthly expenses. If you are using your own data, change this value to your own monthly expenses goal. In cell **B23**, enter a formula using the IFS function to grade yourself on how well you did in meeting your goal for the month. If your total expenses were less than the goal, display **great**. If total expenses were less than or equal to total income, display

ok. If total expenses were greater than total income, display **not great**. Copy the formula to the other cells in the row through **M23**. (*Hint:* Use an absolute reference to the target goal in cell B22 so it stays the same when you copy the formula.)

5. Next we'll look at how quickly you might be able to pay off credit card and other loan debt. Go to the **Credit Card and Loan Debt** worksheet. The worksheet is set up with sample data for two credit cards and a loan. You may choose to use the sample data or modify the data to use actual credit card and loan balances and interest rates.
   a. In cell **G3**, enter a formula using **NPER** to calculate the number of months it would take to pay off the credit card balance in cell **B3** using the new monthly payment in cell **F3**. Remember to express the *Pmt* argument as a negative. The loan balance should be zero at the end and payments are applied at the end of every month, so omit both the *Fv* and *Type* arguments.
   b. Add a function around the formula in cell **G3** to round the calculation result to two decimal places.
   c. Copy the formula in cell **G3** to **G4:G5** to calculate how many months it will take to pay off the other debts based on the new payments.
6. Now that you've calculated how to pay down your debt quicker, let's look at retirement. Go to the **Retirement** worksheet. This part of the project is similar to steps 5b–c in the *Challenge Yourself 6.4* project. The worksheet is set up with sample data for a simple retirement account with a consistent monthly contribution and a consistent annual interest rate. You may choose to use the sample data or modify the data for your own situation.
   a. In cell **B5**, enter a formula to calculate how much money will be in the account when you are ready to retire. Use the appropriate cell references. Remember to use a negative value for the *Pmt* argument and to adjust the *Rate* and *Nper* arguments to reflect monthly payments. There is no money in the account yet and payments are applied at the end of every month, so omit both the *Pv* and *Type* arguments. (*Hint:* Use the **FV** function.)
   b. Once you've saved for retirement, how much can you draw from the retirement account over the next 30 years? In cell **B8**, enter a formula to calculate how much you can pay yourself from the retirement account every month. Assume that at the end of the 30 years, the account balance will be zero and that payments to you will be made at the beginning of every month. Use the appropriate cell references. (*Hint:* Use the **PMT** function to calculate the payments to yourself. Use the ending balance in the retirement account as the *Pv* argument. Enter a negative sign before the formula so the result appears as a positive number.)
7. Save and close the workbook.

projects

Data files for projects can be found by logging into your SIMnet account and going to the *Library* section.

fix it 6.6

In this project, you will work with spreadsheets designed for planning a charity event. In order to determine if the party will meet its fundraising goal, the guest list analysis and expense calculations must be corrected.

Skills needed to complete this project:

- Analyzing Complex Formulas Using Evaluate Formula (Skill 6.21)
- Rounding with Functions (Skill 6.1)
- Using SUMIF and SUMIFS (Skill 6.3)
- Using COUNTIF and COUNTIFS (Skill 6.5)
- Using AVERAGEIF and AVERAGEIFS (Skill 6.4)
- Using Database Functions (Skill 6.19)
- Calculating Totals with SUMPRODUCT (Skill 6.2)
- Finding Data with MATCH and INDEX (Skill 6.18)
- Calculating the Number of Payments with NPER (Skill 6.16)
- Using the IFS Function (Skill 6.12)

1. Open the start file **EX2016-FixIt-6-6** and resave the file as: `[your initials]EX-FixIt-6-6`
2. If the workbook opens in Protected View, click the **Enable Editing** button in the Message Bar at the top of the workbook so you can modify the workbook.
3. Throughout this project, use the Evaluate Formula feature to analyze any formulas you have difficulty troubleshooting.
4. Fix the following errors in the **Guest List** worksheet. Use cell references and named ranges where appropriate. All the named ranges you might need have been defined for you. Refer to the *Named Ranges Reference* sheet for a description of each defined name.
   a. In cell **E3**, the formula to calculate the number of tables should result in a whole number only. Be sure to round the number up so you aren't left with a guess without a seat.
   b. The formula in cell **E4** should calculate the total number of guests from the city listed in cell **D4**.
   c. The formula in cell **E5** should calculate the number of single guests attending from the city listed in cell **D5**.

d. The formula in cell **E6** should calculate the average number of guests attending from the city listed in cell **D6**. The formula should also round up to a whole number.

e. In cell **E7**, use a database function to calculate the number of guests from the **city of Auburn** with a **last name beginning with the letter J**. You will need to correct issues in both the formula and in the criteria data. (*Hints:* DSUM is not the appropriate database function to use in this example. The *Database* arguments should use a named range, but not *GuestList*. Be sure to set the *Criteria_range* argument to include all the column headings so you can change the question and criteria later without having to change the formula. And remember, you are looking for last names that ***begin*** with the letter *J*. There's no problem with using *Last Name* as the *Field* criteria.)

5. Fix the following errors in the **Shopping List** worksheet. Use cell references and named ranges where appropriate. All the named ranges you might need have been defined for you. Refer to the *Named Ranges Reference* sheet for a description of each defined name.

   a. The formula in cell **B2** should calculate the total cost of all the shopping items by multiplying the number of items ordered in the *Quantity* column by the cost of each item in the *TotalCostperUnit* column and then summing the values. Be sure to round the final value to two decimal places. If necessary, apply the *Accounting Number Format.*

   b. The formula in cell **B4** should allow you to look up the vendor for the item listed in cell **B3**. Using a nested INDEX and MATCH formula is the right idea, but the formula is not quite right. Add an IFERROR function to display **item not found** if the formula results in an error. Also, use absolute references so you can copy the formula to cells **B5** and **B6**.

   c. In cell **B5**, copy and paste the corrected nested INDEX and MATCH formula and then update the *Column_num* argument to find the quantity ordered.

   d. In cell **B6**, copy and paste the corrected nested INDEX and MATCH formula and then update the *Column_num* argument to find the item's total cost per unit. Edit the formula to calculate the total cost by multiplying the result of the INDEX formula by the quantity ordered (cell **B5**). (*Hint:* Maintain the IFERROR function as the outermost function in the nested formula.) If necessary, apply the *Accounting Number Format.*

   e. There are three items in the shopping list that are based on the number of guests, but the quantity ordered should be rounded up to the nearest whole number. Add the appropriate rounding function to the formulas in cells **D10**, **D11**, and **D23**.

f. The formula in cell **E4** should calculate how many months it will take to pay off the loan using the total cost in cell **B2** and the loan terms in cells **E2** and **E3**. The formula is using the wrong function and the arguments are in the wrong order. Once you correct this formula, the final cost of the party (cell E5) will be correct as well.

6. Once the guest list analysis and party expenses have been corrected, you can determine whether or not the party will meet the fundraising goal. Go to the **Fundraising Goal** worksheet. The IF formula in cell B10 evaluates whether or not the fundraising goal was met. However, if the goal was not met, the party organizers also want to know if they met at least 75% of the goal.
   a. The formula in cell **B10** should display **Goal met!** if the party income (donations, cell **B6**, **minus** expenses, cell **B8**) is **greater than or equal to** the fundraising goal (cell **B2**). If the income is within 75% of the goal **(greater than or equal to B2*.75)**, then the formula should display this message: **within 25% of goal**. If the income is less than 75% of the fundraising goal, then the formula should display this message: **less than 75% of goal**.
7. Save and close the workbook.

chapter 7

Exploring Advanced Charts and Graphics

In this chapter, you will learn the following skills:

- Create a combination chart
- Work with new Excel 2016 chart types
- Add a data series to a chart
- Apply formatting to charts
- Create and use a chart template
- Use trendlines to analyze and forecast values
- Use Sparklines to visualize data
- Insert and apply formatting to pictures
- Insert and apply formatting to shapes
- Insert and apply formatting to SmartArt graphics

introduction

This chapter expands on Chapter 5's introduction to charts. You will learn to create a combination chart and some of the new chart types that were added to Excel 2016. You will modify charts including adding a data series, applying custom formatting, and working with chart templates. You will add and modify trendlines to forecast data. You will also learn to insert and work with graphic elements, including Sparklines, pictures, shapes, and SmartArt graphics.

Skill 7.1 Creating a Combination Chart

A **combination chart**, or **combo chart**, allows you to specify different chart types for individual data series. The most common combination is a column chart combined with a line chart.

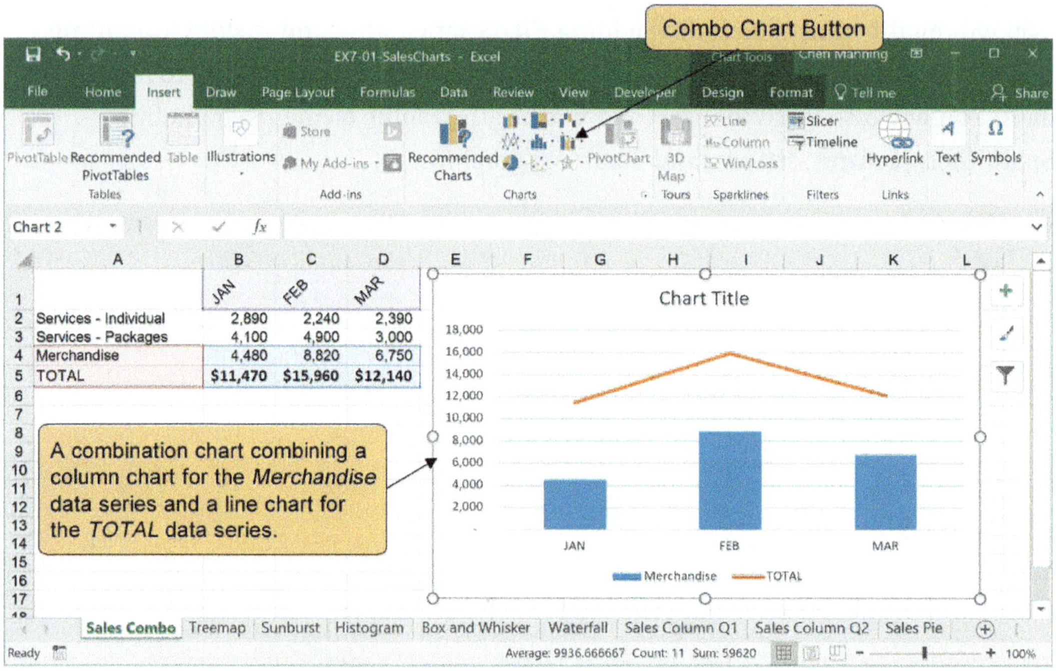

FIGURE EX 7.1

To create a combination chart:

1. Select the data you want to include in the chart.
2. On the *Insert* tab, in the *Charts* group, click the **Combo Chart** button.
3. Click the chart type you want.

You can plot one or more of the data series along a secondary axis. This is useful when you want to illustrate related data that have different scales. In Figure EX 7.2, it is easier to see the relationship between the merchandise data points once the total line has been plotted on the secondary axis.

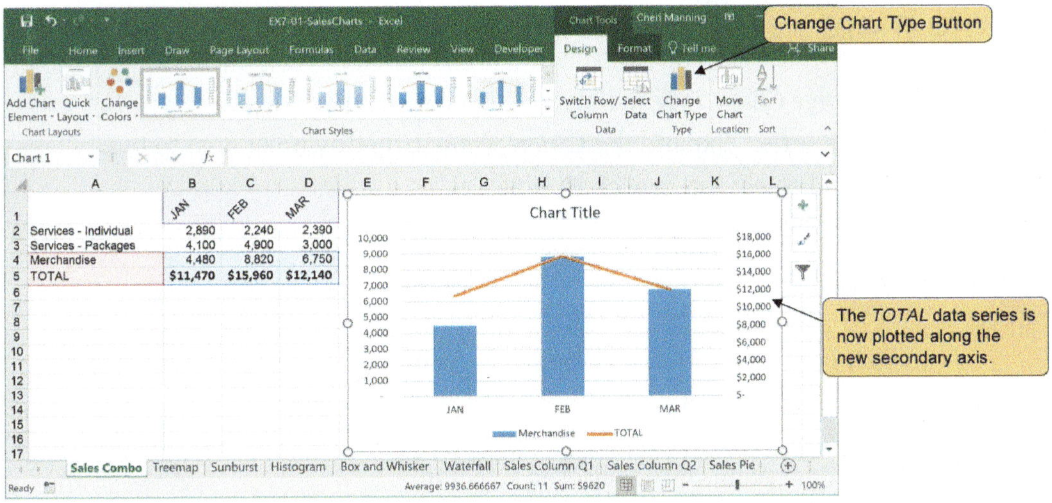

FIGURE EX 7.2

To add a secondary axis to a combo chart:

1. If necessary, click the chart to select it.
2. On the *Chart Tools Design* tab, in the *Type* group, click the **Change Chart Type** button.
3. Click the **Secondary Axis** check box next to the series that you want to plot along the secondary axis.

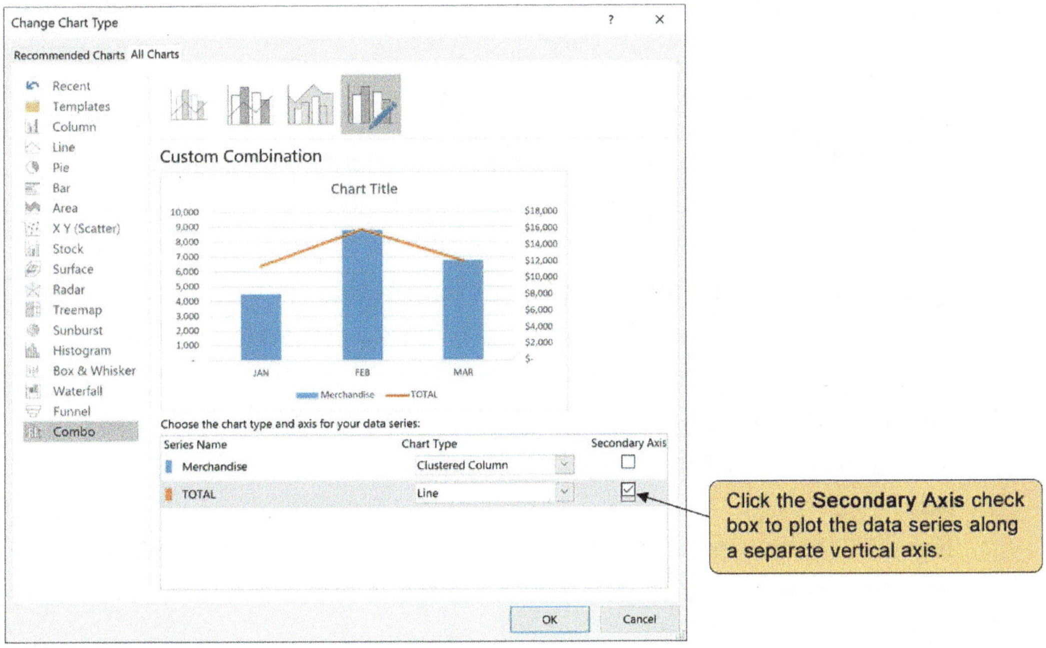

FIGURE EX 7.3

tell me **more**

From the *Change Chart Type* dialog, you can also change the chart type for one of the data series. Expand the **Chart Type** drop-down list next to the series name and select the new chart type.

another method

You can change the axis for a specific series from the *Format Data Series* task pane.

1. Click any data point in the series to select it.
2. On the *Chart Tools Format* tab, in the *Current Selection* group, click the **Format Selection** button.
3. The *Format Data Series* task pane opens to the *Series Options* panel.
4. Click the **Primary Axis** or **Secondary Axis** radio button to change the axis along which the data series is plotted.

let me **try** *Live!*

Open the student data file **EX7-01-SalesCharts** and try this skill on your own:

1. On the *Sales Combo* worksheet, if necessary, select the following cell ranges for your chart: **A1:D1** and **A4:D5** *Hint:* To select non-contiguous cell ranges, select the first cell range, and then press Ctrl and click-and-drag to select additional cell ranges.
2. Insert a **clustered column-line combination** chart based on the selected data. The line chart should represent the *TOTAL* data series. Both data series should be on the primary axis. This is the first chart type in the *Combo Chart* gallery.
3. Modify the chart so the *TOTAL* data series is plotted along the secondary axis.
4. If you will be moving on to the next skill in this chapter, leave the workbook open to continue working. If not, save the file as directed by your instructor and close it.

Skill 7.2 Working with Hierarchy Charts

Hierarchy charts visualize data that are organized into categories (called **branches**) and related subcategories. Excel 2016 includes two types of hierarchy charts—treemap and sunburst.

In a **treemap chart**, each category (branch) is represented as a rectangle and the values for each subcategory are represented as rectangles within the category rectangle. Use a treemap chart when you want to compare the relative size of each branch and then compare the subcategories proportionally within each branch.

In Figure EX 7.4, the treemap chart compares sales for each income category. Each category is then divided into quarters (Q1, Q2, etc.). The rectangle for the largest category (retail) is placed at the left of the treemap, and the largest quarter within that category (Q4) is placed at the top of the *Retail* branch.

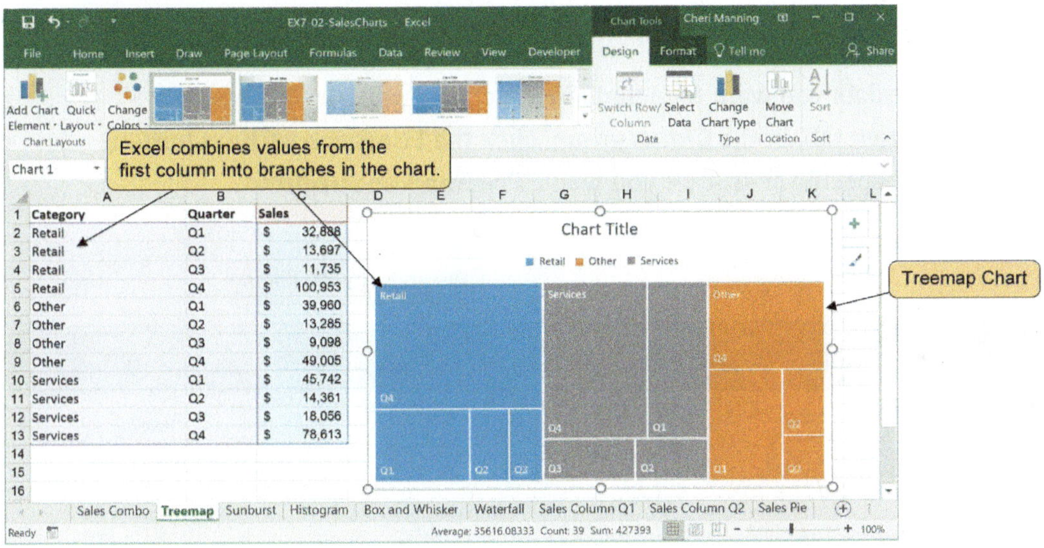

FIGURE EX 7.4

A **sunburst chart** can show more hierarchy levels than a treemap chart because it visualizes the data as a concentric series of rings with the top-level categories as segments of the inner ring. A sunburst chart can include multiple levels of outer rings. Each branch of the sunburst represents all the levels of a category.

In Figure EX 7.5, the sunburst chart includes additional details for retail sales in Q1 and Q4 by month. For the *Retail* branch of the sunburst chart, you can see that *Q1* is the largest segment, and for the *Q1* segment, you can see that *Dec* is by far the largest.

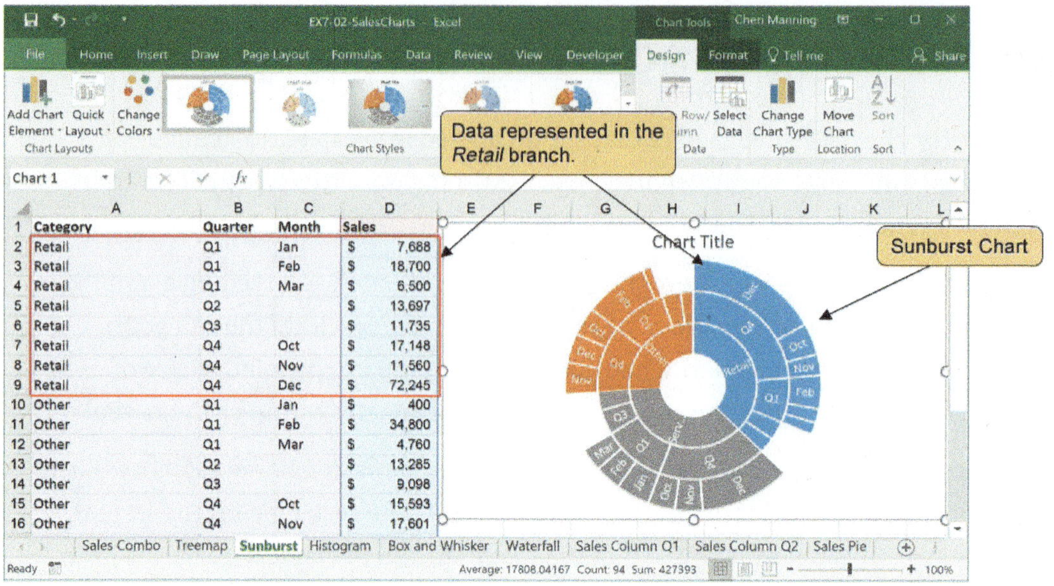

FIGURE EX 7.5

To insert a treemap or sunburst hierarchy chart:

1. Select the data you want to include in the chart.
2. On the *Insert* tab, in the *Charts* group, click the **Hierarchy Chart** button.
3. Select the specific chart type you want: **Treemap** or **Sunburst**.

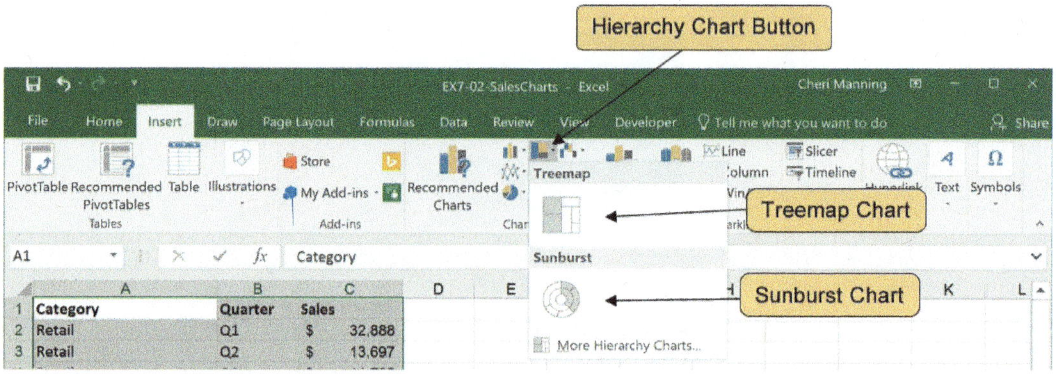

FIGURE EX 7.6

tips & tricks

If your data include more than two levels of hierarchy, a treemap chart will include only the top-level category and the lowest level of subcategory. The middle subcategories will not be represented in the chart. Use a sunburst chart instead if you want to show every level of subcategory.

let me try *Live!*

If you do not have the data file from the previous skill open, open the student data file
EX7-02-SalesCharts and try this skill on your own:

1. Go to the **Treemap** worksheet and select cells **A1:C13**.
2. Insert a **treemap** chart based on the selected cells.
3. Go to the **Sunburst** worksheet and select cells **A1:D25**.
4. Insert a **sunburst** chart based on the selected cells.
5. If you will be moving on to the next skill in this chapter, leave the workbook open to continue working. If not, save the file as directed by your instructor and close it.

Skill 7.3 Working with Statistical Charts

For Excel 2016, Microsoft added three new statistical charts: histogram, Pareto, and box and whisker.

A **histogram chart** is like a column or bar chart except each column represents a range of values instead of a specific data series. In a histogram, each column is called a **bin** and the value range between bins is called the **class interval**. Histograms can be used to visualize **frequency**—how many times a value appears within the range represented on the x axis.

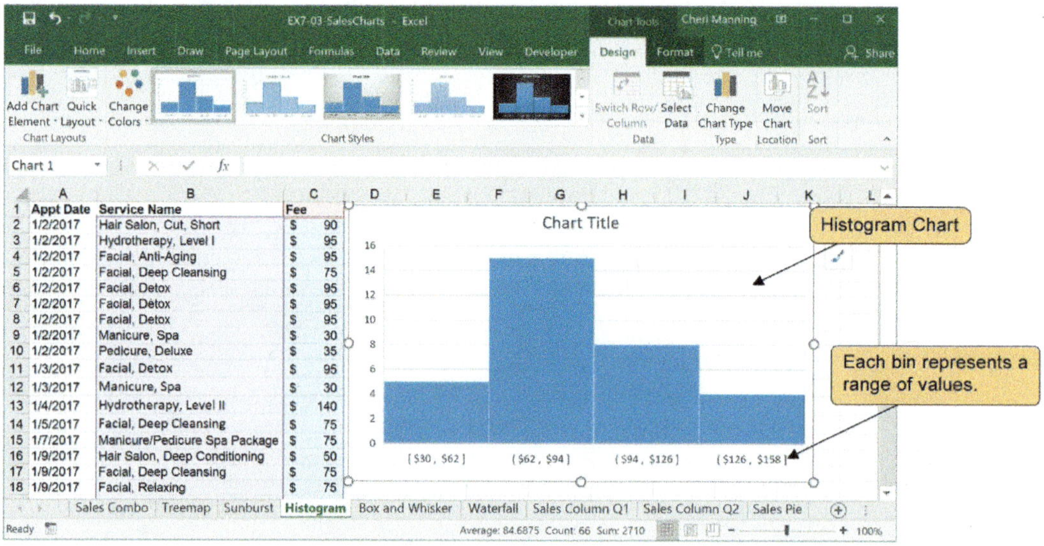

FIGURE EX 7.7

A **Pareto chart** is type of histogram chart where the columns are sorted from largest to smallest with a line chart on a secondary axis showing the cumulative total percentage.

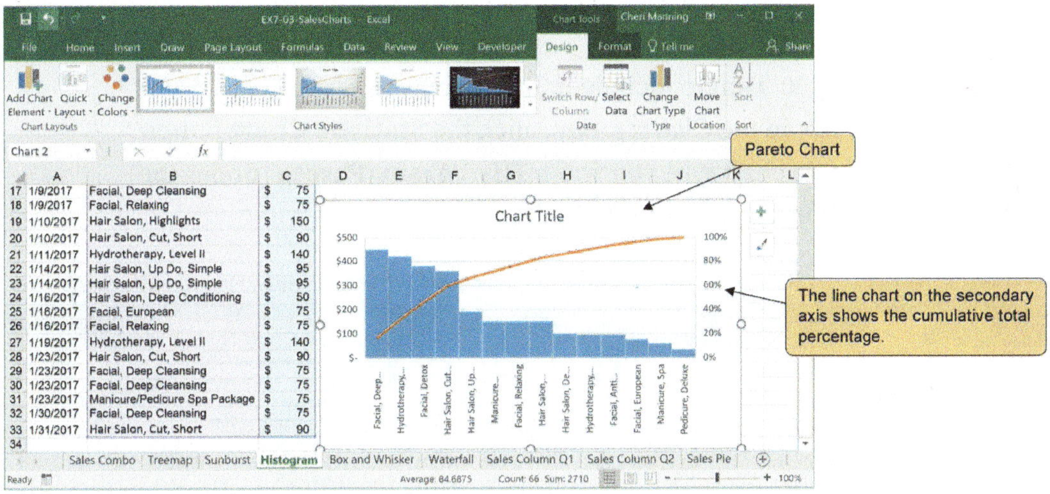

FIGURE EX 7.8

A **box and whisker chart** is another way to represent the range of values for each category based on dividing the values into quartiles.

Quartiles are the values that divide the list of values into four equal parts. Quartile 2 is the median—the middle value that divides the list of values in two. Quartile 1, the **lower quartile**, is the value that divides the first half in half again, and quartile 3, the **upper quartile**, is the value that divides the second (upper) half in half.

In the box and whisker chart, the box represents the range between the upper and lower quartiles (the **interquartile range**) with the X marking the mean (average) value. Lines called **whiskers** extend above and/or below the box to show where there are values outside the quartiles. **Outlier values** (values outside the box by more than 1.5 times the length of the box) are represented by a single dot.

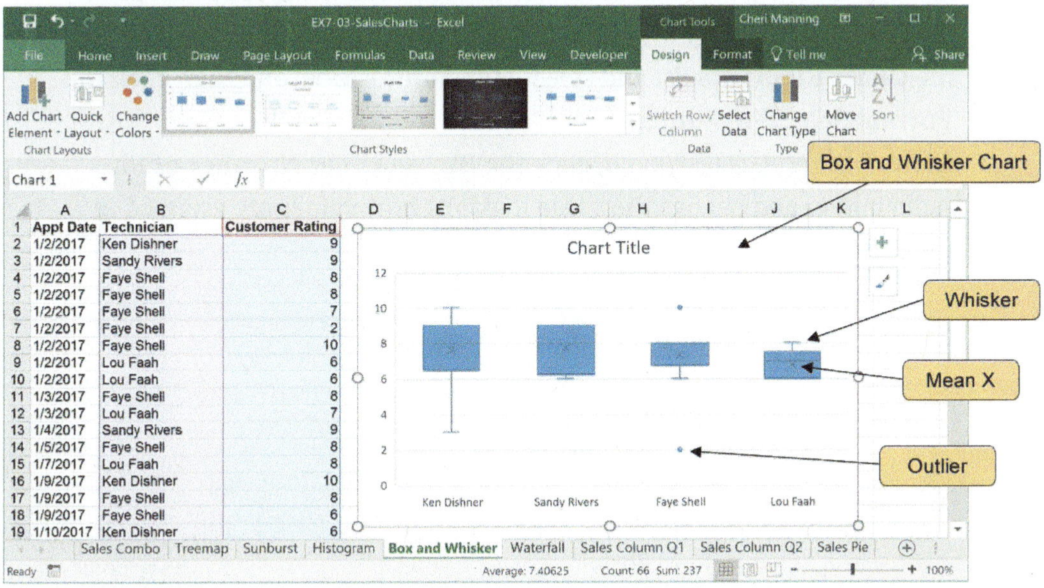

FIGURE EX 7.9

To insert a histogram, Pareto, or box and whisker chart:

1. Select the data you want to include in the chart.
2. On the *Insert* tab, in the *Charts* group, click the **Statistic Chart** button.
3. Select the specific chart type you want: **Histogram, Pareto** (under the *Histogram* section), or **Box and Whisker.**

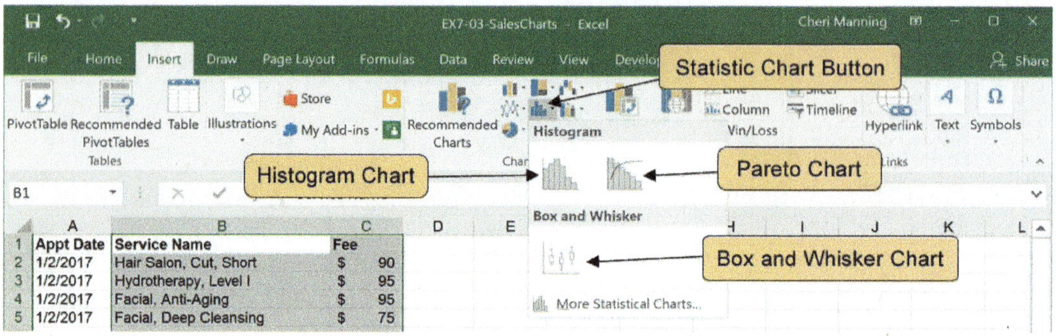

FIGURE EX 7.10

tips & tricks

Pareto histograms are named after Vilfredo Pareto, a pioneer in the field of macroeconomics.

tell me more

To modify the bins in a histogram or Pareto chart:

1. Double-click anywhere on the x axis to open the *Format Axis* task pane or on the *Chart Tools Format* tab, in the *Current Selection* group, expand the **Chart Elements** list and select **Horizontal Axis**, and then click the **Format Selection** button.
2. In the *Format Axis* task pane, click the **Bin width** or **Number of bins** radio button and change the value to adjust how values are grouped in the chart.

let me try *Live!*

If you do not have the data file from the previous skill open, open the student data file
EX7-03-SalesCharts and try this skill on your own:

1. Go to the **Histogram** worksheet and select cells **B1:C33.**
2. Insert a **Histogram** chart based on cells **B1:C33.**
3. If necessary, move the chart to the top of the worksheet to the right of the *Fee* column. Deselect the chart and select cells **B1:C33** again.
4. Insert a **Pareto** chart based on cells **B1:C33.**
5. If the two charts overlap, move the Pareto chart so it is below the histogram chart
6. Go to the **Box and Whisker** worksheet and select cells **B1:C33.**
7. Insert a **box and whisker** chart based on cells **B1:C33.**
8. If you will be moving on to the next skill in this chapter, leave the workbook open to continue working. If not, save the file as directed by your instructor and close it.

Skill 7.4 Working with Waterfall Charts

A **waterfall chart** begins with the first value anchored on the x axis. Subsequent positive and negative values are shown as floating bars adding to or subtracting from a running total. Increases and decreases are color coded so you can clearly see how each data point contributes to the running total. You can set any value as a "total" to anchor that data point on the x axis.

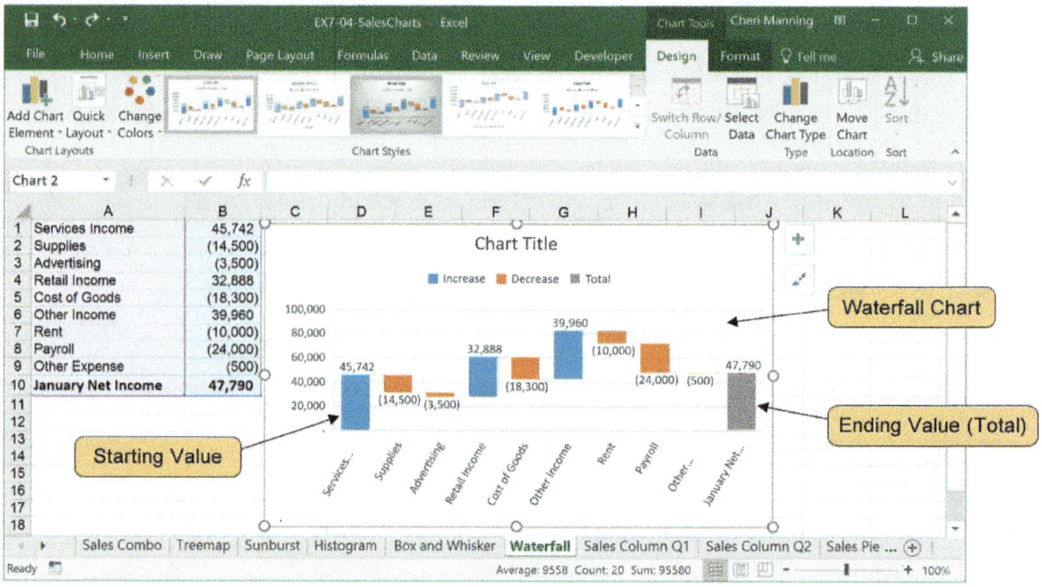

FIGURE EX 7.11

To insert a waterfall chart:

1. Select the data you want to include in the chart.
2. On the *Insert* tab, in the *Charts* group, click the **Waterfall or Stock Chart** button.
3. Select **Waterfall**.

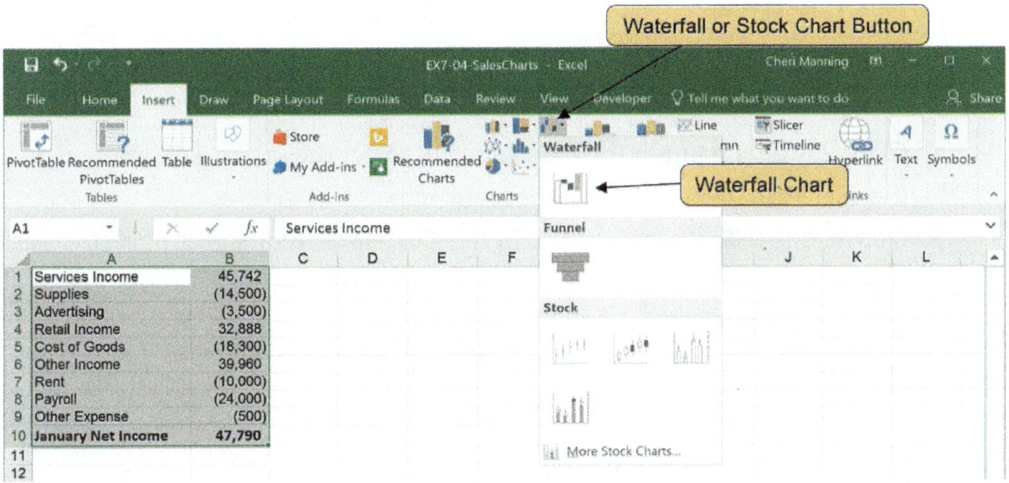

FIGURE EX 7.12

4. If your chart includes a final data point that represents a total, click any data point to select the data series, and then double-click the data point you want to set as a total. In the *Format Data Point* task pane, click the **Set as total** check box.

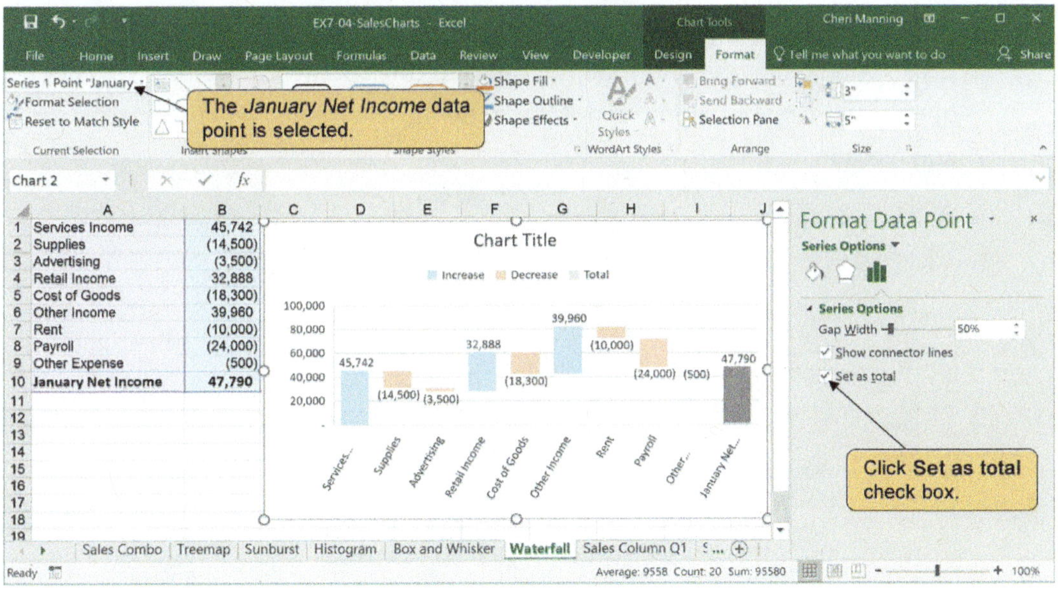

FIGURE EX 7.13

tips & tricks

The waterfall chart will display the values in the order in which they are listed in the data source. Be sure to arrange your values in the best way to tell the story you are trying to convey with the increases and decreases in values.

another method

To open the *Format Data Point* task pane:

1. Click any data point in the data series to select the series, and then click the specific data point you want to format.
2. On the *Chart Tools Format* tab, in the *Current Selection* group, verify that the correct data point is listed in the *Chart Elements* box, and then click the **Format Selection** button.

let me try *Live!*

If you do not have the data file from the previous skill open, open the student data file
EX7-04-SalesCharts and try this skill on your own:

1. Go to the **Waterfall** worksheet and select cells **A1:B10**.
2. Insert a **Waterfall** chart based on cells **A1:B10**.
3. Set the last data point (*January Net Income*) as a total.
4. If you will be moving on to the next skill in this chapter, leave the workbook open to continue working. If not, save the file as directed by your instructor and close it.

Skill 7.5 Adding a Data Series to a Chart

If your worksheet already includes a chart, you can manipulate the data represented without deleting and recreating the chart. The chart in Figure EX 7.14 includes monthly sales data for services. You can add another data series, in this case for gift certificate sales, through the *Select Data Source* dialog.

To add another data series to a chart:

1. If necessary, select the chart.
2. On the *Chart Tools Design* tab, in the *Data* group, click the **Select Data** button.

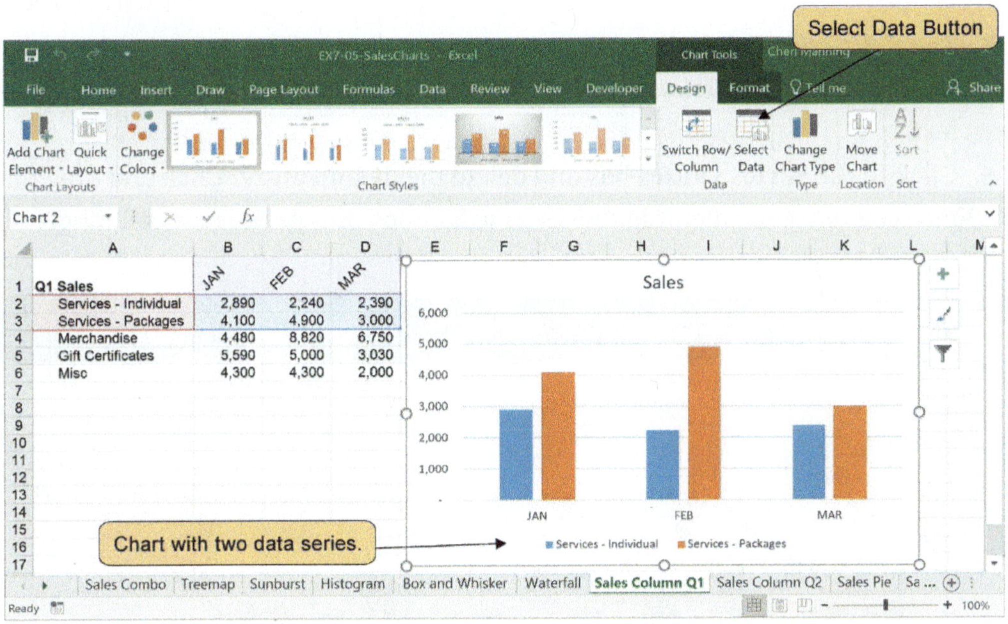

FIGURE EX 7.14

3. The *Select Data Source* dialog opens showing the current data series.
4. Click the **Add** button.

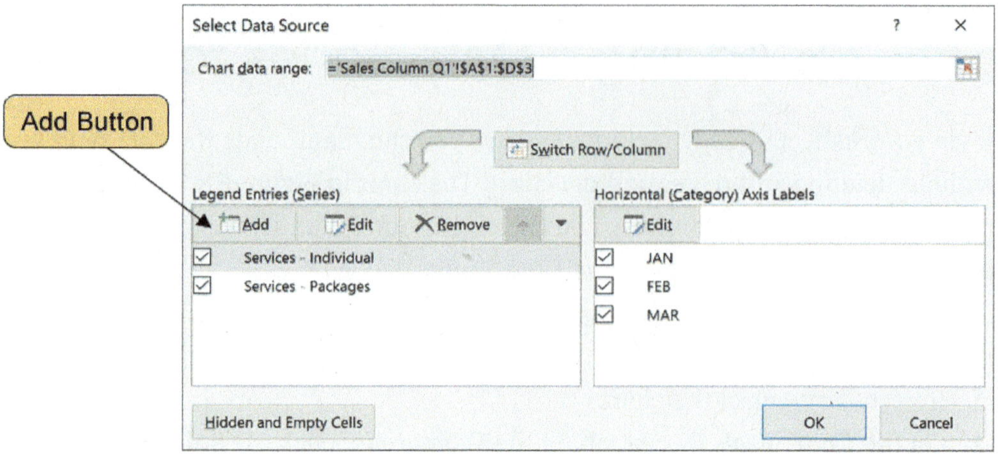

FIGURE EX 7.15

5. The *Edit Series* dialog opens. Enter the appropriate cell reference for the new series name in the *Series name* box. You can type or click a cell reference or enter text.
6. Click in the **Series values** box and delete the default entry. Click and drag the new cell range to enter it in the *Series values* box or type the new cell range.
7. Click **OK**.

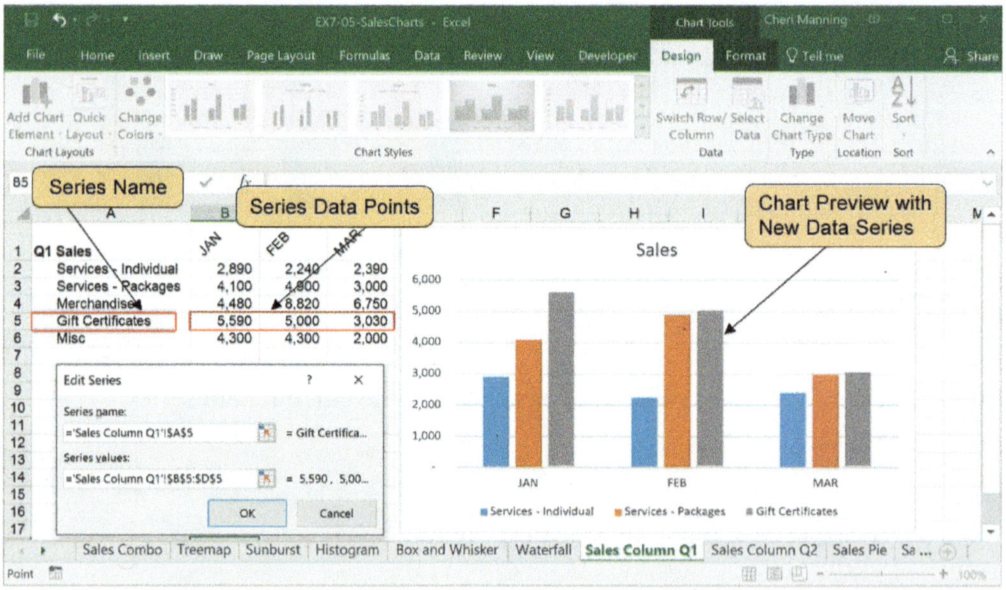

FIGURE EX 7.16

8. The *Select Data Source* dialog opens again with the new data series added. Click **OK** to add the data series to your chart.

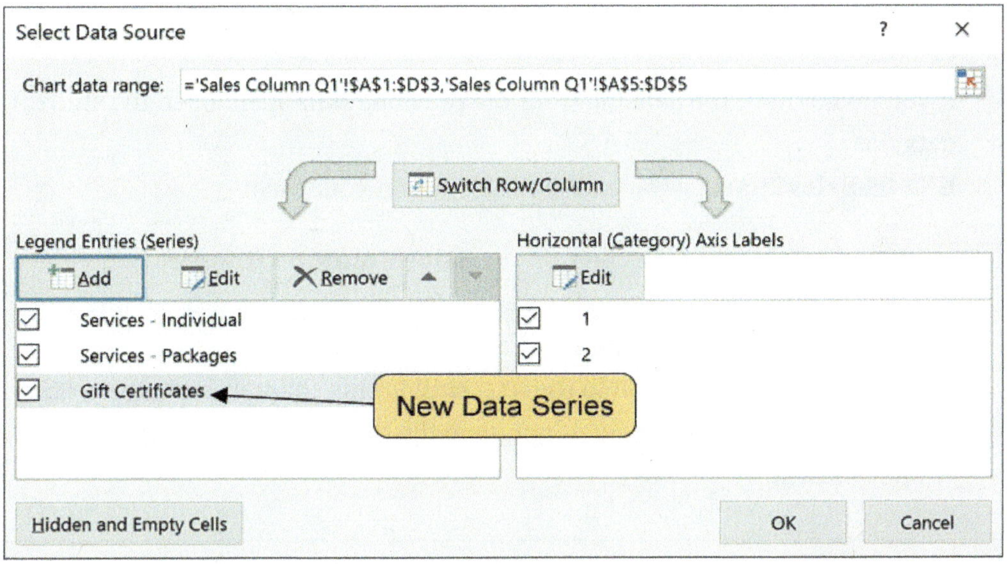

FIGURE EX 7.17

tips & tricks

You can type the cell references into the *Edit Series* dialog instead of clicking the cells in the worksheet, but this method can be tricky. You must include the sheet reference in both the series name and the series values. If you are adding multiple series, you must separate non-contiguous ranges with commas. It is much easier to click the cells to add the references to the dialog.

tell me more

If the source data for your chart are in contiguous cells, you can extend or reduce the source data range for the chart without opening the *Select Data Source* dialog. When the chart is selected, the source data are highlighted. Click one of the resize handles and drag to change the selected cell range.

another method

There are two other methods to open the *Select Data Source* dialog:

- Click the **Chart Filters** button that appears near the top right corner of the selected chart. Click **Select Data...** next to the *Apply* button at the bottom of the *Chart Filters* gallery.
- Right-click anywhere in the chart and click **Select Data...**

let me try *Live!*

If you do not have the data file from the previous skill open, open the student data file
EX7-05-SalesCharts and try this skill on your own:

1. If necessary, select the chart on the **Sales Column Q1** worksheet.
2. Add another data series to the chart. Use cell **A5** as the series name and cells **B5:D5** as the series values.
3. If you will be moving on to the next skill in this chapter, leave the workbook open to continue working. If not, save the file as directed by your instructor and close it.

Skill 7.6 Formatting a Data Point or a Data Series

When you apply a chart style or color from the *Chart Tools Design* tab, *Chart Styles* group, it is applied to the entire chart. If you want to override the formatting for an individual data point or data series, select the data point or data series, and then use the options from the *Chart Tools Format* tab, *Shape Styles* group instead.

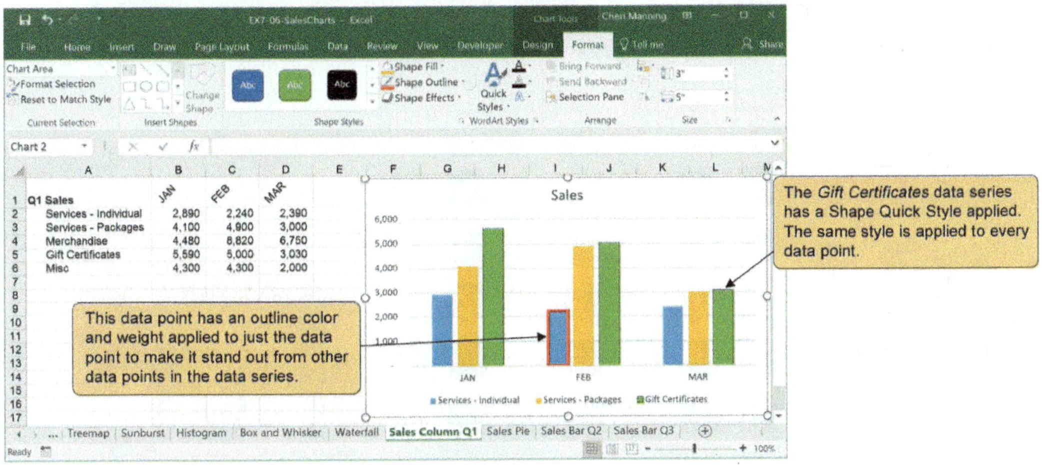

FIGURE EX 7.18

To select a data series, click any data point in the series.

To select a specific data point, click the data point once to select the entire data series, and then click the data point again to select just that data point. Do not double-click. Double-clicking a data point opens the *Data Series* task pane for the entire data series.

Before applying formatting changes, always verify that you have the correct data series or data point selected by checking the *Chart Elements* box on the *Chart Tools Format* tab, *Current Selection* group.

Shape Quick Styles allow you to apply a combination of formatting such as borders, rounded corners, and effects with a single command.

To apply a Shape Quick Style to a data point or data series:

1. Select the data point or data series you want to change.
2. On the *Chart Tools Format* tab, in the *Shape Styles* group, click the **More** button to expand the *Shape Quick Styles* gallery.

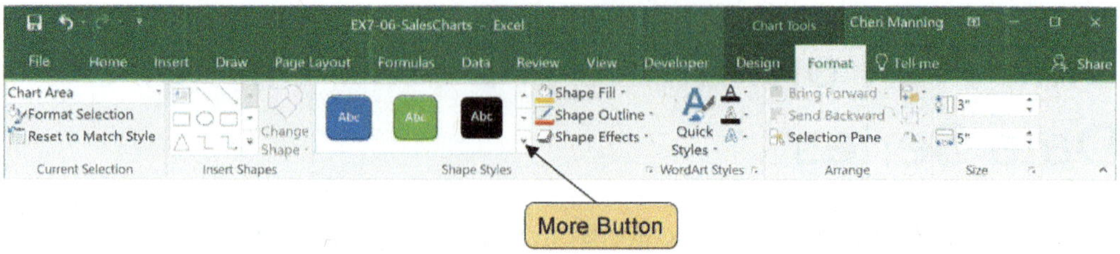

FIGURE EX 7.19

3. Click the style you want.

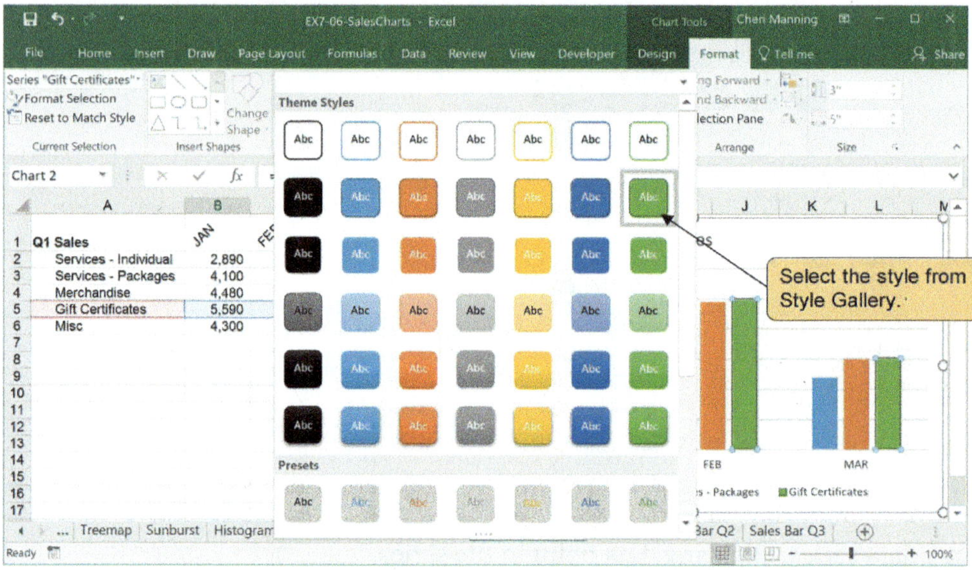

FIGURE EX 7.20

To apply a fill color to a data point or data series:

1. Select the data point or data series you want to change.
2. On the *Chart Tools Format* tab, in the *Shape Styles* group, click the **Shape Fill** button and then click the color you want.

From the *Shape Fill* menu, you can also apply a picture, gradient, or texture to a data series or data point.

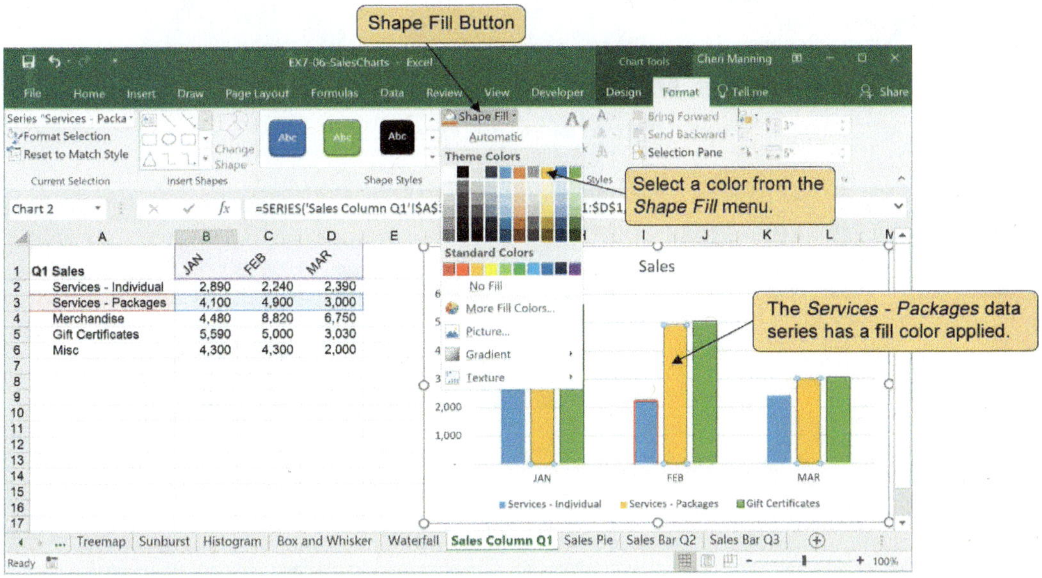

FIGURE EX 7.21

To apply an outline to a data point or data series:

1. Select the data point or data series you want to change.
2. On the *Chart Tools Format* tab, in the *Shape Styles* group, click the **Shape Outline** button, and click the color you want.

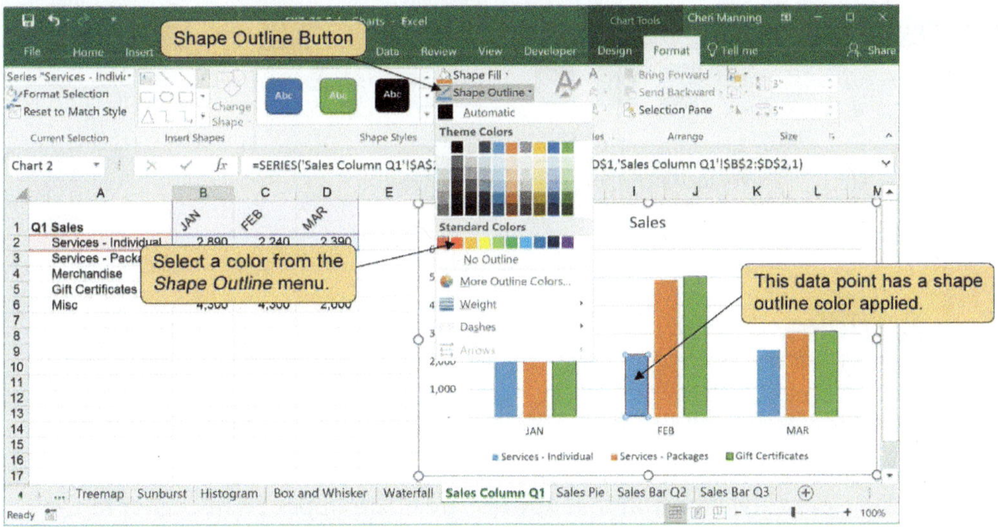

FIGURE EX 7.22

3. To change the outline line width, click the **Shape Outline** button, point to **Weight**, and select the width you want.

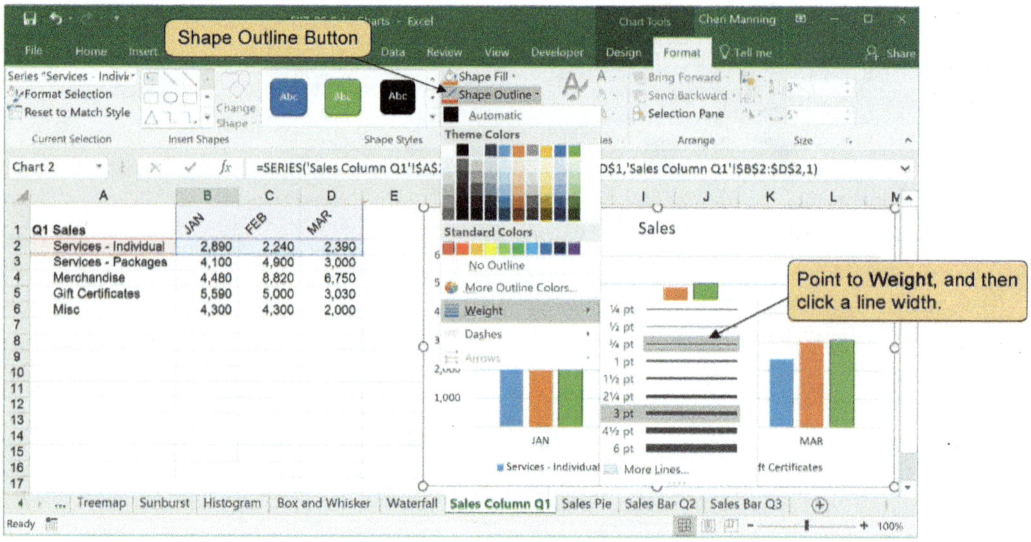

FIGURE EX 7.23

To undo changes and return the selected element to the default chart style:

1. Select the data point or data series to want to revert to the original chart style.
2. On the *Chart Tools Format* tab, in the *Current Selection* group, click the **Reset to Match Style** button.

FIGURE EX 7.24

tips & tricks

- To change the color of a data series in a line chart, change the outline, not the fill.
- The *Chart Styles* button that appears near the upper right corner of the selected chart applies to the entire chart, even if you have a single data series or point selected.

another method

You can change the fill and outline options from the *Format Data Point* or *Format Data Series* task pane:

1. Select the data point or data series, right-click, and select **Format Data Point...** or **Format Data Series...**
2. Click the **Fill & Line** button.
3. To change the fill color or style, click **Fill** to expand that section. Click the **Fill Color** button to open the color palette and then click the color you want. Leave the fill type as *Automatic* unless you want to change to a gradient, picture, or pattern.
4. To change the outline, click **Border** to expand that section. Click the **Outline Color** button to open the color palette and then click the color you want. Click in the **Width** box and adjust the outline weight by typing a value or using the increase/decrease arrows. Leave the line type as *Automatic* unless you want to change to a gradient.

let me try *Live!*

If you do not have the data file from the previous skill open, open the student data file
EX7-06-SalesCharts and try this skill on your own:

1. On the *Sales Column Q1* chart, select the **Gift Certificates** data series and apply the **Colored Fill - Green, Accent 6** shape style (the last style in the second row).
2. Select just the **FEB** data point in the *Services - Individual* data series and change the outline color to **Red** (the second color from the left in the row of standard colors).
3. Change the outline width to **3 pt**.
4. Select the **Services - Packages** data series and change the fill color to **Gold, Accent 4** (the third color from the right in the top row of theme colors).
5. Switch to the **Sales Pie** worksheet and reset the **chart area** to match the chart style.
6. If you will be moving on to the next skill in this chapter, leave the workbook open to continue working. If not, save the file as directed by your instructor and close it.

Skill 7.7 Emphasizing a Data Point in a Pie Chart

Remember that pie charts work best when you want to evaluate data as part of a whole. Each "slice" represents a data point. To emphasize a single data point, you can rotate the pie chart to place the slice where you want it and separate ("explode") that slice from the rest of the pie.

In Figure EX 7.25, the chart has been rotated to place the *Merchandise* data point at the right side of the chart and then that slice has been exploded away from the rest of the pie to give it emphasis.

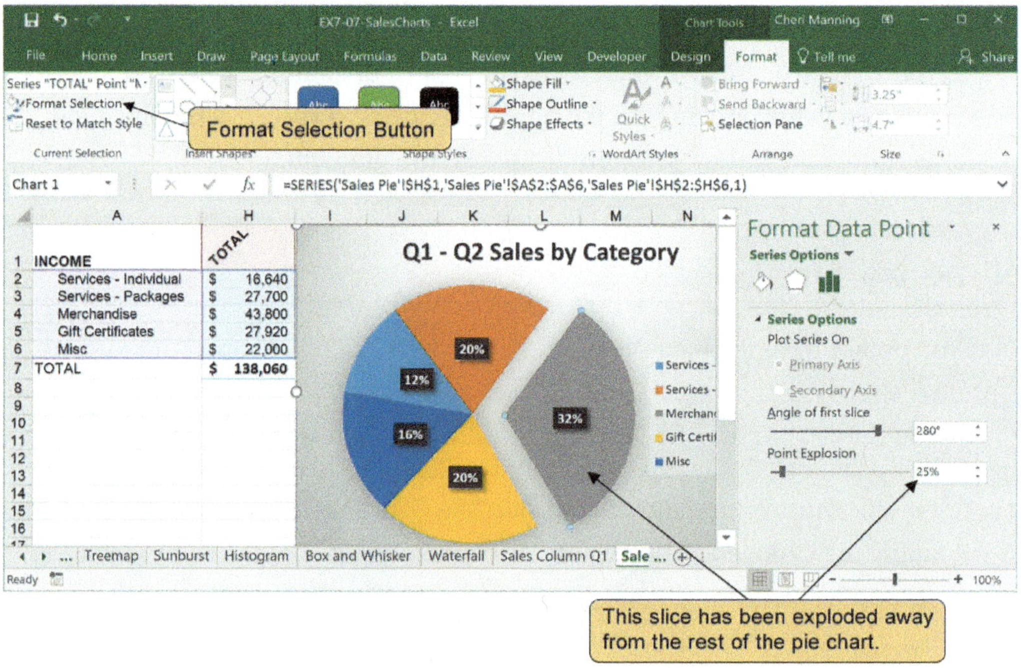

FIGURE EX 7.25

To rotate the pie chart:

1. Click the pie once to select the data series, and then click the data point (slice) you want to emphasize.
2. On the *Chart Tools Format* tab, in the *Current Selection* group, click the **Format Selection** button.
3. The *Format Data Point* task pane opens to the *Series Options* panel. In the *Angle of first slice* box, type the degree of rotation for the chart (from 0 to 360) and press Enter. You can also use the *Angle of first slice* slider to change the rotation, but it can be difficult to select a precise angle.

To explode a single data point:

1. If it is not already open, open the *Format Data Point* task pane.
2. In the *Series Options* panel, type a percentage in the *Point Explosion* box and press Enter. The higher the percentage of explosion, the further away the slice will appear. You can use the *Point Explosion* slider to change the degree of explosion, but it can be difficult to select a precise degree of explosion.

tips & tricks

You can rotate a pie chart without selecting a specific data point first. Double-click anywhere in the pie to open the *Format Data Series* task pane and then use the *Angle of first slice* option to rotate the chart.

tell me more

To apply formatting to an individual data point in a pie chart, use the options in the *Chart Tools Format* tab, *Shape Styles* group or in the *Fill & Line* panel of the *Format Data Series* task pane. Refer to the skill *Formatting a Data Point or a Data Series* for more information.

another method

- If the pie is already selected, double-clicking a single slice will open the *Format Data Point* task pane.
- To format a single data point, right-click the pie slice representing the data point and select **Format Data Point...** to open the *Format Data Point* task pane.
- To explode a data point away from the rest of the pie chart, click the slice once to select it, and then drag the mouse so the slice moves away from the rest of the pie.

let me try *Live!*

If you do not have the data file from the previous skill open, open the student data file **EX7-07-SalesCharts** and try this skill on your own:

1. Go to the **Sales Pie** worksheet and select just the **Merchandise** data point.
2. Rotate the pie chart exactly **280°** so the **Merchandise** data point appears at the right side of the chart near the legend.
3. Explode the *Merchandise* data point by exactly **25%** to move it slightly away from the rest of the pie chart.
4. If you will be moving on to the next skill in this chapter, leave the workbook open to continue working. If not, save the file as directed by your instructor and close it.

Skill 7.8 Formatting Other Chart Elements

Text-specific formatting options are available for chart elements that include text (the title, legend, data labels, and data table). **WordArt** styles are a preset combination of fill, outline, and text effects that can be applied to any text element.

To apply a WordArt style to a text chart element:

1. Click the chart element to select it. (Always double-check the *Chart Elements* box on the *Chart Tools Format* tab, *Current Selection* group to ensure that the correct chart element is selected.)
2. On the *Chart Tools Format* tab, in the *WordArt Styles* group, click the **WordArt Quick Styles** button to expand the gallery. Click the style you want.

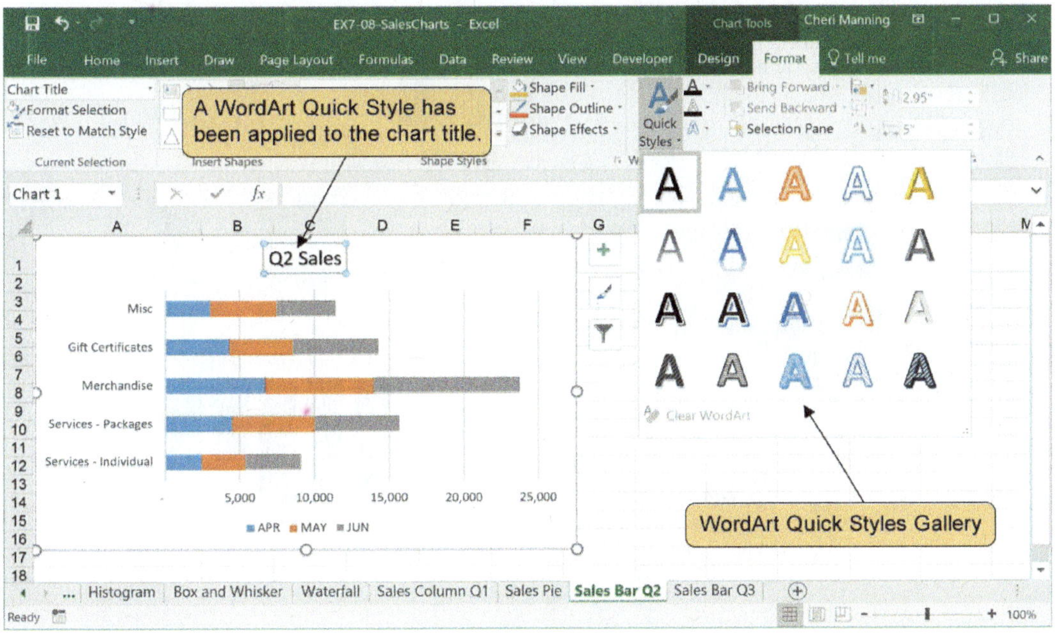

FIGURE EX 7.26

You can apply individual formatting options to text elements using the other buttons in the *WordArt Styles* group:

- To change the font color, click the **Text Fill** button and select a color.
- To apply a border around each text letter or number, click the **Text Outline** button and select a color. To change the outline line width, point to **Width** and select an option. To change the line style, point to **Dashes** and select an option.
- To apply a text effect, click the **Text Effects** button, point to the type of effect you want (**Shadow**, **Reflection**, or **Glow**), and select an option.

If you want to change the font, font size, or other font formatting characteristics, use the options available on the *Home* tab, in the *Font* group.

To add visual interest to the chart, try applying a gradient to the chart background. A gradient transitions the background from a dark shade to light shade of a single color.

1. If necessary, click an empty area of the chart to select the chart area.
2. On the *Chart Tools Format* tab, in the *Shape Styles* group, click the **Shape Fill** button, point to **Gradient**, and select the gradient you want. Be careful to choose a gradient that doesn't overwhelm the chart data.

In Figure EX 7.27, one of the light gradient variations has been applied to the chart area, so the *Gradient* gallery includes only the light variations, not both the light and dark variations as it would if a gradient had not yet been applied.

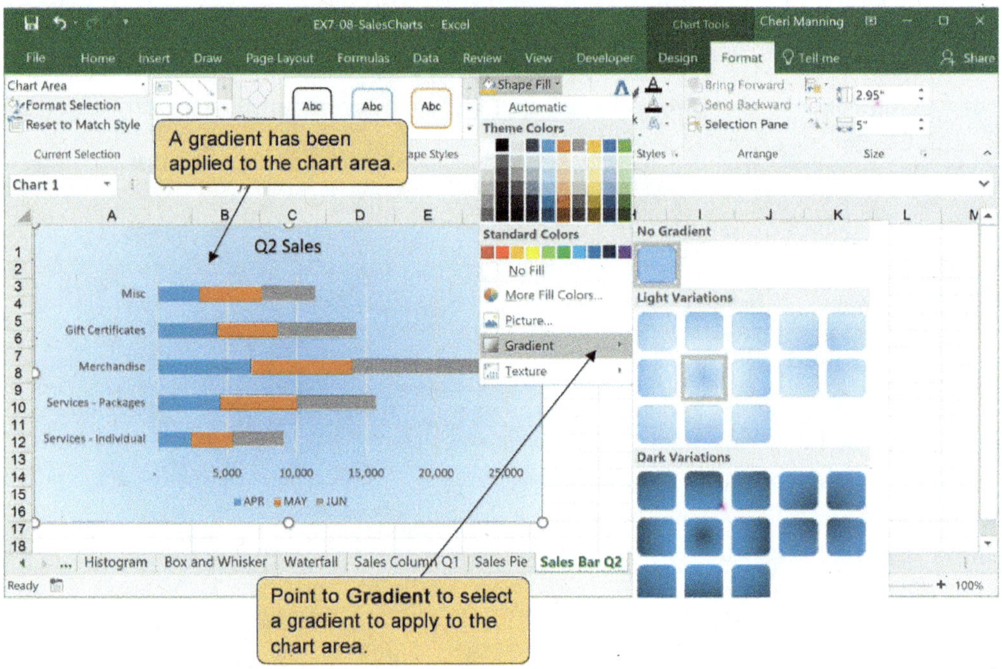

FIGURE EX 7.27

Chart gridlines help the user estimate the values represented by the data markers. They can be an important element in the chart, but they should not be the primary visual focus. Selecting the gridlines can be tricky; it may be easier to use the *Chart Elements* list. In the *Chart Elements* list, the vertical axis gridlines are the lines that run horizontally parallel to the x axis, and the horizontal axis gridlines run up-and-down parallel to the y axis. Pie charts do not have gridlines.

To change the style of the gridlines:

1. On the *Chart Tools Format* tab, in the *Current Selection* group, expand the *Chart Elements* box and select the gridlines.
2. On the *Chart Tools Format* tab, in the *Shape Styles* group, click the **Shape Outline** button and click the color you want.
3. You can also change the style of the lines. Click the **Shape Outline** button again, point to the type of style you want to change (**Width**, **Dashes**, or **Arrows**), and select an option.

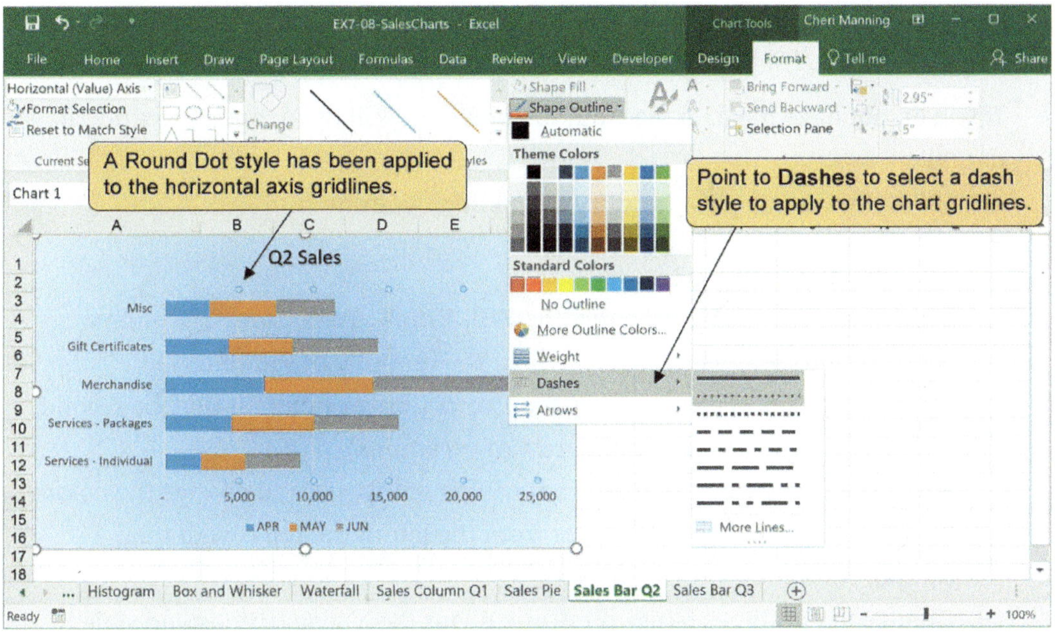

FIGURE EX 7.28

tips & tricks

On the *Chart Tools Format* tab, in the *Current Selection* group, the *Chart Elements* box displays the name of the chart element that is currently selected. This can be helpful if you need to ensure that you have selected the chart area, the plot area, or another chart element. To select a specific chart element, expand the **Chart Elements** list and select the chart element you want to select.

tell me more

From the *Chart Tools Format* tab, *Shape Style* group, *Fill* button, you can apply a texture or a picture to the chart background. Use these options sparingly, as they can distract from the chart data.

another method

You can use the *Format* task pane for any chart element to apply formatting. Select the chart element, and then on the *Chart Tools Format* tab, in the *Current Selection* group, click the **Format Selection** button to open the appropriate *Format* task pane. Each chart element has its own formatting options, but they are all similar.

let me try *Live!*

If you do not have the data file from the previous skill open, open the student data file
EX7-08-SalesCharts and try this skill on your own:

1. Go to the **Sales Bar Q2** worksheet.
2. Select the **chart title** and apply the **Fill: Black, Text Color 1; Shadow** WordArt Quick Style (the first style in the first row of the gallery).
3. Select the **chart area** and apply the **From Center** gradient fill (the second style from the left in the second row of variations).
4. Select the **horizontal (value) major axis gridlines** and change the color to **Blue, Accent 1** (the fifth color from the left in the top row of theme colors).
5. Change the gridlines to use the **Round Dot** dash style (the second style in the list).
6. If you will be moving on to the next skill in this chapter, leave the workbook open to continue working. If not, save the file as directed by your instructor and close it.

Skill 7.9 Creating a Chart Template

Chart templates can be used to quickly apply a set of chart formatting saved from an existing chart. If you find yourself making the same chart formatting changes over and over again, consider saving the chart as a chart template.

To create a chart template:

1. Right-click an empty part of the chart area and select **Save as Template...** to open the *Save Chart Template* dialog.

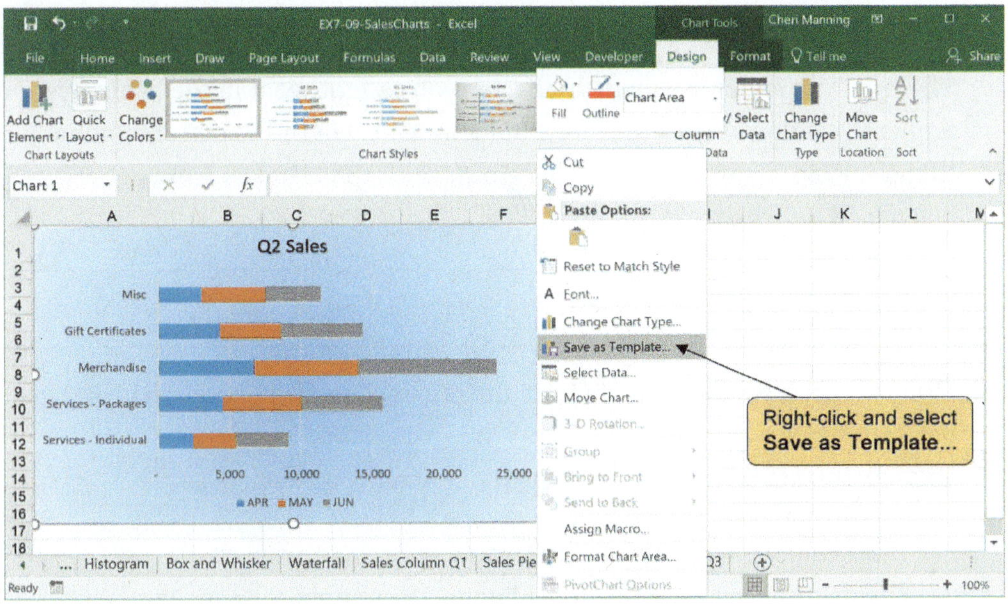

FIGURE EX 7.29

2. Excel automatically sets the location to the correct folder and the file type to *.crtx*. The *Save as type* box displays **Chart Template Files**.
3. Type a meaningful name for the template in the *File name* box.
4. Click **Save**.

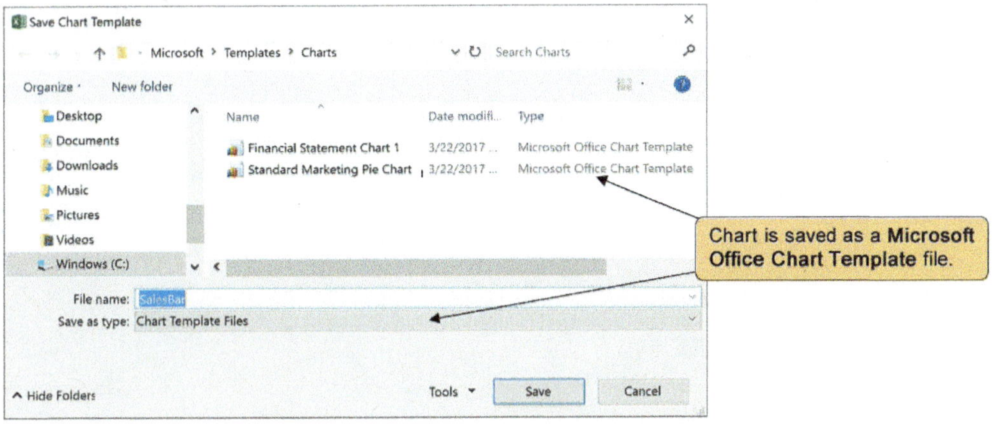

FIGURE EX 7.30

tips & tricks

In Excel 2010, you could create a chart template from a button on the *Chart Tools Design* tab, but this button has been removed in later versions of Excel.

tell me more

By default, Excel saves the chart template file to your local drive in the *Users* folder:

C:\Users*[your user name here]*\AppData\Roaming\Microsoft\Templates\Charts

The *AppData* folder is usually hidden so you cannot see it in the Windows Explorer window unless you show hidden items. On the Explorer window Ribbon, *View* tab, in the *Show/hide* group, click the **Hidden items** check box to add a checkmark.

let me try *Live!*

If you do not have the data file from the previous skill open, open the student data file
EX7-09-SalesCharts and try this skill on your own:

1. If necessary, on the *Sales Bar Q2* worksheet, select the chart.
2. Create a new chart template and name the template: `SalesBar`
3. If you will be moving on to the next skill in this chapter, leave the workbook open to continue working. If not, save the file as directed by your instructor and close it.

Skill 7.10 Applying a Chart Template

Once you have saved a chart template, it is easy to create a new chart with the options and formatting saved in the template. Creating a new chart from a chart template applies the chart type, shows selected chart elements, and applies formatting to the chart. It does not impact the data selected for the chart.

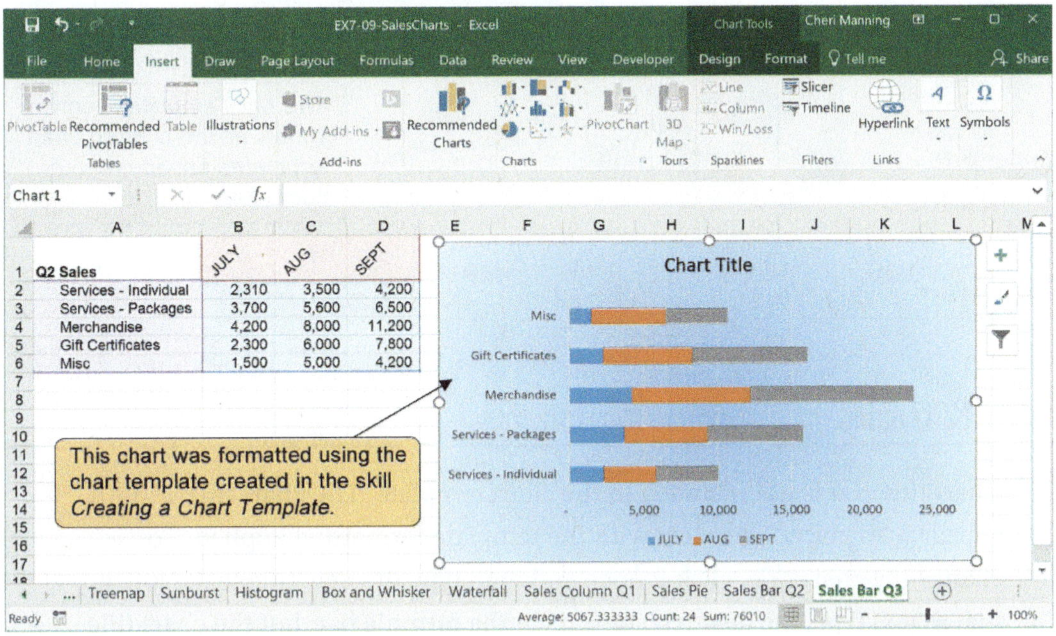

FIGURE EX 7.31

To use the chart template:

1. Select the data you want to visualize in the chart.
2. On the *Insert* tab, in the *Charts* group, click the **Recommended Charts** button to open the *Insert Chart* dialog.
3. Click the **All Charts** tab.
4. Click **Templates** to view the chart templates you have saved.
5. Click the chart template you want and click **OK**.

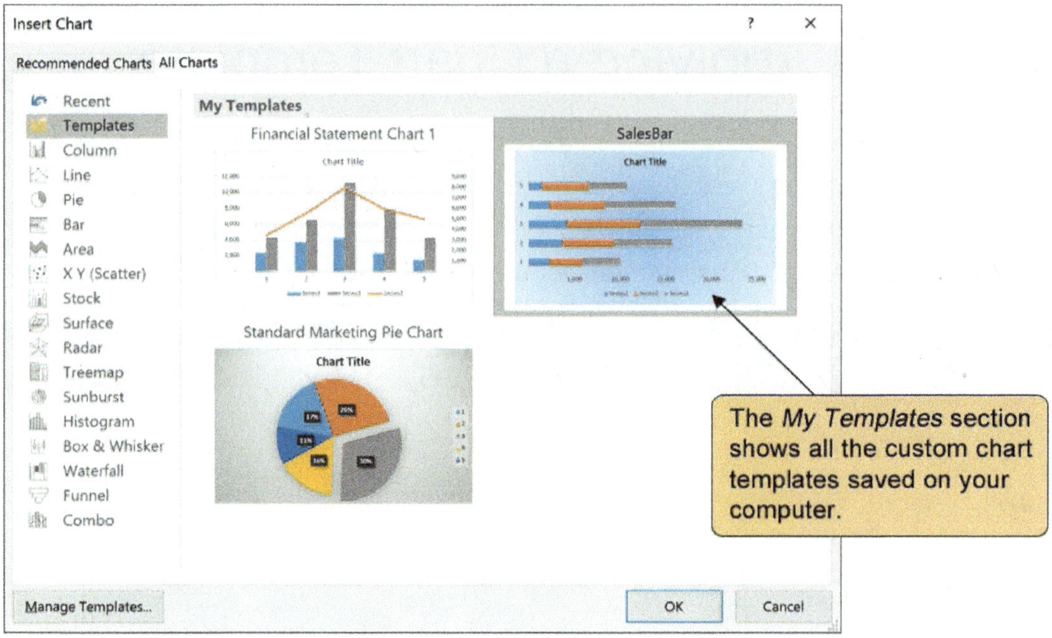

FIGURE EX 7.32

tips & tricks

Chart title text is not included in the chart template. The chart title will appear with placeholder text with the template formatting applied. To change the chart title, click it once and then type the new title text. Notice that as you type, the new text appears in the formula bar, but the chart title text does not change. Press Enter to change the chart title to the new text.

tell me more

You can also apply a custom chart template to an existing chart.

1. On the *Chart Tools Design* tab, in the *Type* group, click the **Change Chart Type** button to open the *Change Chart Type* dialog.
2. Click **Templates.**
3. Select the template you want to apply and click **OK**.

another method

The *Insert Chart* dialog can be opened by clicking any chart button in the *Charts* group, and then selecting the **More Charts** option from the end of the menu.

let me try *Live!*

If you do not have the data file from the previous skill open, open the student data file
EX7-10-SalesCharts and try this skill on your own:

1. Go to the **Sales Bar Q3** worksheet and if necessary, select cells **A1:D6**.
2. Create a chart from the selected cells using the **SalesBar** chart template.
3. Save the file as directed by your instructor and close it.

Skill 7.11 Adding and Removing Trendlines

A **trendline** is a line that overlays the chart and shows the expected data points based on mathematical analysis of the data. A simple linear trendline calculates the difference between the first two data points and can be used to predict future data points based on that difference.

To add a trendline:

1. Click the chart once to select it.
2. Click the **Chart Elements** button that appears near the upper right corner of the chart.
3. Click the **Trendline** check box to add a checkmark.
4. If the chart has more than one data series, Excel will display a dialog and prompt you to select the series to which the trendline should be added. Select the data series for the trendline and then click **OK**.
5. Excel adds the trendline to the chart using the default trendline type and formatting.

To remove a trendline:

1. Click the chart once to select it.
2. Click the **Chart Elements** button that appears near the upper right corner of the chart.
3. Click the **Trendline** check box to remove the checkmark.
4. If the chart has more than one trendline, Excel will display a dialog and prompt you to select the series from which the trendline should be removed.

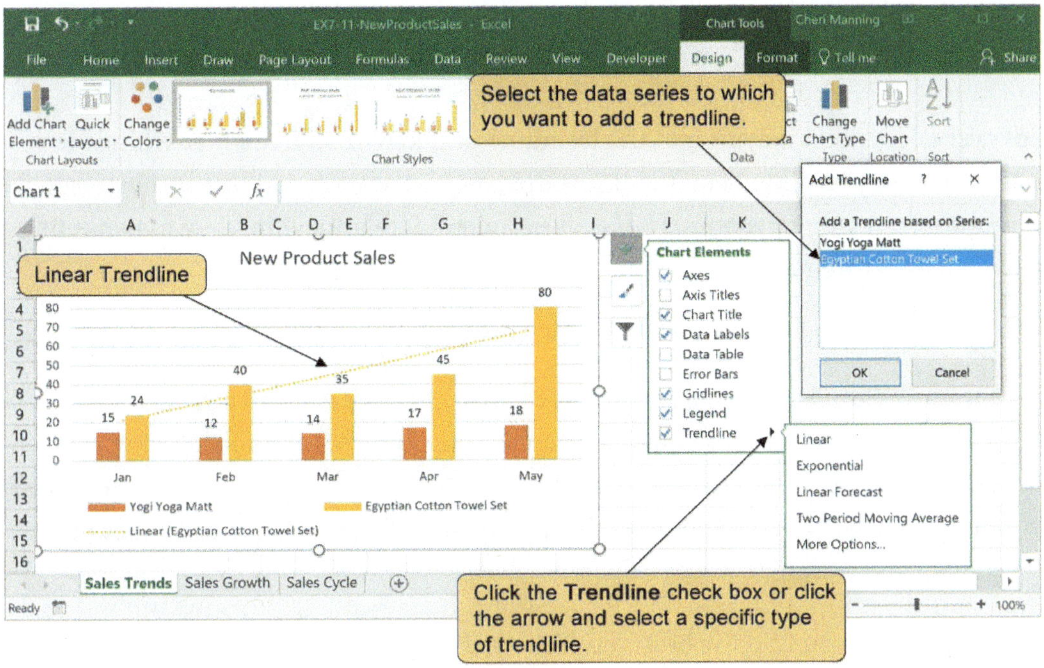

FIGURE EX 7.33

tips & tricks

You can add multiple trendlines to a chart, but you must add them one at a time.

another method

To remove the trendline, right-click the trendline and select **Delete**.

let me try *Live!*

Open the student data file **EX7-11-NewProductSales** and try this skill on your own:

1. On the *Sales Trends* worksheet, select the chart and remove the existing trendline.
2. Add a new trendline for the *Egyptian Cotton Towel Set* data series. Use the default trendline type and formatting.
3. If you will be moving on to the next skill in this chapter, leave the workbook open to continue working. If not, save the file as directed by your instructor and close it.

Skill 7.12 Changing Trendline Options

Not every data point may fit into the trendline perfectly. You'll see that while a few data points may be directly on the line, others will be scattered above and below it. For example, if your data points have an exponential relationship, they may not fit well on a linear trendline.

The trendline types you will use most often are:

- **Linear**—Best suited to data that increase (or decrease) at a steady rate.
- **Exponential**—Used for data that increase (or decrease) at an increasing rate.
- **Logarithmic**—Best fits data that increase or decrease rapidly and then levels off.
- **Moving average**—Use for data that swing up and down. Set the number of periods to average.

One tool to help you find the best trendline type for your data is the R-squared value. The **R-squared value** is a statistical measurement of the how well the data fit the trendline. It is a number between 0 and 1; the closer the trendline's R-squared value is to 1, the better the fit. In Figure EX 7.34, the linear trendline has an R-squared value of *0.7644*. You can see that the points on the trendline do not match the actual data point values very well.

FIGURE EX 7.34

Once you have added a trendline, you can display its R-squared value and change the trendline type through the *Format Trendline* task pane:

1. Click the trendline once to select it.
2. On the *Chart Tools Format* tab, in the *Current Selection* group, click the **Format Selection** button to open the *Format Trendline* task pane.
3. To display the R-squared value, click the **Show R-squared value on chart** check box. (Scroll to the bottom of the task pane if necessary.)
4. To change the type of trendline, click one of the radio buttons at the top of the task pane. Notice that the R-squared value changes when you change the trendline type.

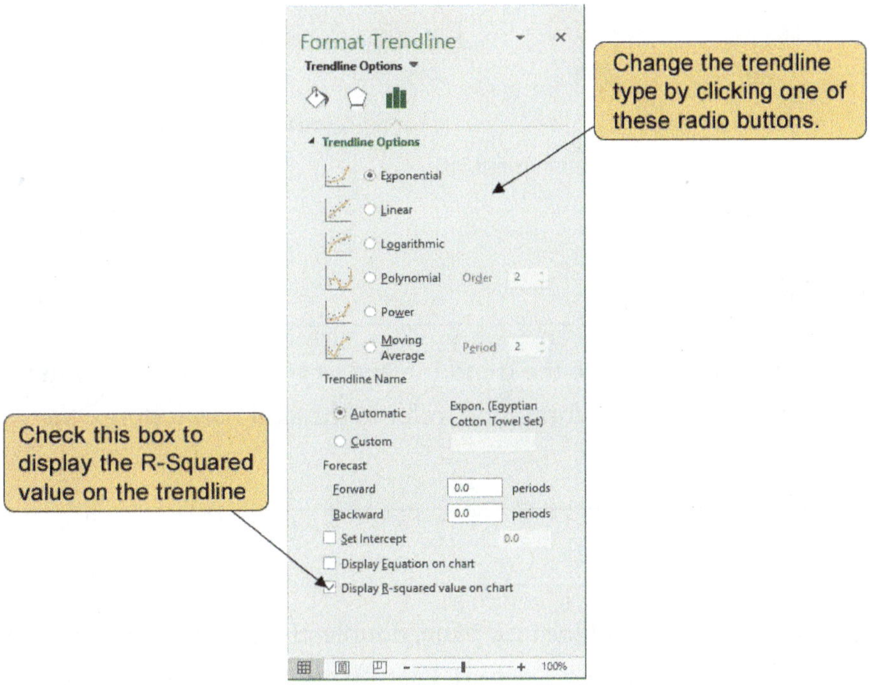

FIGURE EX 7.35

To undo any changes you have made, use the *Undo* command.

In Figure EX 7.36, the trendline has been changed to exponential and new the R-squared value is *0.8311*, indicating a better (although still not great) fit.

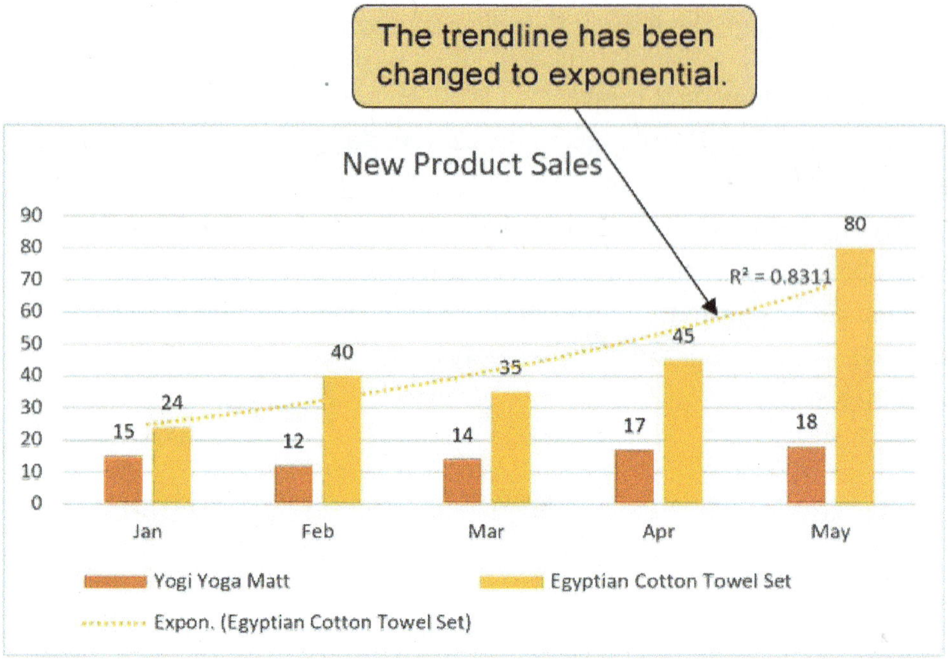

FIGURE EX 7.36

tell me **more**

You can apply formatting to the trendline just as you would to any other chart element. For more information, refer to the skill *Formatting Other Chart Elements*.

another method

To open the *Format Trendline* task pane, double-click the trendline or right-click the trendline and select **Format Trendline...**

let me try *Live!*

If you do not have the data file from the previous skill open, open the student data file
EX7-12-NewProductSales and try this skill on your own:

1. On the *Sales Trends* worksheet, select the trendline.
2. Display the **R-squared** value for the trendline.
3. Change the trendline to **exponential**.
4. If you will be moving on to the next skill in this chapter, leave the workbook open to continue working. If not, save the file as directed by your instructor and close it.

Skill 7.13 Forecasting Values on a Trendline

Trendlines can show the line along which future data points would be expected based on different statistical growth patterns. This forecasting of future values is also known as **regression analysis**.

Once you have added a trendline, you can extend the trendline to estimate values forward or backward through the *Format Trendline* task pane.

1. Click the trendline once to select it.
2. On the *Chart Tools Format* tab, in the *Current Selection* group, click the **Format Selection** button to open the *Format Trendline* task pane.
3. To extend the trendline and forecast future values, enter a value in the **Forward** box for the number of periods you want to forecast forward. (You may need to scroll to the bottom of the task pane.) Press Enter or Tab to accept the value. You can extend the trendline backward to estimate values for previous periods by entering a value in the *Backward* box.
4. To undo any changes you have made, use the *Undo* command.

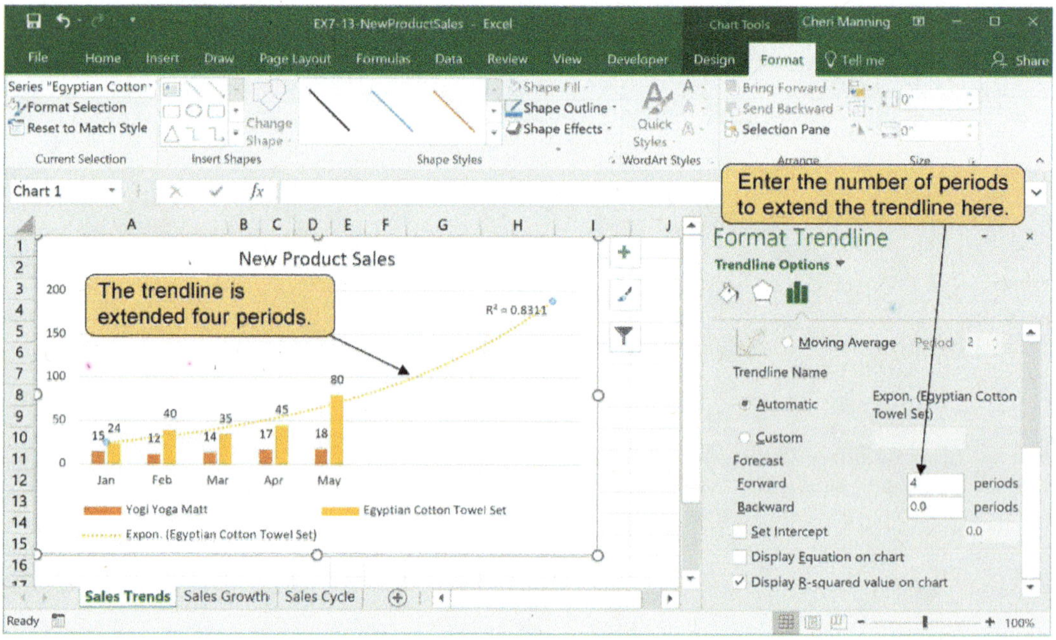

FIGURE EX 7.37

tips & tricks

Mark Twain is often quoted as saying "Facts are stubborn things, but statistics are pliable." As you can see in Figure EX 7.37, forecasting future values with a trendline can be misleading. Accurate forecasting requires having a large enough data set to plot the trendline with a high level of confidence. In this case, five months' sales are probably not enough to accurately predict exponential sales growth for the next three months.

another method

To open the *Format Trendline* task pane, double-click the trendline or right-click the trendline and select **Format Trendline...**

let me try *Live!*

If you do not have the data file from the previous skill open, open the student data file
EX7-13-NewProductSales and try this skill on your own:

1. On the *Sales Trends* worksheet, select the trendline.
2. Extend the trendline to forecast forward three periods.
3. If you will be moving on to the next skill in this chapter, leave the workbook open to continue working. If not, save the file as directed by your instructor and close it.

Skill 7.14 Changing the Sparkline Type

Chapter 5 introduced the concept of Sparklines. Recall that Sparklines represent a series of data values as an individual graphic within a single cell. As you update the underlying data series, the Sparklines update immediately. Sparklines can be helpful in visualizing data patterns. After inserting Sparklines, you may find that you need to change the Sparkline type to present a clearer picture of your data.

To change the Sparkline type:

1. Click one of the cells containing Sparklines to activate the *Sparkline Tools Design* tab. If necessary, click the tab.
2. In the *Type* group, click the **Line**, **Column**, or **Win/Loss** button to change the Sparklines to a new format.

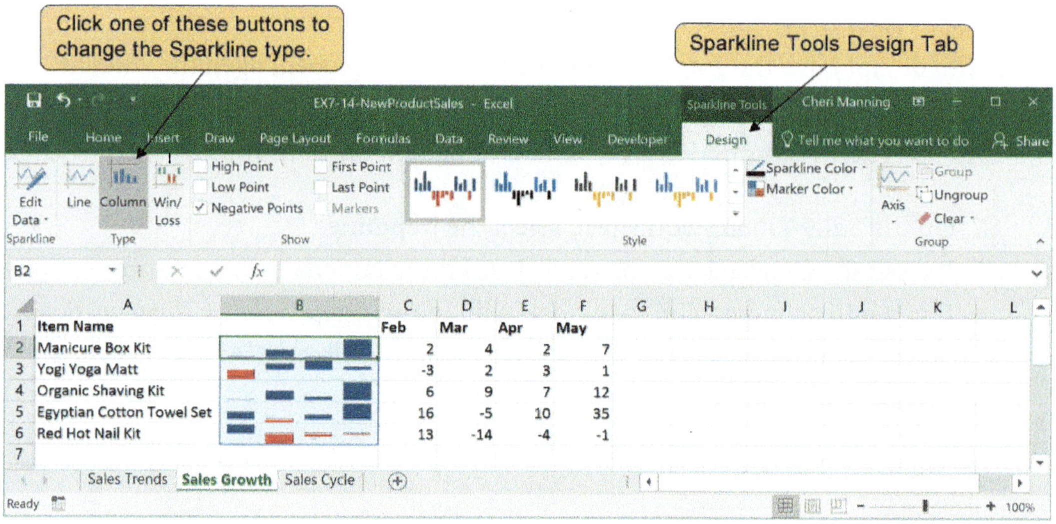

FIGURE EX 7.38

tips & tricks

If you want to know more about the concept of sparklines, check out Edward Tufte's Web site at http://www.edwardtufte.com. Edward Tufte is a pioneer in the field of data visualization and information graphics. He discusses sparklines in depth in his book *Beautiful Evidence*.

tell me **more**

To change the data range or the location range for the Sparklines:

1. Click the **Edit Data** button at the far left side of the *Sparkline Tools Design* tab and select **Edit Group Location & Data**. This opens the *Edit Sparklines* dialog.
2. Edit the cell range in the *Data Range* and *Location Range* boxes as necessary.
3. Click **OK**.

let me try *Live!*

If you do not have the data file from the previous skill open, open the student data file
EX7-14-NewProductSales and try this skill on your own:

1. On the *Sales Growth* worksheet, if necessary, click cell **B2** to select the group of Sparklines.
2. Change the Sparklines from lines to columns.
3. If you will be moving on to the next skill in this chapter, leave the workbook open to continue working. If not, save the file as directed by your instructor and close it.

Skill 7.15 Adding Markers to Sparklines

Markers are visual representations of data points on a Sparkline. Adding markers can help identify the data points or emphasize high or low points.

To add markers to Sparklines, first click anywhere in the Sparklines, and then check the options you want in the *Sparkline Tools Design* tab, *Show* group:

- To add data point markers for every data point, click the **Markers** check box.
- To remove data point markers, click the **Markers** check box again to remove the checkmark.
- To add a marker for just the highest value, click the **High Point** check box.

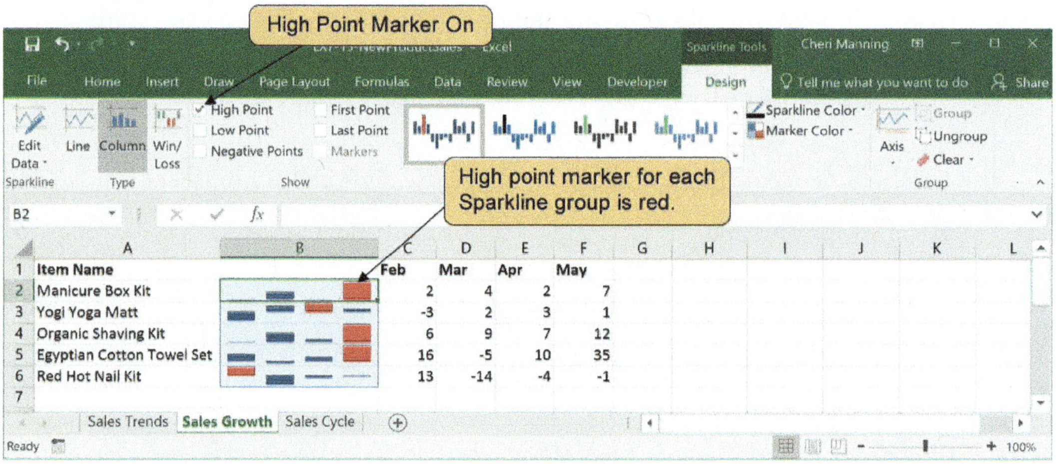

FIGURE EX 7.39

tell me more

For information about formatting Sparklines, refer to the skill *Applying Quick Styles and Other Formatting to Sparklines.*

let me try *Live!*

If you do not have the data file from the previous skill open, open the student data file **EX7-15-NewProductSales** and try this skill on your own:

1. On the *Sales Growth* worksheet, if necessary, click cell **B2** to select the group of Sparklines.
2. Remove the markers for the negative vales.
3. Show markers for just the highest values in this Sparkline group.
4. If you will be moving on to the next skill in this chapter, leave the workbook open to continue working. If not, save the file as directed by your instructor and close it.

Skill 7.16 Applying Quick Styles and Other Formatting to Sparklines

Apply a **Sparkline Quick Style** to change the Sparkline color and marker color(s) at once. You can also specify color for just the Sparklines or individual markers.

To change the Quick Style applied to the Sparklines:

- Click one of the cells containing Sparklines to activate the *Sparkline Tools Design* tab. If necessary, click the tab.
- In the *Style* group, if the Quick Style you want is not visible on the Ribbon, click the **More** button to expand the gallery.
- Click a style to apply it to the Sparklines.

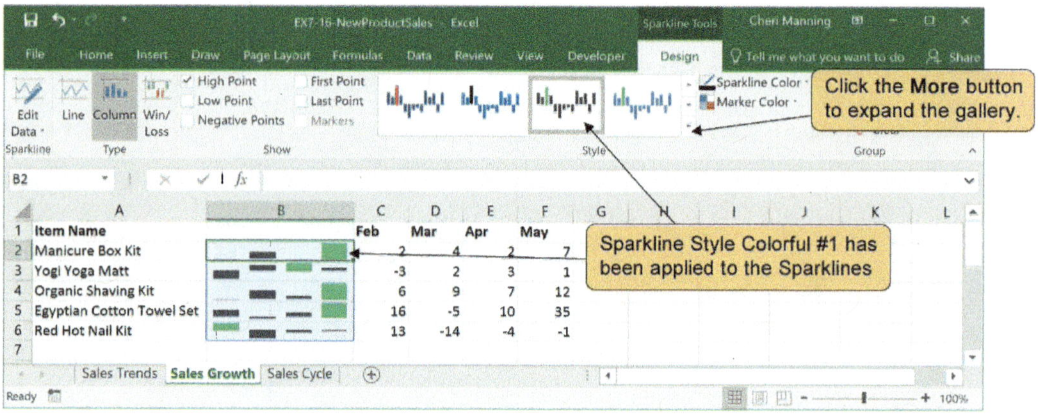

FIGURE EX 7.40

When you create Sparklines, the cells containing the Sparklines are grouped together so any formatting changes you make affect them all. You can remove a single Sparkline from the group to make formatting changes to only that Sparkline.

To change the Sparkline color or the marker color for a single Sparkline:

1. Click the individual Sparkline you want to format separately from the group.
2. On the *Sparkline Tools Design* tab, in the *Group* group, click the **Ungroup** button. Now when you make formatting changes, only the single Sparkline is affected.
3. To change the Sparkline color, on the *Sparkline Tools Design* tab, in the *Style* group, click the **Sparkline Color** button arrow and select the color you want from the color palette.

4. To change the marker color, on the *Sparkline Tools Design* tab, in the *Style* group, click the **Marker Color** button. Point to the marker you want to change (such as **Negative Points**) and then select the color you want from the color palette.

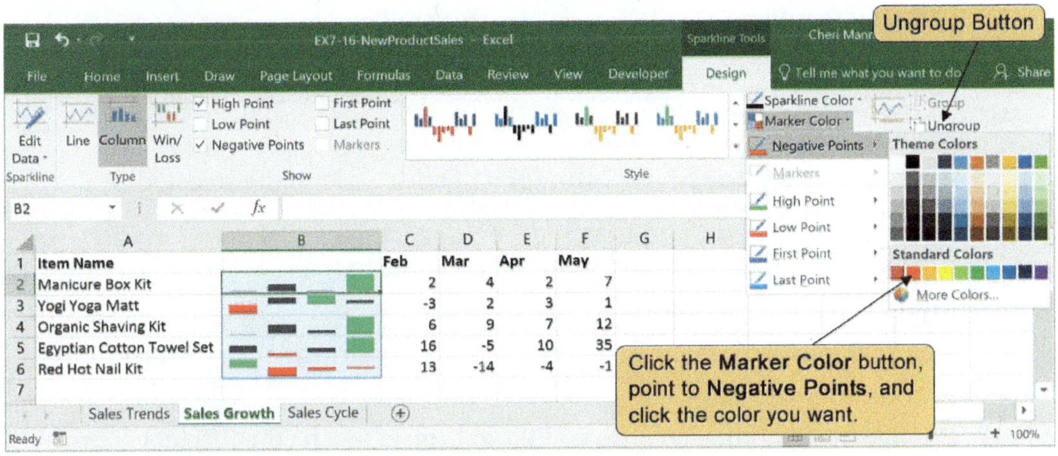

FIGURE EX 7.41

tips & tricks

- If you do not select a single Sparkline and remove it from the group before making changes from the *Sparkline Color* button or the *Marker Color* button, the changes will be applied to all the Sparklines in the group.
- If you click the *Sparkline Color* button instead of the button arrow, the most recently used color will be applied automatically to the selected Sparkline(s).
- The *Ungroup* button appears inactive when the selected Sparkline has already been ungrouped.

let me try *Live!*

If you do not have the data file from the previous skill open, open the student data file **EX7-16-NewProductSales** and try this skill on your own:

1. On the *Sales Growth* worksheet, if necessary, click cell **B2** to select the group of Sparklines.
2. Apply the **Sparkline Style Colorful #1** Quick Style to the selected Sparkline group.
3. Change the marker color for all negative points to red (the second color from the left in the row of standard colors).
4. Ungroup the Sparkline in cell **B5** so you can apply formatting to just that Sparkline.
5. Change the Sparkline color in cell **B5** to **Light Green** (the fifth color from the left in the row of standard colors).
6. If you will be moving on to the next skill in this chapter, leave the workbook open to continue working. If not, save the file as directed by your instructor and close it.

from the perspective of . . .

SPORTING GOODS STORE PURCHASING MANAGER

We chart data from our checkout process using trendlines and Sparklines so we can see which merchandise is in high demand. Our inventory keeps current because we watch the trends over time. We can now better predict which items to order for each upcoming season.

Skill 7.17 Inserting a Picture

You can insert a picture you created in another program into your worksheet. There are many graphic formats Excel will accept, including those commonly used in Web pages such as JPEG, PNG, and GIF. When you insert a picture into an Excel worksheet, the images are embedded objects, meaning they become part of the workbook. Changing the source file will not change or affect the image in the workbook.

You can insert pictures stored on your local hard drive, connected media storage (such as a network drive or a USB key), or from your OneDrive.

To insert a picture from a local file:

- On the *Insert* tab, in the *Illustrations* group, click the **Pictures** button.
- The *Insert Picture* dialog opens.
- If necessary, navigate to the file location. Select the file and click **Insert**.

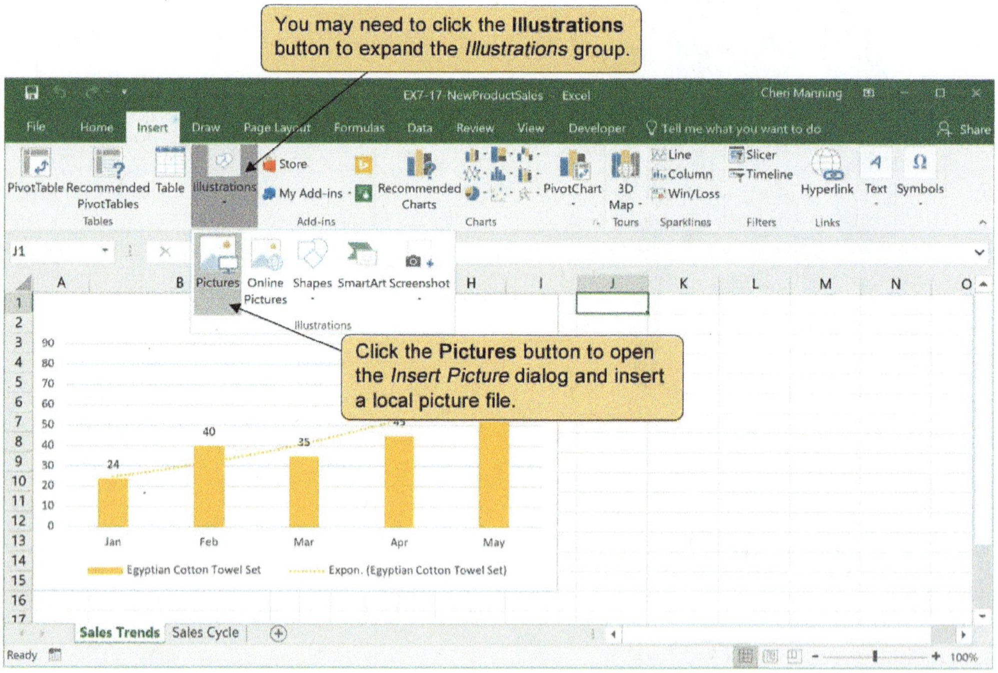

FIGURE EX 7.42

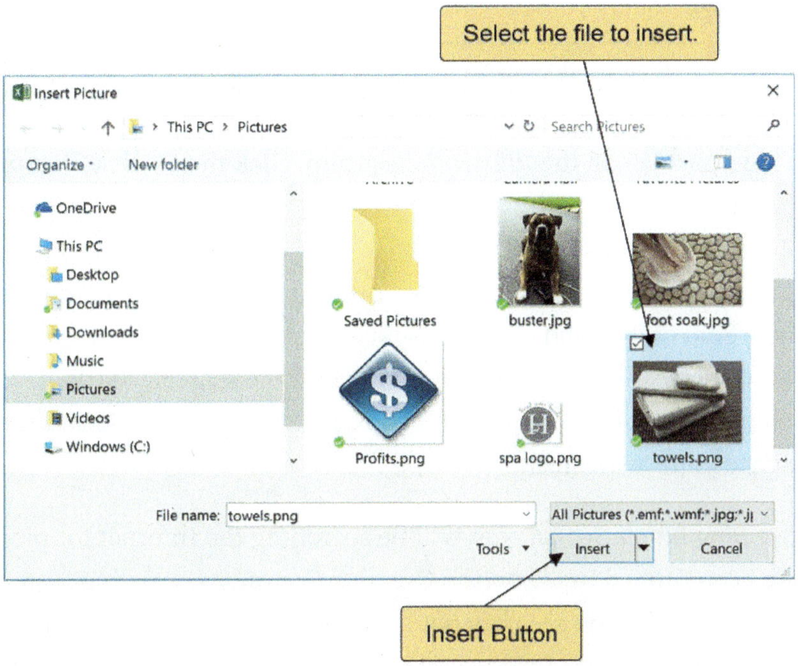

FIGURE EX 7.43

To delete a picture, select the picture and press Delete.

tips & tricks

In Excel, graphic images should be used sparingly and should not distract from the data being presented. Good uses of images in an Excel spreadsheet include inserting a company logo or a picture that helps illustrate the data.

tell me more

You can also insert pictures from online sources using *Bing Image Search*.

1. On the *Insert* tab, in the *Illustrations* group, click the **Online Pictures** button.
2. The *Insert Pictures* dialog opens.
3. Type a word describing the picture you want to search for in the **Bing Image Search** box and click the **Search** button.
4. Excel displays thumbnail results that match the search criteria.
5. Click a thumbnail to select it, and click the **Insert** button to add the image to your worksheet.

If you use *Bing Image Search*, you will be searching the Internet for pictures that have been filtered based on the Creative Commons licensing system. However, the results you see may not include pictures that are royalty free. Always check the source of picture to be sure you only use pictures in your documents that you know you have the proper rights to use.

let me try *Live!*

Open the student data file **EX7-17-NewProductSales** and try this skill on your own:

1. If necessary, click cell **J1** to set the initial position for the image.
2. Insert the **towels** picture into this worksheet. (The *towels* picture is available with the data files for this book. If you do not have that picture available, use a picture of your choice.)
3. If you will be moving on to the next skill in this chapter, leave the document open to continue working. If not, save the file as directed by your instructor and close it.

Skill 7.18 Resizing and Moving Pictures

You can resize an image by either manually entering the values for the size of the picture or by dragging a resize handle on the image to make it larger or smaller. Entering specific width or height values provides more precise control over the size of the picture.

To resize an image by manually entering values:

1. If necessary, click the picture once to select it.
2. On the *Picture Tools Format* tab, in the *Size* group, type a value in the **Width** or **Height** box.
3. Press Enter to accept the change.

When you insert a picture or other graphic object into a worksheet, it is not inserted into a specific cell. You can move it to another place in the worksheet without affecting the underlying data or worksheet structure.

To move a picture, point to the image and when the cursor changes to the move cursor, click and drag the image to the new location.

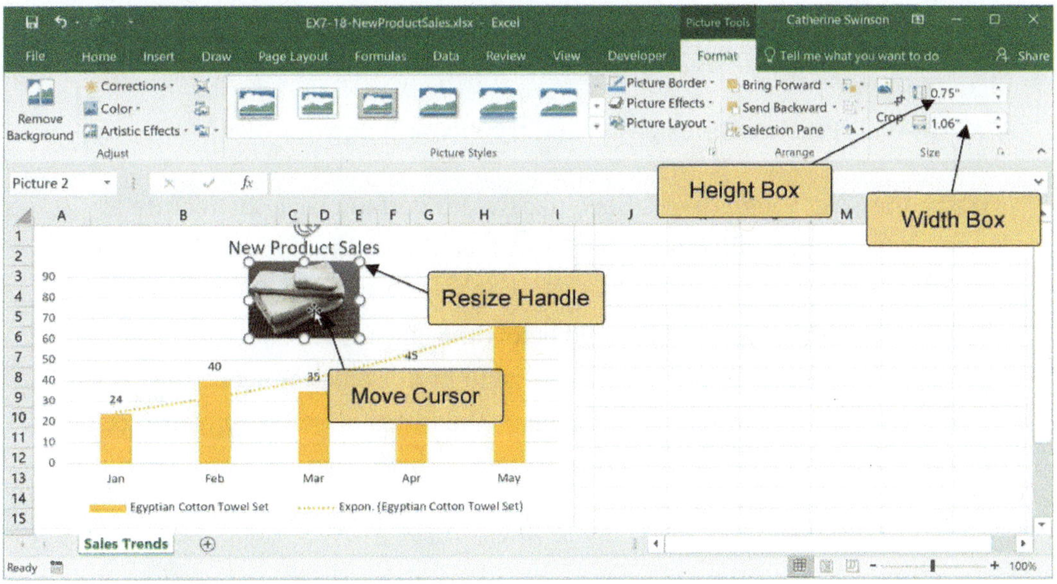

FIGURE EX 7.44

tips & tricks

When you use the *Width* or *Height* box on the *Picture Tools Format* tab to resize a picture, the value in the other box will change automatically to maintain the **aspect ratio**. This means that as the width or height is increased or decreased, the height or width of the image is increased or decreased proportionately. If the aspect ratio did not remain the same, the image would appear stretched or pinched as you resized it.

tell me more

To resize a picture by dragging, click a resize handle, and drag toward the center of the image to make it smaller or away from the center of the image to make it larger. To maintain the aspect ratio of the picture, be sure to use one of the resize handles at the four corners of the picture. If you use a resize handle along one of the sides or the top or bottom, you will be resizing the width or height of the picture only.

let me try *Live!*

If you do not have the data file from the previous skill open, open the student data file
EX7-18-NewProductSales and try this skill on your own:

1. On the *Sales Trends* worksheet, use the Ribbon to resize the picture to exactly **.75** inch tall. Allow Excel to adjust the width to maintain the aspect ratio.
2. Move the image so it is centered below the chart title.
3. If you will be moving on to the next skill in this chapter, leave the document open to continue working. If not, save the file as directed by your instructor and close it.

Skill 7.19 Applying Quick Styles and Other Formatting to Pictures

When you insert a picture in a worksheet, the *Picture Tools Format* tab displays. This Ribbon tab contains tools to change the look of the picture including applying Picture Quick Styles, borders, and effects.

Picture Quick Styles allow you to apply a combination of formatting such as borders, rounded corners, and effects with a single command. To apply a Picture Quick Style:

1. If necessary, click the picture once to select it.
2. On the *Picture Tools Format* tab, in the *Picture Styles* group, click the **More** button to expand the gallery.
3. In the *Picture Quick Styles* gallery, click a style to apply it to the picture.

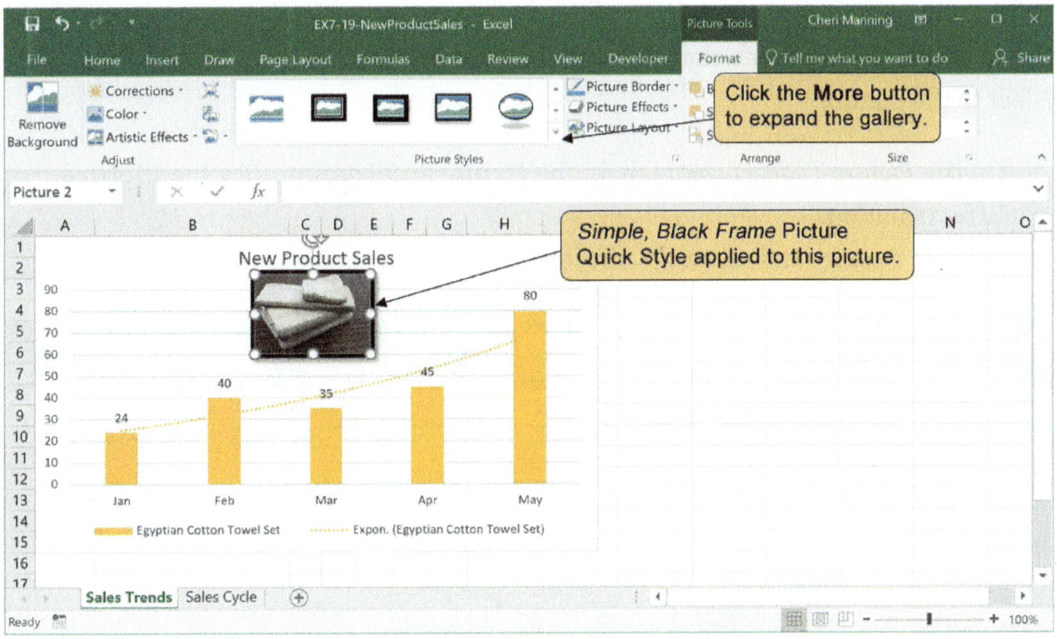

FIGURE EX 7.45

To apply a color border to the picture or change the color of the existing border:

1. On the *Picture Tools Format* tab, in the *Picture Styles* group, click the **Picture Border** button.
2. Select the color you want from the color palette.

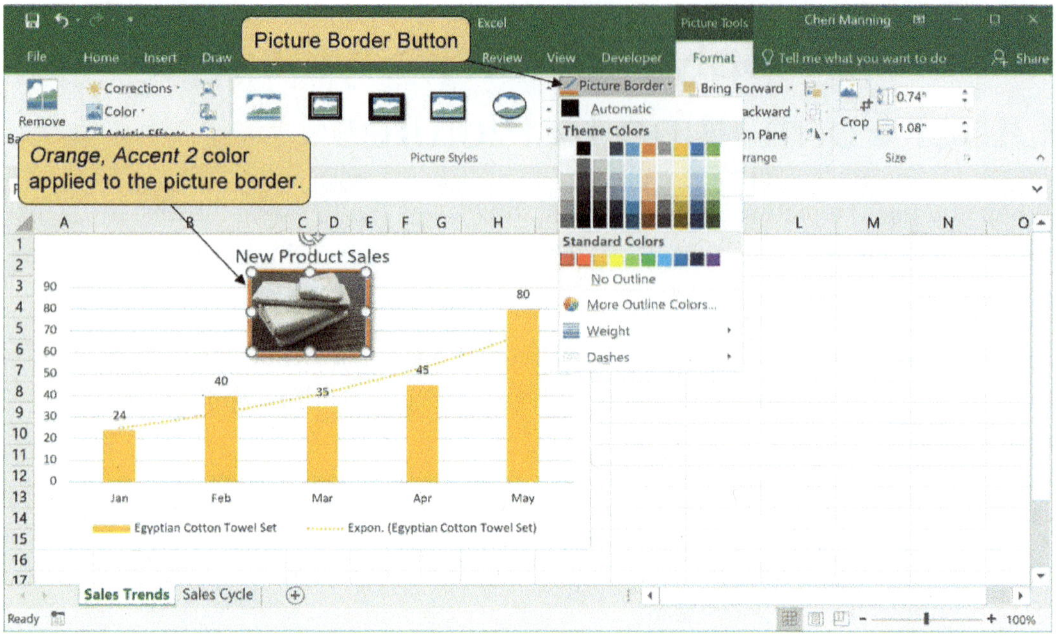

FIGURE EX 7.46

Excel includes a variety of effects you can apply to pictures, including a group of preset effects that combine shadows, reflections, glows, and bevels. To apply a preset effect to the picture:

1. On the *Picture Tools Format* tab, in the *Picture Styles* group, click the **Picture Effects** button.
2. Point to **Preset**, and select the effect you want.

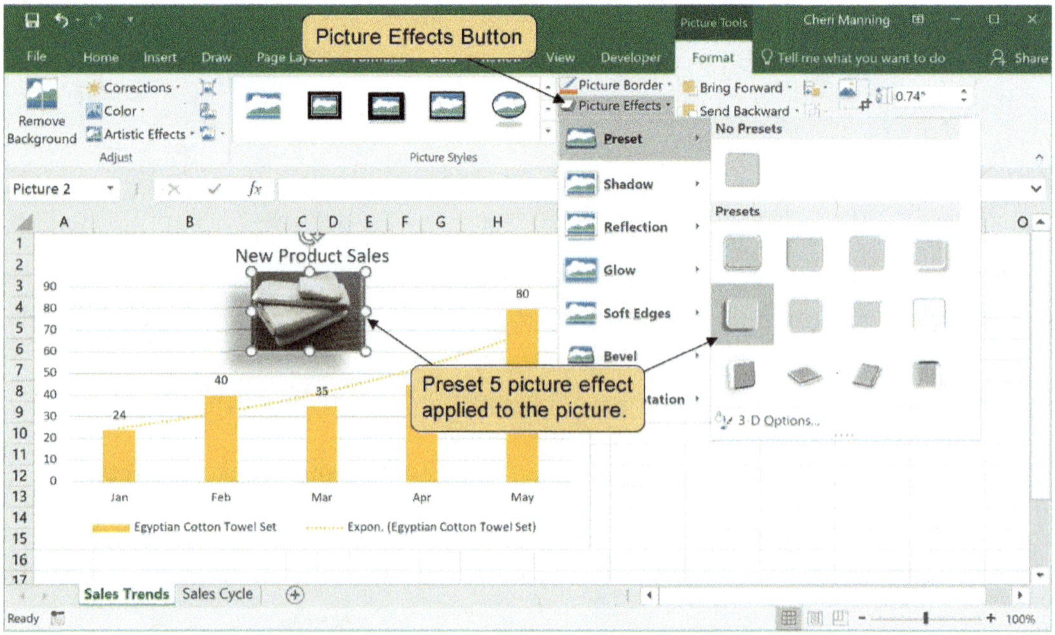

FIGURE EX 7.47

At any time, you can remove formatting and return the image to its original state. On the *Picture Tools Format* tab, in the *Adjust* group, click the **Reset Picture** button.

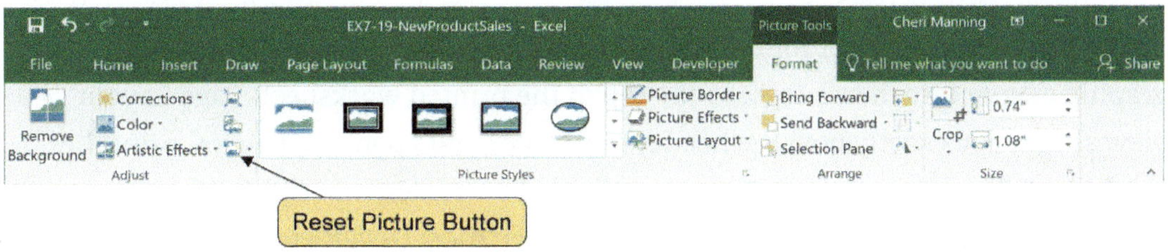

FIGURE EX 7.48

tell me more

Use the tools in the *Adjust* group to color-correct the image, add colorization, and apply a variety of artistic effects.

another method

- The *Picture Quick Styles* gallery is available from the Mini toolbar when you right-click the picture.
- More picture formatting options are available from the *Format Picture* task pane. To open the *Format Picture* task pane, click the **dialog launcher** in any of the groups on the *Picture Tools Format* tab, or right-click the picture and select **Format Picture...**

let me try *Live!*

If you do not have the data file from the previous skill open, open the student data file **EX7-19-NewProductSales** and try this skill on your own:

1. On the *Sales Trends* worksheet, apply the **Simple, Black Frame** Quick Style to the picture.
2. Change the picture border color to **Orange, Accent 2**.
3. Apply the **Preset 5** picture effect to the picture.
4. Reset the picture to its original formatting.
5. If you will be moving on to the next skill in this chapter, leave the workbook open to continue working. If not, save the file as directed by your instructor and close it.

Skill 7.20 Adding a Picture to a Header

When you create a header for a worksheet, you may find that you want to add a graphic element, such as a logo, to the top of the printed worksheet. Page Layout view shows you exactly how the header and footer will appear when you print the worksheet. The header area has three sections: left, center, and right. When you click a header area, the contextual tab *Header & Footer Tools Design* appears. This tab contains commands for working with the header and footer, including adding a picture.

To add a picture to the worksheet header:

1. On the *Insert* tab, if necessary, click the **Text** button to expand the *Text* group.
2. Click the **Header & Footer** button.

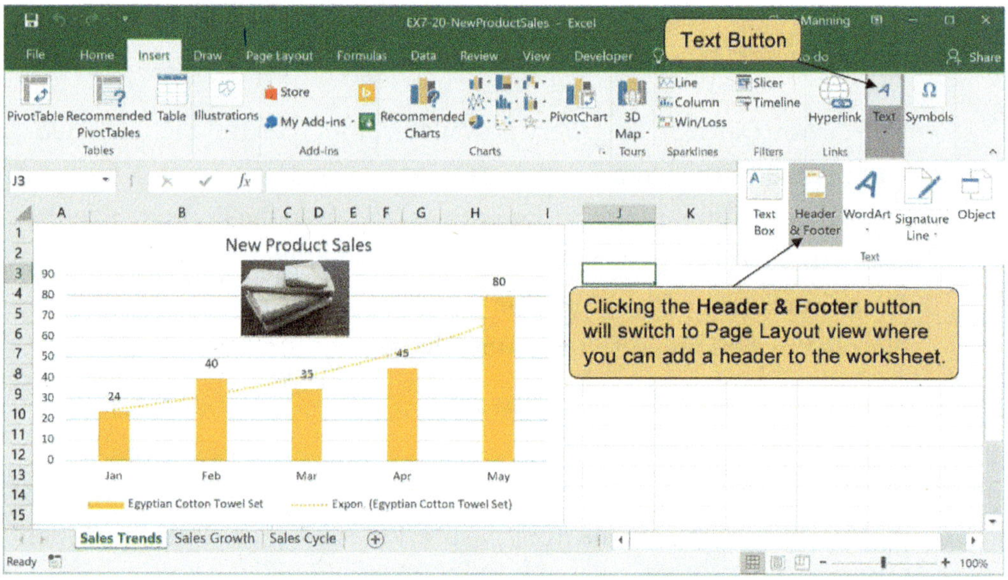

FIGURE EX 7.49

3. Excel switches to Page Layout view with the center section of the header active. If necessary, click the header section where you want the picture to appear.
4. On the *Header & Footer Tools Design* tab, in the *Header & Footer Elements* group, click the **Picture** button.

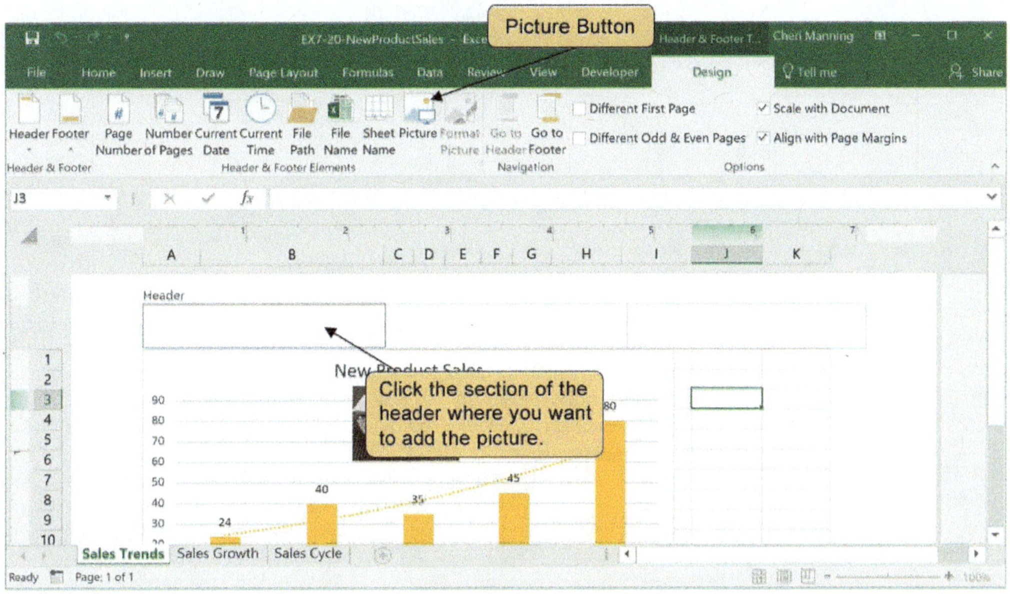

FIGURE EX 7.50

5. Click the **Browse** button next to *From a file* to insert a file from your local hard drive or an attached drive or storage media.
6. Navigate to the file location. Select the file and click **Insert**.

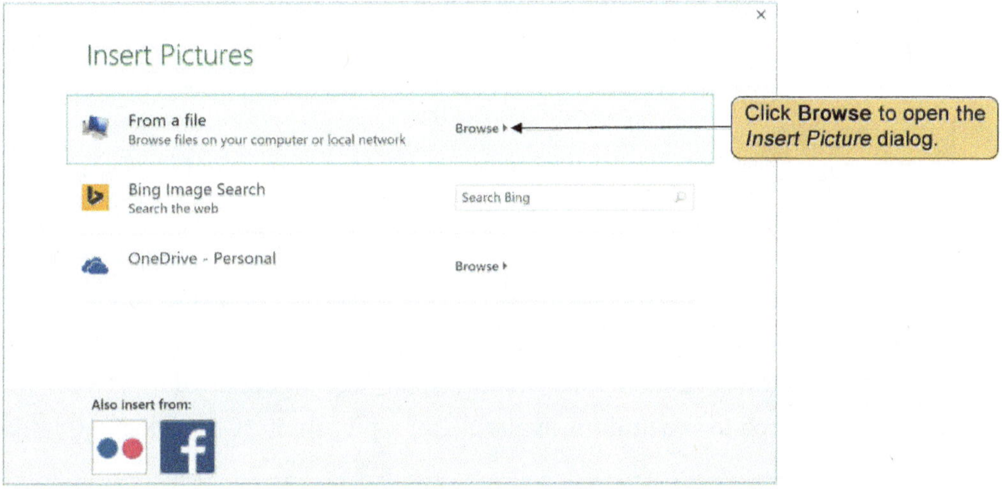

FIGURE EX 7.51

From Page Layout view, when you click the header section where the picture is, you will see the text *&[Picture]* instead of the actual image. When you click outside that header section, the image will appear.

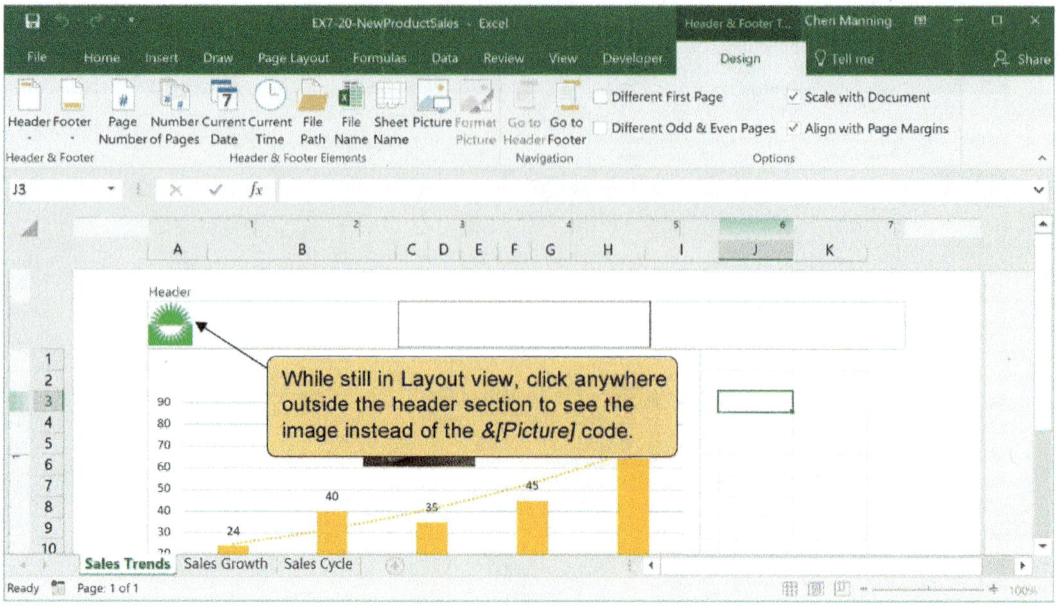

FIGURE EX 7.52

tips & tricks

In Normal view, the picture will not be visible at all because the header is hidden.

tell me more

To format a picture in the worksheet header, select the picture and then on the *Header & Footer Tools Design* tab, in the *Header & Footer Elements* group, click the **Format Picture** button. The *Format Picture* dialog opens. From the dialog, you can resize, rotate, crop, and modify the picture. Note that the formatting options available for a picture in the worksheet header are very limited compared to the options available for a picture in the worksheet.

another method

To add a picture to a header section from the *Page Setup* dialog:

1. On the *Page Layout* tab, in the *Page Setup* group, click the **Page Setup** dialog launcher.
2. In the *Page Setup* dialog, click the **Header/Footer** tab.
3. Click the **Custom Header** button.
4. Click in the section where you want to position the picture.
5. Click the **Insert Picture** button to open the *Insert Picture* dialog.
6. Navigate to the file location. Select the file, and click **Insert**.
7. Click **OK** to close the *Header* dialog, and then click **OK** again to close the *Page Setup* dialog.

let me try *Live!*

If you do not have the data file from the previous skill open, open the student data file
EX7-20-NewProductSales and try this skill on your own:

1. On the *Sales Trends* worksheet, switch to Page Layout view so you can insert a picture into the **left** section of the worksheet header.
2. Add the picture **green logo** to the left section of the worksheet header. (The *green logo* picture is available with the data files for this book. If you do not have that picture available, use a picture of your choice.)
3. If you will be moving on to the next skill in this chapter, leave the workbook open to continue working. If not, save the file as directed by your instructor and close it.

Skill 7.21 Inserting a Shape

A **shape** is a drawing object that you can add to your spreadsheet to call attention to a cell or group of cells. Excel comes with a number of shapes for you to choose from, including lines, block arrows, callouts, and basic shapes such as rectangles and circles. When you insert a shape into a worksheet, it is not inserted into a specific cell. You can move it to another place in the worksheet without affecting the underlying data or worksheet structure.

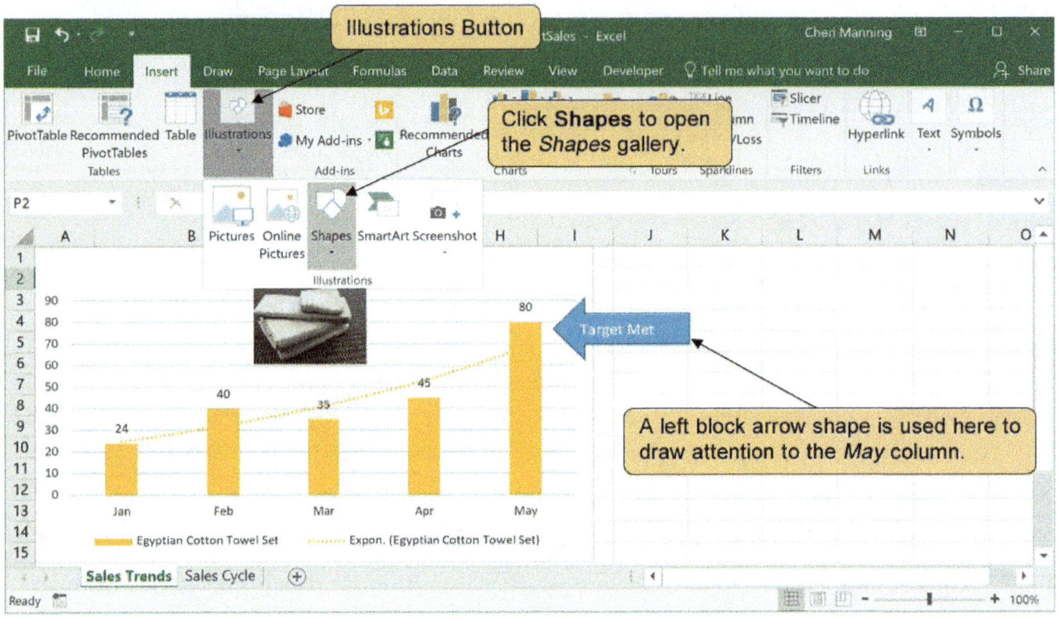

FIGURE EX 7.53

To add a shape:

1. On the *Insert* tab, if necessary, click the **Illustrations** button to expand the *Illustrations* group. Click the **Shapes** button and select an option from the *Shapes* gallery.
2. The cursor changes to a crosshair.
3. Click on the spreadsheet to add the shape. To control the size of the shape more precisely, you can click and drag to draw the shape.

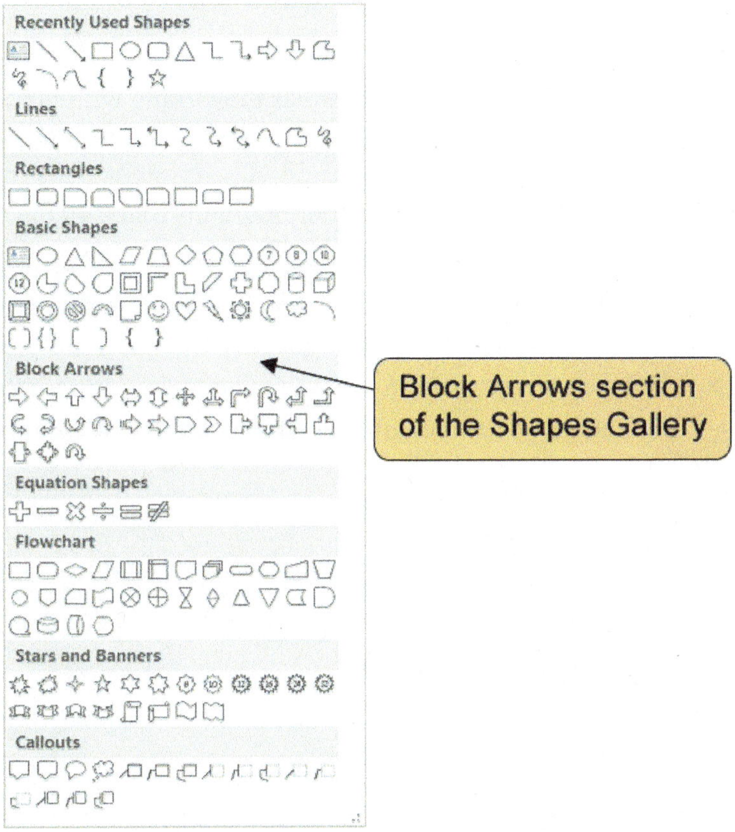

FIGURE EX 7.54

All shapes, except lines, allow you to add text. To add text to a shape:

1. If necessary, click the shape once to select it.
2. Type the text. Click anywhere outside the shape to accept the text.

If you need to edit the shape text, right-click the shape and select **Edit Text**. When you are finished editing the text, you can click outside the shape or right-click the shape again and select **Exit Edit Text**.

tips & tricks

If you have multiple shapes in your worksheet, use the tools in the *Arrange* group to control which image appears on top and group shapes together so they can be manipulated as a single object.

tell me **more**

Resizing and moving shapes is similar to working with pictures. For more information, refer to the skill *Resizing and Moving* Pictures.

- You can resize a shape by either manually entering the values for the size of the shape in the *Width* or *Height* box at the far left side of the *Drawing Tools Format* tab, *Size* group or by dragging a resize handle on the shape to make it larger or smaller.
- To move a shape, point to the shape and when the cursor changes to the move cursor, click and drag the shape to the new location.

another method

If you have a chart selected, you can also insert a shape from the *Chart Tools Format* tab, *Insert Shapes* groups.

If you have a shape selected, you can add more shapes from the *Drawing Tools Format* tab, *Insert Shapes* group.

let me try *Live!*

If you do not have the data file from the previous skill open, open the student data file
EX7-21-NewProductSales and try this skill on your own:

1. On the *Sales Trends* worksheet, if necessary, switch to Normal view.
2. Insert a **Left Arrow** block arrow shape to the right of the *May* column in the chart.
3. Add the text **Target Met** to the shape.
4. Resize the shape as necessary to fit the text.
5. If you will be moving on to the next skill in this chapter, leave the workbook open to continue working. If not, save the file as directed by your instructor and close it.

Skill 7.22 Applying Quick Styles and Other Formatting to Shapes

Shape Quick Styles allow you to apply a combination of formatting such as borders, rounded corners, and effects with a single command. When you insert a shape, Excel applies the default Quick Style for the workbook's theme to the shape. To adjust the formatting of the shape you can choose a new Quick Style from the *Shapes Styles* gallery.

To apply a Quick Style to a shape:

1. Select the shape you want to change.
2. On the *Drawing Tools Format* tab, in the *Shape Styles* group, click a Quick Style in the collapsed gallery on the Ribbon.
3. If the Quick Style you want to use does not appear on the Ribbon, click the **More** button to display the gallery and click a Quick Style in the gallery to apply it to the shape.

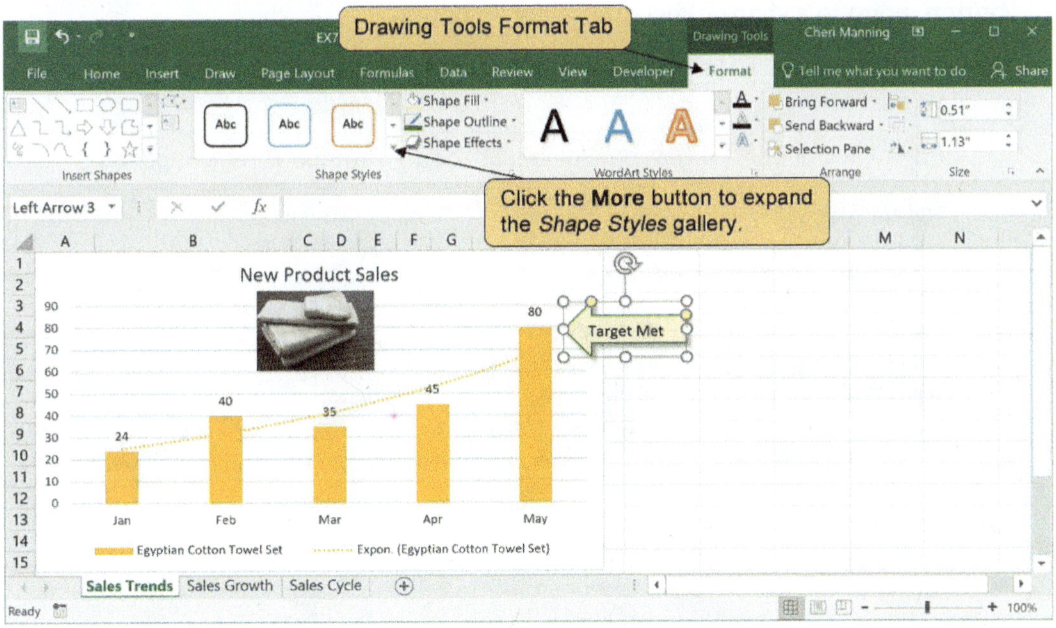

FIGURE EX 7.55

You can further adjust the look of a shape by changing the following:

- **Shape fill**—The color that fills the object. You can choose a solid color from the color palette or fill the color with a gradient or texture.

- **Shape outline**—The line that surrounds the shape. You can further adjust the outline of shapes by changing the color of the outline, width of the outline, and style of the outline.
- **Shape effects**—Graphic effects you can apply to shapes including drop shadows, reflections, glows, and bevels.

To further adjust the formatting of a shape:

1. Select the shape you want to change.
2. Click the **Drawing Tools Format** tab.
3. To change the fill of a shape, in the *Shape Styles* group, click the **Shape Fill** button and select an option from the color palette. To make the shape appear transparent, click the **Shape Fill** button and select **No Fill**.
4. To change the outline of a shape, in the *Shape Styles* group, click the **Shape Outline** button.
   - Select an option from the color palette to change the color of the outline.
   - Point to **Weight** and select a thickness option for the outline.
   - Point to **Dashes** and select a dash style for the outline.
5. To apply a shape effect, in the *Shape Styles* group, click the **Shape Effects** button, point to a shape effect and select an option.

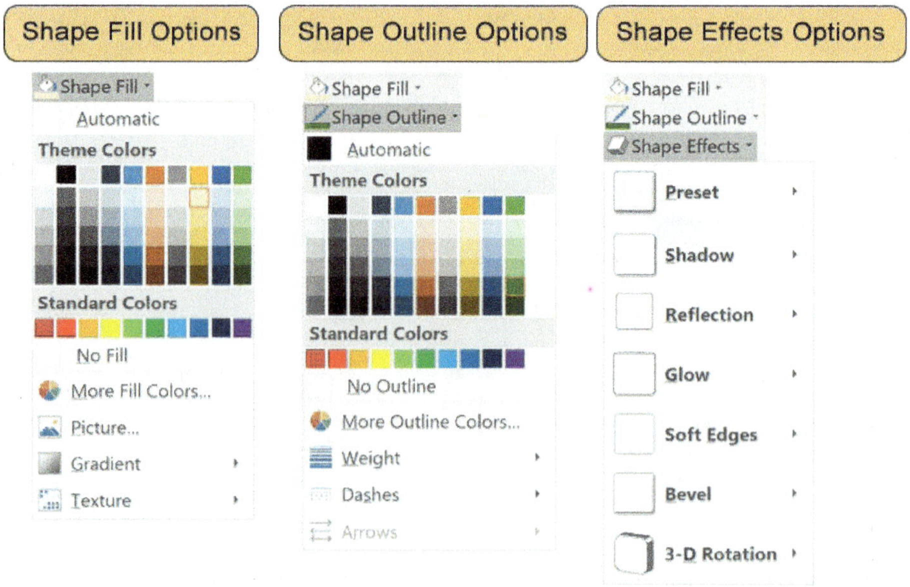

FIGURE EX 7.56

tips & tricks

If the shape includes text, be sure to right-click an empty area of the shape to see the shape formatting options. If you right-click the text area, the right-click menu will show text options instead.

tell me more

More shape formatting options are available from the *Format Shape* task pane. To open the *Format Shape* task pane, click the **dialog launcher** button in any of the groups on the *Drawing Tools Format* tab, or right-click the shape and select **Format Object...**

another method

- To change the Quick Style of a shape, you can right-click the shape and click the **Styles** button on the Mini toolbar.
- To change the fill of a shape, you can right-click the shape and click the **Fill** button on the Mini toolbar.
- To change the outline of a shape, you can right-click the shape and click the **Outline** button on the Mini toolbar.

let me try *Live!*

If you do not have the data file from the previous skill open, open the student data file **EX7-22-NewProductSales** and try this skill on your own:

1. On the *Sales Trends* worksheet, apply the **Colored Outline - Orange, Accent 2** Quick Style to the shape.
2. Change the shape fill color to **Gold, Accent 4, Lighter 80%**.
3. Change the shape outline color to **Green, Accent 6, Darker 25%**.
4. Apply the **Offset Diagonal Bottom Right** shadow effect to the shape.
5. If you will be moving on to the next skill in this chapter, leave the workbook open to continue working. If not, save the file as directed by your instructor and close it.

Skill 7.23 Inserting a SmartArt Graphic

SmartArt images are visual diagrams containing graphic elements with text boxes in which you enter information. There are eight categories of SmartArt for you to choose from:

List—Use to list items that ***do not*** need to be in a particular order.

Process—Use to list items that **do** need to be in a particular order.

Cycle—Use for a process that repeats over and over again.

Hierarchy—Use to show branching, in either a decision tree or an organization chart.

Relationship—Use to show relationships between items.

Matrix—Use to show how an item fits into the whole.

Pyramid—Use to illustrate how things relate to each other with the largest item being on the bottom and the smallest item being on the top.

Picture—Use to show a series of pictures along with text in the diagram.

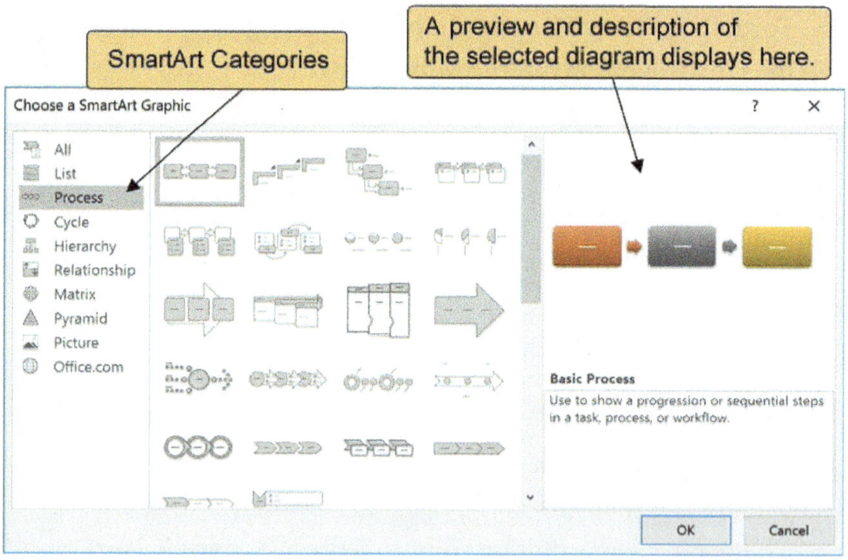

FIGURE EX 7.57

To insert a SmartArt diagram:

1. Click the **Insert** tab.
2. In the *Illustrations* group, click the **Insert a SmartArt Graphic** button.

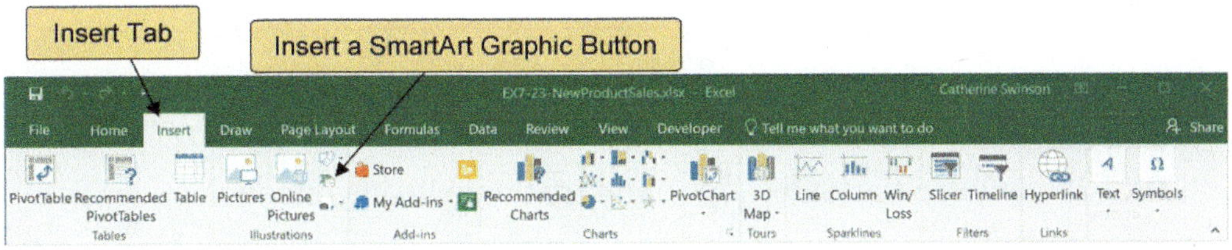

FIGURE EX 7.58

3. In the *Choose a SmartArt Graphic* dialog, click a SmartArt graphic type.
4. Click **OK**.
5. The SmartArt diagram is added to the slide.
6. Each shape in the diagram includes a text placeholder.
7. Click [**Text**] in a shape and enter the text for the item.
8. Enter the text for all the shapes in the diagram.

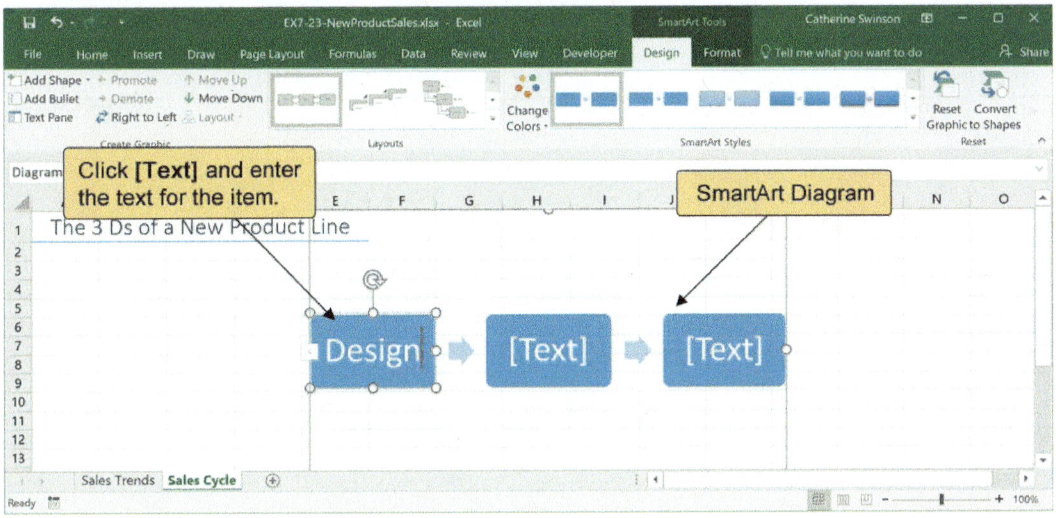

FIGURE EX 7.59

tips & tricks

When choosing a SmartArt diagram, it is important that the diagram type suits your content. In the *Choose a SmartArt Graphic* dialog, click a **SmartArt** type to display a preview of the SmartArt. The preview not only displays what the diagram will look like but also includes a description of the best uses for the diagram type.

let me try *Live!*

If you do not have the data file from the previous skill open, open the student data file **EX7-23-NewProductSales** and try this skill on your own:

1. Verify you are on the Sales Cycle worksheet.
2. Open the **Choose a SmartArt Graphic** dialog.
3. Insert a **Basic Process** SmartArt diagram. It is the first option in the first row of the *Process* category.
4. Enter **Design** as the text for the shape on the right. Add **Develop** as the text for the middle shape. Add **Distribute** as the text for the shape on the left.
5. If you will be moving on to the next skill in this chapter, leave the file open to continue working. If not, save the file as directed by your instructor and close it.

Skill 7.24 Applying Quick Styles and Other Formatting to SmartArt

SmartArt Quick Styles allow you to apply a combination of formatting such as borders, shading, and 3-D effects with a single command. When you add SmartArt to a workbook, the diagram uses the default style and the default colors from the workbook's theme. You can modify the look of SmartArt diagrams by changing the style of the diagram as well as selecting from a variety of color sets.

To change the style of a SmartArt diagram:

1. Select the SmartArt you want to change.
2. Click the **SmartArt Tools Design** tab.
3. In the *SmartArt Styles* gallery, click the **More** button to display the gallery.
4. Click a style to apply to the diagram.

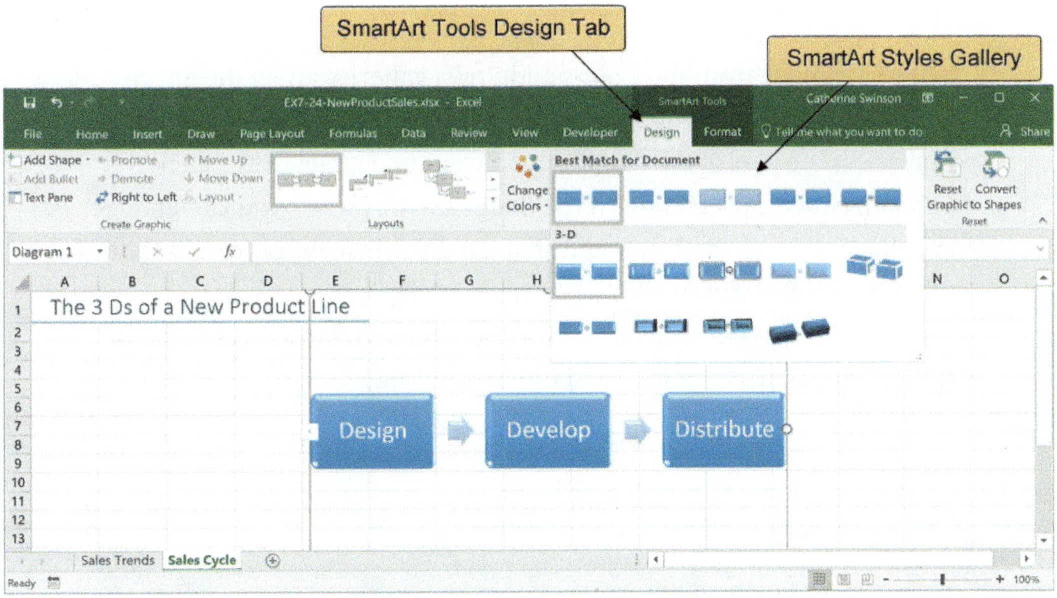

FIGURE EX 7.60

To change the colors of a SmartArt diagram:

1. Click the **SmartArt Tools Design** tab.
2. In the *SmartArt Styles* group, click the **Change Colors** button and select a color set to apply to the diagram.

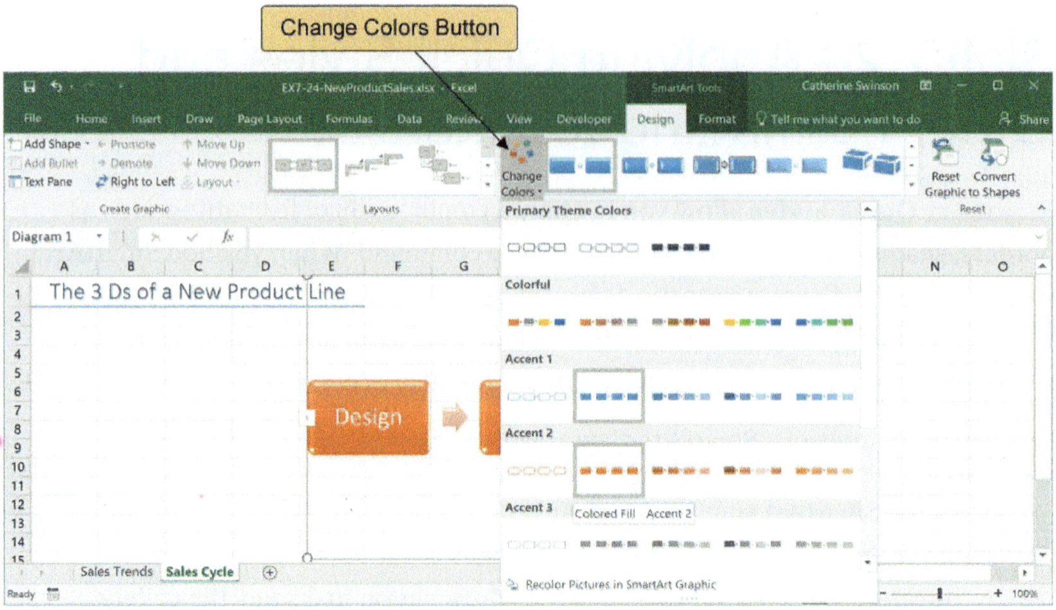

FIGURE EX 7.61

tips & tricks

- Selections made from the *Colors* and *Styles* galleries affect the entire SmartArt diagram. If you want to format a specific shape in the diagram, first select the part of the diagram you want to change. Next, click the *SmartArt Tools Format* tab. In the *Shapes Styles* group, you can change the shape style, shape color, and shape outline just as you would for any other drawing object.
- Click the **Reset Graphic** button on the *SmartArt Tools Design* tab to restore the SmartArt diagram to the original state.

tell me more

There are a variety of SmartArt styles to choose from. These styles include a combination of outlines and effects (such as gradients and bevels) that you can apply with a single command.

another method

- To change the style of SmartArt, you can also right-click an empty area of the diagram, click the **Shape Quick Styles** button on the Mini toolbar, and select an option.
- To change the color of SmartArt, you can also right-click an empty area of the diagram, click the **Shape Fill** button on the Mini toolbar, and select an option.

let me try *Live!*

If you do not have the data file from the previous skill open, open the student data file
EX7-24-NewProductSales and try this skill on your own:

1. Select the SmartArt diagram on the *Sales Cycle* worksheet.
2. Apply the **Polished** SmartArt style to the diagram. It is the first option in the *3-D* section of the gallery.
3. Apply the **Colored Fill - Accent 2** color set to the diagram.
4. Save the file as directed by your instructor and close it.

key terms

- Combination chart
- Combo chart
- Hierarchy chart
- Branch
- Treemap chart
- Sunburst chart
- Histogram chart
- Bin
- Class interval
- Frequency
- Pareto chart
- Box and whisker chart
- Quartiles
- Lower quartile
- Upper quartile
- Interquartile range
- Whisker
- Outlier value
- Waterfall chart
- Shape Quick Style
- WordArt
- Chart template
- Trendline
- Linear trendline
- Exponential trendline
- Logarithmic trendline
- Moving average trendline
- R-squared value
- Regression analysis
- Marker
- Sparkline Quick Style
- Aspect ratio
- Picture Quick Style
- Shape
- SmartArt
- SmartArt Quick Style

concept review

1. Which of these is the most common combination for a combo chart?.
   a. pie and line
   b. column and pie
   c. column and line
   d. column and bar
2. Which of these is a hierarchy chart?
   a. waterfall
   b. box and whisker
   c. histogram
   d. treemap
3. Use the *Chart Styles* button that appears at the upper right corner of a selected chart to change the style for a selected data series or single data point.
   a. true
   b. false
4. Which of these methods allows you to separate a data point in a pie chart?
   a. Move the data point to a secondary axis.
   b. Enter a value in the *Width* box on the *Chart Tools Format* tab, *Size* group.
   c. Enter a value in the *Angle of first slice* box in the *Format Data Point* task pane.
   d. Enter a value in the *Point Explosion* box in the *Format Data Point* task pane.
5. You can apply a chart template that you've saved from which of these methods?
   a. Click the **File** tab. Click **Open** to navigate to the chart templates location.
   b. Click the **File** tab. Click **New** and then type the chart template name in the search box.
   c. On the *Insert* tab, in the *Charts* group, click the **Chart Templates** button.
   d. On the *Insert* tab, in the *Charts* group, click the **Recommended Charts** button, and then click the **All Charts** tab.
6. Use a trendline to
   a. analyze the relationship between data points in a chart.
   b. forecast future values on a chart.
   c. estimate previous values on a chart.
   d. all of the above
7. Which of these would you use for regression analysis?
   a. line Sparklines
   b. line Sparklines with markers
   c. column Sparklines
   d. trendline

8. To change the Sparkline type, you must first clear the existing Sparklines.
   a. true
   b. false
9. When you insert a picture into a worksheet, it is inserted into a specific cell.
   a. true
   b. false
10. When you add a picture to a worksheet header, it is not visible in Normal view.
    a. true
    b. false

projects

Data files for projects can be found by logging into your SIMnet account and going to the *Library* section.

skill review 7.1

In this project, you will analyze U.S. population growth over the last 40 years.

Skills needed to complete this project:

- Applying Quick Styles and Other Formatting to Sparklines (Skill 7.16)
- Changing the Sparkline Type (Skill 7.14)
- Adding Markers to Sparklines (Skill 7.15)
- Adding a Data Series to a Chart (Skill 7.5)
- Creating a Combination Chart (Skill 7.1)
- Formatting Other Chart Elements (Skill 7.8)
- Formatting a Data Point or a Data Series (Skill 7.6)
- Creating a Chart Template (Skill 7.10)
- Inserting a Shape (Skill 7.21)
- Applying Quick Styles and Other Formatting to Shapes (Skill 7.22)
- Applying a Chart Template (Skill 7.10)
- Adding and Removing Trendlines (Skill 7.11)
- Forecasting Values on a Trendline (Skill 7.13)
- Changing Trendline Options (Skill 7.12)

1. Open the start file **EX2016-SkillReview-7-1** and resave the file as: `[your initials]EX-SkillReview-7-1`
2. If the workbook opens in Protected View, click the **Enable Editing** button in the Message Bar at the top of the workbook so you can modify the workbook.
3. Add Sparklines to the data and apply a Quick Style.
   a. On the *Population Data* worksheet, select cells **B4:F13**.
   b. On the *Insert* tab, in the *Sparklines* group, click the **Column** button.
   c. In the *Create Sparklines* dialog, verify that B4:F13 is the *Data Range* and specify **G4:G13** as the *Location Range*. Click **OK**.
   d. On the *Sparkline Tools Design* tab, in the *Style* group, apply the **Dark Blue, Sparkline Style Dark #6** style. Click the **More** button to expand the gallery, then click the first style from the right in the fifth row.
4. Change the Sparklines to lines with markers for all data points and highlight the high point marker in a different color.
   a. On the *Sparkline Tools Design* tab, in the *Type* group, click the **Line** button.
   b. On the *Sparkline Tools Design* tab, in the *Show* group, click the **Markers** check box.

c. On the *Sparkline Tools Design* tab, in the *Style* group, click the **Marker Color** button, point to **High Point**, and select **Red** (the second color from the left in the row of standard colors).

5. Create a column chart to represent the population data for Dallas and then add a second series to represent the overall population of the United States.
   a. Select cells **A3:F3**. Press Ctrl and click and drag to select cells **A12:F12**.
   b. On the *Insert* tab, in the *Charts* group, click the **Column or Bar Chart** button, and choose **Clustered Column** (the first chart type under *2-D Column*).
   c. Click and drag the chart to reposition it immediately below the data.
   d. On the *Chart Tools Design* tab, in the *Data* group, click the **Select Data** button.
   e. In the *Legend Entries (Series)* box, click the **Add** button.
   f. Click cell **A15** to add the cell reference to the *Series name* box.
   g. Click in the *Series values* box and delete the default entry. Click and drag to select cells **B15:F15**.
   h. Click **OK**.
6. Change the chart type to a combination chart with a secondary axis for the national population data.
   a. On the *Chart Tools Design* tab, in the *Type* group, click the **Change Chart Type** button.
   b. In the list of chart types at the left side of the *All Charts* tab, click **Combo**.
   c. Excel automatically suggests a line chart for the *Total US population* series, but the scale difference between the two series makes the Dallas data unreadable. Click the **Secondary Axis** check box next to *Total US population* series.
   d. Click **OK**.
7. Add a legend above the chart and format it by applying a style.
   a. Click the **Chart Elements** button that appears near the upper right corner of the chart. Point to **Legend** and click the arrow that appears at the right. Click **Top**.
   b. Click the legend to select it. On the *Chart Tools Format* tab, in the *Shape Styles* group, click the **More** button to expand the gallery. Select the **Subtle Effect - Yellow, Accent 5** style (the second style from the right in the third row from the bottom in the *Theme Styles* section).
8. Change the fill color of a data point to make it stand out.
   a. Select the data point for *1990* for the series *Dallas, TX* by clicking the **1990** column once to select the series and then clicking it a second time to select just that data point.

b. On the *Chart Tools Format* tab, in the *Shape Styles* group, click the **Shape Fill** button and select **Red, Accent 2** (the fifth color from the right in the first row of theme colors).

9. Save this chart as a new chart template.
   a. Right-click an empty area of the chart and select **Save as Template....**
   b. In the *Save Chart Template* dialog, type **`Population Combo Chart`** in the *File name* box.
   c. Click **Save.**
10. Add a callout to the chart, apply a style to it, and add text.
    a. On the *Chart Tools Format* tab, in the *Insert Shapes* group, click the **More** button to expand the gallery.
    b. Select **Callout: Line** (the fifth shape from the left in the *Callouts* section).
    c. Click anywhere in the chart to insert the shape.
    d. Click and drag the shape to reposition it so it is pointing to the highlighted data point as shown in Figure EX 7.62.
    e. On the *Drawing Tools Format* tab, in the *Shape Styles* group, click the **More** button to expand the gallery. Select the **Subtle Effect - Yellow, Accent 5** style (the second style from the right in the third row from the bottom).
    f. Type: **`What happened here?`** and then click anywhere outside the callout.
    g. If necessary, make the shape slightly larger so all the text is visible.
11. Create a new chart from the template you saved.
    a. Select cells **A3:F4**. Press Ctrl and click and drag to select cells **A12:F12**.
    b. On the *Insert* tab, in the *Charts* group, click the dialog launcher to open the *Insert Chart* dialog.
    c. In the *Insert Chart* dialog, click the **All Charts** tab.
    d. Click **Templates**. If necessary, select the **Population Combo Chart** template.
    e. Click **OK.**
    f. If necessary, move the chart so it is positioned to the right of the first chart as shown in Figure EX 7.62.

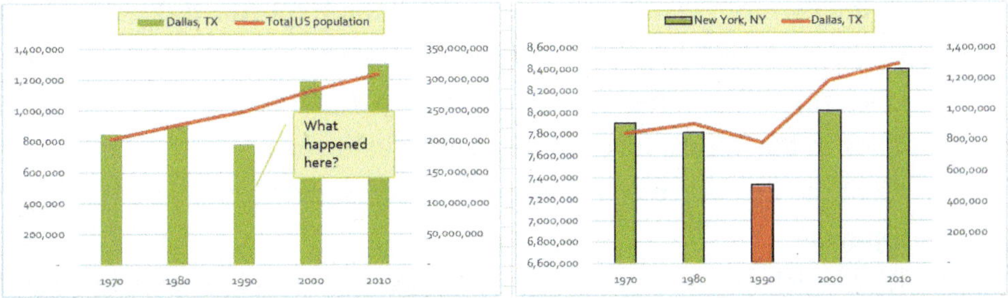

FIGURE EX 7.62

12. Change the outline color of a data series.
    a. Select the *New York, NY* data series by clicking any column in the second

chart.

b. On the *Chart Tools Format* tab, in the *Shape Styles* group, click the **Shape Outline** button, and select **Black, Accent 1** (the second color from the left in the first row of theme colors).

13. Create a clustered column chart for population growth by region. Move the chart to its own chart sheet named *Regional Trends*.
    a. Go to the **Census Data by State** worksheet and select cells **A5:L8**.
    b. On the *Insert* tab, in the *Charts* group, click the **Insert Column or Bar Chart** button and select **Clustered Column** (the first chart under the *2-D Column* section).
    c. If necessary, change the x axis labels to match the column headings. On the *Chart Tools Design* tab, in the *Data* group, click the **Select Data** button. In the *Horizontal (Category) Axis Labels* box, click the **Edit** button, and then click and drag to select cells **B3:L3**. Click **OK**. Click **OK** to accept the changes to the chart.
    d. On the *Chart Tools Design* tab, in the *Location* group, click the **Move Chart** button.
    e. Click the **New Sheet** radio button. Type Regional Trends in the box and click **OK**.
14. Edit and format the chart title.
    a. Click the chart title and type: `Population Trends by Region`
    b. On the *Chart Tools Format* tab, in the *WordArt Styles* group, click the **More** button to expand the gallery, and select one of the WordArt options.
    c. Click anywhere outside the title.
15. Add trendlines to the chart to forecast exponential growth for the next 40 years.
    a. Click the **Chart Elements** button that appears near the upper right corner of the chart. Point to **Trendline**, click the arrow that appears, and click **More Options**.
    b. In the *Add Trendline* dialog, click **OK**. (*Northeast* should be selected by default.)
    c. In the *Format Trendline* task pane, click the **Exponential** radio button.
    d. In the *Forecast* section, type **4** in the *Forward* box.
    e. Click the **Fill & Line** button near the top of the task pane.
    f. Click in the **Width** box and change the value to **4**.
    g. Click the **End Arrow** type box and select **Arrow** (the second option in the top row).
    h. Right-click any data point in the *Midwest* series and select **Add Trendline....** Apply the same formatting options as you applied to the *Northeast* trendline: **exponential**, forecasting forward for **4** periods, **4 pt** width, and arrow type **End Arrow**.

i. Follow the same steps to add a trendline to each of the other data series using the same formatting options (**exponential**, forecasting forward for **4** periods, **4 pt** width, and arrow type **End Arrow**). The final chart should look similar to Figure EX 7.63.

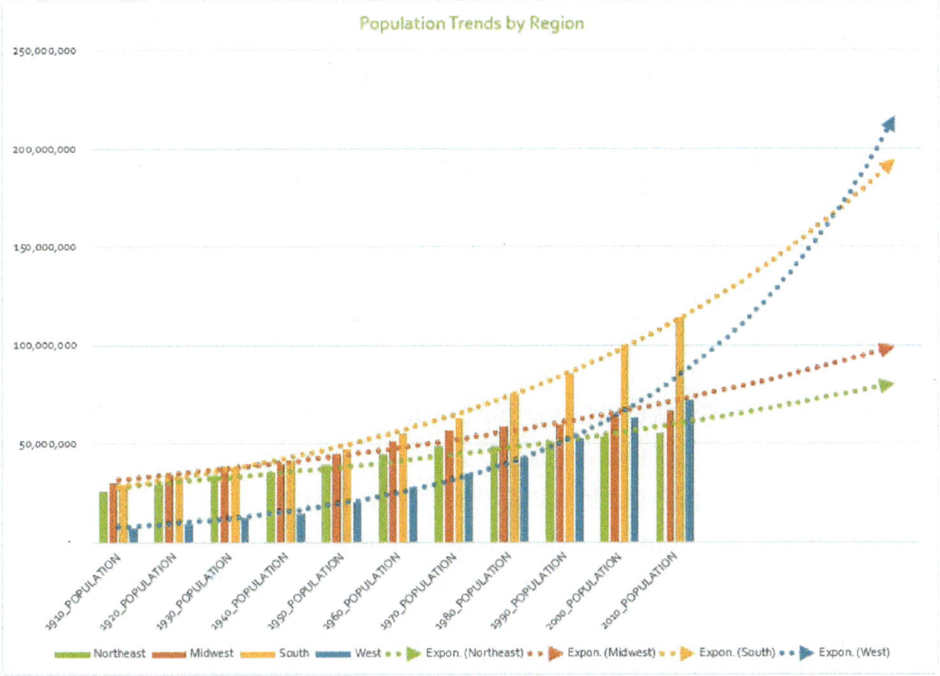

FIGURE EX 7.63

16. Save and close the workbook.

projects

Data files for projects can be found by logging into your SIMnet account and going to the *Library* section.

skill review 7.2

In this project, you will work with regional sales data for a shoe company.

Skills needed to complete this project:

- Changing the Sparkline Type (Skill 7.14)
- Adding Markers to Sparklines (Skill 7.15)
- Applying Quick Styles and Other Formatting to Sparklines (Skill 7.16)
- Inserting a Picture (Skill 7.17)
- Resizing and Moving Pictures (Skill 7.18)
- Applying Quick Styles and Other Formatting to Pictures (Skill 7.19)
- Adding a Picture to a Header (Skill 7.20)
- Emphasizing a Data Point in a Pie Chart (Skill 7.7)
- Formatting a Data Point or a Data Series (Skill 7.6)
- Formatting Other Chart Elements (Skill 7.8)
- Inserting a Shape (Skill 7.21)
- Applying Quick Styles and Other Formatting to Shapes (Skill 7.22)

1. Open the start file **EX2016-SkillReview-7-2** and resave the file as: `[your initials]EX-SkillReview-7-2`
2. If the workbook opens in Protected View, click the **Enable Editing** button in the Message Bar at the top of the workbook so you can modify the workbook.
3. On the *By Region* worksheet, change the Sparkline type to columns and apply a Quick Style.
   a. Click any of the cells containing Sparklines (cells **G3:G7**).
   b. On the *Sparkline Tools Design* tab, in the *Type* group, click the **Column** button.
   c. On the *Sparkline Tools Design* tab, in the *Style* group, apply the **Purple, Sparkline Style Accent 1, (no dark or light)** style. Click the **More** button to expand the gallery, then click the first style in the third row.
4. Change the color of the high point marker for just the Sparkline in the *Flip* row.
   a. Click cell **G7**. On the *Sparkline Tools Design* tab, in the *Group* group, click the **Ungroup** button.
   b. On the *Sparkline Tools Design* tab, in the *Style* group, click the **Marker Color** button. Point to **High Point**, and click **Teal, Accent 3** (the fourth color from the right in the top row of theme colors).

5. Add the *Flip* picture from your local drive, network, or external media storage device, and then resize and move the picture.
   a. On the *Insert* tab, if necessary, click the **Illustrations** button to expand the *Illustrations* group. Click the **Pictures** button.
   b. Navigate to the local or network drive or storage media where you have downloaded the resource files for this project. Select the **Flip** file and click **Insert**.
   c. On the *Picture Tools Format* tab, *Size* group, type .75 in the *Width* box. Press **[Enter]**.
   d. Click and drag the picture so it is in approximately cell **B7** and does not overlap with the picture above it.
6. Add a border to the pictures.
   a. Select all five pictures by pressing [Ctrl] while clicking each picture.
   b. On the *Picture Tools Format* tab, in the *Picture Styles* group, click the **Picture Border** button and click **Purple, Accent 1** (the fifth color in the top row of theme colors).
7. Add the company logo to the left section of the worksheet header.
   a. On the *Insert* tab, if necessary, click the **Text** button to expand the *Text* group. Click the **Header & Footer** button.
   b. Click the left section of the header.
   c. On the *Header & Footer Tools Design* tab, in the *Header & Footer Elements* group, click the **Picture** button.
   d. Click the **Browse** button next to *From a file*. Navigate to the local or network drive or storage media where you have downloaded the resource files for this project. Select the **ShoeLogo** file, and click **Insert**.
   e. Click anywhere outside the worksheet header.
   f. On the status bar, click the **Normal** button to switch back to Normal view.
8. On the *Region 1 Details* worksheet, rotate the chart so the *Flip* slice is at the right side and explode the slice away from the rest of the chart.
   a. Click the **Region 1 Details** worksheet tab.
   b. Click the chart once to select it, and then click the **Flip** slice again to select just that data point.
   c. On the *Chart Tools Format* tab, in the *Current Selection* group, click the **Format Selection** button to open the **Format Data Point** task pane.
   d. In the *Angle of first slice* box, type: **90**
   e. In the *Point Explosion* box, type: **40%**
9. Apply a Quick Style to just the *Flip* data point.
   a. Verify that the *Flip* data point is still selected.

b. On the *Chart Tools Format* tab, *Shape Styles* group, click the **More** button to expand the *Shape Quick Styles* gallery, and click **Intense Effect - Gold, Accent 5** (the second style from the right in the last row of styles in the *Theme Styles* section).

10. Insert, resize, and move and add text to a callout shape.
    a. On the *Chart Tools Format* tab, in the *Insert Shapes* group, click the **More** button to expand the gallery.
    b. Select **Oval Callout** shape (the third shape in the *Callouts* section).
    c. Click anywhere in the chart to insert the shape.
    d. Click and drag the shape to reposition it so it is above the *Flip* slice.
    e. On the *Drawing Tools Format* tab, in the *Shape Styles* group, click the **More** button to expand the gallery. Select the **Colored Outline - Gold, Accent 5** style (the second style from the right in the first row).
    f. Type: `Discontinue this style?`
    g. Make the shape wide enough to view the text by clicking the resize handle in the middle of the right side and dragging to the right until the word *Discontinue* fits on one line without wrapping as shown in Figure EX 7.64.
11. Apply a WordArt Quick Style to the chart title and increase the font size.
    a. Click the chart title once to select it.
    b. On the *Chart Tools Format* tab, in the *WordArt Styles* group, click the **WordArt Quick Styles** button and select one of the WordArt styles.
    c. On the *Home* tab, in the *Font* group, expand the *Font Size* list, and select **20**.

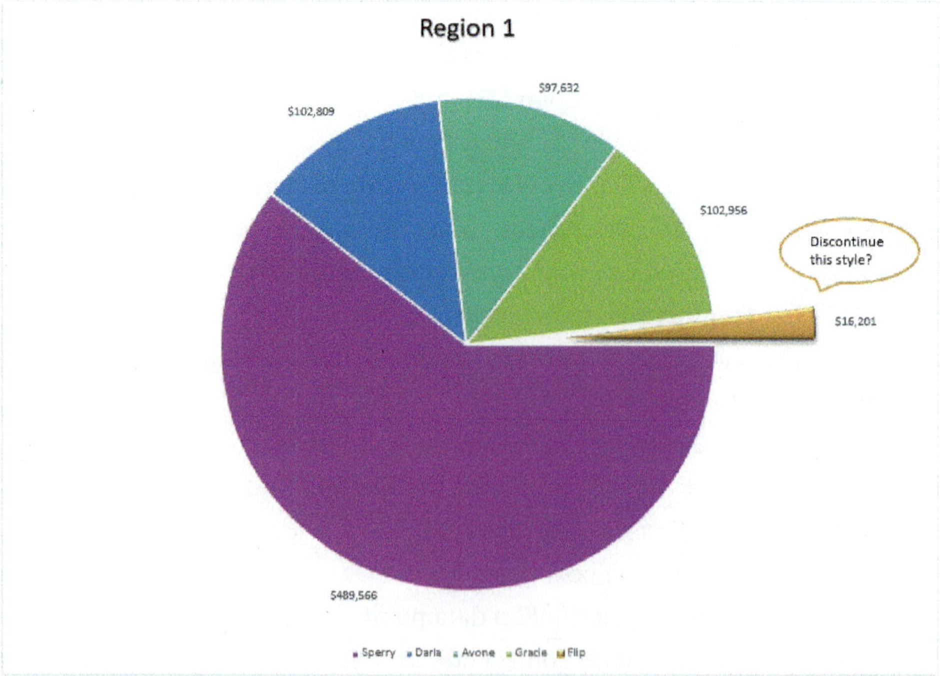

FIGURE EX 7.64

12. Save and close the workbook.

projects

Data files for projects can be found by logging into your SIMnet account and going to the *Library* section.

challenge yourself 7.3

In this project, you will use charts and other graphic elements to analyze carbon dioxide and greenhouse gas emission data from the U.S. Energy Information Administration (https://www.eia.gov/environment/emissions/ghg_report/ghg_gwp.cfm).

Skills needed to complete this project:

- Working with Hierarchy Charts (Skill 7.2)
- Adding a Data Series to a Chart (Skill 7.5)
- Creating a Combination Chart (Skill 7.1)
- Formatting Other Chart Elements (Skill 7.8)
- Formatting a Data Point or a Data Series (Skill 7.6)
- Inserting a Shape (Skill 7.21)
- Applying Quick Styles and Other Formatting to Shapes (Skill 7.22)
- Inserting a Picture (Skill 7.17)
- Resizing and Moving Pictures (Skill 7.18)
- Applying Quick Styles and Other Formatting to Pictures (Skill 7.19)
- Changing the Sparkline Type (Skill 7.14)
- Adding Markers to Sparklines (Skill 7.15)
- Applying Quick Styles and Other Formatting to Sparklines (Skill 7.16)
- Adding and Removing Trendlines (Skill 7.11)
- Forecasting Values on a Trendline (Skill 7.13)
- Changing Trendline Options (Skill 7.12)

1. Open the start file **EX2016-ChallengeYourself-7-3** and resave the file as:
   `[your initials]EX-ChallengeYourself-7-3`
2. If the workbook opens in Protected View, click the **Enable Editing** button in the Message Bar at the top of the workbook so you can modify the workbook.
3. On the *World CO2* worksheet, create a sunburst chart.
   a. Select cells **A4:C19** and cells **H4:H19**.
   b. Insert a sunburst hierarchical chart based on the selected data.
   c. If necessary, make the chart large enough to read the labels.
4. On the *North America CO2* worksheet, add data for Canada to the chart.
   a. Add a new data series to the chart.
   b. Use cell **A4** as the series name and cells **B4:J4** as the series values.
5. Change the chart type to a combination chart.

a. In the combination chart, the **Mexico** and **Canada** data series should be clustered column charts.
b. In the combination chart, the **United States** data series should be a line chart.
c. Place the **United States** data series on the secondary axis.

6. Add a WordArt Quick Style to the chart title.
   a. Change the chart title to: `North America CO2 Emissions`
   b. Apply any WordArt Quick Style.
7. Highlight the *2005 Canada* data point.
   a. Change the outline of the **2005 Canada** data point to **Red** (the second color from the left in the row of standard colors).
   b. Change the outline width to **3 pt**.
8. Add a callout to the chart, apply a style to it, and add text.
   a. Add a **Rectangular Callout** (the first shape in the *Callouts* section of the gallery) to the chart.
   b. Move the callout so it is pointing to the *2005 Canada* data point.
   c. Apply the **Colored Outline - Gray - Accent 3** Shape Quick Style (the fourth style from the left in the first row of the gallery) to the callout.
   d. Add the text: `What caused this increase?`
   e. Increase the size of the callout so the text is visible on two lines as show in Figure EX 7.65.
9. Add the *CanadaFlag* picture from your local drive, network, or external media storage device, and then resize and move the picture.
   a. Deselect the chart.
   b. Insert the **CanadaFlag** picture.
   c. Resize the picture so it is exactly **.5** inch wide. Maintain the picture aspect ratio.
   d. Move the flag pictures so each image is below the appropriate country name in the chart legend as shown in Figure EX 7.65. *Hint:* If you cannot move the *CanadaFlag* picture below the chart, you probably had the chart selected when you inserted it. Delete the picture, and then verify that you do not have the chart selected and try inserting the picture again.

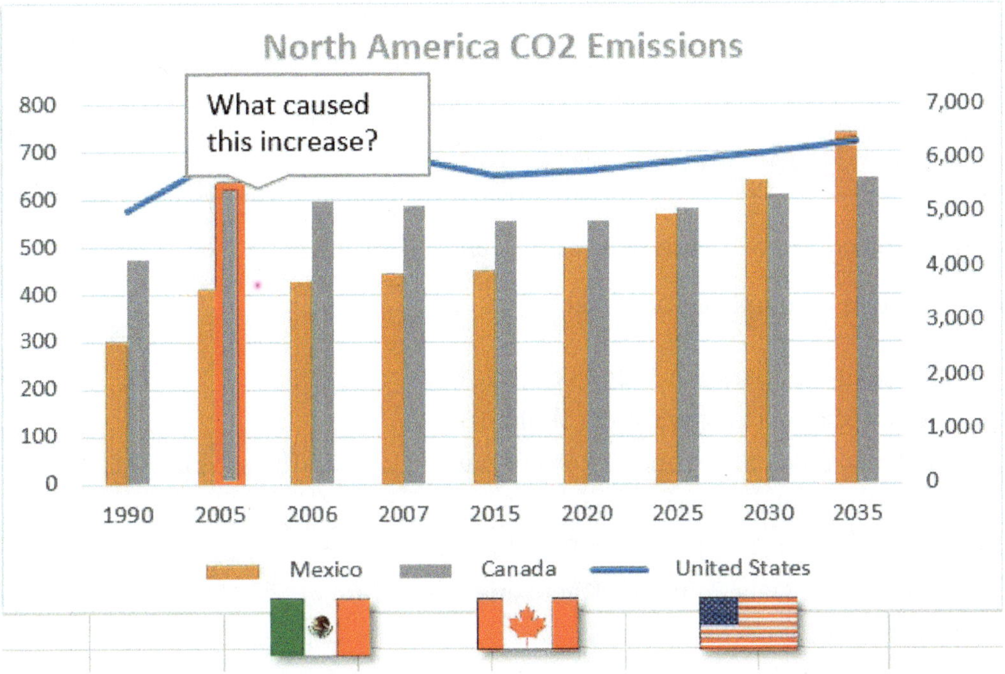

FIGURE EX 7.65

10. Add a shadow effect to the pictures.
    a. Select all three pictures by pressing Ctrl while clicking each picture.
    b. Add the **Offset, Diagonal, Bottom Right** shadow effect (the first effect in the *Outer* section of the gallery).
11. Modify the Sparklines on the *US Greenhouse Gas* worksheet.
    a. Change the Sparkline type to **Line**.
    b. Add markers for the low points and the high points.
    c. Change the color for the low point markers to **Green** (the fifth color from the right in the row of standard colors) and high point markers to **Red** (the second color from the left in the row of standard colors).
12. Add a trendline to the chart to forecast future values.
    a. Add a linear trendline to the chart.
    b. Forecast the trendline forward **5** periods.
    c. Display the **R-squared value** on the trendline.
13. Save and close the workbook.

projects

Data files for projects can be found by logging into your SIMnet account and going to the *Library* section.

challenge yourself 7.4

In this project, you will analyze housing trends using charting tools.

Skills needed to complete this project:

- Changing the Sparkline Type (Skill 7.14)
- Adding Markers to Sparklines (Skill 7.15)
- Applying Quick Styles and Other Formatting to Sparklines (Skill 7.16)
- Formatting Other Chart Elements (Skill 7.8)
- Emphasizing a Data Point in a Pie Chart (Skill 7.7)
- Formatting a Data Point or a Data Series (Skill 7.6)
- Inserting a Shape (Skill 7.21)
- Applying Quick Styles and Other Formatting to Shapes (Skill 7.22)
- Adding and Removing Trendlines (Skill 7.11)
- Changing Trendline Options (Skill 7.12)
- Inserting a Picture (Skill 7.17)
- Applying Quick Styles and Other Formatting to Pictures (Skill 7.19)
- Resizing and Moving Pictures (Skill 7.18)
- Adding a Picture to a Header (Skill 7.20)

1. Open the start file **EX2016-ChallengeYourself-7-4** and resave the file as: `[your initials]EX-ChallengeYourself-7-4`
2. If the workbook opens in Protected View, click the **Enable Editing** button in the Message Bar at the top of the workbook so you can modify the workbook.
3. On the *Summary by Type* worksheet, modify the Sparklines.
   a. Change the Sparklines to columns.
   b. Apply the Quick Style **Green, Sparkline Style Accent 6 (no dark or light)** (the first style at the right in the third row of the gallery).
4. Add a marker to the Sparklines.
   a. Add a marker for the high point.
   b. Change the high point marker color to **Blue** (the third color from the right in the row of standard colors).
5. In the pie chart, change the colors for the individual data labels to match their respective data points and then apply a bevel shape effect to all the data labels. Selecting a single data label is similar to selecting a single data point.

a. Apply the **Blue, Accent 1, Lighter 80%** fill color (the fifth color from the left in the second row of theme colors) to the data label for the **Modern** data point.
b. Apply the **Orange, Accent 2, Lighter 80%** fill color (the fifth color from the right in the second row of theme colors) to the data label for the **Condo** data point.
c. Apply the **White, Background 1, Darker 5%** fill color (the first color at the left in the second row of theme colors) to the data label for the **Ranch** data point.
d. Apply the **Gold, Accent 4, Lighter 80%** fill color (the third color from the right in the second row of theme colors) to the data label for the **Mediterranean** data point.
e. Select all the data labels and apply the **Round** or **Circle** bevel shape effect (the first effect in the *Bevel* section).

6. Emphasize the *Ranch* data point.
   a. Rotate the pie chart **240°** until the **Ranch** data point is at the right side.
   b. Explode the **Ranch** data point away from the pie by **35%**.
   c. Apply the **Round** or **Circle** bevel shape effect (the first effect in the *Bevel* section) to the **Ranch** data point. *Hint:* Do not use the *Format Data Point* task pane to apply the shape effect. Use the option off the Ribbon instead.
7. In the column chart, change the color of each data point to match the corresponding color in the pie chart. You do not need to change the color of the *Modern* data point.
   a. In the column chart, apply the **Orange, Accent 2** fill color (the fifth color from the right in the top row of theme colors) to the **Condo** data point.
   b. In the column chart, apply the **White, Background 1, Darker 35%** fill color (the first color at the left in the fifth row of theme colors) to the **Ranch** data point.
   c. In the column chart, apply the **Gold, Accent 4** fill color (the third color from the right in the first row of theme colors) to the **Mediterranean** data point.
8. Add a callout to the column chart to emphasize the *Ranch* data point.
   a. Add a **Callout: Line** shape (the fifth option in the *Callouts* section of the Gallery) to the chart.
   b. Add the text: `32% of total`
   c. Resize and position the callout so it is pointing to the *Ranch* column as shown in Figure EX 7.66.
   d. Change the shape style **Subtle Effect - Gray, Accent 3** (the fourth style from the left in the fourth row of theme styles).
9. Apply the **Fill: Blue, Accent color 1; Shadow** WordArt style (the second WordArt style) to the column chart title.

10. Apply the **Dash** dashes line option (the fourth option in the list) to the column chart gridlines.

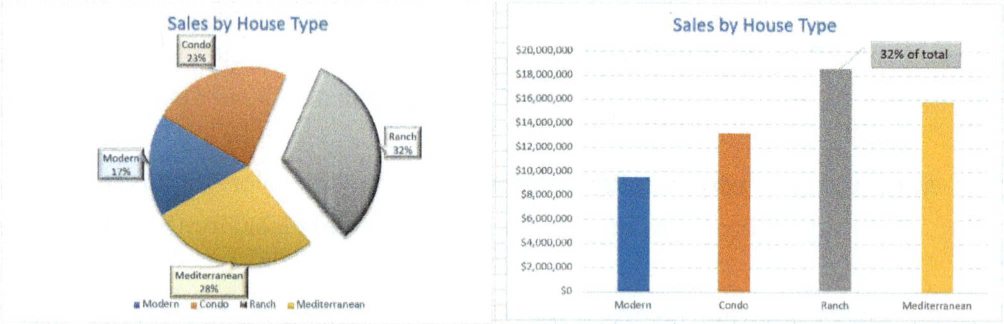

FIGURE EX 7.66

11. Add a trendline to the *1 and 2 Bedroom Condo Sales* chart on the *Condo Sales* worksheet.
    a. Switch to the **Condo Sales** worksheet.
    b. Add a trendline.
    c. Change the trendline type to a two period moving average trendline.
12. Add the *SOLD* picture from your local drive, network, or external media storage device, and then apply a style, resize and move the picture.
    a. Insert the **SOLD** picture.
    b. Apply the **Metal Frame** picture Quick Style (the third style from the left in the top row of the style gallery) to the picture.
    c. Resize the picture so it is **1.5 inches** wide. Do not change the aspect ratio of the picture.
    d. Reposition the picture so it is located near the bottom right corner of the chart as shown in Figure EX 7.67.
13. Add a picture from your local drive, network, or external media storage device to the worksheet header.
    a. Add the **RealtyLogo** picture to the left section of the worksheet header. *Hint:* Because this worksheet is a chart sheet, you cannot switch to Page Layout view. You will need to use the *Page Setup* dialog instead. If you need help with this method, refer to the *another method* box in the *Adding a Picture to a Header* skill.
    b. Preview how the worksheet will look when printed to verify that you inserted the correct picture into the header. It should look similar to Figure EX 7.67.
14. Save and close the workbook.

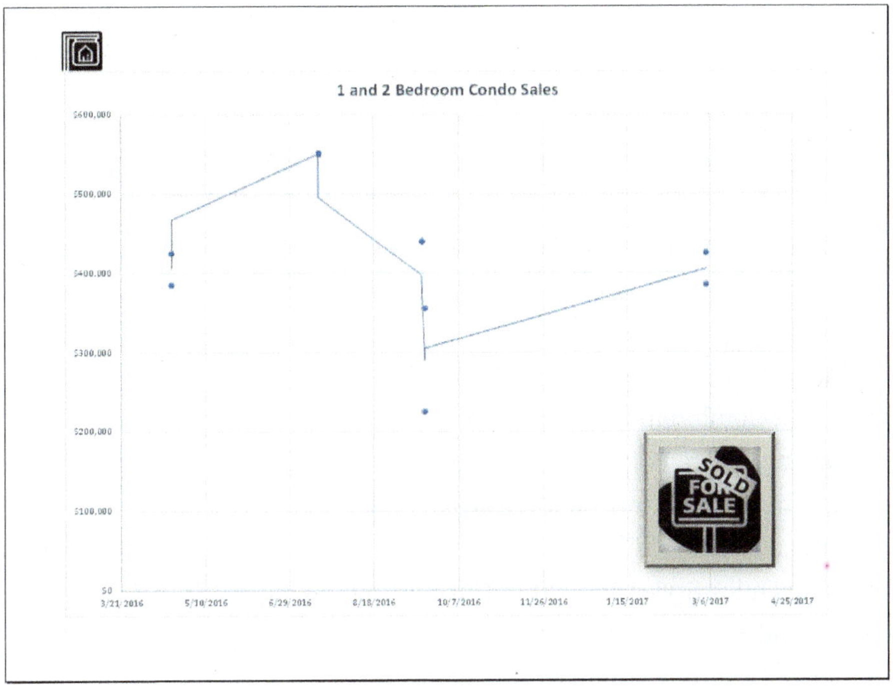

FIGURE EX 7.67

projects

Data files for projects can be found by logging into your SIMnet account and going to the *Library* section.

on your own 7.5

In this project, you will analyze football scores using charting and graphics.

Skills needed to complete this project:

- Adding a Data Series to a Chart (Skill 7.5)
- Creating a Combination Chart (Skill 7.1)
- Formatting a Data Point or a Data Series (Skill 7.6)
- Formatting Other Chart Elements (Skill 7.8)
- Inserting a Shape (Skill 7.21)
- Applying Quick Styles and Other Formatting to Shapes (Skill 7.22)
- Adding and Removing Trendlines (Skill 7.11)
- Changing Trendline Options (Skill 7.12)
- Inserting a Picture (Skill 7.17)
- Resizing and Moving Pictures (Skill 7.18)
- Applying Quick Styles and Other Formatting to Pictures (Skill 7.19)

1. Open the start file **EX2016-OnYourOwn-7-5** and resave the file as: `[your initials]EX-OnYourOwn-7-5`
2. If the workbook opens in Protected View, click the **Enable Editing** button in the Message Bar at the top of the workbook so you can modify the workbook.
3. The *Chart* worksheet contains a scatter chart of the point differences between the winning and losing Super Bowl scores from 1967 through 2017. Add another series to the chart to represent the total scores for the same periods. Use the data on the *Scores* worksheet. *Hint:* Use cell **G2** on the **Scores** worksheet as the **Series name**. Use the data in the *Year* column as the **Series X values** and the data in the *Total Points* column as the **Series Y values**.
4. Change the chart to a combo chart. Use any combination of chart types that works for you. It is not necessary to use a secondary axis.
5. If necessary, change the color of one or both of the data series to make the chart easier to read.
6. Apply other formatting of your choice to the chart. Include at least one WordArt style.
7. Add shapes to the chart to draw attention to the high point for each data series. Add explanatory text of your choice to each shape. Move, resize, and format the shapes as necessary so the text is easy to read.

8. If possible, apply a linear trendline to one of the data series. If necessary, change the color and the width of the trendline so it is clearly visible.
9. Try changing the trendline to different types until you find one that you feel best represents the data trend.
10. Insert a picture of your choice to illustrate the data (from your local drive or use the *Bing Image Search* to find a picture). Resize and move it as necessary.
11. Try applying different formatting options to the picture. Try some of the options from the *Picture Tools Format* tab, *Adjust* group. If you don't like the result, use the *Reset Picture* button to reset the picture back to its original formatting.
12. Save and close the workbook.

projects

Data files for projects can be found by logging into your SIMnet account and going to the *Library* section.

fix it 7.6

In this project, you will fix a salary projections workbook for key departments at a local college.

Skills needed to complete this project:

- Formatting Other Chart Elements (Skill 7.8)
- Changing Trendline Options (Skill 7.12)
- Forecasting Values on a Trendline (Skill 7.13)
- Formatting a Data Point or a Data Series (Skill 7.6)
- Changing the Sparkline Type (Skill 7.14)
- Adding Markers to Sparklines (Skill 7.15)
- Resizing and Moving Pictures (Skill 7.18)
- Adding a Data Series to a Chart (Skill 7.5)
- Adding a Picture to a Header (Skill 7.20)

1. Open the start file **EX2016-FixIt-7-5** and resave the file as:
   `[your initials]EX-FixIt-7-5`
2. If the workbook opens in Protected View, click the **Enable Editing** button in the Message Bar at the top of the workbook so you can modify the workbook.
3. Unfortunately, whoever created this workbook made one of the ugliest charts possible. The first thing to do is fix the chart on the *Salary Projections* worksheet. When you are finished, it should look like the chart in Figure EX7-68.
   a. Change the chart background color to **Green, Accent 1, Lighter 80%** (the fifth color from the left in the second row of theme colors).
   b. Change the gridlines to **Gray, Accent 6** (the first color on the right in the first row of theme colors) and reduce the line width to **½ pt**.
4. The trendline on this chart is wrong. The person who created it chose a logarithmic trendline because it shows the rate of salary increases flattening. However, based on the existing data, that's not the actual trend.
   a. Forecasting forward 10 periods is very misleading when you only have 4 years of data. Change the trendline to forecast **2** periods.
   b. Change the trendline type to the best fit for the existing data. *Hint:* Display the R-squared value and choose the trendline type that has an R-squared value closest to 1.

5. The line representing the *Overall Average Salary* data series should be **Aqua, Accent 4** (the third color from the right in the top row of theme colors). The person who created the chart changed the shape fill color and doesn't understand why the line is still red. Please fix this.
6. It's fine to use a WordArt style for the chart title, but the style chosen makes it difficult to read the text. Use the **Fill: Black, Text color 1; Shadow** WordArt style instead.

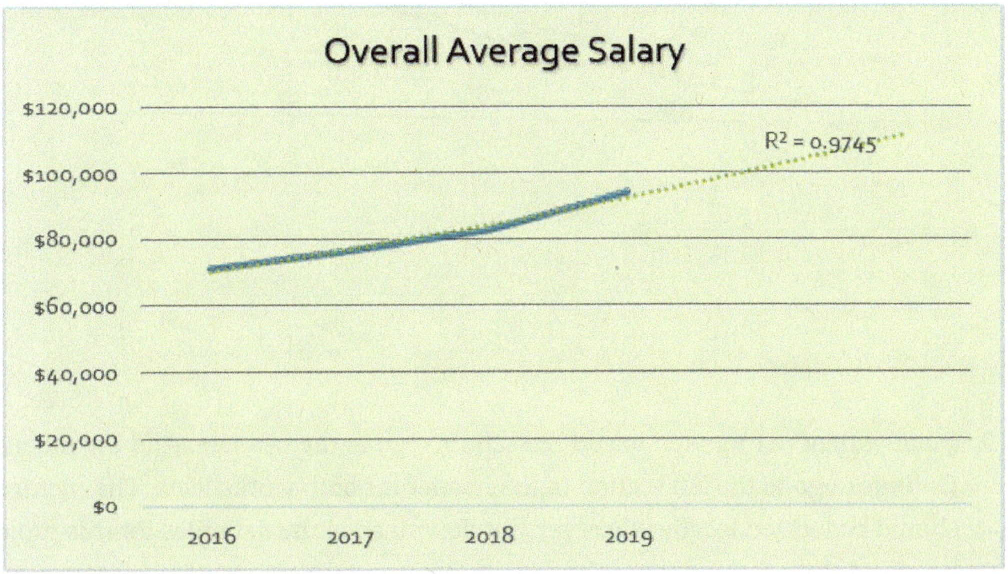

FIGURE EX 7.68

7. The win/loss Sparklines in cells **E12:E18** don't tell us anything about the data.
   a. Change the Sparklines to lines.
   b. Add markers to pinpoint the negative values.
8. The chart on the *Average by Dept* worksheet is better, but it too has a few errors that need correcting.
   a. Someone added the picture of stacked coins to the chart. It is too large and it covers the chart. Move the picture and resize it so it fits below the chart title as shown in Figure EX7-69.
   b. The English department is listed in the chart legend, but the data from the *Salary Projections* worksheet doesn't appear to be represented on the line chart. Can you fix this? *Hint:* You will need to **edit** the series values for the *English* data series through the *Select Data Source* dialog.

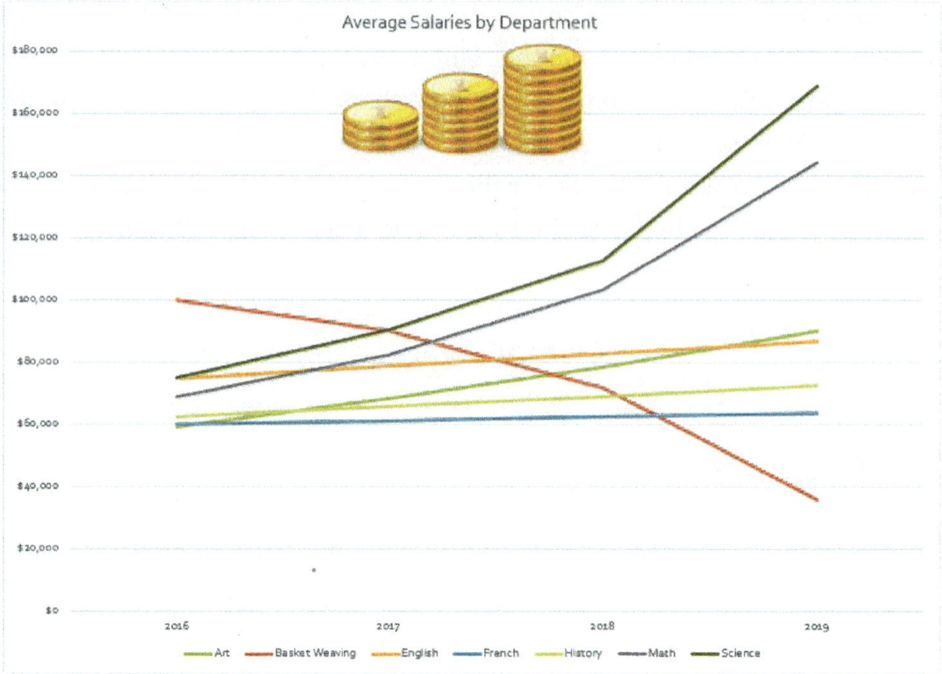

FIGURE EX 7.69

9. Finally, they've forgotten to add the school logo to the headers. Add the picture **CollegeLogo** to the left section of the header for both worksheets. The picture should be located locally wherever you downloaded the data files for this project.
10. Save and close the workbook.

chapter 8

Exploring Advanced Data Analysis

In this chapter, you will learn the following skills:

- Use custom conditional formatting to analyze data
- Use advanced filtering and sorting techniques
- Outline and consolidate data with and without subtotals
- Perform what-if analysis using scenarios, forecast sheets, and Solver
- Use advanced PivotTable and PivotChart techniques

Skill 8.15 Using Solver

Skill 8.16 Refreshing Data in a PivotTable

Skill 8.17 Adding a Calculated Field to a PivotTable

Skill 8.18 Grouping Fields in a PivotTable

Skill 8.19 Filtering PivotTable Data

Skill 8.20 Filtering PivotTable Data with a Timeline

Skill 8.21 Changing the Look of a PivotTable

Skill 8.22 Filtering Data in a PivotChart

Skill 8.23 Changing the Look of a PivotChart

introduction

The material in this chapter builds on your knowledge of conditional formatting, sorting, and filtering. Here you will use custom conditional formatting to highlight and then sort and filter data. You will also learn advanced sorting and filtering techniques. You will summarize and outline data and perform what-if analyses using a variety of methods. Finally, you will expand on the basic PivotTable and PivotChart skills that were covered earlier in this book.

Skill 8.1 Creating New Conditional Formatting Rules

Conditional formatting provides a visual analysis of data by applying formatting to cells that meet specific criteria (conditions). Excel offers a wide variety of conditional formatting options from the *Conditional Formatting* menu (available on the *Home* tab, in the *Styles* group). If one of the prebuilt conditional formatting options does not suit your needs, you can specify your own format through the *New Formatting Rule* dialog. In the *New Formatting Rule* dialog, you first select one of the six rule types, and then specify the conditions and formatting you want.

To create a new conditional formatting rule:

1. Select the data you want to apply conditional formatting to.
2. On the *Home* tab, in the *Styles* group, click the **Conditional Formatting** button.
3. Click **New Rule...** to open the *New Formatting Rule* dialog.

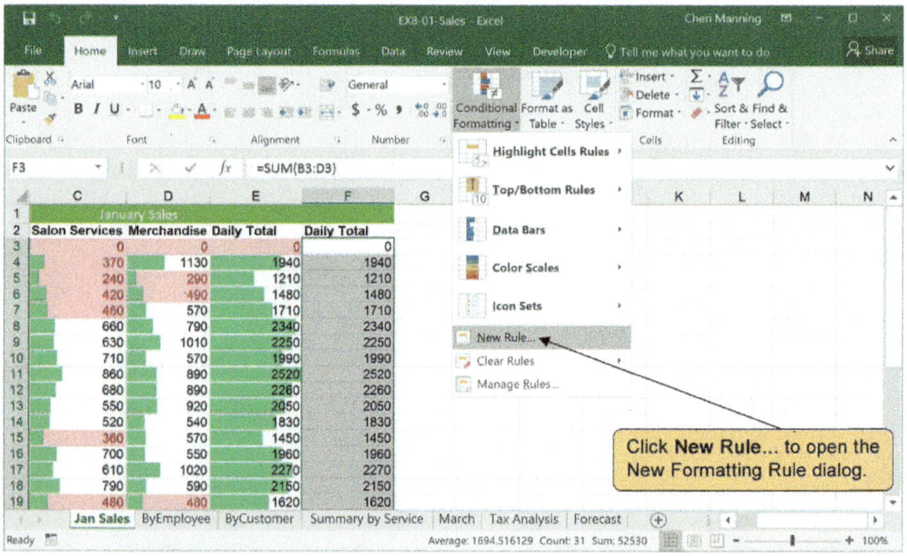

FIGURE EX 8.1

4. Click the type of rule you want to create from the *Select a Rule Type* box.
5. In the *Edit the Rule Description* box, set the rule parameters and formatting options.
6. When you have made all your selections in the *New Formatting Rule* dialog, click **OK** to apply the new conditional formatting rule.

In the *New Formatting Rule* dialog, the options in the *Edit the Rule Description* box are dependent on the type of rule you selected. Each rule type has its own set of rule description values and formatting options.

The first rule type, *Format all cells based on their values*, applies a variable graphic element (color scale, data bar, or icon set) to the cells based on each cell's value relative to the other cells in the selection.

To create a new conditional formatting rule using an icon set:

1. In the *New Formatting Rule* dialog, *Format all cells based on their values* is selected by default.
2. Expand the **Format Style** list and select **Icon Sets**.
3. If necessary, expand the **Icon Style** list and select the icon set you want.
4. To hide the cell value and display only the icon, click the **Show Icon Only** check box.
5. Enter the values to control when each icon is displayed. You can change the comparison operator, the value, and the type. With icon sets, the default comparison operator is >= and the default type is **percent**. Do not use the % symbol when entering values. In Figure EX 8.2, to show the green icon when values are in the top 75% of values, the comparison operator is >=, the value is **75**, and the type is **percent**. To show the red icon when values are below 25%, the value for the *yellow* icon (the middle icon) is set to **>=25 percent**.

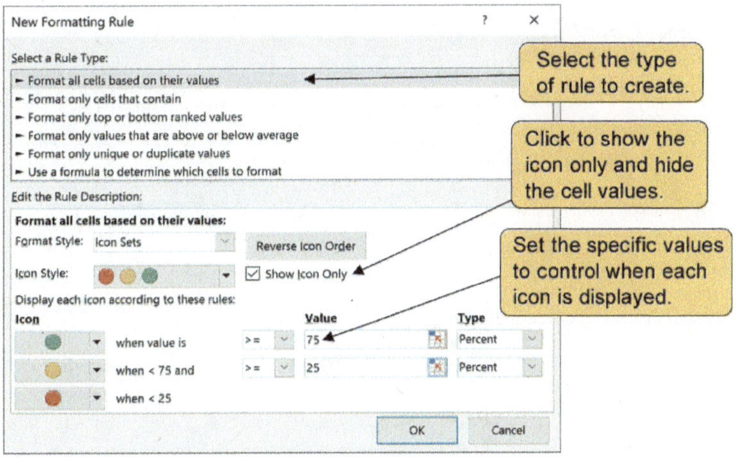

FIGURE EX 8.2

The other rule types all allow you to set cell formatting options instead of applying a graphic element. The options for the rules the cell value must meet change depending on which rule type you select. Setting the cell format is the same for all rule types.

To create a new conditional formatting rule to format cells that are equal to or above the average value:

1. In the *Select a Rule Type* box, click **Format only values that are above or below average**.

2. Expand the **Format values that are** list and select **equal or above.**

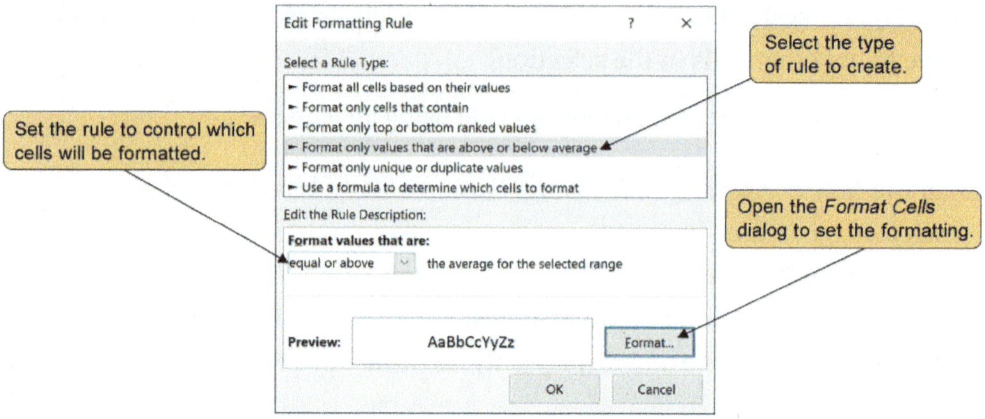

FIGURE EX 8.3

3. Click the **Format...** button to open the *Format Cells* dialog. Notice that this *Format Cells* dialog is slightly different from the one that opens when you format cells in the worksheet.
   a. To apply a specific number format, click the **Number** tab and select the number format to use.
   b. To apply a font change, click the **Font** tab. For conditional formatting, you can change only the font style and the font color. You cannot change the font or font size.

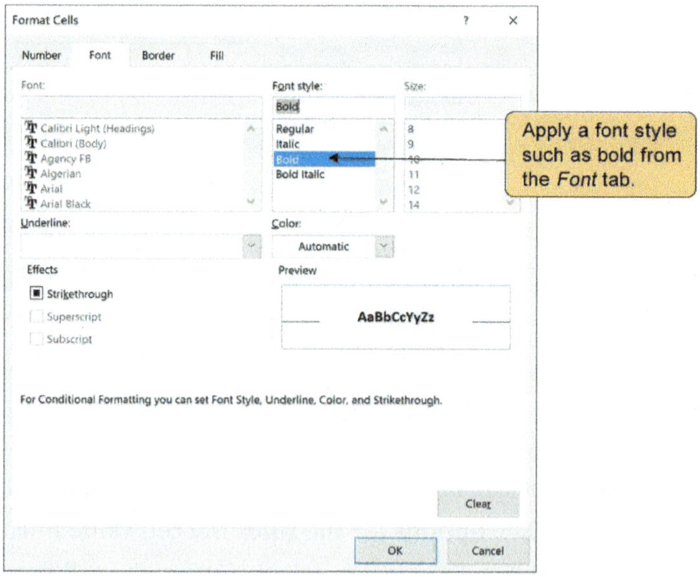

FIGURE EX 8.4

4. To apply a cell border, click the **Border** tab and set the border options.
5. To apply a fill color, click the **Fill** tab and click the color you want.

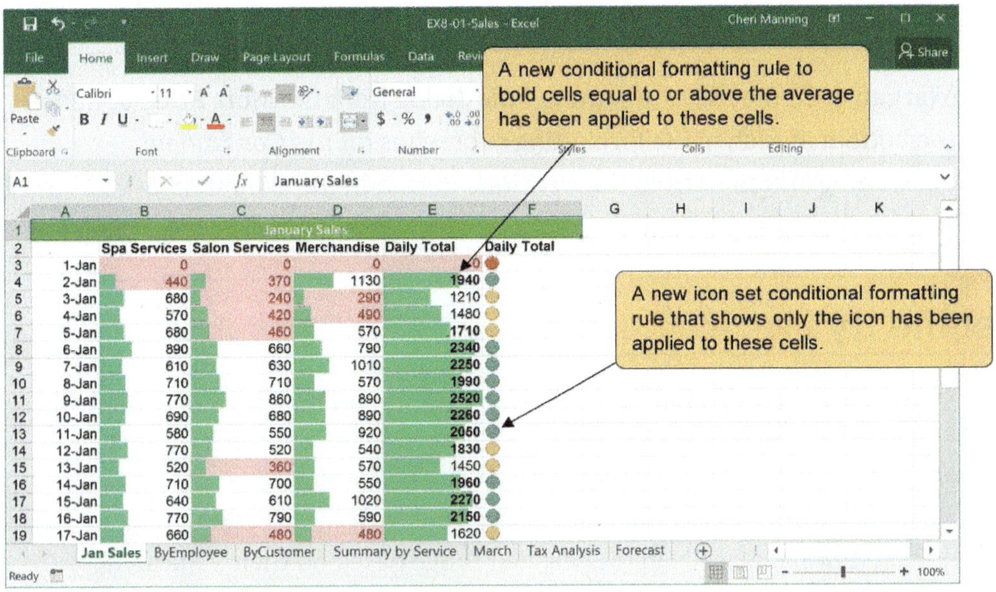

FIGURE EX 8.5

tips & tricks

If you are using conditional formatting with icon sets and your worksheet looks too busy, use this trick:

1. Create a copy of the column of data you want to apply the icon set to.
2. Select the copied data, and create a new conditional formatting rule, using the icon set.
3. In the *New Formatting Rule* dialog, click the **Show Icon Only** check box.

Now you have two columns—one showing the values and one showing only the icon.

tell me more

For a review of conditional formatting, refer to the following skills:

- *Applying Conditional Formatting Using the Quick Analysis Tool*
- *Applying Conditional Formatting with Data Bars, Color Scales, and Icon Sets*
- *Applying Conditional Formatting with Highlight Cells Rules*
- *Applying Conditional Formatting with Top/Bottom Rules*
- *Removing Conditional Formatting*

another method

You can open the *New Formatting Rule* dialog from the *More Rules* option at the bottom of each of the formatting submenus off the *Conditional Formatting* button or from the *New Rule* button in the Conditional Formatting Rules Manager.

let me try *Live!*

Open the student data file **EX8-01-Sales** and try this skill on your own:

1. On the *Jan Sales* worksheet, select cells **F3:F33**.
2. Apply a new conditional formatting rule with these conditions:
   a. Format all cells in the selected range based on their values.
   b. Change the format style to **Icon Sets** and use the **Three traffic lights (unrimmed)** icon set. This is the default icon set.
   c. Show only the icon, not the cell value.
   d. Show the green light icon when the value is **>=75**. Leave the *type* as **percent**.
   e. Show the yellow light icon when the value is **<75 and >=25**. Leave the *type* as **percent**.
3. Select cells **E3:E33**.
4. Apply a new conditional formatting rule with these conditions:
   a. Format only values that are **equal to or above the average** for the selected range.
   b. Cells that meet the rule should be **bold**.
5. If you will be moving on to the next skill in this chapter, leave the workbook open to continue working. If not, save the file as directed by your instructor and close it.

Skill 8.2 Managing Conditional Formatting Rules

When more than one conditional formatting rule is applied to a group of cells, the rules are applied in the order in which they are created. This can sometimes result in conflicts or unexpected results. The **Conditional Formatting Rules Manager** allows you to delete, edit, reorder, and control the way in which conditional formatting rules are applied to your worksheet.

To use the Conditional Formatting Rules Manager:

1. On the *Home* tab, in the *Styles* group, click the **Conditional Formatting** button. Click **Manage Rules...**

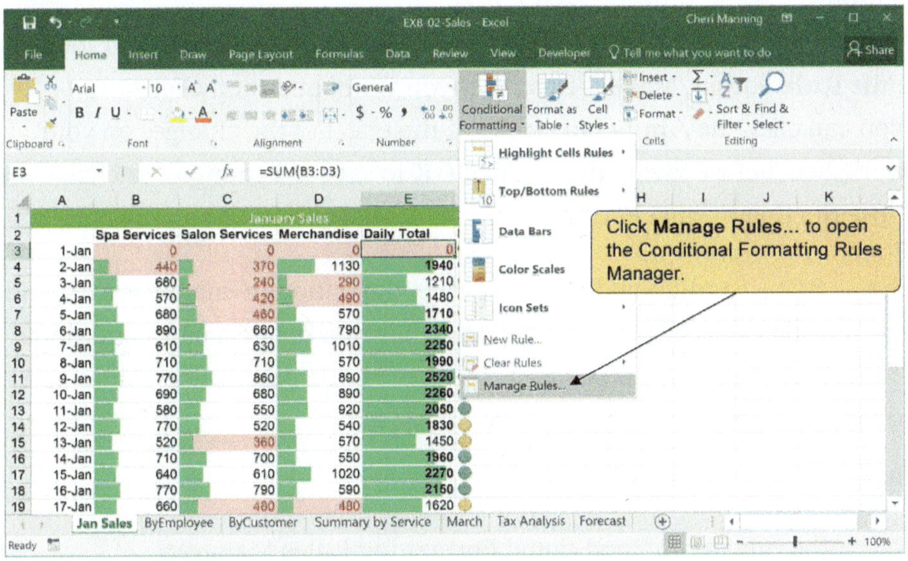

FIGURE EX 8.6

2. If necessary, expand the *Show formatting rule for* list, and select the part of the workbook you want to manage rules for.
3. From the box next to each formatting rule, you can edit the range of cells to which the rule is applied. If the data in your worksheet have changed since you first created the conditional formatting rule, this is an easy way to update the cell range.
4. When there are multiple formatting rules applied to the same set of cells, click the **Stop If True** check box to prevent later conditional formats from being applied to the cells when the selected condition is true.

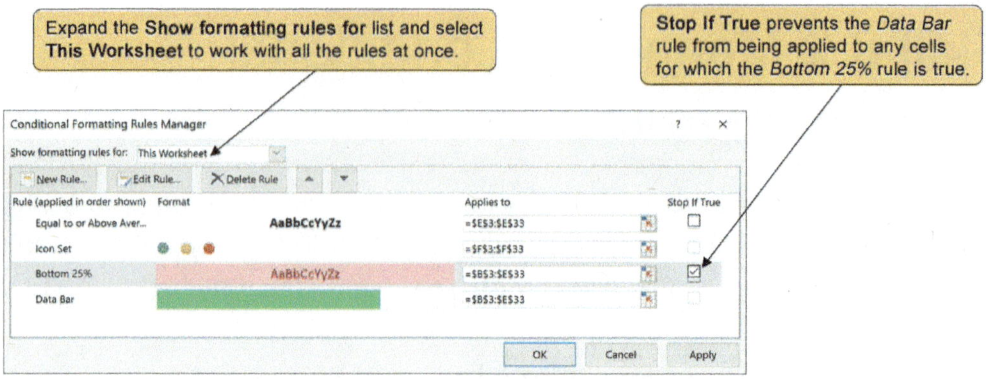

FIGURE EX 8.7

5. To change the order in which rules are applied, click the rule you want to be applied first, and click the **Move Up** button until that rule is at the top of the list.
6. To delete a rule, click the rule you want to delete, and then click the **Delete Rule** button.
7. To modify one of the rules, click the rule you want to change, and then click the **Edit Rule** button. Make the changes you want, and then click **OK**.
8. You can click the **Apply** button to see the effect of the changes on your worksheet before saving them. Click **OK** to save the changes, or click **Cancel** to close the Conditional Formatting Rules Manager without making any changes.

When you edit a conditional formatting rule, the options available are dependent on the type of rule you select, just as they are when you create a new conditional formatting rule. Each rule type has its own set of rule description values and formatting options.

To change formatting for a data bar rule:

1. Select the rule in the Conditional Formatting Rules Manager.
2. Click the **Edit Rule...** button.
3. If you do not want the data bars applied to every cell, expand the **Type** list under *Minimum* and *Maximum* and make a different selection.

   When you change the type to something other than *Automatic*, you can set specific values to use in the *Value* boxes.

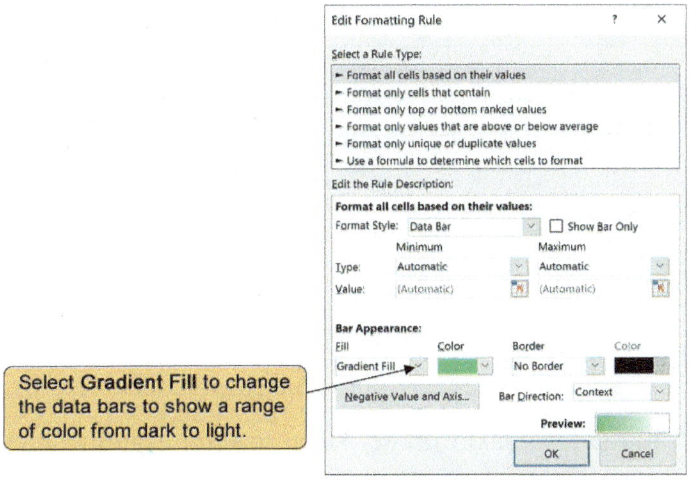

FIGURE EX 8.8

4. To change the fill type for the data bars, expand the **Fill** list and select **Gradient Fill** or **Solid Fill**.
5. To change the color, click the **Color** arrow to display the color palette and select a color.
6. To show only the data bars and hide the cell values, click the **Show Bar Only** check box.
7. Click **OK** in the *Edit Formatting Rule* dialog, and then click **OK** again in the Conditional Formatting Rules Manager to save the changes.

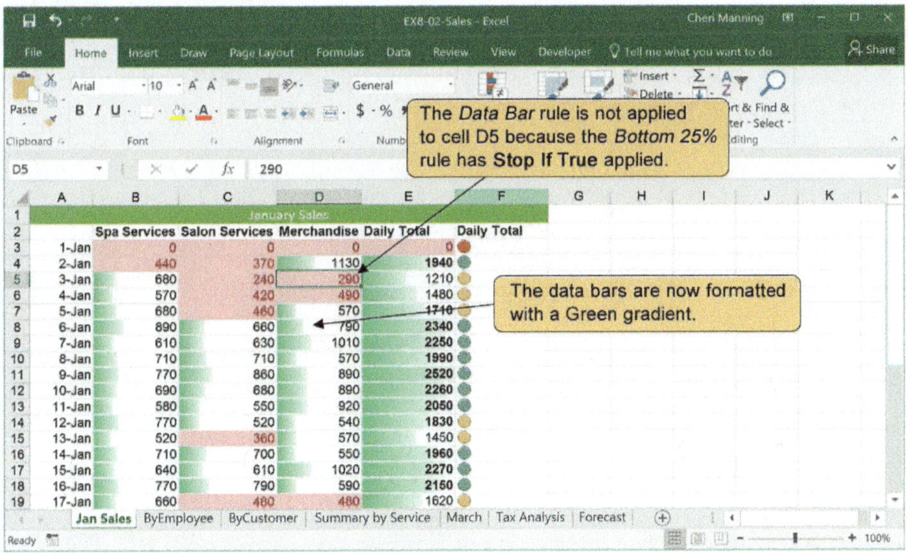

FIGURE EX 8.9

tips & tricks

Using the *Clear Rules* command from the *Conditional Formatting* menu off the Ribbon clears ***all*** the conditional formatting from the selected cells or worksheet. Use the *Delete Rule* command from the Conditional Formatting Rules Manager instead if you want to remove only some of the conditional formatting rules.

tell me more

You can reverse the order of icon sets (for example, reversing the *Three Traffic Lights* icon set applies the red traffic light icon to the highest value instead of the lowest value and applies the green icon to the lowest value instead of the highest value).

1. In the Conditional Formatting Rules Manager, click the *Icon Set* rule you want to reverse.
2. Click the **Edit Rule...** button.
3. In the *Edit Formatting Rule* dialog, click the **Reverse Icon Order** button. Watch carefully in the *Display each icon according to these rules* section to see the change. The button does not change states when the icon order has been reversed.
4. To reverse the icon order again (to put it back to the original order), click the **Reverse Icon Order** button again.

let me try *Live!*

If you do not have the data file from the previous skill open, open the student data file
EX8-02-Sales and try this skill on your own:

1. Select any cell in the *Jan Sales* worksheet.
2. Open the **Conditional Formatting Rules Manager**.
3. Show all the formatting rules in this worksheet.
4. Apply the **Stop If True** option to the *Bottom 25%* rule so cells with a value in the bottom 25% of all values will not have the *Data Bar* rule applied to them.
5. Delete the **Equal to or above average** rule.
6. Edit the *Data Bar* rule and change the data bar fill to a gradient.
7. Save the conditional formatting changes.
8. If you will be moving on to the next skill in this chapter, leave the workbook open to continue working. If not, save the file as directed by your instructor and close it.

Skill 8.3 Filtering and Sorting Using Cell Attributes

You can sort or filter data based on cell color, font color, or icons that were applied with conditional formatting or cell styles. If you need a refresher on sorting and filtering data, refer to the skills *Sorting Data* and *Filtering Data*.

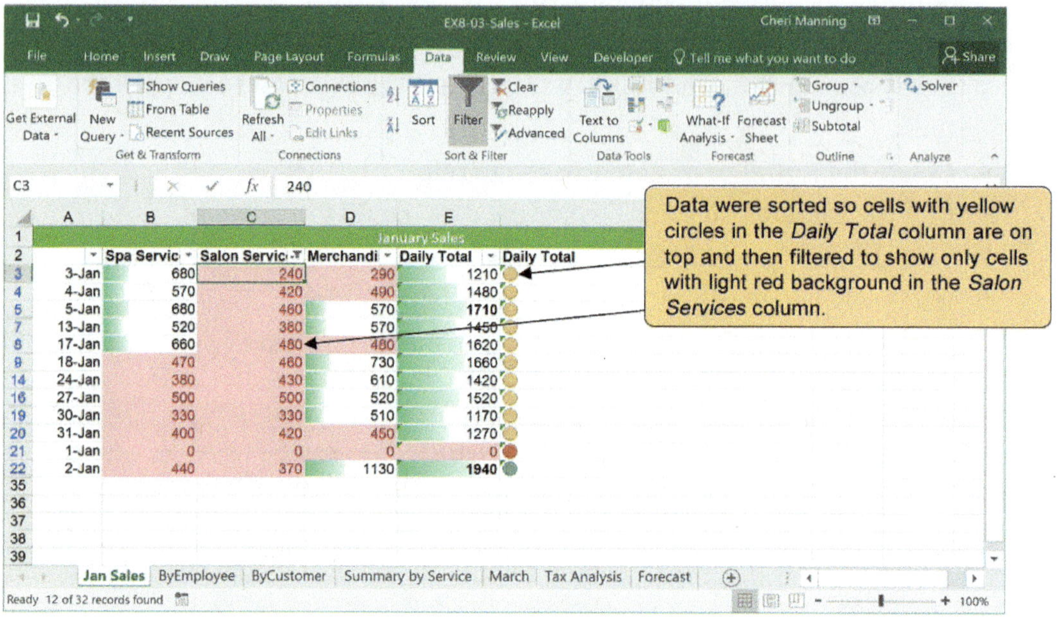

FIGURE EX 8.10

Typically, when you sort data by a single column, you use the *Sort A to Z* or *Sort Z to A* commands available from the *Home* tab, *Editing* group, *Sort & Filter* button or the *Data* tab, *Sort & Filter* group. However, A to Z type sorting does not work with color or icons. Instead, you pick which color or icon appears at the top. Excel moves the rows with the cell attribute you select to the top, and leaves the other rows in their current order.

To sort data by cell attribute:

1. If necessary, on the *Data* tab, in the *Sort & Filter* group, click the **Filter** button to display the AutoFilter arrows at the top of each column. If the data are formatted as a table, these arrows will be available automatically.
2. Click the AutoFilter arrow at the top of the column that includes the cell format you want to sort by.
3. Point to **Sort by Color**, and click the option you want to sort by. Excel automatically displays the options available for that particular column: *Sort by Cell Color, Sort by Font Color,* and *Sort by Cell Icon.*

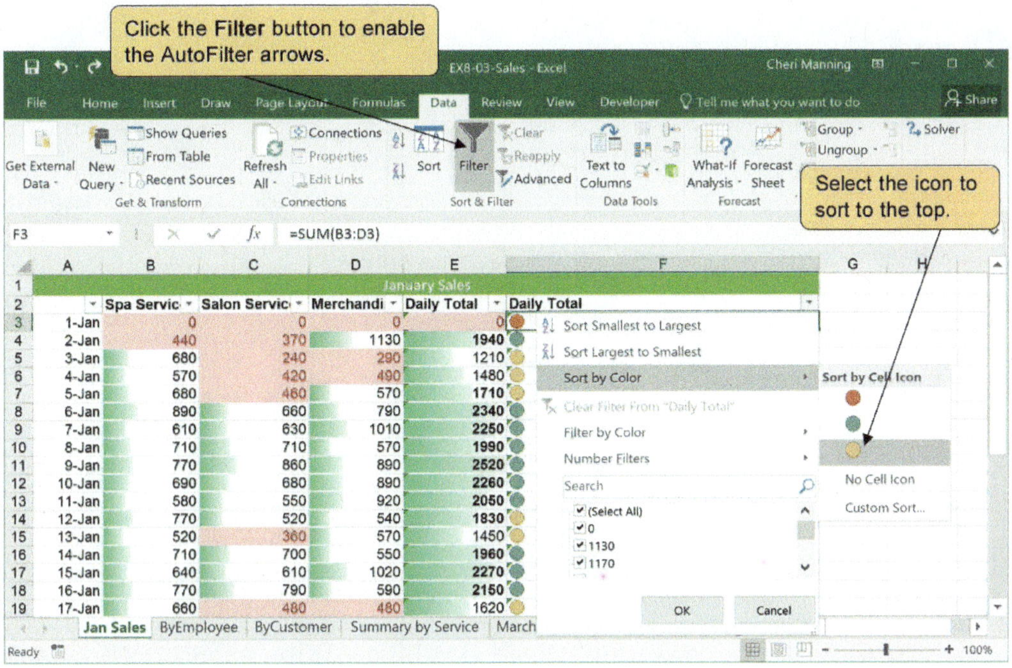

FIGURE EX 8.11

To filter data by cell attribute:

1. If necessary, on the *Data* tab, in the *Sort & Filter* group, click the **Filter** button to display the AutoFilter arrows at the top of each column. If the data are formatted as a table, these arrows are available automatically.
2. Click the AutoFilter arrow at the top of the column that includes the cell format for which you want to filter.
3. Point to **Filter by Color**, and click the option for which you want to filter. Excel automatically displays the options available for that particular column: *Filter by Cell Color*, *Filter by Font Color*, and *Filter by Cell Icon*.

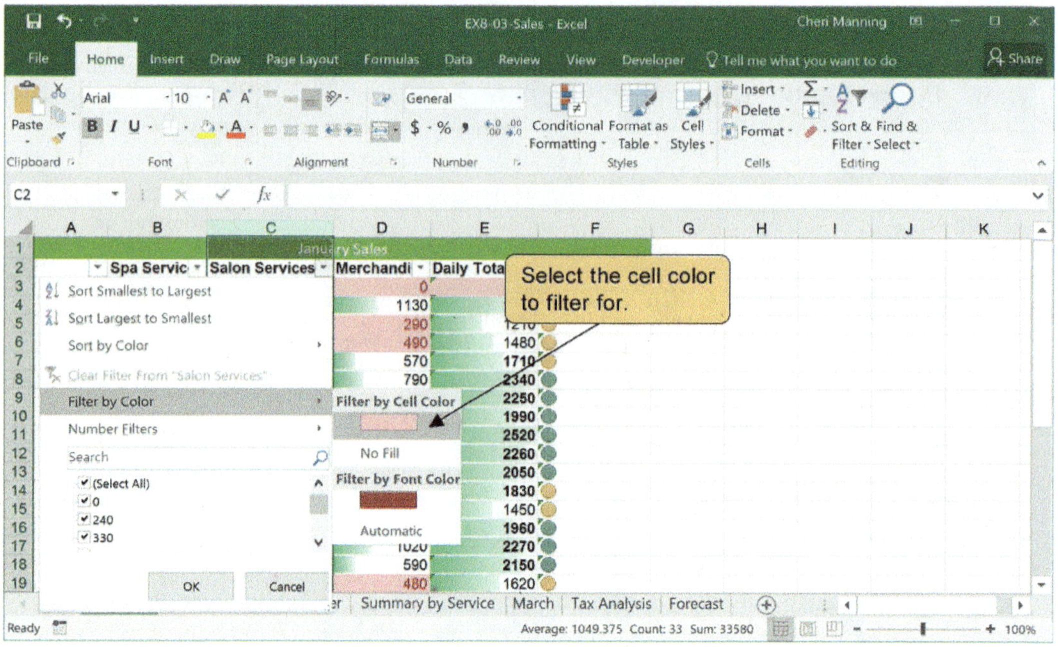

FIGURE EX 8.12

tips & tricks

Excel does not recognize data bars and color scales as icons or as cell colors, so you cannot sort and filter cells using those conditional formatting styles.

tell me more

You can specify that cells with a specific cell attribute appear at the top of the column and cells with another attribute appear at the bottom of the column. From the *Sort* dialog, use the **Add Level** button to create multiple sort levels, and use the *Sort On* list to select **Cell Color**, **Font Color**, or **Cell Icon**. For more information on using the *Sort* dialog, refer to the skill *Sorting Data on Multiple Criteria*.

another method

Right-click a cell that includes the attribute you want to sort or filter by and then point to **Sort** or **Filter** and select the option you want (such as **Put Selected Cell Icon on Top** or **Filter by Selected Cell's Color**).

let me try *Live!*

If you do not have the data file from the previous skill open, open the student data file
EX8-03-Sales and try this skill on your own:

1. Select cell **F3** in the *Jan Sales* worksheet.
2. Sort the data so cells with the yellow circle icon (the last icon in the list) in column F (the second *Daily Total* column) appear on top.
3. Now filter the data to show only cells with the light red background in column C (the *Salon Services* column).
4. If you will be moving on to the next skill in this chapter, leave the workbook open to continue working. If not, save the file as directed by your instructor and close it.

Skill 8.4 Sorting Data on Multiple Critera

Recall that sorting rearranges the rows in your worksheet by the data in a column. If you want to create a multilevel sort so the data are sorted first by one criteria and then sorted again within each group, use the *Sort* dialog. For each sort level, set the column to sort by, the type of sort, and the order in which you want the data sorted.

In Figure EX 8.13, the data are sorted first by values in the *Top Seller* column, so all the rows with *FS* as the top seller come before the rows with *KD*. Next, the rows within each group are sorted by date.

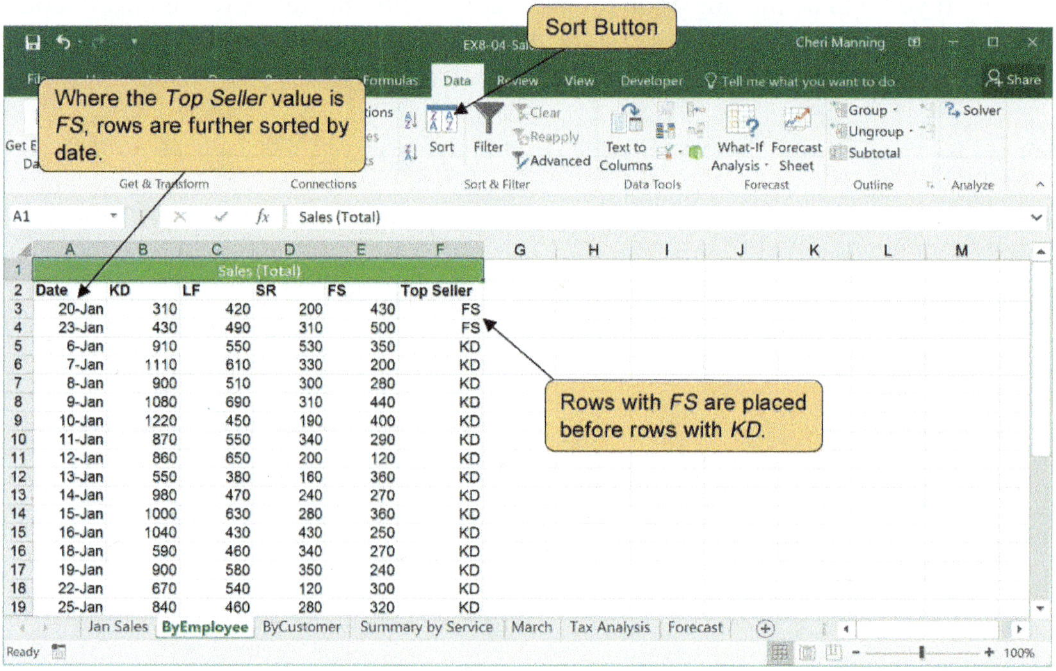

FIGURE EX 8.13

To sort data on multiple criteria:

1. Select any cell in the data range.
2. On the *Data* tab, in the *Sort & Filter* group, click the **Sort** button.
3. If your data include a header row, Excel will usually identify that for you and automatically check the *My data has headers* check box.
4. In the *Sort* dialog, expand the **Sort by** list, and select the column you want to use for the first sort level.
5. The *Sort On* list defaults to **Value**. If you want to sort by a cell attribute instead, expand the **Sort On** list and select **Cell Color**, **Font Color**, or **Cell Icon**.

6. The *Order* list detects what type of data are in the column and displays appropriate options such as *A-Z* for text, *Smallest to Largest* for numbers, and *Oldest to Newest* for dates. To change the sort order, expand the list and select another option.
7. Click the **Add Level** button.
8. Expand the **Then by** list, and select the column you want for the next sort level.
9. Continue adding levels and building the sort criteria until you are finished.
10. To rearrange the order of sort criteria, click the level you want to move, and then use the **Move Up** or **Move Down** arrow.
11. To delete a level from the sort, click the level you want to delete, and then click the **Delete Level** button.
12. When you have built all the levels for the sort, click **OK**.

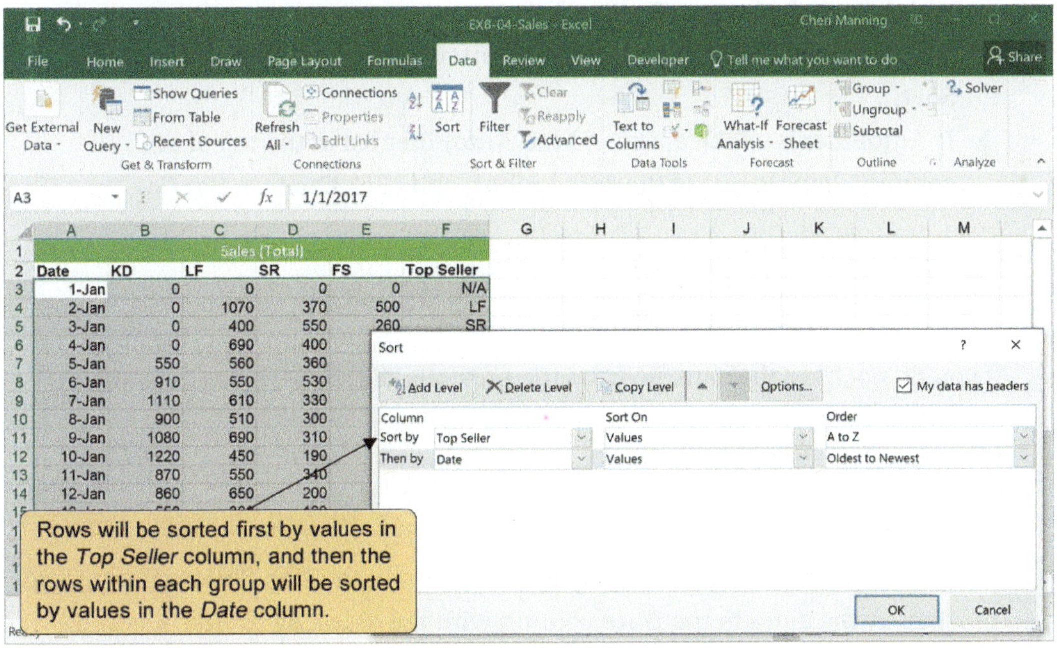

FIGURE EX 8.14

tips & tricks

The *Sort* command ignores hidden rows and columns. Be sure to unhide any hidden rows or columns before sorting the data or you may end up with unexpected results.

tell me **more**

By default, Excel ignores text case when sorting. To enforce case sensitivity, click the **Options** button in the *Sort* dialog, and check the **Case sensitive** check box. When this option is enabled, identical text will be sorted with initial lowercase before initial uppercase (i.e., *shell* will come before *Shell* in the sort order).

another method

To open the *Sort* dialog:

- From the *Home* tab, in the *Editing* group, click the **Sort & Filter** button and then click **Custom Sort...**
- Right-click any cell in the data set. Point to *Sort*, and click **Custom Sort...**
- If AutoFilter is enabled, expand the AutoFilter list at the top of any column. Point to one of the sort options, and click **Custom Sort...**

let me try *Live!*

If you do not have the data file from the previous skill open, open the student data file

EX8-04-Sales and try this skill on your own:

1. Select cell **A3** in the *ByEmployee* worksheet.
2. Sort the data first alphabetically by the values in the **Top Seller** column and then by the dates in the **Date** column with the oldest dates first.
3. If you will be moving on to the next skill in this chapter, leave the workbook open to continue working. If not, save the file as directed by your instructor and close it.

Skill 8.5 Creating a Custom Filter

In addition to filtering by matching exact values or cell attributes, you can filter for values that meet broader criteria. Columns with different data types have different filtering criteria options available.

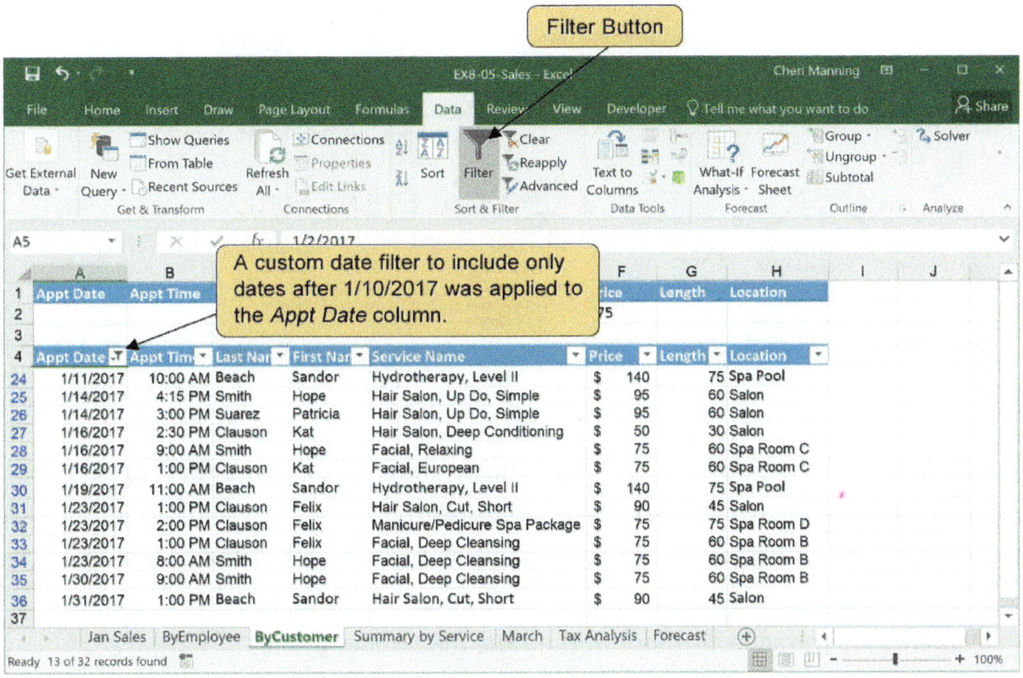

FIGURE EX 8.15

If the data are formatted as a table, filtering is enabled automatically. If your data are not formatted as a table, you must first enable filtering. On the *Data* tab, in the *Sort & Filter* group, click the **Filter** button.

To create a custom date filter:

1. Click the AutoFilter arrow at the top of the column that contains the data you want to filter for, and point to **Date Filters**.
2. Click the filter type you want. There is an extensive list of custom date filter options as shown in Figure EX 8.16.

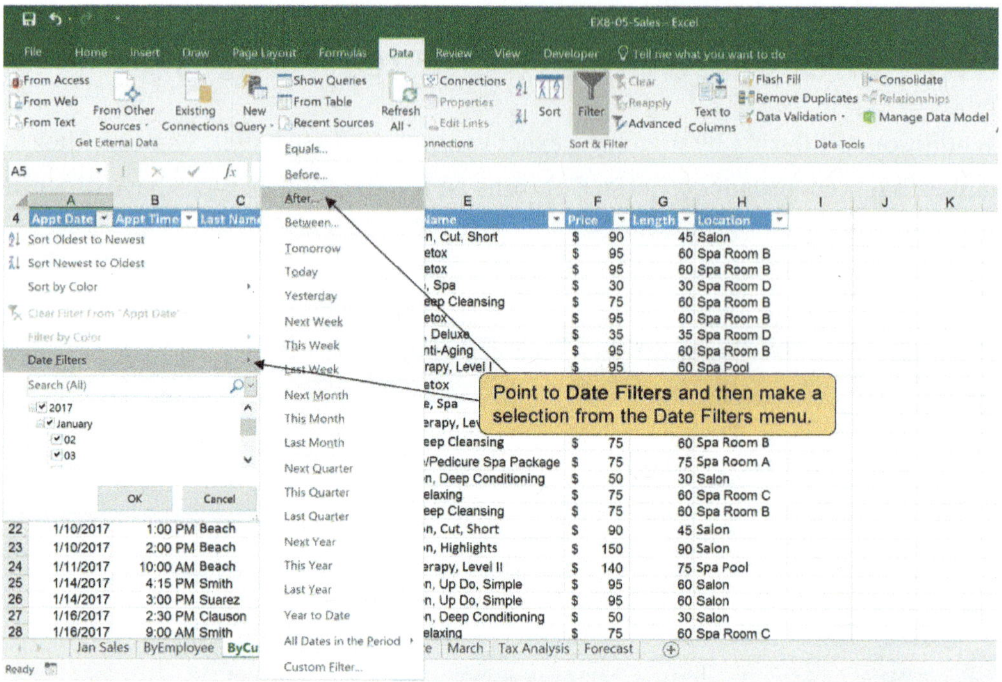

FIGURE EX 8.16

3. The first box in the *Custom AutoFilter* dialog shows the custom filter option you selected. Type the date criteria in the box next to it.
4. You can further refine the filter by expanding the second list and selecting a filter option and then entering the criteria in the box next to it. The filter options available are the same as those in the *Date Filters* menu.
   - The *And* radio button requires that data meet ***both*** criteria in order to be included in the filter.
   - The *Or* radio button requires that data meet ***either*** of the criteria.

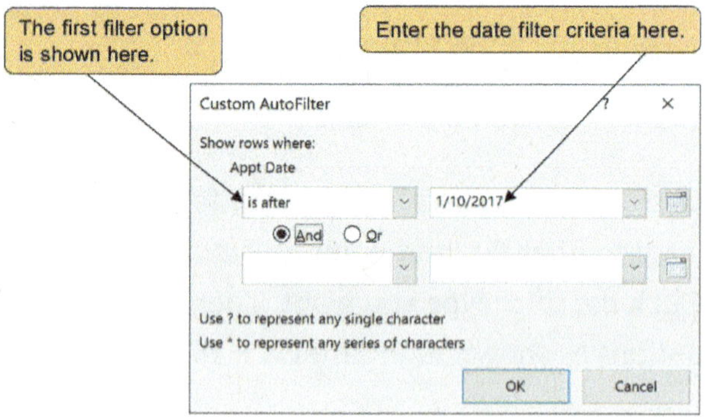

FIGURE EX 8.17

5. Click **OK** to apply the filter.

To create a custom text filter or custom number filter, follow the same steps as shown in Figure EX 8.18 and Figure EX 8.19.

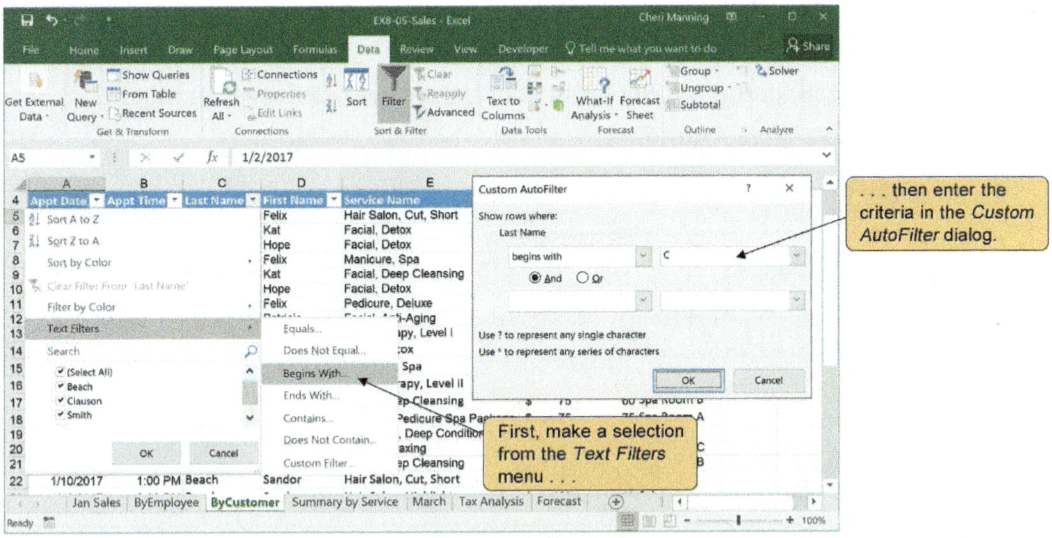

FIGURE EX 8.18

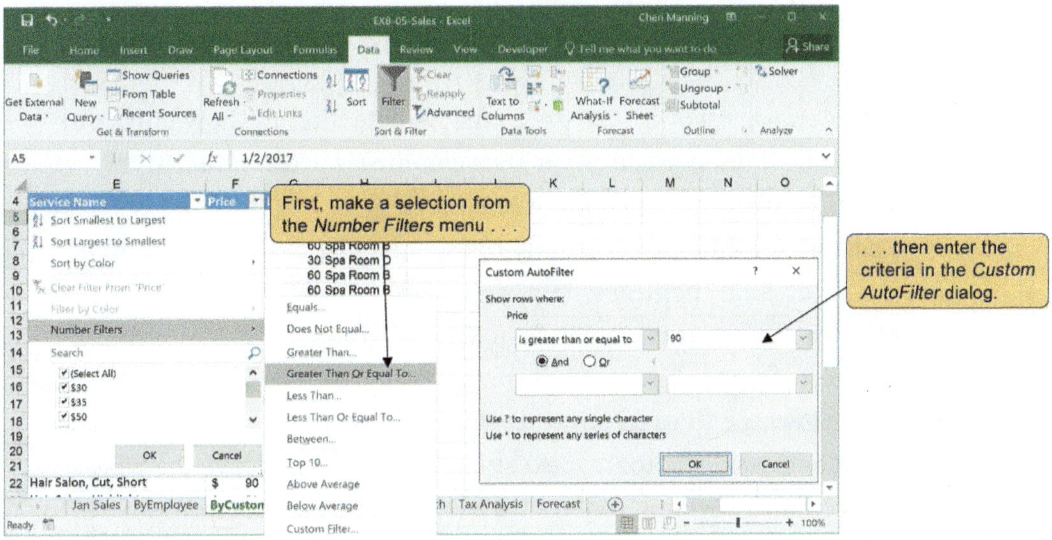

FIGURE EX 8.19

When a filter has been applied to a column, the column header will display a funnel icon: . To clear the filter, click the funnel icon and select **Clear Filter from 'Name of Column'**.

tips & tricks

When a filter has been applied to a column, clicking the **Filter** button again will remove the filter, but it will also remove the AutoFilter arrows.

another method

On the *Home* tab, in the *Editing* group, click the **Sort & Filter** button, and select **Filter** to enable AutoFilter.

To clear the filter:

- On the *Data* tab, in the *Sort & Filter* group, click the **Clear** button.
- On the *Home* tab, in the *Editing* group, click the **Sort & Filter** button, and then select **Clear**.

let me try *Live!*

If you do not have the data file from the previous skill open, open the student data file
EX8-05-Sales and try this skill on your own:

1. On the *ByCustomer* worksheet, use a custom date filter to show only rows where the appointment date (*Appt Date* column) is **after 1/10/2017**.
2. Clear the filter without removing AutoFilter.
3. Use a custom text filter to show only rows where the customer last name (*Last Name* column) **begins with the letter C**.
4. Clear the filter without removing AutoFilter.
5. Use a custom number filter to show only rows where the service price (*Price* column) is **greater than or equal to 90**.
6. If you will be moving on to the next skill in this chapter, leave the workbook open to continue working. If not, save the file as directed by your instructor and close it.

Skill 8.6 Using Advanced Filter

Excel's **Advanced Filter** feature allows you to filter data for criteria in multiple columns using multiple criteria with logical AND and OR operators. If you are familiar with using Excel database functions or creating queries in Access, using Advanced Filter will seem familiar.

Before using Advanced Filter, you must set up the **criteria range**. The criteria range can be on the same worksheet or another worksheet in the same workbook. It must include a row of data labels that match the data labels in the data set you are going to filter and include at least one row below the data labels where you will enter the criteria for the filter.

In the criteria range, type the criteria for which you want to filter.

- If you type criteria in the same row, Excel will use the logical operator AND in the filter—data must meet both criteria.
- If you type criteria in separate rows, Excel will apply the logical operator OR—data must meet either criterion.

The criteria range in Figure EX 8.20 is defined as cells A1:H2. The labels in row 1 match the labels for the data set in row 4. The criterion **Smith** has been entered under the label *Last Name* and the criterion **>75** has been entered in the same row under the label *Price*. When Advanced Filter uses this criteria range, the data are filtered to show only rows where the value in the *Last Name* column is **Smith *and*** the value in the *Price* column is **greater than 75**.

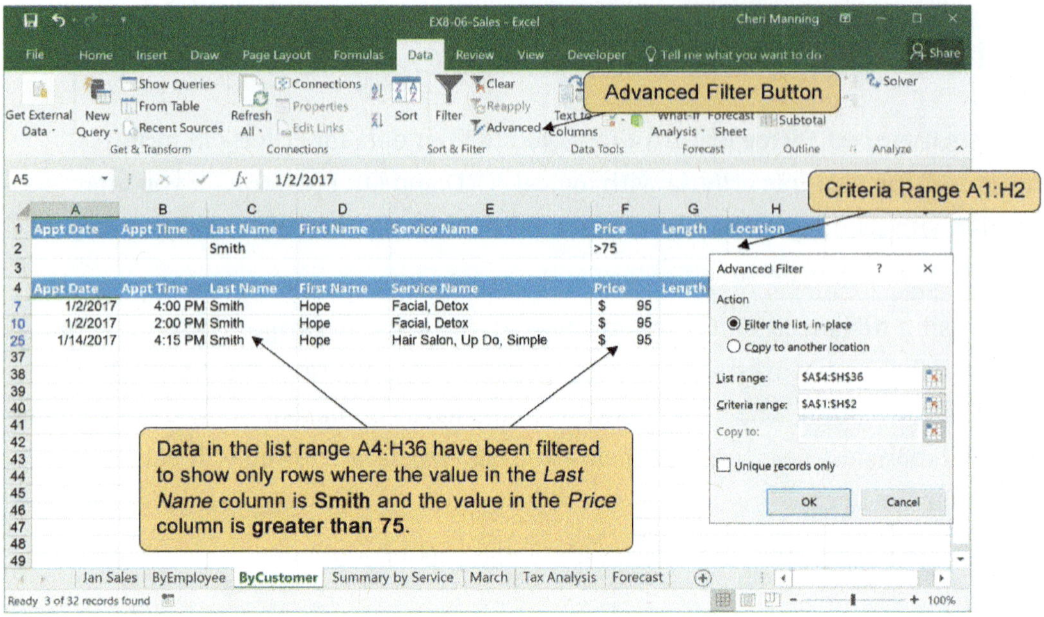

FIGURE EX 8.20

To use Advanced Filter:

1. Click anywhere in the data set you want to filter.
2. On the *Data* tab, in the *Sort & Filter* group, click the **Advanced** button.
3. If necessary, enter the appropriate cell references in the *List range* box. If you begin with a cell in the data set selected, Excel will enter the cell range in the *List range* box for you.
4. Click in the *Criteria range* box and enter the cell references or the name for the criteria range, including the label row. Be careful that your criteria range does not include blank rows.
5. Click **OK**.

To clear the filter from the data, on the *Data* tab, in the *Sort & Filter* group, click the **Clear** button.

tips & tricks

- An easy way to create a criteria range is to insert a few blank rows above the data you want to filter. There should be at least one blank row between the criteria range and the data set. Copy the data label row to the first row of the criteria range and then enter the filter criteria in the row below.
- The first time you define the criteria range, Excel will name the range *Criteria* and then automatically use that criteria range the next time you use Advanced Filter.
- If you name the criteria range *Criteria* before using Advanced Filter, Excel will automatically place the range in the *Criteria range* box for you.

tell me more

By default, Advanced Filter will filter the data in-place. You can also elect to copy the filtered data to another location in the workbook:

1. In the *Advanced Filter* dialog, click the **Copy to another location** radio button.
2. In the *Copy to* box, enter the cell reference for the upper left corner of the range where you want Excel to paste a copy of the data labels and the records that meet the criteria. The location where the filtered records are copied is called the **extract range**.

another method

You can clear the filter from the *Home* tab. In the *Editing* group, click the **Sort & Filter** button, and click **Clear**.

let me try *Live!*

If you do not have the data file from the previous skill open, open the student data file
EX8-06-Sales and try this skill on your own:

1. Continue working with the *ByCustomer* worksheet. If there is a filter applied to the *Price* column, clear it.
2. A criteria range has been set up for you in cells **A1:H2**. Enter criteria in the criteria range to show only rows where the *Last Name* is **Smith** and the *Price* is **greater than 75** and then click any cell in the list range.
3. Filter the data in place using the list range **A4:H36**. The criteria range is **A1:H2**.
4. If you will be moving on to the next skill in this chapter, leave the workbook open to continue working. If not, save the file as directed by your instructor and close it.

Skill 8.7 Adding Subtotals

Adding **subtotals** is an easy way to outline large amounts of data. In order to use subtotals, the data range must be arranged in columns with the first row containing column headings. The columns must be sorted so the rows you want totaled are grouped together. When you add a subtotal, Excel automatically calculates subtotals based on the grouping you selected. Excel inserts formulas using the SUBTOTAL function in a subtotal row for each group and in a grand total row to summarize all the data in the list.

To create an outline automatically using subtotals:

1. Ensure that your data range is organized in rows, with the first row containing column headings.
2. Sort by the column you want to organize into groups.
3. Once the range is sorted into groups, on the *Data* tab, in the *Outline* group, click the **Subtotal** button.
4. In the *Subtotal* dialog, click the **At each change in** arrow, and select the column for which you want to create subtotals—the same column you just sorted by. Excel will create a new subtotal line each time it finds a new value in this column. (That's why you need to sort the data first—so matching values in this column are grouped together before you add the subtotals.)

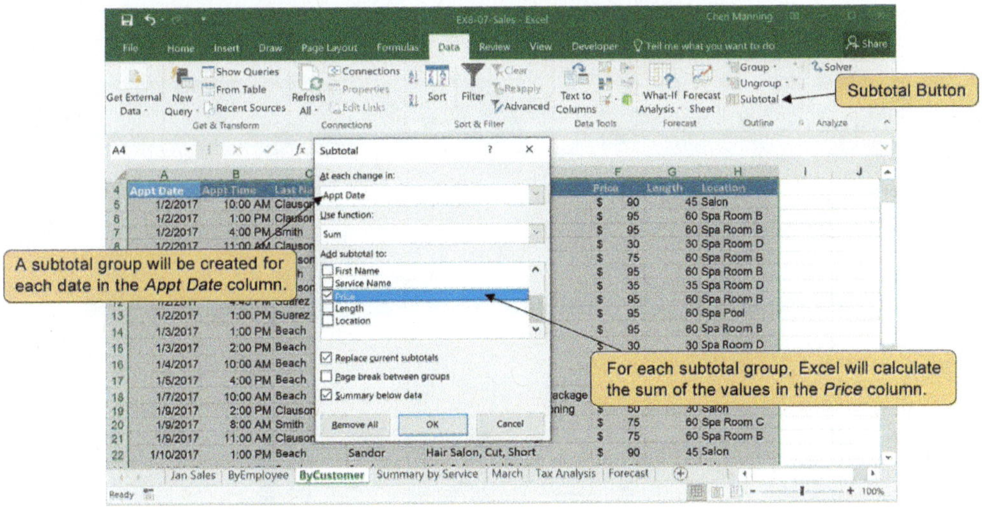

FIGURE EX 8.21

5. Select the function you want to use from the **Use function** drop-down list. Excel can create subtotals with a variety of functions, but SUM and AVERAGE are probably the most common.
6. In the *Add subtotal to* box, check the box(es) for the column(s) containing the data to add subtotals to.

7. Verify that the **Summary below data** check box is selected to place the new subtotal rows below each group. Uncheck this box only if you want the summary row *above* the details instead.
8. Click **OK** to add the subtotals and grouping to your data.

When rows are outlined with subtotals, outline symbols appear to the left of the column headings and row numbers.

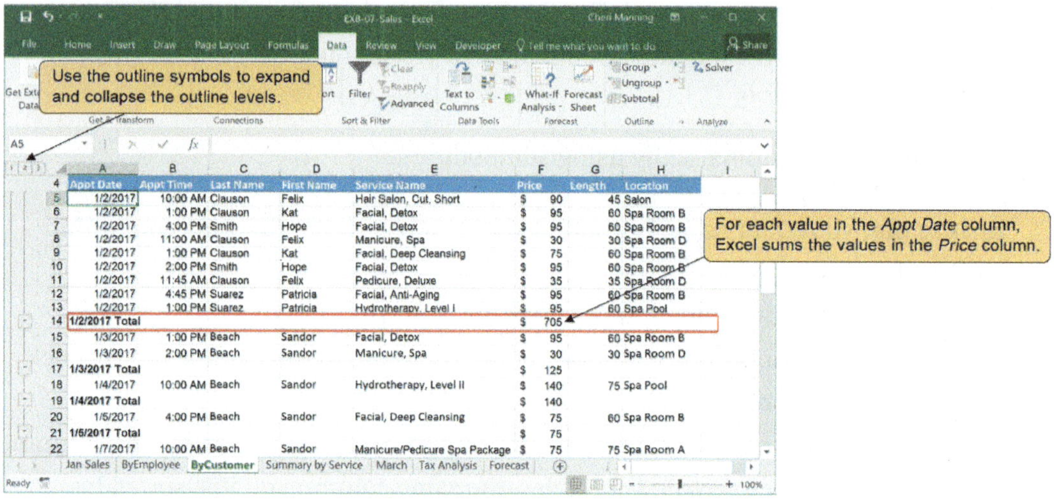

FIGURE EX 8.22

To collapse the outline to show just the subtotals, click the 2 outline symbol at the left of the column headings.

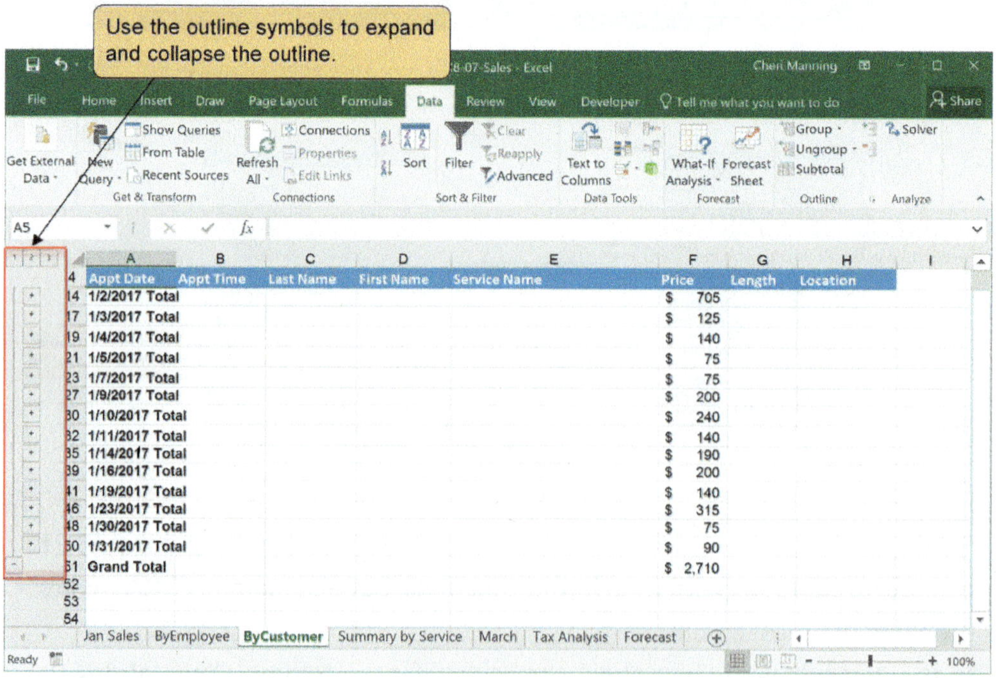

FIGURE EX 8.23

To show the details for a specific outline group, click the plus sign outline symbol next to the row you want to expand.

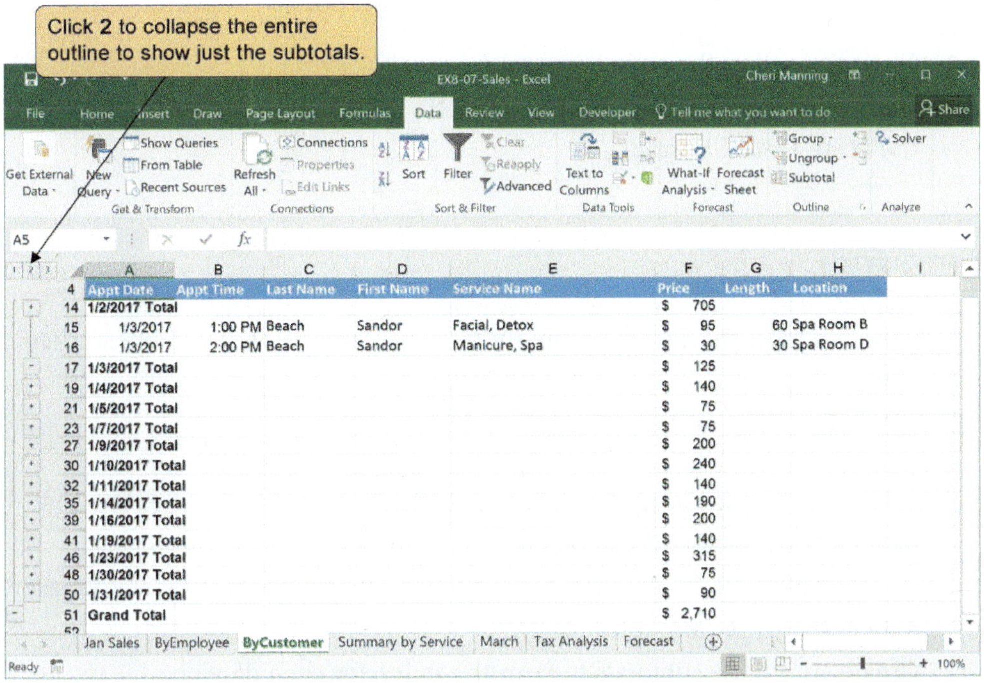

FIGURE EX 8.24

To remove subtotals:

1. On the *Data* tab, in the *Outline* group, click the **Subtotal** button.
2. In the *Subtotal* dialog, click the **Remove All** button.

tips & tricks

To see the SUBTOTAL formulas, click any subtotal cell and look in the formula bar. The SUBTOTAL function requires two arguments. The first argument is a number from 1 to 11 representing the function used to calculate the subtotals. The number 9 is used for the SUM function. The second argument is the range of cells to be subtotaled.

=SUBTOTAL(9,E2:E3)

tell me more

If you add multiple sort levels to your list, you can create subtotals for each level of sorting. Be sure to uncheck the *Replace current subtotals* check box in the *Subtotal* dialog to allow for multiple subtotals.

another method

To expand and collapse outline groups:

1. Click any cell in the summary row or group.
2. On the *Data* tab, in the *Outline* group, click the **Show Detail** button or the **Hide Detail** button.

let me try *Live!*

If you do not have the data file from the previous skill open, open the student data file
EX8-07-Sales and try this skill on your own:

1. Continue working with the *ByCustomer* worksheet. Clear any filters that have been applied to the data.
2. Select any cell in the data range. The data have been sorted by appointment date in the *Appt Date* column.
3. Create automatic subtotals to **sum** the **price** for each date change in the **Appt Date** column.
4. Collapse the entire outline to show just the subtotals.
5. Display the details for just the **1/3/2017** group.
6. If you will be moving on to the next skill in this chapter, leave the workbook open to continue working. If not, save the file as directed by your instructor and close it.

Skill 8.8 Using Consolidate to Create Subtotals

One way to subtotal data without formulas and without including the details in an outline format is to use Consolidate. If the data are organized with labels at the top of each column, you can use Consolidate to summarize data for each unique value in the first column of the cell range defined as the consolidation reference. The data do not need to be sorted in any particular order.

Use **Consolidate** to create subtotals when you want to further manipulate the data or when you do not want or need the details available.

To use Consolidate to create subtotals:

1. Select the cell where you want the upper left corner of the subtotal consolidation to begin. Often this will be cell A1 in an empty worksheet, but it can be an area on the same worksheet as the data you are consolidating. Be sure to leave plenty of room for the summarized data.
2. On the *Data* tab, in the *Data Tools* group, click the **Consolidate** button.
3. In the *Consolidate* dialog, **Sum** is selected in the *Function* list by default. If you want to use another function, expand the list and select the function you want to use.
4. The *All references* box may include references from previous consolidations. If these are not the references you want to use, select each and click the **Delete** button to delete them.
5. Click in the **Reference** box and type the cell range or the range name of the data you want to summarize. If you have only one data range to summarize, you do not need to click the *Add* button. Excel adds the reference to the *All references* box when you click the **OK** button.

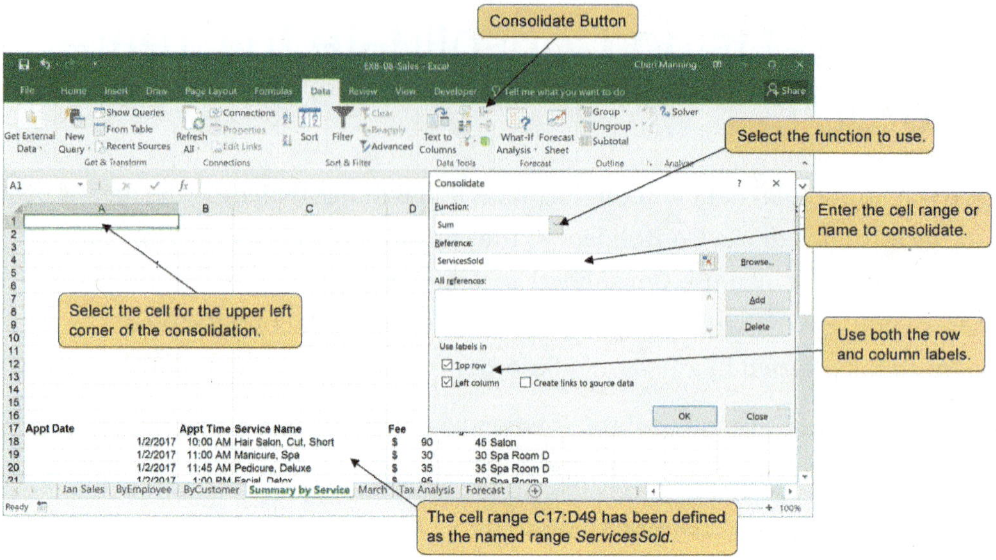

FIGURE EX 8.25

6. Click the **Top row** check box and the **Left column** check box. When the data are organized in rows, you could select just the *Left column* check box as those are the labels used for the consolidation. However, including the *Top row* check box copies the column label above the data that have been subtotaled. This information is often vital to understanding the data.

7. Click **OK**.

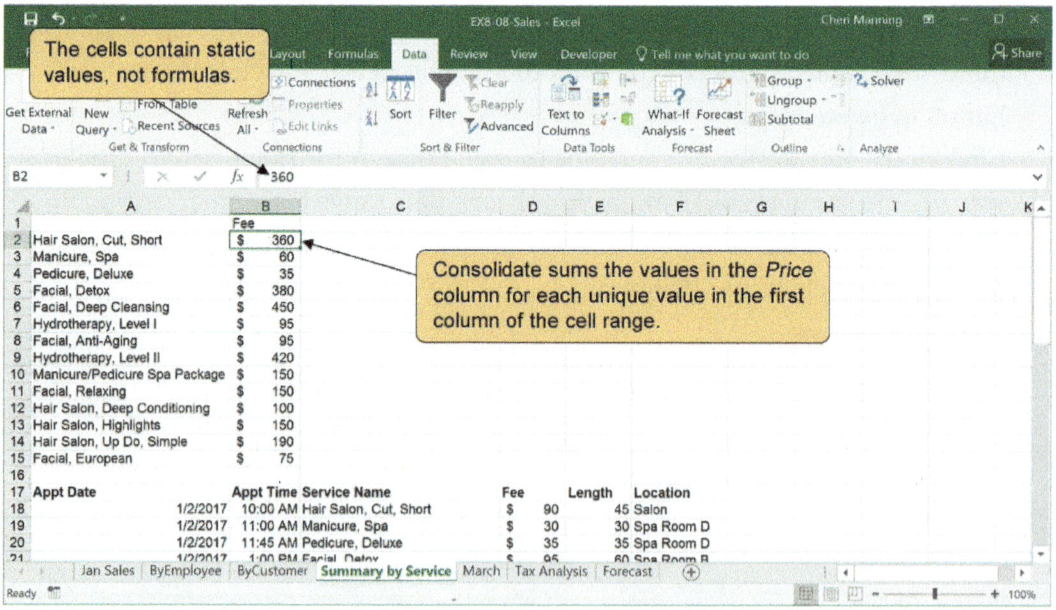

FIGURE EX 8.26

If your consolidation range includes columns with text or dates between first column of data in the reference range and the column with values that are summarized, the consolidation will include blank columns. You can safely delete these columns from the consolidation if you do not want them.

tips & tricks

When using Consolidate as a substitute for the Subtotal command, you do not want to check the **Create links to source data** check box in the *Consolidate* dialog. If you want to summarize a single set of data with subtotals in an outline format, use the *Subtotal* command instead.

tell me more

Another use of Consolidate is to summarize multiple columns of data from worksheets or workbooks with the same data structure. Refer to the skill *Consolidating Data in a Summary Worksheet.*

let me try *Live!*

If you do not have the data file from the previous skill open, open the student data file
EX8-08-Sales and try this skill on your own:

1. Select cell **A1** in the *Summary by Service* worksheet. This is where you will place the consolidated data.
2. Open the *Consolidate* dialog and use the **Sum** function to consolidate prices for the named range **ServicesSold**. Include both the **top row** and **left column** labels. The named range *ServicesSold* has been defined for you for cells C17:D49.

Skill 8.9 Creating an Outline

If your workbook includes a data range organized with summary rows that include formulas, you can use the **Auto Outline** feature to automatically create groups and subgroups of rows that you can expand and collapse. The summary row for each group must include a formula in a consistent location. Auto Outline automatically groups together the rows above each row that includes the formula.

To create an automatic outline based on summary formulas:

1. Click any cell in the data range.
2. On the *Data* tab, in the *Outline* group, click the **Group** button arrow, and click **Auto Outline**.

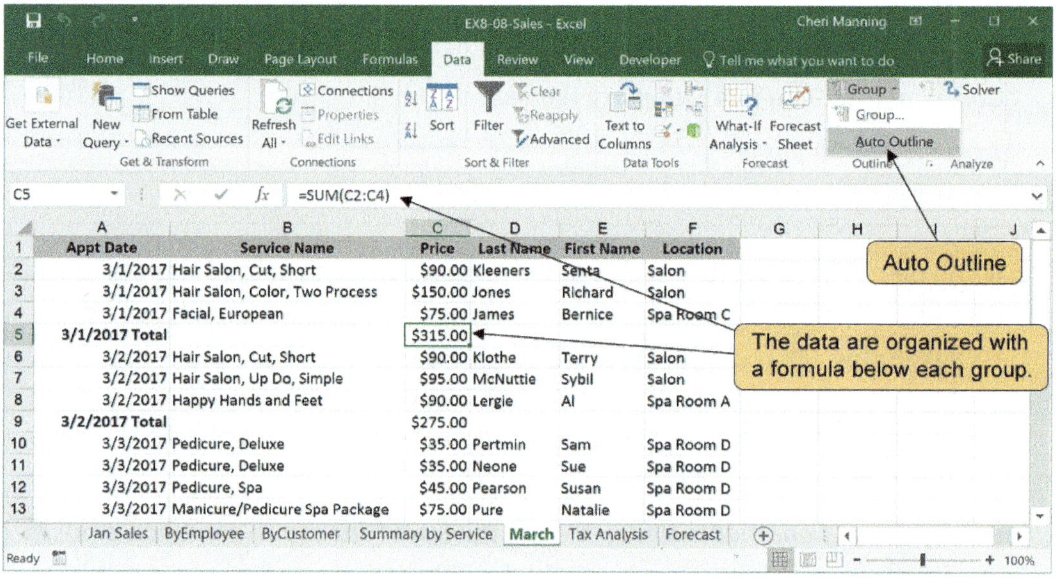

FIGURE EX 8.27

When rows are outlined, outline symbols appear to the left of the column headings and row numbers.

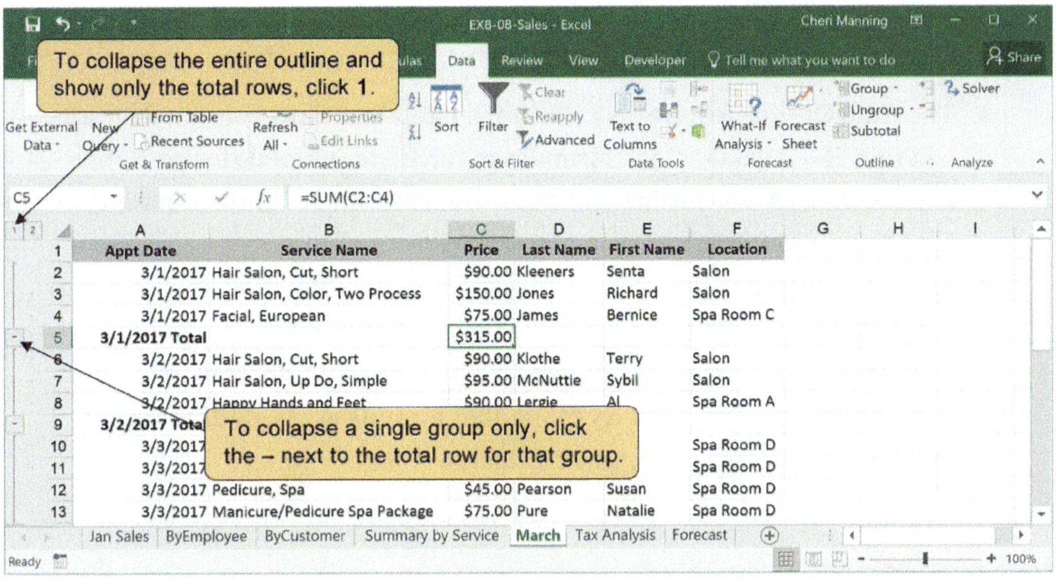

FIGURE EX 8.28

- To collapse the outline to show just the subtotals, click the numbered outline symbols at the left of the column headings to collapse or expand all data at that outline level.
- To show the details for a specific outline group, click the + symbol next to the row you want to expand. Click the – sign symbol to collapse the group.

To remove the entire outline:

1. Select any cell in the outline.
2. On the *Data* tab, in the *Outline* group, click the **Ungroup** button arrow, and select **Clear Outline**.

To ungroup a single group only:

1. Select any cell in the group.
2. On the *Data* tab, in the *Outline* group, click the **Ungroup** button arrow, and select **Ungroup**.

tips & tricks

- The Auto Outline feature also works if subtotals are in a column instead of a row. If the data include formulas to calculate subtotals for both rows and columns, Auto Outline will create both row and column groups based on those formulas.
- Auto Outline is not available if your data range is formatted as a table. To use Auto Outline, first convert the table to a data range.
- Auto Outline can be tricky. If your data include a complicated formula to calculate values, Excel will try to use that formula as the outline point, and Excel may crash (close unexpectedly).

tell me more

If your data do not include rows with summary formulas, you can outline groups of rows manually. This is useful if you have a large amount of data and you usually work with only part of the data at a time. There must be at least one blank row between each group. If you do not have a blank row between groups, the *Group* command will add each subsequent group of rows you define to the initial group (which defeats the purpose of defining the groups in the first place—so you can collapse the data and expand only the rows you need to work with).

1. Select the rows you want to group. Do not include the blank row.
2. On the *Data* tab, in the *Outline* group, click the **Group** button or click the **Group** button arrow, and select **Group...**
3. In the *Group* dialog, **Rows** is selected by default. If you are grouping by columns instead, click the **Columns** radio button.
4. Click **OK**.
5. Repeat steps 1–4 for each group of rows you want to define.

You can use the *Group* command to create multiple levels of groups within each other.

let me try *Live!*

If you do not have the data file from the previous skill open, open the student data file **EX8-09-Sales** and try this skill on your own:

1. Select cell **A2** on the *March* worksheet. Note that the total row for each date uses a SUM function to total the prices.
2. Create an automatic outline from the rows in this data range.
3. Collapse the first group so the details for 3/1/2017 are hidden.
4. If you will be moving on to the next skill in this chapter, leave the workbook open to continue working. If not, save the file as directed by your instructor and close it.

Skill 8.10 Analyzing Changes with the Watch Window

With large or complex workbooks, you will often make changes in one part of the workbook that affect cells you cannot see. The **Watch Window** displays the formulas and current values of the cells you add to it, and it stays open and on top of the Excel window until you close it. As you change values throughout your workbook, the *Value* column in the Watch Window updates to show you the effects on the cells you are watching.

To watch cells using the Watch Window:

1. Select the cells you want to watch.
2. On the *Formulas* tab, in the *Formula Auditing* group, click the **Watch Window** button.
3. In the Watch Window, click **Add Watch**.
4. The cells you selected are automatically entered in the *Add Watch* dialog. Click **Add**.

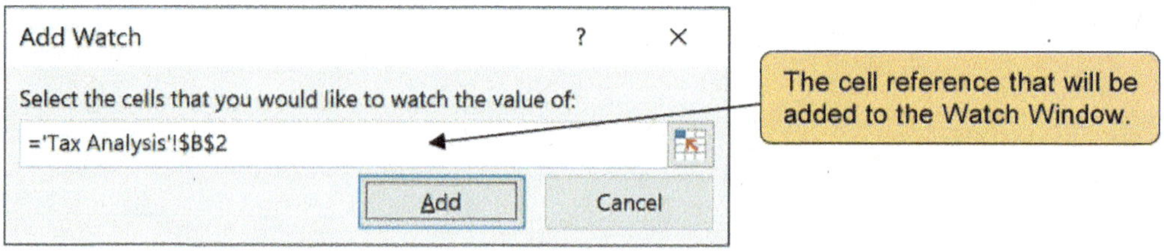

FIGURE EX 8.29

5. Click the main Excel window, and make changes to cells that are referenced by the cells you are watching. The *Value* column in the Watch Window updates as you work.
6. The Watch Window stays on top of the workbook window until you close it.

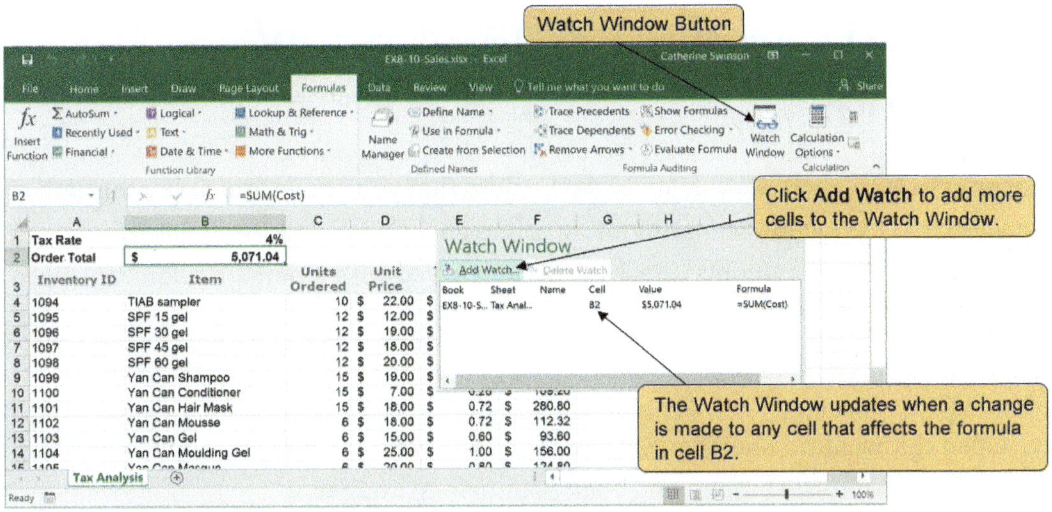

FIGURE EX 8.30

tips & tricks

The Watch Window is really a toolbar. You can drag it to the area beneath the Ribbon, and it will expand to the width of the window and remain anchored there until you move it somewhere else.

tell me more

To remove a watched cell from the Watch Window, click the row in the Watch Window for the cell you want to remove, and then click **Delete**.

let me try *Live!*

If you do not have the data file from the previous skill open, open the student data file
EX8-10-Sales and try this skill on your own:

1. Go to the **Tax Analysis** worksheet.
2. Open the Watch Window and create a new watch for the selected cell (**B2**).
3. Change the value in cell **B1** (the sales tax) to **5%** and note the change to cell B2 in the Watch Window.
4. If you will be moving on to the next skill in this chapter, leave the workbook open to continue working. If not, save the file as directed by your instructor and close it.

Skill 8.11 Creating What-If Analysis Scenarios

A **scenario** is an alternate version of data values that you create and apply through the **Scenario Manager**. Scenarios allow you to analyze the results of changing values in specific cells (inputs). Each scenario is saved with a name, so you can apply it at any time.

To create a scenario:

1. Open the Scenario Manager. On the *Data* tab, in the *Data Tools* group, click the **What-If Analysis** button, and click **Scenario Manager...**

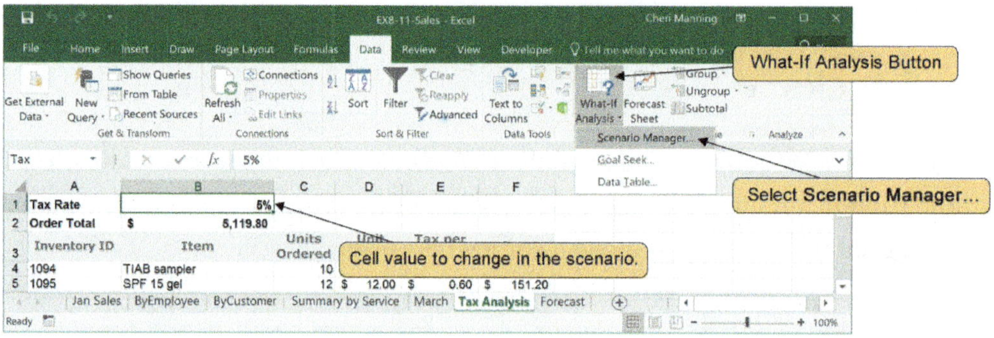

FIGURE EX 8.31

2. To create a new scenario, click the **Add** button.
3. The *Add Scenario* dialog opens. Type a name for the scenario in the *Scenario name* box.
4. Enter the cell, range of cells, or range name of the cells you want to change (the inputs) in the *Changing cells* box. The cell(s) you have selected in the worksheet is (are) entered in the box by default.
5. If you want to add a description for this scenario, type it in the *Comment* box.
6. Click **OK** to continue and add the input values for the scenario.

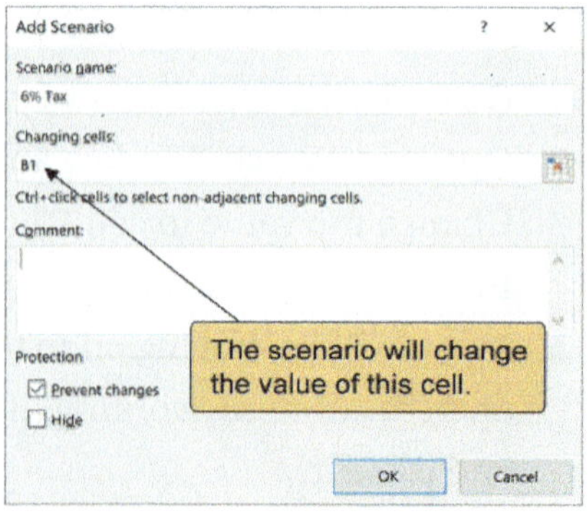

FIGURE EX 8.32

7. In the *Scenario Values* dialog, enter the new value for each input cell.

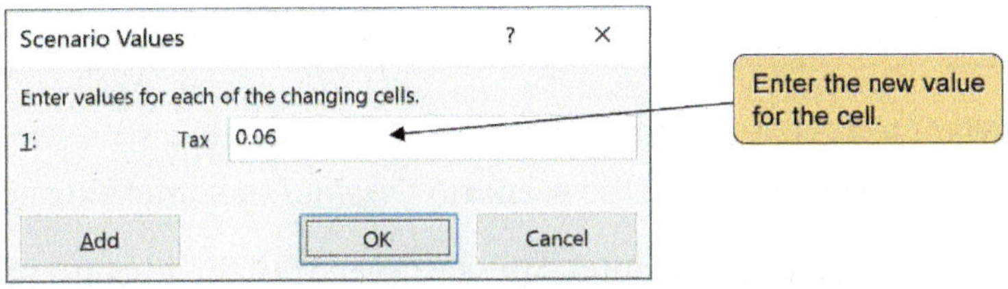

FIGURE EX 8.33

8. Click the **Add** button to open the *Add Scenario* dialog again and add another cell reference to the scenario, or click **OK** to return to the Scenario Manager.
9. Your new scenario is now included in the *Scenarios* list. To apply the scenario, click the name to select it, and then click the **Show** button.
10. To close the Scenario Manager, click the **Close** button.

To delete a scenario:

1. Open the Scenario Manager.
2. Click the scenario name you want to delete.
3. Click the **Delete** button.

Be careful when deleting scenarios! Excel does not ask you to confirm the deletion. Once you click the *Delete* button, the scenario is deleted permanently.

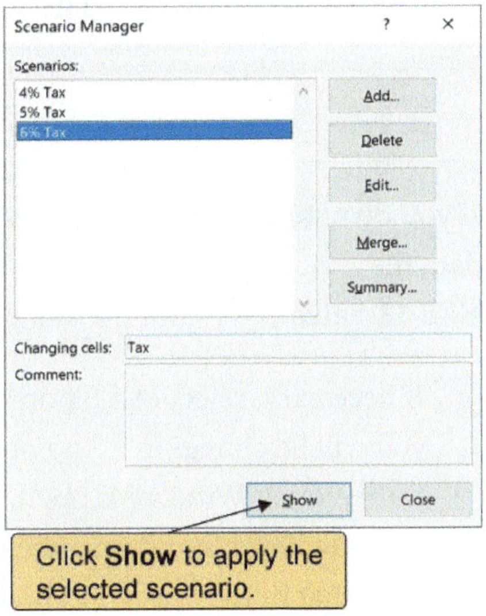

FIGURE EX 8.34

tips & tricks

If you want to keep a copy of your original data, create a scenario without changing any values. Name the scenario *Original* or something similar.

If you include cells with formulas in your scenario, the formulas will be changed to the values specified in the scenario, and you will lose the formula.

tell me more

To edit a scenario:

1. Open the Scenario Manager.
2. Click the scenario you want to edit.
3. Click the **Edit** button.
4. The *Edit Scenario* dialog opens showing the original scenario name and input cells. Make any changes you want, and then click the **OK** button to make changes to the input values.
5. Make any changes you want in the *Scenario Values* dialog, and then click **OK** to return to the Scenario Manager.

let me try *Live!*

If you do not have the data file from the previous skill open, open the student data file
EX8-11-Sales and try this skill on your own:

1. If necessary, select cell **B1** on the *Tax Analysis* worksheet. This is the cell you will be changing in the new scenario.
2. If the Watch Window is open, close it.
3. Create a new scenario named **6% Tax** to change the value of cell **B1** to **0.06**. Note that in the *Scenario Values* dialog, the cell name *Tax* is displayed instead of the cell address *B1*.
4. Show the new **6% Tax** scenario.
5. Close the Scenario Manager.
6. Save the file as directed by your instructor and close it.

Skill 8.12 Creating Scenario Summary Reports

Changing cell values through scenarios affects not only the cells defined in the scenario but also any cells that reference the changing cells. If you create multiple scenarios for the same data, use the Scenario Manager to generate a **scenario summary report** summarizing and comparing the effects of the scenarios. At a glance, you will be able to see the cells each scenario affects and decide which scenario provides the results that best fit your needs.

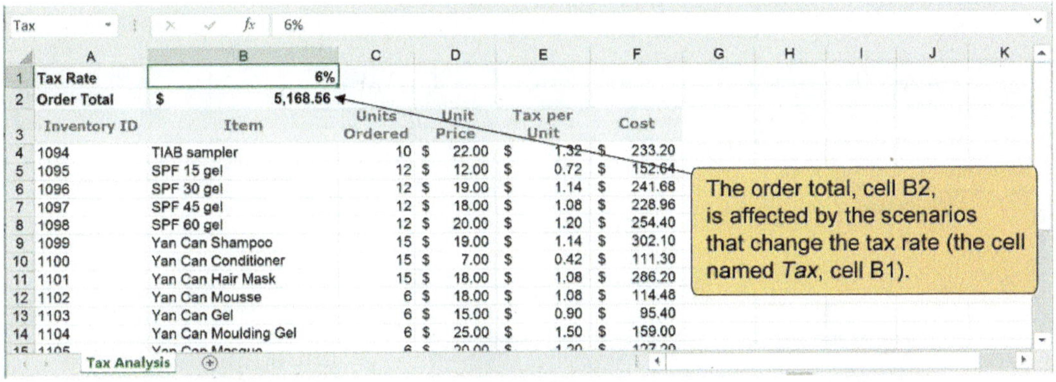

FIGURE EX 8.35

To create a scenario summary report:

1. Open the Scenario Manager. On the *Data* tab, in the *Data Tools* group, click the **What-If Analysis** button, and click **Scenario Manager**.
2. Click the **Summary** button.

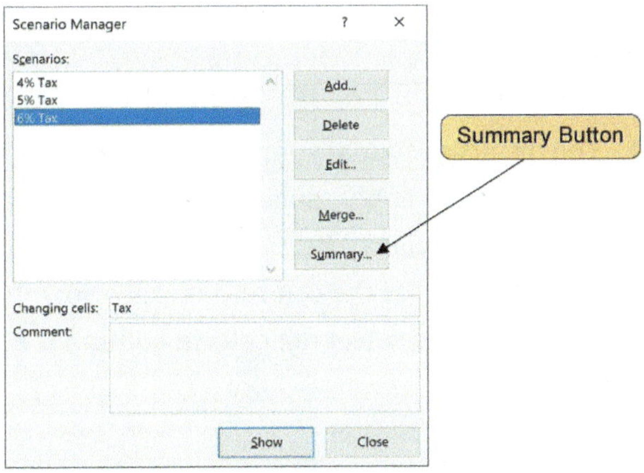

FIGURE EX 8.36

3. In the *Scenario Summary* dialog, select whether you want the summary report to appear as a new worksheet (**Scenario summary** radio button) or a new PivotTable (**Scenario PivotTable report** radio button).

4. In the *Result cells* box, Excel will automatically suggest the cell or cells that contain formulas affected by the changing input values for the scenarios.

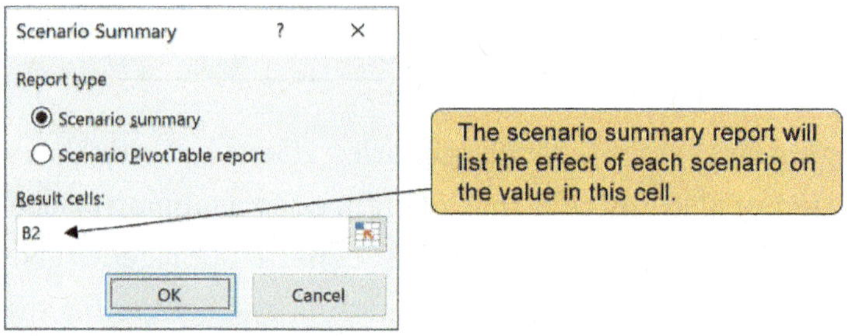

FIGURE EX 8.37

5. Click **OK** to see the scenario summary report. Notice that Excel automatically creates a new worksheet named *Scenario Summary*.

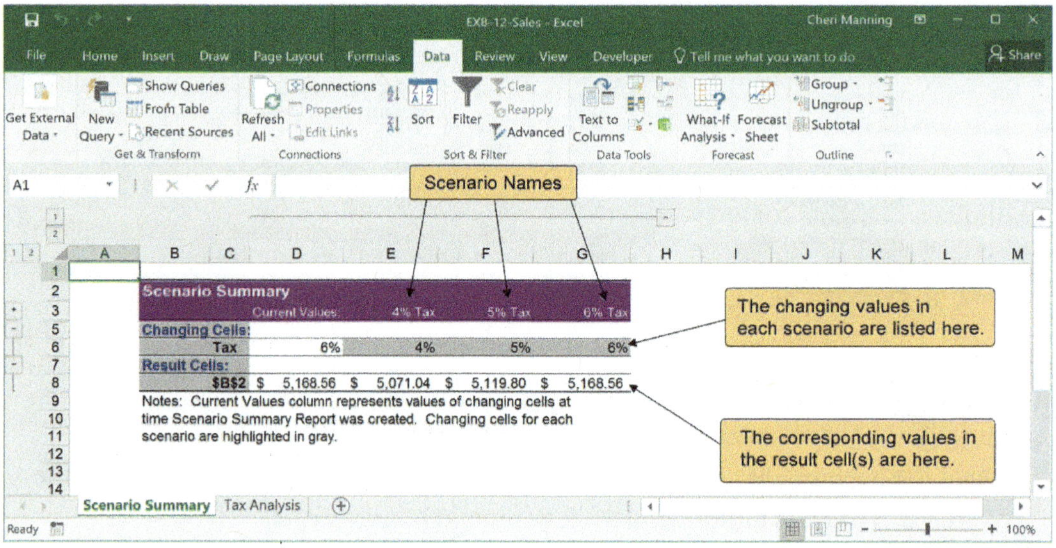

FIGURE EX 8.38

tips & tricks

- The results shown in your scenario summary reports may be easier to analyze if you apply range names to cells. When reviewing a summary report, a cell named *Tax* is easier to identify than one named *B1*.
- If you cannot see the cell references below the *Changing Cells* and *Result Cells* headings, select the cells in column *C* and change the font color.

let me try *Live!*

If you do not have the data file from the previous skill open, open the student data file
EX8-12-Sales and try this skill on your own:

1. Open the Scenario Manager and review the scenarios in this workbook.
2. Create a scenario summary report. Accept the recommended results cells.
3. If you will be moving on to the next skill in this chapter, leave the workbook open to continue working. If not, save the file as directed by your instructor and close it.

from the perspective of . . .

A BOOKING AGENT FOR PROFESSIONAL ATHLETES

I can advise clients and "show them the money" with the Scenario Manager. Understanding the impact of collection fees, commissions, and so on is understandable when looking at scenario summary reports.

Skill 8.13 Forecasting with a Forecast Sheet

One of the most powerful uses of Excel is to identify data trends and forecast future values. You may be familiar with forecasting values with trendlines on a chart. Excel 2016 includes a new feature to analyze time-based data—The **forecast sheet**. The forecast sheet feature creates a new worksheet with a data table and chart predicting future values based on the data you select.

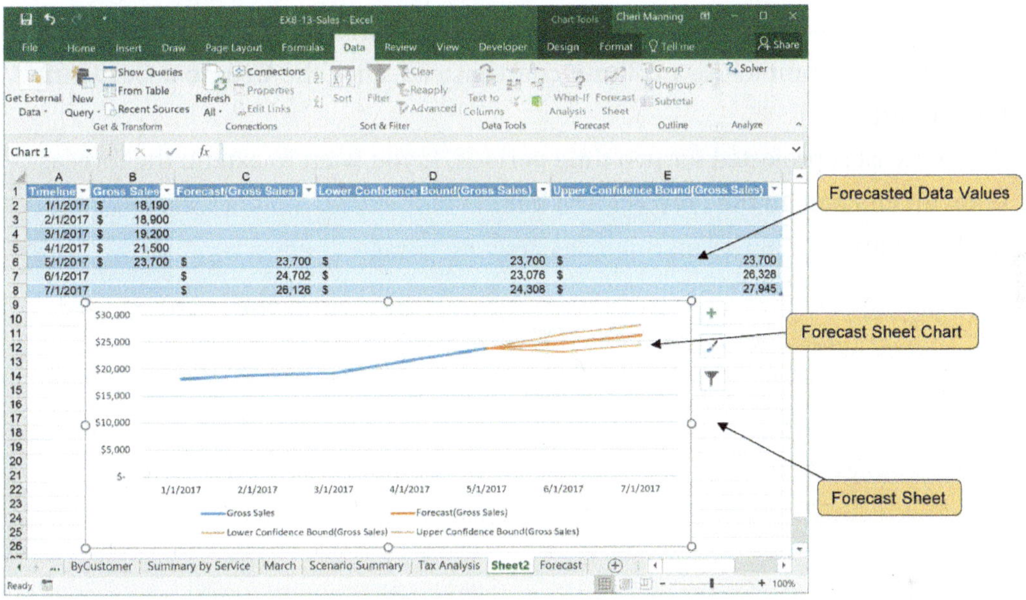

FIGURE EX 8.39

The forecast sheet feature relies on two data ranges: a set of dates in equal increments and a value for each of the dates.

To create a forecast sheet:

1. Select any cell in the data range.
2. On the *Data* tab, in the *Forecast* group, click the **Forecast Sheet** button.

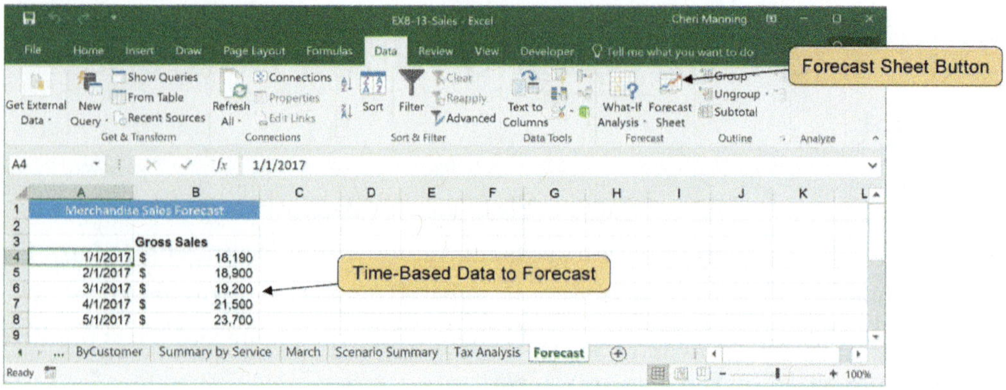

FIGURE EX 8.40

3. In the *Create Forecast Worksheet* dialog, the line chart option is selected by default. If you want to use a column chart instead, click the **Create a Column Chart** button.
4. The forecast is projected for two time periods. If you want to extend the forecast, enter an end date in the *Forecast End* box.
5. Click **Create**.

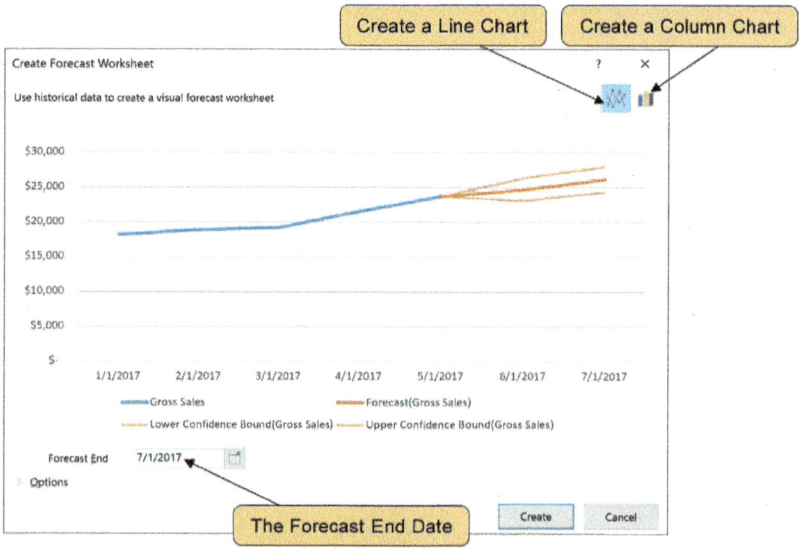

FIGURE EX 8.41

6. Excel adds a new worksheet with the original and forecasted data and chart.

tips & tricks

Using the last day of the month as the time interval does not work with the forecast sheet feature. Excel does not detect the end of month dates as even intervals. Use the first day of the month instead.

tell me **more**

Many businesses have data affected by the time of year—retail sales increase in December, flower sales peak around February 14, and textbook sales have high points in January and September. If your data have highs and lows that can be predicated by the time of year, the forecast sheet incorporates this seasonality automatically. To manually control how the forecast incorporates seasonality:

1. In the *Create Forecast Worksheet* dialog, click **Options**.
2. Under *Seasonality*, click the **Set Manually** radio button.
3. Use the stepper to set the number of time units to use for seasonality intervals.

let me try *Live!*

Open the student data file **EX8-13-Sales** and try this skill on your own:

1. On the *Forecast* worksheet, verify that a cell in the range **A2:B7** is selected.
2. Create a **Forecast Sheet** based on the selected data. Use a line chart and forecast values through **July 1, 2017**.
3. Save the file as directed by your instructor and close it.

Skill 8.14 Activating the Solver Add-In

Solver is a data analysis tool that you will learn to use in the skill *Using Solver*. However, Solver is not available in Excel by default. You must add it through the *Excel Options* dialog.

To install the Solver add-in:

1. Click the **File** tab.
2. Click **Options** to open the *Excel Options* dialog.
3. Click **Add-Ins**.
4. The *Add-ins* list is divided into *Active Application Add-ins* and *Inactive Application Add-ins*. If Solver is listed in the inactive section, you will need to install it.
5. Near the bottom of the window, the *Manage* box should display *Excel Add-ins*. If it does not, expand the list and select **Excel Add-ins**.

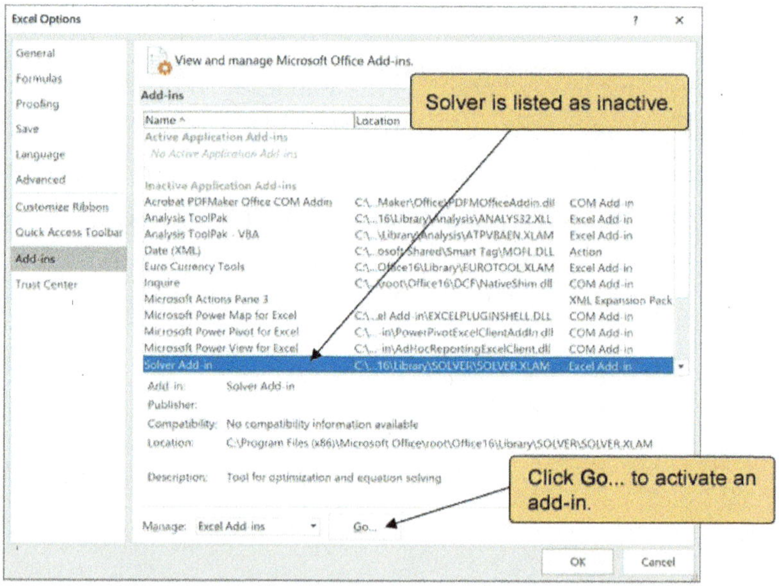

FIGURE EX 8.42

6. Click **Go...** to open the *Add-Ins* dialog.
7. Click the **Solver Add-in** check box and click **OK**.

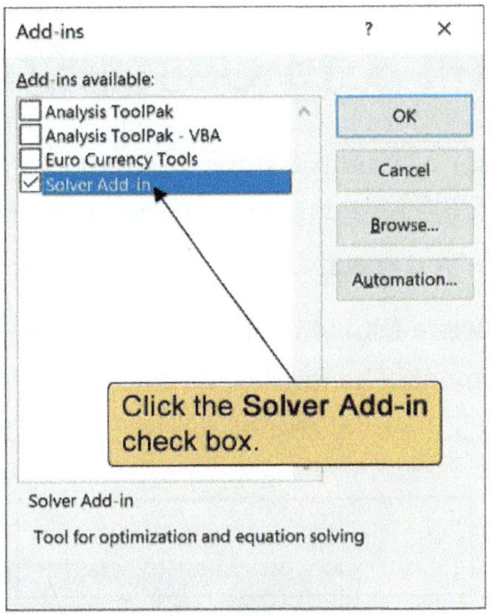

FIGURE EX 8.43

The *Solver* button is now available at the far right side of the *Data* tab in the *Analysis* group.

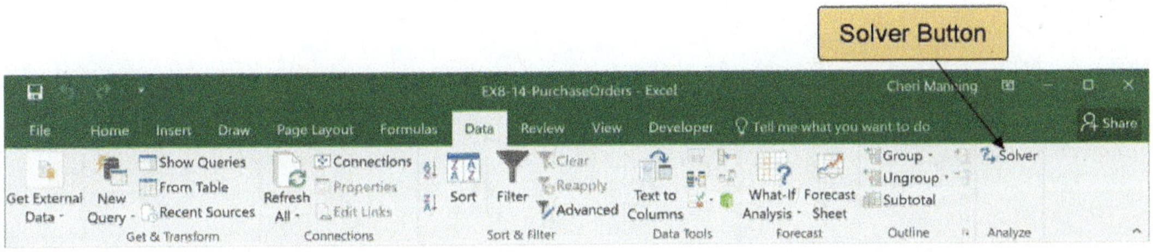

FIGURE EX 8.44

let me try *Live!*

Open the student data file **EX8-14-PurchaseOrders** and try this skill on your own::

1. Open Excel and check to see if the Solver add-in is installed.
2. If the *Solver* button is not available on the *Data* tab, install it.
3. If you will be moving on to the next skill in this chapter, leave the workbook open to continue working. If not, save the file as directed by your instructor and close it.

Skill 8.15 Using Solver

Solver is a data analysis tool that evaluates multiple variables affecting a formula and produces optimal values for those variables within defined constraints to result in a value you specify.

In Figure EX 8-45, we want to find the maximum profit possible from a single shipment. The formula to calculate profit in cell *B1* is the total price of the order minus the total cost of goods. This seems simple enough.

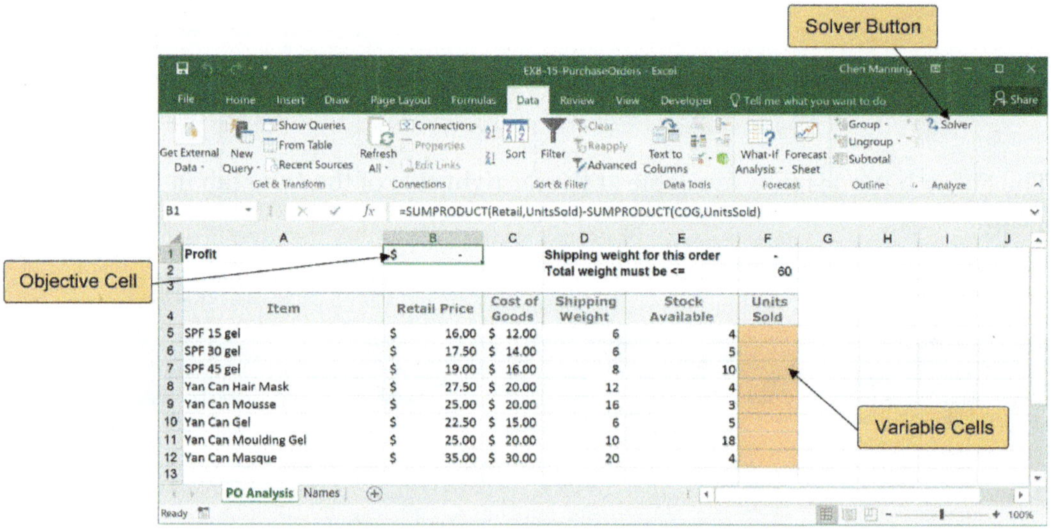

FIGURE EX 8.45

However, there are limitations (**constraints**). The number of units sold must be less than or equal to the number of units in stock, and in this example, the total shipping weight must be less than or equal to 60 ounces. In addition, the units sold must be integers (whole numbers).

How can we find the optimal number of units to ship for each product in order to maximize profits? Use Solver.

To use Solver:

1. On the *Data* tab, in the *Analysis* group, click the **Solver** button.
2. In the *Solver Parameters* dialog, enter the objective cell reference or cell name in the *Set Objective* box. This is the cell containing the formula you want Solver to solve for. In Figure EX 8-46, cell **B2** is the objective cell.
3. Click the radio button to find the **Max** (maximum) or **Min** (minimum) result value for the formula, or click the **Value Of** radio button and enter a specific value to solve for.

4. In the *By Changing Variable Cells* box, enter the cells you want Solver to manipulate to reach the objective target. These cells must be precedents to the formula in the objective cell. In Figure Figure EX8-46, the cells in the named range **UnitsSold** (F5:F12) are the variable cells.

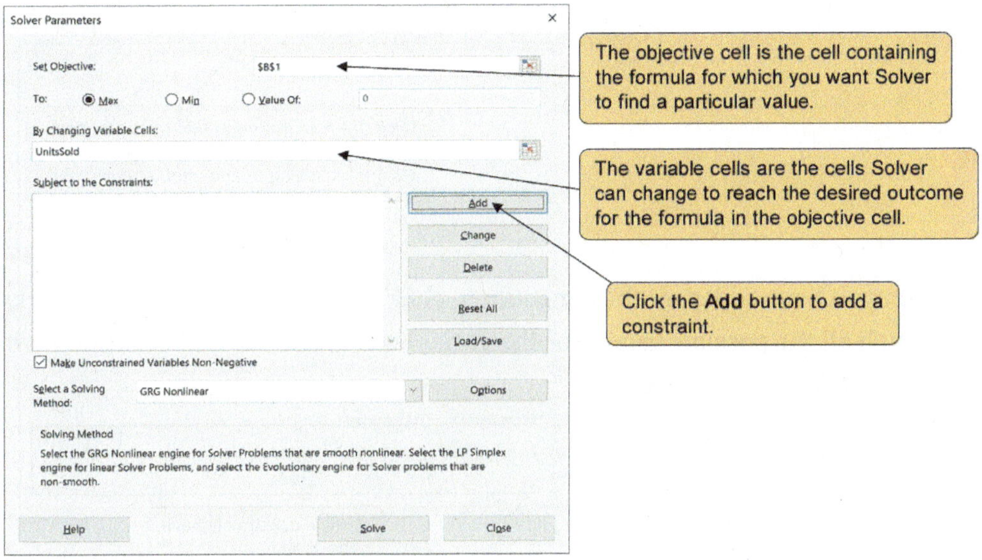

FIGURE EX 8.46

5. The **constraints** are limitations you place on the acceptable values for the variable cells. Solver will not produce a result that violates the rules you set here. To add constraints, click the **Add** button next to the *Subject to the Constraints* box.

   In Figure EX8-47, the value in the *UnitsSold* named range must be *less than or equal to* the parallel value in the *Stock* named range.

   - In the *Cell Reference* box, enter the cell containing the variable you want to place limits on. You can use a cell reference or a named range. The reference must be a precedent to the formula in the objective cell.
   - Expand the drop-down list in the middle box and select an operator. If you want to restrict values to whole numbers, select **Int** from the list.
   - In the *Constraint* box, enter the limit value. This can be a numerical value or a cell reference.
   - Click **OK** to add the constraint, or click **Add** to add the constraint and immediately add another constraint.

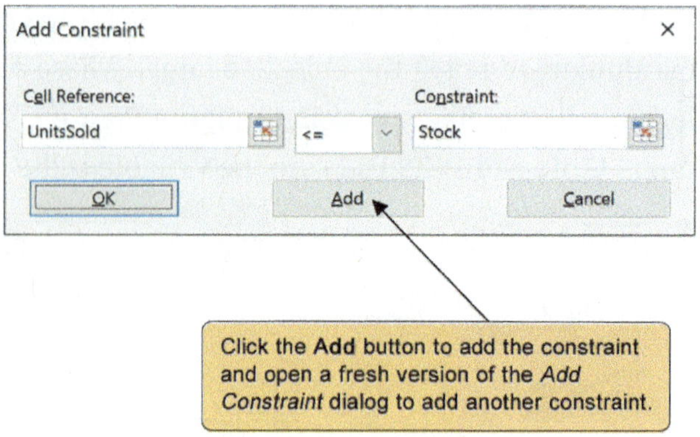

FIGURE EX 8.47

6. When you have added all the constraints, click the **Solve** button. Solver works through all the possible values for the variables and tries to find a solution within the constraints you defined.

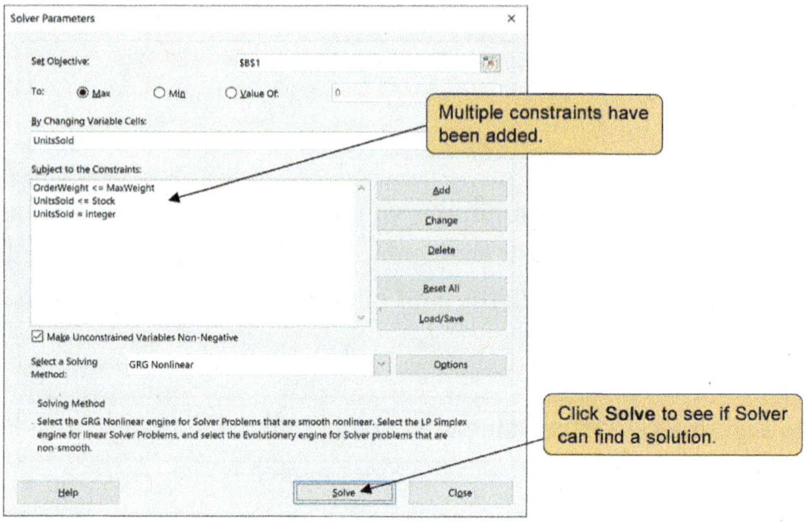

FIGURE EX 8.48

7. If Solver is successful, the values are applied to the worksheet. If necessary, move the *Solver Results* dialog so you can see the results.

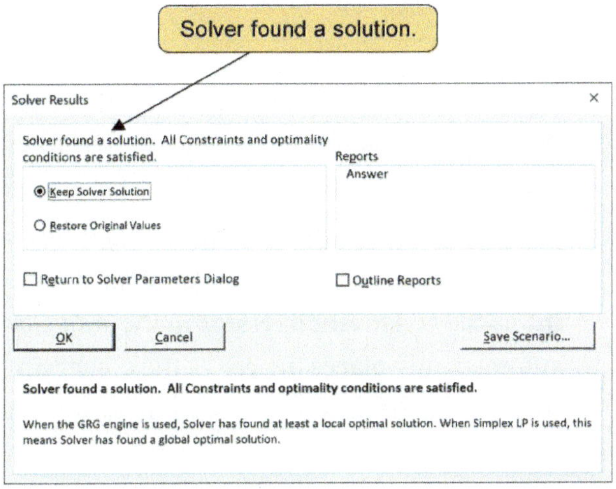

FIGURE EX 8.49

- If you want to keep the solution results, click **OK**.
- If you do not want to apply the Solver solution right away, but may want to come back to it later, you can save it as a scenario. Click the **Save Scenario...** button. Enter a name for the scenario, and click **OK**. You can show the scenario at any time using the Scenario Manager.
- If you want the cells restored to their original values, click the **Restore Original Values** radio button, and then click **OK**.
- If you want to modify the Solver parameters before accepting a change, click the **Return to Solver Parameters Dialog** check box, and then click **OK**.

Figure EX8-50 shows the results of the Solver parameters entered in Figure EX8-15-4. The maximum value for the objective cell is $57.00.

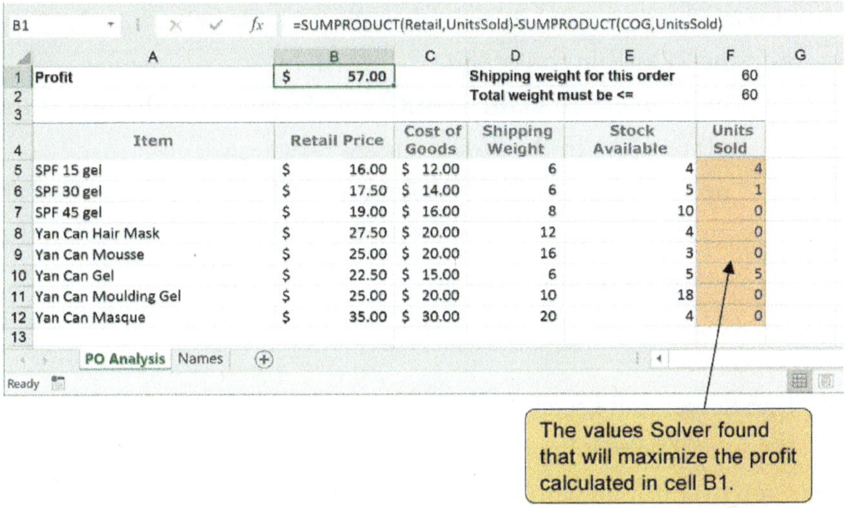

FIGURE EX 8.50

tips & tricks

- Solver may not be able to find a solution that meets the constraints. When this happens, try modifying the variable constraints or the objective target value.
- Some variables, number of units sold or number of people, must be a whole number. If one of the variables must be a whole number, select **int** as the constraint operator in the *Add Constraint* dialog. Solver automatically places *integer* as the constraint value and will only find a solution that returns a whole number for that variable.

tell me more

For more information about Solver, visit the official solver Web site at www.solver.com.

let me try *Live!*

If you do not have the data file from the previous skill open, open the student data file
EX8-15-PurchaseOrders and try this skill on your own:

1. Use Solver to find the combination of units sold for each product that will result in the maximum profit.
2. Set the objective to find the maximum value for cell **B1**.
3. Use the range name **UnitsSold** as the variable cells.
4. Add the following constraints:
    1. The values in the **UnitsSold** named range must be **less than or equal to** the values in the **Stock** named range.
    2. The value in the **OrderWeight** named range must be **less than or equal to** the maximum weight for the order as defined in the **MaxWeight** named range.
    3. The values in the **UnitsSold** named range must be whole numbers only.
5. Run Solver and accept the solution.
6. If you will be moving on to the next skill in this chapter, leave the workbook open to continue working. If not, save the file as directed by your instructor and close it.

Skill 8.16 Refreshing Data in a PivotTable

The skill *Creating PivotTables Using Recommended PivotTables* introduces the concept of PivotTables, how to create them, add fields, and change the function used to summarize the data. Recall that PivotTables do not contain any data themselves—they summarize data from another part of your workbook. After you create a PivotTable, if the underlying data change, you must update or refresh the PivotTable to see the changes.

To refresh the data in a PivotTable:

1. Select any part of the PivotTable.
2. On the *PivotTable Tools Analyze* tab, in the *Data* group, click the *Refresh* button.

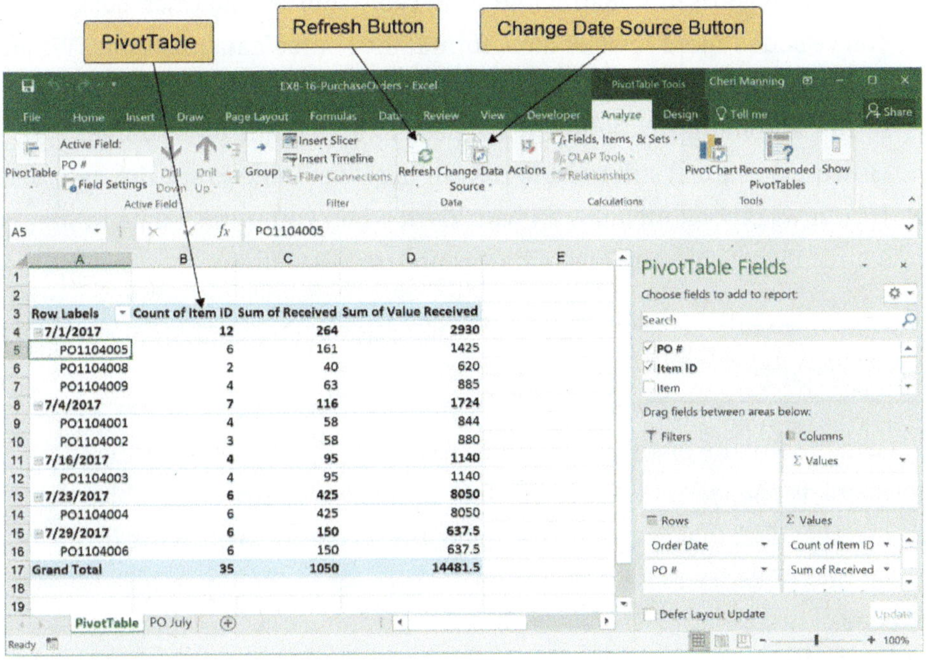

FIGURE EX 8.51

If the source for the PivotTable has been updated with additional rows of data, refreshing the PivotTable is not enough. You will need to update the range of cells used as the PivotTable source:

1. Select any part of the PivotTable.
2. On the *PivotTable Tools Analyze* tab, in the *Data* group, click the Change Data Source button.
3. In the Change PivotTable Data Source dialog, enter the cell range, named range, or table name in the box. You can also click and drag the appropriate cells in the

worksheet to update the cell range.

4. Click **OK**.

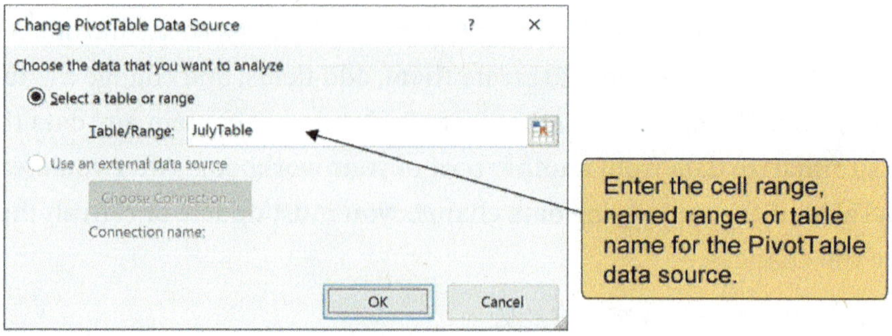

FIGURE EX 8.52

tips & tricks

- If you find yourself updating the PivotTable source data often because you've added more rows of data, format the source data as a table. When new rows are added to the table, they are included in the PivotTable source automatically. You will not need to update the data source. However, you will still need to refresh the PivotTable to see the updates.
- If your workbook includes a PivotChart, when you refresh data in the source PivotTable, the PivotChart is updated as well.

tell me more

You can modify the PivotTable options to refresh the data every time the workbook is opened. This setting is not recommended for PivotTables that use external data that may have changed unexpectedly. By leaving this option unchecked, you have more control over when the PivotTable is updated.

To change the PivotTable option to refresh automatically, select any cell in the PivotTable.

1. On the *PivotTable Tools Analyze* tab, in the *PivotTable* group, click the **Options** button.
2. In the *PivotTable Options* dialog, click the **Data** tab.
3. Click the **Refresh data when opening the file** check box.
4. Click **OK**.

let me try *Live!*

If you do not have the data file from the previous skill open, open the student data file **EX8-16-PurchaseOrders** and try this skill on your own:

1. In the *PO July* worksheet, delete rows **4:5**.
2. Update the PivotTable in the *PivotTable* worksheet.
3. Data were added to the *PO July* worksheet after the PivotTable as created. Update the data source for the PivotTable to use the table named **JulyTable**. Now if more rows are added later, you will not need to update the data source again.
4. If you will be moving on to the next skill in this chapter, leave the workbook open to continue working. If not, save the file as directed by your instructor and close it.

Skill 8.17 Adding a Calculated Field to a PivotTable

Recall that PivotTables summarize data and calculate subtotals using functions like SUM and AVERAGE. PivotTables do not contain any data themselves—they summarize data from another part of your workbook. However, you can add new fields to the PivotTable to perform calculations based on that data.

To add a calculated field to a PivotTable:

1. On the *PivotTable Tools Analyze* tab, if necessary, click the **Calculations** button to expand the *Calculations* group. Click **Fields, Items, & Sets**. Select **Calculated Field...**

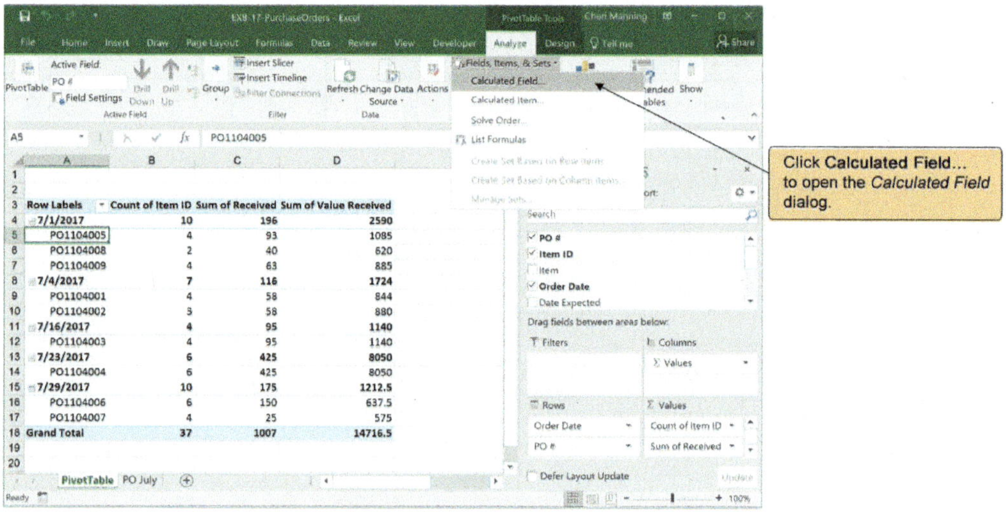

FIGURE EX 8.53

2. In the *Insert Calculated Field* dialog, type a header title for the field in the *Name* box.
3. In the *Formula* box, delete the **0** and type the formula you want to calculate. Do not delete the = sign.
4. To include fields from the PivotTable, double-click the field name in the *Fields* list (or click the field name once, and then click the **Insert Field** button). If the field name includes spaces, Excel will automatically place single quotation marks around the field name. If you type the field name yourself, be sure to include them. This is necessary only for field names that include spaces.
5. Click **OK** to add the calculated field to the PivotTable.

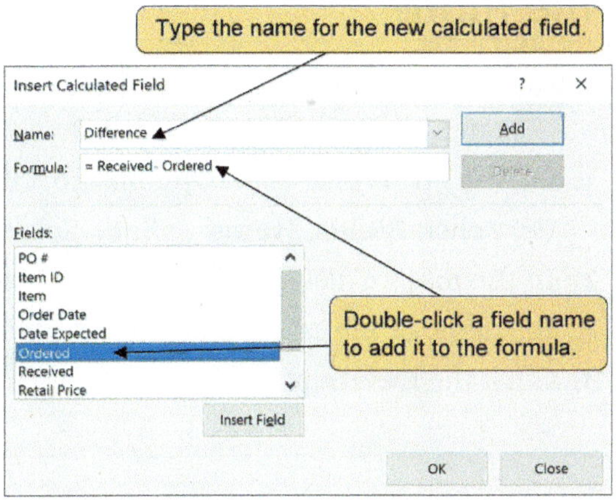

FIGURE EX 8.54

The calculated field is added to the PivotTable at the far right side. It is included in the *PivotTable Fields* pane as well.

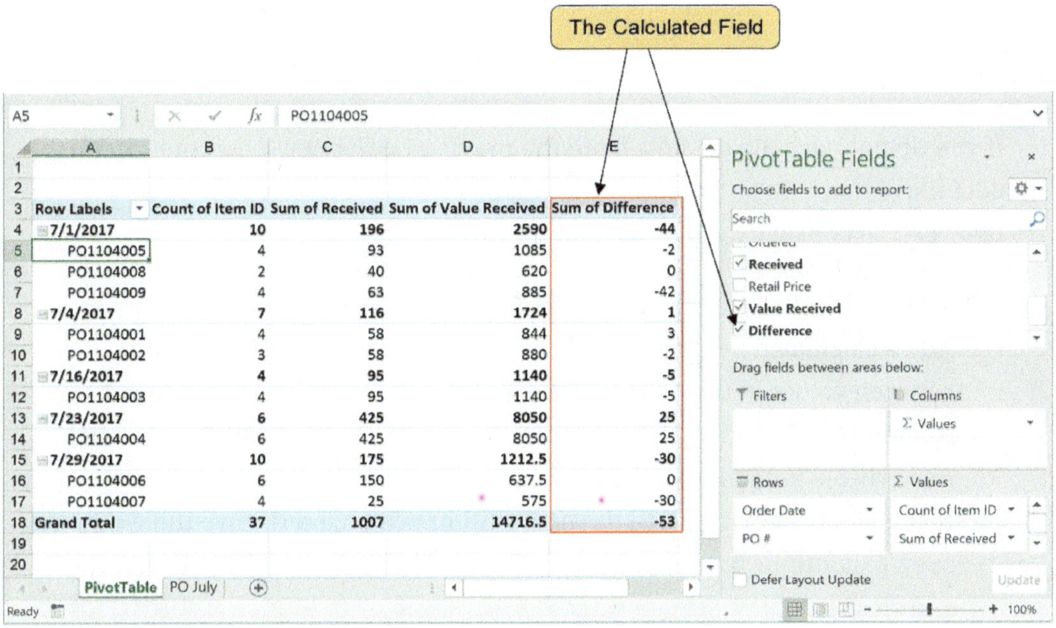

Row Labels	Count of Item ID	Sum of Received	Sum of Value Received	Sum of Difference
7/1/2017	10	196	2590	-44
PO1104005	4	93	1085	-2
PO1104008	2	40	620	0
PO1104009	4	63	885	-42
7/4/2017	7	116	1724	1
PO1104001	4	58	844	3
PO1104002	3	58	880	-2
7/16/2017	4	95	1140	-5
PO1104003	4	95	1140	-5
7/23/2017	6	425	8050	25
PO1104004	6	425	8050	25
7/29/2017	10	175	1212.5	-30
PO1104006	6	150	637.5	0
PO1104007	4	25	575	-30
Grand Total	37	1007	14716.5	-53

FIGURE EX 8.55

tips & tricks

When you create a calculated field, the field name is added to the *PivotTable Fields* pane. To remove the field from the PivotTable, click the check box to uncheck it. This removes the field from the PivotTable display without deleting it, so you can display it later without having to re-create it.

tell me **more**

To delete a calculated field:

1. On the *PivotTable Tools Options* tab, click the **Calculations** button, and then click **Fields, Items, & Sets**. Select **Calculated Field...**
2. In the *Insert Calculated Field* dialog, expand the **Name** list, and select the name of the calculated field you want to delete.
3. Click the **Delete** button.

another method

To build the formula in the *Insert Calculated Field* dialog, *Formula* box, double-click a field name in the *Fields* list to add it to formula or click the field name once and then click the **Insert Field** button.

let me try *Live!*

If you do not have the data file from the previous skill open, open the student data file
EX8-17-PurchaseOrders and try this skill on your own:

1. Select any cell in the PivotTable in the *PivotTable* worksheet.
2. Add a calculated field named `Difference` to summarize the difference between values in the *Ordered* field and the *Received* field (**=Ordered-Received**). Note that it is not necessary for the *Ordered* and *Received* fields to be visible in the PivotTable.
3. If you will be moving on to the next skill in this chapter, leave the workbook open to continue working. If not, save the file as directed by your instructor and close it.

Skill 8.18 Grouping Fields in a PivotTable

PivotTables often contain large amounts of data, making it difficult to find the information you want. **Grouping** adds another level of organization to your PivotTable. You can expand or collapse groups to show or hide details as required.

To add grouping:

1. Click a cell in the PivotTable with the type of data you want to group by (a date or number).
2. On the *PivotTable Tools Options* tab, if necessary, click the **Group** button to display the *Group* group. Click the **Group Field** button.

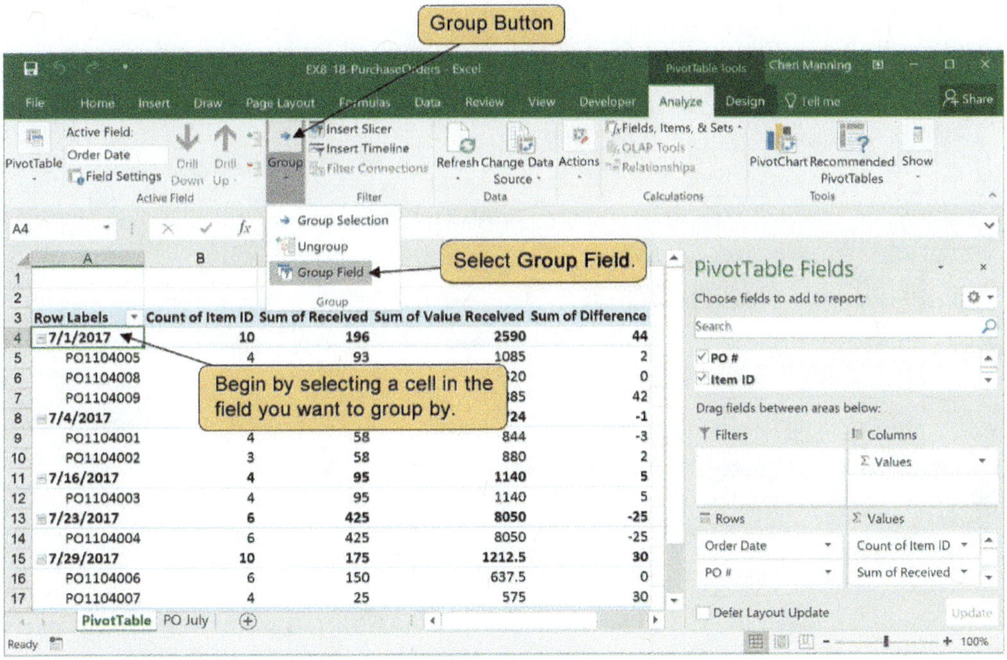

FIGURE EX 8.56

3. In the *Grouping* dialog, Excel automatically detects and enters the start and end values based on the values in the PivotTable.
4. Select how you want the data grouped:
   - For dates, you can select multiple grouping levels, such as months, quarters, and years. Click each grouping level you want to include.
   - For numeric values, enter the increment to group by in the *By* box.

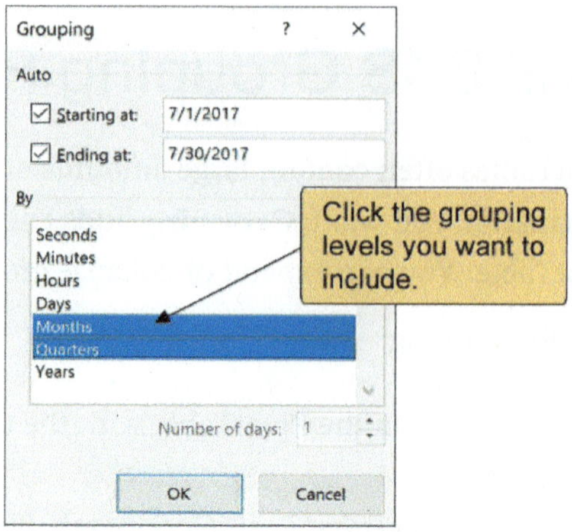

FIGURE EX 8.57

5. Click **OK**.

The PivotTable in Figure EX8-58 has grouping applied by quarter and month.

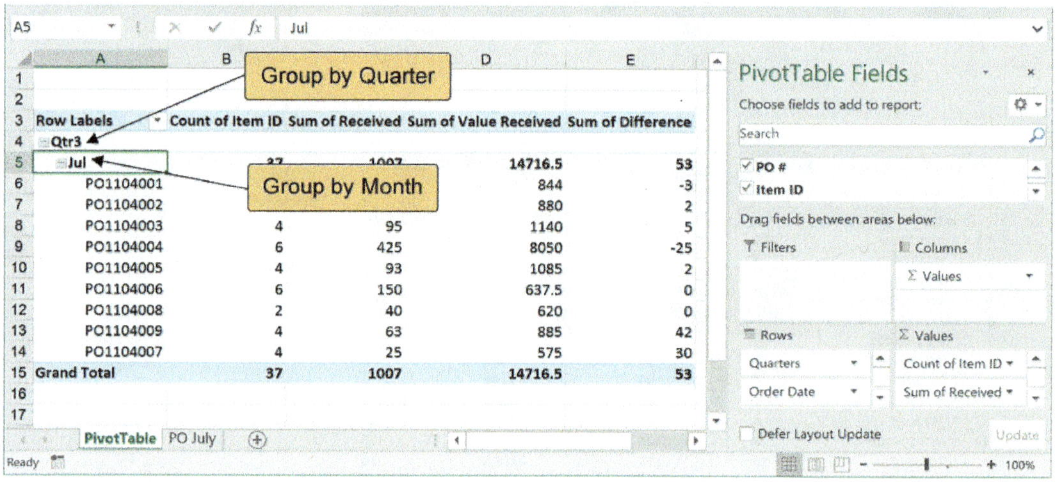

FIGURE EX 8.58

Collapse a grouping level by clicking the collapse icon to the left of the level name. When a group is collapsed, the icon changes to the expand icon. Click the expand icon to expand the group again.

To remove grouping, click one of the grouping level cells, and then on the *PivotTable Tools Options* tab, click the **Group** button to expand the *Group* group, and then click **Ungroup**.

tips & tricks

Depending on your computer's resolution and display settings, the *Group* group may appear collapsed as the *Group* button as shown in the screenshots in this skill. If your Excel window is wide enough, you will see the *Group* group expanded on the Ribbon with buttons for *Group Selection*, *Ungroup*, and *Group Field*.

another method

The *Group* and *Ungroup* commands are also available by right-clicking the cell you want to group or ungroup by.

let me try *Live!*

If you do not have the data file from the previous skill open, open the student data file
EX8-18-PurchaseOrders and try this skill on your own:

1. Select any cell in the PivotTable in the *PivotTable* worksheet.
2. Group the data by both month and quarter.
3. If you will be moving on to the next skill in this chapter, leave the workbook open to continue working. If not, save the file as directed by your instructor and close it.

Skill 8.19 Filtering PivotTable Data

When you create a PivotTable, the column(s) of row labels include(s) an AutoFilter arrow. You can use the options in the AutoFilter menu to filter the PivotTable data just as you would similar data in a table or data range.

To add a filter for a field that is not included in the PivotTable, click the field name in the *PivotTable Fields* pane and drag it to the *Filters* box in the bottom part of the pane. When a field is added to the *Filters* box, a report filter is added to row 1 above the PivotTable. Click the filter arrow to select from the list of values.

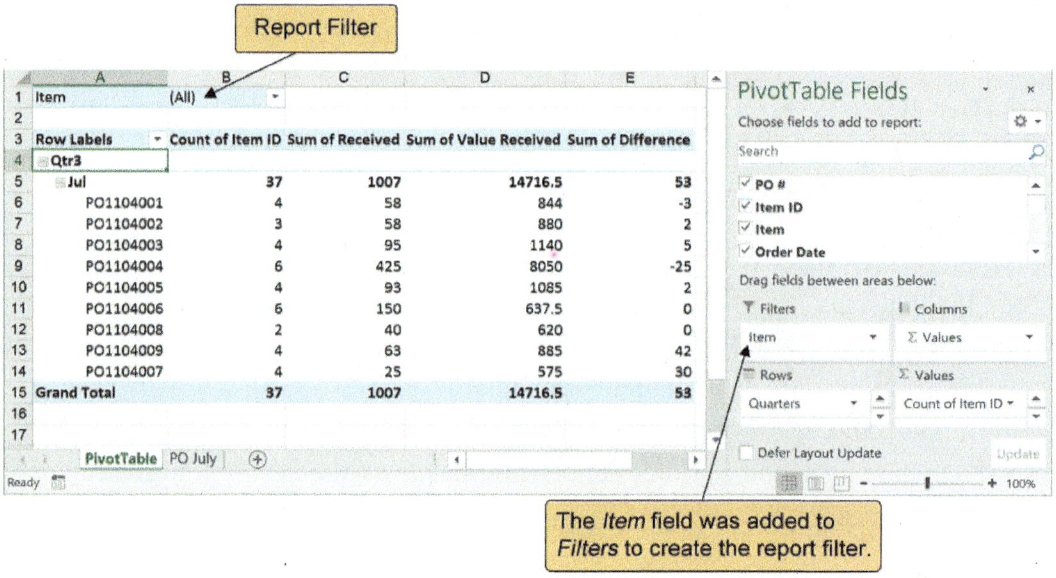

FIGURE EX 8.59

- The report filter is initially set to *(All)* to show all the values.
- To filter for a single value, click the item you want to filter for, and then click **OK**.
- To filter for multiple values, click the **Select Multiple Items** check box, and then click the check box in front of each item you want to include in the filter. Click **OK**.
- To remove a filter, click **(All)** again, and click **OK**.

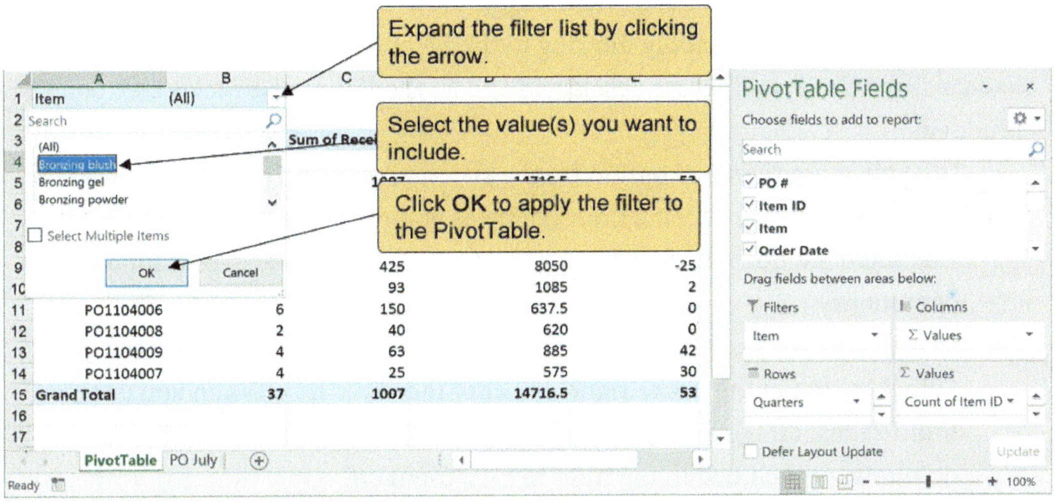

FIGURE EX 8.60

A major limitation to using report filters is that you can't tell when you have multiple items selected. Excel fixed this problem by adding slicers. A **slicer** is a visual representation of a field and the values you can filter by. You can create multiple slicers and filter the PivotTable by multiple values from each.

To add a slicer:

1. On the *PivotTable Tools Analyze* tab, in the *Filter* group, click the **Insert Slicer** button.

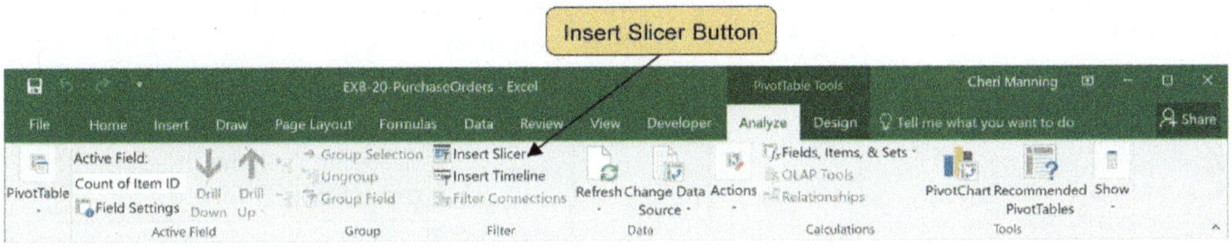

FIGURE EX 8.61

2. In the *Insert Slicers* dialog, click the check boxes for the fields for which you want to create slicers, and then click **OK**.

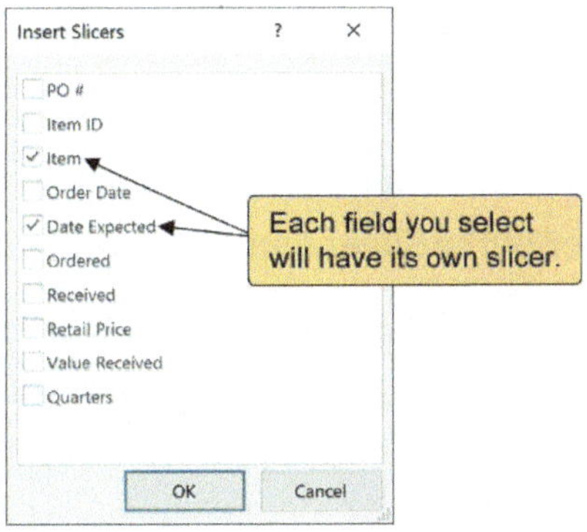

FIGURE EX 8.62

3. A separate slicer opens for each field listing the available values. Click the buttons in each slicer to apply filtering to the PivotTable. Notice that when you add a slicer, the PivotTable is deselected and so the *PivotTable Fields* task pane is hidden.
   - To apply more than one option from a slicer, press **[Ctrl]** as you click. Some slicer buttons may become unavailable as you make selections—indicating that there are no data available for that option under the current filtering conditions.
   - To use more than one filtering option in a slicer, you can also click the **Multi-Select** button at the upper right corner of the slicer box. When you enable multi-select, all the slicer options remain on by default. Click the options you do ***not*** want included in the filter to turn them *off*.

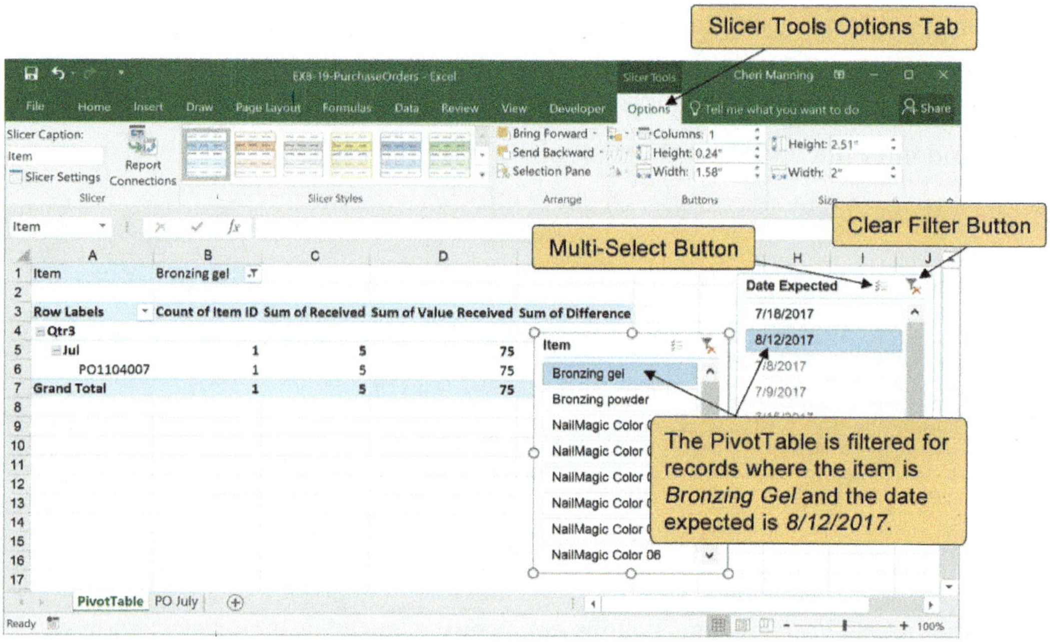

FIGURE EX 8.63

To move a slicer, move your mouse over the slicer. When the cursor changes to the move cursor, click and drag the slicer to the new location.

To clear the selections from a Slicer, click the **Clear Filter** button in the upper right corner of the Slicer window.

To remove a slicer from your PivotTable, click the slicer, and then press the **Delete** key. Deleting the slicer also removes any filtering options applied from that slicer.

tips & tricks

- Slicers are more useful than a report filter because they visually show you which filters are applied to the PivotTable.
- When you add a slicer for a field, a filter icon appears next to the field name in the *PivotTable Fields* pane to indicate that filtering is available.

tell me more

When a slicer is selected, the *Slicer Tools Options* tab becomes available. From this tab, you can apply a style to the slicer and control slicer settings.

another method

- Right-click a field name in the PivotTable Fields pane and select **Add to Report Filter** to create a new report filter for that field.
- When a PivotTable is active, the Slicer button is available from the *Insert* tab, *Filters* group.
- You can also delete a slicer by right-clicking the slicer and selecting the **Remove** option.

let me try *Live!*

If you do not have the data file from the previous skill open, open the student data file
EX8-19-PurchaseOrders and try this skill on your own:

1. Select any cell in the PivotTable in the *PivotTable* worksheet.
2. Add a report filter for the **Item** field.
3. Use the report filter to filter the PivotTable to show only data where the *Item* value is **Bronzing gel**.
4. Add slicers for the **Item** and **Date Expected** fields. Note that the *Item* slicer reflects the filter that was applied through the report filter.
5. Use the slicer to filter the data further to show only data where the *Date Expected* value is **8/12/2017**.
6. If you will be moving on to the next skill in this chapter, leave the workbook open to continue working. If not, save the file as directed by your instructor and close it.

Skill 8.20 Filtering PivotTable Data with a Timeline

A **timeline** allows you to filter data in a PivotTable by segment(s) of time—days, months, quarters, or years. Timelines are similar to slicers except they are limited to PivotTable fields formatted as dates.

To add a timeline filter to a PivotTable:

1. On the *PivotTable Tools Analyze* tab, in the *Filter* group, click the **Insert Timeline** button.

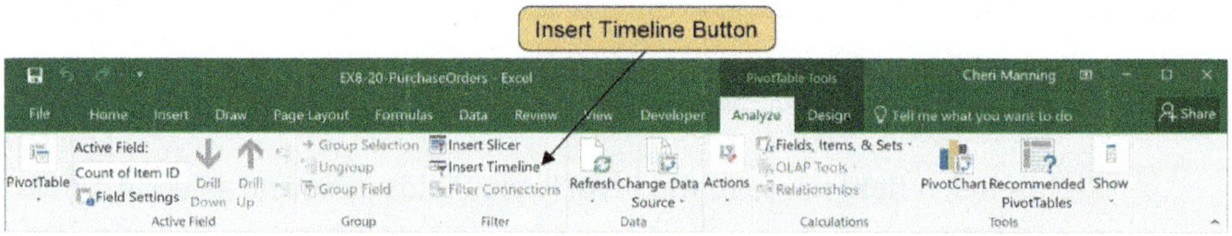

FIGURE EX 8.64

2. In the *Insert Timeline* dialog, click the check box for the field you want to create a timeline for, and then click **OK**. You can include more than one timeline if you have multiple data fields in your PivotTable.

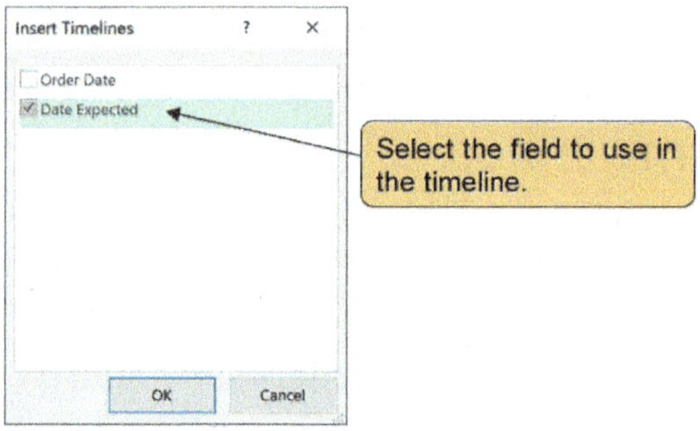

FIGURE EX 8.65

3. A timeline opens for the selected field. By default, the timeline will be segmented by month. To select another time frame for each segment, click the **Months** button and make a selection.
4. Click a time on the timeline to apply filtering to the PivotTable. To apply more than one option from a timeline, press **[Shift]** as you click each button.

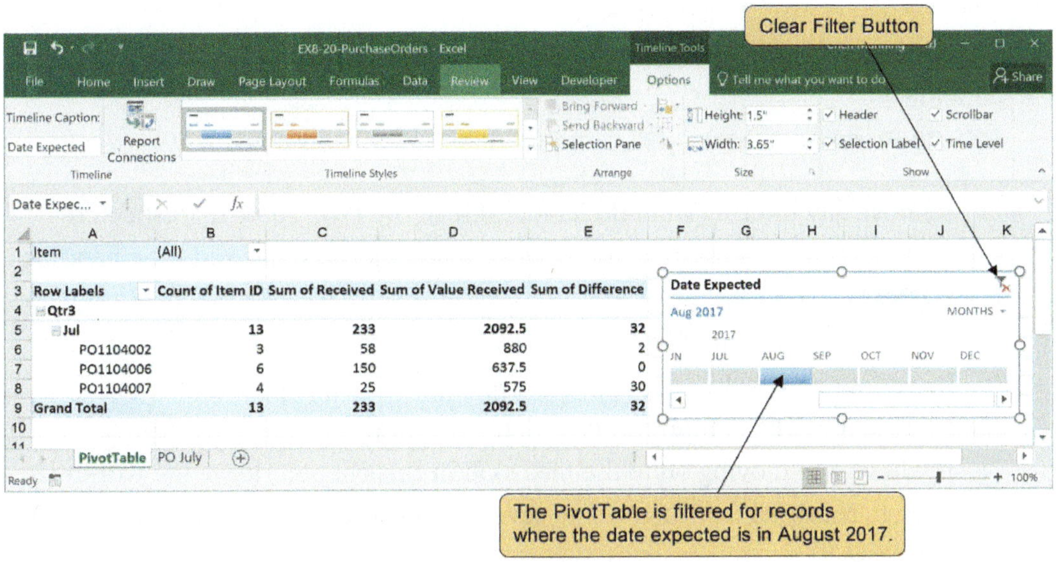

FIGURE EX 8.66

To move a timeline, move your mouse over the timeline. When the cursor changes to the move cursor, click and drag the timeline to the new location.

To clear the selections from a timeline, click the **Clear Filter** button in the upper right corner of the timeline window.

To remove a timeline from your PivotTable, click the timeline, and then press the **[Delete]** key. Deleting the timeline also removes any filtering options applied from that timeline.

tips & tricks

When a timeline is opened, a filter icon appears next to that field name in the *PivotTable Fields* pane to indicate that filtering is available.

another method

- When a PivotTable is active, the *Timeline* button is available from the *Insert* tab, *Filters* group.
- You can also delete a timeline by right-clicking the timeline and selecting the **Remove** option.

let me try *Live!*

If you do not have the data file from the previous skill open, open the student data file

EX8-20-PurchaseOrders and try this skill on your own:

1. Remove any filtering from the PivotTable in the *PivotTable* worksheet. If any Slicers are visible, remove them by selecting the slicer and then pressing **[Delete]**.
2. Add a timeline to the PivotTable to filter the data by values in the **DateExpected** field.
3. Use the timeline to filter the PivotTable to show only dates in **August**.
4. If you will be moving on to the next skill in this chapter, leave the workbook open to continue working. If not, save the file as directed by your instructor and close it.

Skill 8.21 Changing the Look of a PivotTable

You can customize PivotTables in almost any way imaginable. As with other tables, you can apply a Quick Style to a PivotTable to give it a professional, polished appearance.

To apply a Quick Style to a PivotTable:

1. Click anywhere in the PivotTable.
2. On the *PivotTable Tools Design* tab, in the *PivotTable Styles* group, click a style to apply it. To expand the *PivotTable Quick Styles* gallery, click the **More** button.

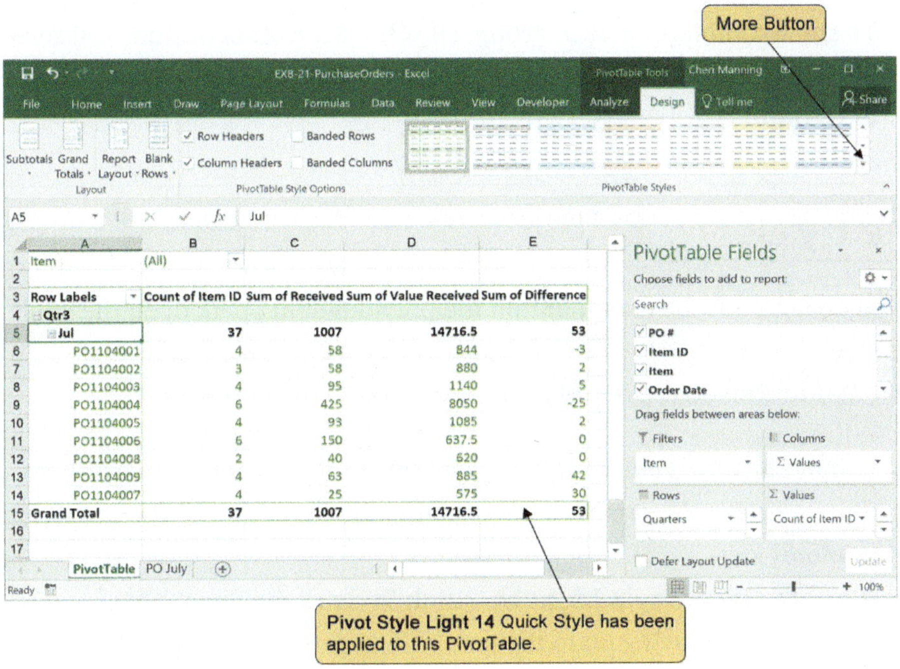

FIGURE EX 8.67

tell me **more**

You can also change the layout of a PivotTable. By default, PivotTables use the compact layout, combining all the row fields in a single column. If you have large groups, you may want to use a tabular layout instead to separate the fields into their own columns.

To change the PivotTable layout:

1. On the *PivotTable Tools Design* tab, in the *Layout* group, click the **Report Layout** button and select **Show in Tabular Form**.
2. Now fields are separated into their own columns, but there will be blank cells to the left of each subgroup item.
3. To repeat the item labels in every row, click the **Report Layout** button again and select **Repeat All Item Labels**.
4. To show subtotals for each group, click the **Subtotals** button, and select **Show all Subtotals at Bottom of Group** or **Show all Subtotals at Top of Group**.

let me **try** *Live!*

If you do not have the data file from the previous skill open, open the student data file
EX8-21-PurchaseOrders and try this skill on your own:

1. Remove any filtering from the PivotTable in the *PivotTable* worksheet. If a timeline is visible, remove it by selecting the timeline and then pressing the **[Delete]** key.
2. Apply the **Pivot Style Light 14 Quick Style** to the PivotTable.
3. If you will be moving on to the next skill in this chapter, leave the workbook open to continue working. If not, save the file as directed by your instructor and close it.

Skill 8.22 Filtering Data in a PivotChart

PivotCharts do not have a *Chart Filters* button like regular charts do. However, you can use slicers to filter data in a PivotChart. Adding a slicer to a PivotChart is the same as adding one to a PivotTable.

To add a slicer to a PivotChart:

1. On the *PivotChart Tools Analyze* tab, in the *Data* group, click the **Insert Slicer** button.
2. In the *Insert Slicers* dialog, click the check boxes for the fields you want to create slicers for, and then click **OK**.

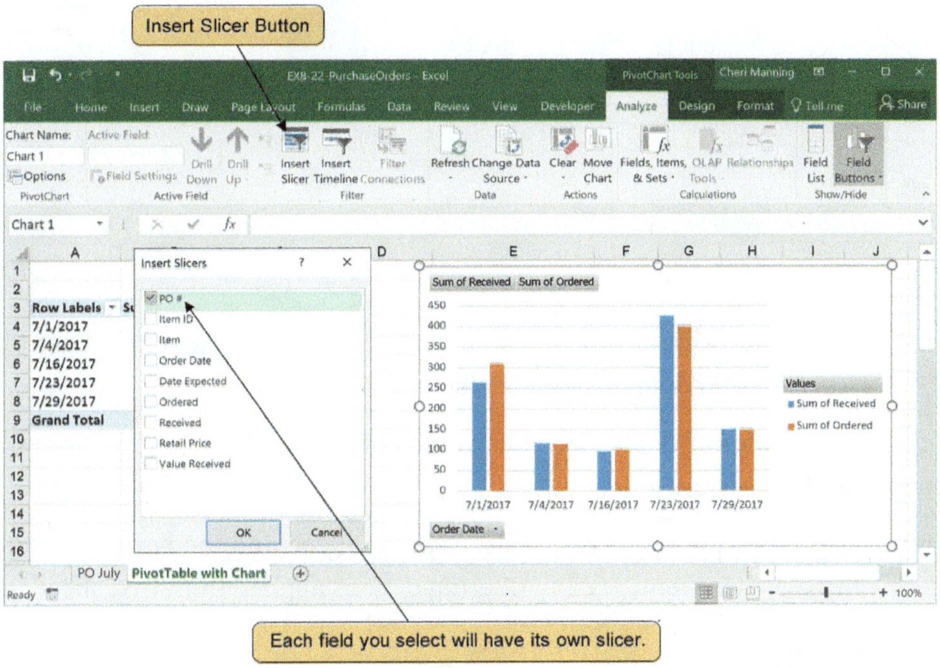

FIGURE EX 8.68

3. A separate slicer opens for each field listing the available values. Click the buttons in each slicer to apply filtering to the PivotChart. As you use the slicer to filter data in the PivotChart, the same changes are applied to the associated PivotTable.
   - To apply more than one option from a slicer, press the **[Ctrl]** key as you click. Some slicer buttons may become unavailable as you make selections—indicating that there are no data available for that option under the current filtering conditions.

- To use more than one filtering option in a slicer, you can also click the **Multi-Select** button at the upper right corner of the slicer box. When you enable multi-select, all the slicer options remain ***on*** by default. Click the options you do ***not*** want included in the filter to turn them ***off***.

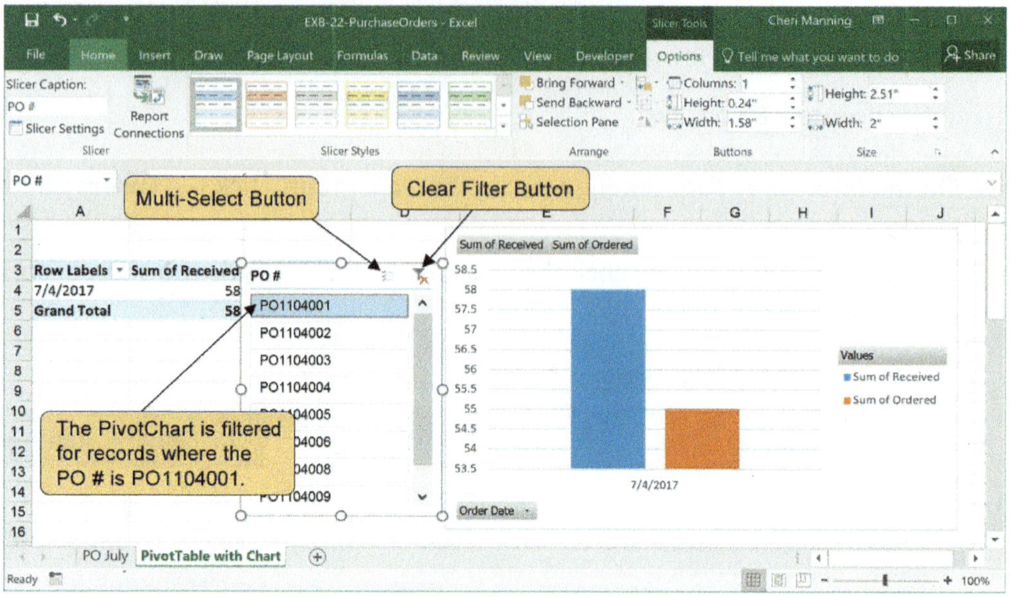

FIGURE EX 8.69

To move a slicer, move your mouse over the slicer. When the cursor changes to the move cursor, click and drag the slicer to the new location.

To clear the selections from a slicer, click the **Clear Filter** button in the upper right corner of the slicer window.

To remove a slicer from your PivotTable, click the slicer, and then press **[Delete]**. Deleting the slicer also removes any filtering options applied from that slicer.

tips & tricks

You cannot add slicers if the PivotChart is located on a chart sheet. For more information about chart sheets, refer to the skill *Resizing and Moving Charts*.

tell me more

When a slicer is selected, the *Slicer Tools Options* tab becomes available. From this tab, you can apply a style to the slicer and control slicer settings.

let me try *Live!*

If you do not have the data file from the previous skill open, open the student data file

EX8-22-PurchaseOrders and try this skill on your own:

1. Select the PivotChart in the *PivotTable with Chart* worksheet. If the *PivotTable Fields* pane covers part of the chart, you can close it.
2. Add a slicer to this PivotChart for the **PO #** field and show only data where the *PO #* value is **PO1104001** (the first button in the slicer).
3. If you will be moving on to the next skill in this chapter, leave the workbook open to continue working. If not, save the file as directed by your instructor and close it.

Skill 8.23 Changing the Look of a PivotChart

When you create a PivotChart, you have many of the same formatting and design options as you have with "regular" charts. All the skills for formatting charts can be applied to PivotCharts.

From the PivotChart Tools Design tab, you can change the chart type and apply chart layouts and chart styles.

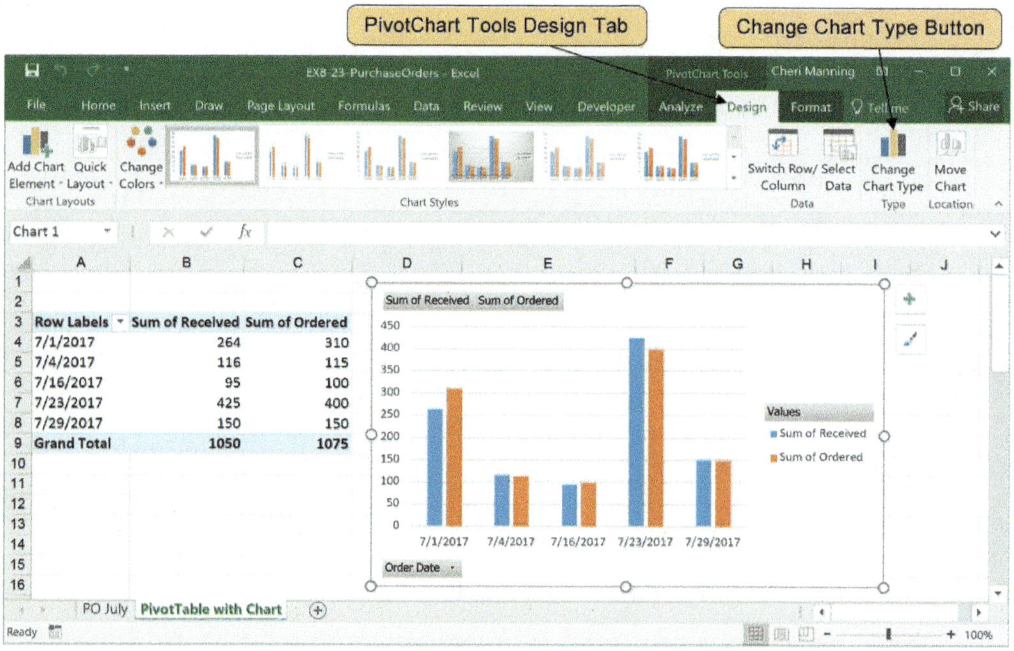

FIGURE EX 8.70

To change the PivotChart chart type:

1. On the *PivotChart Tools Design* tab, in the *Type* group, click the **Change Chart Type** button.
2. In the *Change Chart Type* dialog, click a chart type category to display that category in the right pane.
3. Select a subcategory from the top of the dialog.
4. Click the chart type you want. Notice the dialog shows a preview of how the chart will look.
5. Click **OK**.

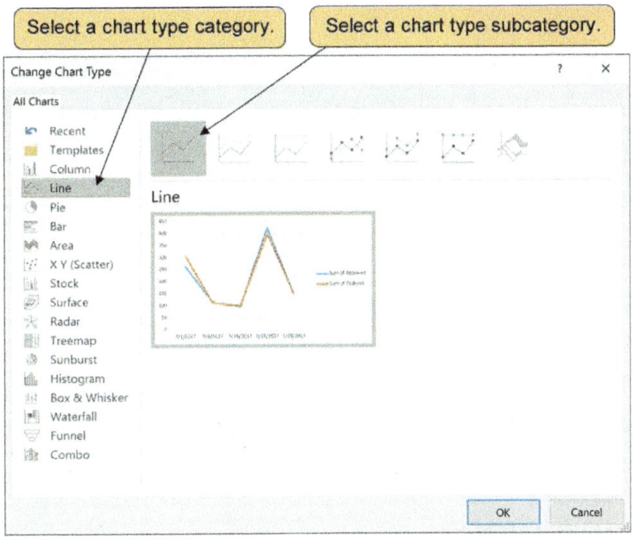

FIGURE EX 8.71

To apply a Quick Style to a PivotChart, on the *PivotChart Tools Design* tab, in the *Chart Styles* group, click the style you want to use, or click the **More** button to see all of the Quick Styles available.

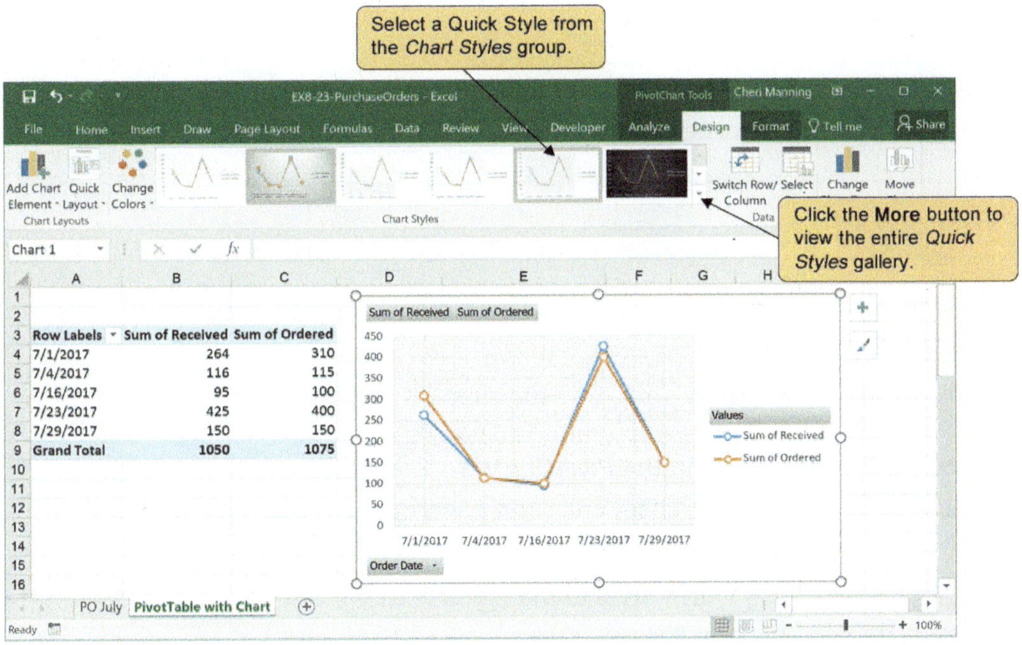

FIGURE EX 8.72

From the *PivotChart Tools Format* tab you can modify the format of specific aspects of the chart including applying fills, outlines, and effects to data series and individual data points. You can also insert and format shapes and apply WordArt Styles to text elements.

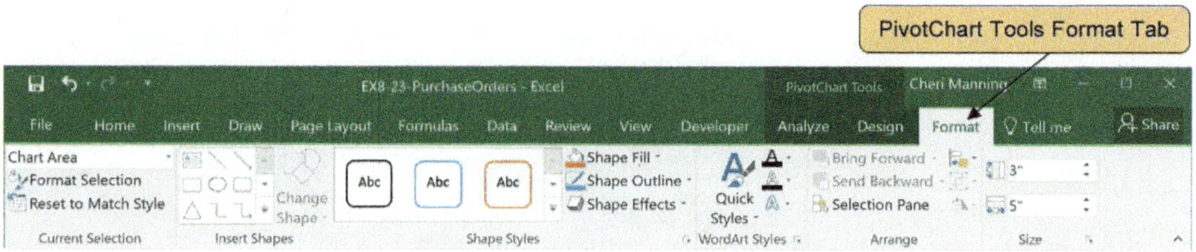

FIGURE EX 8.73

tips & tricks

The PivotChart can display only data visible in the associated PivotTable. To show item details in the PivotChart, expand the field in the PivotTable.

tell me more

For more details on formatting charts, review the skills *Formatting a Data Point or a Data Series* and *Formatting Other Chart Elements*.

another method

Quick Styles are also available from the *Chart Styles* button that appears near the upper right corner of the PivotChart when it is selected.

let me try *Live!*

If you do not have the data file from the previous skill open, open the student data file
EX8-23-PurchaseOrders and try this skill on your own:

1. Select the PivotChart in the *PivotChart* worksheet. Remove any visible slicers by selecting the slicer and then pressing the **[Delete]** key.
2. Change the PivotChart type to the first line chart option.
3. Apply the **Style 5** Quick Style to the PivotChart.
4. Save the file as directed by your instructor and close it.

key terms

- Conditional formatting
- Conditional Formatting Rules Manager
- Advanced Filter
- Criteria range
- Extract range
- Subtotal
- Consolidate
- Auto Outline
- Watch Window
- Scenario
- Scenario Manager
- Scenario summary report
- Forecast sheet
- Solver
- Constraints
- Grouping
- Slicer
- Timeline (PivotTable)

concept review

1. To open the *Sort* dialog,
   a. on the *Data* tab, in the *Sort & Filter* group, click the **Sort** button.
   b. on the *Home* tab, in the *Editing* group, click the **Sort & Filter** button, and click **Custom Sort...**
   c. right-click any cell in the data set, point to **Sort**, and click **Custom Sort...**
   d. do all of the above
2. Which of these options is ***not*** available from the *Text Filters* menu?
   a. *Equals*
   b. *Does Not Equal*
   c. *Greater Than*
   d. *Contains*
3. When setting up the criteria range for Advanced Filter, type criteria in separate rows if data must meet any one of the criteria to be included in the filter.
   a. true
   b. false
4. Before adding subtotals with the *Subtotal* command, you must ________________ the data.
   a. filter
   b. outline
   c. sort
   d. group
5. The *Subtotal* command uses which function to create subtotals?
   a. SUM
   b. SUMIFS
   c. SUBTOTAL
   d. OUTLINE
6. If you want to summarize data without using an outline format or including formulas, you use which command?
   a. *AutoOutline*
   b. *Outline*
   c. *Subtotals*
   d. *Consolidate*
7. When you show a scenario, any changing cells that included formulas originally will be converted to values.
   a. true
   b. false

8. To install Solver, open the *Excel Options* dialog, and go to which section?
   a. *Customize Ribbon*
   b. *General*
   c. *Add-Ins*
   d. *Trust Center*
9. When setting up the Solver parameters, which of these cells must include a formula?
   a. objective
   b. variable cells
   c. constraint
   d. all of the above
10. When a PivotTable's source data updates, the PivotTable and PivotChart update automatically.
   a. true
   b. false

projects

Data files for projects can be found by logging into your SIMnet account and going to the *Library* section.

skill review 8.1

In this project, you will analyze sales data using consolidation, subtotals, outlines, conditional formatting, advanced filters, PivotTables, and PivotCharts.

Skills needed to complete this project:

- Using Consolidate to Create Subtotals (Skill 8.8)
- Sorting Data on Multiple Criteria (Skill 8.4)
- Adding Subtotals (Skill 8.7)
- Creating an Outline (Skill 8.9)
- Creating New Conditional Formatting Rules (Skill 8.1)
- Filtering and Sorting Using Cell Attributes (Skill 8.3)
- Managing Conditional Formatting Rules (Skill 8.2)
- Using Advanced Filter (Skill 8.6)
- Refreshing Data in a PivotTable (Skill 8.16)
- Adding a Calculated Field to a PivotTable (Skill 8.17)
- Changing the Look of a PivotTable (Skill 8.21)
- Filtering PivotTable Data (Skill 8.19)
- Filtering Data in a PivotChart (Skill 8.22)
- Changing the Look of a PivotChart (Skill 8.23)

1. Open the start file **EX2016-SkillReview-8-1** and resave the file as:
   `[your initials]EX-SkillReview-8-1`
2. If the workbook opens in Protected View, click the **Enable Editing** button in the Message Bar at the top of the workbook so you can modify the workbook.
3. Use consolidate to create a summary of the sales data by region. The summary will be located on the *Analysis* worksheet.
   a. Go to the **Analysis** worksheet, and select cell **A2**.
   b. On the *Data* tab, in the *Data Tools* group, click the **Consolidate** button.
   c. Verify that **Sum** is selected in the *Function* box.
   d. If there are any references in the *All references* box, click each and then click the **[Delete]** button to remove them.
   e. Click in the **Reference** box, and then click the **Sales Data** worksheet tab. Click and drag to select cells **C3:E67**.
   f. Click both the **Top row** and **Left column** check boxes.
   g. Click **OK**.

h. On the *Analysis* worksheet, delete cells **B2:B10**, allowing the other cells to shift left.

4. Sort the sales data alphabetically by region and then by last name.
   a. Go to the **Sales Data** worksheet, and click any cell in the data set.
   b. On the *Data* tab, in the *Sort & Filter* group, click the **Sort** button.
   c. In the *Sort* dialog, expand the **Sort by** list, and select **Region**.
   d. Click the **Add Level** button.
   e. Expand the **Then by** list, and select **Last Name**.
   f. Click **OK**.
5. Add subtotals to the data to calculate the total commission earned for each sales associate.
   a. On the *Data* tab, in the *Outline* group, click the **Subtotal** button.
   b. Expand the **At each change in** list, and select **Last Name**.
   c. Verify that **Sum** is selected in the *Use function* box.
   d. Verify that there is a checkmark next to **Commission Earned** in the *Add subtotal to* box.
   e. Click **OK**.
6. Copy the subtotal data to the *Analysis* worksheet.
   a. On the *Sales Data* worksheet, click the outline level **2** button to collapse the list so only the total commission earned for each sales associate is visible. This will make it easier to copy the data.
   b. Select cells **A3:G77** and copy them to the Clipboard. Do not include the *Grand Total* row (row 78).
   c. Go to the **Analysis** worksheet and paste the copied data beginning in cell **A13**.
7. Notice that when you paste the subtotaled data, Excel removes the subtotal grouping, but keeps the subtotal rows and formulas. You can use the *Outline* command to re-create groups based on the subtotal formulas.
   a. Click any cell in the data range.
   b. On the *Data* tab, in the *Outline* group, click the **Group** button arrow, and select **Auto Outline**.
   c. Click the outline level **1** button to collapse the list so only the total commission earned for each sales associate is visible.
8. On the *Commissions* worksheet, create a new conditional formatting rule to apply an icon set to the values in the *Rating* column.
   a. Go to the **Commissions** worksheet and select cells **H3:H66**.
   b. On the *Home* tab, in the *Styles* group, click the **Conditional Formatting** button. Click **New Rule...**
   c. In the *Select a Rule Type* box, verify that **Format all cells based on their values** is selected.

d. In the *Edit the Rule Description* box, expand the **Format Style** list, and select **Icon Sets**.
e. Expand the **Icon Style** list, and select **Three Stars**.
f. Click the **Show Icon Only** checkbox to hide the values in the selected cells.
g. In the *Display each icon according to these rules* section, expand the first **Type** list and select **Number**.
h. In the first *Value* box type `9000` to display a completely filled gold star when the cell value is greater than or equal to 9,000.
i. Expand the second **Type** list and select **Number**.
j. In the second *Value* box, type `4500` to display a partially filled gold star when the cell value is less than 9,000 and greater than or equal to 4,500.
k. Click **OK**.

9. Sort the sales data so cells with the completely filled gold star icon appear first.
   a. Scroll down and find a cell with a completely filled gold star.
   b. Right-click a cell with a completely filled gold star, point to Sort, and select **Put Selected Cell Icon On Top**.
10. On the *Sales Data Filter* worksheet, delete the conditional formatting rule that applies a font format to cells where the value is above average.
    a. Go to the **Sales Data Filter** worksheet.
    b. On the *Home* tab, in the *Styles* group, click the **Conditional Formatting** button. Click **Manage Rules...** to open the Conditional Formatting Rules Manager.
    c. If necessary, expand the **Show formatting rules for** list and select **This Worksheet**.
    d. Select the **Above Average** rule and click the **Delete Rule** button.
    e. Click **OK**.
11. Use the Advanced Filter feature to find sales greater than $110,000 for George Anderson or Xin Zhu.
    a. Insert four new rows above row 3, so the column label row is now row 7 and there are five blank rows between the title and the column labels. If necessary, clear all formatting from the new rows.
    b. Copy the range **A7:G7** (the column labels) and paste in **A3:G3**.
    c. Enter the filter criteria in **A4:G5** as follows:
       i. In **A4**, type: `George`
       ii. In **B4**, type: `Anderson`
       iii. In **E4**, type: `>110000`
       iv. In **A5**, type: `Xin`
       v. In **B5**, type: `Zhu`
       vi. In **E5**, type: `>110000`
    d. Click any cell in the data set.

e. On the *Data* tab, in the *Sort & Filter* group, click the **Advanced** button.
f. Verify that the **Filter the list, in place** radio button is selected.
g. The *List range* box should display $A$7:$G$71. If it does not, click in the **List range** box, and then click and drag to select cells **A7:G71**.
h. Click in the **Criteria range** box. Click and drag to select the range **A3:G5** as the criteria range.
i. Click **OK**.

12. The data in the *Sales Data* worksheet has changed since the PivotTable was created. Refresh the PivotTable to reflect the changes.
    a. Go to the **PivotTable** worksheet and click anywhere in the PivotTable.
    b. On the *PivotTable Tools Analyze* tab, in the *Data* group, click the **Refresh** button.
    c. In the *PivotTable Fields* pane, click **Last Name** to add the *Last Name* field to the *Rows* box.
    d. In the *Rows* box, click **Last Name** and move it above **Client**.
13. Add a calculated field to determine the average commission rate for each row in the PivotTable.
    a. On the *PivotTable Tools Analyze* tab, in the *Calculations* group, click the **Fields, Items, & Sets** button.
    b. Click **Calculated Field...**
    c. In the *Name* box, type: `Average Commission Calculated`
    d. In the *Fields* box, click **Commission Earned**, and then click the **Insert Field** button.
    e. Type: `/`
    f. In the *Fields* box, double-click **Annual Sales**.
    g. The final formula in the *Formula* box should look like this: `='Commission Earned'/'Annual Sales'`
    h. Click **OK** to add the calculated field to the PivotTable.
    i. Click any cell in the new calculated column.
    j. On the *PivotTable Tools Analyze* tab, in the *Active Field* group, click the **Field Settings** button to open the *Value Field Settings* dialog.
    k. In the *Custom Name* box, type: `Average Commission`
    l. Click the **Number Format** button at the bottom left corner of the dialog. In the *Category* list, click **Percentage**. If necessary, type **2** in the *Decimal places* box.
    m. Click **OK**.
    n. Click **OK** again to close the *Value Field Settings* dialog.
14. Apply a Quick Style to the PivotTable.
    a. Click anywhere in the PivotTable.

   b. On the *PivotTable Tools Design* tab, in the *PivotTable Styles* group, click the **More** button to expand the gallery.
   c. Click **Pivot Style Medium 6**.
15. Use slicers to filter the PivotTable by region to show only the NW1 region.
   a. On the *PivotTable Tools Analyze* tab, in the *Filter* group, click the **Insert Slicer** button.
   b. In the *Insert Slicers* dialog, click the **Region** check box. Click **OK**.
   c. In the *Region* slicer, click the **NW1** button.
16. Filter the PivotChart data to show only the NW1 and NW2 regions.
   a. Go to the **PivotChart** worksheet and select the chart.
   b. On the *PivotChart Tools Analyze* tab, in the *Filter* group, click the **Insert Slicer** button.
   c. In the *Insert Slicers* dialog, click the **Region** check box. Click **OK**.
   d. In the *Region* slicer, click the **NW1** button. Press the **[Ctrl]** key and click the **NW2** button.
17. Apply a Quick Style to the PivotChart.
   a. Select the PivotChart.
   b. On the *PivotChart Tools Design* tab, in the *Chart Styles* group, click the **More** button to expand the gallery.
   c. Click **Style 11**.
18. Save and close the workbook.

projects

Data files for projects can be found by logging into your SIMnet account and going to the *Library* section.

skill review 8.2

In this project, you will use what-if analysis to analyze real estate options and inventory problems for a sporting goods store. This project uses named ranges extensively. For your reference, the named range list was pasted in the *Names* worksheet.

Skills needed to complete this project:

- Creating What-If Analysis Scenarios (Skill 8.11)
- Creating Scenario Summary Reports (Skill 8.12)
- Creating New Conditional Formatting Rules (Skill 8.1)
- Managing Conditional Formatting Rules (Skill 8.2)
- Activating the Solver Add-Inn (Skill 8.14)
- Using Solver (Skill 8.15)
- Refreshing Data in a PivotTable (Skill 8.16)
- Adding a Calculated Field to a PivotTable (Skill 8.17)
- Filtering Data in a PivotChart (Skill 8.22)
- Changing the Look of a PivotChart (Skill 8.23)

1. Open the start file **EX2016-SkillReview-8-2** and resave the file as: `[your initials]EX-SkillReview-8-2`
2. If the workbook opens in Protected View, click the **Enable Editing** button in the Message Bar at the top of the workbook so you can modify the workbook.
3. The store owner is considering buying a new building. The current loan terms are listed in cells B2:B7 on the *Building Loan* worksheet. Create a scenario to save the original loan terms and then create two more scenarios for alternate down payments.
    a. On the *Data* tab, in the *Data Tools* group, click the **What-If Analysis** button, and select **Scenario Manager...**
    b. Click the **Add...** button to create a new scenario.
    c. In the *Scenario* name box, type: `Original Loan Terms`
    d. Click in the **By Changing Cells** box, and then click cell **B3** in the *Building Loan* worksheet.
    e. Click **OK**.
    f. For this scenario, leave the *DownPayment* value at 250,000. Click **Add** to add another scenario.
    g. In the *Scenario* name box, type: `Large Down Payment`

    h. Verify that **B3** is listed in the *By Changing Cells* box. Click **OK**.
    i. Enter **`600000`** in the *DownPayment* box. Click **Add** to add another scenario.
    j. In the *Scenario* name box, type: **`Small Down Payment`**
    k. Verify that **B3** is listed in the *By Changing Cells* box. Click **OK**.
    l. Enter **`150000`** in the *DownPayment* box. Click **OK** to return to the Scenario Manager.

4. Show the *Large Down Payment* scenario.
    a. In the *Scenarios* box, select **Large Down Payment.**
    b. Click the **Show** button.
    c. Do not close the Scenario Manager.
5. Create a Scenario Summary Report.
    a. In the Scenario Manager, click the **Summary...** button.
    b. In the *Scenario Summary* dialog, verify that the **Scenario summary** radio button is selected and that only **B8** is listed in the *Result cells* box.
    c. Click **OK**.
    d. Review the results and then return to the **Building Loan** worksheet.
6. The data in B11:M21 show the monthly payments for combinations of interest rates and loan lengths. Add custom conditional formatting to highlight the highest monthly payments.
    a. Select cells **C12:M21**.
    b. On the *Home* tab, in the *Styles* group, click the **Conditional Formatting** button, and select **New Rule...**
    c. In the *Select a Rule Type* box, click **Format only top or bottom ranked values.**
    d. In the *Edit the Rule Description* box, change **10** to **4** to highlight the four largest values.
    e. Click the **Format...** button to define the format.
    f. On the *Font* tab, expand the **Color** palette and select the standard **Red** color (the second color from the left in the row of Standard colors).
    g. On the *Border* tab, expand the **Color** palette and select the standard **Red** color (the second color from the left in the row of Standard colors). Click the **Outline** button.
    h. Click **OK**.
    i. Review the format in the *Preview* box and then click **OK** to apply the new conditional format to the selected cells.
7. Create another custom conditional formatting rule to highlight the lowest monthly payments.
    a. On the *Home* tab, in the *Styles* group, click the **Conditional Formatting** button, and select **New Rule...**
    b. In the *Select a Rule Type* box, click **Format only top or bottom ranked**

values.

c. In the *Edit the Rule Description* box, expand the dropdown list and select **Bottom**. Change **10** to **4** to highlight the four smallest values.

d. Click the **Format...** button to define the format.

e. On the *Font* tab, expand the **Color** palette and select the standard **Green** color (the sixth color from the left in the row of Standard colors).

f. On the *Border* tab, expand the **Color** palette and select the standard **Green** color (the sixth color from the left in the row of Standard colors). Click the **Outline** button.

g. Click **OK.**

h. Review the format in the *Preview* box and then click **OK** to apply the new conditional format to the selected cells.

8. Create another custom conditional formatting rule to apply an icon to all the values.

    a. On the *Home* tab, in the *Styles* group, click the **Conditional Formatting** button. Click **New Rule...**

    b. In the *Select a Rule Type* box, verify that **Format all cells based on their values** is selected.

    c. In the *Edit the Rule Description* box, expand the **Format Style** list, and select **Icon Sets**.

    d. Expand the **Icon Style** list, and select **3 Symbols (Uncircled)**.

    e. Click the **Reverse Icon Order** button.

    f. Click **OK.**

9. On the *Home* tab, in the *Cells* group, click the **Format** button, and select **AutoFit Column Width**.

10. Manage the conditional formatting rules so the icon rule is applied last and will not be applied to cells that meet one of the other conditions.

    a. On the *Home* tab, in the *Styles* group, click the **Conditional Formatting** button. Click **Manage Rules...**

    b. In the Conditional Formatting Rules Manager, expand the **Show formatting rules for** list, and select **This Worksheet**.

    c. Click the **Icon Set** rule and click the **Move Down** button twice so the rule is last in the list.

    d. Click the **Stop If True** check box next to the *Bottom 4* rule.

    e. Click the **Stop If True** check box next to the *Top 4* rule.

    f. Click **OK.**

11. To reduce inventory before moving to the new building, the store wants to run a 20% off sale for a limited number of items in stock. Use Solver to find the optimal number of items to put on sale for the maximum profit possible. If necessary, install the Solver add-in. If Solver is already installed, skip to step 12.

a. Click the **File** tab.

b. Click **Options** to open the *Excel Options* dialog.

c. Click **Add-Ins**.

d. Near the bottom of the window, the *Manage* box should display *Excel Add-ins*. If it does not, expand the list and select **Excel Add-ins**. Click **Go...** to open the *Add-Ins* dialog.

e. In the *Add-Ins* dialog, click the **Solver Add-in** check box.

f. Click **OK**.

12. Before setting up the Solver parameters, review the formulas in the *Inventory* worksheet cells **C1** and **F2:F5**. Solver will find the maximum profit possible (C1) by changing the number of items in the named range *SaleStock* (J10:J34) within the constraints imposed on the formulas in cells F2:F5.

    a. On the *Inventory* worksheet, click cell **C1**. This is the *Objective* cell containing the formula to calculate profit:
    `=SUMPRODUCT(SalePrice,SaleStock)-SUMPRODUCT(Cost,SaleStock)`

    b. On the *Data* tab, in the *Analysis* group, click **Solver**.

    c. If necessary, enter **$C$1** in the *Set Objective* box.

    d. In the *By Changing Variable Cells* box, enter the range **`J10:J34`** or use the named range: **`SaleStock`**

    e. Click **Add** to add the first constraint: The total number of balls on sale (F2) must be less than or equal to the value in cell G2 (25). In the *Add Constraint* dialog, enter **F2** in the *Cell Reference* box. Verify <= as the comparison operator. Enter G2 in the *Constraint* box. Click **Add** to add another constraint.

    f. The total number of shoes on sale (F3) must be less than or equal to the value in cell G3 (50). Enter **F3** in the *Cell Reference* box. Verify < = as the comparison operator. Enter **G3** in the *Constraint* box. Click **Add** to add another constraint.

    g. The total number of items on sale (F4) must be less than or equal to the value in cell G4 (75). Enter **F4** in the *Cell Reference* box. Verify < = as the comparison operator. Enter **G4** in the *Constraint* box. Click **Add** to add another constraint.

    h. Items from the manufacturer Nuke cannot be on sale this week. The value in cell F5 must be equal to the value in cell G5 (0). Enter **F5** in the *Cell Reference* box. Expand the comparison operator list and select =. Enter **G5** in the *Constraint* box. Click **Add** to add another constraint.

    i. The value of each cell in the *SaleStock* range (J10:J34) must be less than or equal to the value in the *Stock* range (I10:I34). Enter **SaleStock** in the *Cell Reference* box. Verify < = as the comparison operator. Enter **Stock** in the *Constraint* box. Click **Add** to add another constraint.

j. The *SaleStock* values must be whole numbers. Enter SaleStock in the *Cell Reference* box. Expand the comparison operator list and select **int**. Click **OK** to return to the *Solver Parameters* dialog.
k. The default solving method, GRG Nonlinear, will not find an appropriate solution. Expand the list and select **Simplex LP** instead.
l. Carefully review all the settings in the *Solver Parameters* dialog, and then click the **Solve** button.
m. Keep the Solver solution. In the *Solver Results* dialog, verify that the **Keep Solver Solution** radio button is selected. Click **OK**.

13. Now that the values in the *Inventory* worksheet have been updated by Solver, you need to refresh the PivotTable and PivotChart.
    a. Go to the **Inventory PivotTable** worksheet, and click anywhere in the PivotTable.
    b. On the *PivotTable Tools Analyze* tab, in the *Data* group, click the **Refresh** button.
14. Add a calculated field to summarize the remaining items in stock after the sale in the PivotTable.
    a. On the *PivotTable Tools Analyze* tab, in the *Calculations* group, click the **Fields, Items, & Sets** button.
    b. Click **Calculated Field...**
    c. In the *Name* box, type: `Remaining Stock`
    d. In the *Fields* box, click **Stock**, and then click the **Insert Field** button.
    e. Type: `-`
    f. In the *Fields* box, double-click **Items on Sale**.
    g. The final formula in the *Formula* box should look like this: `=Stock-'Items on Sale'`
    h. Click **OK** to add the calculated field to the PivotTable.
15. Apply a Quick Style to the PivotTable.
    a. Click anywhere in the PivotTable.
    b. On the *PivotTable Tools Design* tab, in the *PivotTable Styles* group, click the **More** button to expand the gallery.
    c. Click **Pivot Style Light 14**.
16. Filter the PivotChart data to show data for a single manufacturer.
    a. Click the PivotChart to select it.
    b. On the *PivotChart Tools Analyze* tab, in the *Filter* group, click the **Insert Slicer** button.
    c. In the *Insert Slicers* dialog, click the **Manufacturer** check box. Click **OK**.
    d. In the *Manufacturer* slicer, click the **Jackson** button.
17. Change the PivotChart to a stacked column chart.
    a. Select the PivotChart.

b. On the *PivotChart Tools Design* tab, in the *Type* group, click the **Change Chart Type** button.
c. Click **Stacked Column** (the second column type at the top of the *Change Chart Type* dialog).
d. Click **OK**.

18. In the *Manufacturer* slicer, press **[Ctrl]** and click the **Assuage** and **Zinks** buttons to add these manufacturers to the PivotChart.
19. Save and close the workbook.

projects

Data files for projects can be found by logging into your SIMnet account and going to the *Library* section.

challenge yourself 8.3

In this project, you will analyze grades for a spreadsheets class and use conditional formatting to highlight grades where you suspect students are cheating. You will work with a PivotTable and PivotChart to analyze grades by section and create scenarios to compare the effects of changing the grading scale.

Skills needed to complete this project:

- Using Consolidate to Create Subtotals (Skill 8.8)
- Sorting Data on Multiple Criteria (Skill 8.4)
- Using Advanced Filter (Skill 8.6)
- Creating What-If Analysis Scenarios (Skill 8.11)
- Creating Scenario Summary Reports (Skill 8.12)
- Creating New Conditional Formatting Rules (Skill 8.1)
- Filtering and Sorting Using Cell Attributes (Skill 8.3)
- Refreshing Data in a PivotTable (Skill 8.16)
- Adding a Calculated Field to a PivotTable (Skill 8.17)
- Changing the Look of a PivotTable (Skill 8.21)
- Changing the Look of a PivotChart (Skill 8.23)
- Filtering Data in a PivotChart (Skill 8.22)

1. Open the start file **EX2016-ChallengeYourself-8-3** and resave the file as: `[your initials]EX-ChallengeYourself-8-3`
2. If the workbook opens in Protected View, click the **Enable Editing** button in the Message Bar at the top of the workbook so you can modify the workbook.
3. Use Consolidate to create a summary of the grades by section.
   a. Place the summary in cell **A2** the *Summary by Section* worksheet.
   b. Use the **Average** function.
   c. Consolidate data from the cell range **C3:O26** in the **Gradebook** worksheet.
   d. Use labels from both the top row and the left column.
   e. Do not create links to the source data.
   f. If necessary, autofit the columns.
   g. On the *Summary by Section* worksheet, center and merge the title across cells **A1:M1**.
4. Sort the data in the *Gradebook* worksheet alphabetically by section and then by last name.
5. Use Advanced Filter to find students who had less than 80 on the midterm ***or*** had less than 80 on the final.
   a. Copy cells **A3:P3** and paste them starting in cell **A29** for use as the header

row in the criteria range.

b. Enter the criteria in the criteria range to find rows where the value in the **Midterm** column is **<80** ***or*** the value in the **Final** column is **<80.**

c. Use Advanced Filter and copy the filtered data to the range beginning with cell **A34.**

6. Create and show scenarios for different grading scales.

a. Create a scenario named **`Original Scale`**. Include cells **S5, R6, S6, R7, S7, R8, S8,** and **R9.** For this scenario, do not change any of the cell values. Note that these cells currently include formulas that will be converted to values when you show a scenario.

b. Create a second scenario named **`Generous Scale`**. Change the values for the following cells:

	R	S	T
4	**High**	**Low**	**Grade**
5	100	90	A
6	89	80	B
7	79	70	C
8	69	60	D
9	59		F

c. Create a third scenario named **`Difficult Scale`**. Change the values for the following cells:

	R	S	T
4	**High**	**Low**	**Grade**
5	100	95	A
6	94	89	B
7	88	83	C
8	82	77	D
9	76		F

d. Show the **Difficult Scale** scenario.

7. Create a scenario summary report showing the changes to cells **P4:P26** (students' final grades).
8. Apply custom conditional formatting and filtering to the data in the *Suspect Grades* worksheet to find suspicious grades.
   a. Apply custom conditional formatting to the data so duplicate values for each assignment use **Red, Accent 2** (the sixth color from the left in the top row of theme colors) and **bold** formatting. You will need to create 10 separate conditional formatting rules—one for each chapter assignment.
   b. Filter each of the columns to show only cells with the red font color. Notice that as you work through the columns, some columns no longer include *Filter by Color* as an option because all the cells without red text have been hidden by the filters in previous columns.
   c. When you are finished, there should be five rows visible with two groups of students who suspiciously scored the same on every assignment.
9. The source data for the PivotTable have changed. Go to the **PivotTable** worksheet and update the PivotTable.
10. Add a calculated field named `Difference` to the PivotTable to calculate the difference between the final average and the midterm average for each section. The formula in the *Insert Calculated Field* dialog should look like this: `=Final-Midterm`
11. Apply the **Pivot Style Medium 2** Quick Style (the second style in the *Medium* section) to the PivotTable.
12. Change the PivotChart to a combo chart with the **Sum of Difference** series as a line chart on the secondary axis and the other two series as clustered column charts on the on primary axis.
13. Apply the **Style 5** PivotChart Quick Style to the PivotChart.
14. Add a slicer to the PivotChart to filter the data by the **Grade** field. If necessary, move the slicer so it doesn't cover the PivotChart. Display data where the grade is **B** or **C** only.
15. Save and close the workbook.

projects

Data files for projects can be found by logging into your SIMnet account and going to the *Library* section.

challenge yourself 8.4

In this project, you will use scenarios and a scenario summary to analyze car purchasing options. The data for this project were downloaded from: https://www.fueleconomy.gov/feg/download.shtml You will use custom filtering to find the data you are interested in and copy it from this very large data set to another worksheet. You will then use Advanced Filter, conditional formatting, sorting, and subtotals to further analyze this subset of data. You will manipulate a PivotTable created from the main vehicle data set. Finally, you will use Solver to solve a business problem to help you pay for your new car.

Skills needed to complete this project:

- Creating What-If Analysis Scenarios (Skill 8.11)
- Creating Scenario Summary Reports (Skill 8.12)
- Creating a Custom Filter (Skill 8.5)
- Using Advanced Filter (Skill 8.6)
- Creating New Conditional Formatting Rules (Skill 8.1)
- Sorting Data on Multiple Criteria (Skill 8.4)
- Adding Subtotals (Skill 8.7)
- Changing the Look of a PivotTable (Skill 8.21)
- Filtering PivotTable Data (Skill 8.19)
- Activating the Solver Add-In (Skill 8.14)
- Using Solver (Skill 8.15)

1. Open the start file **EX2016-ChallengeYourself-8-4** and resave the file as: `[your initials]EX-ChallengeYourself-8-4`
2. If the workbook opens in Protected View, click the **Enable Editing** button in the Message Bar at the top of the workbook so you can modify the workbook.
3. You want to purchase a new car. Your current car is worth $3,500 as a trade-in. The base sticker price on the car you want is $24,595. The first financing offer from the dealer is 1.9% APR for 24 months, with no cash back. The original financing offer terms are listed in cells A3:B9 on the *Car Loan* worksheet. Cell B10 contains a formula with a PMT function to calculate the monthly payment. Use what-if analysis tools to compare financing options. Create scenarios to compare financing options for the car loan.
    a. Create names for the following cells on the *Car Loan* worksheet to make the scenarios easier to follow:

Name cell **B3**: **`Price`**

Name cell **B4**: **`TradeIn`**

Name cell **B5**: **`CashBack`**

Name cell **B6**: **`Loan`**

Name cell **B8**: **`Months`**

Name cell **B9**: **`APR`**

Name cell **B10**: **`Payment`**

Name cell **B12**: **`TotalCost`**

b. Create a scenario named **`Original Financing`** to save the original values in cells **B3**, **B5**, **B8**, and **B9**.

c. Create a second scenario named **`Intermediate Car`**. Change the values as follows:

Cell **B3**: **`33999`**

Cell **B5**: **`1500`**

Cell **B8**: **`36`**

Cell **B9**: **`2.4%`**

d. Show the **Intermediate Car** scenario to verify your data entry.

e. Create a third scenario named **`Luxury Car`**. Change the values as follows:

Cell **B3**: **`62700`**

Cell **B5**: **`2500`**

Cell **B8**: **`60`**

Cell **B9**: **`3.9%`**

f. Show the **Luxury Car** scenario to verify your data entry.

g. Autofit column.

4. Create a scenario summary report to compare the results for cells **B10** (the monthly payment) and **B12** (the total cost of the car including interest).
5. The data in the *MPG Data* worksheet were downloaded from the Web site https://www.fueleconomy.gov/feg/download.shtml. The greenhouse gas scores range from 0 to 10, where 10 is best. The vehicles with the best scores on both air pollution and greenhouse gas receive the *SmartWay* designation. Use custom filtering to find cars in this data set that meet your criteria and then copy the smaller data set to another worksheet where you can work with it further.

a. Go to the **MPG Data** worksheet, and display the AutoFilter arrows for the data set.

b. Create a custom number filter to show only rows where the greenhouse gas score is greater than **8**.

c. Create another custom number filter to show only rows where the highway MPG is greater than **35**.

d. Create a custom text filter to show only rows where the *Trans* column contains the word **auto**.

e. Create a custom text filter to show only rows where the value in the *Fuel* column equals **Electricity** or **Gasoline**.

f. At this point, the list of more than 2,000 cars should be filtered down to just 48 records.

g. Copy the filtered data to cell **A1** in the **My Car Data** worksheet. Be sure to include the heading row but do not include the *All Models* title. Paste keeping the source columns widths.

6. On the *My Car Data* worksheet, use Advanced Filter to copy a subset of data to another location on this worksheet.

   a. Copy cells **A1:P1** and paste them below the data set in row **52**.

   b. In cell **A51**, type: `Criteria`

   c. Apply the **Accent 4** cell style to cell **A51**.

   d. Set up the criteria in the row(s) below row 52. Find cars where the value in the **Fuel** column is **Gasoline *and*** the value in the **Hwy MPG** column is **greater than 35**.

   e. In cell **A55**, type: `Filtered Data`

   f. Apply the **Accent 4** cell style to cell **A55**.

   g. Autofit column **A**.

   h. Use Advanced Filter to find the rows that meet the criteria and copy the filtered data to another location beginning in cell **A56**.

   i. Sixteen rows should have been copied from the main data set to cells **A57:P72**.

7. Format the filtered data set (cells A56:P72) as a table. Use **Table Style Light 1** (the first table style in the gallery). Be careful ***not*** to include row 55 in the table data range.

8. Insert a new column to the left of the **Greenhouse Gas Score** column. *Hint:* Be sure to add a column to the worksheet, not just the table.

   a. Copy the values from cells **M57:M72** to **N57:N72**.

   b. Type this column label in cell **N56**: `Cmb MPG Icon`

9. Apply a new custom conditional formatting rule to cells **N57:N72** to show the **4 Ratings** icon set. Show the icon only.

10. Continue working with the filtered data that has the conditional formatting applied. Sort the table first alphabetically by the values in the **Model** column and then by icon in the **Cmb MPG Icon** column so the **Signal Meter With Four Filled Bars** icon appears at the top.

11. Go back to the main data set at the top of the *My Car Data* worksheet and add subtotals for each change in **Model** to calculate the **average** for the following: **Air Pollution Score, City MPG, Hwy MPG,** and **Cmb MPG.**

12. Collapse the data to show just the total rows.

13. Go to the **MPG PivotTable** worksheet. This sheet includes a PivotTable created from the data on the *MPG Data* worksheet.
    a. Refresh the PivotTable data.
    b. Apply the **Pivot Style Medium 1** Quick Style to the PivotTable (the first style in the *Medium* section).
    c. Display a slicer for the **SmartWay** field and show only data where the *SmartWay* value is **Elite**.
14. To pay for the new car, you've decided to start a bakery business out of your home kitchen. You have limited capital and capacity, so you need to make wise decisions about which products to bake each day. Go to the **Bakery Business** worksheet. Cell B1 uses a SUMPRODUCT formula to calculate profit. Carefully review the assumptions and formulas in this worksheet before entering the following Solver parameters:
    a. Find the maximum possible profit (cell **B1**) by changing the values in cells **C7:C10**.
    b. The working hours required (**B3**) must be less than or equal to the number of working hours in the day (**D3**).
    c. The total cost of ingredients (**B4**) must be less than or equal to the available capital (**D4**).
    d. For each item in the range **C7:C10**, the number of items baked cannot exceed the maximum capacity available per day as defined in cells **F7:F10**. This restriction requires four separate constraints in the *Solver Parameters* dialog.
    e. The items in the variable cell range **C7:C10** must be whole numbers.
    f. There should be a total of seven constraints.
    g. Run Solver and accept the Solver solution.
15. Save and close the workbook.

projects

Data files for projects can be found by logging into your SIMnet account and going to the *Library* section.

on your own 8.5

In this project, you will update data for selling back textbooks with our own data and then make copies of the worksheet to analyze with a variety of methods.

Skills needed to complete this project:

- Creating What-If Analysis Scenarios (Skill 8.11)
- Creating Scenario Summary Reports (Skill 8.12)
- Refreshing Data in a PivotTable (Skill 8.16)
- Adding a Calculated Field to a PivotTable (Skill 8.17)
- Changing the Look of a PivotChart (Skill 8.23)
- Filtering Data in a PivotChart (Skill 8.22)
- Creating New Conditional Formatting Rules (Skill 8.1)
- Managing Conditional Formatting Rules (Skill 8.2)
- Filtering and Sorting Using Cell Attributes (Skill 8.3)
- Sorting Data on Multiple Criteria (Skill 8.4)
- Adding Subtotals (Skill 8.7)

1. Open the start file **EX2016-OnYourOwn-8-5** and resave the file as: **`[your initials]EX-OnYourOwn-8-5`**
2. If the workbook opens in Protected View, click the **Enable Editing** button in the Message Bar at the top of the workbook so you can modify the workbook.
3. Update the data in the *Book Inventory* worksheet to reflect your own textbook inventory. Update the sell back rate in cell B2 to reflect the average rate that you receive when selling back textbooks.
4. Create a few scenarios using different sell back rates and generate a scenario summary report.
5. Once you've updated the data, you'll need to refresh the PivotTable and PivotChart in the Pivot worksheet.
6. The PivotTable data source includes the total row from the *Book Inventory* data, but it should not. Update the data source.
7. Add a calculated field to the PivotTable to calculate the difference between the book costs and the resell values.
8. Change the PivotChart type to something other than a combo chart. Choose a chart type that is appropriate for the data.
9. Add slicers to filter the PivotChart.
10. Create a copy of the *Book Inventory* worksheet.

a. Create custom conditional formatting rules to highlight the books with the highest or lowest resale values.
b. Create a custom formatting rule using an icon set or data bars to compare resale values.
c. Use the Conditional Formatting Rules Manager as necessary to reorder the rules.
d. Sort the data based on cell attributes applied by the conditional formatting rules.

11. Create another copy of the *Book Inventory* worksheet.
    a. Delete the *Total* row.
    b. Sort the data by subject matter and year published.
    c. Add subtotals to calculate the total cost and resell value at each change in subject matter.
12. Save and close the workbook.

projects

Data files for projects can be found by logging into your SIMnet account and going to the *Library* section.

fix it 8.6

In this project, you will fix errors in financial data for a restaurant chain to find which locations are the lowest performers and correct the Solver parameters to set target sales goals for next year using reasonable constraints. You will create the missing scenario summary report.

Skills needed to complete this project:

- Managing Conditional Formatting Rules (Skill 8.2)
- Filtering and Sorting Using Cell Attributes (Skill 8.3)
- Sorting Data on Multiple Criteria (Skill 8.4)
- Using Advanced Filter (Skill 8.6)
- Creating a Custom Filter (Skill 8.5)
- Refreshing Data in a PivotTable (Skill 8.16)
- Filtering Data in a PivotChart (Skill 8.22)
- Changing the Look of a PivotChart (Skill 8.23)
- Creating What-If Analysis Scenarios (Skill 8.11)
- Activating the Solver Add-In (Skill 8.14)
- Using Solver (Skill 8.15)
- Creating Scenario Summary Reports (Skill 8.12)

1. Open the start file **EX2016-FixIt-8-6** and resave the file as:
   `[your initials]EX-FixIt-8-6`
2. If the workbook opens in Protected View, click the **Enable Editing** button in the Message Bar at the top of the workbook so you can modify the workbook.
3. There are multiple conditional formatting rules applied to cells in the *Financial Data* worksheet. Make changes to the conditional formatting rules on this worksheet only.
   a. There should be three conditional formatting rules: a *Top 2* rule, a *Bottom 2* rule, and an *Icon Set* rule. Delete all the extra rules.
   b. Correct the cell range for the remaining rules. All the rules should be applied to cells **D5:G20**.
   c. Fix the remaining conditional formatting rules so if the value of the cell is in the top 2 values or the bottom 2 values, the icon rule is not applied.

4. Now that the conditional formatting rules have been fixed, sort the data alphabetically by the value in the *Location* column and then by icon in the *Quarter 1* column so rows with the up arrow are at the top and rows with the bottom arrow are at the bottom.
   a. If necessary, be sure to click a cell in the data set to deselect the D5:G20 cell range or the sort will be applied to only the selected cells and your data will be mixed up.
   b. You will need to use the *Sort* dialog as this requires a multilevel sort.
   c. If the sort if performed correctly, the data will be sorted by location, and then within each location, by the icon in the *Quarter 1* column.
5. An advanced filter should be performed to find any locations with a profit/loss for ***any*** quarter less than or equal to 10,000. The results should be copied to cell **I4**.
   a. The criteria range beginning in cell **A23** is set up incorrectly. The criteria for this filter should include values <10,000 in *Quarter 1* ***or*** <10,000 in *Quarter 2* ***or*** <10,000 in *Quarter 3* ***or*** <10,000 in *Quarter 4*.
   b. The previous attempt at using Advanced Filter used the wrong *Criteria range*.
   c. The previous attempt at using Advanced Filter resulted in an incorrect *Copy to* range. Be sure to start the new *Copy to* range in cell **I4**.
   d. AutoFit column **K**.
6. Apply a custom number filter to the main data set to show only stores with a profit greater than $55,000 in *Quarter 4*. You will need to select the data range **A4:G20** before enabling *Filter*.
7. The data underlying the PivotTable have been updated since it was created. Update the PivotTable and PivotChart.
8. A slicer should be visible so the user can filter the data in the PivotChart by *Performance Status*. Use the slicer to show only data where the *Performance Status* is **Below Average**.
9. Change the PivotChart style to use **Style 8**.
10. Conditional formatting rules have been applied to the data on the *Financial Targets* worksheet to highlight the two lowest values for each quarter. However, the values for *Quarter 4* are not highlighted. Use the Conditional Formatting Rules Manager to fix the problem.
11. The *Financial Targets* worksheet has two scenarios for possible sales targets for next year. Show the **20% Increase for All Locations** scenario.
12. The *Financial Targets* worksheet has been set up with Solver parameters to find reasonable target sales goals for the two worst locations for each quarter. Some locations had shown very uneven profit-loss results from quarter-to-quarter. The Solver parameters include constraints to limit the new sales target for each cell to less than or equal to the average quarterly sales for that location.

Fix the Solver parameters to find the **maximum** possible value for the overall average quarter income (cell **G24**) by changing the values in cells **C10, C15, D15, D19, E15, E19, F10,** and **F19** within the following constraints. It may be easier to delete all of the existing constraints and start over.

a. For each quarter, the value of the two variable cells for that quarter must be equal to each another. This requires a total of four constraints.

b. None of the changing cells can have a value greater than half the average for that location (the location average is calculated in column *G*). This requires a total of eight constraints—one for each variable cell where the value is less than or equal to the value in the average cell for that location.

c. Fix the Solver parameters and then run Solver.

d. Keep the Solver solution and create a new scenario named: **`Solver Results`**

13. Create a scenario summary report to show the changing results for cell **G24** only.
14. Save and close the workbook.

chapter 9

Importing Data, Reviewing, and Finalizing the Workbook

In this chapter, you will learn the following skills:

- Import data from external files
- Export data to text formats
- Use Flash Fill and Text to Columns to manipulate data
- Use data validation tools
- Summarize data using Consolidate
- Add, review, and delete comments
- Work with hyperlinks
- Share and protect workbooks and worksheets
- Track and accept or reject changes
- Save a workbook in alternative formats
- Finalize a workbook

Skill 9.15 Checking for Compatibility with Previous Versions of Excel

Skill 9.16 Saving a Workbook in Other Formats

Skill 9.17 Adding a Password

Skill 9.18 Running the Document Inspector

Skill 9.19 Finalizing the Workbook

introduction

This chapter begins with importing data from external sources and exporting the data in text file formats. You will then use Excel's *Flash Fill* and *Text to Columns* features to manipulate the imported data. You will learn how adding data validation can help prevent errors and make the workbook more user-friendly and how to use Consolidate to summarize data. As part of the review process, you will work with comments and hyperlinks and apply sharing and protection options to the workbook. You will check the workbook for compatibility with older versions of Excel and save to file to other formats. Before finalizing the workbook, you will secure the workbook with a password and remove private and hidden data.

Skill 9.1 Importing Data from Access

Microsoft Access is a relational database program. Data are stored in multiple tables that connect to one another via related fields. Through queries based on table relationships, the database can create a specific view of data combining fields from multiple tables. Organizations often use a database to input and store data and then import those data into Excel to perform statistical and what-if analyses.

To import data from an Access database:

1. On the *Data* tab, if necessary, click the **Get External Data** button to expand the *Get External Data* group. Click the **From Access** button.

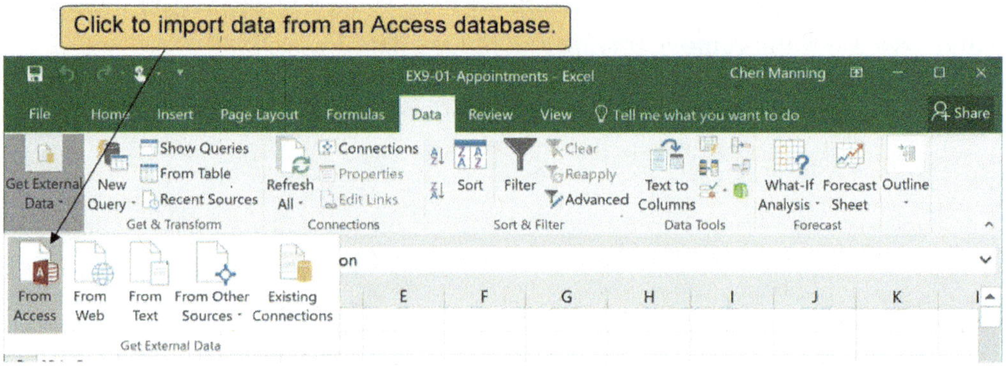

FIGURE EX 9.1

2. In the *Select Data Source* dialog, navigate to the folder where the Access database is stored, select the file, and click the **Open** button.
3. In the *Select Table* dialog, select the table or query view from which you want to import data, and then click **OK**.

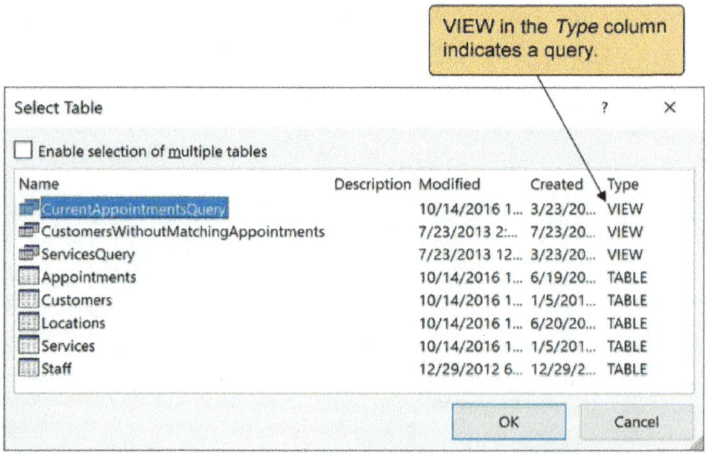

FIGURE EX 9.2

4. In the *Import Data* dialog, select how you would like the data formatted in Excel. Click the **Table**, **PivotTable Report**, **PivotChart**, or **Only Create Connection** radio button. The last option creates the connection but does not import the data.
5. By default, the data will be imported into the selected cell in the current worksheet. You can change the cell reference for the current worksheet or click the **New worksheet** radio button to import the data into a new worksheet.
6. Click **OK** to complete the import.

Once the import is complete, the data in the worksheet remain connected to the database.

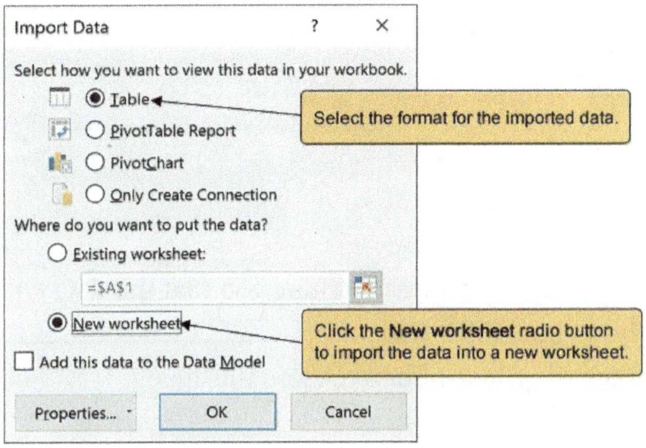

FIGURE EX 9.3

You can refresh the data from the database connection from the *Data* tab, *Connections* group. Click the **Refresh All** button, and either select **Refresh** to update data only in the selected table, PivotTable, or PivotChart or select **Refresh All** to update all connected data in the workbook.

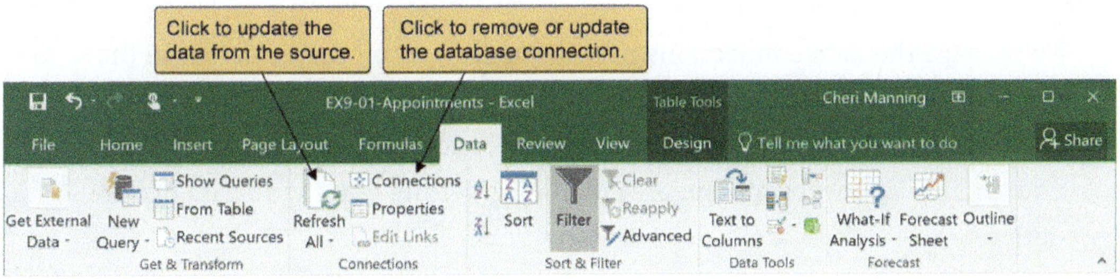

FIGURE EX 9.4

To disconnect the worksheet data from the database:

1. On the *Data* tab, in the *Connections* group, click the **Connections** button to open the *Workbook Connections* dialog.

2. If necessary, click the name of the connection you want to delete. If you are unsure about removing the connection, you can check to see where the connection is used by clicking the **Click here to see where the selected connections are used** link in the *Locations where connections are used in this workbook* box. When you are ready to remove the connection from the workbook, click the **Remove** button.

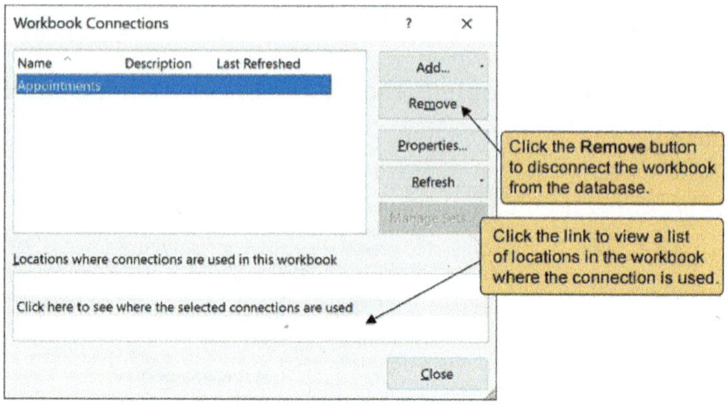

FIGURE EX 9.5

3. A warning box appears telling you that the data will no longer be updated from the source. Click **OK.**
4. Click the **Close** button to close the dialog.

tips & tricks

You do not need to have Access installed on your computer to import data from a database.

tell me more

To manage the data connections in your workbook, on the *Data* tab, in the *Connections* group, click the **Connections** button. From the *Workbook Connections* dialog, you can see where connections are used in the workbook and manage connection properties including setting automatic data update options.

When you open a workbook that has connections to an external data source, the file may open in Protected View. Click the **Enable Content** button in the warning bar to work with the file. For more information about Protected View, refer to the skill *Working in Protected View.*

another method

If you imported the data as a table, tools to manage the connection are included in the Table *Tools Design* tab, *External Table Data* group.

let me try *Live!*

Open the student data file **EX9-01-Appointments** (or open Excel and create a new, blank workbook)and try this skill on your own:

1. Import data from the **CurrentAppointments** query in the **Appointments** Access database.
2. Import the data as a table in a new worksheet.
3. Update the linked worksheet data.
4. Disconnect the worksheet data from the database.
5. If you will be moving on to the next skill in this chapter, leave the workbook open to continue working. If not, save the file as directed by your instructor and close it.

Skill 9.2 Importing Data from a Text File

If you work with data from external sources such as vendors or customers, those data may be available only in plain text format. Text files are common for passing data between organizations because they can be read by many different application programs. A text file that includes multiple data fields may separate the fields with a specific character (a **delimiter**). Common delimiters are commas, tabs, and spaces. When you import data from a text file using a delimiter, each data field is imported into a separate column.

To import data from a text file:

1. On the *Data* tab, if necessary, click the **Get External Data** button to expand the *Get External Data* group. Click the **From Text** button.
2. In the *Import Text File* dialog, navigate to find the file you want to import, select it, and click the **Import** button.

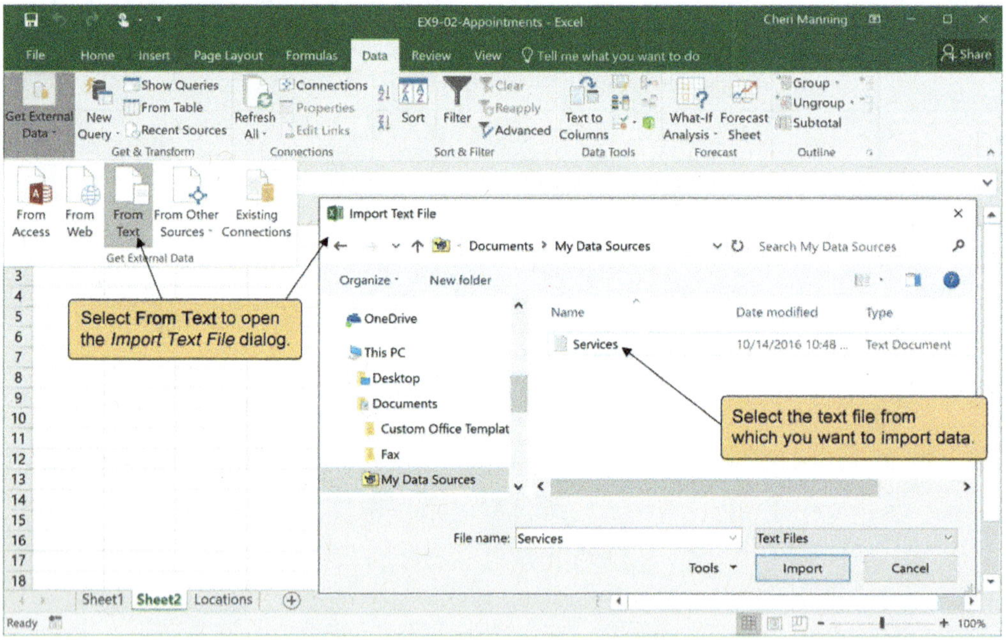

FIGURE EX 9.6

3. The *Text Import Wizard* opens. In Step 1, click the radio button that describes how the data fields are separated—**Delimited** or **Fixed width**. The wizard may detect that the text is delimited and select that option for you. If appropriate, click the **My data has headers** check box.

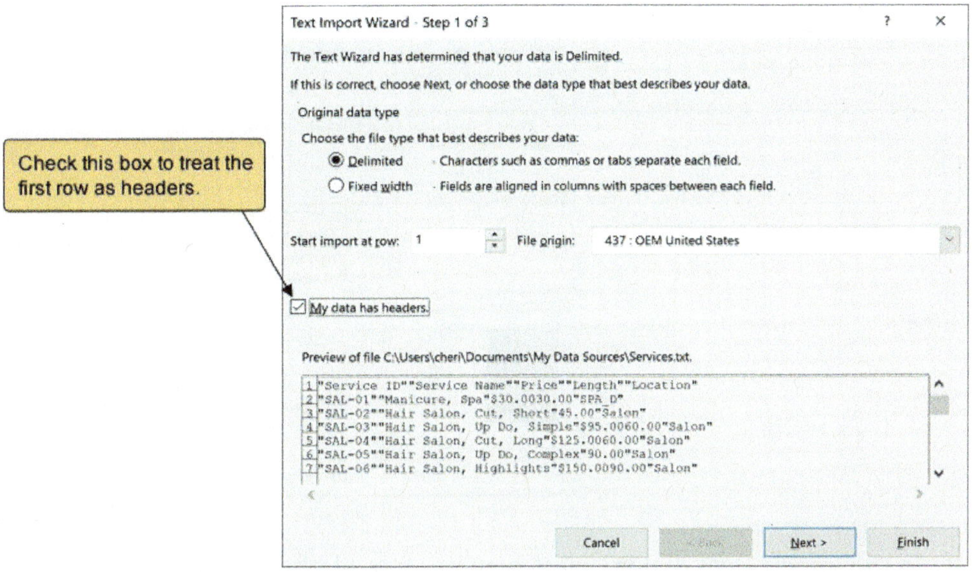

FIGURE EX 9.7

4. Step 2 asks you to select the delimiter character that separates the data fields. Click the appropriate check box. The *Data preview* pane shows how the imported data will be separated into columns.

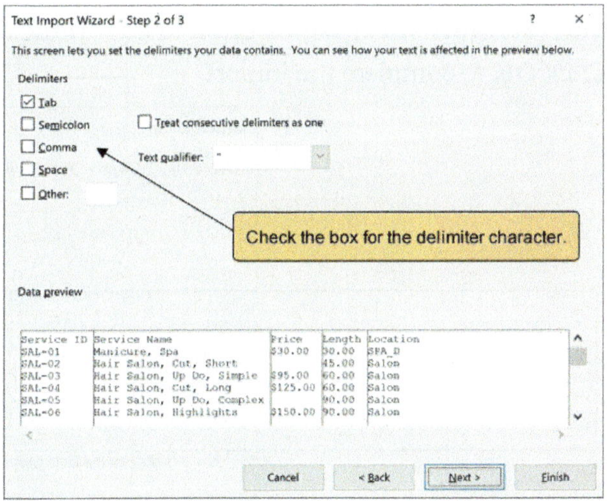

FIGURE EX 9.8

5. In Step 3, if necessary, set the data format for each column. By default, all columns are set to the *General* format. You can always reformat the columns after they have been imported.
6. Click **Finish**.

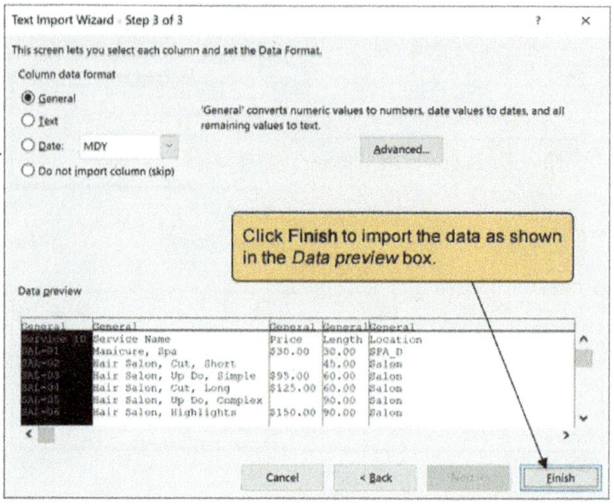

FIGURE EX 9.9

7. In the *Import Data* dialog, select how you would like the data formatted in Excel. Click the **Table**, **PivotTable Report**, **PivotChart**, or **Only Create Connection** radio button. The last option creates the connection but does not import the data.
8. By default, the data will be imported into the selected cell in the current worksheet. You can change the cell reference for the current worksheet or click the **New worksheet** radio button to import the data into a new worksheet.
9. Click **OK** to complete the import.

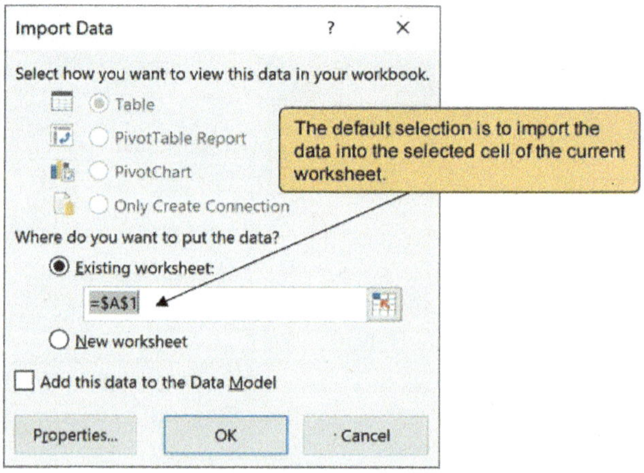

FIGURE EX 9.10

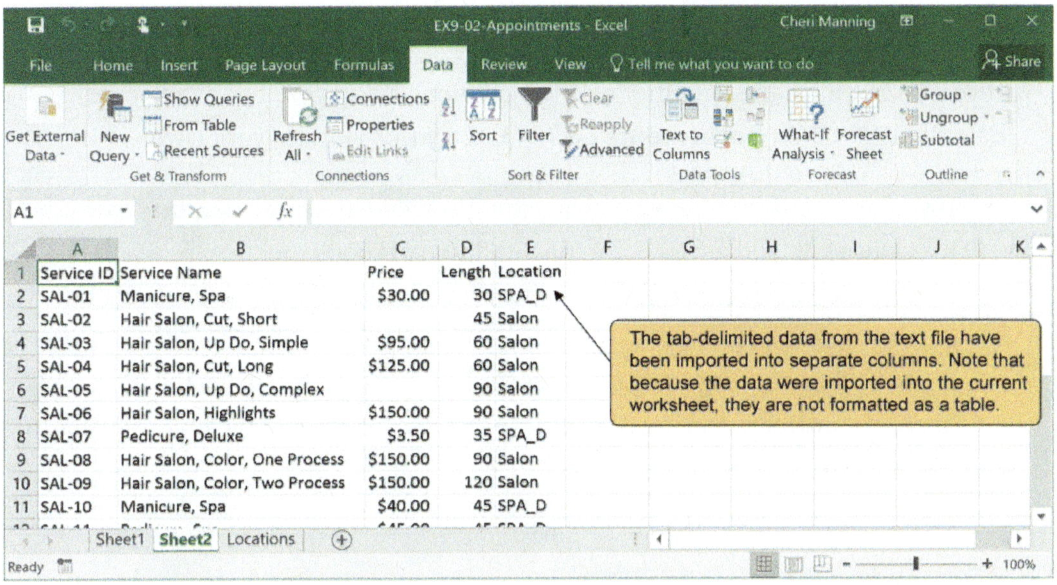

FIGURE EX 9.11

tips & tricks

Text files that contain large amounts of data are usually exported from another program. If you want to import each new batch of data from scratch, there is no need to keep the data in the workbook connected to the original text file. Remove the data connection so users who may not have access to the source file are not confused if they try to refresh the data.

tell me more

To open a text file directly in Excel instead of import it into a new file:

1. Click the **File** tab.
2. Click **Open**.
3. Navigate to find the text file you want to import. Click the file once to select it, and then click the **Open** button.
4. Follow the steps in the *Text Import Wizard*.

The data from the text file now appears in Excel. Notice that this is not a new file. The original text file is simply displaying in Excel. If you want to save the file with formatting, formulas, and other features that are unavailable in a plain text file, use the *Save As* command to save a new copy of the file in the *Excel Workbook* format.

let me try *Live!*

If you do not have the data file from the previous skill open, open the student data file **EX9-02-Appointments** and try this skill on your own:

1. If you are continuing to work with the file **EX9-01-Appointments** from the previous skill, add a new worksheet to the workbook.
2. Import the **Services** tab-delimited text file into the *Sheet2* worksheet. The data include a header row.
3. If you will be moving on to the next skill in this chapter, leave the workbook open to continue working. If not, save the file as directed by your instructor and close it.

Skill 9.3 Exporting to Text Formats

Text file formats allow Excel data to be read by a variety of applications. The most common text file formats are **Text (Tab delimited)** (.txt) and **CSV (comma delimited)** (.csv). When you save in one of the text formats, only the current worksheet will be saved. (Text formats do not support multiple worksheets in the same file.) You will also lose all formatting, and cells with functions will be converted to their current values.

To export a worksheet to a text format:

1. Click the **File** tab.
2. Click **Save As.**
3. On the *Save As* page, click the **Save as type** arrow and select the text format you want.
4. Click **Save**.

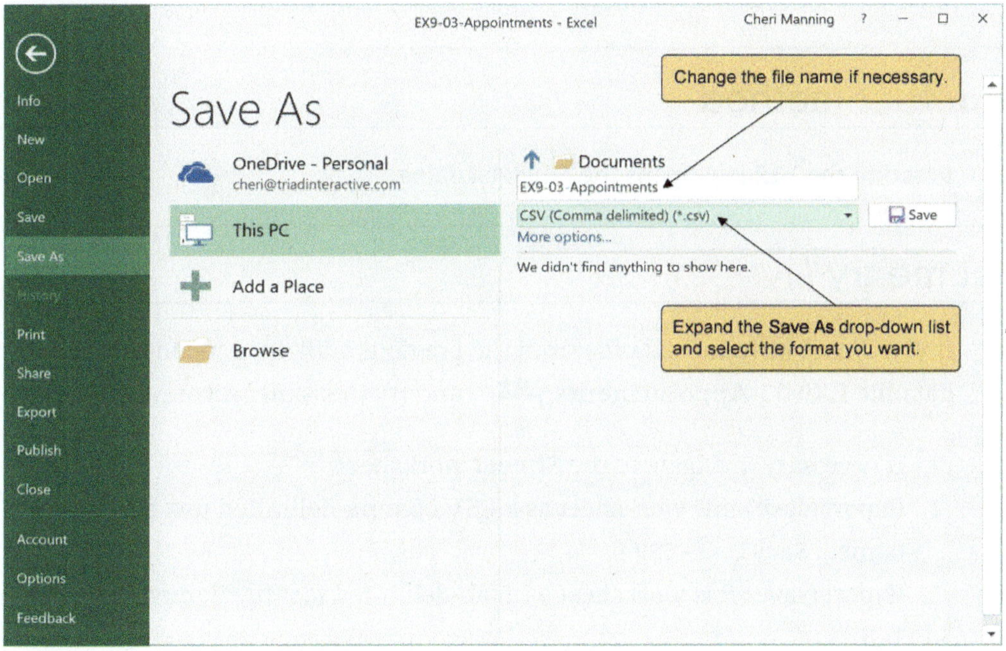

FIGURE EX 9.12

5. If your workbook includes more than one worksheet, Excel displays a message warning that the text file format does not support multiple worksheets. Click **OK** to dismiss the message.

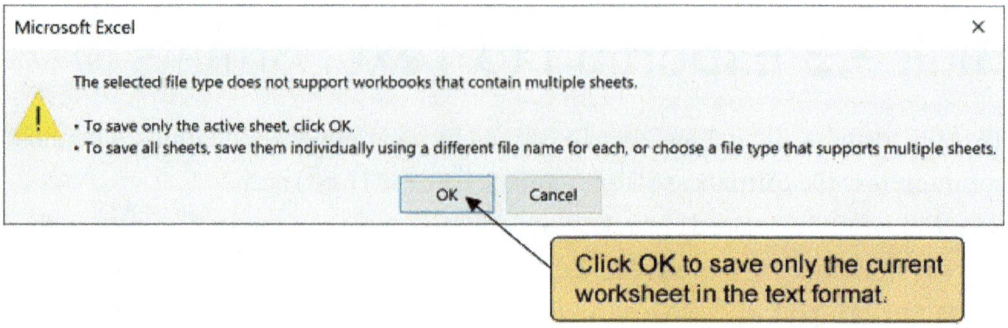

FIGURE EX 9.13

6. Excel may show yet another warning message that some features might be lost if you save in the selected format. Click **Yes** to continue saving the file.

tips & tricks

If you or someone else is going to import the file into another spreadsheet program or database, comma delimited (.csv) is the most common format to use.

another method

Pressing the **F12** key opens the *Save As* dialog.

let me try *Live!*

If you do not have the data file from the previous skill open, open the student data file **EX9-03-Appointments** and try this skill on your own:

1. If necessary, navigate to the **Sheet2** worksheet.
2. Export (save) this worksheet as a CSV comma-delimited text file named: `Services-CSV`
3. Export (save) this worksheet as a tab-delimited text file named: `Services-Tab`
4. Close the file.

Skill 9.4 Inserting Data Using Flash Fill

Flash Fill detects patterns in your data and autofills the remaining cells for you. This feature is useful when you've imported data that aren't formatted quite as you would like. Flash Fill can be used to combine data from contiguous cells into a single cell or to split data from a single cell into multiple cells.

To begin using Flash Fill:

1. Insert a column where you want the new data to appear.
2. In the first cell of the new column below the header row, type an example of how you'd like the data filled. If Flash Fill detects a pattern while you're typing, it will automatically make an autofill suggestion. Sometimes Flash Fill will make a suggestion after you type data in just one cell. Other times, you will need to type two or three examples before Flash Fill recognizes the pattern.
3. Press **Enter** to accept the suggestion. In Figure EX 9.14, Flash Fill made a suggestion as soon as **F** was typed in cell F3.

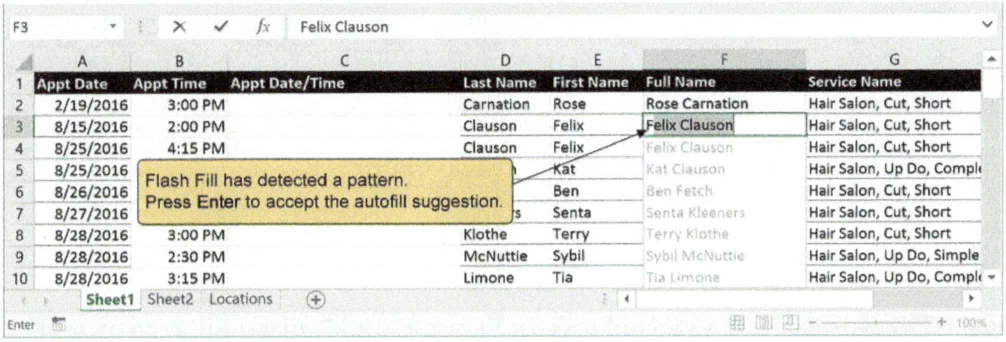

FIGURE EX 9.14

There will be cases when Flash Fill does not recognize the pattern automatically. However, you can invoke the *Flash Fill* command manually.

1. Select the first cell below the cell containing the example you want Flash Fill to copy. In Figure EX 9.15, you would begin by selecting cell C3 as cell C2 contains the pattern you want to use to autofill the rest of the column.
2. On the *Data* tab, in the *Data Tools* group, click the **Flash Fill** button to see if Flash Fill can find a pattern to autofill.

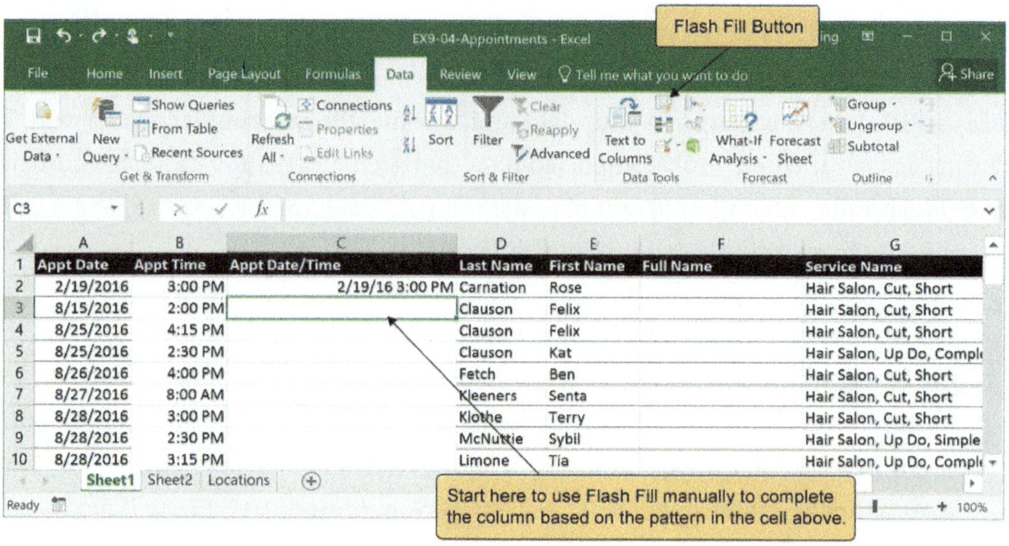

FIGURE EX 9.15

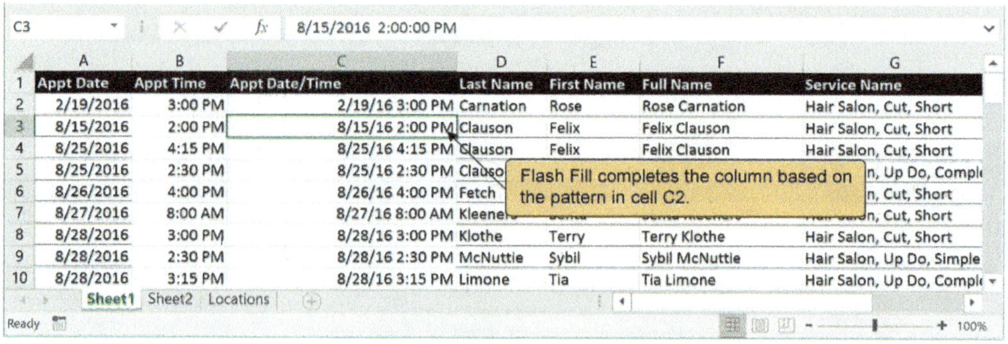

FIGURE EX 9.16

Flash Fill can also be used to add text. In Figure EX 9.17, Flash Fill recognizes that the word *minutes* should be added after the number based on the example in cell E2. Yes, you could accomplish the same result using the CONCATENATE function. However, using Flash Fill fills the cells with static content instead of formulas, making it easier to move and manipulate the data.

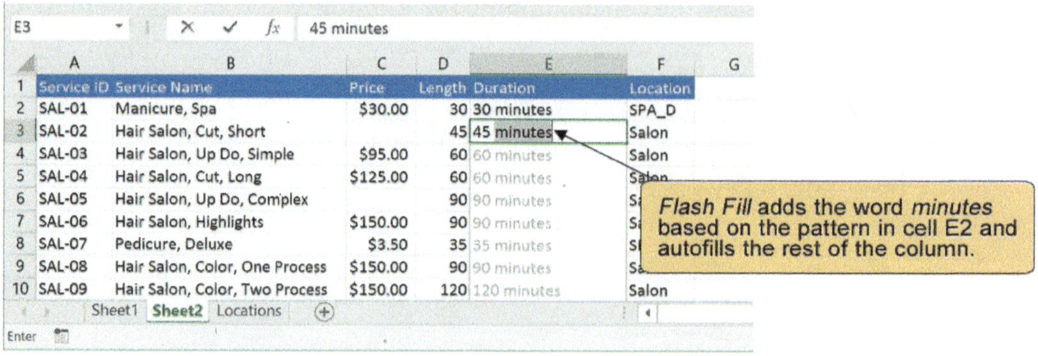

FIGURE EX 9.17

tips & tricks

Flash Fill doesn't always fill the data consistently as you intended. Be sure to check the data after you've accepted Flash Fill's suggestions.

tell me more

Flash Fill works on one column at a time. If you want to split data into multiple columns, first use Flash Fill to fill data in the first column using the first part of the pattern, and then use Flash Fill to fill data in the second column using the second part of the pattern.

another method

On the *Home* tab, in the *Editing* group, click the **Fill** button and select **Flash Fill**.

let me try *Live!*

Open the student data file **EX9-04-Appointments** and try this skill on your own:

1. On *Sheet1*, in cell **F2**, type `Rose Carnation` and press Enter.
2. In cell **F3**, begin typing `Felix Clausen` and when Flash Fill makes an autofill suggestion, accept it. If Flash Fill does not make a suggestion, use the command on the Ribbon.
3. Review the appointment date and time pattern in cell **C2**. Use the Flash Fill command on the Ribbon to autofill the rest of the column based on the pattern in cell **C2**.
4. Go to **Sheet2**, and type `30 minutes` in cell **E2**. Use Flash Fill to autofill the remaining cells in the column.
5. If you will be moving on to the next skill in this chapter, leave the workbook open to continue working. If not, save the file as directed by your instructor and close it.

from the perspective of . . .

INVENTORY MANAGER

One of our main customers sends us purchase orders in Excel with a single column listing the part number followed by a comma and then the part name. Of course, our inventory system expects the part number and the item name to be in separate fields. I use Text to Columns to separate the data into two separate columns.

The customer's system also omits our three-letter company codes from the part numbers. In the past, I used a nested IF formula with CONCATENATE to correct the part numbers. Now with Excel 2016, I use Flash Fill to update the part numbers by typing just a few examples. I'm hiring an assistant soon who doesn't know Excel very well. It will be much easier to show him how to use Flash Fill than to teach him how to use my old formula.

Skill 9.5 Converting Data to Columns

Excel's **Text to Columns** feature allows you to split data into separate columns if there is a consistent character at which Excel can split the data (the **delimiter**) or the data can be split at a specific number of characters. If the column to the right of the column you are splitting contains data, Excel will replace the contents of the destination cells. If you do not want to overwrite the data in the second column, insert enough empty columns to the right of the column you are splitting *before* converting the data.

To split data from one column into separate columns using a delimiter character:

1. Ensure that there are enough empty cells to the right of the selected cells to hold the new columns.
2. Select the data in the column you want to split.
3. On the *Data* tab, in the *Data Tools* group, click the **Text to Columns** button.

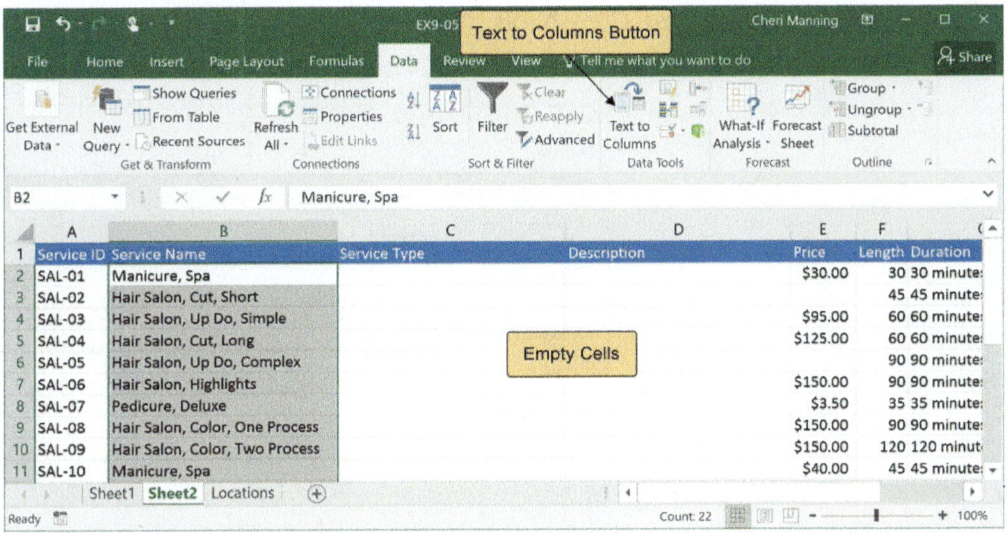

FIGURE EX 9.18

4. The *Convert Text to Columns Wizard* opens.
5. If the data are separated by a common delimiter such as a tab, space, or comma, click the **Next** button to go to Step 2.

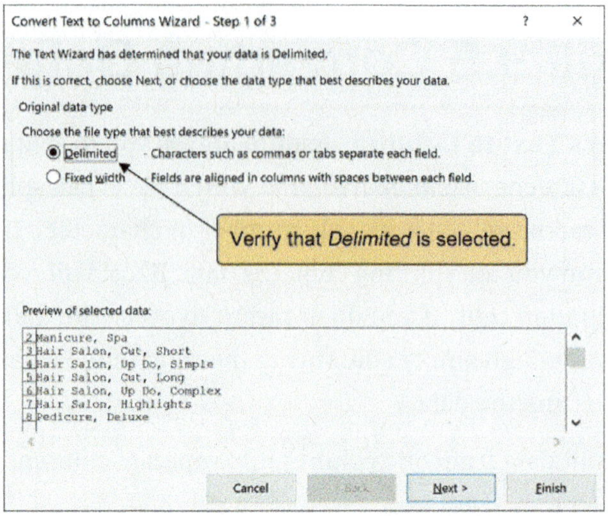

FIGURE EX 9.19

6. Click the check box for one of the common delimiter characters (tab, semicolon, comma, or space) or click the *Other* check box and enter the delimiter character in the box. The *Data preview* box shows how the data will be separated based on the delimiter you selected. Click **Next**.

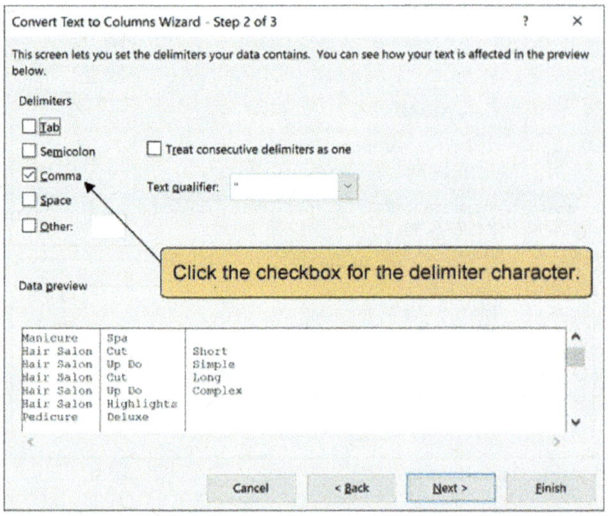

FIGURE EX 9.20

7. If necessary, select the correct data format for each column. The *General* format is selected by default. You can always change the format later.
8. Click **Finish**.

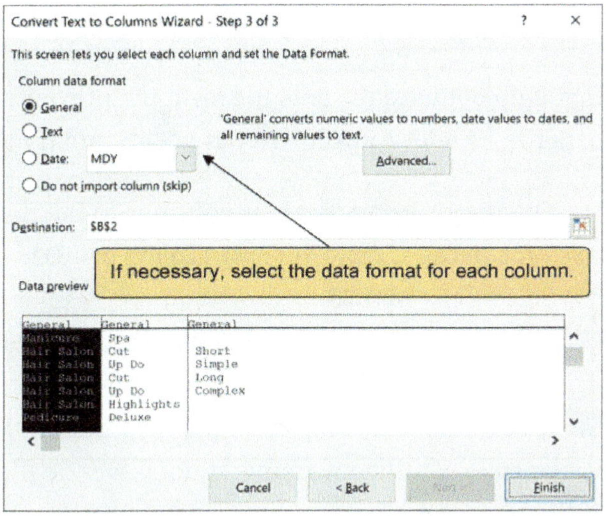

FIGURE EX 9.21

Text to Columns removes the delimiter character and splits the original data into separate columns as shown in Figure EX 9.22.

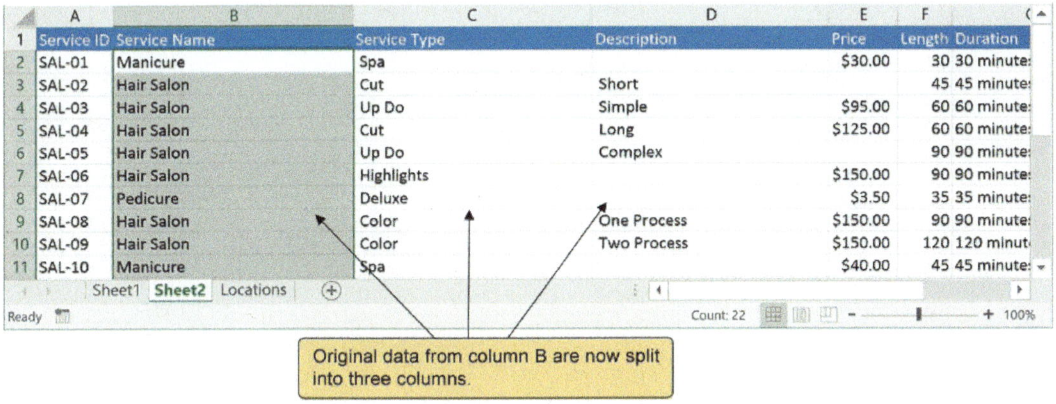

FIGURE EX 9.22

tips & tricks

If you need to maintain the original column, try using Flash Fill instead of Text to Columns to create new columns of data without affecting the original.

tell me more

You can also split cells into columns at specific character intervals. This option works only if the data in the cells you want to split have exactly the same number of characters in each interval in each row.

let me try *Live!*

If you do not have the data file from the previous skill open, open the student data file **EX9-05-Appointments** and try this skill on your own:

1. On *Sheet2*, insert two new columns to the right of column B. Type **`Service Type`** in cell **C1** and **`Description`** in cell **D1**.
2. Select cells **B2:B23**.
3. Split the text in cells **B2:B23** into separate columns. Use the comma as the delimiter.
4. If you will be moving on to the next skill in this chapter, leave the workbook open to continue working. If not, save the file as directed by your instructor and close it.

Skill 9.6 Adding Data Validation

One way to prevent errors in your workbooks is to add **data validation rules**. By requiring data validation, you can prevent users from entering invalid data or data that may cause errors in formulas. Data validation rules can limit cell entries to a specific data type (such as whole number or date) or a list of acceptable values.

To add data validation rules:

1. Select the cells to which you want to apply data validation rules.
2. On the *Data* tab, in the *Data Tools* group, click the **Data Validation** button.
3. To restrict data entries to a specific numeric value or values within a range:
   a. From the *Allow* list, select **Whole number** or **Decimal**.
   b. From the *Data* list, select a comparison operator.
   c. Enter the specific value or the minimum and maximum values.
   d. To require a value in every cell, click the **Ignore blank** check box to uncheck it.
4. When you have completed the data validation settings, click **OK**.

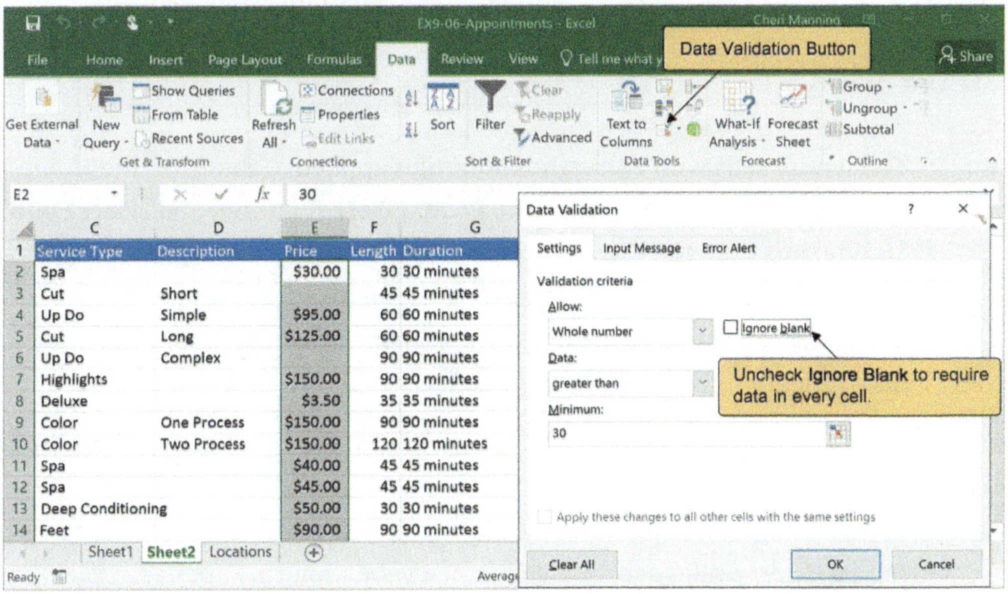

FIGURE EX 9.23

If you added data validation rules after entering data, you may have invalid data in your worksheet. Click the **Data Validation** button arrow, and select **Circle Invalid Data** to identify the invalid data entries in your worksheet. You do not need to select the cells with the data validation rules first.

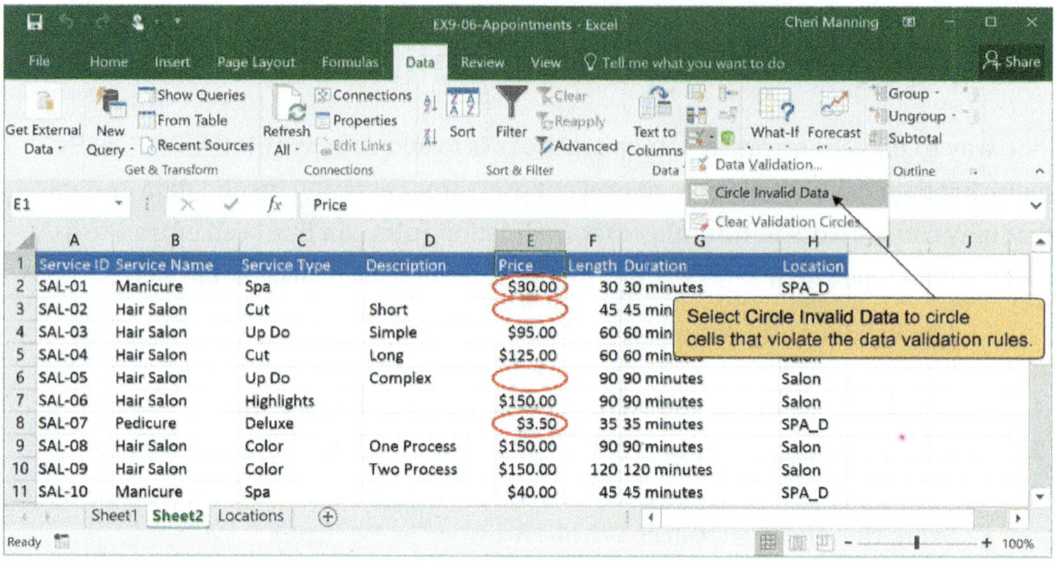

FIGURE EX 9.24

To hide the circles, click the **Data Validation** button arrow and select **Clear Validation Circles**.

Clearing the validation circles does not remove the validation rules. To remove data validation rules, click the **Clear All** button in the *Data Validation* dialog.

tips & tricks

- To identify cells with data validation rules applied to them, on the *Home* tab, in the *Editing* group, click the **Find & Select** button, and select **Data Validation** from the list.
- When you save or close the workbook, Excel hides the validation circles. They will not be visible the next time you open the workbook, but the data validation rules will still be in effect.

tell me more

When you enter invalid data in a cell with a validation rule applied, Excel displays a warning message. You can customize the warning message through the *Validation Rules* dialog. For more information, refer to the skill *Adding an Input Message and Error Alert to Data Validation*.

let me try *Live!*

If you do not have the data file from the previous skill open, open the student data file **EX9-06-Appointments** and try this skill on your own:

1. On *Sheet2*, select cells **E2:E23** if necessary.
2. Every service must have a price listed. Add data validation to the list of prices. Require **whole** numbers greater than **30**. Do not ignore blank cells.
3. Display the circles to find invalid data.
4. Hide the validation circles.
5. If you will be moving on to the next skill in this chapter, leave the workbook open to continue working. If not, save the file as directed by your instructor and close it.

Skill 9.7 Adding an Input Message and Error Alert to Data Validation

When cells have a data validation rule applied, you can add a prompt that will appear every time a user clicks one of the cells requiring data validation. Customizing these messages makes your workbook more user-friendly.

1. If the *Data Validation* dialog is not open, select the cells and on the *Data* tab, in the *Data Tools* group, click the **Data Validation** button.
2. Click the **Input Message** tab.
3. The **Show input message when cell is selected** check box is checked by default. This ensures that the user will always see the input prompt.
4. Enter text for the message title and/or message. Be as brief as possible. A title is not required.
5. Click **OK** to apply the changes.

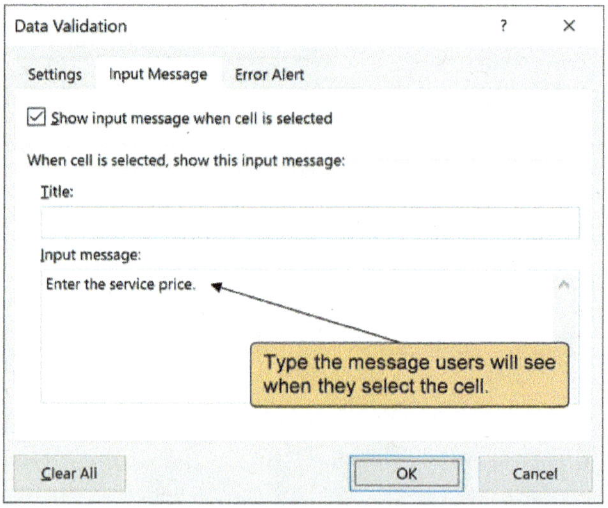

FIGURE EX 9.25

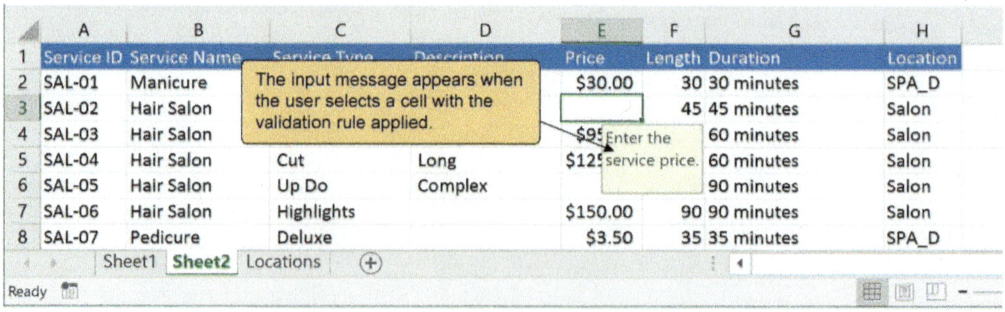

FIGURE EX 9.26

When the user enters data that violate the data validation rule, an error message appears. You can customize the error message from the *Error Alert* tab in the *Data Validation* dialog.

1. If the *Data Validation* dialog is not open, select the cells and click the **Data Validation** button to open it.
2. Click the **Error Alert** tab.
3. The **Show error alert after invalid data is entered** check box is checked by default. This ensures that the error message will display whenever the user attempts to enter data that break the data validation rule.
4. Enter text for the message title and/or message. Be as brief as possible. A title is not required.
5. Click **OK** to apply the changes.

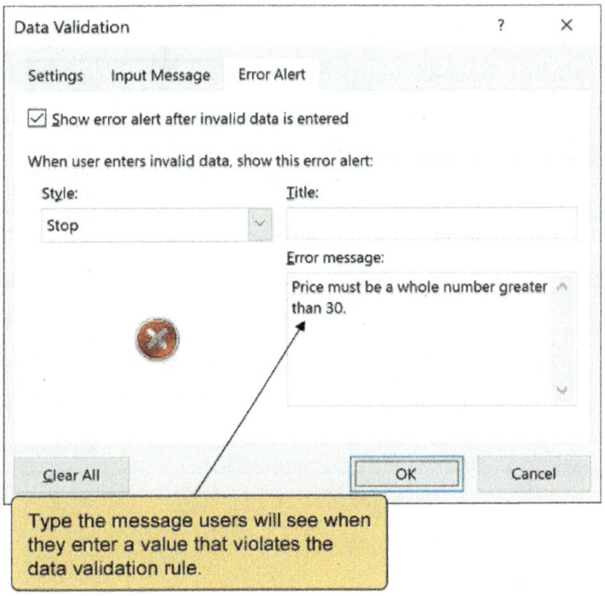

FIGURE EX 9.27

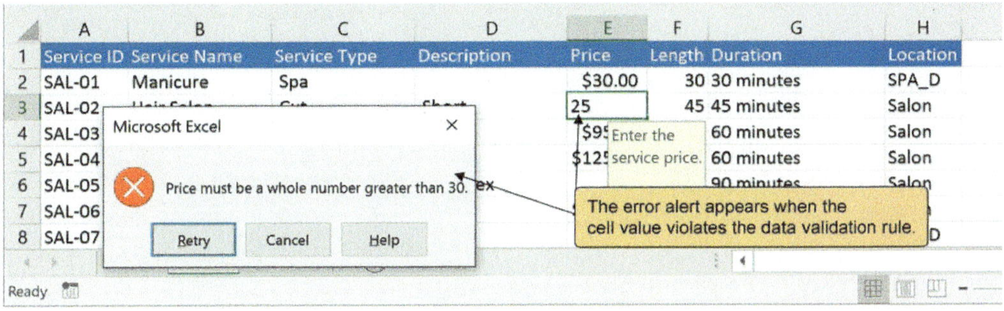

FIGURE EX 9.28

tell me **more**

To change data validation rules, including adding or changing input messages and error alerts:

1. Select at least one of the cells that has the data validation rule applied.
2. On the *Data* tab, in the *Data Tools* group, click the **Data Validation** button.
3. In the *Data Validation* dialog, on the *Settings* tab, click the **Apply these changes to all other cells with the same settings** check box. This step isn't necessary if you've selected all the cells already.
4. Make the changes you want and then click **OK**.

let me try *Live!*

If you do not have the data file from the previous skill open, open the student data file **EX9-07-Appointments** and try this skill on your own:

1. On *Sheet2*, select cells **E2:E23** if necessary.
2. Add this input message: `Enter the service price`
3. Add the same message as the alert that appears if the user attempts to enter invalid data: `Price must be a whole number greater than 30`
4. If you will be moving on to the next skill in this chapter, leave the workbook open to continue working. If not, save the file as directed by your instructor and close it.

Skill 9.8 Creating a Drop-Down List for Data Entry

You can use a data validation rule to limit cell entries to a list of acceptable values and create a drop-down menu for users to choose from.

To create a drop-down list for data entry:

1. Select the cell or range of cells where you want the list to appear.
2. On the *Data* tab, in the *Data Tools* group, click the **Data Validation** button.
3. In the *Data Validation* dialog, from the *Settings* tab, click the **Allow** arrow, and select **List**.
4. In the *Source* box, type the list of acceptable values, separating each value with a comma. You can also reference a named range as the list source. Type = followed by the name.
5. To include a drop-down list of values, ensure that the **In-cell dropdown** check box is checked. When the *Allow* option is set to **List**, this box is checked by default.
6. Click **OK**.

When you click in a cell that has a list data validation rule applied, an arrow appears at the right side of the cell. Click the arrow to expand the list and make a selection.

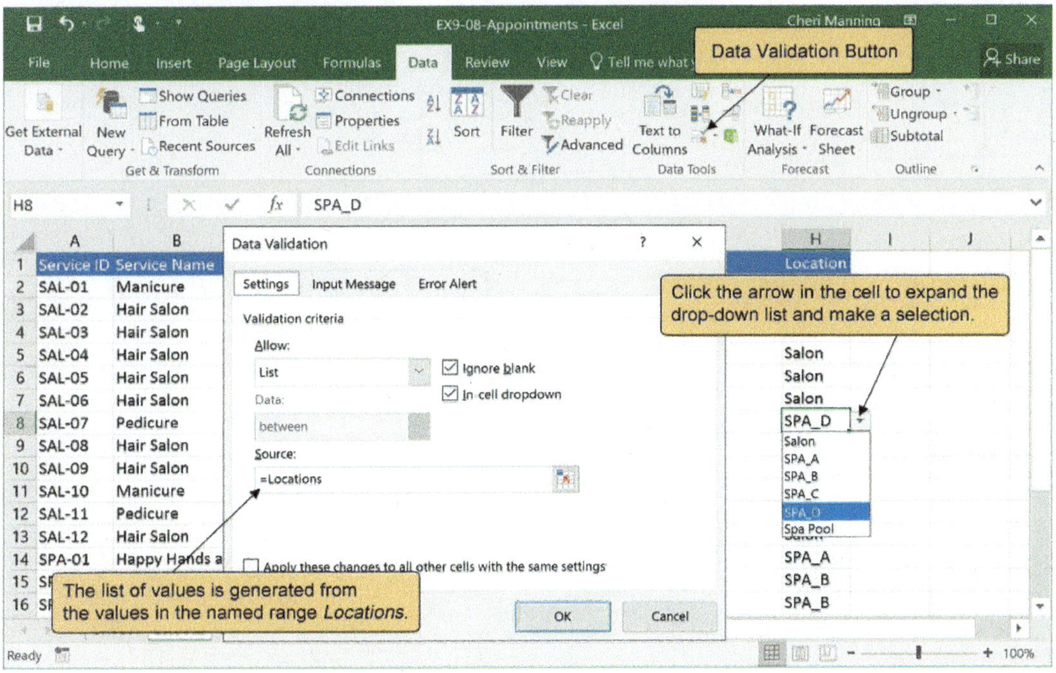

FIGURE EX 9.29

tips & tricks

Using a named range as the list source allows you to add and remove values from the in-cell drop-down list without having to modify the validation rule.

let me try *Live!*

If you do not have the data file from the previous skill open, open the student data file **EX9-08-Appointments** and try this skill on your own:

1. On the *Services* worksheet, select cells **G2:G23** if necessary.
2. Use data validation to display an in-cell drop-down list of values from the named range **Locations**. Allow blanks.
3. Save the file as directed by your instructor and close it.

Skill 9.9 Consolidating Data in a Summary Worksheet

If your workbook contains multiple worksheets with the same data structure, you can create a master worksheet to summarize the data. You may already be familiar with how to do this using formulas that reference cells in other worksheets (see the skill *Creating Formulas Referencing Data from Other Worksheets*). You can also use the **Consolidate** command. Through the *Consolidate* dialog, you can summarize data from multiple worksheets for a range of cells at once.

Unlike regular formula references, Consolidate gives you the option to link to the source data via formulas or insert a static summary—that is, cells that contain only values, not references to other cells. Use *Consolidate* to create summary worksheets whenever you want to share the summary as static values without the details. Be sure to uncheck the **Create links to source data** check box in the *Consolidate* dialog when you create the consolidation.

To create the summary worksheet where the data will be consolidated, copy one of the source worksheets and clear the data from the cells containing the values. The summary worksheet is shown in Figure EX 9.30, and the source worksheets are shown in Figure EX 9.31. Notice the identical data structures. You can change the name of the summary worksheet and modify any text or formatting as long as the rows where the data are consolidated are in the same order as the rows in the source worksheets, with the same columns.

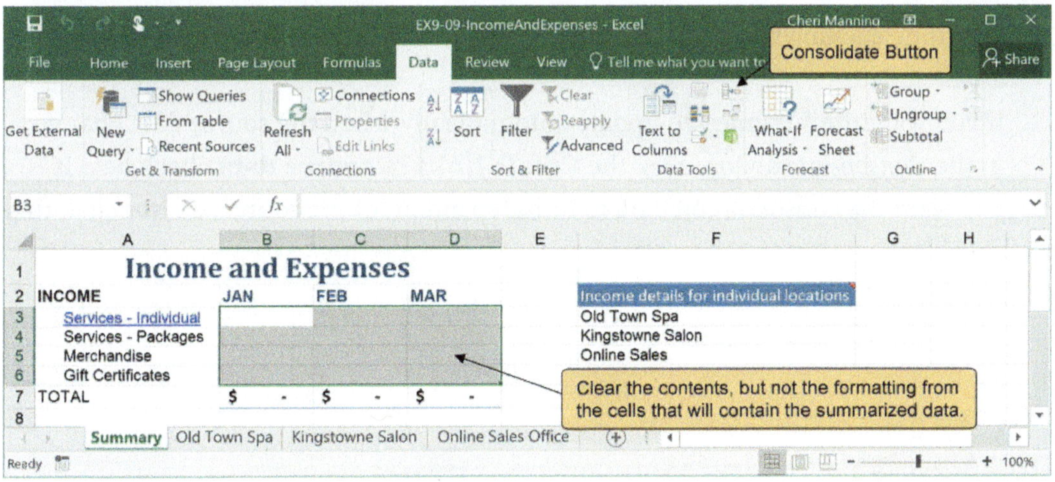

FIGURE EX 9.30

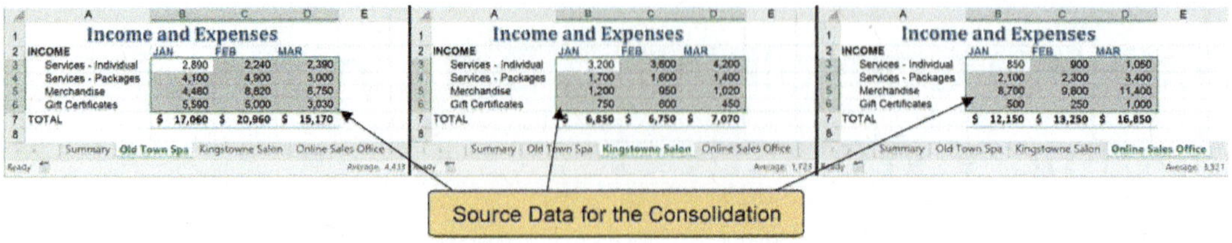

FIGURE EX 9.31

To create a summary totaling data from multiple worksheets:

1. Select the cells that will contain the totals.
2. On the *Data* tab, in the *Data Tools* group, click the **Consolidate** button.
3. In the *Consolidate* dialog, **Sum** is selected in the *Function* list by default. If you want to use another function, expand the list and select the function you want to use.
4. The *All references* box may include references from previous consolidations. If these are not the references you want to use, select each and click the **Delete** button to delete them.
5. If necessary, click in the *Reference* box and then click the tab for the first sheet you want to include.
6. Click and drag to select the cell range. When you release the mouse button, Excel returns to the *Consolidate* dialog.
7. Click the **Add** button.
8. Click the next sheet tab you want to add to the consolidation. Notice that you do not need to select the specific cells in the next worksheet. Excel maintains the same cell range in the *Reference* box, changing only the worksheet name.
9. Click **Add**.
10. Continue clicking sheet tabs and clicking the **Add** button until all the worksheets are included.
11. If you want the summary to update automatically when the source data change, in the *Consolidate* dialog, click the **Create links to source data** check box. If you want the consolidation data to be independent of the source, do ***not*** click this check box.
12. Click **OK**.

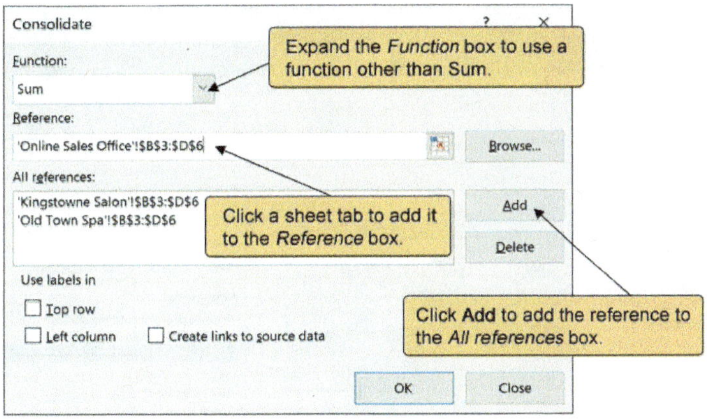

FIGURE EX 9.32

Each cell in the summary sheet displays the total of the values in the corresponding cells in the referenced worksheets. Notice that the cells contain values, not formulas.

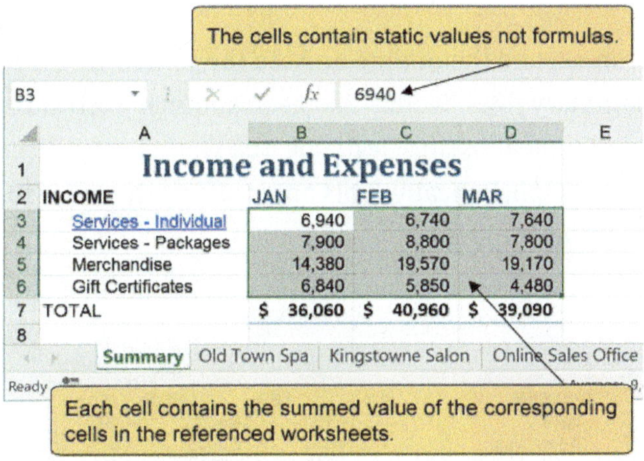

	A	B	C	D
1	Income and Expenses			
2	INCOME	JAN	FEB	MAR
3	Services - Individual	6,940	6,740	7,640
4	Services - Packages	7,900	8,800	7,800
5	Merchandise	14,380	19,570	19,170
6	Gift Certificates	6,840	5,850	4,480
7	TOTAL	$ 36,060	$ 40,960	$ 39,090

FIGURE EX 9.33

When you check the **Create links to source data** check box in the *Consolidate* dialog, Excel creates links to the source data in outline format. Use this option if you want the values in the summary sheet to update when the data in the source worksheets change.

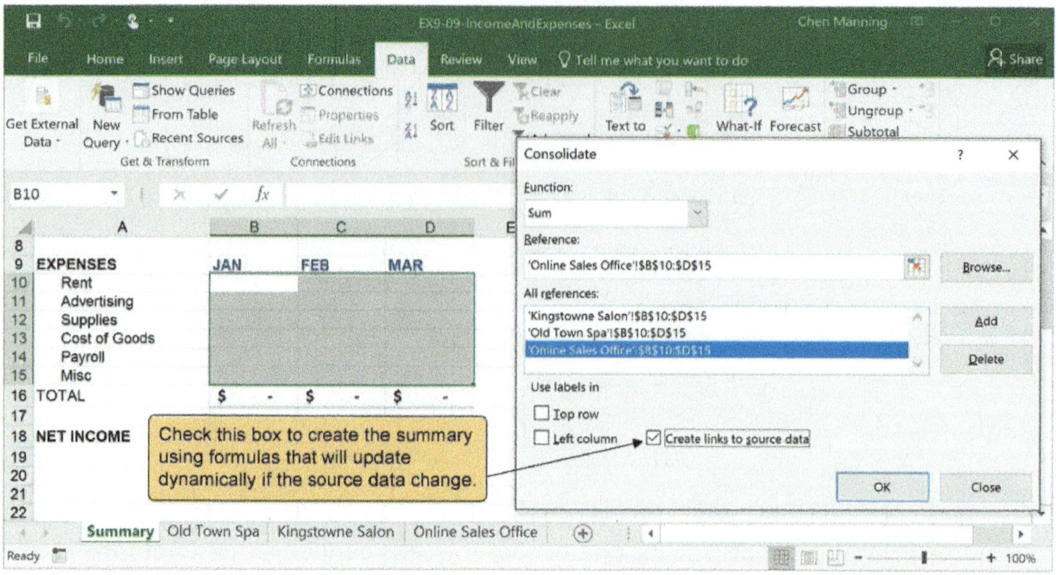

FIGURE EX 9.34

You can expand the outline and see the source values by clicking the + next to one of the summary rows. Notice that each summary cell sums the cells ***above*** it in the outline. In the *Consolidate* dialog, the worksheet references in the *All references* box are sorted alphabetically. This order affects the order in which the references are added in the outline.

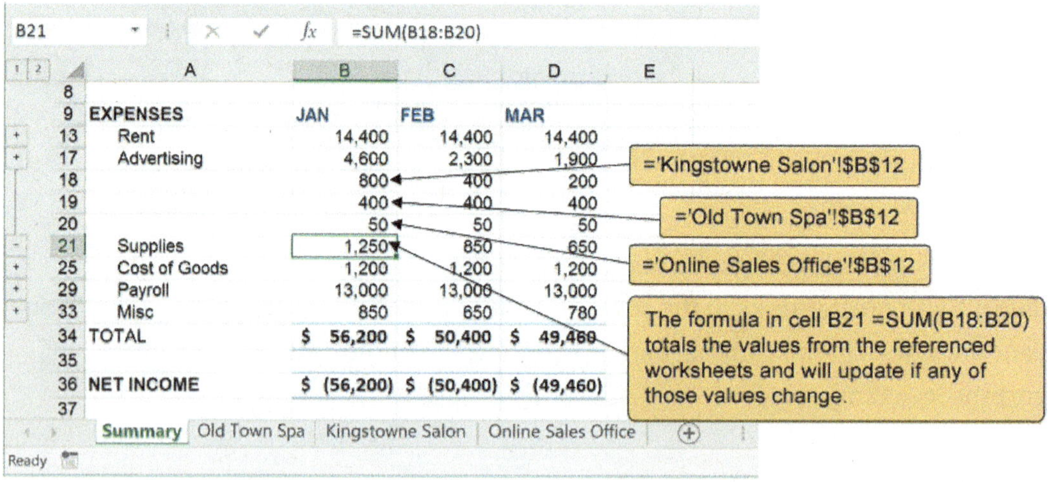

FIGURE EX 9.35

To use Consolidate to summarize data from worksheets in other workbooks:

- In the *Consolidate* dialog, click in the **Reference** box, and then switch to the workbook you want to reference. If the workbook is not already open, click the **Browse...** button next to the *Reference* box to open the workbook.

- In the second workbook, click and drag to select the cells to include in the Consolidate reference. When you release the mouse button, Excel returns to the original workbook.
- If you don't want to create links between the workbooks, remember to verify that the **Create links to source data** check box is ***not*** checked.

tips & tricks

In a consolidation with links to the source data, the details for the first row of the consolidation use the formatting from the row above. Often, this row contains formatting for the heading row. You can select the detail cells and change the formatting without affecting the consolidation.

let me try *Live!*

Open the student data file **EX9-09-IncomeAndExpenses** and try this skill on your own:

1. If necessary, select cells **B3:D6** on the *Summary* worksheet.
2. In the selected cells, use Consolidate to sum data from cells **B3:D6** in the **Old Town**, **Kingstowne Salon**, and **Online Sales Office** worksheets. In the *Consolidate* dialog, *Sum* is selected by default. You do not need to change the function for this exercise. If the *References* box includes references, delete them before adding the new references for this exercise.
3. Select cells **B10:D15** on the *Summary* worksheet.
4. In the selected cells, use Consolidate to sum data from cells **B10:D15** in the **Old Town**, **Kingstowne Salon**, and **Online Sales Office** worksheets. In the *Consolidate* dialog, *Sum* is selected by default. You do not need to change the function for this exercise. If the *References* box includes references, delete them before adding the new references for this exercise. This time include links to the source data to display subtotals.
5. If you will be moving on to the next skill in this chapter, leave the workbook open to continue working. If not, save the file as directed by your instructor and close it.

Skill 9.10 Working with Comments

A **comment** is a note you add to a cell in a worksheet. Use comments to add information, descriptions, or instructions to cells. Add and work with comments from the *Review* tab, *Comments* group.

To insert a comment:

1. Select the cell in which you want to insert the comment.
2. On the *Review* tab, in the *Comments* group, click the **New Comment** button.
3. Type your comment text in the balloon that appears.
4. Click outside the balloon when you are finished.

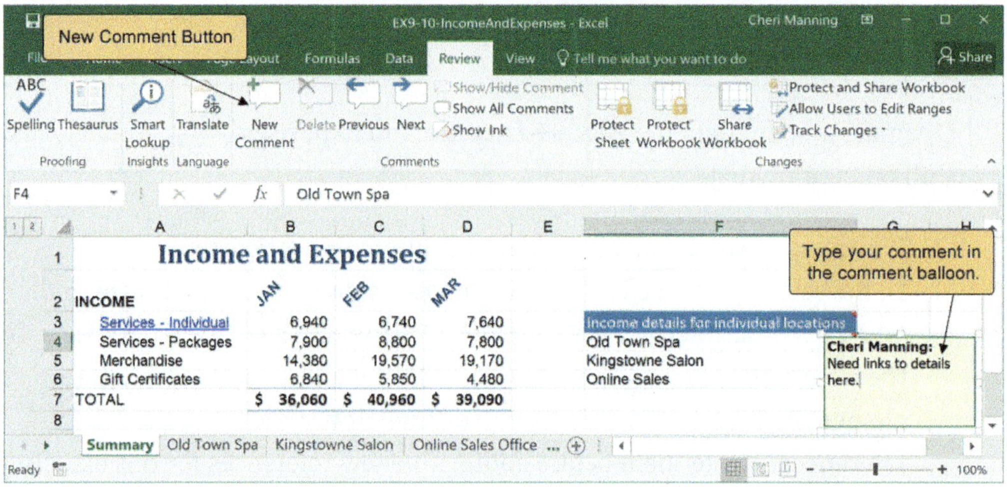

FIGURE EX 9.36

Each cell can have only one comment. When the cell includes a comment, the *New Comment* button changes to *Edit Comment.*

When your worksheet includes comments, there are a few ways to view them:

- A red triangle appears in the corner of a cell that has a comment. Point to the cell to make the comment visible. Move your mouse away from the cell to hide the comment.
- To display all the comments in a worksheet at once, click the **Show All Comments** button.
- To display a specific comment, click the cell, and then click the **Show/Hide Comment** button.
- To browse through all the comments in your worksheet, use the **Previous** and **Next** buttons.

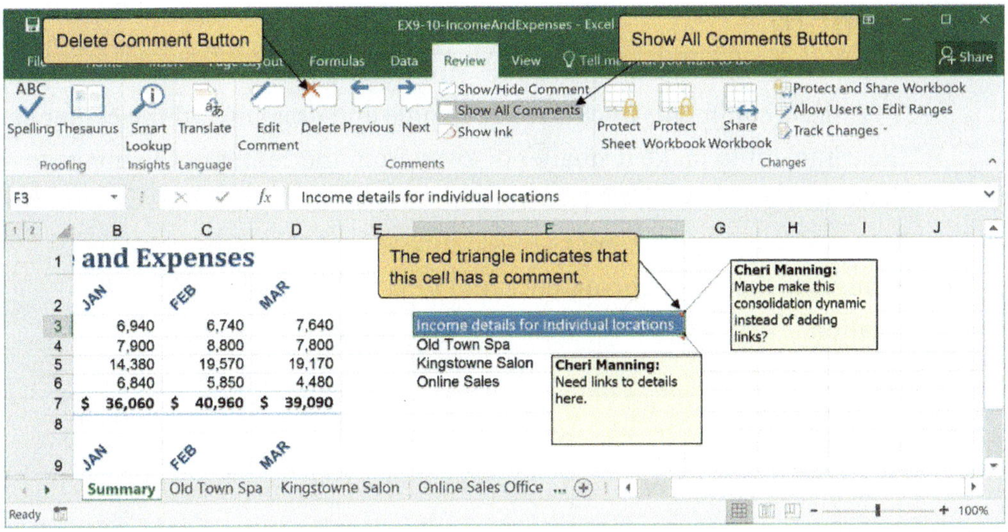

FIGURE EX 9.37

To delete a comment, first select the cell that includes the comment you want to delete, and then on the *Review* tab, in the *Comments* group, click the **Delete** button.

tips & tricks

When you create a comment, Excel automatically inserts your name (the name used when you installed Excel) so other users know who added the comment. You can edit the name or delete it from the comment, but if you find yourself doing this every time you add a comment, change the user name instead.

To change the Excel user name:

1. Click the **File** tab to open Backstage view.
2. Click **Options**.
3. Under *General*, in the *Personalize your copy of Microsoft Office* section, in the *User name* box, type the name you want to appear.
4. Click **OK**.

tell me more

- To resize a comment: Click a resize handle and drag toward the center of the comment to make it smaller or away from the center of the image to make it larger.
- To move a comment: Point to the comment, and when the cursor changes to the move cursor, click and drag the comment to the new location.

another method

- To insert a comment, right-click the cell in which you want the comment, and select *Insert Comment* or press **Shift +F2**.
- If a cell has a comment, the right-click menu includes the following commands: *Edit Comment*, *Delete Comment*, *Hide Comment* (if the comment is showing), and *Show Comment* (if the comment is hidden).
- You can also delete a comment from the *Home* tab, *Editing* group. Click the cell with the comment, then click the **Clear** button and select **Clear Comments**.

let me try *Live!*

If you do not have the data file from the previous skill open, open the student data file **EX9-10-IncomeAndExpenses** and try this skill on your own:

1. If necessary, select cell **F4** on the *Summary* worksheet.
2. Add this comment to the selected cell: `Need links to details here.`
3. Display all the comments on this worksheet at once.
4. View the comment in cell **F3** and then delete it.
5. If you will be moving on to the next skill in this chapter, leave the workbook open to continue working. If not, save the file as directed by your instructor and close it.

Skill 9.11 Inserting Hyperlinks

A **hyperlink** is text or a graphic that can be clicked to open another location in the same file, another file, or a Web page. In Excel, the hyperlink encompasses an entire cell or range of cells rather than text.

When you add a hyperlink to a cell, the text in the cell appears in the *Hyperlink* cell style (usually a color and underlined). Click the link to navigate to the linked location. Once you click the hyperlink, it will appear in the *Followed Hyperlink* cell style (usually a different color and underlined) to indicate that the link has been followed.

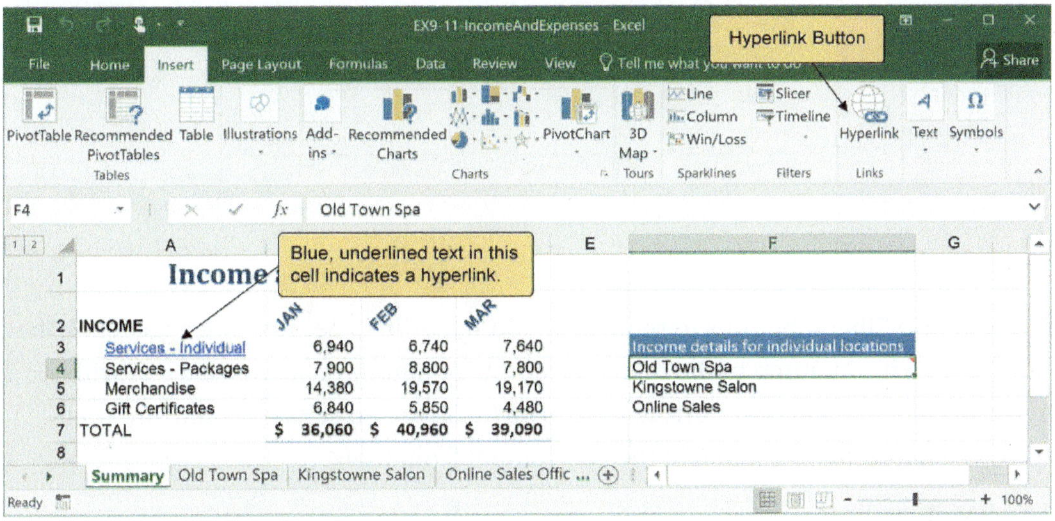

FIGURE EX 9.38

To insert a hyperlink:

1. Select the cell or range of cells where you want to create the link.
2. On the *Insert* tab, in the *Links* group, click the **Hyperlink** button to open the *Insert Hyperlink* dialog.
3. If the cell you selected is empty, type the text you want to appear in the cell in the *Text to display* box. If you selected a cell that contains a value or formula already, the *Text to display* box displays<<*Selection in Document*>>.
4. In the *Link to* section on the left side of the dialog, select the type of location you want to link to, and then enter the link details.
    - Click **Existing File or Web Page**, and then select the specific file or Web page to link to.
    - Click **Place in This Document**, and then select the worksheet or named range to link to. If necessary, edit the cell reference in the *Type the cell reference* box. Cell A1 is selected by default.

- Click **Create New Document**, and then enter the path and file name for the new document.
- Click **E-mail Address**, and then enter the email address to link to and a subject. When this link is clicked, Outlook will open a new mail message.

5. Click **OK** to close the *Insert Hyperlink* dialog and insert the hyperlink into your workbook.

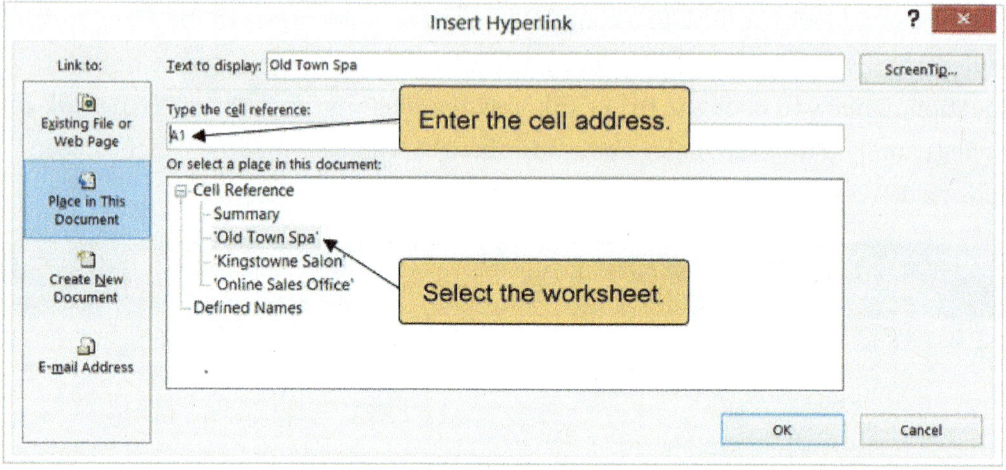

FIGURE EX 9.39

There are no Ribbon buttons to remove or edit hyperlinks because once you click the cell to select it, you jump to the linked location. To edit the *contents* of a cell with a hyperlink, use the keyboard arrow keys to navigate to and select the cell and then click in the formula bar and edit the cell content from there.

To edit a hyperlink:

1. Right-click the link and select **Edit Hyperlink**.
2. Make changes in the *Edit Hyperlink* dialog.
3. Click **OK**.

To delete a hyperlink:

1. Right-click the hyperlinked cell.
2. Select **Remove Hyperlink** from the right-click menu.

Notice when you remove the hyperlink, the cell content is not deleted. Only the hyperlink functionality and cell formatting are removed.

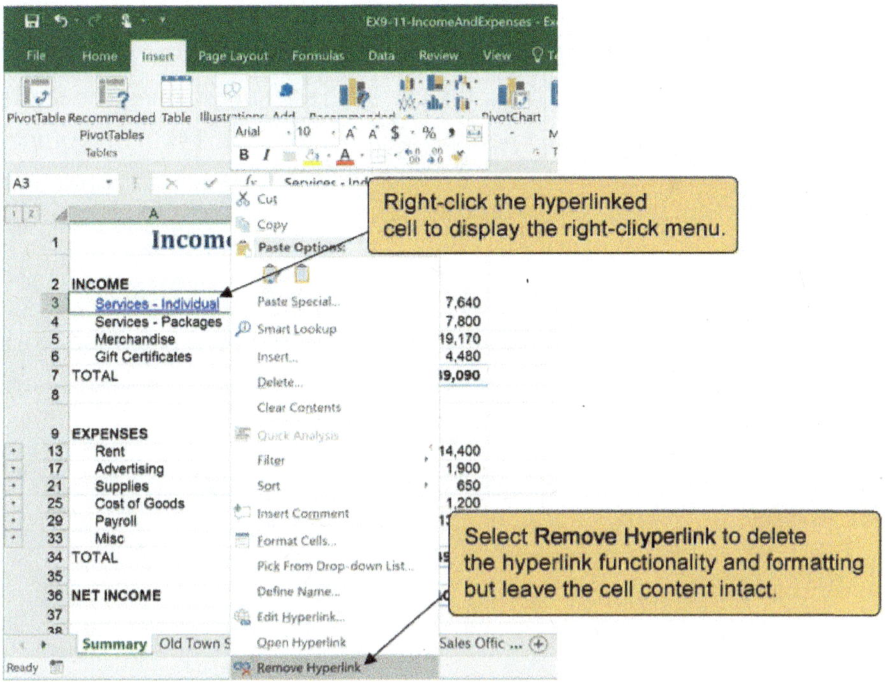

FIGURE EX 9.40

tips & tricks

A **ScreenTip** is a bubble that appears when the mouse pointer is placed over the link. Add a ScreenTip to include a more meaningful description of the hyperlink. In the *Insert Hyperlink* dialog, click the **ScreenTip** button. In the Set *Hyperlink ScreenTip* dialog, enter the ScreenTip text in the box, and then click **OK**.

another method

To open the *Insert Hyperlink* dialog, you can also:

- Right-click the cell and select **Hyperlink...**
- Press **Ctrl + K** on the keyboard.

let me try *Live!*

If you do not have the data file from the previous skill open, open the student data file **EX9-11-IncomeAndExpenses** and try this skill on your own:

1. Add a hyperlink from cell **F4** on the *Summary* worksheet to link to cell **B1** in the **Old Town Spa** worksheet.
2. Remove the hyperlink from cell **A3** on the *Summary* worksheet.
3. If you will be moving on to the next skill in this chapter, leave the workbook open to continue working. If not, save the file as directed by your instructor and close it.

Skill 9.12 Sharing a Workbook

When you share a workbook, you allow several people to view and make changes to the workbook at the same time. **Shared workbooks** are usually saved to a network or cloud location where multiple users have access, so be careful to save your shared workbook to a secure location where only authorized users have access to it.

To share a workbook:

1. On the *Review* tab, in the *Changes* group, click the **Share Workbook** button.

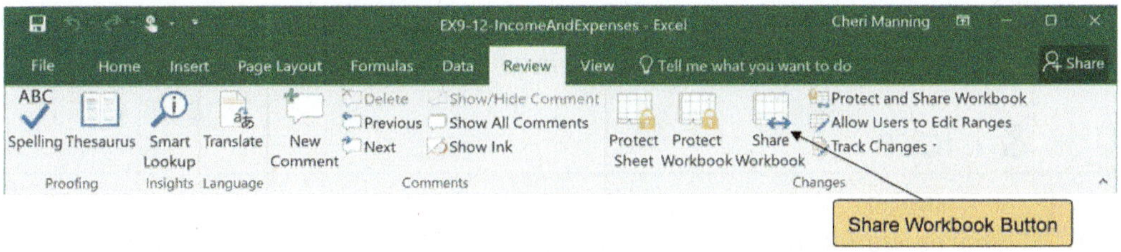

FIGURE EX 9.41

2. In the *Share Workbook* dialog, click the check box to enable sharing. Click **OK**.

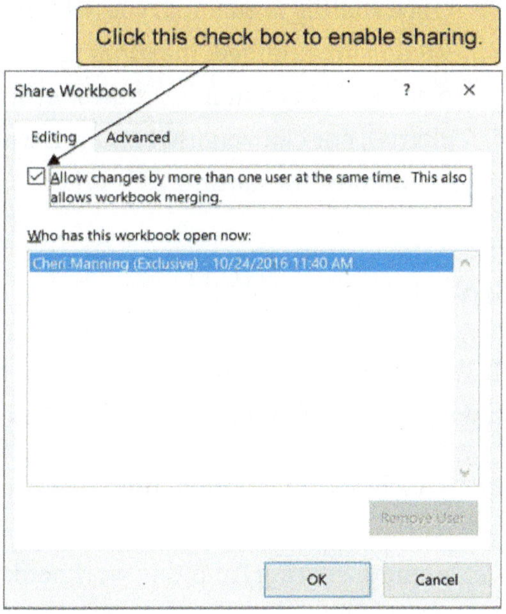

FIGURE EX 9.42

3. A message box appears, asking if you want to save the workbook and continue. Click **OK**.

Once the workbook is shared, *[Shared]* appears after the file name in the title bar.

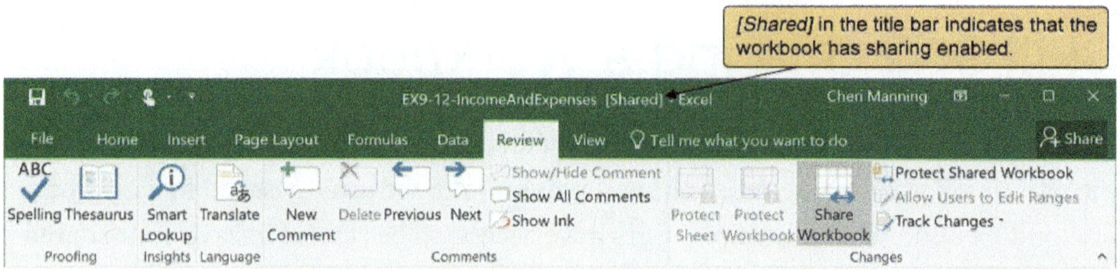

FIGURE EX 9.43

At any point, you can see the list of users who have the workbook open by opening the *Share Workbook* dialog again.

To remove sharing, open the *Share Workbook* dialog again and click the check box to remove the checkmark and disallow sharing.

tips & tricks

- Shared workbooks cannot contain tables. If your workbook contains tables, you will need to convert the tables to named ranges before enabling sharing.
- Once sharing is enabled, you will notice that many of the buttons on the Ribbon are dimmed, meaning you no longer have access to those features. You cannot insert new cells or graphic objects (including charts), nor can you use certain Excel formatting features like conditional formatting.

let me try *Live!*

If you do not have the data file from the previous skill open, open the student data file **EX9-12-IncomeAndExpenses** and try this skill on your own:

1. Enable sharing so more than one person at a time can work on this workbook.
2. Remove sharing from this workbook.
3. If you will be moving on to the next skill in this chapter, leave the workbook open to continue working. If not, save the file as directed by your instructor and close it.

Skill 9.13 Protecting Worksheets and Workbooks from Changes

If you intend to share the workbook, you should set worksheet and workbook protection first. You cannot apply protection after the workbook has been shared.

By default, Excel "locks" all the cells in a worksheet, but this does not affect users until you apply worksheet protection. When you enable worksheet protection, users will not be able to edit or delete any data in the worksheet unless you explicitly ***unlock*** specific cells.

To unlock cells:

1. Select the cells you want users to be able to edit when worksheet protection is enabled.
2. On the *Home* tab, in the *Cells* group, click the **Format** button.
3. Click **Lock Cell** to remove the highlight and unlock the selected cells.

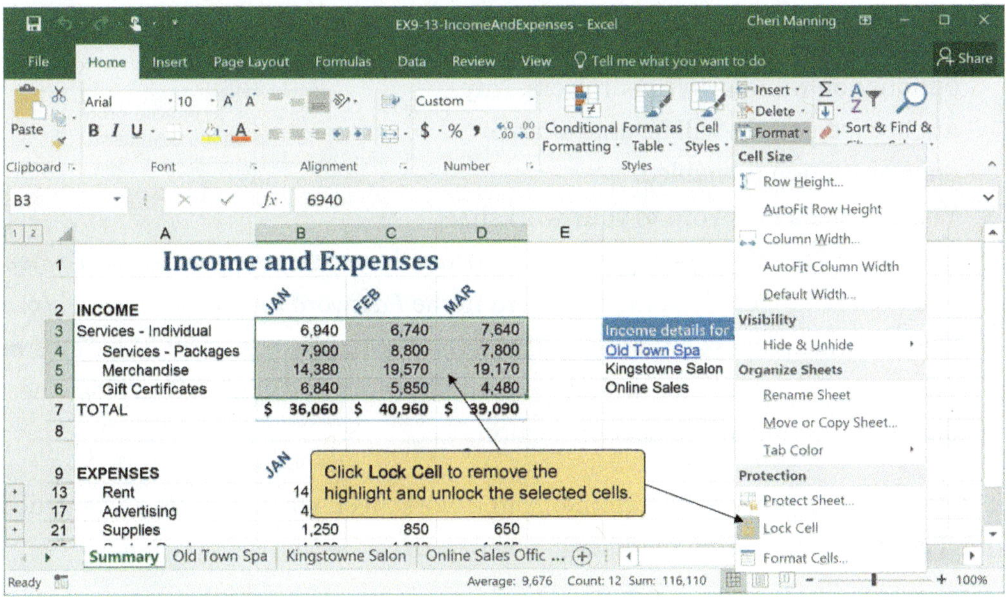

FIGURE EX 9.44

To enable worksheet protection and set protection options:

1. On the *Review* tab, in the *Changes* group, click the **Protect Sheet** button.

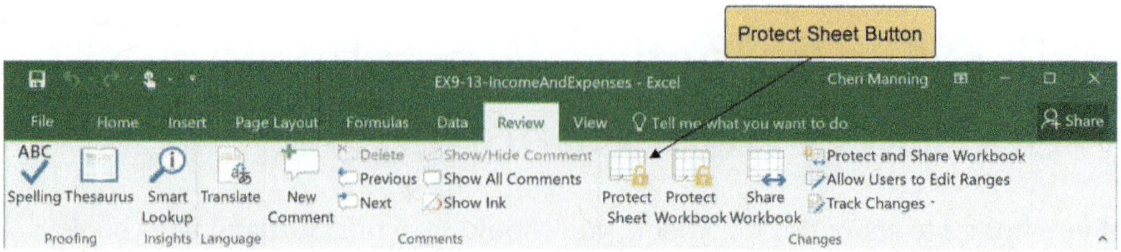

FIGURE EX 9.45

2. In the *Protect Sheet* dialog, notice that the *Select locked cells* option is checked allowing users to select the cells, not edit them. Allowing users to select locked cells can help them understand the worksheet by viewing formulas in the formula bar. The *Select unlocked cells* option is also checked to allow users to select and edit unlocked cells. Users can edit the cells because the cells are *unlocked*.

   Click the check boxes for any other options you want to give your users. Any unchecked options will be unavailable once protection is enabled.

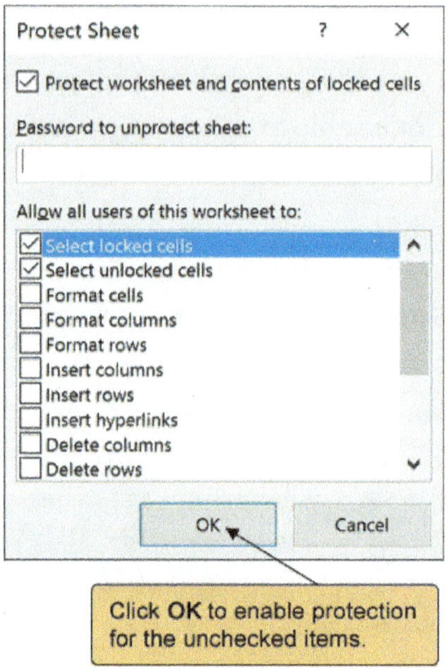

FIGURE EX 9.46

3. You can add a password to your worksheet to require users to enter the password before they can unprotect the worksheet and make changes. Type the password in the *Password to unprotect sheet* box.
4. Click **OK** to accept your changes. If you have entered a password, the *Confirm Password* dialog will appear. Retype your password and click **OK** to close the dialog and enable worksheet protection.

Just as you can protect certain elements in a worksheet, you can protect the structure and display of your overall workbook.

To protect a workbook:

1. On the *Review* tab, in the *Changes* group, click the **Protect Workbook** button.

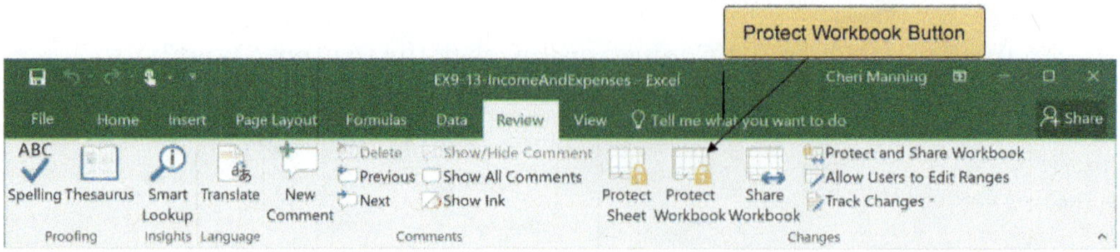

FIGURE EX 9.47

2. In the *Protect Workbook* dialog, notice that the *Structure* check box is checked by default. This prevents users from modifying moving, adding, deleting, and renaming worksheets.
3. Type a password in the *Password* box to require a password to unlock the workbook.
4. Click **OK** to accept your changes. If you have entered a password, the *Confirm Password* dialog will appear. Retype your password and click **OK** to close the dialog and lock your workbook.

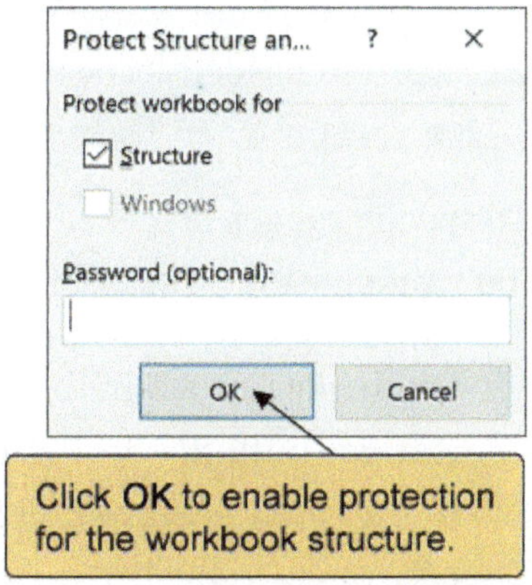

FIGURE EX 9.48

tips & tricks

- If you intend to share the workbook and track changes, you should set worksheet and workbook protection ***first***. You cannot apply protection after the workbook has been shared.
- When a worksheet is protected, the *Unprotect Worksheet* button is unavailable when the workbook is shared. To unprotect the worksheet, you must first remove sharing.
- The *Windows* option in the *Protect Structure and Windows* dialog cannot be used in Excel 2016. It is included only for compatibility with workbooks created in older versions of Excel that have this level of workbook protection enabled.

tell me **more**

Another way to allow users to edit cells in a protected worksheet is to apply a password to the cells. The cells remain locked, but users can unlock them with a password.

To specify ranges of locked cells that users can modify with a password when the worksheet is protected:

1. On the *Review* tab in the *Changes* group, click the **Allow Users to Edit Ranges** button.
2. In the *Allow Users to Edit Ranges* dialog, click the **New** button to add a new range to the list.
3. In the *New Range* dialog, enter a title for the range. The title appears in the *Allow Users to Edit Ranges* dialog.
4. In the *Refers to cells* box, enter = followed by the cell range or the range name.
5. In the *Range password* box, type the password users will have to enter in order to edit the cells.
6. Click **OK**.
7. Excel will ask you to verify the password. Type the password again and click **OK**.
8. Click **OK** to close the *Allow Users to Edit Ranges* dialog and apply the changes to the worksheet.

another method

- To unlock cells from the *Format Cells* dialog, *Protection* tab, click the **Locked** check box to uncheck it.
- To apply protection from the *File* tab, *Info* page, click the **Protect Workbook** button and select **Protect Workbook Structure** or **Protect Current Sheet**.
- To apply protection to the current sheet from the *Home* tab, *Cells* group, click the **Format** button and then click **Protect Sheet**.

let me try *Live!*

If you do not have the data file from the previous skill open, open the student data file **EX9-13-IncomeAndExpenses** and try this skill on your own:

1. If necessary, select cells **B3:D6** on the *Summary* sheet.
2. Unlock the selected cells so the user can edit the cells when the worksheet is protected.
3. Enable worksheet protection for the **Summary** worksheet so users can **select** both locked cells and unlocked cells.
4. The **Old Town Spa** worksheet has been protected. Unprotect it so users can make changes to locked cells.
5. Enable workbook protection so users cannot change worksheet names.
6. Remove workbook protection so users can add new worksheets.
7. If you will be moving on to the next skill in this chapter, leave the workbook open to continue working. If not, save the file as directed by your instructor and close it.

Skill 9.14 Tracking Changes

When you have multiple people working on a shared workbook, tracking the change history can be important. The change history tracks any deletions, insertions, or changes to data (except formatting changes). The change history also displays which user made the change and when.

To track changes to your workbook:

1. On the *Review* tab, in the *Changes* group, click the **Track Changes** button, and select **Highlight Changes....**

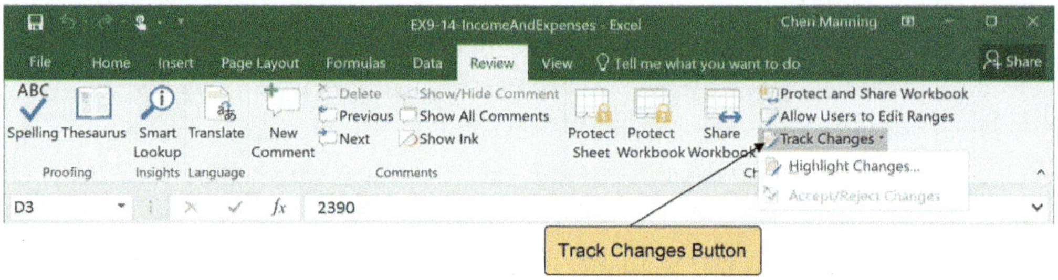

FIGURE EX 9.49

2. In the *Highlight Changes* dialog, click the **Track changes while editing** check box.
3. Specify tracking options, such as highlighting changes since the last time you saved or changes made by a particular user. Click the check box for the type of change you want to highlight, and then select a specific option from the drop-down list.
4. Click the check box to specify where you want to see the changes: **Highlight changes on screen** or **List changes on a new sheet**. (You may be able to select both options.)
5. Click **OK**.
6. Click **OK** again to allow Excel to save the workbook.

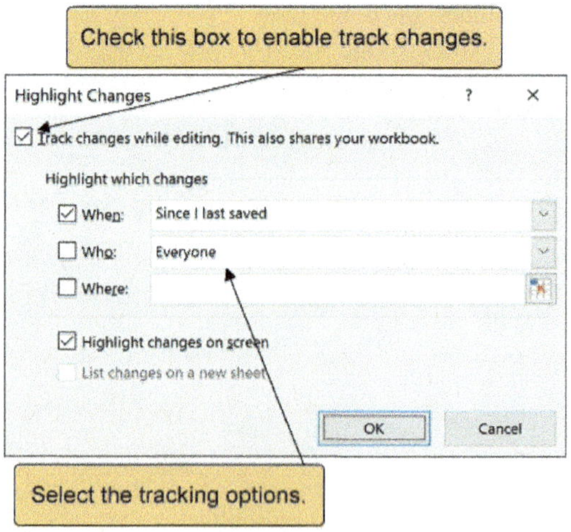

FIGURE EX 9.50

Cells that were changed are highlighted with a dark blue triangle in the upper-left corner. Point to a highlighted cell to see a description of the changes made.

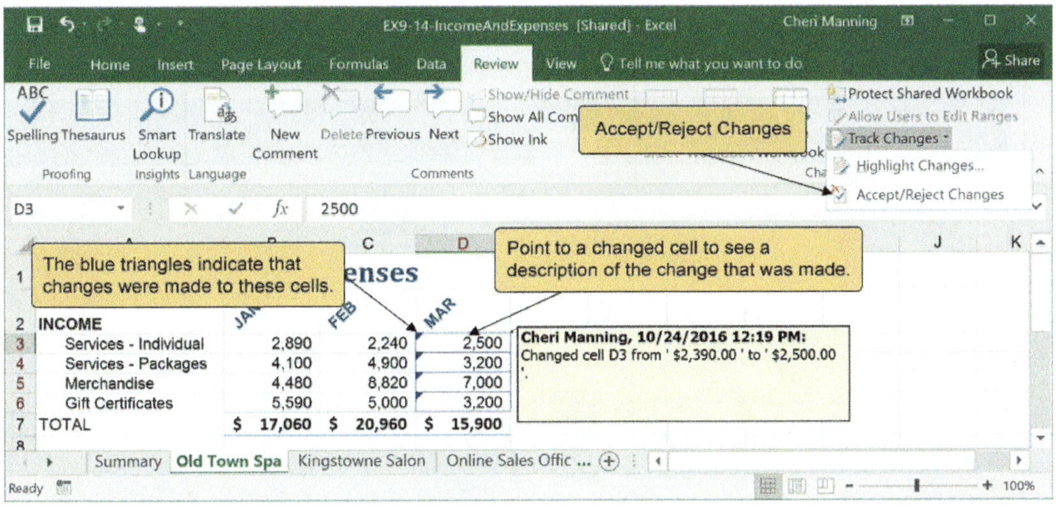

FIGURE EX 9.51

To accept and reject changes in a workbook:

1. On the *Review* tab, in the *Changes* group, click the **Track Changes** button and select **Accept/Reject Changes**.
2. If Excel prompts you to save the workbook, click **OK**.
3. In the *Select Changes to Accept or Reject* dialog, select which changes to review:
   a. **When:** Select changes that have not been reviewed or changes made by a certain date.
   b. **Who:** Select all reviewers or specific reviewers.
   c. **Where:** Enter the cell range or worksheet you want to review. If the *Where* box is empty, the entire workbook will be reviewed.
4. Click **OK** to begin reviewing the changes in the workbook.

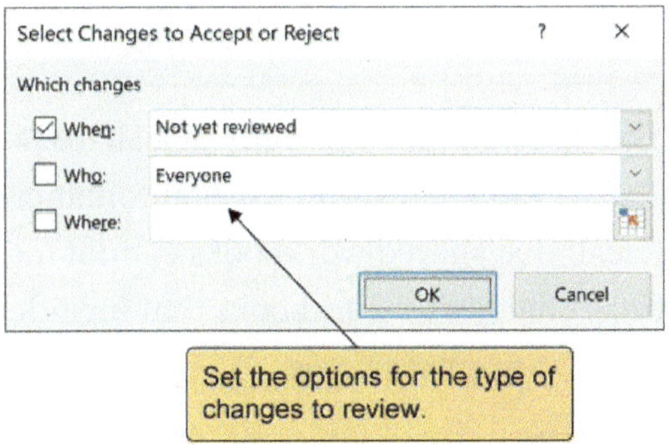

FIGURE EX 9.52

5. The *Accept or Reject Changes* dialog displays information about each change: who made the change, when it was made, and what the change was. You must accept or reject a change before being moving to the next change. Notice the changed cell is highlighted in the worksheet to help you identify the change.
   a. Click **Accept** to accept the current change.
   b. Click **Reject** to reject the current change.
   c. To accept all the changes in the workbook, click **Accept All**.
   d. To reject all the changes in the workbook, click **Reject All**.

6. When all the changes in the workbook have been reviewed, the *Accept or Reject Changes* dialog closes automatically.

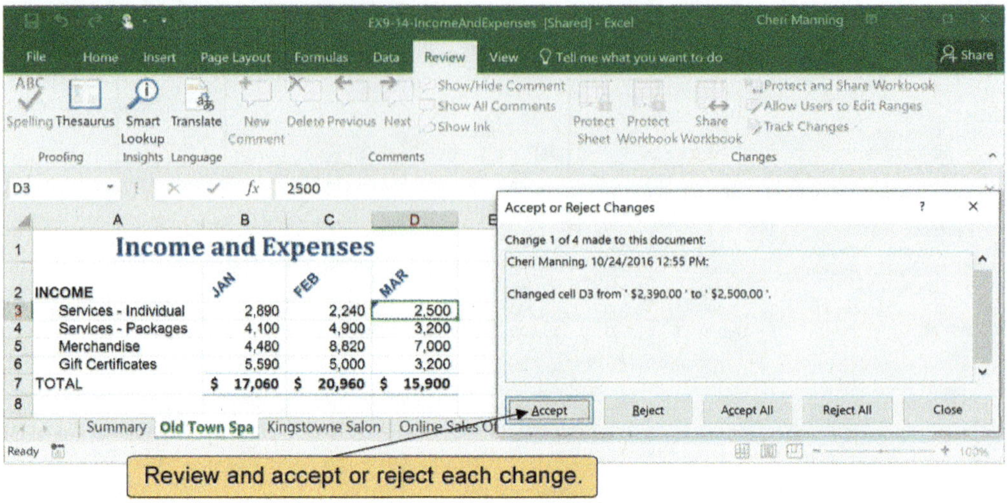

FIGURE EX 9.53

To stop tracking changes:

1. On the *Review* tab, in the *Changes* group, click the **Track Changes** button, and select **Highlight Changes....**
2. In the *Highlight Changes* dialog, click the **Track changes while editing** check box to remove the checkmark.
3. Click **OK.**
4. Click **Yes** again to allow Excel to remove sharing from the workbook.

tips & tricks

You can track changes only in a shared workbook. When you turn on the *Track Changes* feature, Excel automatically enables workbook sharing. Recall that shared workbooks cannot include tables. Therefore, you cannot track changes in workbooks that include tables unless you first convert the tables to normal ranges.

tell me **more**

The change history is kept only for the number of days you specify. The *Advanced* tab in the *Share Workbook* dialog allows you to set the number of days the change history will be kept.

1. On the *Review* tab, in the *Changes* group, click the **Share Workbook** button.
2. Click the **Advanced** tab.
3. Under *Track changes*, select the number of days to keep the change history.
4. Click **OK**.

let me try *Live!*

If you do not have the data file from the previous skill open, open the student data file **EX9-14-IncomeAndExpenses** and try this skill on your own:

1. Turn on Track Changes to highlight all changes made in this workbook since it was last saved.
2. Navigate to the **Old Town Spa** worksheet and make the following changes:

   Change the value in cell **D3** to **2500**
   Change the value in cell **D4** to **3200**
   Change the value in cell **D5** to **7000**
   Change the value in cell **D6** to **3200**

3. Review all changes made to this workbook that have not yet been reviewed.
4. Accept the first change.
5. Accept all the remaining changes at once.
6. Stop tracking changes in the workbook.
7. If you will be moving on to the next skill in this chapter, leave the workbook open to continue working. If not, save the file as directed by your instructor and close it.

Skill 9.15 Checking for Compatibility with Previous Versions of Excel

Some features in Excel 2016 are not available in previous versions of the application. If a workbook uses one of the new features, opening it in a previous version of Excel may cause errors or prevent the workbook from displaying as you intended.

To check your workbook for potential compatibility issues:

1. Click the **File** tab. On *Info* page, click the **Check for Issues** button, and then click **Check Compatibility**.

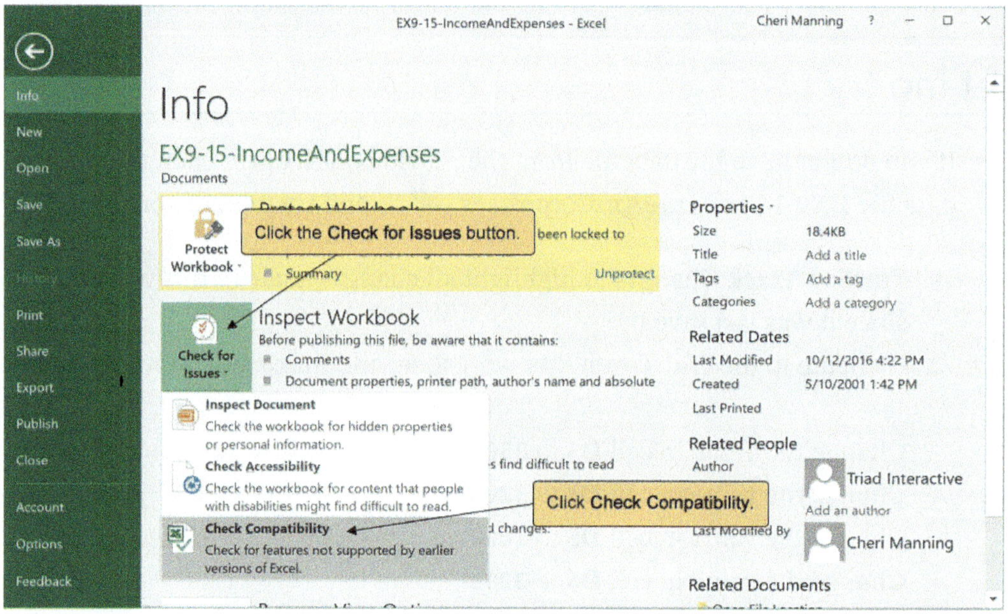

FIGURE EX 9.54

2. The **Compatibility Checker** lists the items in your workbook that may be lost or downgraded if you save the workbook in an earlier Microsoft Excel format. The dialog groups the items by loss of functionality and loss of fidelity (formatting) and lists the number of times each issue occurs in the workbook (occurrences).
   - Click the **Find** link next to an issue to go directly to that cell in the workbook. This closes the *Compatibility Checker* dialog.
   - Excel may be able to offer a fix for some compatibility issues. To remove the incompatible functionality from your workbook, click the **Fix** link. Review the compatibility issue carefully before deciding to "fix" it. Removing the functionality may require you to make other changes to the workbook to maintain data integrity.

- To save a list of the issues found, click the **Copy to New Sheet** button. This closes the *Compatibility Checker* dialog.

3. Click **OK** to close the Compatibility Checker.

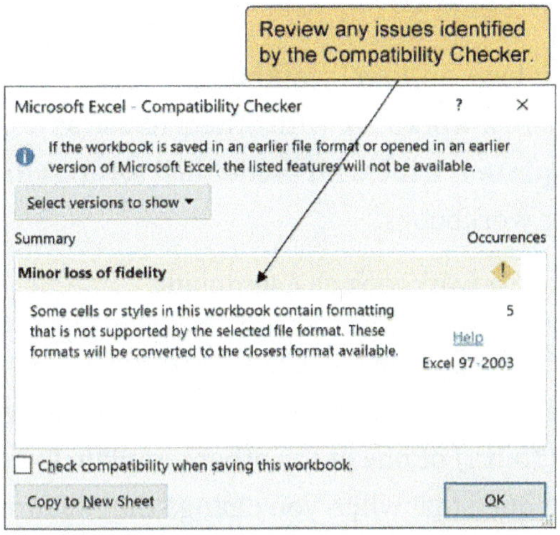

FIGURE EX 9.55

tips & tricks

If you often share a workbook with people using an older version of Microsoft Excel, you can set the Compatibility Checker to run every time you save the workbook. Open the *Compatibility Checker* dialog, and then click the **Check compatibility when saving** check box to add a checkmark. Click **OK**.

let me try *Live!*

If you do not have the data file from the previous skill open, open the student data file **EX9-15-IncomeAndExpenses** and try this skill on your own:

1. Open the Compatibility Checker to check if this workbook contains elements that are not compatible with earlier versions of Excel.
2. Review any issues that are identified, but do not make any changes. Close the Compatibility Checker.
3. If you will be moving on to the next skill in this chapter, leave the workbook open to continue working. If not, save the file as directed by your instructor and close it.

Skill 9.16 Saving a Workbook in Other Formats

If you have an Excel workbook that you make copies of often to reuse, or if you want to share a workbook with others to use as a sample, try saving it as a template. A **template** is a file with predefined settings that you can use as a starting point for other workbooks.

To save a workbook as a template:

1. Click the **File** tab. Click **Save As**.
2. On the *Save As* page, click the **Save as type** arrow and select **Excel Template (*.xltx)** or one of the other template formats.
3. Notice that when you change the file format to Excel Template, the *Save As* location changes to **Documents > Custom Office Templates**. This is the default location for saving new Microsoft Office templates.
4. Click **Save.**

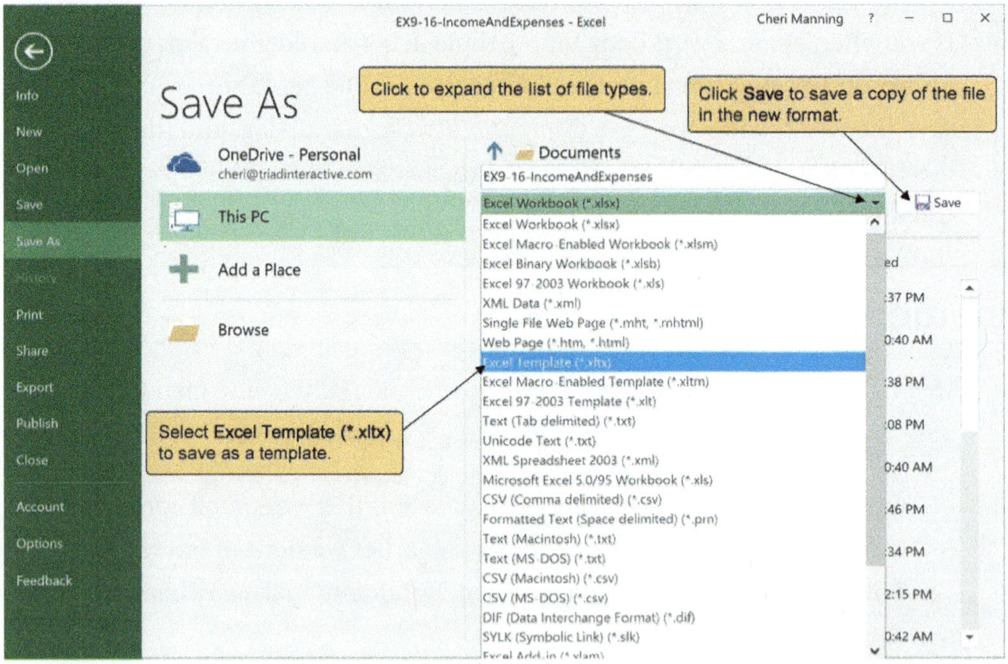

FIGURE EX 9.56

Beginning with Excel 2007, Microsoft changed the default file format for Excel to .xlsx, which is not backward compatible. If you want to share a workbook with people who use an earlier version of Excel, you will need to save the file using the **Excel 97-2003 Workbook** format. Some loss of formatting or functionality may occur.

To save a workbook in a format compatible with older versions of Excel:

1. Click the **File** tab. Click **Save As**.
2. In the **Save As** dialog, click the **Save as type** arrow and select **Excel 97-2003 Workbook (*.xls)**.
3. Click **Save**.
4. If the Compatibility Checker opens, review the issue(s) identified and then click **Continue**.

When saving a workbook, be sure to consider who will use the workbook and how they will use it, and select the most appropriate file format.

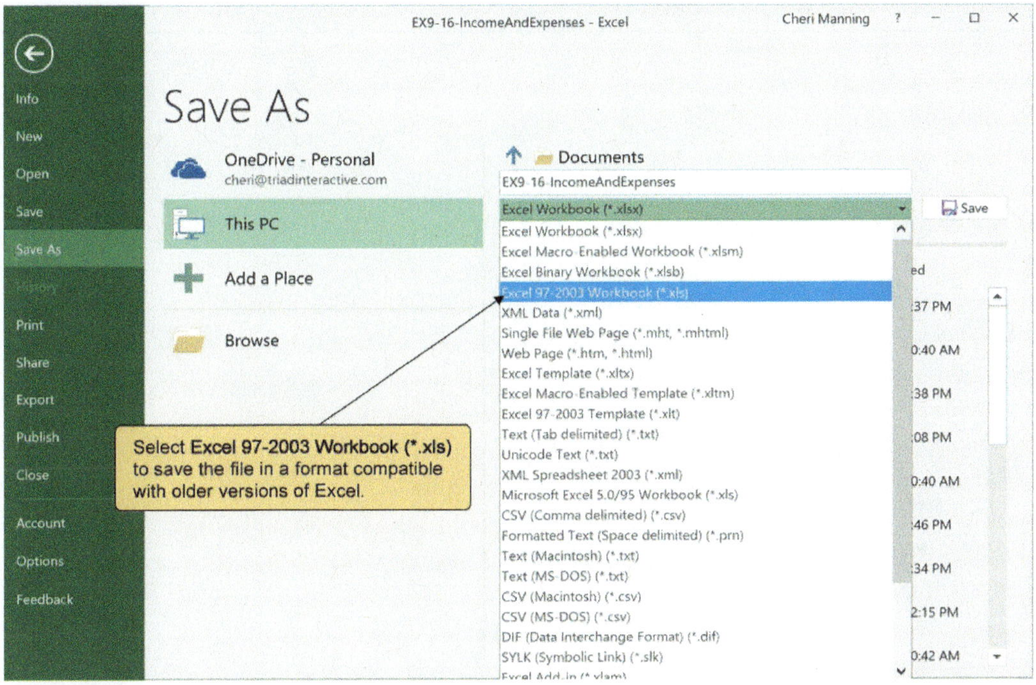

FIGURE EX 9.57

tell me **more**

When you open a workbook created by a version of Excel older than Excel 2007, you will see *[Compatibility Mode]* in the title bar immediately following the name of the workbook. In **Compatibility mode**, some of the new Excel features and formats are not available (in order to maintain backward compatibility). To convert the workbook to the default Excel 2016 format, click the **File** tab, and click the **Convert** button or click **Save As** and select the **Excel Workbook** format.

let me try *Live!*

If you do not have the data file from the previous skill open, open the student data file **EX9-16-IncomeAndExpenses** and try this skill on your own:

1. Save this workbook as an Excel template named **`EX9-16-IncomeAndExpenses_template`**
2. Save the workbook in the format compatible with *Excel 97-2003*. Allow the file to save with compatibility issues. Use the file name **`EX9-16-IncomeAndExpenses_97-2003`**
3. Close the file.

Skill 9.17 Adding a Password

The *Info* tab in Backstage displays the current permissions status of the workbook. By default, workbooks are unsecured—anyone can open, copy, and edit any part of the workbook. One way to secure your workbook is to add a password. Users will need to enter the password before they can open the file to view or edit it.

To add a password to your workbook:

1. Click the **File** tab.
2. On the *Info* page, click the **Protect Workbook** button and select **Encrypt with Password**.

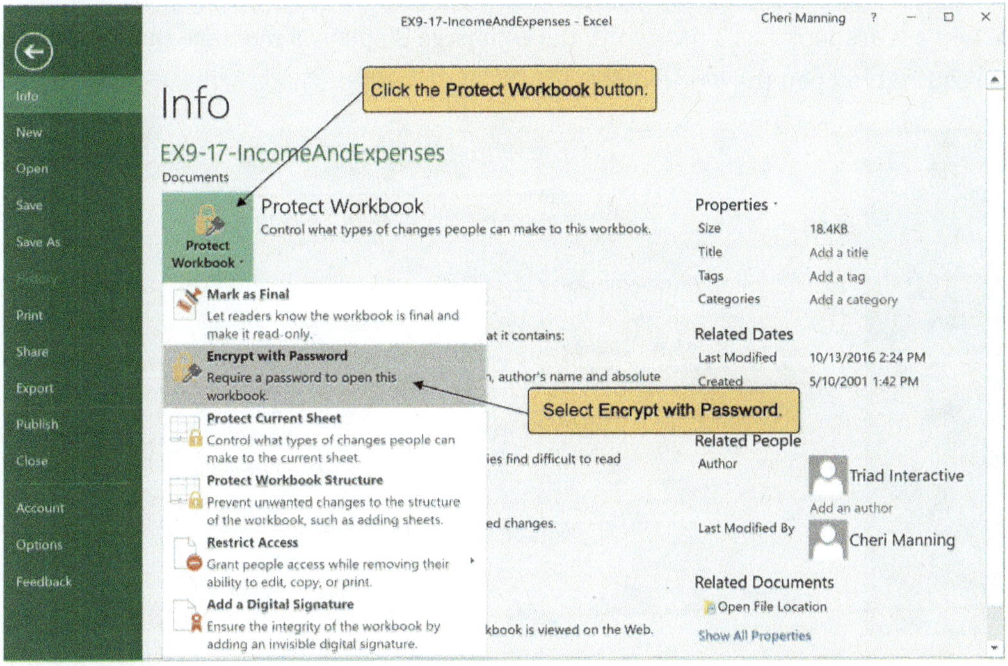

FIGURE EX 9.58

3. Type your password in the *Password* box. Notice that the characters you type are hidden and black dots appear instead. Click **OK**.

FIGURE EX 9.59

4. Retype your password in the *Confirm Password* dialog.
5. Click **OK** to add the password to the workbook.

When a workbook has a password, the *Info* page displays a message that a password is required to open the workbook.

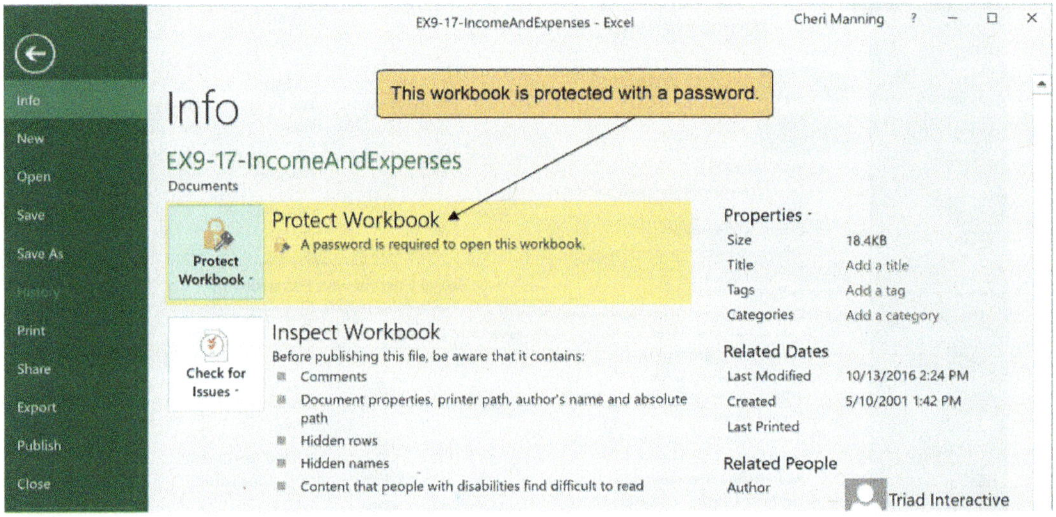

FIGURE EX 9.60

tips & tricks

Adding a password will not lock or unlock data in your workbook. You must set worksheet and workbook protection to prevent users from changing data in the workbook once they have it open. Refer to the skill *Protecting Worksheets and Workbooks from Changes* for more information.

let me try *Live!*

Open the student data file **EX9-17-IncomeAndExpenses** and try this skill on your own:

1. Encrypt the workbook with this password: `eXp3ns$s`
2. If you will be moving on to the next skill in this chapter, leave the workbook open to continue working. If not, save the file as directed by your instructor and close it.

Skill 9.18 Running the Document Inspector

Before finalizing the document, you may want to remove certain elements such as personal information in the document properties, comments and hidden rows, columns, and worksheets. The **Document Inspector** allows you to check your file for hidden data and personal information contained in the workbook properties before you finalize the workbook and send it to others.

To inspect your workbook for hidden data or personal information:

1. Click the **File** tab. Click the **Check for Issues** button, and select **Inspect Document**.

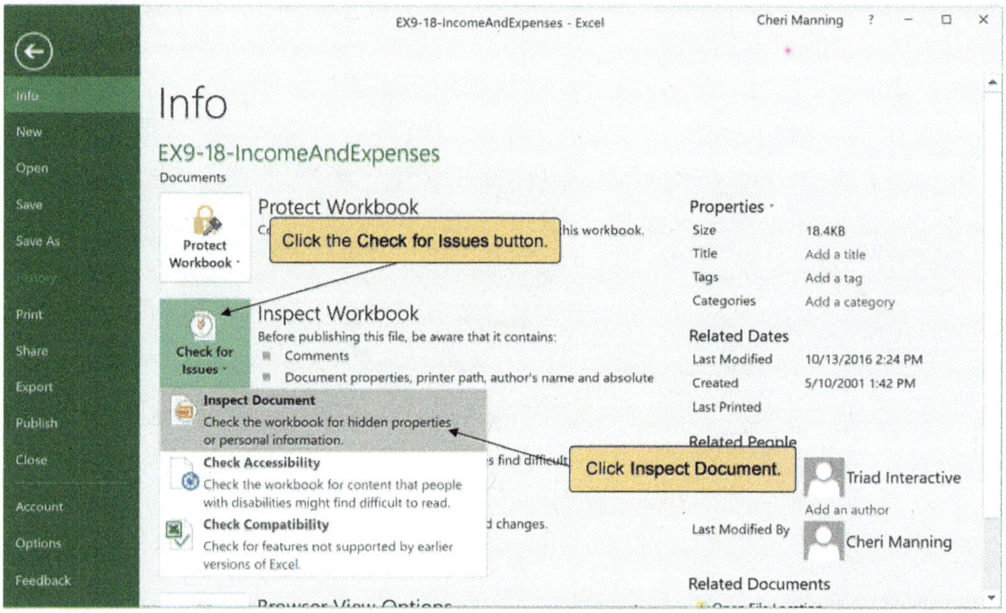

FIGURE EX 9.61

2. Excel will prompt you to save changes before running the Document Inspector. Click **Yes**.
3. Review the list of content types that the Documents Inspector will look for. Uncheck any options you do not want to include.
4. Click the **Inspect** button.
5. Click the **Remove All** button next to the items you want to remove from your workbook.
6. To continue inspecting the workbook, click the **Reinspect** button and then repeat steps 3–5.
7. When you are finished, click the **Close** button to close the Document Inspector.

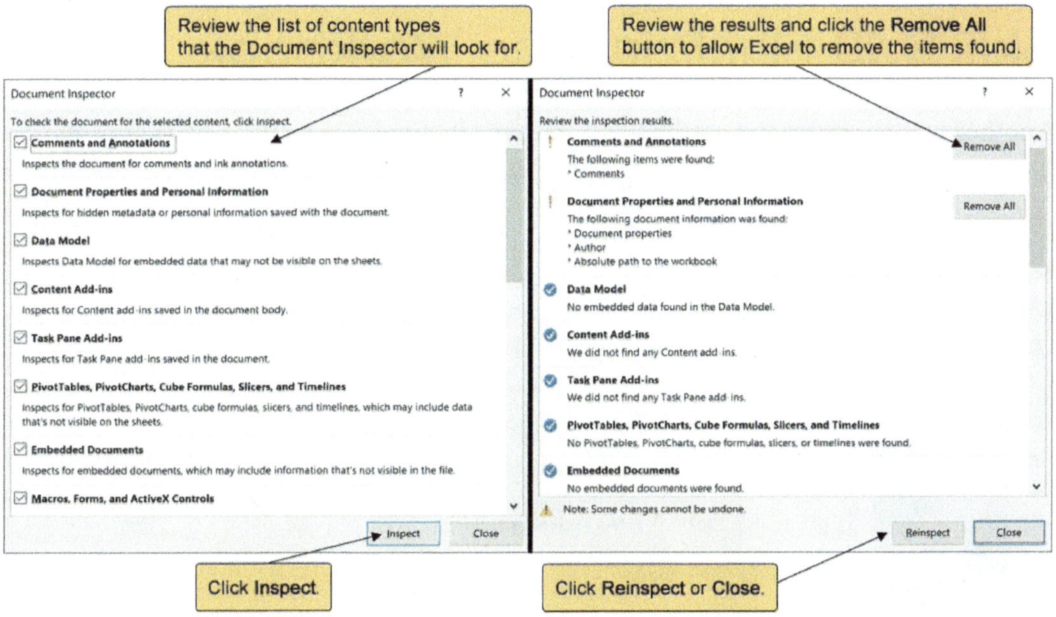

FIGURE EX 9.62

let me try *Live!*

If you do not have the data file from the previous skill open, open the student data file **EX9-18-IncomeAndExpenses** and try this skill on your own:

1. Run the Document Inspector.
2. Remove the **Comments and Annotations** and **Document Properties and Personal Information** identified by the Document Inspector and then close the Document Inspector window.
3. If you will be moving on to the next skill in this chapter, leave the workbook open to continue working. If not, save the file as directed by your instructor and close it.

Skill 9.19 Finalizing the Workbook

Another way to secure the workbook is to mark it "final." Marking a workbook as final indicates that it will not be edited further. The workbook is converted to read-only status.

To mark a workbook as final:

1. Click the **File** tab. On the *Info* page, click the **Protect Workbook** button, and select **Mark as Final**.

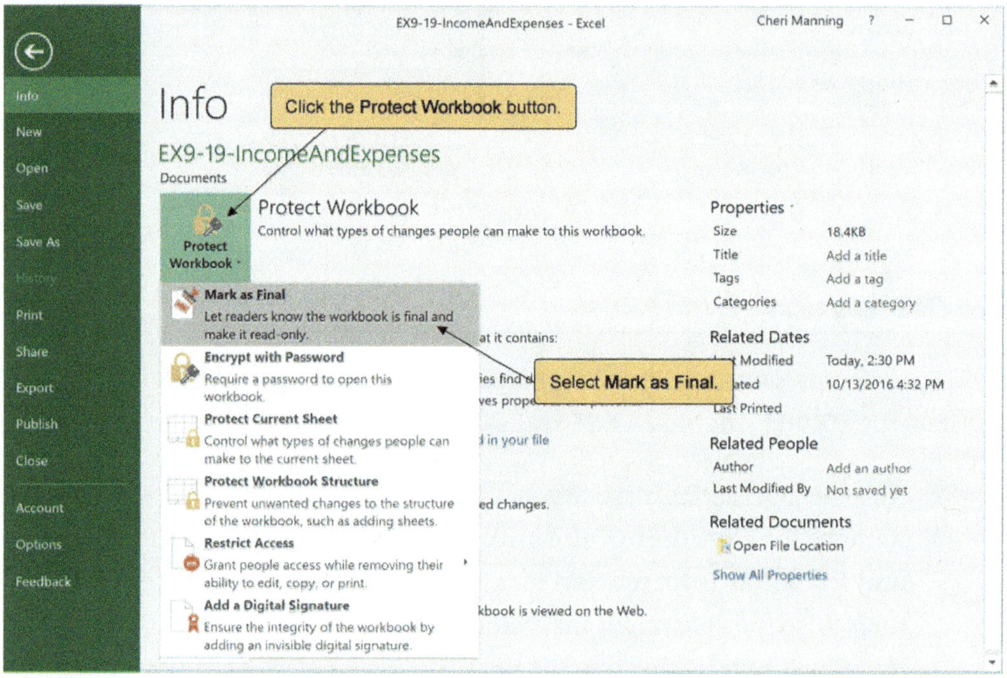

FIGURE EX 9.63

2. A message box appears letting you know the workbook will be marked as final and saved.
3. Click **OK**.
4. Another message box may appear explaining what features are not available when a workbook has been marked as "final." If you do not want to see this message every time you mark a workbook as final, click the **Don't show this message again** check box. Click **OK** to dismiss the message and finalize the workbook.

When a workbook has been marked as final, the *Marked as Final* icon appears in the status bar, and the *Info* page displays a message that the workbook has been marked as final.

Marking a workbook as final does not really prevent another user from editing it. When the workbook is opened, the Message Bar displays a warning that the workbook has been marked as final. Any user can click the **Edit Anyway** button to remove the read-only status from the file.

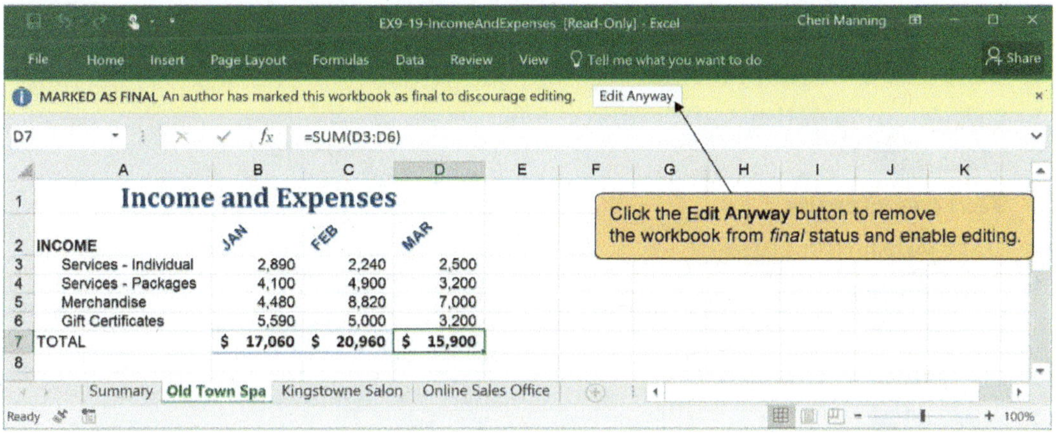

FIGURE EX 9.64

tips & tricks

Files that are marked as final in Microsoft Office 2016 will not be protected with read-only status when opened in Excel 2003 or earlier.

let me try *Live!*

If you do not have the data file from the previous skill open, open the student data file **EX9-19-IncomeAndExpenses** and try this skill on your own:

1. Mark the workbook as final so it opens as read-only to discourage editing.
2. Save the file as directed by your instructor and close it.

key terms

- **Microsoft Access**
- **Delimiter**
- **Text (tab delimited) format**
- **CSV (comma delimited) format**
- **Flash Fill**
- **Text to Columns**
- **Data validation rules**
- **Consolidate**
- **Comment**
- **Hyperlink**
- **ScreenTip**
- **Shared workbook**
- **Compatibility Checker**
- **Template**
- **Excel 97-2003 Workbook format**
- **Compatibility mode**
- **Document Inspector**
- **Mark as Final**

concept review

1. Which of these commands will update data that were imported from a Microsoft Access database?
   a. *Get External Data*
   b. *Refresh All*
   c. *Flash Fill*
   d. *Import Data*
2. Which of these characters is not a common delimiter for a text file?
   a. tab
   b. comma
   c. semicolon
   d. hash tag
3. Which of these formats supports saving a workbook with multiple worksheets?
   a. text (tab delimited)
   b. CSV (comma delimited)
   c. Excel 97-2003 Workbook
   d. all of the above
4. Flash Fill can be used to create multiple columns of data with a single command.
   a. true
   b. false
5. Which of these commands cannot be used for similar purposes?
   a. *Flash Fill* and the CONCATENATE function
   b. *Flash Fill* and *Text to Columns*
   c. *Text to Columns* and the CONCATENATE function
   d. none of the above
6. When you add data validation rules to cells, invalid data are circled automatically.
   a. true
   b. false
7. Using the Consolidate feature always includes links to the source data in an outline format.
   a. true
   b. false

8. Hyperlinks can link to which of these types of locations?
    a. a Web page
    b. an email address
    c. a cell in another worksheet in the workbook
    d. all of the above
9. In order to allow users to edit some cells in a protected worksheet, you must
    a. unlock the cells and verify that **Selected unlocked cells** is checked in the *Protect Sheet* dialog.
    b. verify that **Selected locked cells** is checked in the *Protect Sheet* dialog.
    c. enable the *Track Changes* feature.
    d. verify that the **Structure** check box is checked in the *Protect Structure and Windows* dialog.
10. When a workbook is marked as final, there is no way for a user to edit the workbook.
    a. true
    b. false

projects

Data files for projects can be found by logging into your SIMnet account and going to the *Library* section.

skill review 9.1

In this project, you will import gradebook data from a Microsoft Access database. You will work with the data to create the final gradebook worksheet. Before finalizing the workbook, you will turn on *Track Changes* and check for compatibility issues with earlier versions of Excel.

Skills needed to complete this project:

- Importing Data from Access (Skill 9.1)
- Adding Data Validation (Skill 9.6)
- Consolidating Data in a Summary Worksheet (Skill 9.9)
- Creating a Drop-Down List for Data Entry (Skill 9.8)
- Adding an Input Message and Error Alert to Data Validation (Skill 9.7)
- Working with Comments (Skill 9.10)
- Inserting Hyperlinks (Skill 9.11)
- Converting Data to Columns (Skill 9.5)
- Tracking Changes (Skill 9.14)
- Protecting Worksheets and Workbooks from Changes (Skill 9.13)
- Sharing a Workbook (Skill 9.12)
- Checking for Compatibility with Previous Versions of Excel (Skill 9.15)

1. Open the start file **EX2016-SkillReview-9-1** and resave the file as:
   `[your initials]EX-SkillReview-9-1`
2. If the workbook opens in Protected View, click the **Enable Editing** button in the Message Bar at the top of the workbook so you can modify the workbook.
3. Import student grades from the **WeeklyQuizQry** query (view) in the *Gradebook* Access database.
   a. Go to the **Weekly Quiz** worksheet.
   b. On the *Data* tab, in the *Get External Data* group, click the **From Access** button.
   c. Navigate to the location where the data files for this project were saved. Double-click the **Gradebook** Access database to open it.
   d. In the *Select Table* dialog, click **WeeklyQuizQry**. Click **OK**.
   e. In the *Import Data* dialog, click **OK** to import the data as a table in the existing worksheet.
4. Import student grades from the **HomeworkQry** query (view) in the *Gradebook* Access database.

a. Go to the **Homework** worksheet.
b. On the *Data* tab, in the *Get External Data* group, click the **From Access** button.
c. Navigate to the location where the data files for this project were saved. Double-click the **Gradebook** Access database to open it.
d. In the *Select Table* dialog, click **HomeworkQry**. Click **OK**.
e. In the *Import Data* dialog, click **OK** to import the data as a table in cell A1 in the existing worksheet.

5. Import student grades from the **ExtraAssignmentsQry** query (view) in the *Gradebook* Access database.
   a. Go to the **Extra Assignments** worksheet.
   b. On the *Data* tab, in the *Get External Data* group, click the **From Access** button.
   c. Navigate to the location where the data files for this project were saved. Double-click the **Gradebook** Access database to open it.
   d. In the *Select Table* dialog, click **ExtraAssignmentsQry**. Click **OK**.
   e. In the *Import Data* dialog, click **OK** to import the data as a table in cell A1 in the existing worksheet.
6. Remove the Access database connections.
   a. On the *Data* tab, in the *Connections* group, click the **Connections** button.
   b. In the *Workbook Connections* dialog, click each connection listed and then click the **Remove** button.
   c. When prompted by Excel, click **OK** to remove each connection.
   d. When you have removed all connections, click the **Close** button to close the dialog.
7. Add data validation to the imported data to find any grades that are whole numbers and are less than 0 or greater than 100. You will need to do this for each worksheet.
   a. Select cells **C2:L8** on the **Weekly Quiz** worksheet.
   b. On the *Data* tab, in the *Data Tools* group, click the **Data Validation** button.
   c. In the *Data Validation* dialog, expand the **Allow** list and select **Whole Number**.
   d. Verify that the *Data* box displays **Between**.
   e. Type `0` in the *Minimum* box.
   f. Type `100` in the *Maximum* box.
   g. Click **OK**.
   h. On the *Data* tab, in the *Data Tools* group, click the **Data Validation** button arrow and select **Circle Invalid** data. There should be no invalid data in this worksheet.

8. Repeat steps 7a–h for the **Homework** and **Extra Assignments** worksheets. You should find three invalid entries in the *Homework* worksheet. Fix them as follows:
   a. Edit the values that are negative and remove the – to make the numbers positive.
   b. Edit the value that is greater than 100 and change it to **`100`**
   c. When you have edited the grades, there should be no circles on the worksheet.
9. Use Consolidate to create a single grade for each week averaging the grades from the *Weekly Quiz*, *Homework*, and *Extra Assignments* worksheets.
   a. Go to the **Final Grades** worksheet.
   b. Select cells **B2:K8**.
   c. On the *Data* tab, in the *Data Tools* group, click the **Consolidate** button.
   d. If there are existing references in the *All References* box, remove them by clicking each one and then clicking the **Delete** button.
   e. Expand the *Function* list and select **Average**.
   f. Add the first reference. Click in the **Reference** box.
   g. Click the **Weekly Quiz** worksheet tab and click and drag to select cells **C2:L8**.
   h. Click **Add**.
   i. Click the **Homework** worksheet tab and then click **Add**.
   j. Click the **Extra Assignments** worksheet tab and then click **Add**.
   k. Verify that the **Create links to source data** check box is ***not*** checked.
   l. Click **OK**.
10. Add a drop-down list to limit extra credit to specific values.
   a. On the *Final Grades* worksheet, select cells **N2:N8**.
   b. On the *Data* tab, in the *Data Tools* group, click the **Data Validation** button.
   c. In the *Data Validation* dialog, expand the **Allow** list and select **List**.
   d. In the *Source* box, type: **`10, 25, 50`**
   e. Click **OK**.
   f. Verify that the in-cell drop-down list appears as expected and add the extra credit value 25 to the first student in the gradebook.
11. Add an error alert to the cells with data validation.
   a. On the *Final Grades* worksheet, select cells **N2:N8**.
   b. On the *Data* tab, in the *Data Tools* group, click the **Data Validation** button.
   c. In the *Data Validation* dialog, click the **Error Alert** tab.
   d. In the *Error message* box, type: **`Extra credit must be 10, 25, or 50 points`**
   e. Click **OK**.

f. Verify that the error alert works as expected by typing 35 in cell **O3**. When the alert appears, click **Cancel**.

12. Add a comment about the changed grade.
    a. Select cell **Q2**.
    b. On the *Review* tab, in the *Comments* group, click the **New Comment** button.
    c. In the *Comment* balloon, type: `Grade increased to B with extra credit`
    d. Click outside the balloon.
13. Add a hyperlink to link to the *Grade Scale* worksheet.
    a. Select cell **Q1**.
    b. On the *Insert* tab, in the *Links* group, click the **Hyperlink** button.
    c. Under *Link to*, select **Place in this Document**.
    d. In the *Or select a place in this document* box, click **Grade Scale**.
    e. Verify that the cell reference in the *Type the cell reference* box is **A1**.
    f. Click **OK**.
    g. Test the link by clicking cell **Q1**.
14. Before adding worksheet protection, you should separate the student first and last names into separate columns.
    a. On the *Final Grades* worksheet, insert a new column to the right of the student names.
    b. Change the text in cell A1 to: `First Name`
    c. Press **Tab** and type `Last Name` in cell **B1**.
    d. Select cells **A2:A8**.
    e. On the *Data* tab, in the *Data Tools* group, click the **Text to Columns** button.
    f. In Step 1 of the wizard, verify that **Delimited** is selected. Click **Next**.
    g. In Step 2 of the wizard, if necessary, check the **Space** check box to separate the names at the space between the first name and the last name. Click **Next**.
    h. Review the *Data preview* box to verify that the text will be separated as you expect and then click **Finish**.
15. Unlock the extra credit cells so changes can be made after you apply worksheet protection to the gradebook.
    a. On the *Final Grades* worksheet, select cells **O2:O8**.
    b. On the *Home* tab, in the *Cells* group, click the **Format** button. Click *Lock Cell* to remove the highlight.
16. Apply worksheet protection so users can only select cells that are locked, not edit them.
    a. On the *Review* tab, in the *Changes* group, click the **Protect Sheet** button.
    b. Verify that the **Protect worksheet and content of locked cells** check box is checked.
    c. Verify that **Select locked cells** and **Select unlocked cells** are the only two options checked.

   d. Click **OK**.

17. Recall that shared workbooks cannot include tables. Before turning on *Track Changes* and sharing the workbook, you will need to convert the imported tables to ranges.
    a. Click the **Weekly Quiz** worksheet tab. Select any cell in the table. On the *Table Tools Design* tab, in the *Tools* group, click the **Convert to Range** button. Click **OK**.
    b. Repeat step 16a for the **Homework** and **Extra Assignments** worksheets.
18. Turn on *Track Changes* to highlight any changes to the workbook that have not yet been reviewed.
    a. On the *Review* tab, in the *Changes* group, click the **Track Changes** button and select **Highlight Changes...**
    b. In the *Highlight Changes* dialog, click the **Track changes while editing. This also shares your workbook.** check box.
    c. Expand the **When** box and select **Not yet reviewed**.
    d. Verify that the **Highlight changes on screen** check box is checked.
    e. Click **OK**.
    f. Click **OK** again to save the workbook.
19. Add a 25-point extra credit bonus for Manual Topaz.
    a. On the *Final Grades* worksheet, click cell **O8**.
    b. Click the arrow and select **25** from the list.
    c. Note that you can edit this cell because you unlocked it previously.
20. Accept all changes made to this workbook that have not yet been reviewed.
    a. On the *Review* tab, in the *Changes* group, click the **Track Changes** button and select **Accept/Reject Changes**.
    b. Click **OK** when prompted to save the workbook.
    c. In the *Select Changes to Accept or Reject* dialog, click **OK**.
    d. Review the change and click the **Accept** button.
21. Check for any possible compatibility issues in this workbook.
    a. Click the **File** tab.
    b. Click the **Check for Issues** button and select **Check Compatibility**.
    c. In the Compatibility Checker, review the issues, but do not make any changes.
    d. Click **OK** to close the Compatibility Checker.
22. Close the workbook.

projects

Data files for projects can be found by logging into your SIMnet account and going to the *Library* section.

skill review 9.2

In this project, you will create a summary worksheet to consolidate sales data from different regions. You will import addresses from a text file and manipulate the imported data.

Skills needed to complete this project:

- Consolidating Data in a Summary Worksheet (Skill 9.9)
- Adding Data Validation (Skill 9.6)
- Inserting Hyperlinks (Skill 9.11)
- Working with Comments (Skill 9.10)
- Importing Data from a Text File (Skill 9.2)
- Inserting Data Using Flash Fill (Skill 9.4)
- Converting Data to Columns (Skill 9.5)
- Protecting Worksheets and Workbooks from Changes (Skill 9.13)
- Checking for Compatibility with Previous Versions of Excel (Skill 9.15)
- Finalizing the Workbook (Skill 9.19)

1. Open the start file **EX2016-SkillReview-9-2** and resave the file as: `[your initials]EX-SkillReview-9-2`
2. If the workbook opens in Protected View, click the **Enable Editing** button in the Message Bar at the top of the workbook so you can modify the workbook.
3. Use Consolidate to create a summary sheet totaling sales from the *Northeast*, *Southeast*, *Southwest*, and *Northwest* worksheets. Include links to the source data.
   a. Go to the **Summary** worksheet.
   b. Select cells **B4:E11**.
   c. On the *Data* tab, in the *Data Tools* group, click the **Consolidate** button.
   d. If there are existing references in the *All References* box, remove them by clicking each one and then clicking the **Delete** button.
   e. Verify that **Sum** is selected in the *Function* list.
   f. Add the first reference. Click in the **Reference** box.
   g. Click the **Northeast** worksheet tab and click and drag to select cells **B3:E10**.
   h. Click **Add**.
   i. Click the **Southeast** worksheet tab and then click **Add**.
   j. Click the **Southwest** worksheet tab and then click **Add**.
   k. Click the **Northwest** worksheet tab and then click **Add**.

l. If necessary, click the **Create links to source data** check box to add a checkmark.
m. Click **OK**.

4. Expand the details for the Equipment sales type category and add data validation to find any individual sales less than 65,000.
   a. On the *Summary* worksheet, click the + next to *Equipment*.
   b. Select cells **B4:E7**.
   c. On the *Data* tab, in the *Data Tools* group, click the **Data Validation** button.
   d. In the *Data Validation* dialog, expand the **Allow** list and select **Whole Number**.
   e. Expand the **Data** list and select **greater than**.
   f. Type `65,000` in the *Minimum* box.
   g. Click **OK**.
   h. On the *Data* tab, in the *Data Tools* group, click the **Data Validation** button arrow and select **Circle Invalid** data. There should be one value circled.
5. Add a hyperlink from the circled cell to the cell in the source worksheet.
   a. On the *Summary* worksheet, click cell **B5**. Look in the address bar to see the cell reference for this particular value.
   b. On the *Insert* tab, in the *Links* group, click the **Hyperlink** button.
   c. Under *Link to*, select **Place in this Document**.
   d. In the *Type the cell reference* box, type: `B3`
   e. In the *Or select a place in this document* box, click **Northwest**.
   f. Click **OK**.
   g. Test the link by clicking cell **B5**.
6. Add a comment.
   a. Select cell **B3** in the *Northwest* worksheet.
   b. On the *Review* tab, in the *Comments* group, click the **New Comment** button.
   c. In the *Comment* balloon, type: `Why did sales drop?`
   d. Click outside the balloon.
7. Import sales associate addresses from the tab-delimited text file *SalesAssociateAddressList*. You will create a new worksheet when you import the data.
   a. On the *Data* tab, in the *Get External Data* group, click the **From Text** button.
   b. Navigate to the location where the data files for this project were saved. Double-click the **SalesAssociateAddressList** text file to open it.
   c. In Step 1 of the wizard, verify that delimited is selected. Click **Next**.
   d. In Step 2 of the wizard, click the **Tab** check box if it is not already checked. Click **Next**.
   e. Click **Finish**.

f. In the *Import Data* dialog, click the **New worksheet** radio button under **Where do you want to put the data?**

g. Click **OK**.

8. Double-click the new worksheet tab and rename it: `AddressList`
9. Remove the text file connection.

a. On the *Data* tab, in the *Connections* group, click the **Connections** button.

b. In the *Workbook Connections* dialog, click the connection listed, and then click the **Remove** button.

c. When prompted by Excel, click **OK** to remove the connection.

d. Click the **Close** button to close the dialog.

10. Use Flash Fill to correct the phone number format.

a. On the *AddressList* worksheet, type `Fixed Mobile Phone Format` in cell **D1**. Make the column wider if necessary.

b. Type the new phone number format in cell **D2**: `(916) 555-1324`

c. Press **Enter** or click in cell **D3**.

d. On the *Data* tab, in the *Data Tools* group, click the **Flash Fill** button.

e. Delete column **C**.

11. Use Text to Columns to separate the address into columns for the street address, the city, the state, and the zip code.

a. On the *AddressList* worksheet, insert three columns to the right of the **Address** column.

b. Change the text in cell **B1** to: `Street Address`

c. Press **Tab** and type `City` in cell **C1**.

d. Press **Tab** and type `State` in cell **D1**.

e. Press **Tab** and type `Zip` in cell **E1**.

f. Select cells **B2:B9**.

g. On the *Data* tab, in the *Data Tools* group, click the **Text to Columns** button.

h. In Step 1 of the wizard, verify that **Delimited** is selected. Click **Next**.

i. In Step 2 of the wizard, if necessary, check the **Comma** check box. Click **Next**.

j. Review the *Data preview* box to verify that the text will be separated as you expect and then click **Finish**.

12. Unlock the address and mobile phone cells so changes can be made if you later apply worksheet protection to the workbook.

a. On the *AddressList* worksheet, select cells **B2:F9**.

b. On the *Home* tab, in the *Cells* group, click the **Format** button. Click **Lock Cell** to remove the highlight.

13. Apply worksheet protection so users can only select cells that are locked, not edit them.

a. On the *Review* tab, in the *Changes* group, click the **Protect Sheet** button.

b. Verify that the **Protect worksheet and content of locked cells** check box is checked.

c. Verify that **Select locked cells** and **Select unlocked cells** are the only two options checked.

d. Click **OK**.

14. Close the workbook.

projects

Data files for projects can be found by logging into your SIMnet account and going to the *Library* section.

challenge yourself 9.3

In this project, you will create a summary worksheet to consolidate real estate sales data for different types of properties. You will import sales data from a text file and manipulate the imported data.

Skills needed to complete this project:

- Consolidating Data in a Summary Worksheet (Skill 9.9)
- Importing Data from a Text File (Skill 9.2)
- Creating a Drop-Down List for Data Entry (Skill 9.8)
- Adding an Input Message and Error Alert to Data Validation (Skill 9.7)
- Adding Data Validation (Skill 9.6)
- Working with Comments (Skill 9.10)
- Inserting Data Using Flash Fill (Skill 9.4)
- Inserting Hyperlinks (Skill 9.11)
- Protecting Worksheets and Workbooks from Changes (Skill 9.13)
- Checking for Compatibility with Previous Versions of Excel (Skill 9.15)
- Finalizing the Workbook (Skill 9.19)

1. Open the start file **EX2016-ChallengeYourself-9-3** and resave the file as: `[your initials]EX-ChallengeYourself-9-3`
2. If the workbook opens in Protected View, click the **Enable Editing** button in the Message Bar at the top of the workbook so you can modify the workbook.
3. Use Consolidate to create a summary of real estate sales for all property types. Place the consolidated data on the *Summary* worksheet in cells **B3:C15**. Use the **Average** function to consolidate the data from cells **B2:C14** in the **Condo**, **Townhouse**, and **Single Family** worksheets. Include links to the source data.
4. Import individual sales data from the tab-delimited text file **Select Sales Data 2016-2017**. Import the data as a table in cell **A1** of the **Select Sales** worksheet.
5. Remove the data connection when the import is complete.
6. In the *Select Sales* worksheet, add data validation to restrict values in the *House Type* columns (cells **B2:B139**) to the values in the cell range named **PropertyTypes**. Include a drop-down list of values in the cells to assist in data correction.
7. Add the following input message to cells **B2:B139**: `Select a property type from the list.`
8. Add the following error alert to cells **B2:B139**: `Not a valid property type.`

9. Apply data validation circles to any values that violate the data validation rules you just created.
10. Add a comment to cell **B1** in the *Select Sales* worksheet that reads: **`We need to fix these data.`**
11. Add a hyperlink from cell **B1** in the *Select Sales* worksheet to link to the named range (defined name) **PropertyTypes**. Test the link.
12. Use Flash Fill to add a new column of data to the *Select Sales* worksheet to display the number of bedrooms/the number of bathrooms.
    a. In the *Select Sales* worksheet, cell **F1**, type the heading: **`BR/BA`**
    b. Complete the column of data using this pattern in cell **F2**: **`1 BR/1 BA`**
    You will need to enter at least two samples in order for Flash Fill to suggest the correct autofill data. Check your work carefully.
13. Apply worksheet protection to the *Select Sales* worksheet so users can only select cells, not edit them. Do not unlock any cells.
14. Check for any possible compatibility issues in this workbook.
15. Mark the workbook as final.
16. Close the workbook.

projects

Data files for projects can be found by logging into your SIMnet account and going to the *Library* section.

challenge yourself 9.4

In this project, you will use data validation to identify missing and incorrect data. You will create a summary worksheet to consolidate data about vaccine shipments, and then you will import data from the *Vaccines* Access database and manipulate the data.

Skills needed to complete this project:

- Adding Data Validation (Skill 9.6)
- Working with Comments (Skill 9.10)
- Protecting Worksheets and Workbooks from Changes (Skill 9.13)
- Creating a Drop-Down List for Data Entry (Skill 9.8)
- Inserting Hyperlinks (Skill 9.11)
- Consolidating Data in a Summary Worksheet (Skill 9.9)
- Converting Data to Columns (Skill 9.5)
- Importing Data from Access (Skill 9.1)
- Checking for Compatibility with Previous Versions of Excel (Skill 9.15)
- Finalizing the Workbook (Skill 9.19)

1. Open the start file **EX2016-ChallengeYourself-9-4** and resave the file as: `[your initials]EX-ChallengeYourself-9-4`
2. If the workbook opens in Protected View, click the **Enable Editing** button in the Message Bar at the top of the workbook so you can modify the workbook.
3. Apply data validation rules to cells **F15:F24** on the **2016 Shipments** worksheet and cells **F15:F26** on the **2017 Shipments** worksheet.
    a. Require whole numbers between 500 and 5,000.
    b. Do not allow blanks.
    c. Circle invalid data in both the **2016 Shipments** and **2017 Shipments** worksheets.
4. Add this comment to cell **F20** on the **2017 Shipments** worksheet: **`Look up cost.`**
5. Unlock the blank cells so someone can update the data after the worksheet protection has been applied. *Hint:* There is one cell on the *2016 Shipments* worksheet and one cell on the *2017 Shipments* worksheet. Use the data validation circles to find them.
6. Apply data validation rules to cells **C15:C24** on the **2016 Shipments** worksheet and cells **C15:C26** on the **2017 Shipments** worksheet.

   a. Values for these cells must come from the **Locations** named range.
   b. Include an in-cell drop-down list. Do not allow blanks.
   c. Circle invalid data in both the **2016 Shipments** and **2017 Shipments** worksheets.
7. Add a hyperlink to cell **C16** on the **2016 Shipments** worksheets to link to cell **A26** on the **Locations** worksheet. Test the link.
8. Use Consolidate to create a summary of total units shipped and total cost to date.
   a. Place the consolidated data on the **Summary** worksheet in cells **B2:C10**.
   b. Use the **Sum** function to consolidate the data from cells **B3:C11** in the **2013** and **2014** worksheets.
   c. Include links to the source data.
9. Use Consolidate to create a summary of average total units shipped and total cost to date.
   a. Place the consolidated data on the **Summary** worksheet in cells **B31:C39**.
   b. Use the **Average** function to consolidate the data from cells **B3:C11** in the **2013** and **2014** worksheets.
   c. ***Do not*** include links to the source data.
10. On the **Locations** worksheet, use Text to Columns to separate the city and country names into separate columns.
    a. The city name should remain in column B, and the country name should be moved to column C.
    b. Add the text `Country` to cell **C1**.
    c. Use Format Painter to copy the formatting from cell **B1** to cell **C1**.
11. Import data from the **Vaccines** table in the **Vaccines** Access database to cell **A1** in the **Vaccines** worksheet. The database should be located in the folder where the data files for this project were saved. When you are finished with the import, delete the data connection.
12. Check for any possible compatibility issues in this workbook.
13. Mark the workbook as final.
14. Close the workbook.

Data files for projects can be found by logging into your SIMnet account and going to the *Library* section.

on your own 9.5

In this project, you will work with a university registration workbook. You will import data from an Access database and manipulate the data in workbook to create a summary worksheet.

Skills needed to complete this project:

- Consolidating Data in a Summary Worksheet (Skill 9.9)
- Adding Data Validation (Skill 9.6)
- Adding an Input Message and Error Alert to Data Validation (Skill 9.7)
- Importing Data from Access (Skill 9.1)
- Creating a Drop-Down List for Data Entry (Skill 9.8)
- Working with Comments (Skill 9.10)
- Protecting Worksheets and Workbooks from Changes (Skill 9.13)
- Inserting Hyperlinks (Skill 9.11)
- Exporting to Text Formats (Skill 9.3)
- Checking for Compatibility with Previous Versions of Excel (Skill 9.15)
- Finalizing the Workbook (Skill 9.19)

1. Open the start file **EX2016-OnYourOwn-9-5** and resave the file as: `[your initials]EX-OnYourOwn-9-5`
2. If the workbook opens in Protected View, click the **Enable Editing** button in the Message Bar at the top of the workbook so you can modify the workbook.
3. This workbook includes four worksheets of student GPA and average credit hour data. Create a summary worksheet to calculate average GPA and credit hours for all students for each of the advisors.
4. Apply data validation rules to restrict the credit hours in each worksheet to values appropriate for that level of university student. Add input messages and error alerts to help users enter data correctly.
5. Import the **Class**, **Course**, **Department**, and **Professor** tables from the **University Registration** Access database. The database should be located in the folder where the data files for this project were saved. Remember to remove the data connections when you are finished importing the data.
6. Apply data validation rules to restrict future data entry as appropriate. Try creating a named range of all the department codes and applying a data validation rule wherever department codes are references.

7. Create a hyperlink somewhere in the workbook to link to an appropriate Web page on your school's Web site listing departments or faculty.
8. Save one of the worksheets in a variety of text formats. Be sure to save a copy of the workbook in the default Excel Workbook format before saving as a text file or you will lose your work!
9. Open the Excel Workbook version of your file, and try re-importing data from the text files you saved. How does the imported data compare to the original worksheet you exported?
10. Run Compatibility Checker and Document Inspector before saving the workbook as final.
11. Save the workbook as final and close it.

projects

Data files for projects can be found by logging into your SIMnet account and going to the *Library* section.

fix it 9.6

In this project, you will make corrections to a party planning workbook. Some of the data in this worksheet were imported from other programs and are not formatted correctly for purposes of this workbook.

Skills needed to complete this project:

- Inserting Data Using Flash Fill (Skill 9.4)
- Converting Data to Columns (Skill 9.5)
- Inserting Hyperlinks (Skill 9.11)
- Consolidating Data in a Summary Worksheet (Skill 9.9)
- Adding Data Validation (Skill 9.6)
- Adding an Input Message and Error Alert to Data Validation (Skill 9.7)
- Protecting Worksheets and Workbooks from Changes (Skill 9.13)

1. Open the start file **EX2016-FixIt-9-6** and resave the file as:
   `[your initials]EX-FixIt-9-6`
2. If the workbook opens in Protected View, click the **Enable Editing** button in the Message Bar at the top of the workbook so you can modify the workbook.
3. Use Flash Fill to complete the missing data on the *Guest List* worksheet.
   a. In the *NameTag* column, please complete the list of name. The names should be in all upper case letters similar to the name in cell **C3**. *Hint:* Flash Fill may not complete the data automatically. You may need to use the *Flash Fill* command.
   b. In order to send the addresses to the printer, the city, state, and zip code need to be in a single column in the format **City, State Zip**. Complete the data in column **H**.
4. On the *Places to Shop* worksheet, use Text to Columns and Flash Fill to fix the following issues:
   a. The address should be separated into separate columns for Street, City, State, and Zip.
   b. The phone number should use the format **###-####**. Someone used Flash Fill previously to complete the data, but the phone numbers were not autofilled completely. Delete the data in column I and then redo the Flash Fill using a couple of examples and verify that the autofill works as expected.
5. On the *Week Before* worksheet, the hyperlink in cell **A2** links to the wrong cell in the *Places to Shop* worksheet. It should link to cell **A11**, not cell A12.

6. Add links to the source from the data consolidation in cells **C2:C16** in the **Total Budget** worksheet. When you open the *Consolidate* dialog, the references are there for you. All you need to do is generate the links to the source data.
7. No single budget item should be more than $3,000.
   a. Add data validation to cells **C2:C16** on the *Week Before*, *1 Month Before*, and *2 Months Before* worksheets to require decimal values less than 3,000. Ignore blank cells.
   b. Add the following error alert to the cells with data validation: `Budget must be less than 3,000.`
8. Before saving the file, protect ***all*** the worksheets so no changes can be made and protect the workbook so the structure cannot be modified.
9. Save and close the workbook.

chapter 10

Working with Macros

In this chapter, you will learn the following skills:

- Understand macro security warnings
- Define a trusted location
- Add the Developer tab to the Ribbon
- Use, record, and modify macros
- Work with VBA in the Visual Basic Editor
- Add macros to the Ribbon and the Quick Access Toolbar

introduction

In this chapter you will work with macro-enabled workbooks. First, you will learn to enable and use existing macros, and then you will record and edit a macro on your own. You will add a custom button to the workbook to run a macro. Finally, you will customize the Excel interface by adding a new tab and group to the Ribbon and adding a macro to the Quick Access Toolbar.

Skill 10.1 Opening a Macro-Enabled Workbook

A **macro** is a custom set of programming commands written in the **Visual Basic for Applications (VBA)** language. Macros are often used to simplify repetitive tasks-saving you time and effort. Instead of performing the same set of actions over and over, you can just run the macro. Macros are also useful when other, less-experienced users need to work on the workbook. You can provide them with a set of macros to use instead of expecting them to try to figure out the Excel commands on their own.

Macros are available only in macro-enabled workbooks. A workbook that can include macros has the file extension **.xlsm**; macro-enabled templates use the file extension **.xltm**. Macro-enabled files also use a slightly different file icon as shown in Figure EX 10.1.

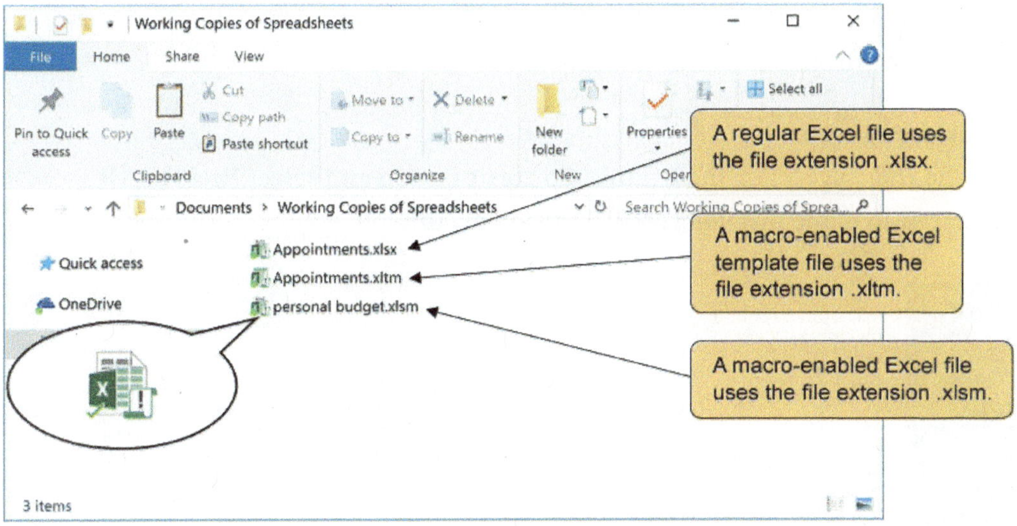

FIGURE EX 10.1

When you open a workbook that contains macros, the Message Bar appears below the Ribbon with a security warning that macros have been disabled. You must click the **Enable Content** button to enable macros in the workbook. Clicking *Enable Content* enables macros for this session only. If you reopen the file later, you will see the same message and will need to click **Enable Content** again.

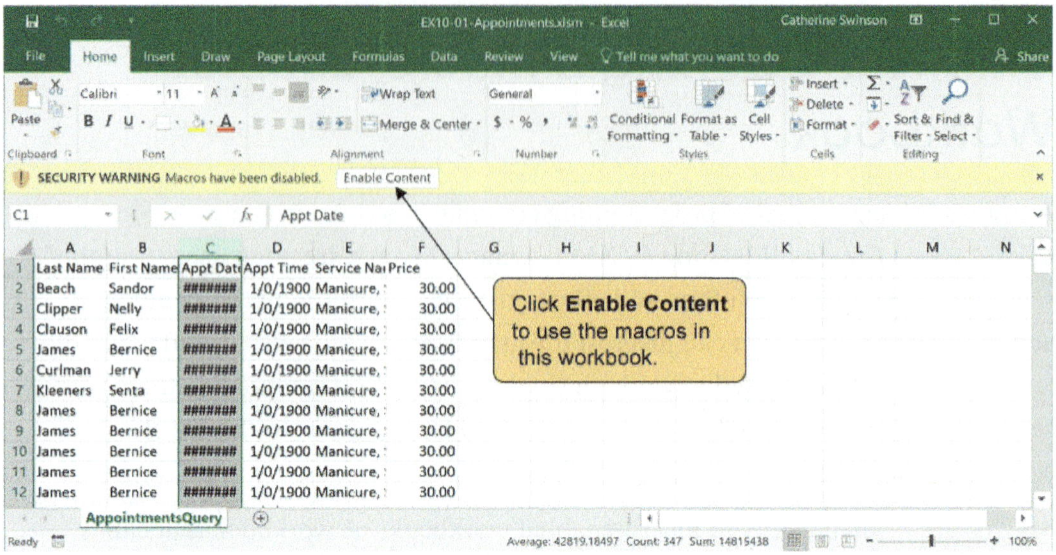

FIGURE EX 10.2

If you do not want this warning to appear every time the workbook is opened, you can make the workbook a **trusted document**. Marking the workbook as trusted allows all active content to run without warning including macros, data connections, and ActiveX controls.

1. Click the **File** tab.
2. On the *Info* page, click the **Enable Content** button and select **Enable All Content** to make this workbook a trusted document.

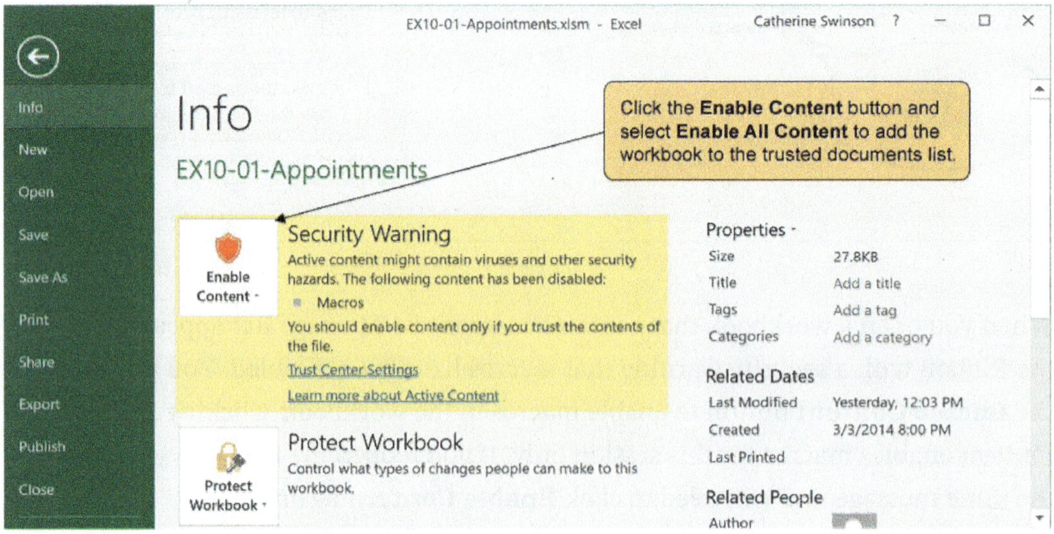

FIGURE EX 10.3

For more information about working with trusted documents, refer to the skill *Changing the Trust Center Settings*.

tips & tricks

- If you begin working without enabling the content, the message disappears, but Excel will not allow you to run macros without first closing the workbook and reopening it with active content enabled.
- If you are working in a computer lab or other environment where the administrator has restricted permissions, you may not be able to enable macros or add the workbook to the trusted documents list.

tell me more

In Windows 10, to display the file name extensions in the Explorer window, on the *View* tab, in the *Show/Hide* group, click the **File name extensions** check box to add a checkmark.

let me try *Live!*

Open the student data file **EX10-01-Appointments** and try this skill on your own:

1. Enable the active content in this workbook for just this session.
2. Close the file without saving it, and then reopen it.
3. Always enable this workbook's active content by making it a trusted document.
4. Save the file.
5. If you will be moving on to the next skill in this chapter, leave the workbook open to continue working. If not, save the file as directed by your instructor and close it.

Skill 10.2 Changing the Trust Center Settings

By default, Excel allows you to open all files that contain macros, but disables the macros unless you explicitly enable the content. If you open a file that you know contains macros, but you do not see the *Enable Content* button on the Message Bar, Excel may be set to disable all macros automatically without warning.

To check the macro security settings, open the **Trust Center**.

1. Click the **File** tab.
2. Click the **Options** button to open the *Excel Options* dialog.
3. Click **Trust Center**, and then click the **Trust Center Settings...** button to open the Trust Center.
4. Click **Macro Settings** and review the current setting. If necessary, click the **Disable all macros with notification** radio button and click **OK**.
5. Click **OK** to close the *Excel Options* dialog.

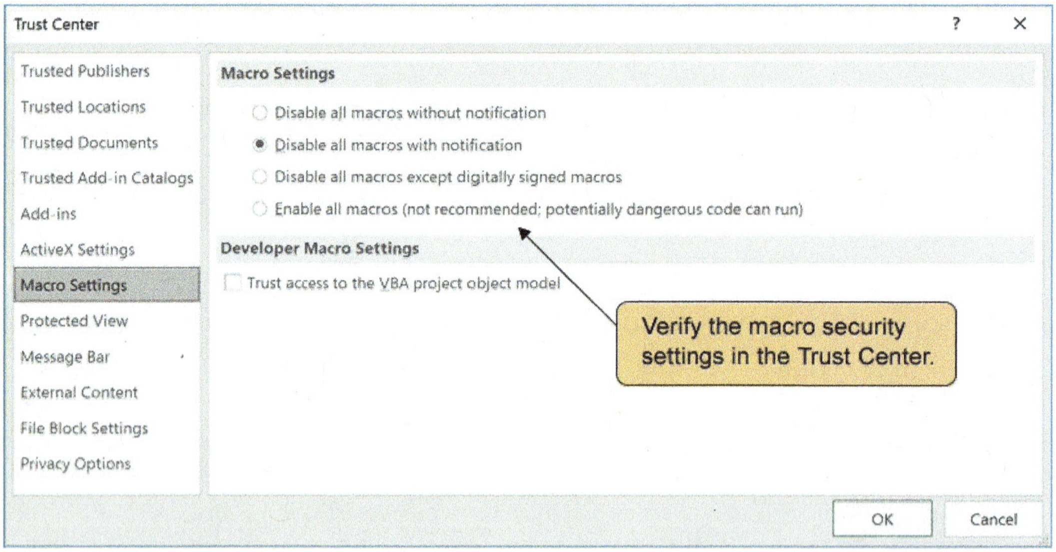

FIGURE EX 10.4

If you work extensively with macro-enabled files, you may want to store them in a folder designated as a trusted location. Files that are opened from a **trusted location** do not use Protected View and active content is allowed without requiring you to enable it each time you open the file. Be careful. Any changes you make to the Trust Center apply to the Excel application, not just the open workbook.

To add a location to the *Trusted Locations* list:

1. Open the Trust Center.
2. Click **Trusted Locations**.
3. Click the **Add new location...** button.
4. Click the **Browse...** button and navigate to the folder you want to use as a trusted location. Select the folder, and click **OK**.
5. Verify the folder location in the *Path* box and click **OK**.
6. The folder is added to the list of trusted locations.
7. Click **OK** to close the Trust Center.
8. Click **OK** again to close the *Excel Options* dialog.

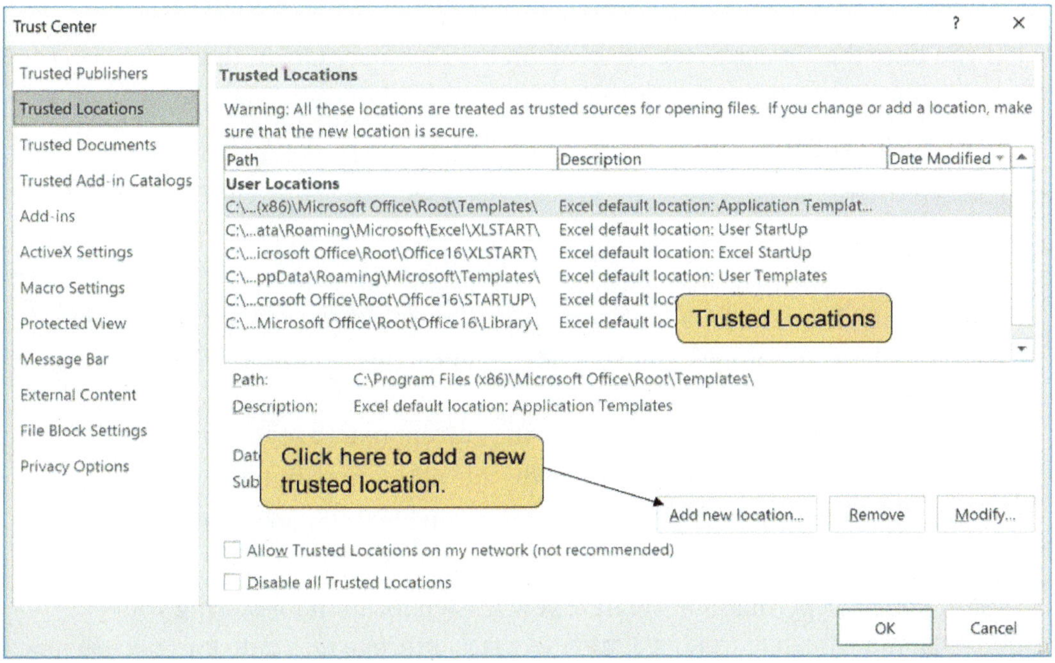

FIGURE EX 10.5

tips & tricks

Macros... what's the danger?

Because a macro runs computer code written in Visual Basic for Applications, it has the potential to contain malicious actions. You should never allow macros to run in files unless you are certain that they come from trustworthy sources.

tell me **more**

To remove a trusted location:

1. Open the Trust Center.
2. Click **Trusted Locations**.
3. Click the path in the *Trusted Locations* list, and click **Remove**.

another method

If there is a security warning active on the Info page, you can click the **Trust Center Settings** link to open the Trust Center.

If you have the *Developer* tab enabled, on the *Developer* tab, in the *Code* group, click the **Macro Security** button to open the Trust Center to the *Macro Settings* page.

let me **try** *Live!*

If you do not have the data file from the previous skill open, open the student data file **EX10-02-Appointments** and try this skill on your own:

1. Open the Trust Center and review the current macro security settings.
2. If necessary, change the setting to disable all macros, but display a warning in the Message Bar so you can choose to enable them on a case-by-case basis.
3. If you have permission, create a new trusted location for storing your macro-enabled workbooks. Be sure to use this location only for files you are certain are safe.
4. If you will be moving on to the next skill in this chapter, leave the workbook open to continue working. If not, save the file as directed by your instructor and close it.

Skill 10.3 Adding the Developer Tab to the Ribbon

Before working with macros, you should add the *Developer* tab to the Ribbon. The **Developer tab** provides easy access to macro tools in the *Code* group. Throughout the macro skills, we use the *Developer* tab as the primary method for working with macros. Most actions are also available from the *View* tab, *Macros* group.

To add the *Developer* tab to the Ribbon:

1. Click the **File** tab.
2. Click **Options** to open the *Excel Options* dialog.
3. Click **Customize Ribbon.**
4. At the right side of the *Customize the Ribbon* window, the *Customize the Ribbon* list shows all the tabs and groups available. Click the **Developer** check box to add the *Developer* tab to the Ribbon.
5. Click **OK.**

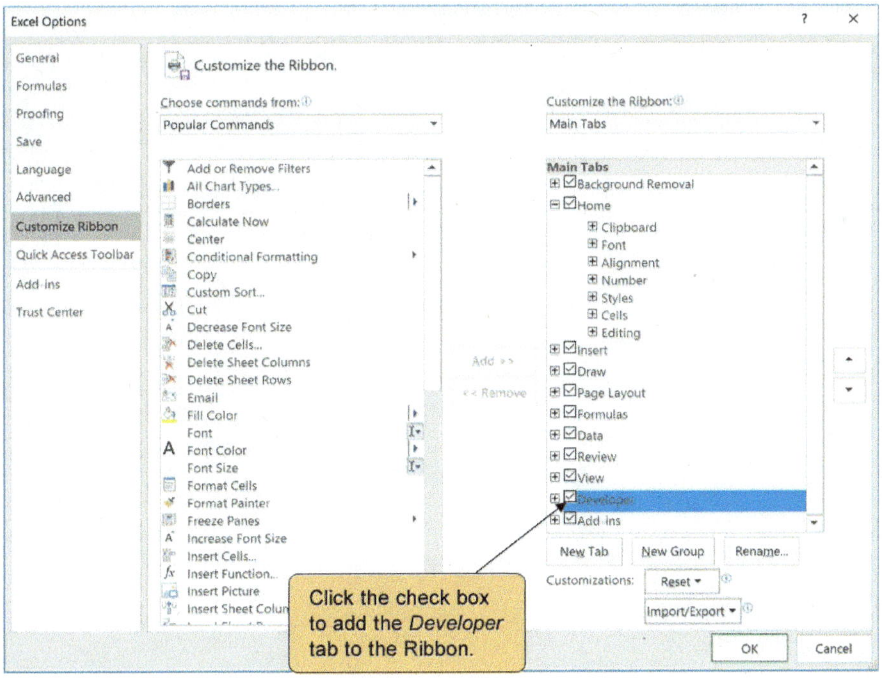

FIGURE EX 10.6

FIGURE EX 10.7

another method

Right-click any area of the Ribbon and select **Customize the Ribbon...** to open the *Excel Options* dialog to the *Customize Ribbon* page.

let me try *Live!*

If you do not have the data file from the previous skill open, open the student data file **EX10-03-Appointments** and try this skill on your own:

1. Add the *Developer* tab to the Ribbon.
2. If you will be moving on to the next skill in this chapter, leave the workbook open to continue working. If not, save the file as directed by your instructor and close it.

Skill 10.4 Running a Macro

Figure EX 10.8 shows data imported from an Access database. The macro named *FormatImport* includes all the steps that must be completed to format the data properly.

To run a macro:

1. If necessary, click the **Enable Content** button in the Message Bar to enable macros in the current workbook.
2. On the *Developer* tab, in the *Code* group, click the **Macros** button.
3. In the *Macro* dialog, click the name of the macro you want to run. Notice that a description of the purpose of the macro appears near the bottom of the dialog.
4. Click the **Run** button.

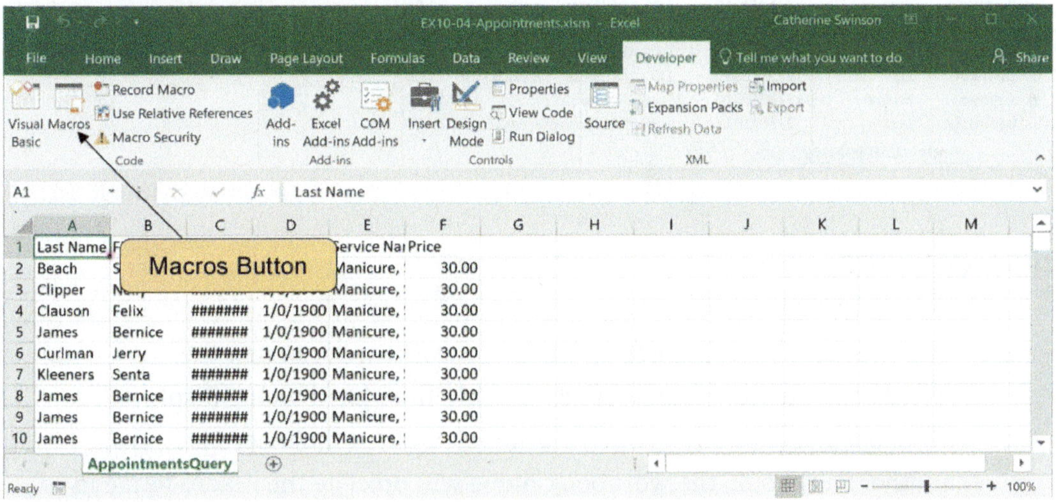

FIGURE EX 10.8

Figure EX 10.10 shows the results after running the macro. The *FormatImport* macro formatted the imported data as a table, applied a time format to column *D*, applied a number format to column *F*, and sorted the data.

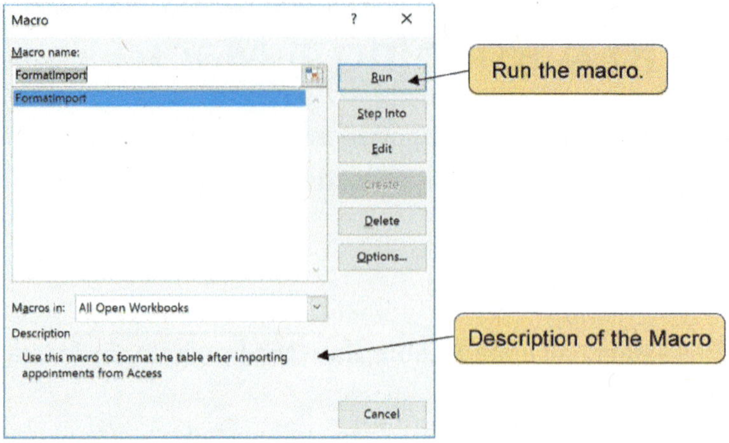

FIGURE EX 10.9

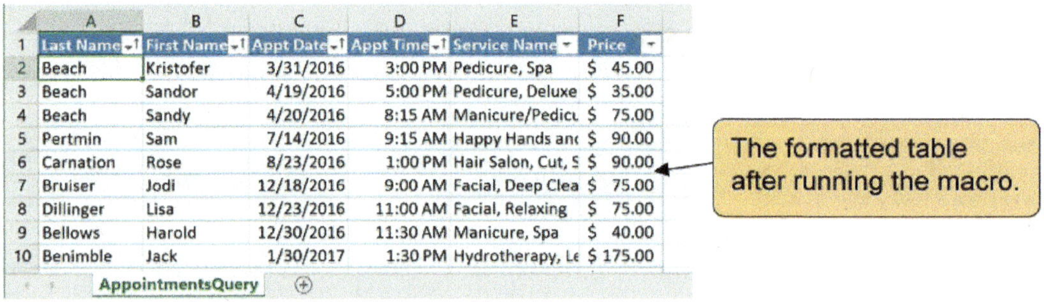

	A	B	C	D	E	F
1	Last Name	First Name	Appt Date	Appt Time	Service Name	Price
2	Beach	Kristofer	3/31/2016	3:00 PM	Pedicure, Spa	$ 45.00
3	Beach	Sandor	4/19/2016	5:00 PM	Pedicure, Deluxe	$ 35.00
4	Beach	Sandy	4/20/2016	8:15 AM	Manicure/Pedicu	$ 75.00
5	Pertmin	Sam	7/14/2016	9:15 AM	Happy Hands anc	$ 90.00
6	Carnation	Rose	8/23/2016	1:00 PM	Hair Salon, Cut, S	$ 90.00
7	Bruiser	Jodi	12/18/2016	9:00 AM	Facial, Deep Clea	$ 75.00
8	Dillinger	Lisa	12/23/2016	11:00 AM	Facial, Relaxing	$ 75.00
9	Bellows	Harold	12/30/2016	11:30 AM	Manicure, Spa	$ 40.00
10	Benimble	Jack	1/30/2017	1:30 PM	Hydrotherapy, Le	$ 175.00

FIGURE EX 10.10

tips & tricks

- You can run a macro stored in any open workbook, not just the workbook you are working on. By default, the *Macro* dialog displays available macros from all open workbooks. When the macro is from another workbook, the workbook name will precede the macro name in the *Macro* dialog.
- To see only the macros contained within a specific workbook, either expand the *Macros in* list and select the workbook file name from the list or select *This workbook* to see only macros in the current workbook.

tell me more

Many macros have a keyboard shortcut associated with them. To find the keyboard shortcut for a macro, open the *Macro* dialog, select the macro you want, and then click the **Options** button.

another method

On the *View* tab, in the *Macros* group, click the **Macros** button arrow, and then click **View Macros** to open the *Macros* dialog.

let me try *Live!*

If you do not have the data file from the previous skill open, open the student data file **EX10-04-Appointments** and try this skill on your own:

1. If necessary, enable the active content in this workbook.
2. Start with cell **A1** selected.
3. Run the **FormatImport** macro.
4. If you will be moving on to the next skill in this chapter, leave the workbook open to continue working. If not, save the file as directed by your instructor and close it.

Skill 10.5 Saving a Macro-Enabled Workbook or Template

If you add macros or other VBA code to the workbook, you will need to save it using the **Excel Macro-Enabled Workbook** (*.xlsm) format. Excel will not save macros or other code in workbooks saved in the regular .xlsx format.

To save the file in a format that supports macros:

1. Click the **File** tab.
2. Click **Save As.**
3. On the *Save As* page, if necessary, navigate to the location where you want to save the file.
4. Click the **Save as type** arrow and select **Excel Macro-Enabled Workbook (*.xlsm)**.
5. Click **Save**.

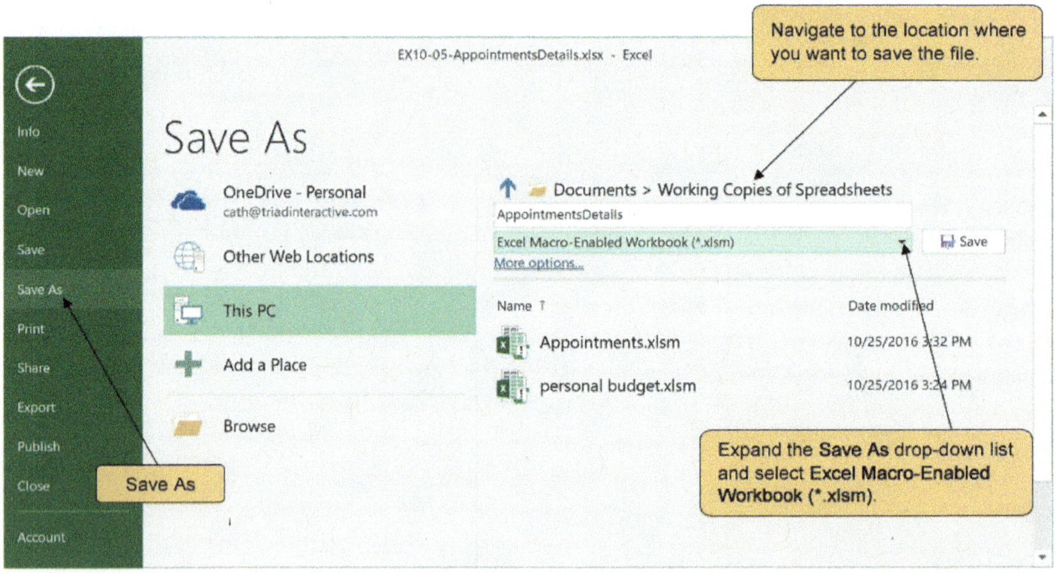

FIGURE EX 10.11

Follow the same steps to save the file as a macro-enabled template. Select the file type **Excel Macro-Enabled Template**. If you have file extensions enabled, you will see the extension ***.xltm**. Notice that when you change the file format to *Excel Macro-Enabled Template*, the *Save As* location changes to **Documents > Custom Office Templates**. This is the default location for saving new Microsoft Office templates. You can navigate to another folder if you want to save the file in another location.

tips & tricks

If you record a macro in a "regular" workbook, when you save or close the file, Excel will display a message stating that the workbook contains a VB project that cannot be saved in a macro-free workbook. Click the **No** button to open the *Save As* page so you can save the workbook in another format.

Before adding macros to a workbook, it is a good practice to save it in the macro-enabled format so you don't accidentally close the workbook without choosing the new format and lose your work.

let me try *Live!*

If you do not have the data file from the previous skill open, open the student data file **EX10-05-Appointments** and try this skill on your own:

1. This file will be used as a template. Save it with the template format that allows macros. Name the file: `Appointments-FormattingMacro`
2. Save the file as directed by your instructor and close it.
3. Open the student data file **EX10-05-AppointmentsDetails** .
4. Save the file as a macro-enabled workbook.
5. If you will be moving on to the next skill in this chapter, leave the workbook open to continue working. If not, save the file as directed by your instructor and close it.

Skill 10.6 Recording a Macro

There are two ways to create a macro. If you are familiar with the VBA programming language, you can open the Visual Basic Editor and write the programming code to instruct Excel to perform each task in the macro. The easier way to create a macro is to record it. When you record a macro, you complete all the actions you want the macro to perform, and Excel converts your keystrokes and mouse clicks to VBA code.

Macro-recording actions are available from the *Developer* tab, *Code* group.

When you have the *Developer* tab enabled, the status bar includes a button to begin recording a new macro. When a macro recording is running, this button changes to a Stop button.

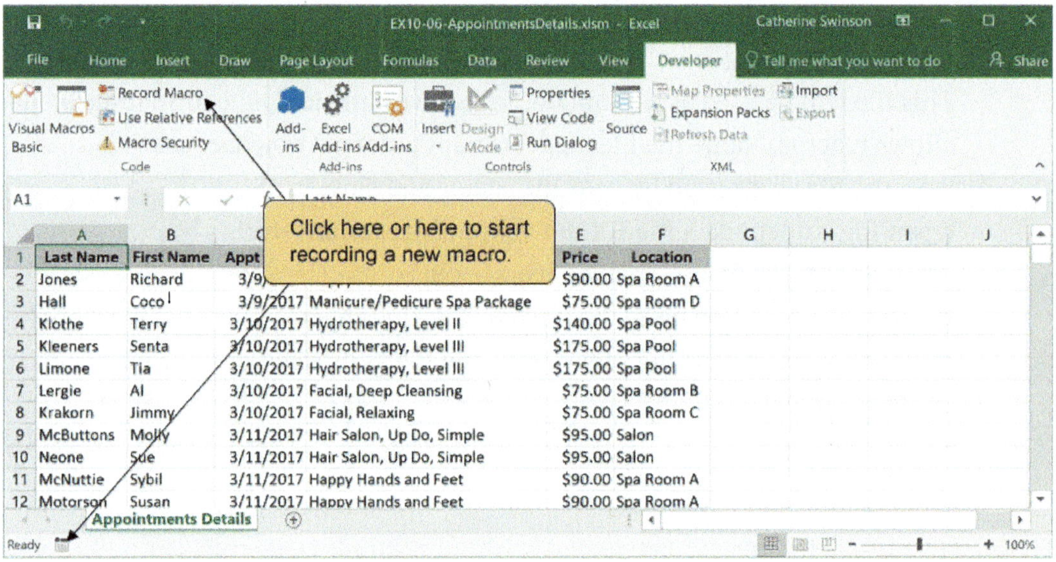

FIGURE EX 10.12

To record a macro:

1. On the *Developer* tab, in the *Code* group, click the **Record Macro** button.
2. In the *Record Macro* dialog, enter a name for the macro in the *Macro name* box.
3. If you want to create a keyboard shortcut for the macro, type the uppercase or lowercase letter in the *Shortcut key* box.
   - If you type a lowercase letter, the keyboard shortcut will be **Ctrl** + the letter you enter.
   - If you type an uppercase letter, the keyboard shortcut will be **Ctrl + Shift** the letter you enter.

4. By default, Excel stores the macro in the current workbook. If you want to store the macro in a new workbook instead, expand the **Store macro in** list and select **New Workbook.** Select **Personal Macro Workbook** to store the macro in a hidden workbook that is available whenever you use Excel. (Refer to the *Tips & Tricks* box for more information about using the personal workbook.)
5. In the *Description* box, enter a description of the tasks the macro will perform and the circumstances under which the macro should be used.
6. Click **OK** to begin recording the macro.

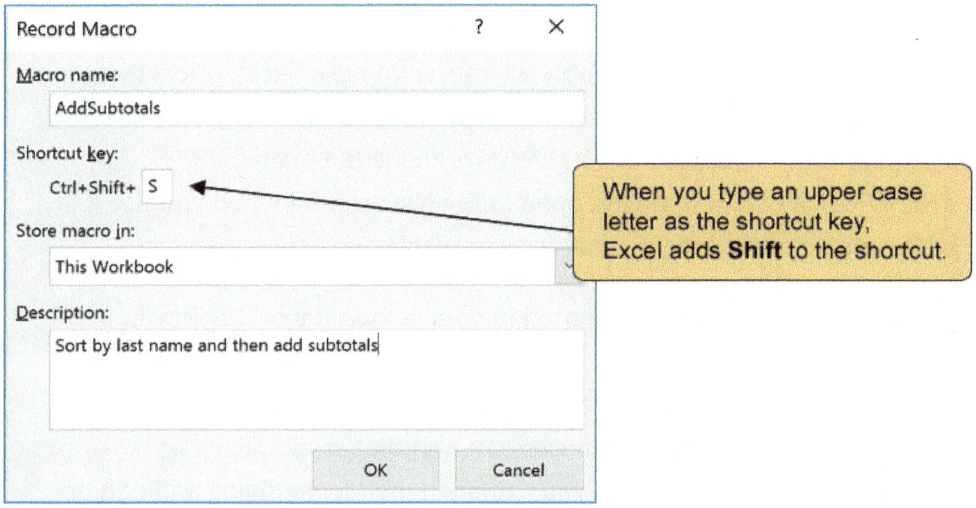

FIGURE EX 10.13

7. Excel is now recording your typing and mouse clicks to create the macro. Perform all the actions you want the macro to perform. If you make minor mistakes, you can correct them in the VBA code later.
8. When you are finished, on the *Developer* tab, in the *Code* group, click the **Stop Recording** button or click the **Stop Recording** button on the status bar.

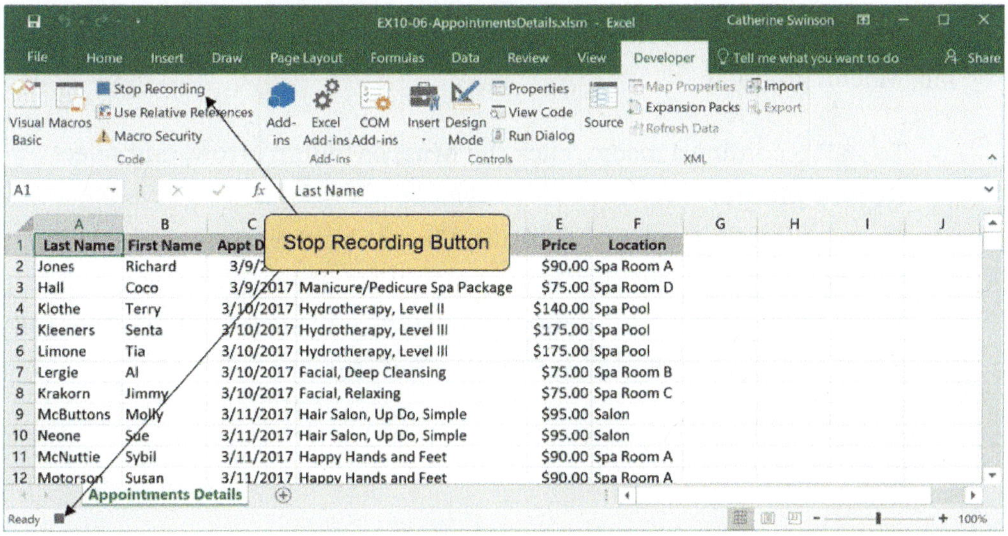

FIGURE EX 10.14

When you record a macro, you can choose whether Excel should capture cell reference as absolute or relative. By default, Excel records macros with absolute references. If you use relative cell references instead, the actions performed by the macro will be relative to the cell you select when you start the macro. On the *Developer* tab, in the *Code* group, click the **Use Relative References** button to enable or disable this option. The button appears highlighted when the option is enabled.

tips & tricks

If you want macros to be available whenever you use Excel, select **Personal Macro Workbook** as the *Store macro in* option in the *Record Macro* dialog. The **personal workbook** is a hidden workbook file named *PERSONAL.XLSB*. It is always open in the background when you use Excel, so the macros stored there are always available.

1. To delete or edit a macro stored in your personal workbook, you first need to unhide the workbook. On the *View* tab, in the *Window* group, click the **Unhide** button. In the *Unhide* dialog, click the **PERSONAL.XLSB** file if necessary, and then click **OK**.
2. Once the file is unhidden, you can open the *Macro* dialog and edit or delete macros as needed.
3. Hide the *PERSONAL.XLSB* workbook when you are finished. Do not close the file. Excel will close it automatically when you exit Excel.

another method

If the *Developer* tab is not available, you can work with macros from the *View* tab, *Macros* group.

- To start recording a macro, click the **Macros** button arrow, and select **Record Macro**.
- To stop recording a macro, click the **Macros** button arrow, and select **Stop Recording**.
- To enable or disable recording with relative references, click the **Macros** button arrow, and select **Use Relative References**.

let me try *Live!*

If you do not have the data file from the previous skill open, open the student data file **EX10-06-AppointmentsDetails** and try this skill on your own:

1. Record a new macro with the following specifications:
   a. Macro name: `AddSubtotals`
   b. Location: `This Workbook`
   c. Shortcut key: `Ctrl+Shift+S`
   d. Description: `Sort by last name and then add subtotals`
2. Record these actions in the macro:
   a. Sort the data from A-Z by the *Last Name* column.
   b. Add subtotals (*Data* tab, *Data Tools* group, **Subtotal** button). At every change in **Last Name, Sum** the values in the **Price** column.
3. Save the file as directed by your instructor and close it.

from the perspective of . . .

SMALL BUSINESS OWNER

Our accountant is an Excel expert. She develops great spreadsheets for us to analyze cash flow and inventory bottlenecks. When I first started working with these spreadsheets, I was extremely intimidated. They are full of fancy macros and complicated formulas! However, as I started recording my own macros and working with the VBA code, I began to understand what was going on behind the scenes. I'm still not a VBA programmer, but I can open the Visual Basic Editor and make simple changes on my own.

Skill 10.7 Modifying a Macro Using VBA

If you need to make a simple change to a macro, there is no need to rerecord it. Instead, you can edit the underlying VBA code in the **Visual Basic Editor (VBE)**.

To edit a macro in the Visual Basic Editor:

1. On the *Developer* tab, in the *Code* group, click the **Macros** button to open the *Macro* dialog.
2. Select the macro you want to edit, and then click the **Edit** button.

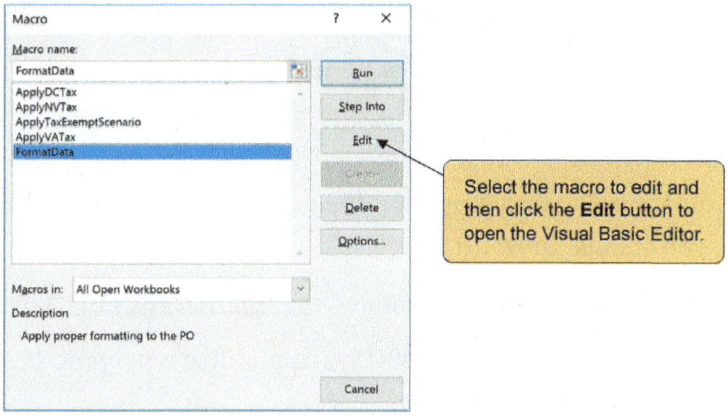

FIGURE EX 10.15

The Visual Basic Editor opens in a new window with the macro code displayed in the **code window**. If there are multiple macros stored in the same module, the VBE will open at the point where the macro you selected starts.

To navigate to the beginning of the code for another macro, if necessary, double-click the module name in the Project Explorer window, and then expand the **Procedure** list in the upper-right corner of the code window, and select the name of the macro you want to go to.

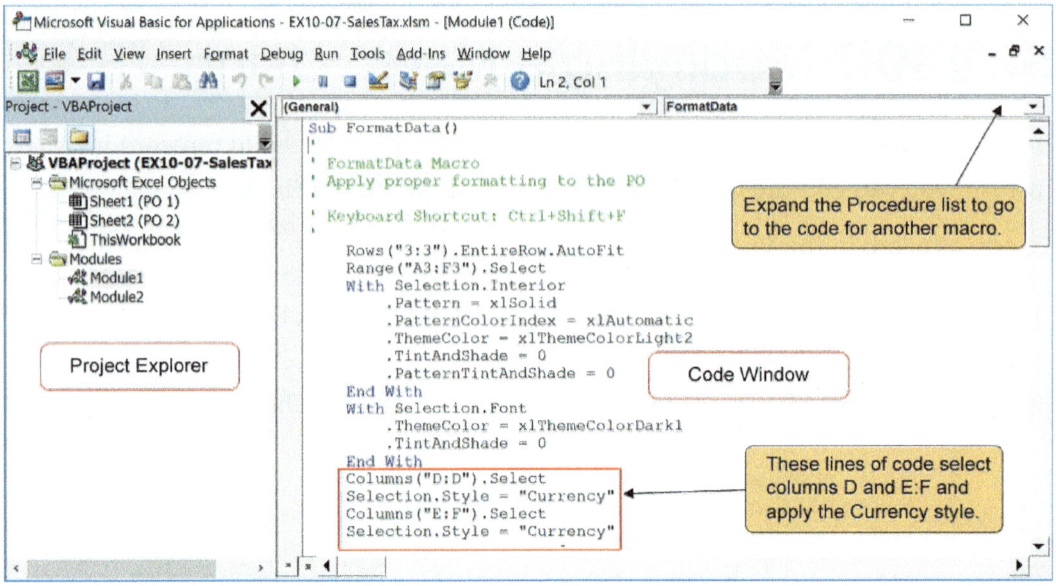

FIGURE EX 10.16

You do not need to be a programming expert to work in the VBE, but there are a few basics you should know first.

The Visual Basic Editor is a separate program that runs in its own window.

Each Excel file has its own set of VBA code called a **project**. Projects are listed in the VBE **Project Explorer** window.

Projects are made up of **modules** and **objects** that contain groups of code called **procedures**. In Excel, objects refer to the individual worksheets and the overall workbook. Procedures in objects are intended for use in that object only. Procedures in modules are usually available to any open Excel workbook. The code for each macro is stored in its own procedure within a ***module*** (not an object). A single module may contain the procedures for multiple macros.

Procedures that perform actions but do not return a value are called **subroutines**. The code for a subroutine procedure begins with the word *Sub* followed by the name of procedure (or macro) and a set of empty parentheses:

```
Sub FormatData()
```

Every programming instruction in a procedure begins on a new line. This makes it easy to find the specific instruction you want to edit. Much of the code is written in such a way that you can figure out what it does by working through it logically.

In Figure EX 10.16, the lines of code to select a column and then apply a number style look like this:

```
Columns("D:D").Select
Selection.Style = "Currency"
Columns("E:F").Select
Selection.Style = "Currency"
```

When the macro was recorded, the user selected column *D*, applied the *Currency* style, and then selected columns *E:F* and applied the *Currency* style again. You can edit the code to combine the instructions and apply the *Comma* style instead.

```
Columns("D:F").Select
Selection.Style = "Comma"
```

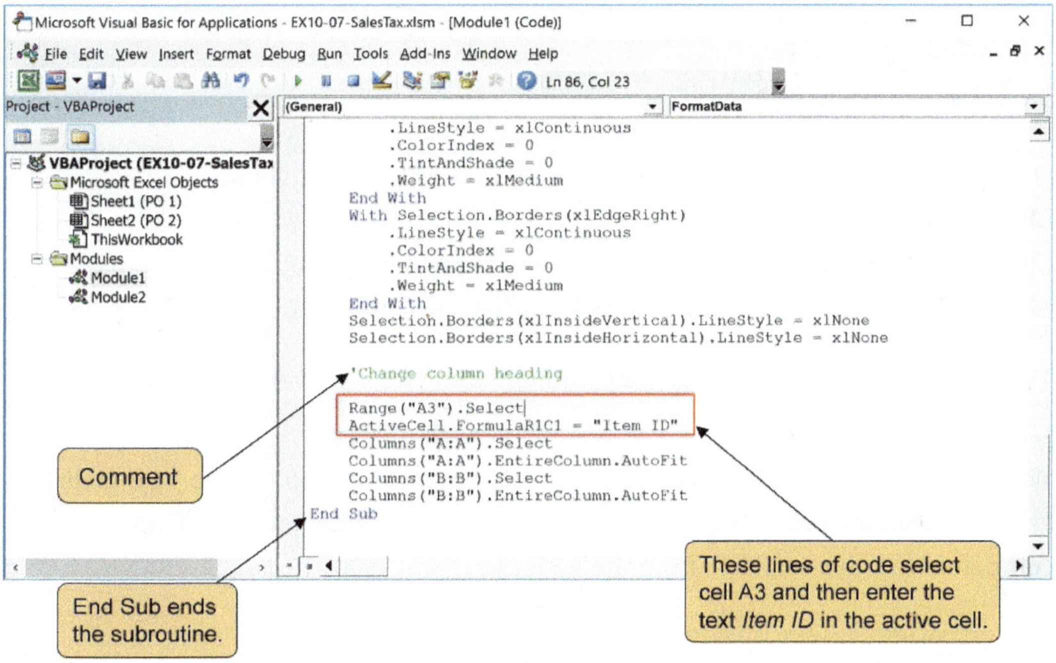

FIGURE EX 10.17

The two lines of code to select a single cell and then enter text look like this:

```
Range("A3").Select
ActiveCell.FormulaR1C1 = "Item ID"
```

To change the text *Item ID* to *Inventory ID*, edit the second line to:

```
ActiveCell.FormulaR1C1 = "Inventory ID"
```

The last line in a subroutine tells Excel that the procedure is finished and to stop executing code:

```
End Sub
```

Comments about the procedure appear in green text, and each line begins with an apostrophe. The apostrophe at the beginning of the line tells VBA to ignore the line—do not execute it as code. When you record a macro, the macro name, keyboard shortcut, and description are automatically added to the beginning of the VBA code as comments.

```
'
' FormatData Macro
' Apply proper formatting to the PO
'
' Keyboard Shortcut: Ctrl+Shift+F
'
```

To add a new comment:

1. Go to the end of the line where you want to insert the comment.
2. Press **Enter** twice to create a new line in the code.
3. Type an apostrophe and then type the comment text.
4. Press **Enter** again to place a blank line after the comment.

The blank lines before and after the comment aren't necessary, but they help break up the code visually.

When you are finished with your changes, click the **Save** button in the VBE toolbar, and then click the red X to close the VBE window and return to Excel. These commands are also available from the VBE *File* menu.

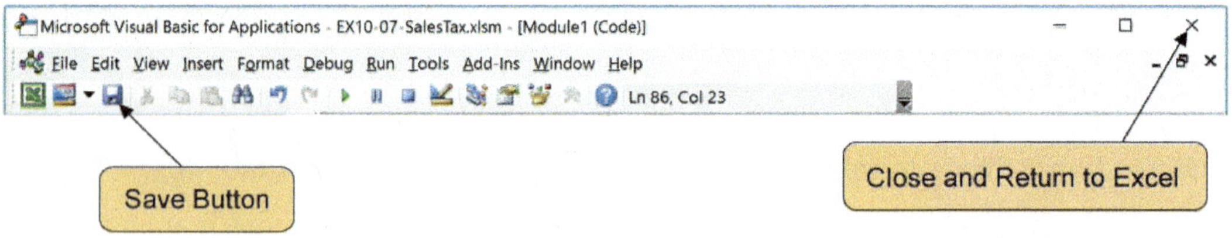

FIGURE EX 10.18

Figure EX 10.19 shows the effect of running the modified macro.

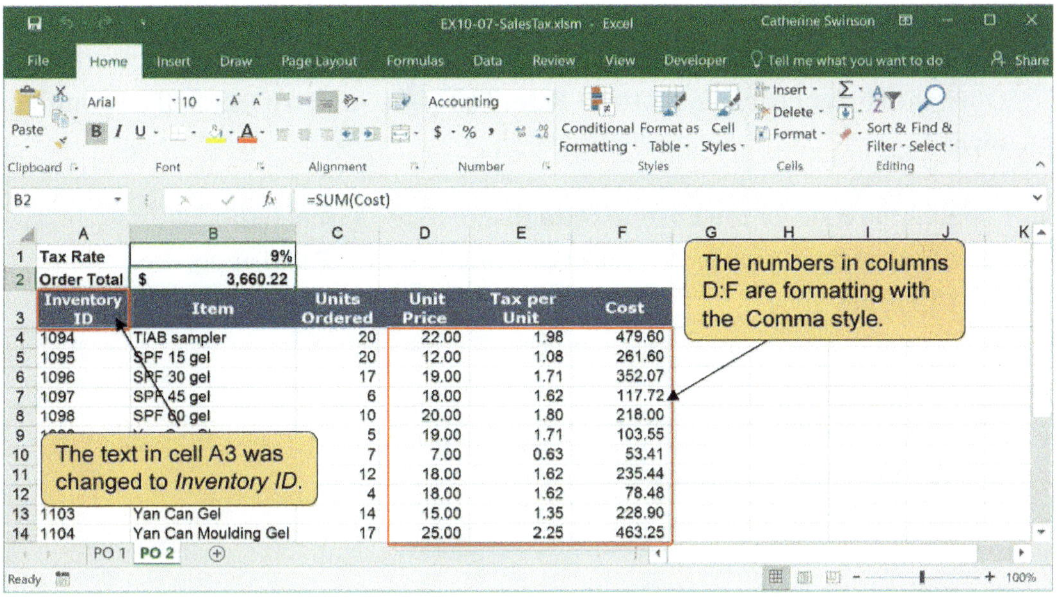

FIGURE EX 10.19

tips & tricks

The Visual Basic Editor may seem intimidating at first. Try creating a few simple macros and then working through the VBA code for each to become familiar with the VBA code for different Excel commands.

tell me more

The *Properties* window in the Visual Basic Editor lists the properties for the selected object or module. Show or hide the Properties window from the VBE *View* menu.

another method

You can also open the Visual Basic Editor and edit macros from the *View* tab.

1. On the *View* tab, in the *Macros* group, click the top half of the **Macros** button to open the *Macro* dialog.
2. Select the macro you want to edit, and then click the **Edit** button.

let me try *Live!*

Open the student data file **EX10-07-SalesTax** and try this skill on your own:

1. Edit the code for the **FormatData** macro in the Visual Basic Editor.
2. Find the lines of code that select columns **D** and **E:F** and apply the **Currency** style.

```
Columns("D:D").Select

Selection.Style = "Currency"

Columns("E:F").Select

Selection.Style = "Currency"
```

3. Modify the code to select columns **D:F** with a single command. (*Hint*: You should end up with two lines of code instead of four.)
4. Modify the code to apply the **Comma** style.
5. Find the lines of code that select cell **A3** and enter the text: `Item ID`

```
Range("A3").Select

ActiveCell.FormulaR1C1 = "Item ID"
```

6. Modify the code to enter the text `Inventory ID` instead of *Item ID*.
7. Insert a new comment `Change column heading` above the block of code you just modified. Include a blank line before and after the new comment.
8. Add other comments throughout the code to identify what each block of code does.
9. Save the changes and close the Visual Basic Editor.
10. Go to the **PO 2** worksheet and run the modified **FormatData** macro.
11. Save the file as directed by your instructor and close it.

Skill 10.8 Adding a Macro to a Form Button Control

If you use a certain macro often, consider adding a **form button control** to the worksheet to call it. Calling the macro from a button is also useful if you are going to use the workbook as a template. You can give the button a friendly name and other workbook users won't need to know which macro to select to run.

To add a form button control to run a macro:

1. On the *Developer* tab, in the *Controls* group, click the **Insert Controls** button, and click the **Command Button (Form Control)** button.
2. Click and drag on the worksheet to draw the button.

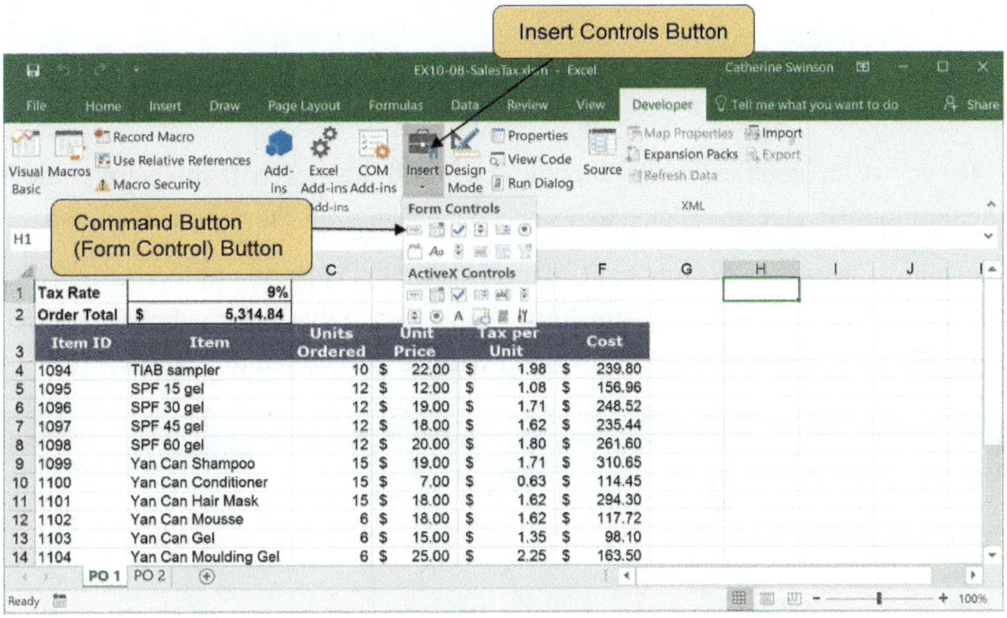

FIGURE EX 10.20

3. When you release the mouse button, the *Assign Macro* dialog opens.
4. Click the name of the macro you want, and then click **OK**.

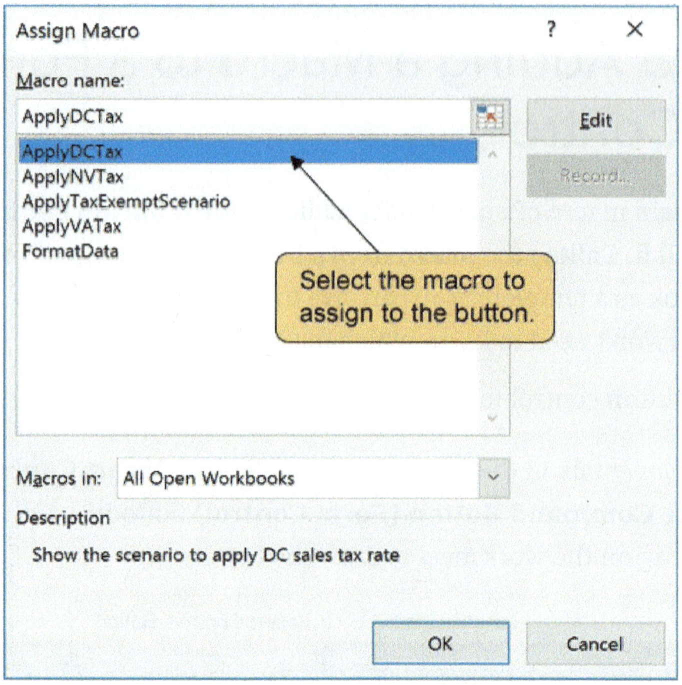

FIGURE EX 10.21

Once you've created the button, clicking it will call the macro. If you want to modify the button instead, right-click it and select an action from the right-click menu.

The button shows the default text **Button [1]** where **[1]** is the number assigned to the button by Excel. To change the button label text, right-click the button and select **Edit Text**. Click outside the button when you are through editing the text.

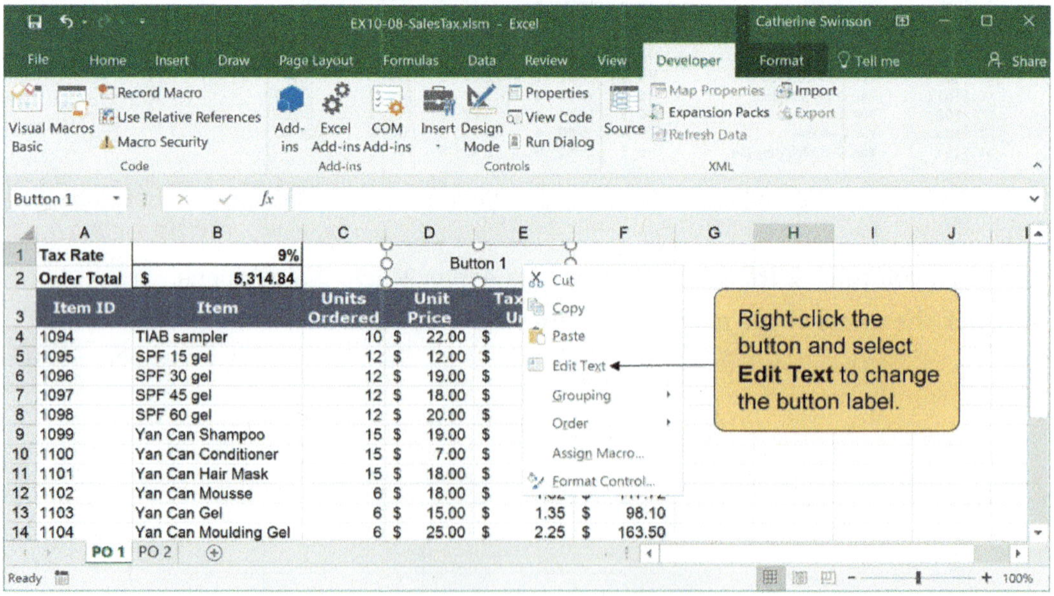

FIGURE EX 10.22

You can modify the look of the button text from the *Format Control* dialog. Right-click the button and select **Format Control...** to open the *Format Control* dialog. From this dialog you can change the look of the button text and change the button properties.

To delete a button control, right-click the button to select it, and then press **Delete**.

tips & tricks

The *Insert Controls* gallery has two groups of buttons: **Form Controls** and **ActiveX Controls**. Form controls can call macros directly. ActiveX controls require that you write the code for the button action directly in the Visual Basic Editor.

tell me more

In the *Assign Macro* dialog, before you select an existing macro to assign to the button, Excel displays a new button name similar to *Button1_Click* in the *Button name* box. This is the default name for the macro or VBA procedure if you want to create a new macro to assign to the button.

- To record a new macro, click the **Record...** button to open the *Record Macro* dialog.
- To write a VBA procedure from scratch, click the **New** button to open the Visual Basic Editor.

let me try *Live!*

If you do not have the data file from the previous skill open, open the student data file **EX10-08-SalesTax** and try this skill on your own:

1. On the **PO 1** worksheet, add a form button control to run the **ApplyDCTax** macro. The button should be placed at approximately cells **D1:E2**.
2. Change the button label text to: `Show DC Tax`
3. If you will be moving on to the next skill in this chapter, leave the workbook open to continue working. If not, save the file as directed by your instructor and close it.

Skill 10.9 Adding a Custom Tab to the Ribbon

If you have a group of macros you use often, consider adding them to a custom Ribbon tab or group.

To add a custom tab and group to the Ribbon:

1. Click the **File** tab.
2. Click **Options** to open the *Excel Options* dialog.
3. Click **Customize Ribbon.**
4. To add a new tab, click the **New Tab** button located below the *Customize the Ribbon* list.
5. A new tab named *New Tab (Custom)* is added with one group named *New Group (Custom).*

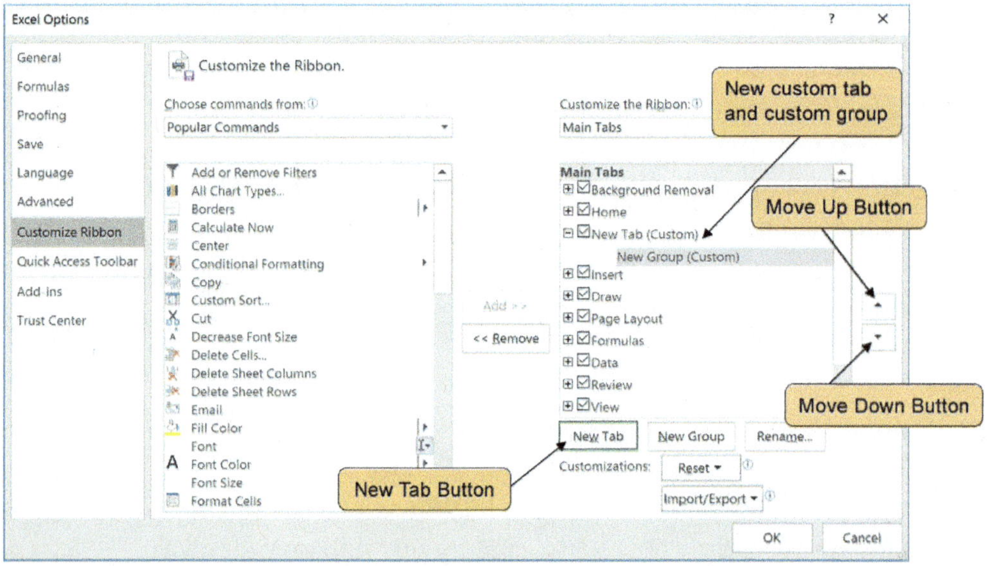

FIGURE EX 10.23

6. To rename the tab, select the tab name in the *Customize the Ribbon* list, and then click the **Rename** button.
7. In the *Rename* dialog, type the new tab name in the *Display name* box, and then click **OK.**

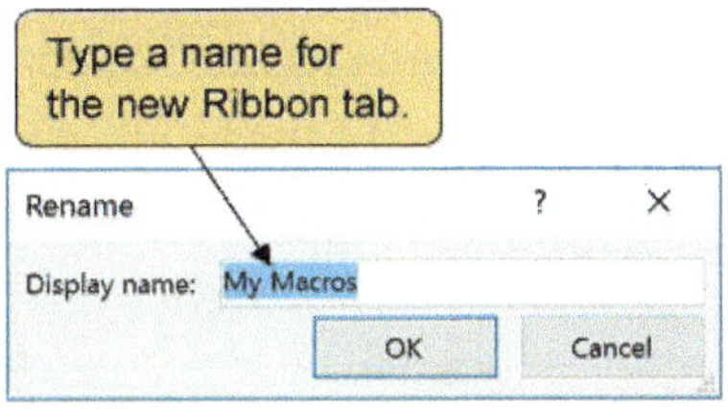

FIGURE EX 10.24

8. Follow the same steps to rename the new group. When you rename a group, you can also select an icon. This is the image that shows on the group button when the Excel window is too narrow to show the group completely.

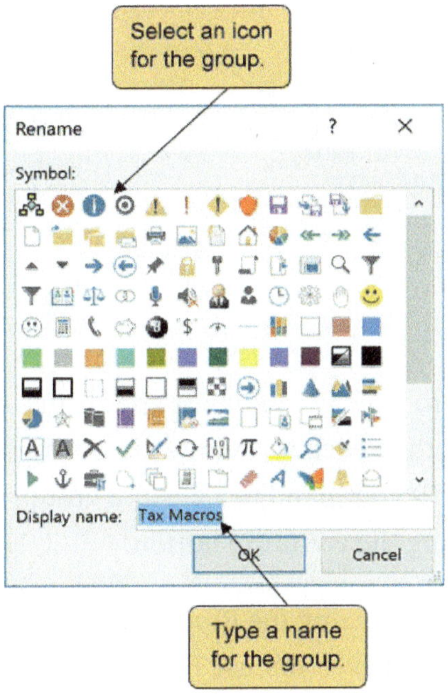

FIGURE EX 10.25

9. To add another group to the tab, select the tab name in the *Customize the Ribbon* list, and then click the **Add Group** button.
10. To change the order in which tabs appear on the Ribbon, select the tab name and then click the **Move Up** or **Move Down** button.

Now that you have a custom tab and group, you need to add commands to the group.

To add a command to a custom group:

1. In the *Customize the Ribbon* list, select the custom group you want to add commands to.

2. At the left side of the *Customize the Ribbon* window, expand the **Choose commands from** list and select the option you want. Select **Macros** to see the list of macros included in all open workbooks. Select the command you want to add and click the **Add** button.

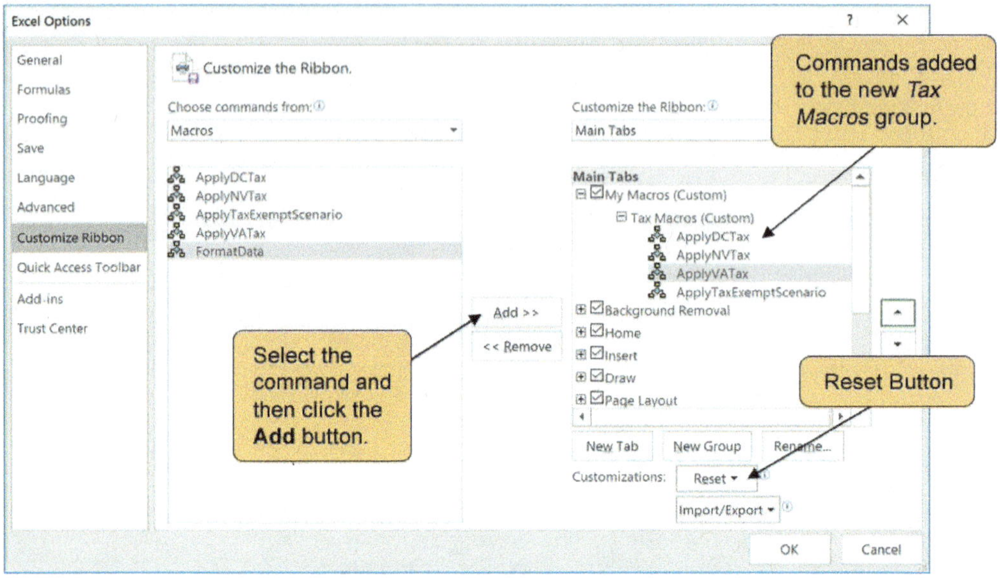

FIGURE EX 10.26

3. To change the order in which commands appear in a custom group, select the command name and then click the **Move Up** or **Move Down** arrow.
4. Once you have added a command to a custom group, you can rename the command button using the **Rename** button.

When you are finished customizing the Ribbon, click **OK**. The custom tab and groups will be available whenever you use Excel.

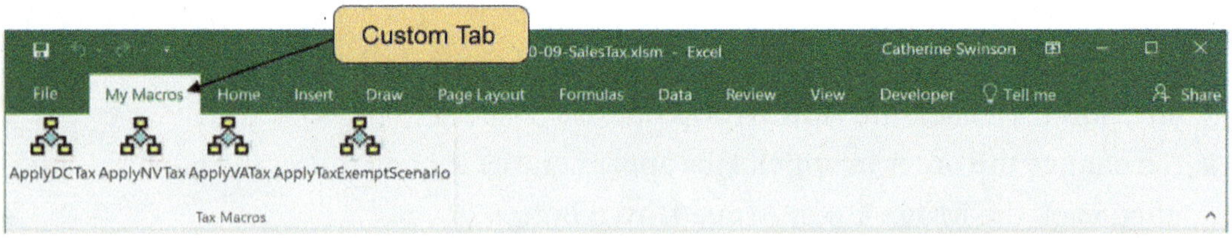

FIGURE EX 10.27

To remove a custom group or tab, select it in the *Customize the Ribbon* list, and then click the **Remove** button. Removing a custom group or tab deletes it permanently. Removing a command from a custom group removes the command only from the group. You cannot delete commands.

To undo all customizations and return both the Ribbon and the Quick Access Toolbar to their original states:

1. In the *Excel Options* dialog, *Customize the Ribbon* page, click the **Reset** button and select **Reset all customizations**.
2. Excel displays a message to verify that you want to reset all Ribbon and Quick Access Toolbar customizations. Click **Yes**.

Caution: Resetting the Ribbon will remove the *Developer* tab. If you need it, you will need to reenable it.

tips & tricks

If you have macros that you want to add to a custom Ribbon tab and group, consider storing them in the Personal Macro Workbook. For more information about working with the Personal Macro Workbook, refer to the *Tips and Tricks* box in the *Recording a Macro* skill.

another method

You can right-click anywhere on the Ribbon and select **Customize the Ribbon** to open the *Customize the Ribbon* window.

let me try *Live!*

If you do not have the data file from the previous skill open, open the student data file **EX10-09-SalesTax** and try this skill on your own:

1. Add a custom tab named `My Macros` to the Ribbon.
2. Rename the new group `Tax Macros` and use the first icon in the list as the group icon.
3. Move the new *My Macros* tab so it appears first in the list.
4. Add the following macros to the **Tax Macros** group in this order: **ApplyDCTax**, **ApplyNVTax**, **ApplyVATax**, and **ApplyTaxExemptScenario**.
5. Click **OK** and review the changes to the Ribbon.
6. Reset all workbook customizations to return the Ribbon to its original state.
7. If you will be moving on to the next skill in this chapter, leave the workbook open to continue working. If not, save the file as directed by your instructor and close it.

Skill 10.10 Customizing the Quick Access Toolbar for the Current Workbook

If you have macros you use often, consider adding them to the Quick Access Toolbar. When customizing the Quick Access Toolbar through the *Excel Options* dialog, you have the option of making the change to just the open workbook.

To customize the Quick Access Toolbar for the current workbook only:

1. Click the **Customize Quick Access Toolbar** button located at the right side of the Quick Access Toolbar.
2. Select **More Commands...**

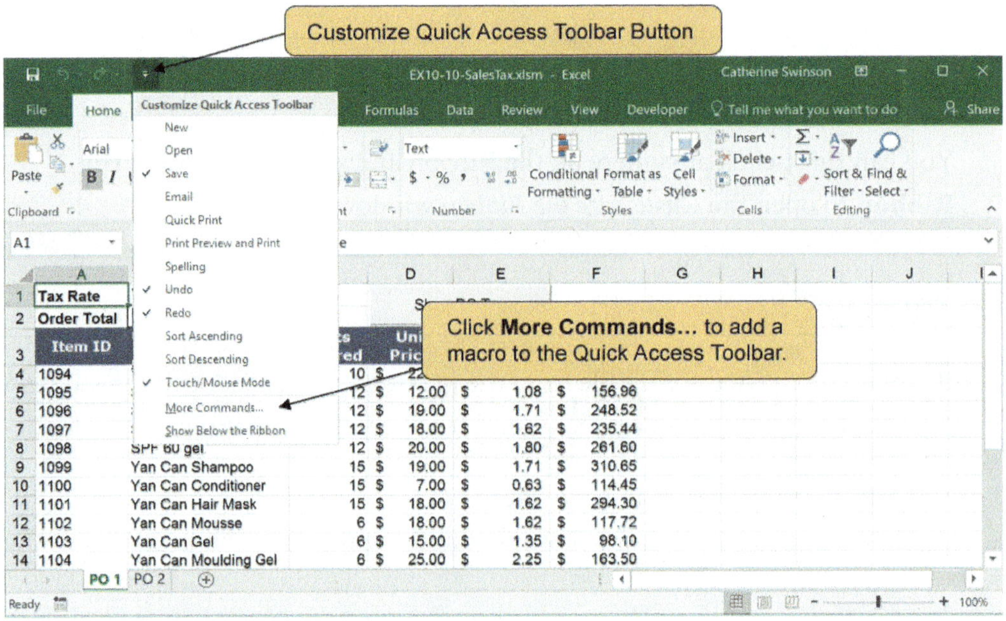

FIGURE EX 10.28

3. The *Excel Options* dialog opens to the *Customize the Quick Access Toolbar* page.
4. To add a macro to the Quick Access Toolbar, expand the **Choose commands from** list and select **Macros**. Select the macro name and click the **Add** button.
5. To limit the customization to the current workbook, expand the **Customize Quick Access Toolbar** list at the right side of the dialog and select the current workbook title.
6. When you are finished customizing the Quick Access Toolbar, click **OK**.

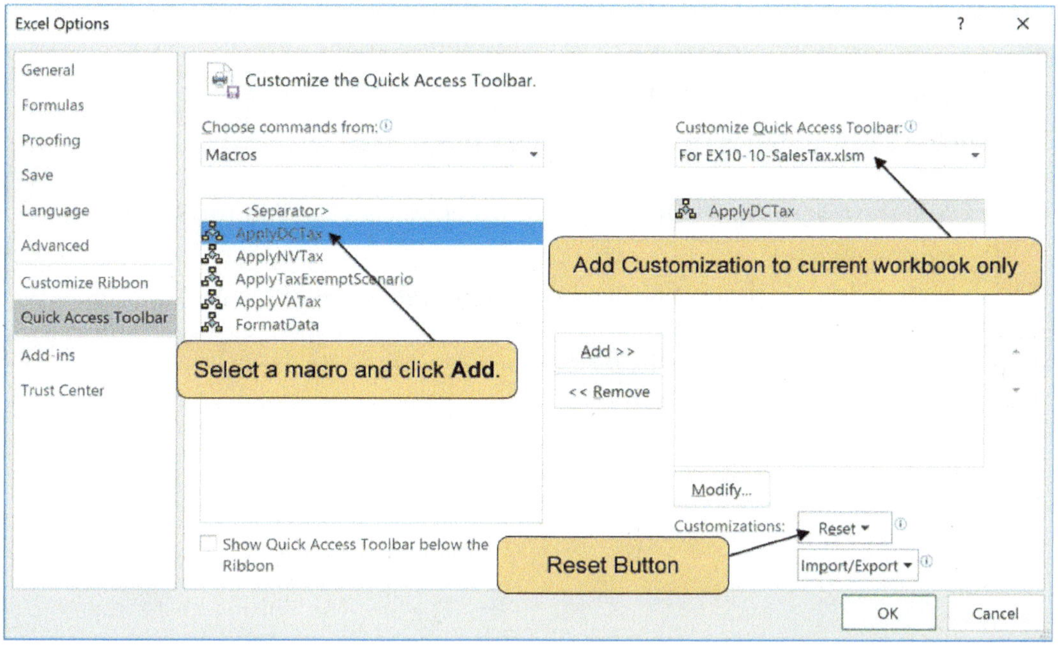

FIGURE EX 10.29

Figure EX 10.30 shows the modified Quick Access Toolbar with the *ApplyDCTax* macro added.

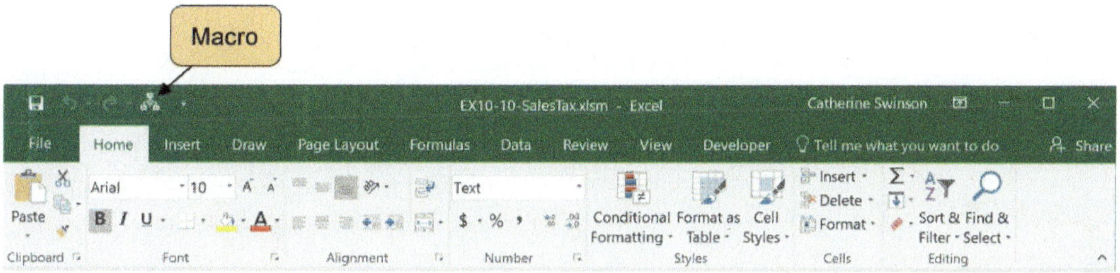

FIGURE EX 10.30

tell me **more**

The skill *Customizing the Quick Access Toolbar* covers the basics of adding commands to the the Quick Access Toolbar.

another method

To open the *Customize Quick Access Toolbar* page:

- Click the **File** tab and click **Options** to open the *Excel Options* dialog. Click **Quick Access Toolbar**.
- Right-click the **Quick Access Toolbar** and select **Customize Quick Access Toolbar...**

let me try *Live!*

If you do not have the data file from the previous skill open, open the student data file **EX10-10-SalesTax** and try this skill on your own:

1. Add the macro **ApplyDCTax** to the Quick Access Toolbar for the current workbook only.
2. Save the file as directed by your instructor and close it.

key terms

- Macro
- Visual Basic for Applications (VBA)
- Trusted document
- Trust Center
- Trusted location
- Developer tab
- Excel Macro-Enabled Workbook
- Excel Macro-Enabled Template
- Personal workbook
- Visual Basic Editor (VBE)
- Project
- Project Explorer
- Module
- Object
- Procedure
- Subroutine
- Comment
- Form button control
- Form Controls
- ActiveX Controls

concept review

1. Macros are written in which programming language?
   a. ASP.net
   b. Visual Basic for Applications
   c. C#
   d. Visual Basic.net
2. A trusted document.
   a. warns the user before running macros and requires the user to allow active content to run.
   b. allows macros to run without warning the user that the workbook contains active content.
   c. disables all macros and other active content.
   d. must be saved in a trusted location.
3. The *Developer* tab must be enabled before you can run a macro.
   a. true
   b. false
4. A macro-enabled workbook uses which file extension?
   a. .xlsx
   b. .xltx
   c. .xlsm
   d. .xltm
5. Where is the command to begin recording a new macro located?
   a. *Developer* tab, *Code* group
   b. *View* tab, *Macros* group
   c. status bar
   d. all of the above
6. Macros are always saved to the personal macro workbook.
   a. true
   b. false
7. In VBA, the code for each macro is stored in its own ________________.
   a. module.
   b. object.
   c. procedure.
   d. project.

8. In VBA, comments must begin with which character?
    a. comma
    b. semicolon
    c. hash tag
    d. apostrophe
9. Which control should you use to add a button to run a macro?
    a. Form Button Control
    b. ActiveX Button Control
    c. Macro Button
    d. None of the above
10. You can add a macro to the Quick Access Toolbar.
    a. true
    b. false

projects

Data files for projects can be found by logging into your SIMnet account and going to the *Library* section.

skill review 10.1

This project begins with data imported from a text file. You will create, edit, and run a macro to format the imported inventory data for three store locations.

Skills needed to complete this project:

- Saving a Macro-Enabled Workbook or Template (Skill 10.5)
- Adding the Developer Tab to the Ribbon (Skill 10.3)
- Recording a Macro (Skill 10.6)
- Modifying a Macro Using VBA (Skill 10.7)
- Running a Macro (Skill 10.4)
- Adding a Macro to a Form Button Control (Skill 10.8)
- Customizing the Quick Access Toolbar for the Current Workbook (Skill 10.10)

1. Open the start file **EX2016-SkillReview-10-1.**
2. If the workbook opens in Protected View, click the **Enable Editing** button in the Message Bar at the top of the workbook so you can modify the workbook.
3. Save the file as a macro-enabled workbook with this file name: `[your initials]EX-SkillReview-10-1`
    a. Click the **File** tab.
    b. Click **Save As**.
    c. Navigate to the location where you want to save the workbook.
    d. Expand the **Save as type** list, and select **Excel Macro-Enabled Workbook**.
    e. Click **Save** to save the workbook with macros.
4. Display the *Developer* tab. (If you already have the *Developer* tab enabled, skip to step 5.)
    a. Click the **File** tab.
    b. Click **Options** to open the *Excel Options* dialog.
    c. Click **Customize Ribbon**.
    d. In the *Customize the Ribbon* list, click the **Developer** check box.
    e. Click **OK**.
5. Start on the *Alexandria* worksheet.
6. Create a macro to format the inventory data and add totals.
    a. On the *Developer* tab, in the *Code* group, click the **Record Macro** button.
    b. In the *Record Macro* dialog, in the *Macro name* box, type: `FormatInventory`
    c. In the *Record Macro* dialog, click in the *Shortcut key* box, press **Shift**, and type: `I`

   d. Verify that *This Workbook* is selected in the *Store macro in* box.
   e. In the *Description* box, type: `Format inventory`
   f. Click **OK**.
7. Record the *Inventory* macro.
   a. Select cells **A1:H1**.
   b. On the *Home* tab, in the *Alignment* group, click the **Merge & Center** button.
   c. On the *Home* tab, in the *Styles* group, click the **More** button to expand the *Styles* gallery. Select the style **Accent 4**.
   d. Select cells **A2:H2**.
   e. On the *Home* tab, in the *Alignment* group, click the **Merge & Center** button.
   f. On the *Home* tab, in the *Styles* group, click the **More** button to expand the *Styles* gallery. Select the style **60%-Accent 4**.
   g. Select cells **A3:H3**.
   h. On the *Home* tab, in the *Font* group, click the **Bold** button.
   i. Click cell **A4**.
   j. On the *Home* tab, in the *Styles* group, click the **Format as Table** button, and select **Table Style Light 12**.
   k. In the *Format as Table* dialog, verify that the cell range *A1:H29* is selected and the *My table has headers* check box is checked. Click **OK**.
   l. Notice that the table includes the titles in cells A1:H2. You will fix this later by editing the macro in the Visual Basic Editor.
   m. On the *Developer* tab, in the *Code* group, click the **Stop Recording** button to stop recording the macro.
8. Fix the errors in the macro by editing the code in the Visual Basic Editor.
   a. On the *Developer* tab, in the *Code* group, click the *Macros* button.
   b. Click the **Edit** button. The *FormatInventory* macro should be selected by default.
   c. In the Visual Basic Editor, scroll down through the code to find the line **Range("A4").Select** and click to place the cursor at the end of the line.
   d. Press **[Enter]** to insert a blank row in the code where you can type a comment.
   e. Type the comment `Fix table cell range` as shown in Figure EX 10.31. Press **[Enter]** after typing the comment text. Remember to type an apostrophe before the comment text.
   f. In the next line of code, correct the cell reference for the table range to `Range("$A$3:$H$29")` as shown in Figure EX 10.31.
   g. Save your changes by clicking the **Save** button on the VBE toolbar.
   h. Click the **File** menu, and select **Close and Return to Microsoft Excel**.

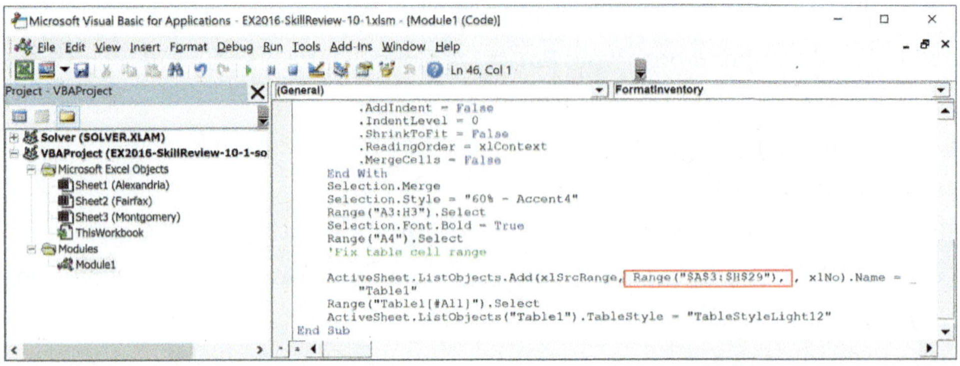

FIGURE EX 10.31

9. Click anywhere in the table. On the *Table Tools Design* tab, in the *Tools* group, click the **Convert to Range** button and then click **Yes** to convert the table back to a regular cell range so you can run the modified macro.
10. Press **Ctrl+Shift+I** to run the modified *Inventory* macro.
11. When you see a message that merging cells keeps only the upper-left cell value, and discards the other values, click **OK**.
12. Look at the last two lines of code in Figure EX 10.31. The two lines of code that apply the table style refer to the table named *Table1*. When the macro was recorded and Excel created the new table, it was automatically named*Table1*. If you run the macro again on another set of data, Excel will name the new table *Table2*, but the macro will look for a table named *Table1* when applying the style. To eliminate this problem, rename the current *Table1* to something else before running the macro on a new set of data.
    a. On the *Formulas* tab, in the *Defined Names* group, click the **Name Manager** button.
    b. The *Table1* name is selected by default. Click the **Edit...** button.
    c. Type `Alexandria` in the *Name* box to rename the table.
    d. Click **OK**.
    e. Click **Close** to close the Name Manager.
13. Add a form button to the *Fairfax* worksheet to run the *Inventory* macro.
    a. Click the **Fairfax** worksheet tab.
    b. On the *Developer* tab, in the *Controls* group, click the **Insert Controls** button, and click the **Button (Form Control)** button.
    c. Click and drag to draw the button to cover cells **J2:K3**.
    d. In the *Assign Macro* dialog, click **FormatInventory** and then click **OK**.
14. Change the button label text.
    a. Right-click the button and select **Edit Text**.
    b. Delete the text **Button 1** and type: `Format Inventory`
    c. Click outside the button.

15. Click the **Format Inventory** button to run the *Inventory* macro on the data in this worksheet.
16. Rename the new *Table1* table.
    a. On the *Formulas* tab, in the *Defined Names* group, click the **Name Manager** button.
    b. Click **Table1** to select it. Click the **Edit...** button.
    c. Type `Fairfax` in the *Name* box to rename the table.
    d. Click **OK**.
    e. Click **Close** to close the Name Manager.
17. Rather than creating a new button for every new sheet of inventory data, it might be easier to access the macro from the Quick Access Toolbar.
    a. Click the **Customize Quick Access Toolbar** button at the far right side of the Quick Access Toolbar.
    b. Select **More Commands...**
    c. Expand the **Choose commands from** list and select **Macros**.
    d. Click the **FormatInventory** macro and click the **Add** button.
    e. Expand the **Customize Quick Access Toolbar** list at the right side of the dialog and select the name of your workbook to save the custom version of the Quick Access Toolbar with this workbook only.
    f. Click **OK**.
18. Go to the **Montgomery** worksheet and click the **FormatInventory** button that now appears on the far right side of the Quick Access Toolbar.
19. Save the workbook.
20. If you are going to submit this project in SIMnet, save a copy of it as a regular Excel workbook (without macros).
21. Close the workbook.

projects

Data files for projects can be found by logging into your SIMnet account and going to the *Library* section.

skill review 10.2

In this project, you will create, edit, and run macros to format the imported hourly billing information for a law firm and consolidate the data.

Skills needed to complete this project:

- Saving a Macro-Enabled Workbook or Template (Skill 10.5)
- Adding the Developer Tab to the Ribbon (Skill 10.3)
- Recording a Macro (Skill 10.6)
- Modifying a Macro Using VBA (Skill 10.7)
- Adding a Macro to a Form Button Control (Skill 10.8)
- Adding a Custom Tab to the Ribbon (Skill 10.9)
- Running a Macro (Skill 10.4)

1. Open the start file **EX2016-SkillReview-10-2.**
2. If the workbook opens in Protected View, click the **Enable Editing** button in the Message Bar at the top of the workbook so you can modify the workbook.
3. Save the file as a macro-enabled workbook with this file name: `[your initials]EX-SkillReview-10-2`
    a. Click the **File** tab.
    b. Click **Save As.**
    c. Navigate to the location where you want to save the workbook.
    d. Click **Save** to save the workbook with macros.
4. Display the *Developer* tab. (If you already have the *Developer* tab enabled, skip to step 5.)
    a. Click the **File** tab.
    b. Click **Options** to open the *Excel Options* dialog.
    c. Click **Customize Ribbon.**
    d. In the *Customize the Ribbon* list, click the **Developer** check box.
    e. Click **OK.**
5. Begin with the *Month1* worksheet active.
6. Create a macro to add totals to the billing data.
    a. On the *Developer* tab, in the *Code* group, click the **Record Macro** button.
    b. In the *Record Macro* dialog, in the *Macro name* box, type: `CalculateTotals`
    c. Do not include a shortcut key for this macro.
    d. Verify that *This Workbook* is selected in the *Store macro in* box.
    e. In the *Description* box, type: `Calculate totals`

f. Click **OK**.

7. Record the *Totals* macro.
   a. Click cell **H1** and type: `Total`
   b. In cell **H2**, enter the following formula: `=SUM(D2:F2)*G2`
   c. Click the AutoFill handle and drag to copy the formula to cells **H3:H14**.
   d. Select cell **D15** and enter the formula: `=SUM(D2:D14)`
   e. Click the AutoFill handle and drag to copy the formula to cells **E15:H15**.
   f. Select cells **G2:H15**.
   g. On the *Home* tab, in the *Number* group, click the **Accounting Number Format** button.
   h. Select cells **A15:H15**.
   i. On the *Home* tab, in the *Font* group, click the **Borders** button arrow, and select **Top and Double Bottom Border**.
   j. Select cells **A1:H1**.
   k. On the *Home* tab, in the *Styles* group, click the **More** button to expand the *Styles* gallery. Select the style **Accent 1**.
   l. On the *Developer* tab, in the *Code* group, click the **Stop Recording** button to stop recording the macro.
8. Edit the macro code to change the number style applied to cells G2:H15 to use the style *Currency [0]* to show zero digits after the decimal.
   a. On the *Developer* tab, in the *Code* group, click the **Macros** button.
   b. Click the **Edit** button. The *CalculateTotals* macro should be selected by default.
   c. In the Code window, locate this line of code:

      `Selection.Style = "Currency"`

      and change it to this:

      `Selection.Style = "Currency [0]"`

      Be sure to include the space after the word *Currency*.

      Hint: If you applied the Accounting Number Format using a method other than the Ribbon button, locate and change this line of code instead:

      ```
      Selection.NumberFormat = "_($* #,##0.00_);_($* (#,##0.00);_($*
      ""_""??_);_(@_)"
      ```
   d. Save your changes by clicking the **Save** button on the VBE toolbar.
   e. Click the **File** menu, and select **Close and Return to Microsoft Excel**.
9. Create another macro to consolidate the data.
   a. Click the **Summary** worksheet.
   b. Click the **Record Macro** button on the status bar.
   c. In the *Record Macro* dialog, in the *Macro name* box, type:
      `ConsolidateTotals`

d. Do not include a shortcut key for this macro.
e. Verify that *This Workbook* is selected in the *Store macro in* box.
f. In the *Description* box, type: `Consolidate totals`
g. Click **OK**.

10. Record the *ConsolidateTotals* macro.
    a. On the *Summary* worksheet, click cell **D2**.
    b. On the *Data* tab, in the *Data Tools* group, click the **Consolidate** button.
    c. In the *Consolidate* dialog, verify that *Sum* is selected in the *Function* box.
    d. Click the **Month1** worksheet tab.
    e. Click and drag to select cells **D2:H14**.
    f. Click the **Add** button.
    g. Click the **Month2** worksheet tab.
    h. Click the **Add** button.
    i. Click the **Month3** worksheet tab.
    j. Click the **Add** button.
    k. Verify that the *Create links to source data* check box is ***not*** checked.
    l. Click **OK**.
    m. Click the **Stop Recording** button on the status bar to stop recording the macro.
11. Add a form button to the *Summary* worksheet to run the *Consolidate* macro.
    a. On the *Developer* tab, in the *Controls* group, click the **Insert Controls** button, and click the **Button (Form Control)** button.
    b. Click and drag to draw the button to cover cells **J2:K3**.
    c. In the *Assign Macro* dialog, click **ConsolidateTotals** and then click **OK**.
12. Change the button label text.
    a. Right-click the button and select **Edit Text**.
    b. Delete the text **Button 1** and type: `Update Data`
    c. Click outside the button.
13. Create a new Ribbon tab and group to display the macros.
    a. Click the **File** tab and click **Options** to open the *Excel Options* dialog.
    b. Click **Customize Ribbon**.
    c. Click the **New Tab** button.
    d. In the list at the right side of the dialog, click **New Tab (Custom)** and then click the **Rename...** button.
    e. Type `My Macros` in the *Display name* box and click **OK**.
    f. If necessary, click the **My Macros (Custom)** tab to select it.
    g. Click the **Move Up** button as many times as necessary so the *My Macros (Custom)* tab appears at the top of the list.
    h. Click **New Group (Custom)** and then click the **Rename...** button.
    i. Click the icon that looks like a pair of scales (the third item in the fourth

row).

j. Type `Billing Summary` in the *Display Name* box and click **OK**.
k. If necessary, click **Billing Summary (Custom)** to select the group.
l. Expand the **Choose commands from** list and select **Macros**.
m. Click **ConsolidateTotals** and then click the **Add** button.
n. Click **CalculateTotals** and then click the **Add** button.
o. Click **OK**.
p. On the Ribbon, click the **My Macros** tab and verify that the two macros are included in the *Billing Summary* group.

14. Run the *Totals* macro on the *Month2* and *Month3* worksheets.
    a. Click the **Month2** worksheet tab.
    b. On the *My Macros* tab, in the *Billing Summary* group, click the **CalculateTotals** button.
    c. Click the **Month3** worksheet tab.
    d. On the *My Macros* tab, in the *Billing Summary* group, click the **CalculateTotals** button.
15. Click the **Summary** worksheet tab and click the **Update Data** button. Notice how the summary data updates to include the totals from the *Month2* and *Month3* worksheets.
16. Remove the custom tab from the Ribbon.
    a. Click the **File** tab and click **Options** to open the *Excel Options* dialog.
    b. Click **Customize Ribbon**.
    c. Click **My Macros (Custom)** in the list at the right side of the dialog.
    d. Click the **Remove** button.
    e. Click **OK** to close the *Excel Options* dialog.
17. Save the workbook.
18. If you are going to submit this project in SIMnet, save a copy of it as a regular Excel workbook (without macros).
19. Close the workbook.

projects

Data files for projects can be found by logging into your SIMnet account and going to the *Library* section.

challenge yourself 10.3

In this project, you will record a macro to calculate grade totals and modify it in VBA. You will then run the macro on a second set of grades.

Skills needed to complete this project:

- Saving a Macro-Enabled Workbook or Template (Skill 10.5)
- Adding the Developer Tab to the Ribbon (Skill 10.3)
- Recording a Macro (Skill 10.6)
- Modifying a Macro Using VBA (Skill 10.7)
- Customizing the Quick Access Toolbar for the Current Workbook (Skill 10.10)
- Adding a Custom Tab to the Ribbon (Skill 10.9)
- Adding a Macro to a Form Button Control (Skill 10.8)
- Running a Macro (Skill 10.4)

1. Open the start file **EX2016-ChallengeYourself-10-3.**
2. If the workbook opens in Protected View, click the **Enable Editing** button in the Message Bar at the top of the workbook so you can modify the workbook.
3. Save the file as a macro-enabled workbook with this file name: `[your initials]EX-ChallengeYourself-10-3`
4. Display the *Developer* tab. (If you already have the *Developer* tab enabled, skip to step 5.)
5. Begin with the *ClassAnalysis* worksheet active.
6. Create a macro to calculate yearly totals and yearly averages for each student.
   a. Name the new macro: `CalculateGrades`
   b. Include the keyboard shortcut: `Ctrl+Shift+G`
   c. Include the description: `Calculate student totals and averages`
7. Record the Grades macro following these steps:
   a. In **G1**, create a column heading: `Total`
   b. In **H1**, create a column heading: `Average`
   c. Click cell **A2**.
   d. Format the data as a table using the **Table Style Medium 7** table style. Be sure to include the table header row.
   e. In the *Total* column, use the SUM function to calculate the yearly total for each student.
   f. In the *Average* column, use the AVERAGE function to calculate the yearly average for each student.

g. Autofit columns **G** and **H**.

8. Edit the **CalculateGrades** macro to use the **Table Style Medium 6** table style instead of **Table Style Medium 7**. *Hint*: Edit this line in the VBA code:
   `ActiveSheet ListObjects("Table1") TableStyle = "TableStyleMedium7"`
9. Add the **CalculateGrades** macro to the Quick Access Toolbar for just this workbook.
10. Create a macro to display the table *Total* row and display the class average for each assignment. *Hint*: To display the table *Total* row, check the **Total Row** check box on the *Table Tools Design* tab, *Table Style Options* group.
    a. Name the new macro: `ShowTotalRow`
    b. Do not include a keyboard shortcut.
    c. Include the description: `Show Total row with averages`
    d. Display the table *Total* row.
    e. Change the text in the first cell of the *Total* row to: `Class Averages`
    f. Select **Average** in the *Total* row for columns **C:H**.
11. Create a macro to hide the table *Total* row. *Hint*: This macro has only one action: Uncheck the **Total Row** check box on the *Table Tools Design* tab, *Table Style Options* group.
    a. Name the new macro: `HideTotalRow`
    b. Do not include a keyboard shortcut.
    c. Include the description: `Hide the Total row`
12. If you have permission, create a new custom Ribbon tab for the macros.
    a. Name the new custom tab: `My Macros`
    b. Name the new custom group: `Challenge Macros`
    c. Add the three macros you created during this project.
13. Add a form button to the **ClassAnalysis** worksheet to run the **CalculateGrades** macro.
    a. Place the button to cover cells **J1:L2**.
    b. Edit the button label text to: `Calculate Grades`
14. Add a form button to the **ClassAnalysis** worksheet to run the **ShowTotalRow** macro.
    a. Place the button to cover cells **J4:L5**.
    b. Edit the button label text to: `Show Assignment Averages`
15. Add a form button to the **ClassAnalysis** worksheet to run the **HideTotalRow** macro.
    a. Place the button to cover cells **J7:L8**.
    b. Edit the button label text to: `Hide Assignment Averages`
16. Test the **Show Assignment Averages** and **Hide Assignment Averages** buttons.

17. Clear all content and formatting from **rows 1:10**. **Caution:** If you delete the rows, you will delete the buttons as well. Instead, use the *Clear All* command from the *Home* tab, *Editing* group.
18. Go to the **Class101B** worksheet and copy the data in cells **A1:F10**.
19. Go to the **ClassAnalysis** worksheet and paste the copied data beginning in cell **A1**.
20. Run the **CalculateGrades** macro using any method.
21. Use the **Show Assignment Averages** button to run the **ShowTotalRow** macro.
22. Save the workbook.
23. If you are going to submit this project in SIMnet, save a copy of it as a regular Excel workbook (without macros).
24. If you added a custom tab to the Ribbon, you may want to remove it before closing the workbook.
25. Close the workbook.

projects

Data files for projects can be found by logging into your SIMnet account and going to the *Library* section.

challenge yourself 10.4

In this project you will work with a macro-enabled workbook that includes three macros. You will edit one of the macros and run it to format data that have been imported into the workbook. You will create form button controls to run the other macros. Finally, you will record your own macro and add it to the Quick Access Toolbar.

Skills needed to complete this project:

- Opening a Macro-Enabled Workbook (Skill 10.1)
- Saving a Macro-Enabled Workbook or Template (Skill 10.5)
- Adding the Developer Tab to the Ribbon (Skill 10.3)
- Adding a Custom Tab to the Ribbon (Skill 10.9)
- Modifying a Macro Using VBA (Skill 10.7)
- Running a Macro (Skill 10.4)
- Adding a Macro to a Form Button Control (Skill 10.8)
- Recording a Macro (Skill 10.6)
- Customizing the Quick Access Toolbar for the Current Workbook (Skill 10.10)

1. Open the start file **EX2016-ChallengeYourself-10-4.**
2. If the workbook opens in Protected View, click the **Enable Editing** button in the Message Bar at the top of the workbook so you can modify it.
3. Save the file as a macro-enabled workbook with this file name: `[your initials]EX-ChallengeYourself-10-4`
4. Display the *Developer* tab. (If you already have the *Developer* tab enabled, skip to step 5.)
5. If you have permission, create a new custom Ribbon tab for the three macros included in this workbook.
   a. Name the new custom tab: `Pet Store Macros`
   b. Name the new custom group: `Custom Macros`
   c. Add the three macros included with this project.
6. The workbook includes a macro to automatically apply formatting after data have been imported. Edit the **Format** macro to change the fill color to the theme color **Accent 5**. *Hint*: Edit this line in the VBA code:
   `ThemeColor = xlThemeColorAccent6`

7. Run the **Format** macro on the data in the *import* sheet. *Hint*: The keyboard shortcut is listed in the comments at the beginning of the macro subroutine procedure code.
8. Add a form button to the **import** worksheet to run the **AddSubtotals** macro.
    a. Place the button to cover cells **H1:J2**.
    b. Edit the button label text to: `Add Subtotals`
9. Add a form button to the **import** worksheet to run the **RemoveSubtotals** macro.
    a. Place the button to cover cells **K1:M2**.
    b. Edit the button label text to: `Remove Subtotals`
10. Test the buttons.
11. Record a new macro to autofit the columns.
    a. Name the new macro: `AutoFit`
    b. Do not include a keyboard shortcut.
    c. Include the description: `AutoFit the columns`
    d. Record the *AutoFit* macro to autofit each of the columns **A:G**.
12. Add the **AutoFit** macro to the Quick Access Toolbar for just this workbook.
13. Go to the **January** worksheet and run the **AutoFit** macro.
14. If you are going to submit this project in SIMnet, save a copy of it as a regular Excel workbook (without macros).
15. If you added a custom tab to the Ribbon, you may want to remove it before closing the workbook.
16. Close the workbook.

Data files for projects can be found by logging into your SIMnet account and going to the *Library* section.

on your own 10.5

In this project you will record macros to format data in a sample personal budget. You will then create your own budget and modify and run the macro to format those data.

Skills needed to complete this project:

- Saving a Macro-Enabled Workbook or Template (Skill 10.5)
- Adding the Developer Tab to the Ribbon (Skill 10.3)
- Recording a Macro (Skill 10.6)
- Adding a Custom Tab to the Ribbon (Skill 10.9)
- Customizing the Quick Access Toolbar for the Current Workbook (Skill 10.10)
- Modifying a Macro Using VBA (Skill 10.7)
- Adding a Macro to a Form Button Control (Skill 10.8)
- Running a Macro (Skill 10.4)

1. Open the start file **EX2016-OnYourOwn-10-5.**
2. If the workbook opens in Protected View, click the **Enable Editing** button in the Message Bar at the top of the workbook so you can modify it.
3. Save the file as a macro-enabled workbook with this file name:
   `[your initials]EX-OnYourOwn-10-5`
4. Display the *Developer* tab. (If you already have the *Developer* tab enabled, skip to step 5.)
5. Record macros to format the budget in the **Sample Budget** worksheet.
   a. Record a macro to apply formatting to the table and calculate annual totals and averages for each budget category. Apply appropriate number formatting where necessary.
   b. Record a macro to calculate total expenses for each month. Apply appropriate number and cell formatting as necessary.
   c. Record a macro to create a chart to display the annual total for each expense category as part of the entire annual budget. Try using a pie chart. Apply a chart style of your choice. If you include a chart title, change the title text.
6. If you have permission, create a new custom Ribbon tab to store the macros you created.
7. Add at least one of the macros to the Quick Access Toolbar for this workbook.

8. Go to the **My Budget** worksheet and update the data to reflect your personal budget. Add new rows as necessary for your budget categories that were not included in the sample.
9. Before working with the VBA code and running the macros on your own data, you might want to copy the worksheet as a backup in case the macros do not work as you intend. This way you'll have a clean copy of the data to try again with.
10. Edit the VBA code as necessary for each of the macros you created so you can run them on the data in the *My Budget* worksheet.
    a. If you added rows to the data, you will need to update the cell ranges where the category totals and averages are calculated. In the example shown in Figure EX 10.32, one row was added to the data. Every reference to row 7 was updated to row 8.

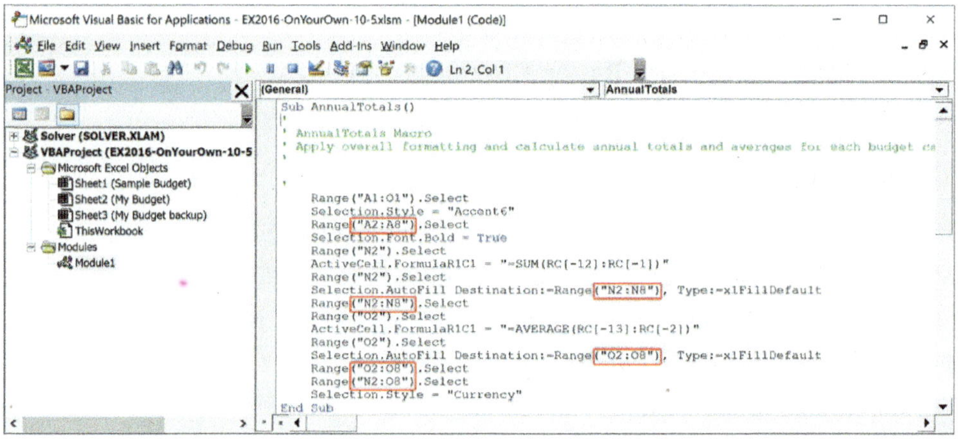

FIGURE EX 10.32

    b. If you added rows to the data, you will need to update the cell range where the monthly totals are calculated. In the example shown in Figure EX 10.33, one row was added to the data. Every reference to row 8 was updated to row 9. We also changed the offset for the SUM function's relative reference range from **"=SUM(R[-6]C:R[-1]C)"** to **"=SUM(R[-7]C:R[-1]C)"** to increase the cell range for the SUM function argument by one.

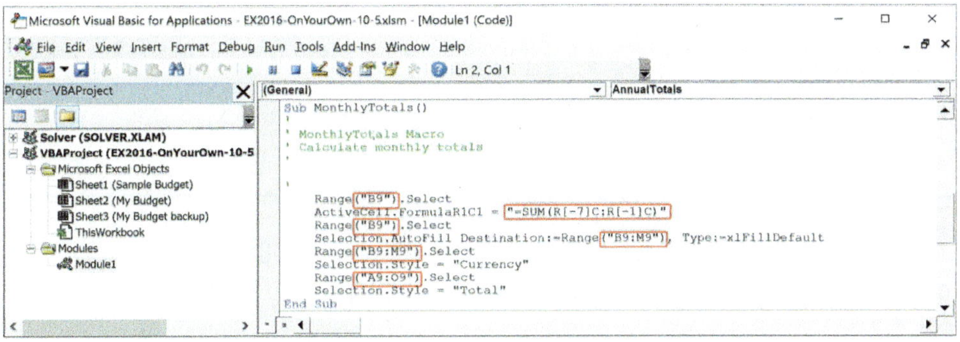

FIGURE EX 10.33

c. If you added rows to the data, you will need to update the cell range for the pie chart. In the example shown in Figure EX 10.34, one row was added to the data. Every reference to row 7 was updated to row 8.

d. Update the sheet name in the code that selects the data source for the chart and update the cell references if necessary as shown in Figure EX 10.34.

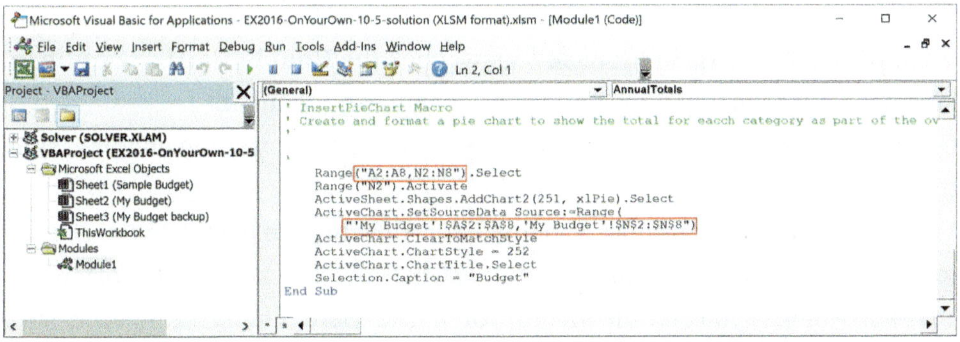

FIGURE EX 10.34

11. Add at least one form button to the **My Budget** worksheet to run one of the macros you created.
12. Run the updated macros on the data in the **My Budget** worksheet.
13. Save the workbook.
14. If you are going to submit this project in SIMnet, save a copy of it as a regular Excel workbook (without macros).
15. Save a copy of the workbook as a macro-enabled template so you can use it again for your personal budget.
16. If you added a custom tab to the Ribbon, you may want to remove it before closing the workbook.
17. Close the workbook.

projects

Data files for projects can be found by logging into your SIMnet account and going to the *Library* section.

fix it 10.6

This project file includes a macro with an error and a missing calculation. Your task is to correct the macro and run it on the data in the file.

Skills needed to complete this project:

- Opening a Macro-Enabled Workbook (Skill 10.1)
- Saving a Macro-Enabled Workbook or Template (Skill 10.5)
- Adding the Developer Tab to the Ribbon (Skill 10.3)
- Modifying a Macro Using VBA (Skill 10.7)
- Running a Macro (Skill 10.4)
- Adding a Macro to a Form Button Control (Skill 10.8)

1. Open the start file **EX2016-FixIt-10-6.**
2. If the workbook opens in Protected View, click the **Enable Editing** button in the Message Bar at the top of the workbook so you can modify it.
3. Display the *Developer* tab. (If you already have the *Developer* tab enabled, skip to step 4.)
4. The workbook contains a macro named **Scholarships** to calculate the number of scholarships in the table named **ScholarshipData**. The keyboard shortcut is **Ctrl+Shift+S**. If you run the macro, you'll find there is an error. Fix the error, and then run the corrected macro.
    a. When you try to run the macro, a message box should appear telling you that there is an application-defined or object-defined error. This means there is a problem with the macro code. Click the **Debug** button to open the Visual Basic Editor with the first line containing an error highlighted.

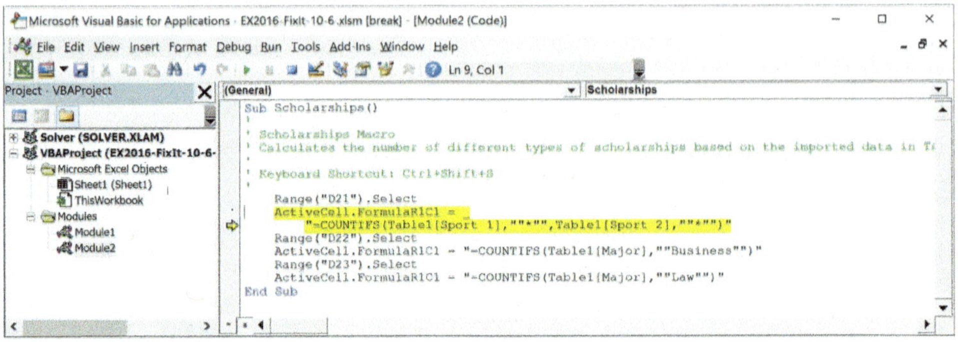

FIGURE EX 10.35

b. Fix the error. *Hint*: The table name is incorrect in the highlighted line of code. The table name is *ScholarshipData* not *Table1*.
c. Save your changes, and then close the VBE window. A message will appear telling you that closing the VBE window will stop the debugger. Click **OK**.
d. Run the modified macro to test your work and continue debugging the macro until all the table name errors have been fixed.

5. The macro does not include a calculation to find the number of communications majors (cell **D24**). Edit the VBA code for the **Scholarships** macro subroutine procedure to include this calculation.
   a. Copy the two lines of code that calculate the number of law majors and then change the code to select cell **D24** and count the number of cells with the word **Communications**.
   b. Run the **Scholarships** macro again. This time it should calculate values for cells **D21:D24**. If you encounter an error, run the debugger again and find and fix your error.
6. The form button to run the **Scholarships** macro should display the label text **Count Scholarships**. Edit the button text.
7. Save the workbook.
8. If you are going to submit this project in SIMnet, save a copy of it as a regular Excel workbook (without macros).
9. Close the workbook.

Online Supplements

Mc Graw Hill Education

SIMnet Keep IT SIMple!

SIMnet for Office 2016, Manning SIMbook, Single Module Registration Code, Excel Complete

As a learning science company, McGraw-Hill Education is dedicated to offering the best digital solutions to unlock the full potential of every student by accelerating learning through intuitive, engaging, efficient and effective experiences – grounded in research. As our leading digital solution for Computer Information Technology,

SIMnet for Office 2016 is redefining student learning at its core by being easy to use, focused on personalized, life-long learning, and committed to measurable results. SIMnet for Office 2016 is reliable, flexible and a culmination of our detailed development. SIMnet's community has grown exponentially during the previous Office version releases as a direct result of extensive customer feedback that has shaped our development. Our unique development partnership with our customers, combined with our agility, responsiveness, and support provides an advantage unmatched in the industry that only McGraw-Hill Education can deliver. Join our community and discover how your needs will be met in an evergreen world where change is constant!

The following steps are for new users registering with SimNet for the first time. (If you already have a SimNet account, simply go to the unique URL provided by your instructor. Enter your login name and password and click on "LOGIN.")

IMPORTANT: You will need to obtain the url from your instructor.

1. Go to https://www.(unique school name)/simnetonline.com
2. If you do not already have a SimNet account, click on "**I have a code**"
3. Check that your school name is accurately displayed in upper left side of screen. "Continue."
4. Verify the course information and click on "Continue."
5. Enter the access code located on either the back cover of your Create printed textbook or located on the user's Create eBookshelf and click on "Continue."
6. Answer the questions to complete your registration.

Visit: http://support.connectmath.com or Call: (949) 390-2095

Monday – Thursday | 7:00 A.M. – 1:00 A.M.

Friday: 7:00 AM – 9:00 P.M.

Sunday: 4:00 PM – 1:00 A.M.
(All times Eastern)